U0666839

金融的力量

田国立 / 主编

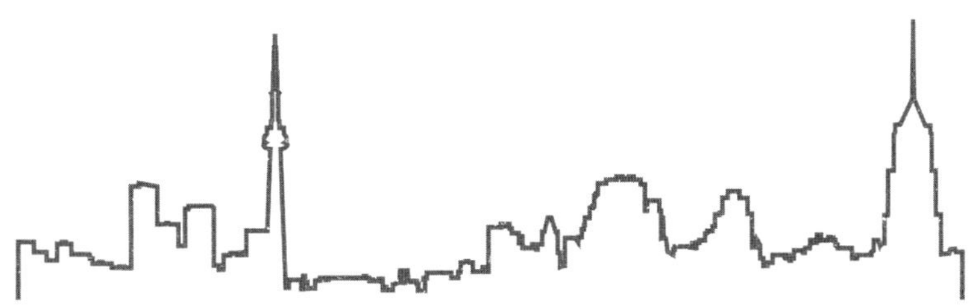

中信出版集团 | 北京

图书在版编目（CIP）数据

金融的力量 / 田国立主编. -- 北京：中信出版社，
2020.1
ISBN 978-7-5217-1134-9

Ⅰ. ①金… Ⅱ. ①田… Ⅲ. ①银行业务－中国－文集
Ⅳ. ①F832.2-53

中国版本图书馆CIP数据核字（2019）第277506号

金融的力量

主　　编：田国立
出版发行：中信出版集团股份有限公司
（北京市朝阳区惠新东街甲4号富盛大厦2座　邮编　100029）
承 印 者：北京通州皇家印刷厂

开　　本：787mm × 1092mm　1/16　　印　　张：37.25　　字　　数：725千字
版　　次：2020年1月第1版　　印　　次：2020年1月第1次印刷
广告经营许可证：京朝工商广字第8087号
书　　号：ISBN 978-7-5217-1134-9
定　　价：175.00元

编委会

主编

田国立

主任

黄　毅

成员

杜要忠　朱　勇　李　昊
宋　伟　王秋霞　赵　熙

序一

新时代　新金融　新担当

当今的中国日益走向世界舞台中央，从主动融入经济全球化转变为经济全球化的推动者，从资本流入国转变为资本输出国，逐步承担起为人类面临的共同难题提供中国方案的责任。十八大以来，我国改革开放和社会主义现代化建设取得了历史性成就，中华民族迎来了从站起来、富起来到强起来的伟大飞跃，中国特色社会主义进入了新时代。

大国崛起需要大国金融，国有金融乃国之重器。国有金融企业作为党在金融领域的重要支柱和依靠力量，必须在时代大潮中更多地承担起自己的责任，在服务国家战略中更多地做出积极贡献。

纵观世界经济金融发展历史，回顾一次次“大危机”“大萧条”，从20世纪以前的荷兰郁金香危机、英国南海泡沫事件、美国金融恐慌，到20世纪初的美国银行业危机、美国股市大崩盘，再到1987年席卷全球股市的黑色星期一、1995年墨西哥金融危机、1997年亚洲金融危机以及2008年美国次贷危机，17世纪以来，全球范围内发生了9次波及范围巨大、影响深远的金融危机，且负外部性显著，给整个社会都造成了巨大混乱。特别是最近一次发生的美国次贷危机，被公认为20世纪30年代“大萧条”以来最严重的金融风暴，其涉及范围及程度远超以往，给社会带来了难以估量的负面影响。

古语有云：“上善若水，水善利万物而不争。”由股市、房市、P2P（个人对个人）等领域的大起大落可见，金融的能量是客观现实，是一种自然动能，怎样善治这种动能，值得深思。金融若水，需以善念之本、善治之道，善加引导，才能润泽万物、利于百姓。引导得好，便是上善若水；引导不好，脱离本源，或将成为洪水猛兽、贻害四方。因此，金融的宏大并不是目标，金融的伟大才值得追求。

新时代标注新坐标。金融机构不能继续陶醉于“灰犀牛”背上的狂欢，留恋于“躺着赚钱”的美好时光，面对新时代经济社会矛盾的新变化，金融是时候该做出改变了。习近平总书记在第五次全国金融工作会议上指出了做好金融工作应把握的重要原则，第一条就是要“回归本源，服从服务于经济社会发展”。这为新时代金融发展指明了方向，人民对美好生活的向往就是新时代金融人的奋斗目标。因此，金融要回归到服务社会的本源，为实现人民对美好生活的向往贡献一分力量。

金融是社会经济的血脉。金融从业者要跳出金融工作本身，必须深入社会、了解社会、读懂社会，以更宽广的视野、更长远的眼光理解社会现象，把握社会发展的总体趋势和方向。如果金融工作者把社会问题看透了，那么金融就是解决社会难点、痛点最温柔的、无痛的手术刀，虽然其他办法最后也能解决问题，但都会有不同程度的副作用，付出的代价和社会痛苦会比较大。随着现代金融深度融入社会生产生活，金融将变成随时、随地、随需的“永远在线的服务”。社会属性赋予了金融机构解决社会问题的责任，现代科技和金融服务深度融合则使提供专业化金融解决方案成为可能。金融将通过创新，以多种形态与社会各行各业深度联结，成为推动社会发展变革、守护社会公义的重要力量，促进“现代经济核心”的作用在社会治理、环境保护、公益事业和人文关怀等各领域得到新的展现。

新时代提出新召唤。习总书记在2014年对建设银行做出重要指示，要求我们进一步增强服务国家建设能力、防范金融风险能力、参与国际竞争能力。建设银行作为中国金融业的主力军，更须提高站位、做出表率，积极响应党中央的号召，将习近平新时代中国特色社会主义思想和中央经济金融方针政策创造性地转化为金融的生动实践。

金融是现代经济的核心。建设银行必须要有强烈的家国情怀、强烈的责任担当，主动为国分忧，当好国家的顶梁柱。国有大型银行是我国金融领域的重要支柱和力量，要有大格局大担当，决不能只一门心思想着赚钱，但凡金融以自我为中心不断虚拟化、泡沫化，必然要误入歧途。要当好顶梁柱，主动融入大局，为服务国家经济与社会发展贡献金融力量，同时还要成为社会主义核心价值观的倡导者。我们既是市场化商业主体，又是社会主流价值观的承载者和守护者，有责任也有能力在新时代担负起弘扬社会主义核心价值观和先进文化的使命。

新时代催生新金融。新金融必然产生并服务于新时代。新金融是以数据为关键生产要素，以科技为核心生产工具，以平台生态为主要生产方式的现代金融供给服务。新时代下，我国社会主要矛盾发生了重大变化，人民日益增长的物质文化需要同落后的社会生产之间的矛盾逐渐转化为人民日益增长的美好生活需要和不平衡不充分的发展之间的矛盾。新金融强调的以人民为中心的发展思想、实现人民对美好生活向往的目标导向、聚焦解决社会民生领域难点和痛点的问题意识，以及科技性、普惠性、共享性的内在特征，都体现了促进国家治理体系和治理能力现代化、提升社会治理效能的目标导向。

新金融是金融回归本源的抓手。西方金融是以资本为中心，为的是实现资本的价值最大化；新金融则是以人民为中心，为的是实现人的最终解放和自由全面发展。新金融的出发点和落脚点是为了实现人民对美好生活的向往，新金融探索是国有大型银行在新时代不忘初心、牢记使命的具体体现。面对新的形势和挑战，金融要自我革命，摒弃以资本为中心的自我循环模式，回归初心和本源。

近年来，建设银行实施了住房租赁、普惠金融、金融科技“三大战略”，建设劳动者港湾和建行大学，以“开启第二发展曲线”的新路径，全面推进新金融行动。我们在新金融模式上的先行探索，从深层次看正是新时代大潮中推动治理体系和治理能力现代化的生动实践。新金融的路径选择，赋予银行格局和视野、情怀和担当，让金融能够真正成为解决社会问题、整合社会资源的耦合剂。建设银行致力于用金融“温柔的手术刀”，努力化解社会难点、痛点。

住房租赁。习近平总书记在党的十九大报告中强调房子是用来住的、不是用来炒的，要求加快建立多主体供给、多渠道保障、租购并举的住房制度。2019 年中央经济工作会议将大力发展租赁住房列为 2020 年重点工作。建设银行作为国有大行、住房金融领域最专业的银行，有责任先行一步、主动作为，履行好政治责任和社会责任。据此，建设银行启动了“蓝海项目”，成立建信住房服务公司，目的就是为了破解社会痛点问题，用金融的力量特别是创新手段疏通房地产市场循环不畅的梗阻。这也契合了中央经济工作会议提出的“促进形成金融和房地产的良性循环”的总体思路和要求，更是十九届四中全会强调构建住有所居的国家基本公共服务制度、推进统筹城乡的民生保障制度的具体实践。“要租房，到建行”“房子是用来住的，租挺好”“长租即长住，长住即安居”，实际上是在引导市场、引领居民消费习惯，传递新时代的新观念、新文化。

普惠金融。十九届四中全会鲜明地提出，要健全具有高度适应性、竞争力、普惠性的现代金融体系，这凸显了新时代的新金融以民为本、普惠共享的方向定位。普惠金融围绕小微、双创、扶贫、涉农等领域，涵盖范围广泛，关系国民经济质量和效益，关系就业和民生改善，是解决新时代发展不平衡不充分的社会主要矛盾、实施乡村振兴、打好脱贫攻坚战、支持实体经济补短板、降低社会融资成本，推动全面建成小康社会的迫切需要，是商业银行践行创新、协调、绿色、开放、共享新发展理念的战略要地。为此，建设银行提出普惠金融战略行动计划，即迅速实施“双小”（小行业、小企业）战略。用“双小”与“住房租赁”“金融科技”相互形成战略支持，用“双小”连接和承接“双大”（大行业、大企业），用住房租赁连接和承接住房按揭，用金融科技连接和承接对公对私业务，从而充分融合原有优势，紧密连接外部市场，造就建设银行差异性和综合性的竞争优势。

金融科技。科技赋能加速着行业的跨界，未来银行想要生存，就一定要成为高科技型的金融企业。建设银行启动“金融科技”战略，以科技支撑普惠金融、住房租赁，历时六年打造“新一代”系统并形成技术优势，融现代科技、客户洞察、金融场景、产品运营于一体，由过去技术应用者向行业引领者、标准制定者跨越。我们成立了建信金融科技公司，启动金融科技“TOP+”战略——强化科技驱动，为金融发展创新深度赋能；推动能力开放，为社会提供技术和信息共享服务；拓展平台生态，为客户和合作伙伴营造生态圈。我们努力以共享的理念整合资源，以科技的力量造福大众，以金融的智慧回馈社会。

劳动者港湾。我们在1.4万个物理网点开设“劳动者港湾”，为快递小哥、环卫工人、出租车司机等户外劳动者提供歇歇脚、喝喝水、上厕所的地方，让老百姓感受到金融服务的温度，以细微行动推动着基层社会治理新格局的建设。未来我们将积极适应社会治理和服务重心向基层下移等政策要求，依托覆盖全国的劳动者港湾，着眼基层社会治理特别是社区治理的新趋势新要求，不断创新服务方式、丰富服务内涵，并影响和带动更多的金融同业、合作伙伴参与到这个事业中来，形成多方合力推动社会治理体系建设的新气象。

建行大学。我们走出金融街，建立以企业为主体、以市场为导向、产学研深度融合的技术创新体系，与科研院所、大专院校结合，共同研究、共同面对鲜活的金融案例。我们走到普罗大众中间，推动新金融与教育深度融合，让更多人了解并学会使用金融工具，让新金融“甜水”如涓涓细流，融入老百姓的日常生活中，随拿随用，应享尽享。在这样的时代背景下，建设建行大学和产教融合联盟成为我们的必由之路。作为国有大行，我们主动尝试跨前一步，承担起推动构建新金融生态的社会责任。

新金融的探索实践，让我们深切认识到，金融说到底是社会实践活动，金融的宗旨就是为实体经济服务。金融的本真模样不是为了追求虚假的繁荣，而是要扎扎实实地贴近社会、源于生活、聚焦问题；金融机构不仅要服务金字塔塔尖上的荣耀，更要去“滋润”金字塔底层的中小企业和个人，这也是一个国家长治久安的根本之道。新金融唯有回归服务本源，根植实体经济，关注民生百姓，才能与时代发展同方向、同步调，方能行稳致远。

新金融的探索实践，让我们深切认识到，客户行为因科技而变，提升金融服务也必须以科技驱动。新金融的科技属性外在表现为金融工具属性的变化和延伸，其深层逻辑则在于通过科技手段将金融服务做到极致。我们改变传统科技附属于银行业务和流程的定位，以金融科技思维重新武装和再造，使金融科技本身成为产品和服务，成为价值创造活动。

新金融的探索实践，让我们深切认识到，金融本源和初心的回归之路，绝非金融机构单枪匹马、孤军作战所能成就。未来的组织和个人都是万物互联中的一个节点，联网才能整合资源、携手并进；断网就会孤舟难行、事倍功半。当我们沿着“以人民为中心”的理念，走出银行自身框架，想要越来越主动地发挥作用、承担更多社会责任，就需要与更多社会机构、高校、企业携手共建。

新金融的探索实践，让我们深切认识到，新时代下的新金融有大量的已知要更新，有大量的未知要探究。基于金融业实际和前瞻的理论研究、学术研究、实务研究愈发重要。

本书是建设银行 2018 年部分学术研究论文选编，是我们探索实践新金融首年全行员工对新金融的理论思考和实践总结。结集成书，以期为新时代中国金融发展贡献微薄智慧，也请专家和从业人士指正。

田国立

Preface Ⅰ

New Finance and New Responsibilities in the New Era

Today, China is moving close to the center of the world stage as it shifts its role from an embracer to a driver of economic globalization, from a recipient to a supplier of capital, providing more and more proposals to address global challenges along the way. Since the 18th CPC National Congress, China has scored even more remarkable historic achievements in reform, opening up and the drive of socialist modernization, and realized a historic leap forward from national independence to national prosperity and strength; the construction of socialism with Chinese characteristics has ushered into a new era.

We need a financial sector that is competent enough to match China's status as a rising global power and state-owned financial enterprises are playing a key role in it. As an important, reliable source of support for the CPC in the financial sector, state-owned financial enterprises must take on more responsibilities and contribute more to the implementation of national strategies in the new era.

In retrospect, since the 17th century the world has been hit by nine massive, catastrophic financial crises whose prominent negative externalities threw the world into unimaginable chaos: the tulip crisis of the Netherlands, the South Sea Bubble in Britain and the financial panic in the United States before the 20th century; the U. S. banking crisis and stock market collapse in the early 20th century; the Black Monday that cast shadow on global stock markets in 1987; the Mexico financial crisis in 1995; the Asian financial crisis in 1997; and the U. S. subprime crisis in 2008. In particular, the last — the 2008 U. S. subprime crisis was considered the worst since the Great Recession in the 1930s, due to the unseen breath and depth of its immeasurable damages to the society.

Laozi, a great Chinese philosopher, once remarked, "The highest excellence is like that of water; the excellence of water appears in its benefiting all things without competing with them." The rise and fall of stock markets, the real estate market, the P2P market and so on all tell that the energy of the financial sector exists objectively; how to harness the energy in our favor is a question worth pondering. Finance is like water; only when it is governed by goodwill and in the right way can it benefit the society and the people. Well-governed, the financial sector will realize its highest excellence; poorly-governed, it will deviate from its original aspiration and might even end up like floods, spreading damages as it goes out of control. Therefore, we are not after the volume, but the greatness of the financial sector.

Along with a new era comes new coordinates. In the new era, facing new economic and social conflicts, financial institutions must wake up from the revelry on the back of "grey rhino" and say goodbye to the days of easy money; it's time to make a change. At the Fifth National Working Conference on Financial Affairs, Chinese President Xi Jinping laid down some key principles, the first of which is that the financial sector should "return to its original purpose that is to serve economic and social development." This is the direction for financial development in the new era — to meet the people's needs for a better life. Therefore the financial sector should come back to its original purpose: to serve the society and help people live a better life.

Finance holds the bloodline of the society and economy. Financial professionals should go beyond their deskwork, reach out to the wider society to gain a better understanding of it, develop a broader, far-sighted vision and better grasp the general trend and direction of social development. With a thorough, insightful knowledge of social issues, financial professionals can turn financial instruments into the gentlest, painless scalpel to address all sorts of difficulties and pain points in the society. Of courses, there are other solutions than financial ones to these issues, but they will cause side effects of varying degrees, such as greater cost and social pain inflicted. Now financial services are more and more indispensable in every aspect of society and will be "always online," whenever, wherever and whatever you need. Financial institutions have the social responsibility to address social issues, and the modern technology has made it possible for them to come up with specialized financial solutions. Through financial innovation, the financial industry will seek deep connection with other industries in various forms, advance social progress and reform and safeguard social justice, and give bigger play to its role as the "core of modern economy" in social governance, environmental protection, public charity and humanistic care.

Along with a new era come new requirements. In 2014, President Xi expressed his expectation that we should sharpen our abilities to serve national development, guard against financial risks and compete with international rivals. As a leading financial institution in China,

China Construction Bank must set an example in responding to the call of the CPC Central Committee and in translating the Xi Jinping Thought on Socialism with Chinese Characteristics for a New Era and the central government's guidelines and policies governing economic and financial affairs into innovative financial practices.

The finance industry is the core of modern economy, and in the Chinese finance industry, state-owned major banks are a key force and should have the country's general interest in mind, instead of focusing on profit seeking. Any financial institution that is self-centered and goes after virtual assets and bubbles is doomed to go astray. As a state-owned major bank, we must be strongly responsible to our country and people, take the initiative to shoulder our due responsibilities as a pillar force of national development and to fit into the national development strategies, and contribute to the country's economic and social development. As a market entity, we should also advocate socialist core values, live and safeguard the mainstream values in Chinese society, and be responsible for and capable of promoting socialist core values and advanced culture in the new era.

A new era calls for new finance which must serve the new era into which it is born. New finance refers to modern financial services with data as the key production element, science and technology as the central tools, and platform ecosystems as the main means of production. In the new era, the principal contradiction facing Chinese society has evolved. Previously the principal contradiction was described as one between "the ever-growing material and cultural needs of the people and backward social production". What we now face is the contradiction between unbalanced and inadequate development and the people's ever-growing needs for a better life. What new finance stresses is the people-centered development philosophy, the goal to meet people's needs for a better life, the awareness to concentrate on addressing the difficulties and pain points concerning people's livelihood, and that it should be high-tech, universal and for all. All this points to one direction: the modernization of state governance system and capabilities and the improved efficiency and effects of social governance.

To direct the financial industry to its original purpose, new finance has a key role to play. In the West, the financial industry is capital-centered, aimed to maximize the value of capital; in China, new finance is people-centered, aspiring for the eventual liberation and free, all-round development of mankind. All the new finance is about and after is to meet the people's needs for a better life, and by fumbling into the unknown realm of new finance, state-owned major banks, including CCB, are telling the world that we remain true to our original aspiration and keep our mission firmly in mind in the new era. Facing the new circumstances and challenges, the financial industry should revolutionize itself, discard the capital-centered self-repeating mode and go back to its original aspiration and mission.

In recent years, CCB have launched housing rental, inclusive finance and fintech strategies and built Workers' Harbors and the CCB University to explore a new path towards "the second development curve" and advance new finance on all fronts. Our pioneering exploration with the mode of new finance represents, deep down, our effort to drive the modernization of governance system and capabilities. While seeking and selecting the right path for new finance, the banks will develop a broad vision and a strong sense of responsibility and financial services will truly become the coupling agent to address social issues and integrate social resources. CCB have been committed to solving difficulties and pain points in the society by applying the "gentle scalpel" of finance.

First, home rental. In his report to the 19th CPC National Congress, President Xi made it clear that housing is for living, not for speculation and demanded the establishment of a housing system involving diverse suppliers, diverse channels and providing both home rental and purchase services. Among the priority tasks listed for 2020 at the 2019 Central Economic Work Conference, one is to vigorously develop housing rental. As a state-owned major bank with apparent specialty and advantage in housing finance, CCB has the responsibility to take the initiative to fulfill its political and social responsibilities. To this end, CCB has launched the Blue Sea Program and founded the CCB Housing Service Co., Ltd., trying to employ financial services, especially financial innovation, to stimulate the goods and capital flow in the real estate market. This is in line with the guideline and requirement proposed at the Central Economic Work Conference: "to form a virtuous mutually reinforcing cycle between finance and real estate." This is also a vivid case of us contributing to a national public service system that ensures people's right to housing and an urban-rural social protection system, as stressed at the fourth plenary session of the 19th CPC Central Committee. "Want to rent a home? Ask the CCB." "Home rental is good." "Long-term rental brings you long, comfortable stay." All these slogans are delivering new messages to shape the market and consumer behavior in the new era.

Second, inclusive finance. Again at the fourth plenary session of the 19th CPC Central Committee, it was made clear to build a modern financial system that is highly adaptive, competitive and inclusive, highlighting that new finance in the new era should be people-centered, inclusive and for all. Inclusive finance covers a wide range of areas such as micro and small enterprises, mass entrepreneurship and innovation, poverty reduction and agriculture, and is vital for the quality and efficiency of national economy and for the improvement of employment and people's living standards. It is badly needed to address the current principal contradiction caused by unbalanced, insufficient development, vitalize the countryside, reduce poverty, make up for the weak links in the real economy, lower the financial cost, and contribute to building a moderately prosperous society in all respects. It also represents a strategic highland for commercial banks to pursue innovative, coordinated, green, open and inclusive development. It is in this context that CCB comes up with the inclusive finance strategic action plan which targets small industries and enterprises. Starting with small industries and enterprise, we hope to form mutual strategic support between home rental products and fintech and then extend to big industries and enterprises. We also hope to supplement home mortgage products with home rental ones, apply fintech to both institutional and personal banking services, then fully integrate our existing strengths, closely follow external markets, and build up our differentiated, comprehensive competitive edge.

Third, fintech. Technology is enabling cross-sector development at a faster pace. To survive the future competition, banks must transition into high-tech financial enterprises. CCB has launched the fintech strategy and developed technologies to support its inclusive finance and home rental products. After six years of efforts, we have developed a new-generation technology system and superior technical know-how based on modern technology, customer insights, financial scenarios and product operation. We are shifting our role from a technology user to a market leader and standard setter. We have founded the CCB Fintech Co., Ltd. and launched the "TOP+" fintech strategy, to give technology a bigger role in enabling innovative financial development; to share our technologies and information with the society; to build platform ecosystems for partners and clients. We are working hard to integrate and share resources, benefit the general public with technology and give back to society through financial solutions.

Fourth, the Workers' Harbors. We have set up the Workers' Harbor in 14,000 physical outlets, with free chairs, drinking water and toilets open to ordinary workers such as deliverymen, sanitary workers and taxi drivers. It is a small step to bring financial institutions closer to ordinary people and form a new pattern of social governance at the primary level. In the future, as the gravity of social governance and services moves downward, we will respond to the new trend and requirements in social governance at the primary level, especially community governance, and keep introducing innovative services to diversify our service package through our nationwide network of Workers' Harbors. At the meanwhile, we hope to attract more peer institutions and partners to join us and form a synergy to build a sound social governance system.

Fifth, the CCB University. We have gone beyond the Financial Street to form a market-oriented technology innovation system where CCB plays the leading role and integrates deeply with universities and research institutes. We have partnered up with research institutes and institutions of higher education to study typical financial cases in reality. We have promoted new finance among the ordinary people, raised their financial literacy and taught them how to use financial instruments, so that new finance will trickle endlessly into every aspect of their daily life, at their disposal whenever they need. It is against such a background that the CCB University and the Industry-Education Integration Alliance for New Financial Talents become inevitable choices. As a state-owned major bank, we have taken a step ahead of others and shouldered our social responsibility for building a new finance ecosystem.

All these explorations in new finance have brought home to us several things. First, financial services are in the end social practice, whose purpose is to serve the real economy. Financial services are provided not to fuel bogus boom; instead, they should be problem-oriented, as relevant to people's everyday life as possible. Financial institutions should not only serve the few privileged sitting at top of the pyramid, but also "nurture" the vast number of individuals and small and medium-sized enterprises at the bottom. This is the ultimate way leading to sustained stability of a nation. Only when it refocuses on the original purpose of serving the real economy and the ordinary people can new finance keep aligned and pace with the times and achieve steady, sustainable growth.

Second, considering the impact of technology on consumer behavior, we must employ technology to improve financial services. New finance should be technology-driven, as shown in the functional changes and extension of financial instruments. The underlying belief is that technology can maximize the value of financial services. Therefore, we think out of the box where technology is an affiliate of banking services and procedures, and turn the fintech thinking into products and services that can create value.

Third, to redirect the focus of the financial industry to its original aspiration and mission, financial institutions alone are not enough. In the future, all organizations and individuals will become nodes in the Internet of Things. Only when you are connected with others can you seek common progress by integrating resources; disconnected, you will find it difficult to navigate alone and get less for more. As we become more and more people-centered and go beyond our role as a banking institution, we will want to play a bigger role and shoulder more social responsibilities. To do that, we need to work with more social groups, institutions of higher education and other businesses.

Last but not least, facing new finance in the new era, we have a lot of knowledge to update and unknown to explore. Hence theoretical research, academic research and real-world research based on the reality and prospects of the financial industry are gaining importance.

This book collects selected academic papers by our CCB colleagues in 2018 and sums up our thoughts on and practice in new finance in the first year of its birth. We hope this book will do its part to serve China's financial development in the new era and we look forward to your comments.

Tian Guoli

序二

会天下智识　应百年变局

百年变局　风起云涌

“放眼世界，我们面对的是百年未有之大变局。”这是习近平总书记对世界发展大势做出的重大战略判断。如何正确理解和把握这个“大变局”？我们首先应该深刻思考世界和中国发生了怎样的变化，认清世界格局和中国社会演进的趋势，才能在“大变局”中应对全新挑战，把握发展机遇，为全球治理体系创新贡献中国智慧。

当前，全球格局深度调整。气候变化、政治冲突、贸易摩擦、金融危机等全球性议题的广泛性、综合性和复杂性，使得各国之间政治经济的相互联系日趋紧密。伴随着科技革命及由此引发的产业变革，世界经济重心开始由西向东、由北向南转移，新兴经济体和发展中大国地位不断上升，世界政治舞台上出现的非西方国家主导的全球性国际机制，对全球地缘政治和经济格局产生重大影响，传统的西方主导的国际体系呈现出非西方化与多极化并行的演变趋势。在风云变幻的世界格局中，中国共产党团结和带领中国人民锐意进取、不懈奋斗，实现了从站起来、富起来到强起来的伟大飞跃。在经济实力、国防实力、综合国力进入世界前列，国际影响力、感召力和塑造力得到前所未有的提升过程中，中国正日益走近世界舞台中央，努力为解决世界难题提供中国方案，发出愈发坚定而响亮的中国声音。

“前景十分光明，挑战也十分严峻。”在“三期叠加”、经济新常态和中美贸易摩擦的大背景下，国内外风险挑战显著增多，中国社会稳定大局和经济持续健康发展的基础持续承压。各种因素相互交织，给金融业的发展也带来巨大挑战，商业银行躺着都能赚钱的日子已然远去。

作为全球系统性重要银行之一，建设银行不应只关注资产负债表上的数据变化，局限于利润增长、规模扩大的追求，更应有大视野、大胸怀及忧患意识，应当有所为有所不为，要行其然还要知其所以然，承担起金融业领军企业的社会责任。2018 年年初，建设银行党委做出“着眼长远发展，打造新型智库”的重大战略安排，决定打造建行研究院，建立一个国际化、开放性的思想汇聚平台。这既是积极落实党的十九大精神、建设中国特色新型智库的重大举措，也是推进业务高质量发展，打造独特竞争优势的战略部署。诞生和成长于这样的时代背景下，研究院工作开展的内在遵循理应立足当下，提前谋划，剥开问题的表象，找准问题的核心，运用经济金融的专业思维求解国家发展和社会运行的痛点、难点问题。

柳暗花明　且行且探

“金融服务无所不在，就是不在银行网点。”这是美国创新银行家布莱特·金对银行业的未来做出的判断。

技术革命的浪潮席卷各行各业，金融科技业已覆盖到客服、风控、营销和授信等金融业务的核心流程，重塑着金融业的产业链、供应链和价值链。区块链、数字货币等新生事物会如何发展？金融科技未来又会催生出哪些更新更好的金融产品、业务流程及商业模式？

当前，中国正由商品和要素流动型开放转向规则等制度型开放，多项金融对外开放重大政策密集出台，金融业对外开放迈开实质性脚步。金融开放是为了解决中国现在的经济，特别是金融领域中的哪些问题？将给现在的金融体系带来哪些改变？国内的商业银行是否已经做好了应对准备？

随着金融自由化、全球化以及金融创新的发展，商业银行的风险呈现更加多样化、复杂化的趋势。在《巴塞尔协议Ⅲ》推进实施，国内外监管政策日趋严格的背景下，银行如何提升全面风险管理水平？金融法制环境建设和监管体系还存在哪些薄弱环节？

……

众多关乎社会经济发展、科技进步，甚至银行业生死存亡的课题摆在我们面前，有待我们去追根溯源，问诊破局。这些问题当中，或许有些能够通过已有的经验和办法暂时应对，但有些则必须以更高远的站位审视，以更先进的研究理论和方法提出预见性的判断。这一方面凸显了金融业加强研究力量、重视研究投入的重要性和急迫性，同时也对研究工作的前瞻性和有效性、研究人员的能力和素养提出了更高的要求。

习近平总书记曾说：“调查研究是谋事之基、成事之道。没有调查，就没有发言权，更没有决策权。”做好调查研究并非易事。作为银行业的研究人员，特别是青年研究人员，面对纷繁复杂的局势变化，更要“咬定青山不放松，任尔东西南北风”，以“不变”的研究态度应对“万变”的外部形势。

过去我曾长期从事研究工作，对研究工作的辛苦和不易深有体会。结合我自己的经验，我认为一个优秀的研究人员应该抱有以下几个“不变”的态度。首先要有心怀家国、志存高远的心态。古人云：“凡作传世之文者，必先有可以传世之心。”其实讲的就是写文章、做学问“立意”要高远，“胸怀”要宽广。具体到研究工作上，就是要找到真正有意义的研究主题，多思考一些对建行、对社会、对国家发展有价值的事情，在发现、分析、解决真问题的过程中，努力成为建行企业精神的践行者、社会责任的承担者、国家命运的开创者。其次，要有开放包容、开拓创新的心态。社会发展进入数字时代，“世界无边界”的趋势愈发明显，研究人员更要扩宽视野和格局，善于发现行业领域出现的新问题、新事物，拥抱研究领域的新理论、新方法，学会利用科技和数据的力量为研究赋能；在学术交流中应有“和而不同”的理念，乐于在知识的共享和思维的碰撞中接受检验，共同提升。再次，要有淡泊名利、久久为功的心态。从事研究工作，光有兴趣、有能力是不够的，还得耐得住寂寞，坐得住冷板凳，以持之以恒的精神坚持钻研。好的研究离不开接地气的实地调研、客观的数据分析、理性的解读视角，以及不懈的知识积累。为了发表文章而写，为了出名谋利而写，肯定做不出好的研究。

金融新风　百花齐放

新时代呼唤新金融。近年来，建设银行秉持善念之本和善治之道，坚持以习近平新时代中国特色社会主义思想为引领，聚焦“三个能力”建设，推动金融供给侧结构性改革，创造性地实施住房租赁、普惠金融、金融科技“三大战略”，开启“第二发展曲线”，在发挥传统金融优势的基础上，积极探索新时代金融价值取向与功能作用：建立住房租赁平台，缓释社会住房刚需；推动普惠金融落地，创新模式引领市场；发力金融科技创新，海纳百川汇聚新动能；温情打造“劳动者港湾”，引起社会同频共振；开放建设建设银行大学，打造产教融合新模式……通过一系列卓有成效的探索，建设银行打开了新局面，在解决痛点、服务民生中抓住了发展新机遇，赢得了社会大众的尊重与肯定。

新金融的创新实践是全行发展的战略导向，自然也是全行研究工作开展的坚定指引。2018 年秋，研究院围绕“三个能力”建设和“三大战略”实施，开展了研究成果征集活动。全行上下热烈响应，总行各部门、分行、子公司、海外机构精心组织，积极支持，员工踊跃投稿，577 篇研究论文纷至沓来。在论文评选中，研究院坚持“公平、公开、公正”的原则，经过初选、学术查重、交叉初审等环节后，共选出 279 篇进入复审环节。经过人民银行、双一流高校及总行相关业务部门专家的匿名评审，60 余篇论文从中脱颖而出。这些获奖论文涉及宏观经济、建行战略、风险管控、业务发展等诸多方向，既有宏观视野下的实证分析和顶层设计，也有微观视角切入的业务思考和政策建议，在观点、内容或方法上具有较好的前瞻性、实效性和创新性，充分体现出建行员工的经济金融理论和研究功底，基于业务实践的深入思考和立足建行、放眼世界的全球眼光。

“奇文共欣赏、疑义相与析。”我们从此次众多优秀研究成果当中选取部分论文汇编成集，一方面希望在全行营造重研究、求创新、谋发展的氛围，鼓励员工热爱研究、投身研究，通过研究推动建行业务发展，助力新金融理念深入落地；另一方面，我们也希望搭建一个学术研究与业务实践的交流平台，与同行同业共享经验智慧，碰撞思想火花，争取让这些成果对银行业务决策、金融业改革发展产生促进影响，对金融研究体系的完善建设起到积极的推动作用。

研究工作倡导“百家争鸣，百花齐放”，建行研究院“会聚之道，和而不同”的立院宗旨也鼓励不同思想的交汇、不同观点的碰撞、不同智慧的共享。借本书的出版，我们期冀与同道一起“立足本业，建言国家”，为中国经济金融理论与实务研究、为中国经济的高质量发展、为百年大变局中的国家命运贡献金融人的智慧和力量。

黄　毅

Preface II

Gather Brainpower Worldwide to Respond to a Changing World

A Changing World

"Looking at the world at large, we're facing a period of major change that's rarely seen in a century," noted President Xi Jinping about the world development as a whole. Then how to correctly understand and respond to the "major change"? First of all, we should reflect on what changes have occurred in China and the world at large, grasp the development trend in China and worldwide. Only then can we deal with all the new challenges and seize opportunities that follow the "major change" and contribute Chinese wisdom to building a more innovative global governance system.

The global pattern is experiencing profound changes. Inter-state political and economic ties are increasingly cemented as they join hands to tackle such global issues as climate change, political conflicts, trade frictions and financial crisis, which are becoming more and more widespread, comprehensive and complicated. The technology revolution and the ensuing industry reforms are driving the gravity of the world economy from west to east, north to south. The global status of emerging economies and major developing countries is on the rise. As a result, non-Western-dominated international mechanisms have emerged on the world political stage, and become a major force to reshape the global geopolitical and economic landscape. The international governance system, once dominated by Western powers, is shifting to two parallel directions: de-westernization and polarization. Despite all the external changes, the Communist Party of China has united and led Chinese people in a tireless struggle, propelling China into a leading position in terms of economic and technological strength, defense capabilities, and composite national strength. The Chinese nation has stood up, become rich and grown strong. Its international influence and appeal are growing as never before. China is approaching the world stage center, strives to come up with proposals for global challenges and makes its loud and firm voice heard by the world.

"The prospects are bright, but the challenges daunting." We are facing more and more risks and challenges at home and abroad: we have to deal simultaneously with the slowdown in economic growth, making difficult structural adjustments, and absorbing the effects of the previous economic stimulus policies as we enter into the new normal of economic growth, in addition to the ongoing trade frictions with the U. S. All these have added to the pressure on China to maintain a stable society and a sustainable, healthy economy. The pressure is also felt by the financial industry; for commercial banks, the days are long gone when the money could pour in even in their sleep.

A global systemically important bank (G-SIB), China Construction Bank should not be only interested in the balance sheet, profits or business scale, but should aim high, see far and wide, and be risk-conscious. We should know what to do and what not to, do the right thing and know why it is right, and assume our social responsibility as a leading financial institution. To this end, in early 2018, the CCB Party Committee proposed to "focus on long-term development and build a new-type think tank" and decided to build the CCB Research Institute and make it an international, open platform gathering top brains. This is a major step to implement the guiding principles of the 19th CPC National Congress and develop new-type think tanks with Chinese characteristics, and a strategic move to advance high-quality development and build up our unique competitive edge. Born in such a context, the Research Institute should plan in advance, focus on current issues, especially the pain points and difficulties with national development and social operation, and apply economic and financial thinking to see through the surface and reach the core of these issues.

Charting the Unknown Water

"Banking everywhere, never at a bank," American banking innovator Brett King said of the future banking industry.

As the technology revolution sweeps across all sectors, fintech has reached the core of financing industry such as client services, risk control, marketing and credit extension, reshaping its industry chain, supply chain and value chain. Moreover, what's the future for novelties such as blockchain and digital currency? What more financial products, service process and business model will fintech bring about?

As the Chinese market is transitioning from an open market with free flow of goods and factors to one with more institutional openness, the Chinese government has rolled out several policies on opening up the financial industry to foreign capital, marking a solid step toward a more open financial industry. By opening up the financial industry, what problems with the economy, especially in the financial sector, are we targeting? How will it change the current financial system? Are Chinese commercial banks ready for the changes?

Commercial banks are facing more diversified, complicated risks that arise from financial liberalization, globalization and financial innovation. What should they do to better guard againstrisks on all fronts, especially in the context of the Basel III and tightening regulation at home and abroad? What are the weak links with the legal environment and regulatory system for the financial industry?

...

All these questions concerning the socioeconomic development, technological advancement and even the survival of banking are awaiting an answer. To answer some of these questions, existing experience and approaches may suffice; but for others, we must climb high, gaze far, and apply advanced theories and methods to come up predictive conclusions. That requires financial institutions to step up research efforts and inputs as soon as possible and make sure that their research results are forward-looking and valid and their researchers competent for the tasks.

President Xi once remarked that, "Investigation and study are the foundation for success. He who makes no investigation and study has no right to speak, not to mention to decide." But investigation and study are not easy work. Banking researchers, especially young researchers, should develop serious working attitudes that won't bend to the ever-changing world.

I am a researcher for a long time and know how hard it is. In my experience, I find good researchers share the following "fundamentals" that distinguish them from others. First, they have the country's best interests in mind and their ambition is lofty. As an ancient saying goes, "Anyone who writes something that can be passed down to later generations must first have later generations in his mind." It is telling us to aim high and far in our writing and academic study. In the case of specific research projects, we must work on meaningful topics, think about which are valuable for CCB, the society and the whole country, and as we identify, analyze and solve real problems, we should put CCB's corporate spirit into practice, assume our social responsibility and be the pioneer in creating a better future for China. Next, they are open-minded, inclusive and they are pioneers and innovators. In this digital age, the world is becoming more and more "borderless," which requires the researchers to broaden their horizon, identify new problems and things in their respective area of research, embrace new research theories and methods and employ technology and data tools to support their research. In academic exchanges, they should agree to disagree, enjoy knowledge sharing and the clash of minds, and seek for common progress. Third, they are indifferent to fame and profits and persistent in their hard work. Research requires more than interest and talent, but also patience and persistence. A good research project must be based on honest field survey, objective data analysis, rational interpretation and relentless knowledge learning. Research for the sake of authorship, fame and profits is doomed to fail.

Encouraging Different Schools of Thoughts to Contend with Each Other

The new era is calling for new finance. In recent years, CCB has upheld goodwill and sound corporate governance, followed the Xi Jinping Thought on Socialism with Chinese Characteristics for a New Era, focused on developing three capabilities, and helped advance the structural reform of financial supply side. Through such innovations as home rental, inclusive finance and fintech, CCB has mapped out the "secondary development curve" to explore the orientation and functions of finance in the new era by giving play to the advantages of traditional finance. Specifically, we have built the home rental platform to meet the rigid housing demand; launched inclusive finance projects and introduced innovative models to lead the market; stepped up efforts in fintech innovation and attracted innovators from all over the world to forge a new momentum; set up Workers' Harbors to serve the ordinary workers; and opened the CCB University to explore a new mode of business-education integration... All these fruitful attempts have opened up a new situation, and allowed CCB to seize development opportunities and win public respect and recognition as it tries to address social pain points and serve the general public.

The innovative practice of new finance is the strategic orientation for our across-the-board development, and naturally the solid guide for all our research work. In the fall of 2018, the Research Institute started to solicit research papers on the building of the "three capabilities" and the implementation of the "three strategies." The call for papers was warmly answered, receiving a total of 577 papers from the head office, branches, subsidiaries and overseas affiliates alike. After preliminary evaluation, duplicate checking and preliminary cross examination based on the principles of equality, transparency and fairness, 279 papers made it to the review round. Then after the blind review by experts from the People's Bank of China, universities participating in the "Double First-Class" university project, and head office departments concerned, eventually over 60 papers were announced winners. These winning papers touch upon topics ranging from macroeconomics, CCB strategies, risk management & control and business development. Some provide empirical analysis and top-level design from a macro perspective while others offer business thinking and policy recommendations from a micro perspective. But they are all forward-looking, practical and innovative in their viewpoints, contents or methods, showing our employees' theoretical knowledge and research capabilities, what they have learnt from their actual work, and their global vision that starts from and goes beyond CCB.

We selected some of the outstanding research papers to make this book, hoping to create an atmosphere where research, innovation and development are valued and sought after, encourage employees to do research, drive our business development through research, and turn concepts of new finance into concrete actions. We also want to build a platform for academic research and business practice, where we can share experience and wisdom with peers, learn from each other, and contribute our research findings to banking decision making, financial reform, and the improvement of the financial research system.

In research, we should allow different thoughts to contend with each other and go in full bloom. The CCB Research Institute believes that "the key to attracting the best brains is to agree to disagree", and encourages different thoughts and viewpoints to fully express themselves and clash with each other. With this book, we hope to attract the likeminded to contribute our expertise to national development, in other words, our financial knowledge and strength to China's research on economic and financial theories and business, to China's high-quality economic development, and to securing China's future ina period of major change that's rarely seen in a century.

Huang Yi

目 录

宏观经济篇

普惠金融篇

住房租赁篇

金融科技篇

业务研究篇

风险管控篇

宏观经济篇

中国经济增长与杠杆率调控的逻辑关系

——基于货币政策传导的分析

江苏省分行　产　俊

一、对中国经济杠杆率水平的测算

（一）宏观层面杠杆率处于历史高位

宏观层面杠杆率一般使用总货币水平和名义 GDP（国内生产总值）的比率来衡量。本文同时测算了广义货币供应量（M2）、社会融资规模存量、银行贷款余额与同期名义 GDP 的比值。

1. 宏观杠杆率逐年走高，但趋势放缓

从近年数据来看，上述 3 项杠杆率指标呈现逐年上升趋势。2017 年年末，我国 M2 余额 169 万亿元、社会融资存量规模 175 万亿元，银行各项贷款 120 万亿元，与同期 GDP 比值分别达到 204%、211% 和 145%，均处于历史高位，分别较 2008 年提高了 56、92 和 50 个百分点。与全球 M2/GDP 相比①，我国经济杠杆率处于高位。同时，随着去杠杆和供给侧结构性改革的深入，2016 年以来杠杆率过快攀升的势头得到初步遏制。以 M2/GDP 来看，2017 年较上年下降 4 个百分点。在 2018 年 1 月的达沃斯论坛上，中国政府表示将争取用 3 年左右时间将杠杆率控制在合理水平。

2. 社会融资规模/GDP 上升速度最快

随着金融结构多元化和监管范围的扩展，银行贷款在社会融资总规模中的占比先降后升。2013 年年末，银行贷款占社会融资总量比例为 54.7%，较 2002 年下降 41 个百分点。2014 年以来影子银行监管趋严，使 2017 年贷款渠道占比回升至 71.2%。与之相对应的是，社会融资规模/GDP 曲线最为陡峭（见图 1.1 和表 1.1）。

---

① 从全球范围看，M2/GDP 也呈现不断走高的态势。1960 年全球 M2/GDP 为 52.84%，2013 年增至 126.72%，复合增长率为 1.64%。受量化宽松货币政策影响，2009 年美国 M2/GDP 达到历史最高值 90.41%。

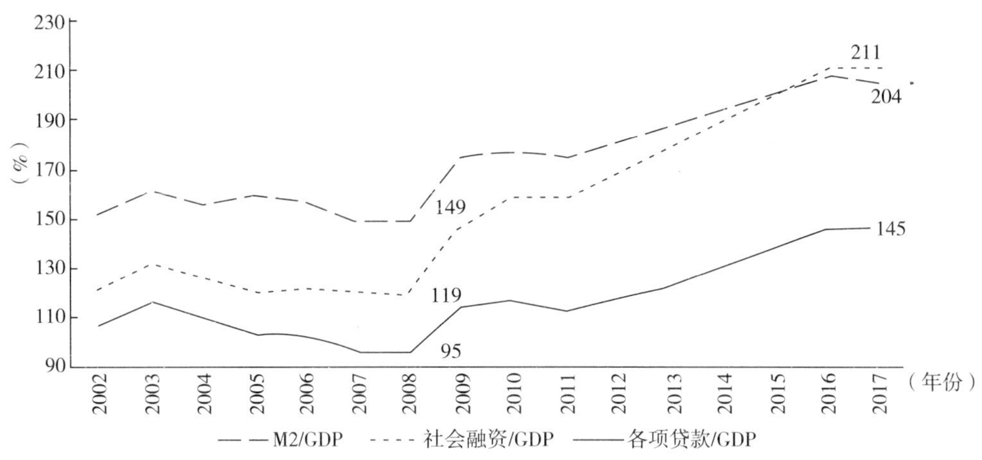

图 1.1 宏观经济杠杆率变化趋势（2002—2017）

资料来源：万得资讯。

表 1.1 我国社会融资渠道占比 （%）

年份	当年社会融资规模（亿元）	1. 银行贷款占比	2. 直接融资占比	其中：2.1 股票占比	其中：2.2 债券占比	3. 影子银行占比
2002	20 112	95.5	4.9	3.1	1.8	2.3
2003	34 113	87.9	3.1	1.6	1.5	8.2
2004	28 629	84.3	4.0	2.4	1.6	9.9
2005	30 008	83.2	7.8	1.1	6.7	6.7
2006	42 696	77.2	9.0	3.6	5.4	11.7
2007	59 663	67.4	11.1	7.3	3.8	19.8
2008	69 802	73.1	12.7	4.8	7.9	12.1
2009	139 104	75.7	11.3	2.4	8.9	11.3
2010	140 191	60.2	12.0	4.1	7.9	25.7
2011	128 286	62.7	14.0	3.4	10.6	19.7
2012	157 631	57.9	15.9	1.6	14.3	22.9
2013	173 169	54.7	11.7	1.3	10.5	29.8
2014	164 571	61.6	17.4	2.6	14.7	17.6
2015	154 086	68.9	24.0	4.9	19.1	3.7
2016	178 022	66.7	23.8	7.0	16.9	6.1
2017	194 430	71.2	6.8	4.5	2.3	18.4

资料来源：万得资讯。

（二）企业部门和金融部门杠杆运用出现分化

1. 国有企业负债率上升，经营效益下滑

以全国国有企业为样本考察企业杠杆运用情况。2008 年以来，国有企业资产负债率中枢抬升，2016 年年末资产负债率为 65.5%，较 2008 年提升了 4 个百分点。在扩大负债的同时，国企资产收益率出现明显下降，与负债率上升相背离（见图 1.2）。

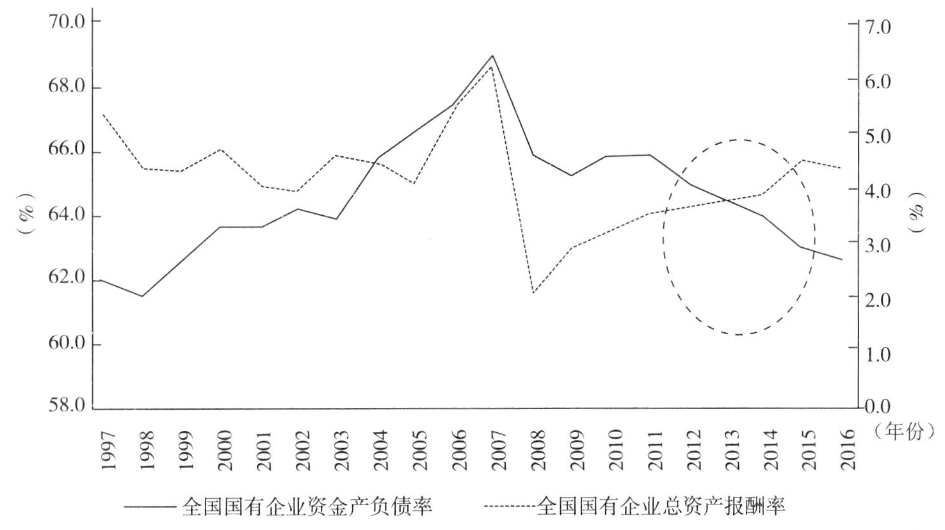

图 1.2 国有企业盈利与负债水平变化趋势

资料来源：万得资讯。

2. 商业银行总体资本充足，杠杆率较低

本文以资本充足情况衡量商业银行杠杆水平。商业银行作为中国金融体系的主体，一直受到严格的资本监管，国内主要银行也将资本管理上升到战略高度，资本充足率保持在较高水平。2018 年 6 月末，我国商业银行资本充足率为 13.57%，一级资本充足率为 11.20%，核心一级资本充足率为 10.65%，表明我国主要金融部门资本充足状况良好，且主要是损失吸收能力最强的核心一级资本，其中大型银行资本充足性最好。值得关注的是，近年股份制银行和城商行发展金融市场和资管业务较为激进，非标业务占比多超过 10%，在资管新规下表外非标转回表内将对资本充足率直接造成冲击，这也是银行体系杠杆的最主要风险之一（见表 1.2 和图 1.3）。

我国宏观经济、企业部门和金融部门的杠杆率呈现不同特征，其中，企业负债率上升而效益下滑是去杠杆的主要风险；银行体系整体资本充足则为协调稳增长和去杠杆奠定了较好基础，中小银行杠杆风险值得关注。

表 1.2　我国商业银行资本充足率　（%）

年份	资本充足率	一级资本充足率	核心一级资本充足率
2009	11.40	—	9.40
2010	12.20	—	10.10
2011	12.70	—	10.20
2012	13.25	—	10.62
2013	12.19	9.95	9.95
2014	13.18	10.76	10.56
2015	13.45	11.31	10.91
2016	13.28	11.25	10.75
2017	13.65	11.35	10.75
2018/6/30	13.57	11.20	10.65

资料来源：万得资讯。

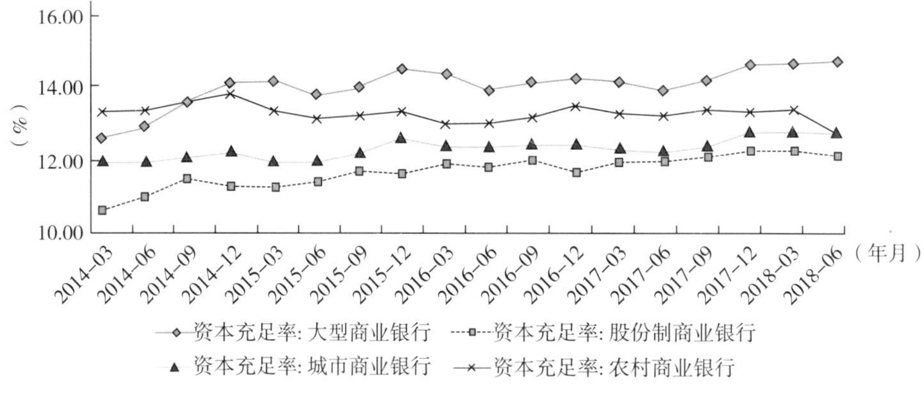

图 1.3　我国各类银行资本充足率情况

二、对稳增长和杠杆率调控的总体判断

主流货币经济理论和实践均表明，货币政策的有效性在很大程度上取决于微观主体对基准利率变化的敏感性和响应程度，同时货币政策效力具有典型的非对称性。

（一）单纯加杠杆对经济增长的拉动效益减弱

货币宽松与经济增长具有正相关性，适度宽松的货币环境和畅通的融资渠道是经济持续稳定增长的必要条件。2010 年以来，我国上市公司（非银行等）的资产收益率开始下降，整个企业部门的经营效益不容乐观，并且宏观经济景气指数的先行指标开始一路走低。实际上，自 2014 年 11 月央行启动本轮降息以来，货币宽松政策已经持续较长时间，但受制于实体经济高债务杠杆、低投资回报的困境，货币政策提振实体经济的效果并不明显，单纯的货币宽松对经济增长的拉动作用下降。

（二）货币政策非对称性会加剧去杠杆的风险

杠杆率（总债务/GDP）=（总债务/总资产）/（GDP/总资产）。分子可理解为资产负债率，分母为以增加值表示的资产收益率。这表示如果负债率下降，但收益率下降得更快，杠杆率仍会上升。紧缩政策去杠杆总体上会降低企业融资的可得性，并增加财务成本。目前我国企业整体资产负债率居高不下，根据金融加速器原理，短时间内快速去杠杆将对企业资产负债表造成明显冲击，企业账面价值的下降会进一步降低其融资能力，从而加剧去杠杆风险，不利于经济平稳运行。因此，理性去杠杆应该建立在企业经营状况见底回升的基础之上。

（三）保持稳定增长有助于降低杠杆率水平

从宏观层面看，去杠杆和稳杠杆的核心是遏制杠杆率快速上升势头，使总债务水平、总价格水平、货币总量等保持在可控范围内，守住不发生系统性风险的底线，这既要防止总货币过快扩张，也要防止 GDP 增长失速。与此同时，经济稳步增长也有助于提升对总债务的承受能力和消化杠杆。从微观角度看，去杠杆要促进金融资源流向生产效率更高的企业，降低金融资源的无效沉淀；也要尤其关注去杠杆可能导致的企业经营困难，带来盈利较负债以更大幅度下降。

三、相关建议

稳增长和去杠杆并不矛盾，稳定增长，提升长期偿债能力，有助于降低杠杆率水平；而合理的去杠杆或称稳杠杆，又往往伴随着金融资源的优化配置，可提升微观主体活力，有利于宏观经济稳定增长。

（一）继续保持适宜的货币环境

当前中国经济企稳回暖现象增多，但未来一段时间内经济增长仍面临较大压力，回暖企稳的基础尚不稳固。从稳增长和去杠杆的关系看，现阶段单靠货币政策稳增长难以取得良好效果，同时收缩银根加速去杠杆则会加剧实体经济运行的困难，存在较大的不确定性和风险隐患。因此，要继续保持稳健的货币政策，维持适度宽松的货币环境，并搭配积极的财政政策和产业政策，提高经济活力，夯实微观基础，增强债务消化能力，进而降低杠杆水平。

（二）通畅货币政策传导机制

从本质上看，杠杆率调控也属货币政策调控范畴，需畅通货币政策传导机制。目前各市场主体对货币政策的敏感性主要存在两方面梗阻：一是国有企业和地方政府融资预算软约束问题仍然存在，对利率反应钝化；二是对于众多小微企业来说，融资可获得性的重要程度远远超过融资成本问题，而目前监管层面对于银行小微企业贷款价格的控制较为严格，这种出于引导贷款价格下行的政策可能会进一步加剧融资难的问题。针对上述情况，建议从严规范政府融资，要保持高度定力和韧劲儿，对违规举债从严问责、终身追责，真正解决预算软约束；对解决小微企业融资问题，应首先从融资可获得性着手，对银行贷款价格的控制不宜过度，让小微企业贷款真正走向商业可持续，提高商业银行发展小微金融业务的积极性和内生性。

（三）拓宽实际经济融资渠道

深入推进利率市场化改革，加快直接融资发展。加快资本市场发展是我国金融改革的重要内容，一方面要防止金融风险过度集中于银行体系，另一方面要让有能力的企业从公开市场融资，并接受市场监督。同时，直接融资的发展会冲击商业银行传统的盈利模式，逼迫商业银行深耕细作，主动调整业务结构，加大对优质中小客户的信贷供给，促进金融资源的优化配置。此外，股权融资（包括公开上市、私募股权融资等）的健康发展也能直接拉低整个社会的负债水平。

（四）加强重点领域金融监管

在杠杆率快速上升的背景下，保持金融部门的资本充足至关重要。金融监管在克服顺周期性的同时，还需继续引导促进各类金融机构稳健经营。将盲目扩张的资管同业等影子银行业务纳入更加广泛的严监管范畴，遏制无序增长，维护市场持续，压缩资金在金融体系内部空转空间，让金融更好地服务于实体经济发展。

双支柱监管周期下的利率走势研究

总行金融市场部　郑天乐

一、传统利率走势研究三因子模型

传统的利率研究框架基于“名义增长决定名义利率”的基本逻辑，将经济增长率、通货膨胀率作为分析利率的基点，结合货币政策、信贷政策等因素分析利率的走势和波动。

根据传统利率分析模型，市场上常用“经济增速因子、通胀因子、货币因子”三因子模型对利率进行定价。本文选取“工业增加值”作为经济增速因子，“CPI”（居民消费价格指数）作为通胀因子，“银行间 R007”回购利率加权值作为货币政策因子，选取 2010 年 1 月 ~2018 年 9 月月度数据进行线性回归分析，获得如下回归方程式：

$$\begin{aligned}10\text{年期国债收益率} = &2.8385 + 0.02104 \times \text{工业增加值当月增速} + \\ &0.1054 \times \text{CPI 当月同比} + \\ &0.1163 \times \text{R007 加权利率月均值}\end{aligned}$$

回归结果如图 1.4 所示。

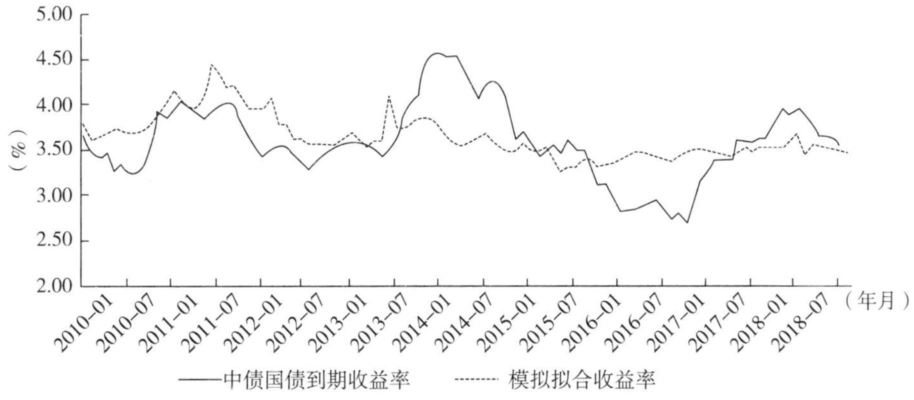

图 1.4　中债国债 10 年期到期收益率真实值与拟合值

资料来源：万得资讯。

如图 1.4 所示，2010 年至 2013 年前半期，拟合值能够较好地反映真实值的预期走势，但自 2013 年 5 月以后，拟合值较为平坦，而真实值则经历大起大落。该模型的拟合程度较弱，拟合曲线难以反映真实的收益率曲线。

分析其中原因，从 2013 年开始，在监管收紧和资产回表过程中，国内经济发展的转型、金融监管带来的货币金融环境变化，使传统框架并不能完整解释利率水平的走势和波动。尤其是 2016 年以后，在名义经济增长较为平稳或温和上行的背景下，10 年期国债收益率却快速上行。名义增长率与名义利率走势的分化，说明经济基本面对债市的影响出现了弱化。央行《2017 年第三季度中国货币政策执行报告》指出：传统货币政策盯住物价稳定，但即使 CPI 较为稳定，资产价格和金融市场的波动也可能很大。所以价格稳定并不等于金融稳定（见图 1.5）。

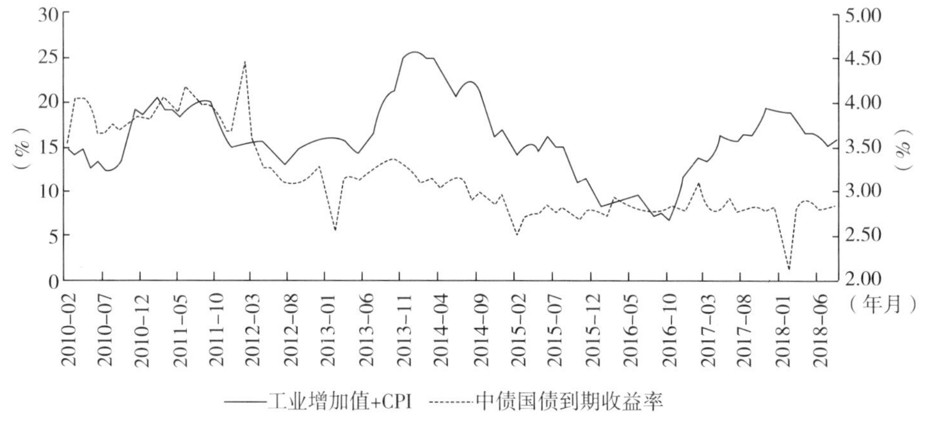

图 1.5　中国名义经济增长与名义利率走势变化

资料来源：万得资讯。

中国在经历 2008 年金融危机后，通过宽松的货币与财政政策迎来经济回升，通货膨胀率大幅提升，成为影响债市的重要因素。而 2013 年以后，债券市场主要逻辑已经开始发生转变，此时的通胀水平下降，宏观经济也未出现回升，国债收益率却大幅上行。分析其中原因，2013 年政府管控影子银行体系，货币条件收紧；2016 年下半年以来，以金融去杠杆为目标的金融监管政策不断加码，货币政策目标转向稳增长、去杠杆和防风险，数量型调控转向价格型调控。宏观审慎双支柱框架不断完善，前期银行表外业务无序扩张，使其在监管收紧后面临较大回表压力，又因货币基金等存款替代类产品的发展，银行负债荒问题凸显，存贷款基准利率存在加息的可能性，对利率水平也有一定影响。

综上所述，在分析 2013 年以后的利率周期时，除了考虑传统的经济增长、通胀和货币政策因素以外，还要考虑宏观审慎政策因素。宏观经济和双支柱调控成为本文分析利率走势的逻辑框架。

二、双支柱调控下的四因子模型

根据上述分析逻辑，本文选用四因子驱动分析框架来分析长端利率。基本面因素仍从“工业增加值”和“通货膨胀”进行分析，而货币政策升级为“货币政策和宏观审慎双支柱调控”后，单一货币政策因子无法描述“双支柱”。本文将采取其他存款性公司资产负债表中对“金融机构债权（不含央行）的增速贡献”作为宏观审慎因子，与“货币市场利率”一同作为政策因子。

商业银行“对金融机构债权”在一定程度上反映的是扣除居民、企业和政府融资需求后商业银行的可配置的资金投向，也在一定程度上反映了商业银行资产端的富余程度。2012—2013 年的非标业务创新，以及 2015—2016 年的同业理财和委外业务的创新，均表明了当监管政策约束不到位时，商业银行会在信贷以外的资产科目进行监管套利和业务扩张，从而导致“对金融机构债权”总量的扩张。

当监管政策约束不到位时，“对金融机构债权（不含央行）”会快速扩张，增速上行；监管政策收紧后，“对金融机构债权（不含央行）”增速则快速下行。因此，本文将“对金融机构债权（不含央行）”对资产端的增速贡献作为“宏观审慎政策”的映射因子。图 1.6 展示了“对金融机构债权（不含央行）”对资产端的增速贡献与 10 年期国债（右轴，逆序）之间的相关性。相关性背后反映的是宏观审慎监管政策的缺失与填补，通过商业银行资产配置行为，在长端利率上产生的定价影响。

图 1.6 “对金融机构债权（不含央行）”增速拉动与 10 年期国债

资料来源：万得资讯。

通过对上述微观因子的选取，我们来进行回归分析和四因子利率定价。经济增速因子为工业增加值当月增速，通货膨胀因子为 CPI，货币政策因子为 R007 加权利率月均值，宏观审慎因子为对金融机构债权（不含央行）的增速拉动。

线性拟合公式如下：

10 年期国债收益率 = 3.001408 + 0.029173 × 工业增加值当月增速 +
0.041698 × CPI 当月同比 +
0.172304 × R007 加权利率月均值 -
0.05538 × 对金融机构债权的增速拉动

回归结果如图 1.7 所示。在加入宏观审慎因子后，回归结果在细节上更加完善，能够较好修正局部的背离。尤其是 2017 年以来，经济基本面因素变动小，三因子模拟结果维持在 3.5% 左右，但真实市场利率却持续走高。加入宏观审慎因子后的四因子模型则展示出较好的拟合结果。由此，本文得出结论：2017 年以来，影响长端利率的重要定价因素之一是“宏观审慎政策”的实施力度。

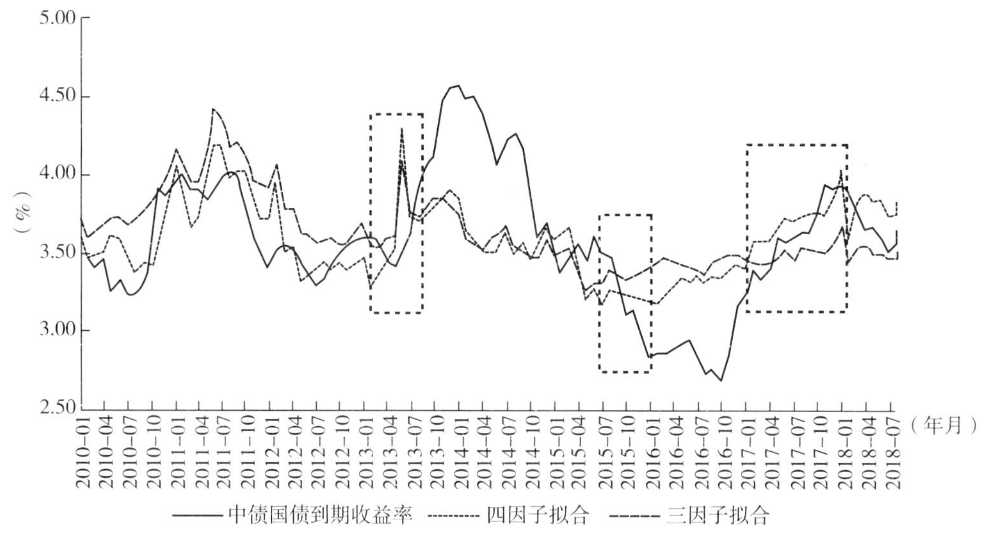

图 1.7　10 年期国债收益率曲线与三因子、四因子拟合示意

资料来源：万得资讯。

三、基于四因子对 2013—2018 年利率走势的回顾性分析

根据 2013—2018 年债券市场的实际走势，用上述因子复盘债券收益率长端变动，并结合相关因素分析收益率曲线变动情况，2013—2017 年可划分为以下四个阶段。

第一阶段，2013 年年初至 2013 年 10 月——“平坦化上行”。伴随着美国、欧洲经济日益明显的复苏态势，美联储退出量化宽松政策的预期对国内债券市场承压，中国经济继续保持弱复苏，维持平稳和缓增长惯性。国内继续实行积极的财政政策和稳健的货币政策，并逐步推出大规模财政刺激举措，同时 CPI 稳步提升至超 3%。6 月，在准备金备付、国内外流动性收缩、财政缴款延后及季末等多重因素影响下，流动性高度紧张，市场上称为“钱荒”。同业杠杆高企的问题引发监管层高度关注和控制。央行在《2013 年第三季度中国货币政策执行报告》中以专栏形式专章论述了商业银行的同业业务，银监会在 2013 年 11 月上报《商业银行同业融资管理办法》，并于 2014 年 2 月开始实施。市场监管力度之大使得流动性弥足珍贵，货币市场利率一年内出现两次大幅波动，短端上升更为明显，使得期间内收益率平坦化上行。10 年期国债收益率上行 57bp（基点），1 年期国债收益率上行 106bp。

第二阶段，2013 年 10 月至 2015 年 3 月——“陡峭化下行继而平坦化下行”。世界经济出现较为显著的分化，美国经济强劲复苏，欧洲经济萎靡，美联储开启退出 QE（量化宽松）序幕，对国内债市承压。然而，中国经济下行压力增大，CPI 逐步向下，至 2015 年 1 月下行至阶段低点 0.76，成为期间内收益率下行的重要支撑。2014 年 5 月，央行又联合银监会等五部委发布《关于规范金融机构同业业务的通知》，意图控制同业业务超常规的规模膨胀，以防控风险。从 6 月份开始，短期限利率受此影响大幅抬升，收益率曲线平坦化，在此之后，同业杠杆出现了一段时间的平稳。10 年期国债收益率下行 79bp，1 年期国债收益率下行 93bp。

第三阶段，2015 年 3 月至 2016 年 10 月——“陡峭化下行”。国内经济基本面未见起色，宏观经济下行压力难言改善，央行出于稳增长和防控潜在系统性金融风险的目的，大幅放松货币政策，连续的降准降息操作使得流动性总量非常充裕，市场利率大幅下行至历史低位附近。2015 年股票大跌、2016 年年初熔断使得充沛资金进入债券市场，至其收益率不断下行。在低利率环境下，各类资金嵌套套利模式呈爆发式发展，银行理财余额快速飙升。虽然自 2016 年金融去杠杆监管政策不断加码后，银行理财余额和同业业务规模都有所下行，但规模的绝对值仍在上升，存量问题亟待解决，高杠杆、低超储、期限错配造成的金融风险不断上升。10 年期国债收益率下行 70bp 至 2.68%，1 年期国债收益率下行 90bp 至 2.15%。

第四阶段，2016 年 11 月至 2017 年 12 月——“平坦化上行”。11 月国际环境变化，预期新当选的美国总统特朗普将实行扩大基建和财政刺激政策，促使美国经济复苏带动美债收益率上行，中美利差缩窄也成为利率上行的支撑。2016 年年底以来国内一线城市的房价不断攀升，带动楼市回暖，客观上促进了经济的回暖和通胀上行压力，GDP 增速高于去年同期。货币政策由中性转为稳健中性，略为收紧，央行锁短放长，短期资金利率的抬升使得杠杆套利行为无以为继。国家的监管思路从“稳增长”向

“防风险”转变。2016 年年底的中央经济工作会议首次提出“去产能、去库存、去杠杆、降成本、补短板”五大任务，将同业去杠杆概括纳入了“防范化解金融风险”的总体任务中。2017 年 3 ~4 月银监会密集出台多个文件，加强对债券投资、同业、理财资管等业务监管，金融去杠杆强势推进，推动 3 ~5 月收益率快速上行。11 ~12 月又相继发布资管新规和银行流动性管理新规的征求意见稿，提升市场对严监管预期，使 10 ~11 月债券收益率大幅上行，短端受监管影响更甚。10 年期国债收益率上行 120bp 至 3. 88%，1 年期国债收益率上行 164bp 至 3. 79%。

根据上述四个阶段的历史走势来看，宏观审慎监管周期在金融过热时防控严格，对利率影响大；经济下行时期管控略有放松，此时影响较小。这也是宏观审慎对经济逆周期调节功能的实现（见图 1. 8 和图 1. 9）。

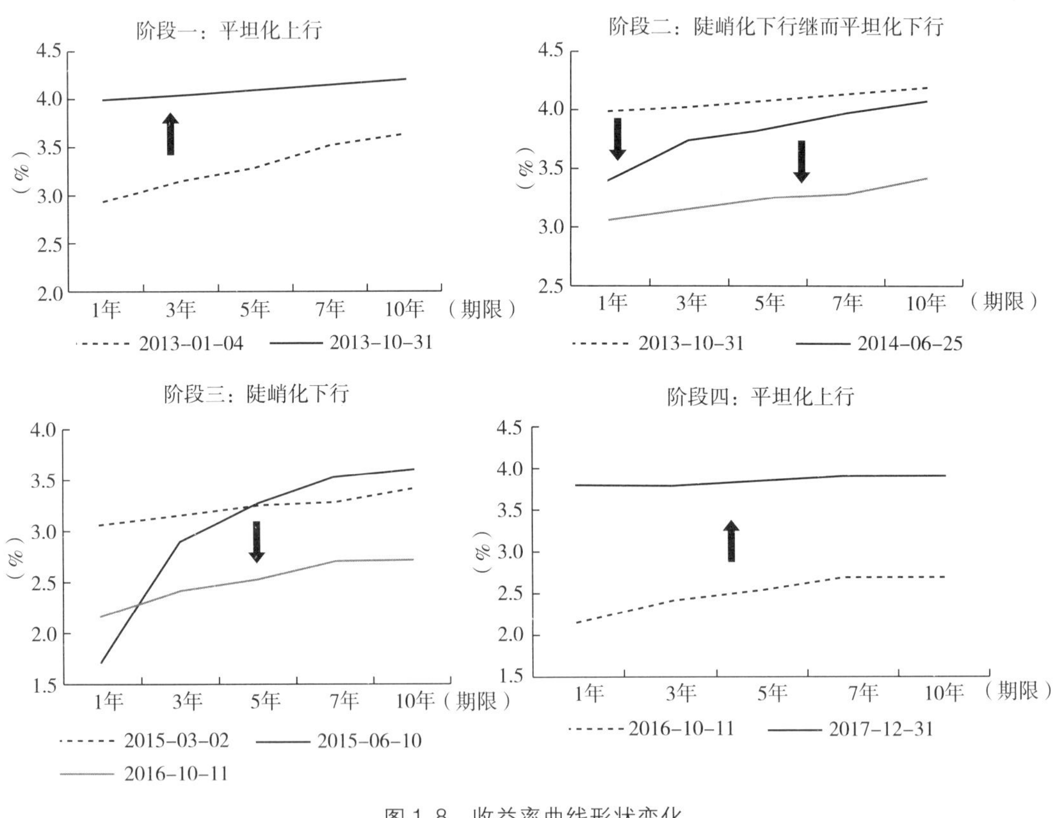

图 1. 8　收益率曲线形状变化

资料来源：万得资讯。

四、未来利率走势判断及风险提示

2018 年，市场表现和预期表现纠结，多空双方信心不足，利率震荡下行。虽然金融“三大攻坚战”政策走向不变，但力度松紧仍是判断利率走势的重要因素。2018 年

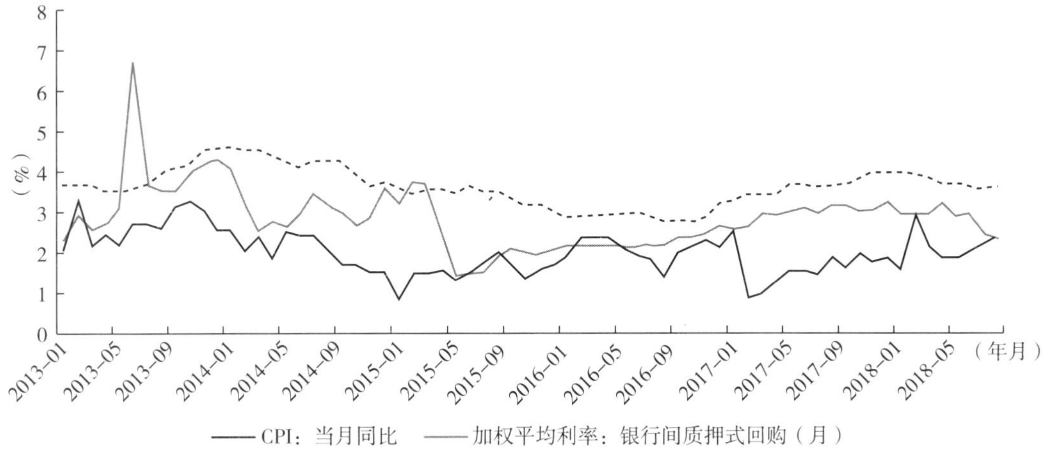

图 1.9　2013—2018 年 CPI 月同比及 7 天回购加权平均利率走势

资料来源：万得资讯。

上半年，强监管、去杠杆效果显现，市场分化明显，信用债违约爆发，国债收益率需求提升，利率下行。受货币政策缓和、资金面改善、贸易摩擦等因素影响，机构对利率债券的投资意愿上升。下半年以来，政策面发生一些重要的指向变化。7 月 23 日国常会强调实施积极的财政政策、加大基建投资补短板力度，使市场对经济基本面预期改善，中长端收益率开始进入震荡上行阶段。1 月、4 月、7 月、10 月央行分别降准，利率曲线短端变动显著。在流动性合理充裕的背景下，短端市场利率锚定政策利率并处于相对低位，而长端利率受制于金融监管收缩、通胀预期和美债约束，利率曲线呈现陡峭化下行态势。

我个人对 2019 年的主要因子情况分析如下所述。

在消费走弱的情况下，通货膨胀受供给端冲击，面临抬升压力。猪周期一般以 4 ~ 5 年为一周期，现在刚结束 2015 年至 2018 年 5 月的下跌周期，转入上涨周期，同时叠加“非洲猪瘟”疫情，补栏量下降，供给端使得通胀预期抬升。预计 2019 年 CPI 会达到 3% 的高点后回落，年内中枢在 2.4% 左右。

在经济增长方面，由于宽货币向宽信用的传导出现阻碍，且中国经济正处于新旧动能转换时期，尚未出现明显的新的增长极，此外，民营企业与中小企业在去杠杆背景下融资困难，中美贸易摩擦对国内经济的冲击不容小视，且经历史上最长扩张周期后房地产未来面临下滑压力，导致工业增加值在 2019 年预计将有所下降，中枢在 6.2% 左右。

在宏观审慎相关政策方面，监管压力边际放缓，监管周期开始进入更偏重“稳”的层面，去杠杆工作开始着重力度和节奏的把握。这是因为国内财政政策预计会延续 2018 年第三季度的更加积极的态势，且资管新规补充通知及配套细则较预期放缓，同业杠杆可控。因此，上一利率周期中的宏观审慎监管因素对于利率短端走势的强影响将逐步削弱。现阶段该增速负增长，但存量规模快速下降的可能性也不大，因此，预计对金融机构债权增速拉动在 -0.2% 左右。

在货币政策方面，目前狭义流动性处于高位，狭义向广义的传导困难，叠加中美利差因素影响，货币政策进一步放松的可能性较小。因此，短端收益率难下，也不会骤升，预期将处于平稳震荡。R007 中枢预计在 2.8% 左右（见图 1.10）。

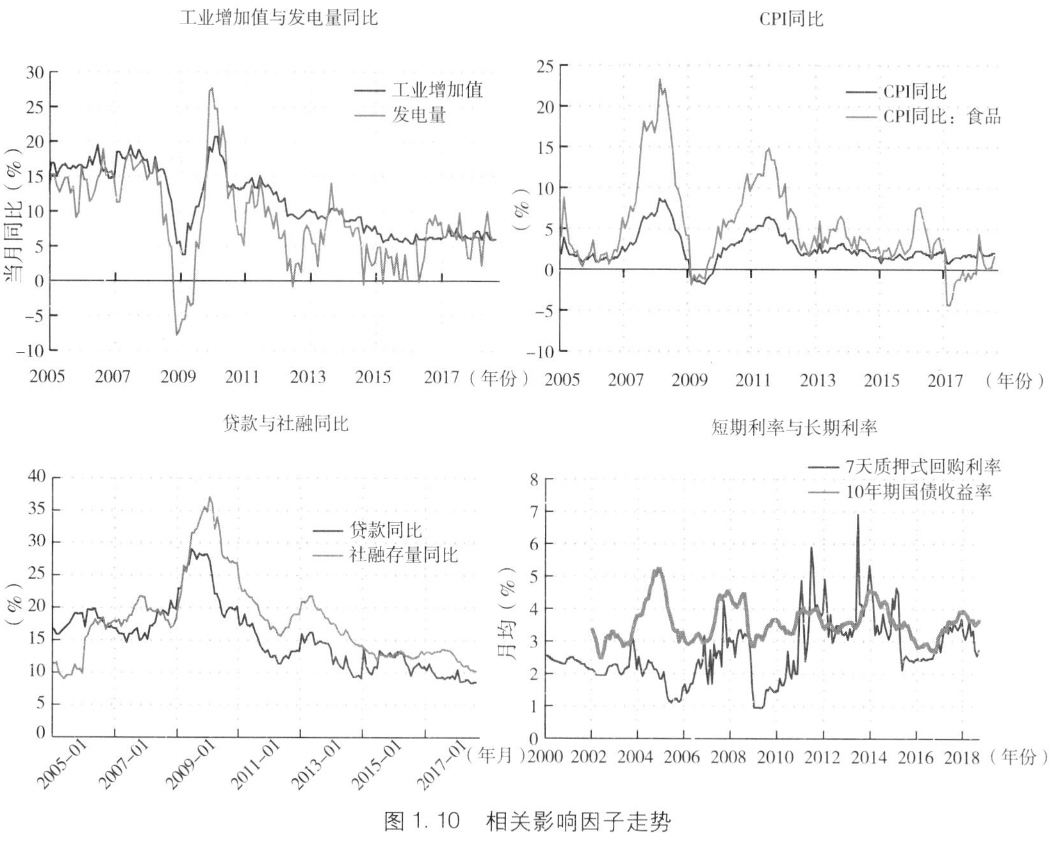

图 1.10　相关影响因子走势

资料来源：万得资讯。

基于上述因子预测，四因子模型输出的 10 年期国债收益率拟合值为 3.77%，三因子模型输出的 10 年期国债收益率拟合值为 3.54%。基于当前市场形势，经济下行风险较大，因此宏观审慎因子影响偏弱，中枢在此基础上向三因子模型拟合结果靠近，预计长端收益率将在 3.6% 左右的中枢震荡下行，低点为 3.2% ~3.3%。

风险可能会在以下几种情况中出现：经济超预期上行或下行；金融去杠杆进程放缓带来的潜在扩张可能，使得债市关键逻辑发生变化；中美贸易摩擦加剧，影响国内经济政策取向超预期变化；美国国债收益率持续上升，中美利差对国内收益率形成支撑等。

央行预期管理与银行风险承担[①]

——基于中国银行业的经验证据

湖北省分行　付英俊

一、引言

2008 年金融危机以来，金融稳定成为各国货币政策当局和金融监管部门最为关注的问题之一。货币政策与金融稳定的关系问题也引起了学者们的关注，人们开始反思货币政策除了影响经济稳定外是否也会影响金融稳定，并重新审视货币政策传统的传导机制。越来越多的研究表明，货币政策与金融稳定有着密切的关系。为了解释这种密切关系，学术界提出了货币政策的银行风险承担渠道。

货币政策的银行风险承担渠道（Risk-taking Channel of Monetary Policy），是指货币政策会影响银行等金融机构的风险容忍度，进而影响其所选资产组合的风险水平、贷款定价以及其他非价格条款（Borio and Zhu，2008）。货币政策的银行风险承担渠道表明，货币政策会影响银行风险承担，并对金融稳定造成影响。随后的许多研究证实了货币政策的银行风险承担渠道的存在性（Adrian and Shin，2010；Altunbas and Gambacorta，2010）。

我国的金融体系属于银行主导型，银行的稳定是金融稳定的核心，因此我国货币政策的银行风险承担问题尤其值得关注和研究。国内已有一些学者对这一问题开展了研究，江曙霞、陈玉婵（2012），徐明东、陈学彬（2012）等实证研究了我国货币政策的银行风险承担渠道的存在性。在已有的研究文献中，货币政策变量选取的主要是利率这一传统货币政策工具。考虑到我国货币政策工具运用的实际情况，国内也有一些学者在研究中选取了法定存款准备金率这一货币政策工具。近些年来，预期管理已成为许多国家央行重要的货币政策手段，央行沟通成为央行预期管理的重要工具。既然传统的货币政策工具如利率能影响银行的风险承担行为，作为一种新型货币政策工具

① 本文已在《云南财经大学学报》2019 年第 10 期发表。

的央行沟通是否也会影响到银行的风险承担呢？如果能产生影响，其影响机理是什么？国内外鲜有文献对这一问题进行研究。

本文的贡献在于：第一，已有的文献主要研究传统货币政策工具（利率、存款准备金率）对银行风险承担的影响，而本文从一个崭新的视角研究了作为预期管理重要工具的央行沟通对银行风险承担的影响；第二，本文对莫里斯和星（Morris and Shin，2002）模型进行扩展，从理论上分析了央行沟通对银行风险承担的作用机制，并提供了来自中国银行业的经验证据；第三，基于银行的异质性特征，本文研究了央行沟通对不同类型商业银行风险承担的影响，并研究了央行沟通对银行风险承担影响的非对称性。

二、相关文献综述

传统上，依据货币与债券之间替代性的不同，货币政策的传导渠道可以分为货币渠道（贷款与债券可以完全替代）和信贷渠道（贷款与债券不可完全替代）。金融危机爆发后，博里奥和茹（Borio and Zhu，2008）最先提出货币政策银行风险承担，分析了货币政策对金融稳定的影响。

（一）货币政策影响银行风险承担的机理

货币政策是通过何种渠道和路径影响银行风险承担的，两者之间有着怎样的逻辑关系呢？本文通过梳理相关文献，总结了货币政策对银行风险承担影响的路径与机理。

1. 收入估值效应

较低的利率会通过影响收入、估值和现金流，进而影响银行的风险承担。长期低利率的货币政策会提高抵押物的价值，降低企业的财务费用，增加其现金流。这会使银行对贷款风险过于乐观，从而降低信贷审查标准，积极增加贷款，风险承担意愿提高（Adrian and Shin，2009）。

2. 收益搜寻动机

低利率会使无风险资产相对风险资产的收益率下降更多，由于行为、心理或者契约、制度等方面的原因，银行等金融机构会进行资产替代，降低无风险资产需求，增加对高风险资产的需求，导致风险承担上升（Rajan，2006）。

3. 中央银行的沟通反馈机制

中央银行的沟通策略也会影响到商业银行的风险承担。较高的货币政策透明度和可信性降低了未来的不确定性，使银行对未来通胀水平和远期利率水平有着较准确的预测和判断，从而降低了风险溢价，最终导致银行低估风险，产生“透明度效应”（Borio and Zhu，2012）。中央银行的透明度效应是本文研究的逻辑出发点。

（二）货币政策对银行风险承担影响的理论研究

对于货币政策的风险承担渠道的理论研究目前还比较少。在货币政策的银行风险承担渠道的理论研究上，莱温和德拉里恰（Laeven and Dell'Ariccia，2011）的研究发现，低利率的货币政策会导致银行的杠杆率上升，风险承担意愿增加。银行杠杆率和资本充足率会影响货币政策银行风险承担行为。巴伦西亚（Valencia，2014）的研究认为政策利率下降会降低银行的融资成本，使银行积极放贷，增加其自身的风险承担。莫里斯和星（2014）通过建立一个博弈模型，分析了货币政策的风险承担渠道。雅维耶（Javier Bianchi，2014）在一个包含银行部门的DSGE模型框架下，研究了不同的利率规则对金融部门风险承担的影响。夏仕龙和付英俊（2017）用公司金融中的资本结构理论重新构建了货币政策的风险承担模型。

（三）货币政策对银行风险承担影响的实证研究

阿尔通巴什和甘巴科尔塔（Altunbas and Gambacorta，2010）通过采用欧元区及美国上市银行的季度数据研究发现，长期的超低利率特别是低于泰勒规则基准值的利率将导致银行风险承担的增加。德利斯和考雷塔斯（Delis and Kouretas，2011）通过采用欧元区国家银行年度数据发现，较低的短期利率增加了银行的风险承担，并发现银行表外业务的增加会加剧货币政策对银行风险承担的负向影响。比什、艾克迈尔和普列托（Buch，Eickmeier and Prieto，2011）的实证研究发现，货币政策对美国小型银行、大型银行、外资银行的风险承担影响不同。德拉里恰等（2016）运用美国银行业内部评级数据，提供了对美国银行系统货币政策银行风险承担的经验证据。张雪兰和何德旭（2012）提供了我国货币政策银行风险承担的实证证据，并发现市场结构、银行资产负债特征对银行风险承担存在重要影响。徐明东和陈学彬（2012）发现资本充足率、资产规模等银行特征变量会对货币政策的银行风险承担渠道产生影响。牛晓健、裘翔（2013），刘生福和李成（2014）等也提供了我国货币政策银行风险承担渠道存在的经验证据。

此外，关于预期管理对银行风险承担和金融市场稳定的影响方面，汪莉和王先爽（2015）研究了央行的预期管理政策对通货膨胀和银行风险承担的影响，发现央行的预期管理政策会通过影响通胀预期的波动，进而影响银行的风险承担行为。李云峰等（2014）基于我国的《金融稳定报告》，分析了央行沟通对金融市场波动的影响，认为央行沟通是维护金融市场稳定的一种重要手段。弗拉茨克等（Fratzscher et al.，2008）研究了央行沟通在维护外汇市场稳定中的重要作用。博恩等（Born et al.，2014）认为中央银行的金融稳定性沟通对维护金融稳定有着积极作用。

综合国内外相关文献来看，一些文献通过构建理论模型研究了货币政策的银行风险承担，但此类文献尚比较少。大多数文献从实证角度研究了货币政策银行风险承担渠道的存在性，主要研究利率对银行风险承担的影响，但鲜有文献关注央行预期管理对银行风险承担的影响。本文与汪莉和王先爽（2015）的文献不同的是，前者是在“信息黏性”模型基础上分析有无预期管理信息情形下通胀预期波动的不同，进而实证研究通胀预期的波动对银行风险承担产生的影响，间接研究了央行预期管理对银行风险承担的影响，而本文是通过最新统计方法构建央行沟通指数来测度央行预期管理，直接考察央行预期管理与银行风险承担的关系。

三、央行沟通影响银行风险承担的理论分析

货币政策的风险承担渠道的“央行透明度效应”为我们提供了研究思路，它表明央行沟通会影响银行风险承担水平。从本质上讲，即央行释放的公共信息会影响商业银行的行动决策。莫里斯和星（2002）的模型研究了公共信息对社会福利的影响，是研究信息社会价值的经典文献。本文借鉴莫里斯和星（2002）模型并进行扩展，分析央行沟通对商业银行风险承担的影响。假设存在一个连续集的商业银行个体 i，i 服从［0，1］均匀分布。p_i 表示单个商业银行的风险承担，R 表示全体商业银行的风险承担集，$p_i \in R$。p 表示所有商业银行的风险承担，θ 表示经济基本状态，商业银行 i 的支付函数为：

$$u_i(p,\theta) = -(1-w)(p_i-\theta)^2 - w(L_i-\bar{L}) \tag{1}$$

其中，ω 是一个常数，且 $0 \leqslant \omega \leqslant 1$，$L_i = \int_0^1 (p_j - p_i)^2 dj$，$\bar{L} = \int_0^1 L_j dj$。支付函数分为两项，第一项是银行的风险承担 p_i 与经济基本状态 θ 之间的偏差，该部分权重为 $(1-\omega)$。第二项是“凯恩斯选美竞赛”项，它表示商业银行 i 风险承担与所有商业银行平均风险承担之间的差异，表明商业银行 i 希望与其他商业银行保持行动一致，这一部分的权重为 ω。ω 越大，表明商业银行更看重与其他商业银行行为保持一致，体现从众动机；ω 越小，表明商业银行更看重其行为与经济基本面保持一致。对于商业银行 i，其最优的风险承担可由其效用最大化的一阶条件得出：

$$p_i^* = (1-\omega)E_i(\theta) + \omega E_i(\bar{p}) \tag{2}$$

其中 $\bar{p}$ 是所有商业银行的平均风险承担，$E_i(\cdot)$ 表示商业银行 i 的条件期望 $E(\cdot \mid Y, X_i)$。关于 θ，所有商业银行面临不确定性，但商业银行 i 能依据央行披露的公共信息 Y 和其拥有的私人信息 X_i 对 θ 进行预期。公共信息 $Y = \theta + \eta$，私人信息 $X_i = \theta + \varepsilon_i$，$\eta \sim N(0,\sigma_\eta^2)$，$\varepsilon_i \sim N(0,\sigma_\varepsilon^2)$，$\theta$ 与 η 相互独立，ε_i 与 θ、η 相互独立，$E(\varepsilon_i\varepsilon_j) = 0(i \neq j)$。

我们把公共信息的精确度记为α，私人信息的精确度记为β。其中，$\alpha = \frac{1}{\sigma_\eta^2}$，$\beta = \frac{1}{\sigma_\varepsilon^2}$。根据所获得的公共信息 Y 和私人信息 X_i，商业银行 i 对经济基本状态 θ 的期望值为：

$$E_i(\theta \mid Y, X_i) = \frac{\alpha Y + \beta X_i}{\alpha + \beta} \tag{3}$$

为了求得均衡解，假设商业银行的最优风险承担 p_i^* 可以表示为央行披露的公共信息 Y 和商业银行拥有的私人信息 X_i 的一个线性组合，并且假设存在唯一均衡。商业银行 i 的最优风险承担为：

$$p_i^* = kX_i + (1-k)f(\sigma_\eta^2)Y \tag{4}$$

其中，$f(\sigma_\eta^2)$ 表示中央银行的信誉度函数，$0 \leqslant f(\sigma_\eta^2) \leqslant 1$。本文研究认为，中央银行沟通是一个双向的过程，中央银行沟通的效用不仅取决于中央银行向公众所披露信息的精确度，也取决于公众对中央银行的信任度。这也是本文与莫里斯和星（2002）模型的主要不同之处。

所有商业银行平均风险承担的条件期望为：

$$E_i(\bar{p} \mid Y, X_i) = k\frac{\alpha Y + \beta X_i}{\alpha + \beta} + (1-k)f(\sigma_\eta^2)Y \tag{5}$$

将（3）式和（5）式代入（2）式化简得到：

$$p_i^* = \frac{\beta[1-\omega(1-k)]}{\alpha + \beta}X_i + \frac{\alpha + \omega\beta(1-k)}{\alpha + \beta}f(\sigma_\eta^2)Y \tag{6}$$

比较（4）式和（6）式的系数，可以解得：$k = \frac{\beta(1-\omega)}{\beta(1-\omega)+\alpha}$，由此得到商业银行的最优风险承担为：

$$p_i^* = f(Y) = \frac{\alpha f(\sigma_\eta^2)Y + \beta(1-\omega)X_i}{\alpha + \beta(1-\omega)},\ \frac{\partial f(Y)}{\partial Y} > 0 \tag{7}$$

由（7）式可知，商业银行的最优风险承担 p^* 与央行沟通信息 Y 之间呈正向关系。央行沟通释放的宽松信号越强烈，商业银行风险承担水平越高。当 $\alpha \to \infty$，$f(\sigma_\eta^2) = 1$ 或者 $\beta = 0$，$f(\sigma_\eta^2) = 1$ 时，$p^* = Y$ 则表明当公共信息非常精确、中央银行声誉很高时，或者私人信息极不精确、央行有着很高的声誉时，商业银行的风险承担行为将完全依赖于央行公共信息，而不会受私人信息的影响。据此，我们得出结论：央行沟通会影响商业银行的风险取向，央行沟通释放货币政策宽松的信号越强烈，商业银行的风险承担意愿就越高。

四、变量与数据说明

（一）央行沟通指数的构建

央行沟通分为书面沟通和口头沟通，《中国货币政策执行报告》是央行重要的书面沟通方式。欧阳志刚（2013）发现，央行口头沟通与《中国货币政策执行报告》具有高度一致性。因此本文主要以《中国货币政策执行报告》为央行沟通的研究对象，借鉴海涅曼和乌尔里克（Heinemann and Ulrich，2005）的文本分析法构建央行沟通指数。第一，将货币政策分为扩张期、中性期和紧缩期。第二，提取出反映货币政策倾向的关键措辞。本文综合卞志村（2012）与林建浩（2015）的方法，选择了通胀、紧缩、流动性偏多等 19 种措辞类型。第三，筛选出在不同货币政策时期出现频率具有显著差异的措辞。第四，在第三步筛选出措辞的基础上，进一步筛选出在不同货币政策时期出现频率满足单调性的措辞。第五，构建央行沟通指数。借鉴海涅曼和乌尔里克（2005）的方法，构建沟通指数的公式为：

$$CB_t = \sum_{i=1}^{k} \frac{nobs(x_{i,t}) - mnobs(x_i)}{stdv(x_i)} \cdot sign(x_i) \cdot \omega(x_i) \tag{8}$$

其中，CB_t 为我国央行沟通指数，$nobs(x_{i,t})$ 表示措辞 i 在 t 时期出现的频率，$mnobs(x_i)$ 表示措辞 i 在每期出现频率的均值，$stdv(x_i)$ 表示措辞 i 在每期出现频率的标准差，$\omega(x_i)$ 为措辞 i 所占的权重，$sign(x_i)$ 指的是措辞 i 的符号。当货币政策信号为宽松时措辞符号为正，当货币政策信号为紧缩时措辞符号为负。图 1.11 显示了我国央行沟通指数的走势。

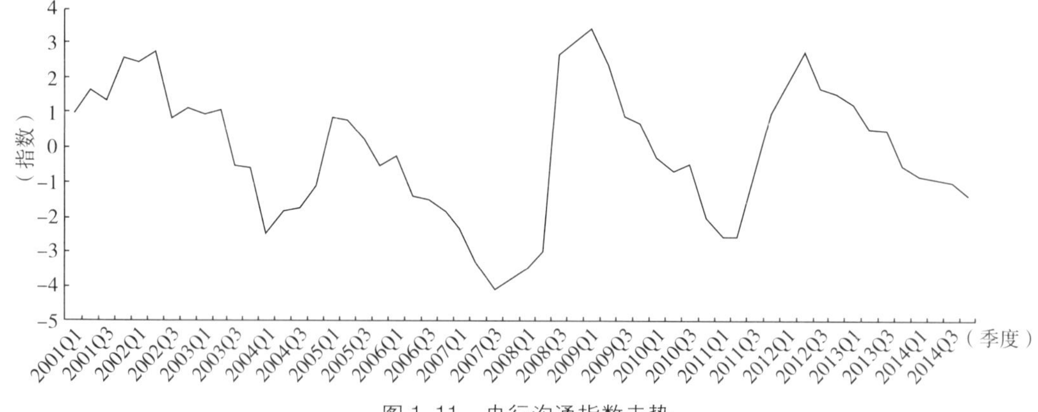

图 1.11　央行沟通指数走势

（二）银行风险承担变量（RISK）

关于银行风险承担指标的选择，目前的文献主要选用预期违约率（EDF）、Z 值、不良贷款率、加权风险资产比率等来衡量银行风险承担。由于我国缺乏违约率数据，所以银行业的 EDF 数据难以获得。我国银行业贷款按风险实行五级分类，不良贷款余额可操作空间大，而且由于监管部门对商业银行的不良贷款问题十分重视，导致商业银行对不良贷款率的重视程度远高于对利润率的重视程度。风险加权资产较难获得，计算方法也各异，误差较大。因此综合分析后，本文选择 Z 值[①]作为银行风险承担的衡量指标，同时在稳健性检验中，以不良贷款率（NPL）作为考察指标。

（三）货币政策代理变量（MP）

国外学者多以短期利率作为货币政策的代理变量，考虑到我国货币政策调控的实际特征和本文的研究目的，除了选用央行沟通（CB）作为货币政策代理变量外，还选取 1 年期贷款基准利率（RATE）和法定存款准备金率（RE）分别作为价格型货币政策工具和数量型货币政策工具的代理变量。

（四）控制变量

为了有效识别央行沟通对银行风险承担的影响，还需控制其他可能影响银行风险承担的变量。根据已有的相关文献，本文引入银行层面控制变量为资本充足率（CAP）、银行规模（SIZE）和资产收益率（ROA），其中银行规模用银行总资产的对数来表示。宏观层面控制变量为名义 GDP 的增长率（GDPN）和通货膨胀率（CPI）。

考虑到央行沟通指数数据的季度性特征和银行业季度数据的可获得性，本文选择的样本为 2007 年第一季度至 2014 年第四季度我国 14 家上市银行的平衡面板数据。样本始于 2007 年，主要是因为大部分上市银行在 2007 年才开始公布季度数据。样本银行包括中国银行、工商银行、建设银行、交通银行 4 家大型国有商业银行，招商银行、中信银行、华夏银行、民生银行、平安银行、浦发银行、兴业银行 7 家全国性股份制商业银行，还有南京银行、北京银行、宁波银行 3 家城市商业银行。数据来自 Bankscope 数据库、万得数据库、人民银行和国家统计局网站。表 1.3 为主要变量的描述性统计结果。[②]

---

① Z 值定义为：$Z_{it}=(ROA_{it}+EA_{it})/\sigma_i(ROA_{it})$，$ROA$ 表示资产收益率，EA 表示资本资产比率，$\sigma(ROA)$ 表示资产收益率的标准差。Z 值表示每一单位资产风险有多少资产收益与自有资本来弥补。Z 值越高，银行破产概率越小。由于 Z 值偏度较高，借鉴莱温和莱维纳（Laeven and Levine，2009）的做法，对其进行对数化处理。同时，由于 Z 值与银行风险承担水平负相关，为了在回归中和其他风险承担代理变量的系数解读保持一致，取 Z 值得相反数进入实证分析。参考以往文献做法，本文使用了第三季度滚动数据来计算 ROA 的标准差，为检验滚动期选择可能产生的影响，我们还计算了第二季度和第四季度的滚动数据，发现对基本结论影响不大。

② 农业银行和光大银行由于在 2010 年才上市，数据缺失严重，因此不包括在样本中。此外考虑到季节性因素的影响，我们对 GDP 等部分变量进行了季节性调整。

表 1.3　主要变量的描述性统计

变量	变量含义	均值	标准差	最小值	最大值
Z	Z 值	2.95	0.24	2.14	3.62
NPL	不良贷款率（%）	1.14	0.83	0.34	7.00
CB	中央银行沟通指数	-1.80	2.25	-4.10	3.46
RATE	1 年期贷款基准利率（%）	6.18	0.69	5.31	7.47
RE	法定存款准备金率（%）	17.37	3.12	9.83	21.50
CAP	资本充足率（%）	12.09	2.43	3.88	30.14
SIZE	银行总资产的自然对数	14.35	1.34	11.11	16.76
ROA	资产收益率（%）	0.75	0.35	0.09	1.73
GDPN	名义 GDP 的增长率（%）	5.60	1.73	1.89	9.48
CPI	通货膨胀率（%）	3.43	2.40	-1.53	8.03

五、模型构建与实证检验

（一）实证模型的构建

1. 不同货币政策工具对银行风险承担影响的基准模型

根据前文的分析，同时考虑到银行风险承担行为的持续性特征，本文在德利斯和考雷塔斯（2011）研究的基础上建立动态面板基准模型（9）：

$$RISK_{it} = \alpha_0 RISK_{i,t-1} + \alpha_1 MP_t + \alpha_2 CAP_{it} + \alpha_3 SIZE_{it} + \alpha_4 ROA_{it} + \alpha_5 GDPN_t + \alpha_6 CPI_{t\ i} + \varepsilon_{it} \tag{9}$$ [①]

货币政策代理变量的系数 α_1 的符号和显著性是本文重点关注的问题。前文的理论分析表明，正向的央行沟通会提高银行的风险承担水平，因此当货币政策代理变量为央行沟通时，α_1 应显著为正。现有的实证文献大都表明，宽松的货币政策操作（降低利率或法定存款准备金率）会鼓励银行风险承担，反之，紧缩的货币政策操作（提高利率或法定存款准备金率）会抑制银行风险承担，因此当货币政策代理变量为基准贷款利率（RATE）或法定存款准备金率（RE）时，α_1 应显著为负。

2. 考虑央行沟通对银行风险承担影响是否依赖于银行资本充足率

随着我国从 2004 年开始实施《巴塞尔协议》，资本充足率监管成为制约我国银行

---

① 因为《中国货币政策执行报告》发布滞后，当货币政策代理变量是央行沟通时，采用滞后一期值 CB_{t-1}。即 t-1 期值的央行沟通会影响 t 期商业银行的风险承担。

行为的重要因素。不同资本状况的银行其风险承担行为和抵御货币政策冲击的能力可能存在异质性。为了考察央行沟通对银行风险承担的影响是否取决银行资本充足率，本文设定模型（10）：

$$
\begin{aligned}
RISK_{it} = & \alpha_0 RISK_{i,t-1} + \alpha_1 CB_{t-1} + \alpha_2 CAP_{it} + \alpha_3 SIZE_{it} + \\
& \alpha_4 ROA_{it} + \alpha_5 GDPN_t + \alpha_6 CPI_t + \\
& \alpha_7 CB_{t-1} \times CAP_{it} + \varepsilon_{it}
\end{aligned} \tag{10}
$$

3. 考虑央行沟通对银行风险承担影响是否依赖于银行系统重要性

国际金融危机后，金融稳定理事会等国际监管机构提出了“系统重要性金融机构”的概念，认为系统重要性金融机构对整个金融体系的稳定起到至关重要的作用。金融稳定理事会将我国的“中、农、工、建”四大行列入全球系统性重要银行名单。我国银保监会根据“规模、关联度、不可替代性（金融基础设施）、复杂性”的不同，将“中、农、工、建、交”划分为我国的系统重要性银行。由于农业银行不包括在样本内，本文定义“中、工、建、交”为我国四大系统重要性银行。为了考察银行系统重要性是否会影响银行的风险取向，我们对基准模型进行扩展，得到模型（11）：

$$
\begin{aligned}
RISK_{it} = & \alpha_0 RISK_{i,t-1} + \alpha_1 CB_{t-1} + \alpha_2 CAP_{it} + \alpha_3 SIZE_{it} + \\
& \alpha_4 ROA_{it} + \alpha_5 GDPN_t + \alpha_6 CPI_t + \\
& \alpha_7 SYS_{it} + \alpha_8 SYS_{it} \times CB_{t-1} + \varepsilon_{it}
\end{aligned} \tag{11}
$$

其中，SYS 表示系统重要性虚拟变量，当样本银行属于系统重要性银行时，SYS 取值为1；当样本银行是非系统重要性银行时，SYS 取值为0。

4. 考虑央行沟通与银行风险承担是否存在非线性关系

博里奥和茹（2008）研究认为，当出现流动性过剩或者银行等金融机构存在较强的政府救助预期时，货币政策与银行风险承担之间并非是简单的线性关系，而可能存在非线性关系。为了检验我国央行沟通与银行风险承担之间是否存在非线性关系，设定模型（12）：

$$
\begin{aligned}
RISK_{it} = & \alpha_0 RISK_{i,t-1} + \alpha_1 CB_{t-1} + \alpha_2 CAP_{it} + \alpha_3 SIZE_{it} + \\
& \alpha_4 ROA_{it} + \alpha_5 GDPN_t + \alpha_6 CPI_t + \\
& \alpha_7 CYCLE_t + \alpha_8 CYCLE_t \times CB_{t-1} + \varepsilon_{it}
\end{aligned} \tag{12}
$$

其中，$CYCLE$ 表示货币政策周期虚拟变量。我们依据央行沟通指数划分货币政策周期，如果央行沟通指数 $CB_t > 0$，则视为货币政策扩张期，$CYCLE$ 取值为1；反之，若央行沟通指数 $CB_t < 0$，则视为货币政策紧缩期，$CYCLE$ 取值为0。

（二）实证结果与分析

在模型（9）（10）（11）（12）中，由于有被解释变量的滞后项作为解释变量，若采用传统的估计方法（如OLS方法、固定效应估计等），得到的参数估计将是有偏差和不一致的，因此我们采用GMM估计。GMM分为系统GMM和差分GMM，由于系统GMM损失的信息比差分GMM更少，估计偏差更小，故本文采用系统GMM估计。系统GMM估计又包括一步GMM和两步GMM，两步GMM估计的权重矩阵受估计参数影响，标准差存在向下偏离，并没有明显提高估计效率且估计量不可靠，一步GMM估计虽然效率有所下降但估计是一致的，因此本文最终选择一步系统GMM方法。

1. 不同货币政策工具对银行风险承担影响检验

表1.4为模型（9）对不同类型的货币政策影响商业银行风险承担的估计结果。二阶序列相关检验和Sargan检验结果均不能拒绝原假设，表明工具变量的选择是有效的。回归结果显示，银行风险承担变量的一阶滞后项Z（-1）的系数显著为正，表明我国银行风险承担具有惯性特征。央行沟通对银行风险承担具有显著正向影响，说明央行

表1.4　不同货币政策工具对银行风险承担影响检验

变量	央行沟通	基准贷款利率	存款准备金率
Z（-1）	0.2655** （0.020）	0.2491** （0.030）	0.3088** （0.030）
MP	0.0112*** （0.000）	-0.0173** （0.031）	-0.0048** （0.050）
CAP	-0.0289*** （0.002）	-0.0275*** （0.001）	-0.0251** （0.012）
SIZE	-0.1752* （0.072）	-0.1680** （0.034）	-0.0605** （0.036）
ROA	-0.1792*** （0.000）	-0.1799*** （0.000）	-0.1809*** （0.000）
GDPN	0.0004 （0.803）	-0.0013 （0.402）	-0.0033** （0.020）
CPI	-0.0002 （0.970）	-0.0127** （0.045）	-0.0097 （0.228）
观测值	327	327	327
AR（2）（p值）	0.318	0.687	0.307
Sargan（p值）	1.000	1.000	1.000

注：括号内为p值，*表示10%的显著性水平下显著，**表示5%的显著性水平下显著，***表示1%的显著性水平下显著。

沟通释放的宽松信号鼓励了银行的风险承担，与预期一致。基准贷款利率（RATE）和法定存款准备金率（RE）对银行风险承担具有显著负向影响，表明货币政策宽松时，银行愿意承担更多风险。货币政策紧缩时，银行风险承担受到约束，和预期相符。比较 3 种类型货币政策代理变量的系数可以发现，不同类型货币政策工具对银行风险承担行为影响存在差异性。在同等条件下，价格型货币政策对银行风险承担的影响最大，其次是央行沟通，最后是数量型货币政策，这表明目前我国银行风险承担对价格型货币政策反应最敏感。价格型货币政策对银行风险承担的影响大于数量型货币政策，这与江曙霞和陈玉婵（2012）、徐明东和陈学彬（2012）的研究结论一致。

从银行层面的控制变量来看，资本充足率（CAP）、资产规模（SIZE）、资产收益率（ROA）变量的系数均显著为负。银行资本充足率与银行风险承担呈现负相关关系，表明银行资本充足率越高，自有资本越多，银行的股东和债权人之间的代理问题越小，经营冒险可能性变小，风险承担意愿会更低；相反，资本充足率低的银行因为股东和债权人之间的代理问题更大，经营冒险可能性变大，风险承担意愿会更高。银行规模变量的系数显著为负，可能的合理解释是大银行受到的监管更加严格，迫于较大的监管压力，其经营更趋保守稳健，不愿意过度承担风险。贝尔特拉蒂和斯塔尔茨（Beltratti and Stulz，2011）的研究也发现，不同的银行监管密度会引起银行风险承担意愿的差异。资产收益率的系数显著为负，表明盈利能力越强的银行风险承担意愿越低，反之风险承担意愿越高。宏观层面控制变量的系数不显著，表明经济增长率和通货膨胀率对银行风险承担的影响并不明显。

2. 央行沟通对银行风险承担行为的异质性检验

表 1.5 为模型（10）和模型（11）对央行沟通对银行风险承担影响的异质性检验结果。银行资本充足率与央行沟通的交叉项（CB × CAP）系数显著为负，表明央行沟通对银行风险承担的影响会因银行资本充足率的不同而存在差异，银行资本充足率越高，抵御央行沟通对其风险承担冲击的能力也越强，换言之，银行资本充足率的提高会降低央行沟通对其风险承担的影响。系统重要性虚拟变量（SYS）的系数显著为负，表明系统重要性银行与非系统重要性银行的风险承担行为存在差异，系统重要性银行的风险承担意愿相对更低。央行沟通变量与系统重要性虚拟变量的交叉项（CB × SYS）系数显著为负，表明央行沟通对非系统重要性银行风险承担的影响更大。可能的原因是系统性重要银行受到监管部门更加严厉的监管，各项监管指标要求均高于非系统重要性银行，因而其风险承担意愿更低。例如 2011 年我国银监会[①]规定，正常时期系统重要性银行的资本充足率不得低于 11.5%，高于非系统重要性银行 1 个百分点，并对

① 现为银保监会。

系统重要性银行提出附加资本要求。还有一个可能的原因是，系统性重要银行有着政府的隐性担保，能以更低利率吸收存款，资金运用渠道也更广；而非系统性重要银行融资成本相对较高，资金运用渠道有限，只能将大部分资金投向信贷资产，风险承担意愿相对较高。

表 1.5　央行沟通对银行风险承担影响的异质性检验

变量	资本充足率	系统重要性
Z（-1）	0.2477*** (0.001)	0.2376* (0.000)
CB	0.0009** (0.044)	0.0774** (0.013)
SYS		-1.6463** (0.037)
CB×SYS		-0.1945** (0.017)
CAP	-0.0379*** (0.001)	-0.0287*** (0.000)
CB×CAP	-0.0005** (0.032)	
SIZE	-0.1124** (0.020)	0.0074** (0.040)
ROA	-0.1792*** (0.000)	-0.1646*** (0.000)
GDPN	0.0013 (0.488)	-0.0007 (0.675)
CPI	-0.0036 (0.432)	-0.0064 (0.201)
观测值	327	327
AR（2）（p值）	0.726	0.259
Sargan（p值）	1.000	1.000

注：括号内为p值，*表示10%的显著性水平下显著，**表示5%的显著性水平下显著，***表示1%的显著性水平下显著。

3. 央行沟通对银行风险承担影响的非对称性检验

表1.6为模型（12）对央行沟通对银行风险承担影响的非对称性检验结果。货币政策周期虚拟变量（CYCLE）的系数显著为正，表明宽松货币政策环境下银行的风险承担水平高于紧缩环境下银行的风险承担水平。央行沟通变量与货币政策周期虚拟变

表 1.6　央行沟通对银行风险承担影响的非对称性检验

变量	央行沟通
Z（-1）	0.2098*** (0.010)
CB	0.0247** (0.032)
CAP	-0.0285*** (0.001)
SIZE	-0.2675** (0.030)
ROA	-0.1865*** (0.000)
GDPN	0.0028 (0.203)
CPI	-0.0031 (0.329)
CYCLE	0.0294** (0.033)
CB×CYCLE	-0.0209** (0.029)
观测值	327
AR（2）（p 值）	0.756
Sargan（p 值）	1.000

注：括号内为 p 值，* 表示 10% 的显著性水平下显著，** 表示 5% 的显著性水平下显著，*** 表示 1% 的显著性水平下显著。

量交叉项（CB×CYCLE）系数显著为负，表明在同等条件下，释放紧缩信号的央行沟通对银行风险承担的抑制作用强于释放宽松信号的央行沟通对银行风险承担的激励作用，这与传统货币政策的非对称性是一致的。传统货币政策的非对称性指出：在经济下行阶段，宽松性货币政策对经济的刺激作用小于在经济上行阶段相同幅度紧缩性货币政策对经济的抑制作用。央行沟通通过对银行风险承担影响的非对称，进而对银行的信贷产生非对称影响，在一定意义上可以说，央行沟通对银行风险承担的非对称性对我国传统货币政策的非对称性具有放大效应。关于央行沟通对银行风险承担影响的非对称性，一个可能的解释是，商业银行主体在不同的经济运行状态下信心和预期不同。在经济下行阶段，商业银行主体对未来经济增长缺乏信心，预期下降，再加上企业经营状况和财务状况的恶化，使得商业银行会采取更加保守的信贷策略，贷款时会更加谨慎，此时释放宽松信号的央行沟通对银行风险承担的刺激作用会大打折扣。而在经济上行阶段，商业银行主体对经济预期比较乐观，常常会降低信贷审批标准，采取激进的信贷策略，贷款大幅增长，风险承担随之提高。而一旦央行释放紧缩性的政策信号，商业银行为了防范流动性风险和信用违约风险，会提高信贷审批标准，缩减信贷规模，风险承担意愿大幅降低。

（三）稳健性检验

为了保证上述回归结果的稳健性，我们以不良贷款率作为银行风险承担的另一代理变量，对模型（9）（10）（11）（12）进行重新估计，所得的主要结论与前文得到的结论基本保持一致，因此本文的基本结论是稳健的（见表 1.7、表 1.8 和表 1.9）。

表 1.7　不同货币政策工具对银行风险承担影响检验（稳健性检验）

变量	央行沟通	基准贷款利率	存款准备金率
NPL（-1）	0.9688*** (0.000)	0.7960 (0.000)	0.9890 (0.000)
MP	0.0364** (0.050)	-0.1504** (0.016)	-0.0300*** (0.003)

表 1.8　央行沟通对银行风险承担影响的异质性检验（稳健性检验）

变量	资本充足率	系统重要性
NPL（-1）	0.8305*** (0.000)	0.9731*** (0.000)
CB	0.3452** (0.015)	0.0603** (0.010)
SYS		-0.3401** (0.047)
CB×SYS		-0.0332** (0.042)
CAP	-0.0412* (0.075)	-0.0463*** (0.007)
CB×CAP	-0.0238** (0.016)	

表 1.9　央行沟通对银行风险承担影响的非对称性检验（稳健性检验）

变量	央行沟通
NPL（-1）	0.9907*** (0.000)
CB	0.0064* (0.073)
CYCLE	0.0465** (0.023)
CB × CYCLE	-0.0036** (0.037)

六、结论与启示

货币政策风险承担渠道的"央行透明度效应"为我们研究央行预期管理对银行风险承担的影响提供了思路。基于这一效应，本文借鉴莫里斯和星的思想，从理论上分析了央行沟通对银行风险承担的影响，并运用 2007—2014 年 14 家上市商业银行的微观面板数据检验了我国央行沟通对商业银行风险承担行为的影响。研究发现：（1）央行沟通对银行风险承担具有显著的正向影响，央行沟通释放宽松的货币政策信息越多，银行风险承担越高；（2）央行沟通对银行风险承担的影响具有异质性特征，因银行资本充足率和系统重要性的不同而存在差异，资本充足率越高的银行，其风险承担行为对央行沟通反应的敏感性越低，非系统重要性银行风险承担行为对央行沟通反应的敏感性强于系统重要性银行；（3）释放紧缩信号的央行沟通对银行风险承担的抑制作用强于相同程度的释放宽松信号的央行沟通对银行风险承担的激励作用；（4）不同货币政策工具对银行风险承担行为影响具有差异性，银行风险承担对价格型工具反应最为敏感，其次是央行沟通，再次是数量型工具。

预期管理已成为许多发达国家央行重要的货币政策手段，我国政府和央行也愈加认识到预期管理在宏观调控中的重要性，作为预期管理重要工具的央行沟通将在未来我国货币政策调控中发挥重要而积极的作用。我国央行应重视沟通的预期引导作用，提高货币政策的透明度和可信度，不断完善沟通渠道，提高沟通技巧，充分发挥央行沟通的效用。中央银行应关注央行沟通对金融机构风险取向的影响以及进而对金融稳定产生的影响，充分考虑央行沟通对不同商业银行风险承担行为的差异性，以及央行沟通对银行风险承担行为影响的非对称性。货币政策（利率、法定存款准备金率、央行沟通）和宏观审慎政策都会影响银行的风险承担，进而影响金融稳定。中央银行在调整货币政策（利率、法定存款准备金率）和运用沟通引导公众预期的过程中，应当注意传统货币政策工具的调整、央行沟通释放的信号对银行风险承担和金融稳定可能产生的影响，加强传统货币政策工具、新型货币政策工具（央行沟通）与宏观审慎管理工具的协调配合，以维护金融体系的稳定。

机构投资者行为与市场效率的实证分析

甘肃省分行　魏海波

一、选题的背景和研究意义

维护市场稳定是国际证监会组织和我国证监会的监管目标。作为新兴证券市场，中国股市具有不成熟与不稳定性，其特征之一就是受投资者情绪影响股价波动剧烈，市场经常呈现震荡状态。虽然经历了2006—2008年的大起大落与金融危机的冲击，但是在超常规发展机构投资者的战略指导下，我国股票市场的机构投资者队伍依旧迅速壮大起来。

2012年3月30日，中国证监会新批准了3家QFII（合格境外机构投资者）进入A股市场，至此，取得QFII资格的机构已增至158家①，使我国机构投资者队伍得到扩大。我国机构投资者经过近几年来的不断发展，逐步形成了包括证券投资基金、社保基金、保险资金、QFII及企业年金等专业化机构投资者共同发展的格局。

截至2011年年底，沪深A股总市值21.38万亿元，流通市值合计16.49亿元，我国拥有证券投资基金915只，股票有效账户数为14 050.37万户，交易所上市证券投资基金成交额达6 365.80亿元②。而在2012年，广东千亿元养老金入市的消息令业界兴奋良久。2012年3月下旬，全国社保基金理事会发布消息称，经国务院批准，社保基金理事会受广东省政府委托，投资运营广东城镇职工基本养老保险结存资金1 000亿元③。这一系列数据表明了我国机构投资者取得了一定的发展成果。

管理层不遗余力地发展机构投资者队伍，其出发点就是希望机构能理性投资，成为稳定市场的重要力量。但证券公司的违规操作行为、基金坐庄操纵股价事件的普遍存在，使得机构投资者稳定市场的作用一再受到质疑。分析机构投资者与证券市场稳定两者之间的逻辑关系，进而探索发展成为这种关系所需的市场条件，并对照我国证

① 资料来源：中国证监会。

② 资料来源：中国证监会。

③ 资料来源：凤凰网。

券市场的实际情况完善市场条件，以上所述的这些工作对于我们寻求一条机构投资者发展的正确道路及制定相关的政策而言具有现实意义。因此，研究机构投资者与股票价格波动的关系就成为很有现实意义的一个课题。

二、国内外研究现状及分析

1965 年，法马（Fama）的博士论文全文发表，他回顾了关于股价行为的已有文献，并指出有足够证据证明股价随机游走理论。而且在萨缪尔森和哈利·罗伯茨（Samuelson and Harry Roberts）的研究基础上，法马最终确立了有效市场假说，即资本市场有效是指无法利用信息来获取高于平均的报酬。在他看来，资本市场的效率在于资本市场能否完全反映各种与市场有关的信息，即股票的市场价格能否消化和反映市场中的所有信息，通过定价机制来提高投资者的理性预期能力，规范其投资行为，客观上为资本市场进行资金配置提供重要参照。有效市场理论在 20 世纪 70 年代达到顶峰，直到 20 世纪 80 年代后期，有效市场理论无法解释市场中越来越多的异常现象，这些现象包括价值效应、规模效应、新发效应及日历效应等。即使有学者对有效市场理论进行了修正、放宽了一些假设条件，但仍然无法对市场的一些异象给出合理解释。

市场不断发生的异象表明许多金融理论还不完善，再加上期望理论得到广泛认可和经验证明，行为金融在这一时期有了突破性进展，基于行为金融的研究也随之兴盛。行为金融从人的角度来解释市场行为，充分考虑市场参与者的心理因素的作用，为人们理解金融市场提供了一个新的视角。按照行为金融理论分析，应以真实的决策行为——有限理性重新界定市场有效性，基于“人是有限理性的”这样一个观点，学者们对股票价格的异常波动、股市中的“羊群效应”、反应过度和反应不足切换机制等方面的探索论证陆续展开，试图从不同的角度来解释投资者的行为。

对于机构投资者是否能够稳定市场，学术界一直存在着较大的争议。目前，部分学者和业界人士认为机构投资者对资本市场有明显的积极作用，如稳定市场、价格发现等；也有一些学者对机构投资者的作用提出了疑问；还有一部分学者认为机构投资者与稳定股价之间没有必然联系。

（一）国外研究现状

国外学者对机构投资者与市场效率关系的研究方兴未艾，他们以发达国家的证券市场为实证基点，从不同的角度研究机构投资者与市场效率两者的关系。夏斯（Sias，1996）以 1977—1991 年纽交所所有上市公司为样本，分析了股价波动与机构投资者持股比例的关系，得出以下结论：在控制公司规模的情况下，机构投资者持股比例与股价波动之间存在正相关关系，持股比例的增加导致股价波动的加剧。兰考尼肖科、施莱费尔和维什尼（Lakonishok，Shleifer and Vishny，1991）指出，机构投资者不存在羊群效应和正反馈交易现象，机构投资者的存在至少不会导致市场的不稳定。科埃内特（Cohenetal，2002）通过考察1983—1998年总共16年的年度数据，实证研究发现：美国的机构投资者通常会买入具有正现金流信息的股票，卖出没有信息却引发价格上涨的股票，从而使股价向其价值回归，进而产生稳定市场的作用。奇亚尚塔纳（Chiyachantana，2004）采用37个国家的机构投资者在1997年第四季度、1998年第一季度及2001年前三个季度的交易数据研究了机构投资者的交易行为对价格的影响，结果发现机构投资者对价格的影响与市场状况有关。

（二）国内研究现状

虽然我国的证券市场起步晚、发展程度不及国外，但是我国学者对国内证券市场的探索研究从未间断过，学者们一直在努力通过理论及实证研究发现我国证券市场在发展过程中存在的问题，寻找解决的方法途径，以提高市场的整体质量，加快证券市场的市场化进程。

就近10年来说，其中，李国正和杜贺亮（2003）利用2003年第三季度基金的10大重仓股数据，研究了基金持股比例与股价波动的关系，发现基金投资行为对股价波动没有显著影响。但该研究只是针对2003年第三季度的数据进行的，应该说得出的结论不具有全面性。姚姬和刘志远（2005）就此问题运用Fama-MacBeth回归方法进行了研究，发现基金公司持股比例越高的股票的季度流动性和收益率越高、波动性越低，他们由此得出基金作为机构投资者确实发挥了稳定市场的作用的结论。何佳和何基报（2005）针对国内市场的情况，以2003—2005年12个季度证券投资基金的数据作为样本，建立了投资者结构与股价波动关系的理论模型并进行研究，结果表明：在市场产品结构、交易制度和规则体系等要素给定的情况下，股价波动是投资者结构参数的函数，机构投资者与稳定股价没有必然联系，股价波动的大小与市场中复杂的投资者结构、市场环境和制度等均有关。即使在相当理性的市场上，随着投资者结构的变化，既出现了股价波动随着机构投资者比例增加而增加的情况，也出现了股价波动随着机构投资者比例增加而减少的情况，从而否定了国内的主流研究思想。祁斌、黄明和陈卓思（2006）选取了2001年1月1日至2004年12月31日在上交所上市的451只股票为样本进行分析，将股票按照机构投资者持股比例高低分为不同子集，分别研究惯性和反转现象的发生情况。研究发现，不同投资者群体主导的股票子集表现出来截然不同的特征。机构投资者持股比例比较低的股票存在着比较明显的反转现象，而机构投资者持股比例比较高的股票存在着比较明显的惯性现象。在这之后，何佳、何基报、王霞及翟伟丽（2007）在他们前期研究的基础上，利用2003年至2007年4月机构投资者的季末持股和交易数据，对机构投资者是否起到了稳定股市的作用进行实证研究。结果表明，机构投资者对整个市场价格波动的影响很小，而以证券投资基金为代表的机构投资者随市场环境和结构的变化对股价波动会产生不同的影响，有时增加股价波动，有时减少股价波动，不能得出“机构投资者一定能够稳定股市”的结论。盛军锋、邓勇和汤大杰（2008）利用 GARCH 事件模型和条件波动方程，采用上海、深圳及香港证券市场数据，从市场整体角度出发检验中国机构投资者对市场的影响，实证发现机构投资者的进入在一定程度上起到了稳定市场的作用。总体来看，机构投资者发挥了稳定市场的功能，与发展机构投资者的政策预期相符。在每次大力推动机构投资者发展的政策时间点之后，机构投资者的壮大都对市场起到了明显的稳定作用，且机构投资者对深圳证券市场的稳定性作用更强更明显。后来的研究中，蔡庆丰和宋友勇（2010）运用 TARCH 模型（从宏观层面）和面板数据模型（从微观层面）来研究我国基金业跨越式发展对市场波动率的影响，实证研究发现我国基金业的跨越式发展并没有促进市场的稳定和理性，反而加剧了机构重仓股的波动。

纵观学者们的文献，他们从不同角度对机构投资者行为与市场效率两者间的关系进行了研究。在我国证券市场上，机构投资者的产生和发展在很大程度上都是由政府出于自己的某种需要而推动的，是一种明显的政府行为。这主要来自两方面的需要：一方面是希望机构投资者能够起到稳定和规范证券市场发展的作用，且这种意图在有关的法规中都有非常明确的表述；另一方面则是为了与证券市场迅速扩容相适应，期望机构投资者的扩容能够带来市场资金的迅速增加。那么在政策的引导下，机构投资者是否发挥了它应有的作用呢？由此看来，随着我国经济及证券市场的进一步发展，对机构投资者的行为进行“与时俱进”的研究具有现实意义。

三、样本数据与研究设计

（一）样本的选取与数据来源

考虑到中国股票市场在过去的若干年里数次经历了从熊市到牛市的转折，同时为了能集中考察基金持股行为对股价波动的影响，本文特意选取了 2005 年 1 月 1 日至 2011 年 12 月 31 日的上海 A 股市场近 7 年来公司利润均居前的 10 家基金公司交叉持有的股票，在筛选个股时以持有该股的基金公司个数及各个公司持有该股的时期长短为衡量指标。考虑到数据的可获得性，在选出基金公司后，我只通过各基金公司的开放式基金选取各基金公司的重仓股，最终选取了 50 只个股。本文的数据频率为季度，主要数据来源于国泰安数据库，分析所用软件为 Eviews 6.0。需要说明的是，下文中缺失的相关数据用横线表示。

（二）研究思路

基金公司的持股是稳定了股价还是加剧了股价的波动？基金公司的持股对大盘而言是起到稳定大盘的作用还是加剧大盘的波动？带着这两个疑问，本文中我主要通过以下两方面来对基金公司的行为与市场效率的关系进行探讨：（1）基金持股波动与样本收益波动的关系；（2）上证指数波动与样本收益波动的相关性。

四、实证检验与结果分析

本章内容主要有三部分，第一部分为对总样本区间的划分，第二部分为模型的设定，第三部分则为对模型的回归估计及检验分析，具体内容见下文。

（一）市场周期的划分

图 1. 12 为上证指数的月度波动图，从图中可以看出，在总样本区间里市场既存在牛市又存在熊市。根据大盘的趋势可将总样本区间划分为四个阶段，其中包括两个牛市阶段（2005 年第三季度至 2007 年第三季度、2008 年第四季度至 2009 年第二季度）和两个熊市阶段（2007 年第四季度至 2008 年第三季度、2009 年第三季度至 2011 年第四季度）。虽然最初的总样本区间的起始日期设定为 2005 年 1 月 1 日，但在 2005 年 6 月大盘有个低点，因此我将 2005 年 6 月作为市场周期划分的时间起点。这样的样本区间划分可以在考虑市场制度的巨大变革的基础上，对在不同市场周期机构投资者和市场定价效率的关系做出研究。

图 1. 12　上证指数波动

（二）模型的设定及对各变量的说明

各种不同类型的资产均要面临系统性风险，股票也不例外。股票价格波动会导致股价收益率的变化，从而作用于基金持股行为，使得基金改变了对个股的持仓量。那么基金的持仓量和系统性风险这两个量对于股票的收益率的影响如何？鉴于此，我建立了下面的二元回归模型：

$$R_{i,t} = \alpha_{i,t} + \beta_{1i,t} \triangle S_{i,t} + \beta_{2i,t} SZZS_{i,t} + \mu_{i,t}$$

在模型中，各变量所代表的含义如下：

$S_{i,t}$为基金持股比例，即所有基金在季度 t 内对股票 i 所持的股票市值占该股票流通市值的比重。

$\triangle S_{i,t}$为基金持股比例的季度变化，以所有基金对该只股票的持股总和计算，就是对股票 i 而言，所有基金在季度 t 的持股总比例减去上一季度（即季度 $t-1$）基金的持股比例，它反映了基金的持股行为。

$R_{i,t}$代表股票价格的季度收益率，就是股票 i 在季度 t 内价格涨跌的幅度，它反映了股价的波动。

$SZZS_{i,t}$为上证指数在季度 t 内的波动幅度。

$\alpha_{i,t}$为常数项，$\beta_{1i,t}$及 $\beta_{2i,t}$为自变量系数，$\mu_{i,t}$为随机误差项。

（三）模型的检验

1. 时间序列的平稳性检验

我对 50 只样本股票各自的时间序列运用散点图、自相关函数及单位根检验进行了平稳性检验。平稳性检验表明绝大多数样本股票的时间序列是平稳的，因为个体较多，在此我只列示了 12 号股票的相关情况。

如图 1.13 所示，从 12 号股票的收益率、持股比例的变动及上证指数的波动率 3 个

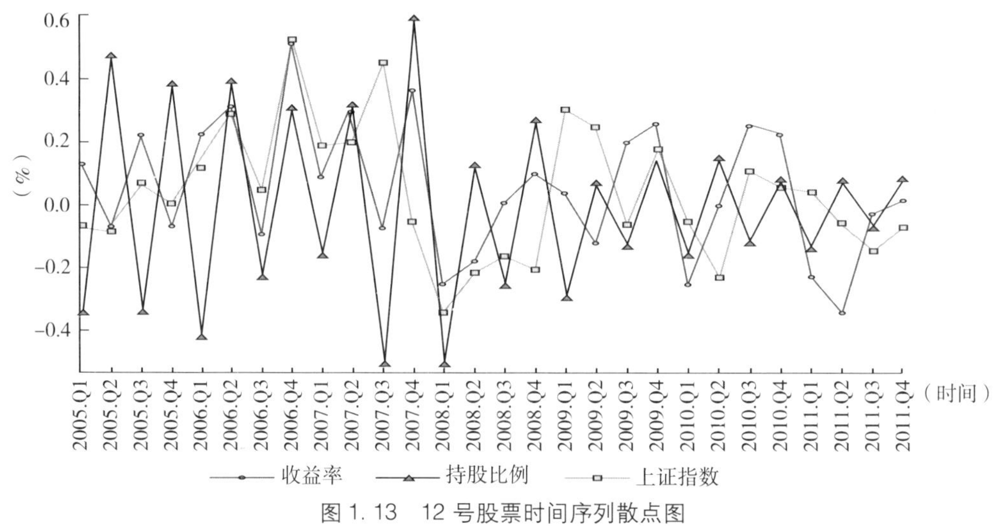

图 1.13　12 号股票时间序列散点图

变量的时间序列的散点图可以看出，各变量均围绕其对应的平均值上下波动，这说明时间序列是平稳的。

图1.14列示了12号股票的持股比例的时间序列自相关性，可看出相关系数是迅速衰减的，表明序列是平稳的。

样本：2005.Q1~2011.Q4
包含观察结果：28个

自相关	偏相关		AC	PAC	Q-Stat	Prob
		1	−0.094	−0.094	0.2743	0.600
		2	0.009	0.001	0.2772	0.871
		3	−0.045	−0.045	0.3456	0.951
		4	0.241	0.235	2.3714	0.668
		5	−0.039	0.003	2.4270	0.787
		6	−0.284	−0.309	5.4991	0.482
		7	0.117	0.100	6.0445	6.535
		8	−0.010	−0.037	6.0484	0.642
		9	−0.054	−0.093	6.1794	0.722
		10	−0.137	−0.010	7.0523	0.721
		11	−0.127	0.000	7.8535	0.726
		12	0.165	0.129	9.2818	0.679

图1.14　12号股票时间序列R12的自相关图

2. 第一阶段检验结果分析

根据前文对市场的划分，总样本期间内2005年第三季度至2007年第三季度为第一阶段，对各只股票该阶段的时间序列数据用最小二乘法进行估计，估计结果如表1.10所示。

表1.10　2005年第三季度至2007年第三季度检验结果

股票序号	时序个数	常数项	β_1	显著性水平	β_2	显著性水平	R^2	F检验值
1	9	-0.085	-1.385	-1.053	2.032	4.511	0.780	10.663
2	9	-0.151	0.758	1.158	1.721	4.037	0.867	19.620
3	4	-0.255	-0.514	-1.123	1.756	2.162	0.851	2.852
4	—	—	—	—	—	—	—	—
5	4	2.001	-13.709	-4.618	-4.665	-4.309	0.956	10.792
6	9	0.165	0.585	0.683	0.467	0.468	0.130	0.449
7	9	0.056	1.121	1.975	1.005	1.562	0.519	3.240
8	3	-0.403	0.361	—	1.578	—	1.000	—
9	9	-0.078	0.095	0.078	1.133	1.894	0.410	2.089
10	9	0.141	2.344	4.646	1.021	4.118	0.883	22.552
11	9	-0.061	-0.029	-0.073	0.781	1.981	0.401	2.008
12	9	0.057	0.214	1.163	0.494	1.299	0.358	1.675
13	9	0.180	0.968	2.286	0.536	0.933	0.510	3.123

（续表）

股票序号	时序个数	常数项	β_1	显著性水平	β_2	显著性水平	R^2	F 检验值
14	9	-0.007	0.955	0.700	1.042	1.870	0.418	2.150
15	—	—	—	—	—	—	—	—
16	—	—	—	—	—	—	—	—
17	7	0.256	1.068	3.280	0.907	1.807	0.803	8.177
18	9	0.126	0.282	0.678	0.455	0.597	0.133	0.460
19	6	0.262	1.005	1.139	0.791	0.589	0.414	1.060
20	4	1.083	-0.917	-0.502	-0.986	-0.322	0.203	0.127
21	9	0.167	2.507	0.956	0.581	0.644	0.186	0.688
22	9	-0.106	-1.904	-1.210	1.249	2.309	0.524	3.302
23	9	0.007	0.832	0.973	1.160	2.442	0.594	4.396
24	9	0.039	1.789	4.033	1.154	3.097	0.851	17.079
25	9	0.076	1.473	4.252	0.573	2.286	0.813	13.014
26	5	0.083	0.624	0.323	1.011	1.870	0.799	3.971
27	5	0.129	1.003	0.915	0.370	0.303	0.302	0.432
28	9	-0.202	0.266	0.409	1.865	2.490	0.549	3.654
29	9	0.187	0.788	1.506	-0.133	-0.276	0.274	1.135
30	9	0.074	0.819	0.804	1.154	1.883	0.395	1.961
31	9	0.202	0.898	3.215	0.368	0.910	0.659	5.787
32	9	0.041	1.111	1.996	0.511	1.205	0.498	2.981
33	9	-0.078	0.574	0.652	1.662	2.496	0.529	3.371
34	9	-0.020	0.426	0.476	1.941	1.911	0.391	1.924
35	—	—	—	—	—	—	—	—
36	9	0.186	1.147	2.220	0.077	0.149	0.453	2.485
37	9	0.133	0.358	1.213	0.479	1.293	0.346	1.585
38	9	0.058	0.309	2.195	0.329	1.660	0.576	4.083
39	9	0.035	0.170	0.603	0.350	0.762	0.160	0.569
40	9	-0.064	0.478	1.139	0.917	3.908	0.769	9.993
41	9	0.015	1.013	1.318	1.067	3.777	0.739	8.479
42	9	-0.114	1.205	1.705	1.406	3.948	0.770	10.065
43	—	—	—	—	—	—	—	—
44	—	—	—	—	—	—	—	—
45	—	—	—	—	—	—	—	—
46	9	0.087	1.154	0.889	0.597	3.664	0.697	6.887
47	—	—	—	—	—	—	—	—
48	9	0.093	0.366	0.993	0.101	0.426	0.143	0.500
49	8	0.132	1.304	1.483	1.367	2.350	0.749	7.460
50	9	0.041	0.591	2.471	1.149	2.852	0.741	8.573

在2005年第三季度至2007年第三季度的这段牛市行情中，选取的50只个股中，有8只股票是在该考察期之外发行上市的，故而无相关数据，还有2只股票在考察期内时间序列样本数太少，将这两种情况的股票剔除后，剩余40只股票。从表1.10中可见，这40只股票的回归方程的决定系数$R^2<30\%$的只有6只，说明回归方程的拟合优度高，该模型可以对基金持股比例与个股价格波动的关系、大盘波动与个股价格波动的关系进行说明。在0.05的显著性水平下，F检验量的值表明回归方程部分显著；参数β_1绝大多数不显著，没有太多的参考价值；β_2回归系数部分显著，具有一定的参考价值。下面我们就这40只股票的估计结果进行分析。

（1）考察基金持股比例与个股价格波动关系的参数是β_1。40只股票中，$\beta_1<0$的有6只股票，表明对于这6只股票而言，股价波动与基金持股比例成反比例关系，也就是说牛市行情中，在影响股价波动的其他因素不变的情况下，基金持股比例的增加将抑制股价的上涨，基金持股比例的减少将加剧股价上涨。然而有34只股票$\beta_1>0$，这表明牛市行情中，在影响股价波动的其他因素不变的情况下，基金持股比例的增加促使股价进一步上涨，基金持股比例的减少将抑制股价的上涨。

所以总体来说，在牛市行情中，基金持股比例的增减对股价的波动作用表现为增量价升，减量价跌。关于这一点我个人认为，以基金公司为代表的机构投资者的行为存在操纵股价的嫌疑。在我国股票市场上，与上市公司有特定联系的机构投资者往往利用资产重组、资产置换等可以直接操纵股票基本面价值的行动来操纵股价。虽然并不是所有的机构投资者都能使用此类操纵手法，但是由于此类操纵行为完全可能在合法范围内进行，所以要完全杜绝此类操纵是很困难的。从这方面来说，我国证券市场的法制监管仍有待加强。还有一种情况是在市场中最为常见的，它的表现形式是：庄家拉起股价—散户跟风买入—庄家出逃。这种操纵股价的行为往往仅通过买卖证券来进行，没有采用任何公众可以察觉的非交易行动来改变公司股票的价值，也没有散布虚假信息，只是由于交易者是大户，又有较大的市场影响力，因此他们的买卖行为能在某种程度上影响股票的价格。在这个过程中，只能说他们“引导”了投资者的投资方向，以牺牲其他个体的利益换取了自己的收益，加剧了市场波动。

（2）考察大盘波动与个股波动的关系的参数是β_2，其实β_2代表了系统性风险。

①在40只股票中，$\beta_2<0$的有3只股票，表明这3只股票的收益增减波动与整个市场呈反向变动关系。即当影响股价波动的其他因素不变的情况下，大盘处于正收益状态时，这3只股票却处于负收益状态；大盘处于负收益状态时，这3只股票却处于正收益状态。

②在40只股票中，有19只股票$0<\beta_2<1$，表明这19只股票的收益低于整个市场，对大盘而言它们起到了稳定作用。

③在 40 只股票中，有 18 只股票 $\beta_2>1$，表明这 18 只股票的收益高于整个市场，即基金公司持有的这些股票对大盘上涨下跌起到推波助澜的作用。

以上分析显示，从总体来看，这些股票在牛市的表现说明基金公司持有的重仓股对大盘的作用并不能够明显地界定，部分由基金公司持有的重仓股对大盘起稳定作用，而部分则起相反的作用。

我个人认为，现阶段代理投资模式下基金经理或基金管理公司可能的道德风险行为以及基金投资者处置效应所强化的基金管理费收入盈亏报酬不对称的激励模式的存在，导致了现阶段“稳定市场”不会成为基金“自发”或“自觉”的行为目标。当股市快速下跌而导致基金净值在短时间内大幅缩水，基金投资者往往会由于“处置效应”而不愿意中止亏损，这样的行为使得即使基金净值最终的缩水幅度一样，但由于基金份额赎回较少，那么基金公司的资产规模相对缩水较少，相应的基金管理费收入的减少也会较少。因此，对于缺乏信托责任，只追求自身利益最大化的开放式基金而言，在股市上涨阶段“火上加油”（追涨），而在股市下跌阶段“雪上加霜”（快速杀跌），是其作为“经济人”的理性选择。而这种投资行为无疑会加剧市场的波动性，并直接损害基金投资者利益。

而且，在证券市场中，机构投资者同样不可避免地存在着“羊群效应”。由于竞争激烈及业绩压力，一般的机构投资者也会十分关注“领头羊”机构投资者的动向，一买俱买，一卖俱卖。机构投资者的这种行为恰恰没有起到稳定市场的作用，反而加剧了市场的波动。

3. 第二阶段检验结果分析

根据上文对市场的划分，总样本期间内 2007 年第四季度至 2008 年第三季度为第二阶段，对各只股票该阶段的时间序列数据用最小二乘法进行估计，估计结果如表 1. 11 所示。

表 1. 11　2007 年第四季度至 2008 年第三季度检验结果

股票序号	样本个数	常数项	β_1	显著性水平	β_2	显著性水平	R^2	F 检验值
1	4	-0. 185	0. 073	0. 276	0. 560	1. 183	0. 772	1. 692
2	4	-0. 014	-0. 140	-0. 526	1. 003	2. 155	0. 829	2. 430
3	4	0. 558	-1. 240	-24. 029	4. 327	32. 204	0. 999	520. 778
4	4	-0. 271	1. 509	2. 830	-0. 577	-0. 911	0. 903	4. 657
5	4	0. 139	-0. 168	-1. 505	1. 488	5. 551	0. 927	20. 166
6	—	—	—	—	—	—	—	—
7	4	-0. 367	0. 697	0. 969	-0. 946	-0. 438	0. 536	0. 578
8	4	0. 230	-0. 093	-0. 017	1. 633	1. 058	0. 804	2. 048

（续表）

股票序号	样本个数	常数项	β_1	显著性水平	β_2	显著性水平	R^2	F 检验值
9	4	0.191	1.279	0.662	1.206	0.509	0.770	1.678
10	4	-0.223	0.324	0.912	0.112	0.199	0.599	0.747
11	4	-0.014	-0.203	-0.187	1.008	0.409	0.149	0.088
12	4	0.402	-0.006	-0.016	2.181	1.318	0.871	3.362
13	4	0.109	-0.970	-1.619	2.217	1.256	0.730	1.352
14	4	0.146	-0.640	-0.875	1.786	1.562	0.764	1.622
15	4	-0.004	2.645	1.841	0.746	2.244	0.965	13.650
16	4	-0.092	7.155	1.176	0.342	0.239	0.934	7.078
17	4	-0.345	-0.388	-0.494	0.143	0.058	0.218	0.140
18	4	0.608	-1.646	-9.770	4.001	8.820	0.990	50.133
19	4	0.215	-0.529	-0.496	1.885	0.864	0.428	0.373
20	4	-0.448	0.379	1.496	-0.671	-0.757	0.691	1.120
21	4	-0.011	-0.726	-0.245	1.039	0.426	0.155	0.092
22	4	0.019	-0.814	-0.524	1.238	0.967	0.485	0.470
23	4	-0.114	1.083	0.485	0.612	0.451	0.694	1.133
24	4	-0.475	1.609	6.762	-1.274	-2.892	0.988	42.880
25	4	0.462	-1.021	-4.666	3.112	6.463	0.977	21.279
26	4	-0.058	0.041	0.052	0.788	0.913	0.630	0.852
27	4	0.042	0.348	11.836	0.854	7.124	0.997	197.402
28	4	-0.333	1.343	1.275	-0.272	-0.187	0.657	0.958
29	4	0.689	-1.150	-3.279	3.788	7.573	0.987	37.566
30	4	-0.225	1.196	0.312	-0.006	-0.003	0.112	0.063
31	4	-0.118	0.340	3.084	0.019	0.047	0.934	7.115
32	4	0.026	-1.438	-0.607	1.335	0.552	0.273	0.188
33	4	0.256	-0.456	-7.986	2.312	39.997	1.000	2 028.850
34	4	-0.586	1.064	19.689	-1.872	-9.218	0.997	194.740
35	4	-0.039	-0.195	-0.261	1.231	0.518	0.439	0.391
36	4	-0.160	-0.027	-0.045	0.354	0.354	0.040	0.021
37	4	1.016	-1.328	—	3.328	—	1.000	—
38	4	-0.209	0.442	0.683	0.239	0.292	0.378	0.303
39	4	0.197	-0.180	-0.473	1.126	1.180	0.593	0.729
40	4	-0.171	1.389	—	-0.258	—	1.000	—
41	4	0.522	-5.671	-1.277	4.122	1.516	0.766	1.632
42	4	0.322	-0.513	-0.215	2.257	1.065	0.726	1.327

（续表）

股票序号	样本个数	常数项	β_1	显著性水平	β_2	显著性水平	R^2	F 检验值
43	4	0.078	0.802	0.619	1.663	5.248	0.931	20.124
44	3	-0.102	2.273	—	0.655	—	1.000	—
45	—	—	—	—	—	—	—	—
46	4	0.448	-1.114	-0.399	2.795	4.155	0.983	28.396
47	3	0.186	-0.178		2.033		1.000	
48	4	-0.411	1.598	3.936	-1.343	-1.795	0.941	7.913
49	4	0.081	-1.230	-0.444	2.029	0.992	0.508	0.516
50	4	0.699	-0.859	-0.983	4.227	1.468	0.684	1.081

在 2007 年第四季度至 2008 年第三季度这段熊市行情中，选取的 50 只个股中，1 只股票是在该考察期外发行上市的，无相关数据，还有 1 只股票无统计数据，将这两只股票剔除，再剔除无参数显著性统计值的 4 只股票，剩余 44 只股票。从表 1.11 可见，对于各只股票，回归方程的决定系数绝大多数均很高，说明回归方程的拟合优度高，该模型可以对基金持股比例与股价波动的关系、大盘波动与个股波动的关系进行简单说明。在 0.05 的显著性水平下，F 检验量的值表明回归方程绝大多数不显著；参数 β_1 绝大多数不显著，没有太多的参考价值；β_2 回归系数绝大多数也不显著。

得出这样的回归结果可能是因为样本容量太少，也可能是因为影响股价波动的因素很多，而模型没有将部分重要因素在研究中考虑进来。由于估计结果存在不可靠性，在此便不进行详细分析。

4. 第三阶段检验结果分析

根据上文对市场的划分，总样本期间内 2008 年第四季度至 2009 年第二季度为第三阶段，对该阶段各只股票的时间序列数据用最小二乘法进行估计，估计结果如表 1.12 所示。

表 1.12　2008 年第四季度至 2009 年第二季度检验结果

股票序号	样本个数	常数项	β_1	β_2	R^2
1	3	-0.031	1.842	1.351	1.000
2	3	-0.114	0.643	1.241	1.000
3	3	0.230	-0.477	0.579	1.000
4	3	0.184	0.225	0.547	1.000
5	3	-0.144	0.585	1.455	1.000
6	3	0.075	-0.436	0.123	1.000
7	3	0.216	-1.366	-0.992	1.000

（续表）

股票序号	样本个数	常数项	β_1	β_2	R^2
8	3	-0.039	8.706	1.024	1.000
9	3	0.088	3.787	2.363	1.000
10	3	0.147	-0.473	0.436	1.000
11	3	0.031	-0.655	-0.914	1.000
12	3	0.094	-0.547	-0.729	1.000
13	3	0.151	0.105	1.620	1.000
14	3	0.120	-1.611	0.378	1.000
15	3	-0.019	8.105	0.848	1.000
16	3	0.000	3.545	1.150	1.000
17	3	0.334	-0.310	0.913	1.000
18	3	-0.002	0.717	1.528	1.000
19	3	-0.082	0.319	1.331	1.000
20	3	-0.082	0.319	1.331	1.000
21	3	-0.076	0.716	1.366	1.000
22	3	-0.103	1.368	1.727	1.000
23	3	-0.182	14.027	1.783	1.000
24	3	0.218	-2.241	1.132	1.000
25	3	-0.115	-0.494	0.873	1.000
26	3	0.224	-2.937	1.381	1.000
27	3	0.114	0.169	-0.313	1.000
28	3	0.014	-0.415	-0.318	1.000
29	3	2.287	-19.354	-21.014	1.000
30	3	0.030	1.693	1.129	1.000
31	3	-0.161	0.291	1.307	1.000
32	3	0.079	-8.929	-0.010	1.000
33	3	-0.031	0.594	1.031	1.000
34	3	0.131	0.716	1.800	1.000
35	3	0.121	0.865	1.482	1.000
36	3	0.307	-2.929	-1.830	1.000
37	—	—	—	—	—
38	3	0.190	-1.207	1.107	1.000
39	3	0.124	-0.362	-0.671	1.000
40	—	—	—	—	—
41	3	0.001	0.001	1.443	1.000
42	3	0.652	2.195	1.084	1.000

（续表）

股票序号	样本个数	常数项	β_1	β_2	R^2
43	3	0.711	-13.108	-0.014	1.000
44	3	-0.061	0.395	1.010	1.000
45	3	-0.106	2.364	1.632	1.000
46	3	-0.096	-0.104	1.196	1.000
47	3	0.009	-0.588	1.713	1.000
48	3	-0.020	-2.044	0.075	1.000
49	3	-0.115	5.790	1.497	1.000
50	3	0.224	-1.408	1.346	1.000

可能是因为可观察的样本较少，该阶段的估计结果不理想，所以并没有多大的分析价值，故此不做详细分析。

5. 第四阶段检验结果分析

根据上文对市场的划分，总样本期间内2009年第三季度至2011年第四季度为第四阶段，对该阶段各只股票的时间序列数据用最小二乘法进行估计，估计结果如表1.13所示。

表1.13　2009年第三季度至2011年第四季度检验结果

股票序号	样本个数	常数项	β_1	显著性水平	β_2	显著性水平	R^2	F检验值
1	10	-0.031	0.499	2.134	1.610	7.502	0.920	40.164
2	10	0.022	1.551	2.020	1.337	4.714	0.856	20.735
3	10	-0.051	-0.041	-0.130	1.161	2.750	0.519	3.783
4	10	-0.031	0.003	0.013	0.725	2.873	0.542	4.136
5	10	-0.017	0.638	0.935	0.618	3.532	0.648	6.436
6	10	0.110	0.335	1.066	0.442	0.907	0.229	1.039
7	10	0.032	0.487	1.016	1.120	2.192	0.513	3.682
8	10	0.010	2.419	0.935	0.776	4.002	0.710	8.584
9	10	0.055	0.314	0.303	0.758	2.030	0.371	2.068
10	10	0.027	-0.758	-0.918	2.699	4.939	0.786	12.826
11	10	-0.016	-0.314	-0.610	1.656	3.915	0.687	7.694
12	10	0.028	0.371	0.635	0.791	1.275	0.220	0.985
13	10	-0.065	-0.273	-0.919	0.998	1.867	0.361	1.973
14	10	0.015	0.352	1.096	0.714	2.412	0.495	3.432
15	10	0.002	4.203	1.724	0.579	4.398	0.766	11.489
16	10	-0.030	4.152	1.797	0.753	4.956	0.821	16.091
17	10	-0.051	0.095	0.374	1.378	3.756	0.677	7.332

（续表）

股票序号	样本个数	常数项	β_1	显著性水平	β_2	显著性水平	R^2	F 检验值
18	10	-0.049	0.488	2.227	0.508	2.006	0.576	4.754
19	10	0.067	0.179	1.470	1.277	5.939	0.841	18.467
20	10	0.042	0.235	0.413	1.888	2.390	0.485	3.292
21	10	0.064	-0.558	-1.924	2.039	7.192	0.882	26.162
22	10	-0.010	0.363	1.168	0.490	1.613	0.402	2.350
23	10	-0.063	-0.306	-0.390	0.979	2.827	0.552	4.314
24	10	-0.014	-1.564	-1.323	1.897	2.769	0.550	4.280
25	10	0.016	0.291	0.898	1.175	4.545	0.769	11.682
26	10	-0.004	0.429	1.763	0.689	3.355	0.691	7.844
27	7	0.048	0.148	0.386	0.590	0.860	0.268	0.732
28	10	-0.008	-0.218	-0.503	1.587	3.779	0.671	7.143
29	10	-0.041	-0.679	-1.371	1.429	3.434	0.631	5.984
30	10	-0.013	0.655	1.796	0.931	3.956	0.744	10.154
31	10	0.043	-0.047	-0.154	0.528	1.014	0.140	0.568
32	10	0.225	0.130	0.411	2.626	5.473	50.814	15.292
33	10	0.090	1.432	1.824	1.429	3.683	0.696	8.017
34	10	-0.001	-0.084	-0.339	1.766	4.665	0.757	10.907
35	10	-0.049	-0.332	-0.251	1.307	2.368	0.454	2.907
36	10	0.049	-0.438	-1.445	1.889	6.015	0.840	18.432
37	10	0.009	0.189	0.617	1.427	2.371	0.477	3.192
38	10	0.097	-0.285	-0.501	0.788	0.960	0.162	0.678
39	10	0.055	0.234	0.403	0.085	0.166	0.024	0.086
40	10	-0.058	0.924	1.422	-0.092	-0.266	0.251	1.176
41	10	-0.012	3.633	3.325	0.631	2.614	0.808	14.723
42	10	-0.010	0.501	1.013	0.549	2.872	0.589	5.012
43	10	0.008	1.908	1.929	0.725	2.879	0.600	5.245
44	10	-0.020	1.824	0.997	0.389	1.122	0.297	1.480
45	10	0.026	1.119	1.333	0.960	4.557	0.765	11.385
46	10	-0.004	-1.090	-0.189	1.106	3.755	0.733	9.614
47	10	0.009	0.315	0.772	0.602	2.934	0.558	4.412
48	10	0.026	-0.881	-0.985	1.820	3.609	0.660	6.809
49	10	-0.027	0.597	0.518	1.583	3.946	0.748	10.398
50	10	-0.051	0.042	0.082	0.942	1.434	0.249	1.163

从表 1.13 可见，在 2009 年第三季度至 2011 年第四季度这段熊市行情中，选取的 50 只个股中只有 9 只股票的回归方程的决定系数 $R^2<30\%$，说明回归方程的拟合优度高，该模型可以对基金持股比例与个股价格波动的关系、大盘波动与个股波动的关系进行说明。在 0.05 的显著性水平下，F 检验量的值表明大多数回归方程显著；参数 β_1 不显著，没有太多的参考价值；β_2 回归系数绝大多数显著，具有极强的参考价值。下面就这 50 只股票的估计结果进行分析。

（1）考察基金持股比例与个股价格的波动关系的参数是 β_1。

①50 只股票中，其中 $\beta_1<0$ 的有 25 只，表明对于这 25 只股票而言，股价波动与基金持股比例成反比例关系，也就是说熊市行情中，在影响股价波动的其他因素不变的情况下，基金持股比例的增加将加速股价的下跌，基金持股比例的减少将减弱股价下跌。

②50 只股票中，同时有 25 只股票 $\beta_1>0$，这表明牛市行情中，在影响股价波动的其他因素不变的情况下，基金持股比例的增加将使得股价上涨，基金持股比例的减少将使得股价下跌。

通过以上两种情况的分析，可以发现总体来说，在熊市行情中，基金持股比例的增减对股价的作用不是绝对的，对于部分股票来说，在熊市中基金公司的持股对该股的价格起稳定作用，而对于部分股票则不然。

熊市中基金公司持股对市场的稳定作用是令人欣喜的，然而，熊市中基金公司的整体表现令人喜忧参半。我认为，这种现象的存在是必然的，人是有限理性的，基金公司作为一个财力、人力强大的个体，它的投资行为无论如何仍是由人做出的，必然逃脱不了趋利避害的本性，在某些时刻难免将自己的行为由“投资”转为“投机”。机构投资者并不一定买进长期持有性股票，更不一定始终持有，机构投资者也必须在一定时期内达到一定的业绩标准，否则，将会面临大量偿付的风险。当它们认为风险收益前景马上就要恶化时，没有任何理由认为它们仍将会大量持有证券资产，面临这种状况减少证券资产的持有量是趋利避害的唯一正确选择。此时，希望机构投资者违背自身的利益原则而大发善心来拯救证券市场是不切实际的。除非其认为，若短期内抛售过多过快会使自身难以全身而退，才会暂时不加以抛售，以换取相对稳定；否则，只要能够比其他投资者较早觉察风险，它们一定会抢先抛售。

（2）考察大盘波动与个股波动的关系的参数是 β_2。

①在 50 只股票中，$\beta_2<0$ 的仅只有 1 只股票，表明这只股票的收益增减波动与整个市场呈反向变动。即在影响股价波动的其他因素不变的情况下，大盘处于正收益状态时，这只股票却处于负收益率；大盘处于负收益状态时，这只股票却处于正收益率。

显然在熊市中这样的股票太少了，也表明熊市中基金持有该种性质的股票较少，不能发挥稳定市场的作用。

②在 50 只股票中，有 26 只股票 $0 < \beta_2 < 1$，表明这 26 只股票的收益低于整个市场。这类股票对大盘起稳定的作用。

③在 50 只股票中，有 23 只股票 $\beta_2 > 1$，表明这 23 只股票的收益高于整个市场。即基金公司持有的这些股票在该熊市行情中对股价起加剧下跌的作用。

经过对 50 只样本股票的 β_2的分析，我发现在熊市中基金公司持有的重仓股能够对大盘起到一定的稳定作用。这样的验证结果说明发展机构投资者还是产生了应有的效应。在这一点上，我对部分机构投资者在其中扮演的角色给予肯定。机构投资者拥有先进的分析技术和专门的研究人才，假设该机构投资者注重价值投资、对公司证券内在价值会进行严格分析和研究，在进行投资决策时，也会考虑到上市公司的绩效水平，会“用脚投票”。机构投资者作为外部人，对上市公司持股比例的提高，必然会对解决我国上市公司“内部人控制”问题起到积极作用。当机构投资者持股达到一定规模后，退出成本超过参与治理成本，会选择长期持有该公司的股票，并且积极地介入上市公司治理，参与公司经营管理，提高公司绩效水平。显而易见，这样的行为带来的是公司股票价格的真实上涨，即使在熊市中，机构也会维持对该公司股票的持有，这便在一定程度上起到了稳定市场的作用。

五、实证小结及建议

（一）小结

本文对基金公司持股比例与股价波动的关系、上证指数波动与股价波动的相关性进行定量建模分析，得到以下两点结论。

第一，在牛市行情中，基金持股比例的增减对股价波动的作用表现为增量价升，减量价跌，而基金公司持有的重仓股对大盘的作用并不能够明显地界定。

第二，在熊市行情中，基金持股比例的增减对股价的作用不是绝对的，对于部分股票，在熊市中基金公司的持股对该股的价格起稳定作用，而对于部分股票则不然；基金公司持有的重仓股则对大盘起到积极的稳定作用。

综合看来，以证券投资基金为代表的机构投资者，对股价波动的影响随市场环境的变化会有所差异。机构投资者有时加剧股价波动，有时减弱股价波动，所以不能得出“机构投资者一定能够稳定股市”或者“机构投资者一定会扰动股市”的结论，也就是说，机构投资者在市场中的作用不是绝对正面或绝对反面的。

我在进行定量建模分析时，将总样本区间分为 4 个小样本区间，在回归方程的估计结果中，有些小样本区间的参数估计及模型估计不显著，这可能与小样本区间的样本观察个数较少有关，也可能是由于最初样本的选取太少，还有可能是模型估计在方法的选择上欠妥当。究竟是什么原因导致在定量研究中出现这些不尽如人意的状况？我将在以后进一步探讨研究。虽然本文的实证模型不能用于经济预测，但在对机构投资者行为对市场效率的影响这一问题的说明上仍是具有一定意义的。

（二）建议

本文通过实证探讨，发现以基金公司为代表的机构投资者的投资行为对市场效率的影响在市场周期的不同阶段的表现不同，由此看出我们大力发展机构投机者的初衷还没有得到很好的实现，但发展机构投资者对我国资本市场的发展至关重要。我认为应该从以下 3 点着手不断改进，以逐步全面实现发展机构投资者的初衷。

1. 加强证券市场的改革发展

证券市场的发展是其自身稳定的先决条件，也是发挥机构投资者稳定功能的先决条件。一方面，随着证券市场的发展，当机构投资者有更多的投资组合时便有更多的选择，其投资组合也随之变得更加科学合理，同时机构投资者的盈利能力得以增强。另一方面，证券市场向宽度和深度方面的发展对机构投资者驾驭风险的能力提出了更大的挑战，进而可以提升机构投资者管理资产的能力。从这两方面可以看出，证券市场的进一步改革发展对机构投资者大有裨益。

2. 坚持构建公平、竞争的金融生态环境，促进机构投资者发挥稳定市场的功能

发展机构投资者不是直接目标和宗旨，机构投资者是在建立和完善金融体系甚至社会经济体系的过程中发展起来的中间产物。在公平的规则体系下，自由市场的制度安排在机构投资者发展中有着至关重要的作用。放松管制和加强有效监管为机构投资者的长期发展奠定了基础，这将充分释放机构投资者的能量，促进机构投资者业务范围的拓展和创新，促进机构投资者规模的扩大，并且能够在增强机构投资者竞争的过程中实现机构投资者的整合。

3. 不断进行制度创新

进行制度创新是市场发展的必然要求，已有成绩及经验表明，允许卖空以及各种金融衍生品的使用，使机构投资者资产配置及风险分散的能力大大提升，同时也增强了对个人投资者的吸引力。在机构投资者的成长过程中，制度的创新为其提供了可持续发展的生命源泉。

4. 加强机构投资者信托责任观念及长期投资理念的培养

基金经理和基金管理公司的道德风险行为将损害基金投资者的利益，危及这一行

业的健康发展。加强基金治理，减少代理人的道德风险行为，提高委托人素质和改善委托人结构，培养基金投资者的长期投资理念，这些都是未来我国基金业努力的方向。要不断减少基金凭借资金实力通过市场操纵等道德风险行为牟取暴利的可能性，使其只能通过规范的投资活动获利，使基金能够更有效地贯彻长期投资和价值投资的理念，而不是去追求短期收益。

影子银行信用扩张的非对称传导效应研究

——基于 NARDL 模型的分析

总行内控合规部　王光远

一、引言和综述

不同国家的金融体制不同，影子银行的存在形态也不同，因此当前对影子银行的定义也不尽相同。从机构的角度理解，影子银行为非银行信用中介，在商业银行体系之外行使类银行职能，表外操作证券化贷款（McCulley，2007）。从功能来讲，影子银行具有期限、信用及流动性转换功能（FSB，2011）。从监管来说，影子银行是规避监管的金融工具创新，通过非银行渠道进行短期市场融资，购买大量的高风险、低流动性的长期资产（Geithner，2008）。从流动性担保来讲，影子银行运作无法获得央行的流动性支持或公共部门信贷担保（Pozsar，2013）。影子银行与商业银行在资金链上的联系密不可分（袭翔、周强龙，2014）。发达国家的影子银行往往包括一系列复杂的非银行信贷中介活动和实体，且体系庞大；而发展中国家的影子银行信贷中介链相对直接，其总量占比也相对较小。例如，截至 2016 年，美国的广义影子银行占其 GDP 的比重达 145.6%，占全球影子银行的比重为 27%；欧盟地区的影子银行占全球比重为 32%；中国的影子银行占全球比重为 10%，占我国 GDP 的比重为 89%（FSB，2017）。

西方国家的影子银行体系是金融市场发展到一定程度的产物，其影子银行业务更多的是基于金融衍生品。美式的影子银行主要由投行和经纪商组成，通过资产支持商业票据（asset-backed commercial paper，简称 ABCP）、资产支持证券（asset-backed security，简称 ABS）、担保债务凭证（collateralized debt obligations，简称 CDO）、回购协议（repos）等手段将信贷资产出表并转移风险（Pozsar et al.，2012）。同时基于同业回购协议和庞大的回购交易市场吸收大量的短期、低成本资金，为证券化资产的发行融通资金，反过来又以资产支持证券作为抵押物，进一步扩大融资和发行规模。这一循环模式抵抗流动性冲击的能力较弱（Gorton and Metrick，2012）。商业银行介入影子银行业务的发展，除了可以扩展表外业务削减金融交易成本外，还可以改善银行的信贷约束，达到灵活调节银行资金流动性的目的（Gertler et al.，2012）。

中国的影子银行是提供信用、期限和流动性转换的信用中介，其业务模式与商业银行的经营模式在本质上类似，却属于正规的银行体系之外，存在引发系统性风险或监管套利的可能（《中国金融稳定报告2013》）。我国的影子银行主要包括银行理财产品、信托业务和委托融资平台等（黄益平等，2012）。中国特色的影子银行主要依附于银行体系，是银行利用其他机构作为通道，将信贷资产转移至表外，或打包成表内其他资产。中国的影子银行是商业银行传统信贷业务的线性延伸，开展“银信合作”的基础是银行为了规避金融监管和行政管制（巴曙松，2013）。2013 年，我国推行了更严厉的“中国版《巴塞尔协议Ⅲ》”，对银行业的存贷款比有特殊的规定。银行无法在资产负债表内发放高风险贷款，于是开展“类贷款业务”，开展银信合作、银证合作等银行与金融机构之间的合作，称为中国式影子银行（万晓莉，2016）。影子银行不能吸收存款（缺乏流动性供给）、缺乏监管、无“最后贷款人”，其流动性来源主要是商业银行。

影子银行的融资渠道加速了金融系统性风险的传递，高杠杆操作增加了金融市场的流动性风险，系统性风险被放大（Baily et al.，2008）。顺周期时，金融市场的流动性十分充裕，影子银行的循环模式可持续，杠杆率上升，资产负债表扩张；但危机到来时，投资者认识到风险问题，会抛卖大量资产，资产价格下跌，流动性迅速枯竭，资产负债表收缩（Adrian and Shin，2010）。美国银行大量使用信用风险转移工具，导致银行与金融机构间的关联性加强，遇到负面冲击时会引发银行风险传染的连锁反应（Hakenes and Schnabel，2010），金融危机中银行所依赖的非银行融资规模大幅收减（Singh and Aitken，2010）。中国的影子银行将短期理财产品资金配置于长期资产中，存在严重的期限错配，会加剧银行对银行间市场的依赖（Song and Hachem，2015）。

影子银行是否像银行一样扩大了信用？是对信用的直接创造还是间接创造？这些是分析影子银行的关键问题，因为只有真正扩大的信用，才能带来真正的风险，而信用转换带来的风险是可控的（瞿强，2013）。尽管当前对影子银行的研究甚多，但鲜有从影子银行的信用扩张的角度对影子银行不同于传统银行的信用创造功能进行分析和研究。本文将尝试从此角度，对中美影子银行的兴起原因与运作机制的不同之处进行分析，并重点探讨影子银行的信用扩张功能，实证研究了影子银行规模的缩减对社会信用扩张与收缩存在的非对称传导效应影响。

二、影子银行的信用扩张

（一）影子银行的信用创造过程

首先，通过经典的银行货币乘数问题简单地梳理了一下影子银行的信用扩张过程。假设 t = 0 时，基础货币量为 M，传统商业银行体系内的基础货币比例为 αM，受利益驱动的影响，商业银行准备将可贷资金的（$1-\beta$）比例进行资产证券化（通过 SPV、CDO 等），或经过“银信合作”等通道业务，将信贷资产出表，则这部分资金将流入影子银行体系进行信用扩张，称为 A 类影子银行，资产比例为（$1-\beta$）αM。传统银行体系内剩余 $\beta\alpha M$ 资金比例进行货币信用创造。另外，美国的资金托管机构、P2P（个人对个人）贷款等非银行信用中介，称为 B 类影子银行，直接从公众吸收存款，行使类银行职能。B 类影子银行资金占总基础货币的比例为（$1-\alpha$）M。

$t=1$ 时，商业银行将按照存款准备金率 r，把留存准备金外的所有吸收存款用于放贷，此时商业银行体系内的可贷资金数量为 $\beta(1-r)\alpha M$，这部分资金将通过传统的商业银行贷款扩张信用，不考虑超额准备金。商业银行准备流入影子银行体系（A 类影子银行）的可贷资金量为（$1-\beta$）（$1-r$）αM。类似于传统的银行信用创造过程，影子银行在信用扩张时不受法定存款准备金的限制，所以可选用与银行不同的准备金率 r_s，则 B 类影子银行的可贷资金数量为（$1-r_s$）（$1-\alpha$）M。

$t=2$ 时，商业银行传统信用扩张后的信贷总量为 $\beta(1-r)^2\alpha M+\beta(1-r)\alpha M$，其中 $\beta(1-r)\alpha M$ 是初始银行的信用量（可贷资金），$\beta(1-r)^2\alpha M$ 为银行贷给企业后，企业又将款项存入银行，银行新增的信用。值得一提的是，此时经济体内商业银行持有的实际基础货币量仅为 $\beta\alpha M$，而信用量扩张为 $\beta(1-r)^2\alpha M+\beta(1-r)\alpha M$，则 $\beta\alpha M-[\beta(1-r)^2\alpha M+\beta(1-r)\alpha M]=\beta[r-(1-r)^2]\alpha M$ 部分为银行通过基础货币扩张后的信用部分。$t=2$ 时，商业银行流入影子银行体系的可贷资金将采用影子银行的准备金率 r_s 扩张，A 类影子银行扩张后的信用总量变为：$(1-\beta)(1-r)(1-r_s)\alpha M+(1-\beta)(1-r)\alpha M$。另外，B 类影子银行体系内扩张的信用量由（$1-r_s$）（$1-\alpha$）M 变为 $(1-r_s)^2(1-\alpha)M+(1-r_s)(1-\alpha)M$。整个体系的各期信贷扩张路径如表 1.14 所示。

表 1.14　影子银行的信贷扩张路径

期数	商业银行		影子银行（B 类）
$t=0$	$\beta\alpha M$	$(1-\beta)\alpha M$（A 类）	$(1-\alpha)M$
$t=1$	$\beta(1-r)\alpha M$	$(1-\beta)(1-r)\alpha M$	$(1-r_s)(1-\alpha)M$
$t=2$	$\beta(1-r)^2\alpha M+$ $\beta(1-r)\alpha M$	$(1-\beta)(1-r)(1-r_s)\alpha M+$ $(1-\beta)(1-r)\alpha M$	$(1-r_s)^2(1-\alpha)M+$ $(1-r_s)(1-\alpha)M$
…	…	…	…
$t=n$	$\Sigma(1-r)^{n-1}\beta\alpha M$	$\Sigma(1-r_s)^{n-2}(1-\beta)(1-r)\alpha M$	$\Sigma(1-r_s)^{n-1}(1-\alpha)M$

如表 1.14 所示，当 $n\to\infty$ 时：

$$\sum_{n=1}^{\infty}(1-r)^{n-1}\beta\alpha M=\frac{1}{r}\beta\alpha M$$

其中，$0<r<1$，$\frac{1}{r}$ 为商业银行传统信用扩张乘数；同理可得商业银行将部分贷款表外操作后的“类贷款”影子银行业务（A 类）的信用扩张乘数 $\frac{1-r}{r_s}$：

$$\sum_{n=2}^{\infty}(1-r_s)^{n-2}(1-\beta)(1-r)\alpha M=\frac{1}{r_s}(1-\beta)(1-r)\alpha M$$

以及从期初开始就通过银行理财、信托、P2P 贷款等直接流入影子银行体系资金（B 类）的信用乘数为 $\frac{1}{r_s}$：

$$\sum_{n=1}^{\infty}(1-r_s)^{n-1}(1-\alpha)M=\frac{1}{r_s}(1-\alpha)M$$

综上所述，影子银行的信用扩张路径可以分别总结如下：

其一，A 类影子银行分流了传统商业银行的信贷扩张资金，使（$1-\beta$）αM 比例的基础货币通过影子银行进行信用扩张，$\beta\alpha M$ 留在商业银行体系内进行传统的信用扩张。当商业银行面临影子银行高额收益率的诱惑时，就有激励减少留在体系内的资金比例 β，导致更多资金通过证券化等过程流入影子银行体系。

其二，影子银行在信用扩张时会留存比率为 r_s 的资金作为准备金，以维护流动性的需要。由于 r_s 不受法定存款准备金率的限制，影子银行往往选择留存更少的准备金，即 $r_s<r$，所以影子银行的信贷扩张倍数将大于商业银行的信贷扩张倍数，即 $1/r_s>1/r$。当影子银行机构的风险偏好变得更强时，r_s 变小，导致其信贷扩张乘数 $1/r_s$ 变大。所以，在相同社会资金量的情况下，影子银行的存在导致了社会信用扩张的倍数增加。

其三，从制度变迁的角度来看，当社会体制内的非银行信用中介（B 类影子银行）增多时，基础货币 M 将更多地分流至影子银行体系内，留在商业银行的高能货币占总货币的比例 α 降低。例如，美国的非银行信用中介、影子银行的发达程度高于中国，其信用扩张的程度也高于中国，当经济形势向好时，人们对未来社会繁荣的预期增加，投资增加，风险偏好也会增加，也会导致（$1-\alpha$）比例的增加，进一步扩大了影子银行的信用扩张能力；当投资人风险偏好增加时，金融体系内的系统性风险升高，资本的信用扩张乘数越高，危机来临时的信贷收缩也会越急剧。

（二）美国影子银行的信用创造过程

1. 从资产证券化的角度陈述（SPV 打包贷款评级）

资产证券化过程是美国影子银行信用扩张的核心内容之一。本文从影子银行资产证券化的角度分析美国的信用扩张路径，以考察其对我国影子银行分析的借鉴意义。

资产证券化允许银行将贷款进行表外操作，通过 SPV（special purpose vehicle，特殊目的机构）等机构对贷款打包评级，以回购协议的方式出售给货币市场基金，获得融资（Gorton and Metrick，2010）。这一过程将银行原本持有的信贷风险也转移出去了。SPV 的打包评级过程转移了银行原本持有的信贷风险，期限转换功能满足了不同的信贷需求，有助于进一步吸引资金。1990 年，美国的资产证券化的现金池仅为 1 000 亿美元，到 2007 年增长到超过 2. 5 万亿美元（Claessens，2012）。

对资产证券化的信用创造过程描述如下。假设整个经济体只存在一家银行 D，持有基础货币 M，可贷资金为（1－r）M，r 为存款准备金。贷款资金（1－r）M 或贷给不同风险级别的企业用于投资固定资产，或贷给不同信用等级的居民购买房产。D 银行资金流出，资产负债表的负债方记长期或短期贷款，贷款总额度为（1－r）M。

如果按照正常的货币扩张路径，居民和企业购买固定资产的资金会由售卖者得到后重新存入银行，银行再将（1－r）2M 部分进行贷款，循环 n 期后，原本的 M 量基础货币扩张为 M/r。

如果银行在 t＝1 期时就将全部的贷款 β 比例进行资产证券化，则原本手中的 β（1－r）M 量账面贷款出表，出售给 SPV，SPV 将贷款打包成证券化产品，并进行评级，银行将证券化产品出售给货币市场基金等资金池，或进行同业操作，以吸收回购资金。在这一过程中，银行 β（1－r）M 量的账面贷款又重新以回购资金的形式流回银行，银行则可将回购资金的 β（1－r）2M 量作为可贷资金。这样，由 SPV 打包评级的证券化贷款吸引的回购资金 β（1－r）M 将按照货币乘数量扩张为 $\beta\frac{1-r}{r}M$。则 D 银行的 M 量基础货币创造的信用扩张为 $\beta\frac{M}{r}[1+(1-r)]$。如果银行将 t＝2 期的账面贷款也进行 β 比例的证券化操作，则信用将扩张为 $\beta\frac{M}{r}[1+(1-r)+(1-r)^2]$。如果 D 银行将每一期的账面贷款的 β 比例都进行资产证券化操作，则信用货币量 $\beta\frac{M}{r}$ 可以扩张至：

$$\beta\frac{1}{r}M[(1-r)+(1-r)^2+\cdots+(1-r)^n]=\beta\frac{1}{r^2}M$$

如果将证券化的资产再进行 p 轮的证券化操作，信用甚至可以无限扩张至 $\beta\frac{1}{r^p}M$。可以看到，资产证券化过程的信用创造能力非常强大。SPV 的证券化评级过程激活了银行手中原本持有的贷款，资产证券化的环节越多，信贷扩张网络的分布范围越大，整个体系的抗风险能力也越弱，风险冲击可能导致银行与其他金融机构的串联式破产。

美国的资产证券化环节要比中国强大得多，表现为 p 更大。资产证券化的信用创造循环模式如下图 1.15 所示。

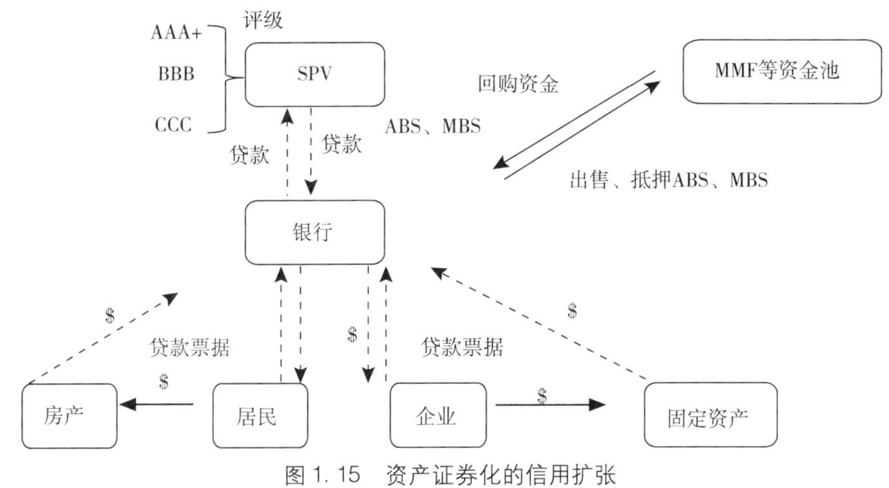

图 1.15　资产证券化的信用扩张

资料来源：作者整理。

2. 抵押担保债务（CDO）的信用扩张

假设 $t=1$ 期时，经济体中居民和企业持有的房产和固定资产总量为 $(1-r)M$，此时居民和企业将拿出其中的一定比例进行抵押，则获得额外融资 $\theta(1-r)M$，并将这一部分继续存入银行（假设经济体内只存在一家银行 D），银行获得额外的 $\theta(1-r)M$ 用于信用扩张，循环 n 期得到扩张后的信用量 $\theta\frac{1-r}{r}M$。如果银行创造的所有信用贷款 $\frac{1}{r}M$ 都被用来投资房产和固定资产，所有房产和固定资产的 θ 比例都用来抵押再融资，则经济体的信用将扩张至 $\theta\frac{1}{r^2}M$。当抵押再融资的资产继续用来抵押融资 q 轮时，信用甚至可以无限扩张至 $\frac{1}{r^q}M$。

假设经济体内仅有银行传统信贷、资产证券化和抵押担保 3 种信用扩张方式，则与仅有传统银行信用扩张的方式相比，M 量的基础货币由创造 $\frac{1}{r}M$ 量的信用，增加至 $\frac{1}{r}M+\beta\frac{1}{r^2}M+\theta\frac{1}{r^2}M$，最多扩张至 $\frac{1}{r}M+\beta\frac{1}{r^p}M+\theta\frac{1}{r^q}M$。

当资产证券化产品可以交易的时候，盘活了本身具有价值但不易流通的资产，提高了价值商品的流动性，充当了“货币”的交易功能。人们因为相信、肯定了资产证券化产品背后的固定资产的未来变现价值，因而赋予了资产证券化产品信用创造的功能，增加了整个社会体系的信用扩张。所以结论是，证券化和担保债务过程都赋予了原本不具有信用扩张功能的价值商品作为价值资产继续扩张信用的功能。

（三）中国影子银行的信用扩张

中国影子银行的信用扩张渠道不同于美国影子银行体系，我国的资产证券化业务发展并不成熟，而主要是通过银行理财产品、银行与信托公司合作和银行进行委托贷款等这些“通道业务”，通过货币的转移而非货币的创造来满足社会融资需求、扩张信用活动。因此我国的影子银行主要是 A 类影子银行，B 类影子银行的规模相对较小，例如，据埃勒斯（Ehlers，2018）统计，截至 2016 年，我国的 P2P 贷款总量为 8 000 亿元，仅占影子银行信贷总量的 1.4%，占 GDP 的比例为 1.1%。且我国的资产证券化和担保债务凭证的市场相较美国仍不发达，银行通过证券化和担保债务扩张信用的环节很少。

由于我国目前没有相对成熟的类似 SPV 的证券化评级机构，无法对出表后的贷款打包产品进行分级，从业者也缺乏对投资项目的风险识别，所以我国利用 WMP 影子银行产品投资股市、地产项目的风险较高。在金融市场尚未健全的体制下，中国影子银行的表外信用扩张环节透明度低，不易监测，因此不宜过度纵容影子银行发展。

信托公司是我国影子银行的特有部分，其代表客户进行资产管理活动，将资产投资于债券和股票等金融工具，或以贷款的形式直接向非金融企业提供贷款，再将打包好的信托贷款出售给商业银行、同业市场进行融资。银行通过与信托公司合作将原贷款资产转变为“类贷款”，在资产负债表上记作非保本理财产品（表外）或隐藏于表内的买入返售等科目。在这里，信托公司只是起到规避政策监管目的的“通道”机构，创造的信用只是由于银行因受到“监管挤压”而损失的那一部分。从这一层面来看，中国的影子银行不同于美国资产证券化产品的信用创造功能。WMP 主要投资于股票、债券等“非标准信贷资产”，收益率高于银行存款利率。从微观角度考虑，理财产品的出现满足了不愿承受股市风险，又愿意为理财产品高于无风险存款的风险溢价选择储存更多货币的个人投资者的需求。如此看来，我国的银信合作和理财产品并没有赋予价值资产继续扩张信用的这一功能，只是商业银行进行传统信用扩张的通道工具，或银行通过影子银行对信用扩张的投向板块起到调节分配的作用（见图 1.16）。

我国的银行同业业务是向影子银行体系提供资金的途径之一。主要通过商业银行之间、银行与其他金融机构之间的资金融通业务不占用银行贷款额度，不影响存贷比（祝继高，2016）。同业业务的信贷投向透明度低、不受监管，且要求的风险资产权重较低。同业拆借业务的投资期限往往较短，很多在 1 年期以内，属于临时性资金融通业务，资金通过非银行融资渠道的流转速度更快。影子银行满足了相当一部分无法通过正常银行贷款渠道获得满足的超额信贷需求，或许这部分信贷扩张蕴含更高的风险，同业业务的发展为影子银行的这一功能提供了流动性。

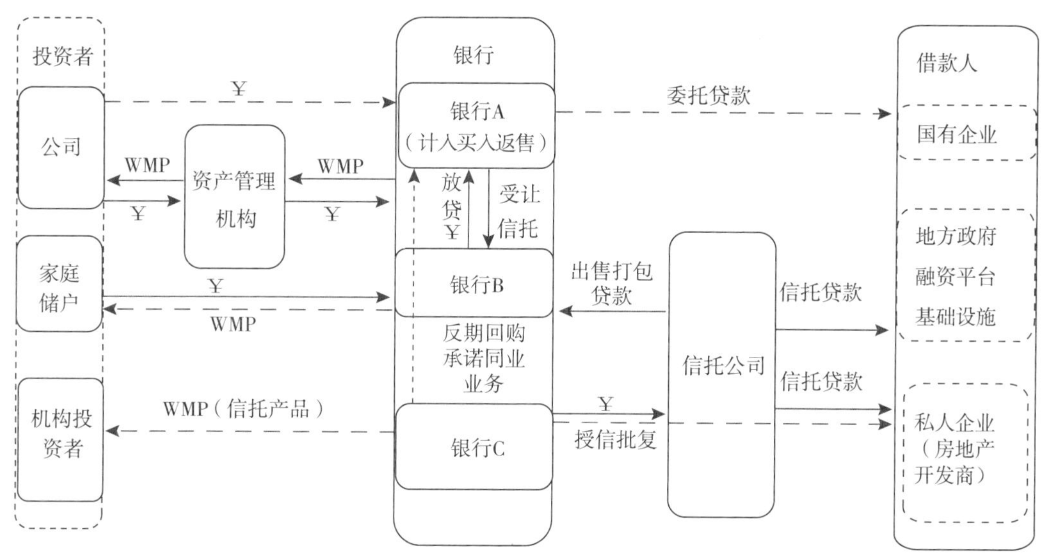

图 1.16　中国影子银行体系的运作

资料来源：根据 FBS（2015）和祝继高（2016）相关研究整理得出。

三、中国影子银行信用扩张的实证检验

（一）模型设定

米什金（Mishkin，2010）认为宏观经济具有高度的非线性特征，很多宏观经济变量在经济周期中的表现并不是对称的。影子银行对信用扩张的传导可能存在长期和短期的非对称性，而且影子银行的正向冲击和负向冲击也可能对信用扩张存在非对称传导。基于此种考虑，本文选用非线性自回归分布滞后模型（NARDL）对解释变量的正负项进行分解，这样可以分析正负冲击对于被解释变量影响的差异性。同时，信贷扩张和影子银行的规模存在滞后效应，该模型滞后项的引入可对变量间的依赖关系和动态调整路径做出很好的刻画，可以更清晰地分析非对称效应和长短期均衡关系。传统的自回归分布滞后模型（ARDL）有如下形式：

$$\Delta y_t = \alpha_0 + \rho y_{t-1} + \theta x_{t-1} + \sum_{j=1}^{p-1} \alpha_j \Delta y_{t-j} + \sum_{j=0}^{q-1} \pi_j \Delta x_{t-j} + \varepsilon_t \tag{1}$$

通过把 ARDL 模型的解释变量拆分为正负项变动的积累以考察长期与短期传递效应的非对称性。NARDL 模型（Shin et al.，2014）的一般形式为：

$$\Delta y_t = \rho y_{t-1} + \theta^+ x_{t-1}^+ + \theta^- x_{t-1}^- + \sum_{j=1}^{p-1} \varphi_j \Delta y_{t-j} + \sum_{j=0}^{q-1} (\pi_j^+ \Delta x_{t-j}^+ + \pi_j^- \Delta x_{t-j}^-) + \varepsilon_t \tag{2}$$

其中，x_t^+ 是 x_t 的正向累积增量 $x_t^+ = \sum_{j=1}^{t} \Delta x_j^+ = \sum_{j=1}^{t} max(\Delta x_j, 0)$。$x_t^-$ 是 x_t 的负向累积增量，$x_t^- = \sum_{j=1}^{t} \Delta x_j^- = \sum_{j=1}^{t} min(\Delta x_j, 0)$，自变量分解为 $x_t = x_0 + x_t^+ + x_t^-$。

为了考察影子银行规模（Sh）对信贷扩张（Cre）的影响，建立 NARDL 模型如下：

$$\Delta Cre_t = \rho Cre_{t-1} + \theta^+ Sh_{t-1}^+ + \theta^- Sh_{t-1}^- + \sum_{j=1}^{p-1} \varphi_j \Delta Cre_{t-j} + \sum_{j=0}^{q-1} (\pi_j^+ \Delta Sh_{t-j}^+ + \pi_j^- \Delta Sh_{t-j}^-) + \varepsilon_t \tag{3}$$

其中，π_j^+ 为影子银行规模增加对信贷的短期传递效应，π_j^- 为影子银行规模缩减对信贷的短期传递效应，当 $\sum_{j=0}^{q-1} \pi_j^+ \neq \sum_{j=0}^{q-1} \pi_j^-$ 时，说明影子银行规模的正负变动对信贷的短期传递存在着非对称性。对于 Sh_t 的正负一单位冲击，Cre_t 的累积动态乘数效应分别为：

$$m_h^+ = \sum_{j=0}^{h} \frac{\partial\ Cre_{t+j}}{\partial\ Sh_t^+},\ m_h^- = \sum_{j=0}^{h} \frac{\partial\ Cre_{t+j}}{\partial\ Sh_t^-},\ h = 0,1,2\cdots \tag{4}$$

可以证明，当 $h \to \infty$时，$m_h^+ \to -\frac{\widehat{\theta}^+}{\widehat{\rho}} = \widehat{\beta}^+$，$m_h^- \to -\frac{\widehat{\theta}^-}{\widehat{\rho}} = \widehat{\beta}^-$。所以，$\widehat{\beta}^+$ 代表了影子银行规模增加对信贷的长期传递效应，$\widehat{\beta}^-$ 代表了影子银行规模减小对信贷的长期传递效应。当 $\widehat{\beta}^+ \neq \widehat{\beta}^-$ 时，说明影子银行规模的正负变动对信贷的长期传递存在着非对称性。

为了验证和描述长期和短期非对称性，对方程（3）的参数施加了以下不同约束：

（1）令 $\theta = \theta^+ = \theta^-$，且 $\sum_i \pi_i^+ = \sum_i \pi_i^- (i = 0,1\cdots q-1)$，同时约束 NARDL 模型的长、短期非对称性，模型回归为对称的自回归分布滞后 ARDL，其中影子银行对信贷扩张的长期与短期传递效应都是线性且对称的。

（2）仅令 $\theta = \theta^+ = \theta^-$，约束长期非对称性，模型回归为短期非对称分布滞后，记为 NARDLS。

（3）令 $\sum_i \pi_i^+ = \sum_i \pi_i^+ (i = 0,1\cdots q-1)$，仅约束短期非对称性，模型回归为长期非对称分布滞后，记为 NARDLL。

（4）无约束模型，长短期均存在非对称性，即 NARDL。

（二）数据选取和处理

参考穆迪投资公司对中国核心影子银行的检测指标，本文选用社会融资规模中的委托贷款、信托贷款和未贴现银行承兑汇票之和衡量影子银行规模；选用彭博中国信贷脉搏指数来衡量中国的信用扩张程度，该指标衡量了新增信贷扩张占 GDP 的比重；选用影子银行同比增长率①考察影子银行的规模增速，表示影子银行的信贷扩张较上一年同期水平的扩张规模大小。以上数据均选取 2006—2017 年的月度数据（见图 1.17 和图 1.18）。

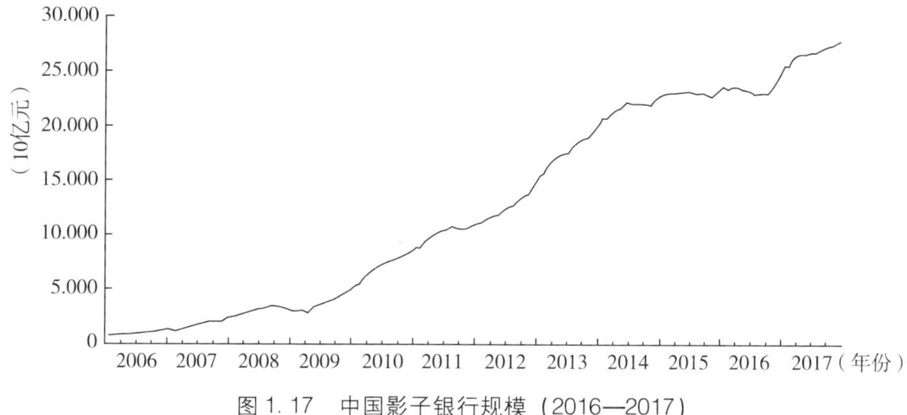

图 1.17　中国影子银行规模（2016—2017）

资料来源：彭博数据库。

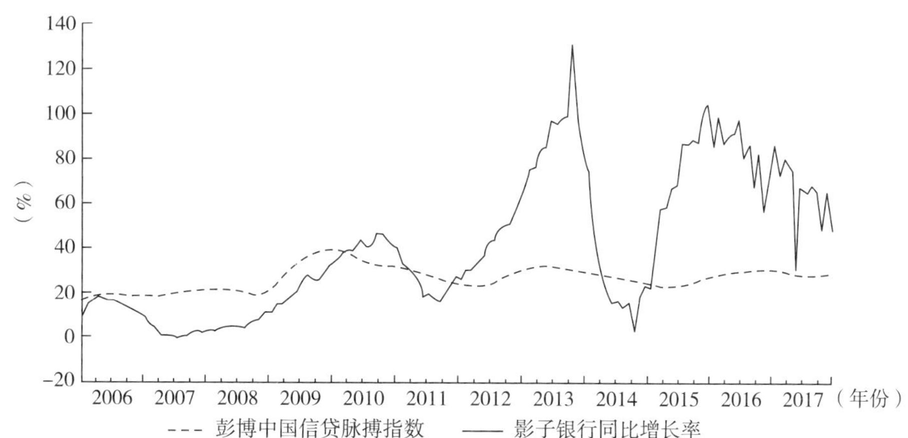

图 1.18　彭博中国信贷脉搏指数和影子银行同比增长率（2006—2017）

资料来源：彭博数据库。

① 同比增长率 = 本期发展水平/去年同期水平 ×100%。

由图 1. 17 可以看出，我国影子银行的规模总体处于不断扩大的趋势，从 2006 年 1 月的 7 070 亿元增长到 2017 年 12 月的 278 330 亿元，增长了 38 倍多。从图 1. 18 可以看出，以彭博中国信贷脉搏指数衡量的信用扩张总体平稳，略有起伏。相反，影子银行的同比增长率波动较大。2008 年金融危机爆发后，影子银行的同比增速急剧下降到零。2009 年至 2010 年中期，受国家 4 万亿元救市计划及相对宽松的货币政策影响，影子银行的信贷规模又出现了短期的急剧上升。2010 年"紧缩"政策出手，影子银行的信贷扩张开始逐步放缓，随后又急剧上升。2013 年"钱荒"事件发生后，国家对影子银行的监管更加严格和重视，导致影子银行的同比增长速度急剧下降，随后开始回升。近两年，影子银行的同比增速在震荡中下降。通过对比可以发现，影子银行的同比增速波动更大，呈现出"缓慢上升、急速下降"的特点，这反映了影子银行扩张与收缩速度存在非对称性。

（三）估计结果

我们利用 2006—2017 年的彭博中国信贷脉搏指数、影子银行规模数据对方程（3）进行估计。为了减少异方差的影响，变量均作对数化处理。ADF 单位根检验显示信贷扩张波动 ΔCre_t 与影子银行规模波动 ΔSh 均为平稳序列，可在 1% 的显著性水平下拒绝不平稳的原假设。根据系数的显著性选择 NARDL 模型滞后期为（12，6，2），实证结果见表 1. 15。

表 1. 15　NARDL 及约束条件模型的估计结果

NARDL		NARDLL		NARDLS		ARDL	
变量	系数	变量	系数	变量	系数	变量	系数
Cre_{t-1}	0. 114*** (0. 04)	Cre_{t-1}	-0. 102** (0. 04)	Cre_{t-1}	-0. 027 (0. 024)	Cre_{t-1}	-0. 032 (0. 023)
Sh^+_{t-1}	-0. 017 (0. 012)	Sh^+_{t-1}	-0. 025** (0. 011)	Sh_{t-1}	-0. 001 (0. 01)	Sh_{t-1}	-0. 006 (0. 006)
Sh^-_{t-1}	-0. 293** (0. 116)	Sh^-_{t-1}	-0. 267** (0. 124)				
ΔCre_{t-3}	0. 304*** (0. 082)	ΔCre_{t-3}	0. 324*** (0. 085)	ΔCre_{t-3}	0. 268*** (0. 089)	ΔCre_{t-3}	0. 324*** (0. 087)
ΔCre_{t-5}	-0. 21** (0. 085)	ΔCre_{t-5}	-0. 244*** (0. 086)	ΔCre_{t-5}	-0. 216** (0. 087)	ΔCre_{t-5}	-0. 23*** (0. 087)
ΔCre_{t-6}	0. 208** (0. 088)	ΔCre_{t-6}	0. 226** (0. 088)	ΔCre_{t-6}	0. 235** (0. 09)	ΔCre_{t-6}	0. 228** (0. 09)
ΔCre_{t-7}	0. 22** (0. 09)			ΔCre_{t-7}	0. 219** (0. 093)		

（续表）

NARDL		NARDLL		NARDLS		ARDL	
变量	系数	变量	系数	变量	系数	变量	系数
$\Delta\ Cre_{t-12}$	-0.23*** (0.081)	$\Delta\ Cre_{t-12}$	-0.192** (0.081)	$\Delta\ Cre_{t-12}$	-0.271*** (0.082)	$\Delta\ Cre_{t-12}$	-0.216*** (0.08)
ΔSh_t^+	0.388*** (0.131)	ΔSh_t	0.312*** (0.098)	ΔSh_t^+	0.386*** (0.134)	ΔSh_t	0.36*** (0.096)
ΔSh_{t-3}^+	-0.281** (0.117)	ΔSh_{t-2}	-0.261*** (0.092)	ΔSh_{t-3}^+	-0.326*** (0.118)	ΔSh_{t-2}	-0.306*** (0.09)
ΔSh_{t-5}^+	0.362*** (0.12)	ΔSh_{t-3}	-0.284*** (0.098)	ΔSh_{t-4}^+	-0.251** (0.121)	ΔSh_{t-3}	-0.34*** (0.094)
ΔSh_{t-6}^+	0.333*** (0.121)	ΔSh_{t-5}	0.244** (0.1)	ΔSh_{t-5}^+	0.31** (0.12)	ΔSh_{t-5}	-0.26*** (0.093)
ΔSh_{t-2}^-	-0.816*** (0.26)	ΔSh_{t-6}	0.205** (0.098)	ΔSh_{t-2}^-	-0.91*** (0.265)		
Const.	0.288*** (0.099)	*Const.*	0.299*** (0.1)	*Const.*	0.097 (0.086)	*Const.*	0.164*** (0.06)
R^2	0.59		0.54		0.57		0.52
$\overline{R}^2$	0.49		0.44		0.47		0.43
F_{pss}	5.86***		5.73***		5.43***		5.61***
W_{LR}	8.46**		9.18**				
W_{SR}	40.38***				54.22***		
EG	-10.97***		-11***		-11.05***		-10.83***

注：F_{pss}统计量检验长期影响的存在性；W_{LR}和W_{SR}为Wald检验统计量，分别用来检验长短期的非对称效应；***和**分别代表在1%和5%的显著水平统计显著；EG表示Engle-Granger两步法的ADF检验结果。

结果汇报中剔除了短期动态滞后系数不显著的变量。无论从系数的显著性还是拟合优度来看，非对称的ARDL模型估计结果是最优的。Wald检验结果的显著性也证实了影子银行对社会信贷扩张的短期与长期影响均存在非对称效应，长期对称性W_{LR}检验与短期对称性W_{SR}检验均在1%显著性水平下拒绝原假设。模型的EG两步法的检验结果均拒绝了1%显著性水平下不存在协整关系的原假设，说明影子银行的规模变动与社会信用的扩张及收缩变动之间存在稳定的非对称协整关系。

（四）非对称传导效应分析

从短期来看，正向波动ΔSh_t^+、ΔSh_{t-5}^+、ΔSh_{t-6}^+的系数分别为0.388、0.362、0.333，

负向波动 ΔSh_{t-2}^{-} 的系数为 -0.816。可以看出，影子银行规模的正向波动对社会信用的扩张具有持续的正向影响，滞后 6 期的影响仍显著。负向波动对社会信用的扩张具有负向影响，但持续期较短，破坏力较大，其系数的绝对值远大于正向波动。中国的影子银行主要体现为商业银行通过“理财产品”“银信合作”“银证合作”“同业业务”将信贷资产出表，以满足无法通过正常渠道获得商业银行贷款的机构和企业的贷款需求。所以在短期内，影子银行规模的正向波动扩张了社会信用。而当央行采取紧缩政策或监管部门加强对影子银行的监管时，影子银行的增速会急剧下降，对社会信用的扩张产生不利影响。在图 1.18 中，影子银行的增速体现出“缓慢上升、急剧下降”的特点。这种特点在 NARDL 模型中就体现为负向波动系数的绝对值远大于正向波动。

从长期来看，Sh_{t-1}^{-} 的系数为 -0.293，Sh_{t-1}^{+} 的系数为 -0.017。这说明影子银行规模的负向累积和正向累积均不利于信用扩张，而且负向累积的负面影响更加显著。根据前面的分析，影子银行扩张了社会信用，影子银行的负向累积必然会缩减信用扩张。值得注意的是，在长期中，影子银行规模的正向累积系数也为负，竟然不利于信用扩张。究其原因，影子银行的融资体系中包含更多的风险偏好者，且机构不受存款准备金、存贷比等政策的监管限制，所以影子银行的信用扩张比例增大会导致金融体系的不稳定增加，系统性风险增强，进而不利于社会信用的扩张。虽然正向累积系数的绝对值较小，但其中包含的风险值得注意。

对比短期和长期可以发现，影子银行规模的正向波动在短期内有利于信用扩张，在长期内不利于信用扩张；负向波动在短期和长期内都不利于信用扩张。通过累计动态乘数图可以更加清楚地看到这种长短期的非对称性。在图 1.19 中，Sh^{+} 表示影子银行的正向冲击带来的累积影响乘数，Sh^{-} 表示影子银行的负向冲击带来的累积影响乘数。对于影子银行一单位的正向冲击，社会信用的扩张的响应在前 5 期为正向且逐渐减少，之后转变为负向响应，说明了我国目前的“通道式”影子银行业务的健康循环性较差，流向房地产和地方融资平台的模式存在一定的风险，并不利于整个社会的长期良性信用扩张。“通道式”影子银行的规模越大，对社会信用的良性扩张的负向作用就越大，这与影子银行的系统性风险积累在于它的顺周期性（Claessens，2012）的结论类似。对于影子银行收缩的一单位负向冲击，社会信用的响应为负向，且在短期内急剧波动后逐渐平稳，说明影子银行的规模缩小会导致社会信用的急剧收缩，其负向影响在短期内很显著。

四、研究结论和政策建议

通过对比，本文发现美国与中国的影子银行体系本质上都提供了信用和流动性转换。不同的是，美国影子银行的信贷扩张基于强大的证券化、抵押担保业务和具有公

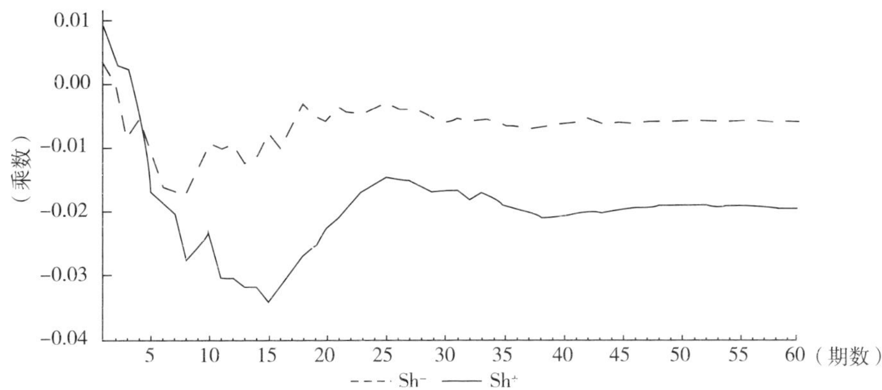

图 1.19　影子银行非对称传导效应的累积动态乘数

信力的评级机构；中国影子银行涉及相对较少的资产证券化产品，也不主要依靠证券化产品吸引回购资金来融资，而主要依靠银行间同业业务互相融通资金。中国影子银行主要是依附于占主导体系的商业银行的“通道业务”。

通过实证研究，本文发现，不论是在短期还是长期内，影子银行规模的正负项波动对信用扩张的影响均存在显著的不同；影子银行规模的正向波动在短期内有利于信用扩张，在长期内不利于信用扩张；负向波动在短期和长期内都不利于信用扩张。这都体现了影子银行信用扩张的非对称性。实证结果表明，影子银行有利有弊，在扩张信用的同时，也积聚了系统性风险，应当注意平衡两者之间的关系。对此，本文提出以下政策建议。

第一，通过规范影子银行的业务范围和业务细则，引导和发挥影子银行扩张信用的有利影响。影子银行的规模扩张，在一定程度上弥补了银行信用的不足，具有满足融资需求、提高金融效率等积极作用，同时也推动了商业银行转型创新，促进了实体经济发展，昭示了金融体系内在缺陷及未来发展方向。从我国的实际情况来看，2008年我国政府为了应对金融危机投放了过多的流动性，房地产和地方融资平台的需求量过大是催生中国影子银行迅速发展的前提条件。我国“以钱生钱”的能力要远远低于欧美等国的金融市场，而货币流通速度慢，表现为实体信贷需求与信贷配给之间的不匹配性。如果社会融资规模需要不断扩大，而正规的银行贷款等企业融资渠道不能满足所有的信贷需求，那么影子银行规模的扩张将是必然的趋势，所以需要合理的“阳光化”引导，使其在正规体系内发挥良性信用扩张的作用。

第二，加强对影子银行的监管，建立风险监测和预警制度，有效防范影子银行规模过大所带来的系统性风险。由于我国的影子银行信贷资产更多地流向房地产和地方政府融资平台等领域，其业务的健康可持续循环性较差，并不利于整个社会的长期良性信用扩张。从冲击响应的长期均衡水平来看，我国的“通道式”影子银行业务的规模不宜持续扩大，其对社会信贷收缩的冲击具有短期剧烈的特征，相较传统的商业银行体系的信贷扩张融资更加不稳定、风险更大。对于监管当局来说，要逐步完善影子银行监管的法律体系，制定合理的信息披露办法、信用评级制度；推动建立防火墙制度，有效隔离商业银行与影子银行，避免影子银行的风险传染到商业银行体系中。对于影子银行来说，要注意加强内部风险控制，做好投资项目的风险评估，避免把信贷投资到产能落后、产能过剩等高风险行业。

中国对外贸易成本变动及其影响因素研究

陕西省分行　米嘉伟

一、研究综述

运输成本是国际贸易理论中贸易成本重要的构成要素和早期研究的切入点。保罗·萨缪尔森（Paul A. Samuelson，1954）最早提出了“冰山型运输成本”，即在进行国际货物贸易时为运达商品，始终会有一部分额外的“商品”在运输过程中“消融”。随后贸易成本逐渐成为国际贸易领域研究的热点问题，是新贸易理论和新新贸易理论从企业异质性角度研究出口增长动力的重要突破口。安德森和温库（Anderson and Wincoop，2003）认为贸易成本是产品除生产成本之外的从生产者到达最终消费者过程中发生的需要支付的所有成本，包括信息成本、运输费用、时间成本、边界成本（关税及非关税壁垒）、合同成本（履约成本）、汇率成本（汇兑差额）、法律合规成本以及目的市场分销成本。张蕙（2013）在回顾了马克思主义经济学中的流通费用、新制度经济学中的交易成本、新兴古典经济学中的交易费用后，从中观层面给出了对贸易成本的定义，认为贸易成本是产品从生产者转移到消费者过程中经历所有贸易环节需要支付的成本。

在近年来，我国学者在研究贸易成本测度问题方面主要沿用了诺维（Novy）的测算方法。钱学锋、梁琦（2008）利用其测度模型对中国同部分贸易伙伴的贸易成本进行了测度，结果显示我国同这些贸易伙伴的双边贸易成本呈下降趋势，我国的贸易自由化进程取得了一定的成效。方虹（2010）对 1992—2007 年中国与 28 个主要贸易伙伴的双边贸易成本进行了测算。梁俊伟（2015）借助投入产出表中一国生产总量数据代替 GDP 数据，计算了中国与日本和韩国的双边贸易成本。

二、中国与主要贸易伙伴双边贸易成本测度

（一）测度方法

现有研究文献对贸易成本测算所使用的方法主要为基于引力模型的间接测算方法。

引力模型是国际贸易领域研究国际贸易流量潜力、评估贸易集团效应、估计贸易成本大小的重要研究工具。国际贸易研究中被广泛使用的引力模型最早是由廷贝亨（Tinbergen，1962）引入使用的，灵感来自物理学中的“万有引力”定理：两物体之间的引力大小与其质量的乘积成正比，与其距离成反比。与之进行类比，国际贸易中贸易双方之间的贸易流量大小与两国的经济总量的乘积成正比，与两国之间的距离成反比。其具体的表现形式为：

$$Tflow_{ij} = A\frac{(Y_iY_j)^{\theta_1}}{(dist_{ij})^{\theta_2}} \tag{1}$$

其中，$Tflow_{ij}$ 表示 i 国向 j 国出口的贸易流量，Y_i 和 Y_j 分别代表 i 国和 j 国的经济总量，常以两国的 GDP 总量进行表示，$dist_{ij}$ 表示两国之间的地理距离，实证研究中多以两国首都或经济中心之间的距离进行表示，A 代表的是一个比例常数。从经济意义的角度进行理解：Y_i 表示 i 国产品的生产能力和供应能力，Y_j 则表示 j 国对进口商品的需求结构的丰富度和需求能力，$dist_{ij}$ 表示 i 国和 j 国进行双边贸易时所受到的阻碍。在引力模型基础上诺维（2013）推导出被广泛使用的贸易成本测算模型：

$$\tau_{ij} = [(t_{ij}t_{ji})/(t_{ii}t_{jj})]^{\frac{1}{2}} - 1 = [(X_{ii}X_{jj})/(X_{ij}X_{ji})]^{\frac{1}{2(\sigma-1)}} \tag{2}$$

其中，τ_{ij} 为本文所要计算的关税当量，其实质上度量了双边贸易成本 $t_{ij}t_{ji}$ 与贸易双方国内贸易成本 $t_{ii}t_{jj}$ 的相对大小，当我们从贸易流量角度观测到一国的对外贸易流量相对于国内贸易流量增加时，这很有可能就是双边贸易成本下降所带来的效应。X_{ii} 和 X_{jj} 是 i 国和 j 国的国内贸易流量，X_{ij} 和 X_{ji} 分别为 i 国对 j 国的出口量和 j 国对 i 国的出口量，σ 为国内外商品间的替代弹性。

（二）数据来源

本文所使用的中国与贸易伙伴各年的双边进出口数据、贸易伙伴各年的进出口总额数据均取自联合国 UNComtrade 数据库，世界各年进出口总额数据来自世界银行数据库（World Bank Database）。依照以往的研究经验，本文将两国间的商品替代弹性取值为 8。

（三）测算结果

图 1.20 呈现了中国总体及与不同区域贸易伙伴的双边整体贸易成本变动趋势。结果显示中国同各区域双边贸易成本都呈下降趋势，同不同区域的贸易成本存在差异。

从总体角度来看，中国整体的贸易成本在 1995—2016 年处于下降状态，从 1995 年的 0.861 下降至 2016 年的 0.649，下降了 24.59%。分区域来看，在观测时间范围内，

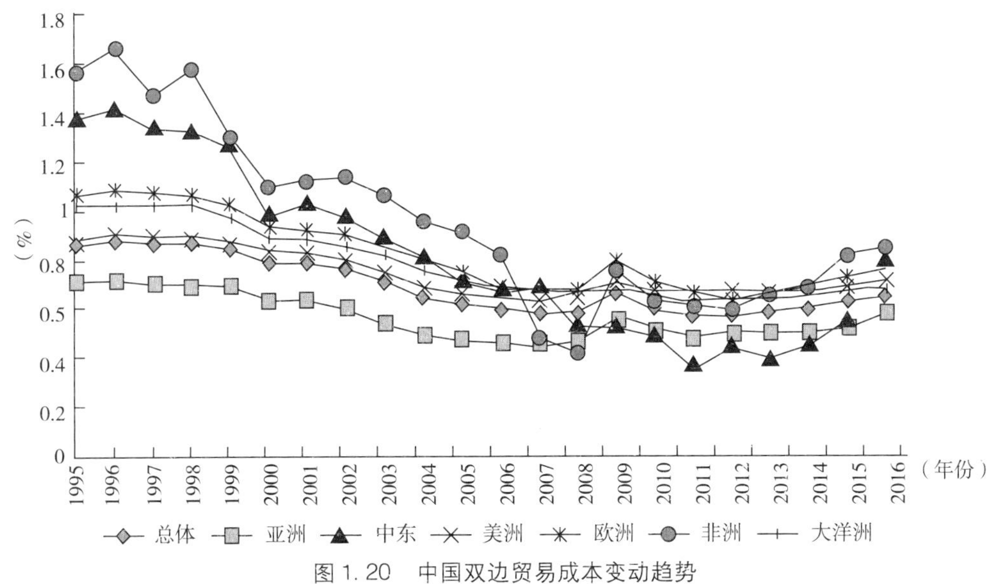

图 1.20　中国双边贸易成本变动趋势

中国与非洲、中东国家双边贸易成本降幅最大，较 1995 年分别降低了 42.40% 和 46.11%，中国同亚洲及美洲贸易伙伴的双边贸易成本降幅最小，分别下降了 18.68% 和 18.17%，同欧洲贸易伙伴的双边贸易成本下降了 27.74%，同大洋洲贸易伙伴的双边贸易成本下降了 32.76%。从变化的整体趋势来看，2007 年之前，中国与各区域双边贸易成本按照绝对值由高到低依次排名为非洲、中东、欧洲、大洋洲、美洲以及亚洲，2007 年后中国与不同区域双边贸易成本的数值范围较 1995 年明显收窄，说明同不同区域的贸易伙伴的贸易成本有趋同集中的倾向。

表 1.16　中国与各贸易伙伴双边贸易成本　（%）

成本组别	区域	贸易伙伴	2016 年双边贸易成本	较 1995 年变动幅度
高成本	亚洲	巴基斯坦	1.06	-13.35
		孟加拉国	1.19	-16.26
		哈萨克斯坦	1.71	24.59
	中东	以色列	1.08	-32.65
		埃及	1.37	-24.98
		土耳其	1.16	-25.06
	欧洲	西班牙	1.03	-19.98
		瑞典	1.07	-13.68
		丹麦	1.05	-25.88
	美洲	阿根廷	1.14	-26.29
		哥伦比亚	1.15	-51.05
	非洲	尼日利亚	1.33	-17.50

（续表）

成本组别	区域	贸易伙伴	2016 年双边贸易成本	较 1995 年变动幅度
中等成本	亚洲	缅甸	0.82	-29.30
		印度	0.92	-34.60
		印度尼西亚	0.79	-15.71
	大洋洲	新西兰	0.97	-25.28
	中东	沙特阿拉伯	0.75	-32.85
		伊拉克	0.82	-44.71
		阿曼	0.80	-39.95
		科威特	0.88	-42.42
	欧洲	英国	0.87	-22.27
		俄罗斯	0.74	-23.64
		法国	0.93	-20.13
		瑞士	0.84	-35.28
		意大利	0.91	-14.93
		波兰	0.99	-37.59
	美洲	巴西	0.84	-38.18
		加拿大	0.87	-13.07
		墨西哥	0.83	-51.84
		智利	0.73	-43.41
		秘鲁	0.90	-32.46
	非洲	南非	0.73	-33.55
		安哥拉*	0.76	-49.12
低成本	亚洲	日本	0.60	-9.80
		韩国	0.43	-34.36
		越南*	0.31	-69.06
		泰国	0.45	-47.91
		菲律宾	0.68	-42.58
	中东	阿联酋*	0.48	-63.00
		伊朗*	0.67	-54.71
	欧洲	德国	0.62	-31.72
		荷兰	0.57	-41.66
		比利时	0.66	-43.82
		捷克*	0.56	-63.28
		匈牙利*	0.58	-63.04
	美洲	美国	0.64	-18.99
	大洋洲	澳大利亚	0.66	-33.33

注：将中国同各国的双边贸易成本按照（0，0.7]、(0.7，1)、[1，+∞）划分为低、中等、高成本组别；标注 * 的国家，表示由于数据的缺失，这些国家 2016 年的贸易成本取值为可测得的最近年份的数值；由于无法估计中国香港、新加坡和马来西亚的贸易流量，故将这三者剔除。

表1.16列示了中国同不同贸易伙伴2016年的双边整体贸易成本计算结果，和其较1995年的贸易成本的变化幅度，并按照贸易成本的高低不同将不同水平的贸易成本国家分为3组，高成本国家、中等成本国家以及低成本国家。从计算结果可知，中国同不同贸易伙伴的双边贸易成本均呈下降的趋势，具体的贸易成本绝对数值大小存在差异。3个组别中各区域的贸易伙伴均有分布，其中处于高成本组别的有12个国家，处于中等成本组别的有21个国家，处于低成本组别的有14个国家。中国同2016年中国贸易份额的前17位贸易伙伴的双边贸易成本均处于中低等水平，其中有8个国家处于中等成本组别（法国、印度、英国、加拿大、巴西、瑞士、印度尼西亚以及俄罗斯），剩余的9个国家处于低成本组别（菲律宾、澳大利亚、美国、德国、日本、荷兰、韩国、泰国、越南）。

此外，本文将50个样本国家（地区）划分为发达国家（地区）、新兴经济体及其他发展中国家3个组别。以是否为OECD（经合组织）成员国家（除智利、墨西哥、土耳其）作为是否为发达国家的判断标准，对新兴经济体的确认沿用博鳌亚洲论坛《新兴经济体发展报告》中选择的11个国家。按上述方法分组后还有中国香港、新加坡、韩国未确定分组，依据经济总量及人均收入水平，本文将这3个国家（地区）归入发达国家（地区）组别。

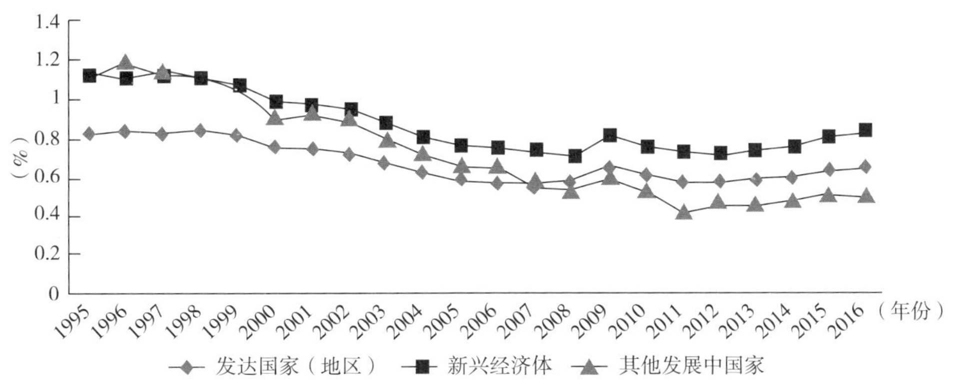

图1.21　中国同发达国家（地区）、新兴经济体及其他发展中国家双边贸易成本变动

图1.21为中国同发达国家（地区）、新兴经济体及其他发展中国家的双边贸易成本变动情况。可以看到1995—2008年中国同发达国家（地区）的双边贸易成本最低，同新兴经济体和其他发展中国家的双边贸易成本较为接近。2008—2016年中国同其他发展中国家的双边贸易成本最低，其次为同发达国家（地区），同新兴经济体国家的双边贸易成本最高。从变化趋势来看，中国同这3个组别贸易伙伴的双边贸易成本均呈下降趋势，同其他发展中国家的双边贸易成本下降速度最快。从变化幅度来看，1995—2016年中国同其他发展中国家的双边贸易成本降幅最大，达56.31%，同新兴经

济体国家的双边贸易成本降幅达25.95%，同发达国家的双边贸易成本降幅达19.67%。

三、中国与主要贸易伙伴双边贸易成本影响因素的实证分析

（一）模型设定

本文借鉴其他学者关于贸易成本影响因素实证建模经验（孙瑾、杨英俊，2016；熊立春、程宝栋，2017），基于传统引力模型构建面板数据模型如下：

$$Ln\tau_{ij}^{t} = \beta_0 + \beta_1 FTA_{ij}^{t} + \beta_2 Lndist_{ij} + \beta_3 Lnopen_{j}^{t} + \beta_4 Lngdpgap_{ij}^{t} + \beta_5 Comlan_{ij} + \beta_6 Lntrain + \beta_7 WTO_{j} + \varepsilon_{ij}^{t} \quad (3)$$

其中，t 为所选的样本时间，β 为所选各变量的系数，ε_{ij}^{t} 为随机误差项。对各变量的具体说明见表1.17。

表1.17　变量说明

变量名	预期符号	变量含义	说明
$Ln\tau_{ij}^{t}$	无	被解释变量，双边贸易成本取对数	依据诺维（2013）计算得到的双边整体贸易成本
FTA	负	虚拟变量，与中国签订自由贸易协定后取值为1，其余为0	双边自由贸易协定可直接降低关税水平，促进双边经贸文化交流
$Lndist_{ij}$	正	经两国主要城市人口比例加权平均后的两国地理距离取对数	源于引力模型，地理距离是天然的贸易壁垒
Lnopen	负	t年样本国家的贸易开放度取对数	外贸开放程度越高贸易流量越大，贸易成本越小
Lngdpgap	正	t年贸易伙伴国与中国人均GDP差值的绝对值取对数	人均GDP既反映两国经济发展水平的差异，又反映两国人民需求结构的差异，差异越大，贸易难度越大
Comlan	负	CEPII组织计算所得的两国间的共同语言（Common Spoken Language）指数	共同语言指数在一定程度上反映了两国贸易商之间沟通交易信息的难易程度和对双方文化的了解认同程度，代表文化因素
Lntrain	负	贸易国国内铁路密度（铁路总公里/国土面积）取对数	铁路运输是一种经济的陆上运输方式，贸易国铁路网络越发达，其运输成本可能越低，可减少运输过程带来的时间成本
WTO	负	虚拟变量，中国与贸易伙伴均不是WTO（世贸组织）成员时取值为0，只有一方为成员时取值为1，双方均为成员时取值为2	WTO成员享受成员间的最惠国关税待遇，发生贸易争端时可在WTO框架下进行争端的解决

（二）数据来源

$Lndist_{ij}$数据来自 CEPII 数据库所提供的根据中国与各国的经主要城市人口比重进行加权平均后的地理距离数据。Lnopen 和 Lngdpgap 所需要的各国每年的进出口贸易额、GDP、人均 GDP 数据以及计算 Lntrain 需要的铁路总公里数、国土面积的数据均来自世界银行数据库。中国和贸易伙伴国加入 WTO 的情况来自世贸组织官方网站公布的世贸组织成员名单。由于存在变量数据缺失的问题，本文在前文选择的 50 个样本国家（地区）的基础上，剔除了中国香港、新加坡、马来西亚及伊拉克，将剩余的 46 个国家（地区）作为回归的样本国家（地区），样本时间为 1995—2016 年。

（三）计量回归结果

本文使用 Stata 12. 0 软件对模型（3）进行固定效应回归，并采用逐步回归的方法进行计量分析，回归结果如表 1. 18 所示。

表 1. 18　固定效应模型回归结果

变量	方程（1）	方程（2）	方程（3）	方程（4）	方程（5）	方程（6）
FTA	-0. 319*** (-5. 22)	-0. 299*** (-5. 67)	-0. 221*** (-3. 68)	-0. 182** (-2. 47)	-0. 131** (-2. 27)	-0. 259*** (-5. 61)
Lnopen		-0. 649*** (-5. 62)	-0. 835*** (-9. 25)	-0. 783*** (-8. 65)	-0. 568*** (-2. 27)	-0. 165*** (-5. 78)
Lntrain			-0. 187** (-2. 39)	-0. 189** (-2. 60)	-0. 111* (-1. 98)	0. 060*** (6. 79)
Lngdpgap				-0. 065** (-2. 60)	-0. 017 (-0. 92)	-0. 079*** (-1. 79)
WTO					-0. 463*** (-11. 61)	-0. 227*** (-10. 97)
$Lndist_{ij}$						0. 232*** (11. 71)
Comlan						-2. 951* (-1. 70)
_cons	-0. 046*** (-6. 93)	-0. 513*** (-6. 15)	-1. 448*** (-4. 54)	-0. 838** (-2. 16)	-0. 463 (-1. 59)	-. 906*** (-5. 27)
时间效应	未控制	未控制	未控制	未控制	未控制	未控制
地区效应	控制	控制	控制	控制	控制	未控制
F 统计量	27. 2 P > F = 0. 000	35. 95 P > F = 0. 000	42. 02 P > F = 0. 000	27. 37 P > F = 0. 000	52. 33 P > F = 0. 000	71. 69 P > F = 0. 000
R^2	0. 08	0. 33	0. 50	0. 53	0. 64	0. 42

注：解释变量下方括号中的数值为 t 值，*、**、*** 分别表示 10%、5% 和 1% 的显著性水平，每个方程均采用了以地区为聚类变量的聚类稳健标准误差。

方程（1）～（5）为使用固定效应模型逐步回归得到的计量结果。由于地理距离和共同语言两个变量不随时间发生变化，在固定效应模型中会被视为样本的不随时间改变的个体特征而被自动剔除，所以为了探究这两个变量对中国对外贸易成本的作用效果，使用混合回归对模型（3）进行回归，得到方程（6）。

对表1.18的计量回归结果分析如下。

FTA对中国对外贸易成本有着显著的负向作用。在方程（5）中其估计系数为-0.131，通过了5%的显著性检验，说明中国与贸易伙伴之间签订FTA有助于降低双边贸易成本，其作用强度仅次于贸易伙伴的开放程度和是否为WTO成员。方程（1）～（5）中，FTA的估计系数逐渐变小，说明随着其他解释变量的加入，其对于贸易成本的作用效果会被分散到其他影响因素上。

贸易伙伴对外贸易越开放，双边贸易成本越低。从方程（2）～（5）可以看到贸易开放度的估计系数的绝对值始终大于0.5，且均通过了1%的显著性检验，说明贸易伙伴的贸易开放度对中国对外贸易成本作用效果明显。从方程（5）的回归结果来看，贸易伙伴的外贸开放度每提高一个百分点，双边贸易成本就会下降0.568个百分点。

贸易相关基础设施越完善，双边贸易成本越低。以贸易伙伴内部铁路密度变量为代表的基础因素回归结果显示，在方程（3）（4）（5）中，铁路密度变量对双边贸易成本的作用效果较大，分别通过了5%和10%的显著性检验。实证结果与理论预期相符，基础设施的完善有助于降低双边贸易成本。

人均GDP差距对双边贸易成本的作用方向与理论预期相反，且作用力度很小。方程（4）（5）中人均GDP差距的估计系数绝对值分别为0.065和0.017，还不到铁路密度估计系数的1/2。其估计系数在方程（4）中通过了5%的显著性水平检验，在方程（5）中未通过显著性检验。与中国的人均GDP水平差距较大的国家（地区）往往具有较大的经济规模，经济规模越大，贸易流量越大，会引起贸易成本的降低，所以有可能是经济规模的负向作用掩盖了人均GDP差距的正向作用。

成为WTO成员对降低中国对外贸易成本有显著的作用。从方程（5）中可以看到其估计系数的绝对值为0.463，通过了1%的显著性检验。地理距离也依然对双边贸易成本有着显著的阻碍作用，共同语言对于降低双边贸易成本具有促进作用，通过了10%的显著性检验。

综上，除人均GDP差距外，各变量对中国对外贸易成本的影响与理论预期基本一致。

四、结论与建议

（一）结论

从测算结果来看，1995—2016 年中国与不同区域贸易伙伴的双边整体贸易成本都呈下降趋势，且下降速度放缓。2007 年之前中国与各区域双边贸易成本按照绝对值由高到低依次排名为非洲、中东、欧洲、大洋洲、美洲以及亚洲，2007 年后中国与不同区域双边贸易成本的数值范围较 1995 年明显收窄，说明同不同区域的贸易伙伴的贸易成本有趋同集中的倾向。从贸易伙伴的发达程度来看，在 1995—2016 年中国同新兴经济体国家双边贸易成本一直最高，2007 年以前与发达国家（地区）的双边贸易成本最低，2007 年之后与其他发展中国家的双边贸易成本最低。

从计量回归结果来看，签订自由贸易协定（FTA）、成为 WTO 成员、增强贸易伙伴的贸易开放度以及完善贸易相关的基础设施建设均有助于中国同其贸易伙伴之间贸易成本的降低。同时计量结果显示地理距离依然对双边贸易成本有着显著的阻碍作用，共同语言对于降低双边贸易成本具有促进作用。

（二）建议

首先，要积极探索地区内的贸易制度安排。从实证检验结果看到自由贸易协定的签订、成为 WTO 成员以及贸易开放度的提高均有助于贸易成本的降低，所以通过构建行之有效的贸易制度安排来推动区域内的贸易自由化进程，对于降低中国对外贸易成本，促进中国对外贸易的发展具有重要意义。其次，面对复杂多变的国际政治经济形势，中国应该在持续对外开放的同时努力发展国内贸易市场。从双边整体贸易成本测算结果可以看出，近年来中国同各区域国家（地区）贸易伙伴的双边贸易成本降速放缓，且双边贸易成本变化呈现趋同的倾向，说明中国与各贸易伙伴的双边贸易成本降低的边际在减小。若要继续减少双边贸易成本，需要比以往付出更多努力，而通过降低国内省际或市际之间的贸易成本来实现国内贸易促进经济增长的边际作用可能会更多，所需付出的边际成本可能较少。最后，国际贸易的完成离不开金融机构的支持，银行作为我国金融体系的重要组成部分，应积极探索更加优化便捷的贸易融资路径，同时为贸易企业寻找成本更低的融资渠道，从完善金融服务角度为降低我国企业贸易成本做出努力。

银行关联、非效率投资与企业价值

——基于沪深 A 股上市公司的实证研究

福建省分行　何　凯

一、引言

企业价值最大化是现代企业所追求的目标，企业能否持续稳定地创造价值也是衡量一家企业经营成功与否的标志。企业的经营要获得持续稳健的发展，必然需要充足的资金作为支撑。虽然，随着金融市场的发展，我国企业的融资渠道得到拓宽，我国人民币贷款占全社会融资规模的比例也从 2002 年的 91.9% 下降到 2017 年的 68.1%①，但银行贷款仍然占据了半壁江山以上，是我国大部分企业获取资金的主要来源。许多企业在申请银行贷款时经常面临银行严苛的贷款条件，甚至难以获取贷款。为了缓解融资难的问题，越来越多的企业寻求与银行建立关联关系这一非正式的制度安排［主要包含两种形式：企业聘请具有银行工作背景的人员的高管银行关联形式，企业持股银行或银行持股企业的持股银行关联形式，而且该关联关系也越来越普遍（张敏等人，2012）］。近几年以来，银行关联关系研究开始成为学术界的一个热点，不过，对于银行关联关系对企业价值的影响研究鲜有提及，相关文献侧重于研究银行关联关系对企业融资、投资效率与企业风险方面的影响，这些研究为本文提供了基础。

从银行关联与企业融资的关系来看，结论比较一致，认为银行关联关系能有效缓解融资约束，帮助企业获得银行贷款（Booth and Deli，1999；Burak et al.，2008；唐建新等人，2011），而且有助于获得更高额度的信贷（陈仕华和马超，2013）。恰马拉（Ciamarra，2012）研究发现，当企业董事有银行工作背景时，企业能得到更多的银行信贷，而且债务融资成本也低，会缓解企业的融资约束。邓建平和曾勇（2011）以民营上市公司为研究样本，研究银行关联关系对企业债务融资的影响，发现企业高管的银行工作背景会提高企业长期银行信贷额度，且该作用相比金融生态好的地区，在金

① 资料来源：中国人民银行官网公布的各年社会融资规模。

融生态环境差的地区更为显著。另外，张薇薇（2014）也发现民营企业的“软信息”，如与银行的关系维护与非财务信息也会影响到民营企业的融资。从银行关联关系对企业投资效率的关系来看，迪特曼等人（Dittmann et al.，2010）认为企业董事有银行工作经历会显著降低投资现金流敏感度。翟胜宝（2014）以我国民营上市公司为研究样本，银行关联关系会提高企业投资效率，该影响在市场化程度较低的地区更为显著。李文贵（2013）以1999—2010年的我国非金融类上市公司为研究样本，研究发现高管银行关联关系提高了投资水平对投资机会的敏感性，进而提高了资本配置效率，该作用主要存在于低市场化程度地区。从银行关联关系与企业风险的关系来看，翟胜宝（2014）实证研究表明，银行关联关系会提高企业风险水平，且不论是高管银行关联形式还是持股银行关联形式，银行关联企业的风险均显著高于非银行关联企业。

综上所述，本文在前人的基础上，做了如下两个方面的扩展研究：首先，目前关于银行关联关系的相关文献主要集中于研究银行关联对企业债务融资约束、投资效率与企业风险的影响，而本文进一步研究了银行关联对企业价值的影响，这为银行关联领域研究提供了新的视角；其次，大多数文献只是从总体上研究银行关联对投资效率的影响，并没有将非效率投资区分为过度投资和投资不足，本文在此基础上进行了扩展研究。因此，本文基于沪深A股所有上市公司的相关数据，研究银行关联关系这一特殊的非正式制度对企业非效率投资和企业价值的影响，将有利于识别银行关联关系这一非正式的制度安排是否合理。

二、研究设计

（一）理论分析与研究假设

在我国特殊的金融市场环境下，虽然随着我国金融市场改革的日益深化，我国企业的融资渠道也得到拓宽，但银行贷款仍然是我国大部分企业获取资金的主要来源，而且企业融资难、融资成本高仍然是突出的问题。在该情况下，许多企业积极建立和维护好与银行的关系来寻求获得贷款便利。布斯和德利（Booth and Deli，1999）研究发现，银行关联关系这一非正式的制度安排能帮助企业获取贷款融资便利，增加信贷额度，布拉克等人（Burak et al.，2008）和唐建新等人（2011）也得到了相同的结论。在企业财务决策中，企业的投融资决策占有重要地位且具有紧密的联系，二者相互作用。在企业实际经营中，企业投资常受到融资约束、信息不对称以及委托代理问题的扭曲，这容易导致企业出现过度投资与投资不足等非效率投资。过度投资常常投资一些净现值小于零的项目，投资不足则无法投资有价值性的项目，这会降低企业资源配置效率，降低投资效率，进而降低企业价值（刘红霞和索玲玲，2011；杜兴强等人，

2011；詹雷和王瑶瑶，2013）。银行关联有助于企业从银行获得负债融资，童盼和陆正飞（2005）认为负债融资会从负债的治理机制对企业投资产生正向影响。本文认为，作为非正式的制度安排的银行关联关系可能在一定程度上降低融资约束、信息不对称以及委托代理问题对企业投资效率的不利影响，从而有助于提高企业价值。原因如下所示。

首先，企业在面临融资约束时，即使有好的投资机会也无计可施，无法获取充足的资金投资好的项目，只能放弃净现值为正的投资项目，导致投资不足（Whited，2006），这也会降低企业投资效率。因而，企业有动力积极建立银行关联关系获取融资来改善投资效率。一方面，企业通过聘请具有银行背景人员担任董事或管理人员，利用他们与银行在信息交流、关系维护和行业经验方面的优势，从银行获得融资便利（Burak et al.，2008；Dittmann et al.，2010；邓建平和曾勇，2011），缓解融资约束，进而可抓住有利的投资机会。另一方面，企业通过持股银行或银行持股企业建立股权关系，银行可列席企业董事会会议，这能够帮助银行了解企业的实际经营情况，减少银行发放贷款所需要信息的搜寻成本，降低银企双方的信息不对称程度，从而使企业更容易获得贷款。因而，银行关联关系能有效缓解企业面临的融资约束问题，改善投资不足的境遇，抓住有价值增值性的投资项目，这有助于提高企业的投资效率，进而提高企业价值。

其次，企业代理问题往往会导致管理层为获取私人收益而出现“经理帝国主义”（empire-building）和“职位固守行为”（entrenchment）等不利于企业价值最大化的行为，企业也往往投资了非最优的投资项目，特别是投资一些净现值小于零的项目，出现过度投资（Shleifer and Vishny，1989；Chen et al.，2009），这将会降低资本配置效率，降低企业价值（蒋东升，2011；詹雷和王瑶瑶，2013）。企业无论是在面临内部还是外部充分的监督和激励机制下，只要贷款问题得到有效缓解，管理层就会积极地进行投资决策以实现企业价值最大化，积极选择那些净现值为正的投资项目（John et al.，2008）。一方面，企业聘请银行家加入董事会，而银行家作为行业专家，其对企业所选择的投资项目的风险和收益有着深刻的理解，这能为企业在投资决策中提供优质建议，帮助企业选择更好的投资项目。另一方面，银行家加入企业董事会可以提高银行对企业管理层的监督程度（Ciamarra，2012），这样可以督促企业管理层积极努力工作，并减少企业管理层为实现个人收益而不利于企业价值最大化的资源转移行为，加入企业董事会的银行家作为债权人，会积极监督贷款投向和企业选择的投资项目，防止银行债权遭受损失（何进日和周艺，2004），从而抑制企业过度投资，提高企业投资效率，提高企业价值。

基于上述分析，本文提出如下两个假设。

假设一：银行关联会改善企业投资不足，抑制企业过度投资，提高投资效率。

假设二：银行关联不仅会改善企业投资不足对企业价值的负面影响，而且还会抑制过度投资对企业价值的负面影响，提高企业价值。

（二）变量定义与数据来源

1. 企业价值

本文借鉴默克等人（Morck et al.，1988）、白重恩等人（2005）以及姜付秀和黄继承（2011）的方法，将托宾Q值（TQ）和市净率（MB）作为企业价值的代理变量。其中，托宾Q值等于年末市场价值除以重置成本，年末市场价值等于年末流通股市场价值加年末非流通股账面价值（净资产）再加年末负债账面价值，重置成本等于年末总资产。市净率等于每股股价与每股净资产的比率。本文将市净率作为企业价值的代理变量进行稳健性检验。

2. 银行关联关系

在衡量银行与企业的关联关系时，翟胜宝等人（2014）认为主要存在为两种方式，即高管银行关联（企业高管具有银行工作背景）和持股关联（包括企业持股银行和银行持股企业）。本文借鉴其方法，设立银行关联虚拟变量，当企业存在高管银行关联或持股银行关联时，则取1，否则取0。

3. 非效率投资

理查森（Richardson，2006）提出了衡量投资效率的一种方法，该方法在学术界应用较为广泛，认为企业存在的最优投资规模会受到企业规模、投资报酬率、投资机会、财务杠杆以及现金持有量等因素的影响，当企业实际投资规模低于最优规模时，即为投资不足，反之即为过度投资。本文参考理查森（2006）、詹雷和王瑶瑶（2013）的研究，用以下模型度量投资效率：

$$Invest_{it} = \delta_0 + \delta_1 TQ_{it-1} + \delta_2 Lev_{it-1} + \delta_3 Cash_{it-1} + \delta_4 Age_{it-1} + \delta_5 Size_{it-1} + \delta_6 \mathrm{Ret}_{it-1} + \delta_7 Invest_{it-1} + \sum Year + \sum Industry + \kappa_{it}$$

其中投资规模$Invest_{it}$代表企业i在第t年实际新增的固定资产、在建工程和长期投资。TQ_{it-1}、Lev_{it-1}、$Cash_{it-1}$、Age_{it-1}、Ret_{it-1}分别表示企业i在第$t-1$年的托宾Q值、年末资产负债率、持有现金比率、公司上市年限、公司资产规模以及年度股票投资报酬率。此外，模型中还加入了年度虚拟变量（Year）和行业虚拟变量（Industry），以控制年度和行业效应。对该模型回归得到的残差κ_{it}为样本公司在t年的实际投资偏离理想投资部分。设定变量Overinv、Underinv以及虚拟变量Oinv，剔除掉$\kappa_{it}=0$的样本，当$\kappa_{it}>0$时，则为过度投资，$\text{Overinv}=\kappa_{it}$，且Oinv取1；当$\kappa_{it}<0$时，则为投资不足，为方便研究，取其绝对值作为投资不足的代理变量，$\text{Underinv}=|\kappa_{it}|$，且Oinv取0。

4. 控制变量

本文参考杜兴强等人（2011）、刘红霞和索玲玲（2011）的研究，控制企业规模（Size）、成长性（Growth）、杠杆水平（Lev）、盈利能力（Roa）的作用，另外，还控制了年度虚拟变量（Year）和行业虚拟变量（Industry）。企业规模用报告期总资产的自然对数表示，企业成长性用企业主营业收入增长率表示，资产负债率反映企业负债水平，用企业负债与资产的比值表示，资产报酬率表示企业的盈利能力。此外，考虑到企业所在行业以及年度的影响，分别设立年度虚拟变量和行业虚拟变量，用来控制年度和行业效应。根据证监会 2001 年颁布的《上市公司行业分类指引》，将样本公司的行业类型分为 13 类，并以综合类上市公司为参照系，由于剔除了金融行业上市公司，故上市公司样本只覆盖 12 个行业，因此设置 11 个行业控制变量，本文以 2009 年为参照系，设置 7 个年度虚拟变量。

本文选择 2008—2016 年在沪深交易所主板市场上市的所有 A 股上市公司作为初选样本，并在初选样本的基础上进行如下筛选：首先，剔除金融行业企业的样本观测值；其次，剔除资产负债率大于 1 的样本观测值；再次，剔除存在数据缺失的样本观测值；最后，由于在计算非效率投资时，使用了滞后一期的数据，故剔除 2008 年的数据，同时剔除掉 $\kappa_{it}=0$ 的样本，最终经过处理得到 2009—2016 年共计 8 568 个样本观测值。同时，为消除异常值的影响，本文对所有变量在 1% 和 99% 分位上进行了 winsorize（缩尾）处理。另外，本文的银行关联数据由手工收集整理而得，其他企业特征数据来源于 CSMAR 数据库。

（三）模型设定

本文基于上述理论分析与假设，首先设定模型来检验银行关联关系对企业非效率投资的影响，设定模型如下：

$$INV_{it} = a_0 + a_1 \mathrm{Relation}_{it} + a_2 Size_{it} + a_3 Growth_{it} + a_4 Roa_{it} + a_5 Lev_{it} + \sum_{i=1}^{7} b_i Year_i + \sum_{j=1}^{11} g_j Industry_j + \varphi_{it}$$

其中，INV_{it} 为非效率投资，根据虚拟变量 Oinv 将样本分为投资过度组和投资不足组，非效率投资分别用 Overinv 和 Underinv 表征；$Relation_{it}$ 为银行关联关系，$Size_{it}$ 为企业规模的自然对数，$Growth_{it}$ 为企业成长性，Roa_{it} 为资产报酬率，Lev_{it} 为资产负债率，*Year* 和 *Industry* 分别为年度和行业虚拟变量。

此外，分别在企业投资过度组与投资不足组中检验银行关联关系对企业价值的影响以及银行关联在非效率投资影响企业价值过程中的作用，模型设定为：

$$Value_{it} = \beta_0 + \beta_1 \mathrm{Relation}_{it} + \beta_2 INV_{it} + \beta_3 \mathrm{Relation}_{it} \times INV_{it} + \beta_4 Size_{it} + \beta_5 Growth_{it} + \beta_6 Roa_{it} + \beta_7 Lev_{it} + \sum_{i=1}^{7} \beta_i Year_i + \sum_{j=1}^{11} \gamma_j Industry_j + \varepsilon_{it}$$

其中，$Value_{it}$ 为企业价值，用 TQ 表示，并用 MB 进行稳健性检验。

三、实证研究结果分析

（一）描述性统计分析

从表 1.19 中可以得知，企业的托宾 Q 值（TQ）的均值为 1.5826，最大值与最小值分别为 5.2731、0.9025，市净率（MB）的均值为 3.8109，最大值与最小值分别为 52.2533、0.6924，说明不同企业的市场价值存在较大差异。银行关联关系（Relation）的均值为 0.3724，占样本企业的 37.24%，说明银行关联关系在我国上市公司中比较普遍。非效率投资虚拟变量（Oinv）的均值为 0.34，说明过度投资的观察值在样本中占比 34%，相比企业过度投资，投资不足更为普遍。过度投资（Overinv）的均值为 0.1679，平均过度投资额为总资产的 16.79%，投资不足（Underinv）的均值为 0.0516，平均投资缺口占总投资的 5.16%。

表 1.19　主要变量的描述性统计

变量	观测值数目	均值	标准差	最小值	最大值
TQ	8 568	1.5826	0.7073	0.9025	5.2731
MB	8 568	3.8109	2.8947	0.6924	52.2533
Relation	8 568	0.3724	0.4583	0	1
Oinv	8 568	0.3400	0.5301	0	1
Overinv	2 943	0.1679	0.1324	0.0001	0.7802
Underinv	5 625	0.0516	0.7124	0.0001	0.3827
Size	8 568	22.1054	1.4051	10.7232	27.2978
Growth	8 568	0.5817	2.2911	-0.7864	16.6262
Roa	8 568	0.0524	0.0747	-0.3522	0.2697
Lev	8 568	0.5633	0.3122	0.0812	1.5218

（二）研究结果分析

在表 1.20 中，模型（1）和模型（2）分别为以过度投资和投资不足为因变量。模型类型选择结果表明，F 检验值结果都显著地拒绝了混合 OLS 模型，都应采用固定效应模型；LM 检验结果都显著地拒绝了混合 OLS 模型，都应采用随机效应模型；Hausman 检验结果表明两个模型都拒绝随机效应模型，应采用固定效应模型。因此，为消除可能存在的异方差和序列相关，本文采用广义最小二乘方法（GLS）对其进行修正。模型（1）和模型（2）的 Wald chi2 值分别为 85.23 和 83.37，都在 1% 的置信水平下显著，说明模型回归结果稳健。

在模型（1）中，银行关联的系数为 -0.0106，在 1% 水平下显著，说明银行关联能有效抑制企业过度投资，在模型（2）中，银行关联系数也显著为负，为 -0.0189，说明银行关联能改善企业投资不足，从而验证了假设一。

从其他控制变量来看，在模型（1）中，企业规模（Size）的系数显著为正，说明企业规模越大，企业过度投资越严重，模型（2）中，Size 的系数显著为负，说明企业规模越大越能缓解投资不足。可能的原因在于，规模越大的企业，获取资金的渠道也多，同时往往会进行多元化发展，投资需求较强，这与杜兴强等人（2011）的结论一致。模型（1）中，企业成长性（Growth）的系数显著为正，模型（2）中其系数显著为负，说明企业成长性越好，企业越有可能投资过度，但会改善投资不足，这与申等人（Chen et al.，2011）的结论一致。模型（1）中，Roa 的系数显著为正，说明盈利能力越强，企业越容易发生过度投资，而在模型（2）中，Roa 的系数显著为负，说明盈利能力能改善投资不足。原因在于，企业盈利能力越强，企业的自由现金流越多，从而企业越可能进行过度投资，并改善投资不足情况，这与姜付秀和黄继承（2011）的结论一致。模型（1）~（2）中的资产负债率（Lev）的系数显著为负，说明企业高负债比例能约束企业的过度投资，并能改善投资不足。原因在于：一方面，企业负债率越高，企业面临的债务约束越强，越能约束企业的过度投资冲动；另一方面，企业通过负债途径获得的资金越多，越能缓解企业投资不足。

表 1.20　银行关联对非效率投资的影响结果

变量	投资过度组 Overinv（1）	投资不足组 Underinv（2）
常数项	-0.0742 （-1.21）	-0.0371* （-1.72）
Relation	-0.0106*** （-3.08）	-0.0189*** （-4.23）
Size	0.0034*** （4.69）	-0.0019*** （-3.54）
Growth	0.0021* （-1.88）	-0.0008** （-2.67）
Roa	0.0006*** （3.77）	-0.0015*** （3.65）

（续表）

变量	投资过度组 Overinv（1）	投资不足组 Underinv（2）
Lev	-0.0295*** （-3.39）	-0.0142*** （-4.01）
Industry	控制	控制
Year	控制	控制
N	2 943	5 625
F 检验	2.55***	3.21***
LM 检验	70.34***	79.26***
Hausman 检验	8.26***	11.57***
模型设定形式	固定效应模型	固定效应模型
Wald chi2 值	85.23***	84.37***

注：（1） ***、**、*分别表示在1%、5%、10%的置信水平下显著。
（2）括号中数字为对应系数的t值。

在表1.21中，模型（3）~（6）的模型类型选择结果表明，都应采用固定效应模型。本文采用广义最小二乘方法（GLS）对模型进行回归，各模型的Wald chi2值都在1%的置信水平下显著，说明模型回归结果稳健。

在模型（3）~（4）中，TQ和MB分别与过度投资（Overinv）显著负相关，系数分别为-0.1261、-0.1398，说明企业过度投资会降低企业价值，这与詹雷和王瑶瑶（2013）的结论一致。而TQ、MB与Relation×Overinv的系数分别显著为负，为0.1022、0.1105，说明相比无银行关联关系的企业，具有银行关联关系的企业能有效抑制过度投资对企业价值的伤害。在模型（5）~（6）中，投资不足（Underinv）的系数分别为-0.2107、-0.1982，都在1%水平下显著，说明企业投资不足也会降低企业价值。而Relation×Overinv的系数分别显著为负，为0.1391、0.1722，说明相比无银行关联关系的企业，具有银行关联关系的企业能有效改善投资不足对企业价值的负向作用。在模型（3）~（6）中，银行关联的系数都显著为正，均在5%水平下显著，说明银行关联能有效提升企业价值。因此，银行关联关系能有效缓解企业过度投资和投资不足对企业价值的负向影响，提高企业价值，从而验证了假设二。

从其他控制变量来看，在模型（3）~（6）中，TQ、MB与Size在1%置信水平下显著负相关，说明企业规模越大，企业市场价值越低，大规模的企业发展潜力有限，而规模较小的企业则拥有较大的发展空间，具有“规模效应”，从而使得市场价值越高，这与鲁海帆（2007）的结论一致。TQ、MB与Roa在1%置信水平下显著正相关，说明企业盈利能力越强，企业的股票价值越大。TQ、MB与Growth在10%置信水平下显著正相关，说明企业成长性越好，投资者越会看好该企业的股票，从而提高企业的市场价值。TQ、MB与Lev在1%置信水平下显著负相关，说明企业的负债比例越大，企业的市场价值越低。杜兴强等人（2011）认为在中国的股票市场中，企业的资产负债率往往成为一个负信号，资产负债率越高，投资者越不看好该企业的股票，从而导致企业市场价值越低。

表1.21 银行关联、非效率投资与企业价值

变量	投资过度组		投资不足组	
	TQ（3）	MB（4）	TQ（5）	MB（6）
常数项	0.1902*** （8.32）	0.2067*** （6.14）	0.0231 （0.74）	0.0562** （2.21）
Relation	0.0139*** （3.62）	0.0088** （1.99）	0.0111** （2.49）	0.0177*** （3.99）
Overinv	-0.1261*** （-3.32）	-0.1398*** （-3.39）		
Underinv			-0.2107*** （-5.24）	-0.1982*** （-4.57）
Relation × Overinv	0.1022*** （4.27）	0.1105*** （4.73）		
Relation × Underinv			0.1391*** （5.74）	0.1722*** （4.97）
Size	-0.0801*** （-4.22）	-0.0990*** （-4.05）	-0.0268*** （-4.93）	-0.0281*** （-4.33）
Growth	0.0026* （1.32）	0.0053** （2.26）	0.0021** （2.34）	0.0011** （2.06）
Roa	0.6543*** （3.43）	0.7066*** （4.28）	0.0809*** （4.25）	0.0712*** （3.24）
Lev	-0.0039 （-1.58）	-0.0025** （-2.31）	-0.0187*** （-3.49）	-0.0196*** （-4.59）
Industry	控制	控制	控制	控制
Year	控制	控制	控制	控制
N	2 943	2 943	5 625	5 625
F检验	6.21***	5.37***	4.67***	2.92***
LM检验	54.58***	60.29***	87.64***	67.22***
Hausman检验	12.68***	11.36***	10.34***	9.54***
模型设定形式	固定效应模型	固定效应模型	固定效应模型	固定效应模型
Wald chi2值	63.89***	65.77***	78.89***	69.44***

注：（1）***、**、*分别表示在1%、5%、10%的置信水平下显著。
（2）括号中数字为对应系数的t值。

四、研究结论

银行关联关系是中国资本市场上市公司中存在的较为普遍的现象，本文通过收集整理上市公司 2008—2016 年银行关联数据，实证研究了银行关联关系对上市公司非效率投资和企业价值的影响。研究结果表明：银行关联显著抑制了企业的过度投资，改善了企业投资不足，从而提高了投资效率。进一步研究发现，银行关联关系分别抑制和改善了过度投资与投资不足对企业价值的伤害，进而提高了企业价值。因此，基于非正式的银行关联机制对企业价值的提高提供了解释，这有助于企业寻求银行关联关系以改善投资效率和提高企业价值。

人民币国际化的比较分析与路径研究

湖北省分行　罗　霄

一、人民币国际化的逻辑背景

货币国际化是指一种货币超出自身国家主权地域限制，在国际范围内被广泛流通使用，发挥部分或全部货币职能的过程。货币国际化是一国经济金融实力的综合体现，要求在经济规模、对外贸易、金融市场等方面，同时具有较高的国际地位和较强的竞争实力。加入世贸组织以来，中国通过不断坚持发展对外贸易、深化金融体制改革，国内经济连续实现快速稳定增长，GDP 年均增长率达到 9% 以上。目前，中国已成为仅次于美国的世界第二大经济体，世界第一大货物贸易国，以及世界第一大国家外汇储备国，具备了发展人民币国际化的经济金融基础。

2008 年世界金融危机爆发后，美国经济金融遭受明显重创，并开始推行量化宽松的货币政策。美元相应发生了大幅度的贬值，美元资产价值大幅缩水，美元的国际地位和货币信誉也受到严重负面影响。世界金融危机的爆发突出反映了以美元为中心的国际货币体系的固有内在缺陷，并推动国际货币体系开始向多元化方向发展。全球货币“去美元化”发展为人民币登上国际舞台提供了良好契机。

二、主要国际化货币的比较分析

当前，世界主要的国际化货币有美元、欧元和日元，分别对应美洲、欧洲和亚洲地区的代表性发达经济体，但三者的国际化路径设计存在一定差异。按照历史研究经验，货币国际化路径可主要分为“周边化—区域化—国际化”的使用范围路径，以及“结算货币—投资货币—储备货币”的货币职能路径。

（一）美元国际化路径

自 1894 年超越英国后，美国成为世界最大经济体，并随后成为世界最大的贸易出口国和对外投资国。经过 1914 年和 1944 年两次以欧洲为主战场的世界战争，英国、德国、法国等国家经济大幅衰退，英镑、德国马克、法郎等欧洲国家货币的国际地位日益下滑。1945 年，美国经济规模占世界总量一半以上，进出口贸易额占世界总额 1/3 以上，黄金储备更是高达资本主义世界国家总量的 75%。1944 年，美国主导建立了世界货币制度布雷顿森林体系，开始了美元与黄金挂钩，其他国家货币与美元挂钩的“双挂钩”机制，也标志着美元确立了世界第一大国际货币的地位。

由于“特里芬难题”和“不可能三角”的存在，币值稳定要求与被动贸易逆差存在天然矛盾，固定汇率制度、独立货币政策与资本自由流动不可能三者同时成立，因此布雷顿森林体系存在天生的缺陷，必然走向失败。布雷顿森林体系崩溃后，国际货币基金组织提出了牙买加体系，各国货币发行不再受黄金储备约束，国际汇率制度出现了固定汇率制与浮动汇率制并存的现象。但美元依然凭借美国作为世界第一经济与军事强国的地位，在国际贸易、国际投资、国际储备，以及各国货币汇率盯住对象中占据主导地位，其驻锚货币的地位特征依然显著。美国拥有世界最大的股票、债券、金融衍生品市场，并在海外拥有庞大的欧洲离岸美元市场。目前，美元在 SDR（特别提款权）货币篮子中的占比依然高达 41.73%。截至 2018 年第二季度，美元在全球外汇储备中占比为 62.25%。

从使用范围和路径来看，美元没有经历周边化和区域化的过程，而是借助世界货币体系的制度变迁，直接成为国际货币。从货币职能路径来看，美元经历了从国际结算货币到国际投资货币，再到国际储备货币的过程。

（二）欧元国际化路径

1947 年，欧洲经济委员会成立，并同时提出了欧洲货币联盟的概念。1991 年 12 月，欧共体的 12 国首脑签署了《马斯特里赫特条约》，建立欧洲货币联盟。经过 10 年过渡期，2002 年欧元区正式成立，欧元随后成为世界第二大国际货币。在 2008 年世界金融危机期间，欧元区开始暴露自身固有的内在制度缺陷，即欧元区内部的货币政策统一，但区内各个国家的财政政策独立。货币政策与财政政策的分离，导致部分经济实力较弱的成员国出现国家债务偿还风险。受此影响，欧元的国际地位略有下滑。但欧元区在世界金融危机期间暴露出来的问题，并未能阻止欧元区的继续扩展。截至 2016 年，欧元区成员国已扩大至 19 个[①]。目前，欧元在国际货币基金组织的 SDR 中占比为 30.93%，仅次于美元。截至 2018 年第二季度，欧元在全球外汇储备中占比为 20%。

---

① 包括德国、法国、意大利、荷兰、比利时、卢森堡、爱尔兰、希腊、西班牙、葡萄牙、奥地利、芬兰、希腊、塞浦路斯、马耳他、斯洛伐克、爱沙尼亚、拉脱维亚、立陶宛。

从使用范围路径来看，欧元自诞生起就是区域货币。而且，由于欧元区庞大的经济规模，欧元顺利在世界范围内被广泛接受和使用，因此欧元也同时成为世界货币。从货币职能路径来看，欧元同样经历了“国际结算货币—国际投资货币—国际储备货币”的过程。

（三）日元国际化路径

日元的国际化进程始于第二次世界大战之后。20 世纪 50 年代，日本制定“贸易立国”的出口导向型战略，通过低价的人力成本优势，促进劳动密集型出口产业发展。1968—1972 年，日本陆续成为世界第二大经济体和世界第三大贸易国。

在建立了良好的经济基础后，日元的国际化进程主要依托日本金融体系开放而展开，包括四个方面。一是自 1964 年加入国际货币基金组织后逐步放松外汇管制，在 20 年内先后实现了经常项下和资本项下可兑换。二是 1979—1994 年完成了利率市场化改革。三是自 20 世纪 70 年代开始建立离岸的欧洲日元市场。四是自 20 世纪 80 年代开始逐步开放国内股票、债券市场。自 20 世纪 80 年代以来，日元在国际外汇储备和外汇交易市场中的占比基本稳定在第三位。

1985 年，美、英、法、日、德 5 国签订“广场协议”。随后，日元逐步大幅升值，不但对日本以制造业出口为导向的经济发展产生了不利影响，而且导致国际热钱大量涌入，造成资产泡沫化。20 世纪 90 年代，日本资产泡沫破裂，经济遭受重大影响，金融产业也随之出现大幅衰退。在此期间，日本年均 GDP 增长率一直徘徊在 1.5% 左右。1997 年亚洲金融危机后，日本政府对日元的国际化定位开始从国际化向区域化转移。目前，日元在国际货币基金组织的 SDR 中占比为 8.33%，排在美元、欧元和人民币之后。截至 2018 年第二季度，日元在全球外汇储备中占 5 225.9 亿美元，占比自 1990 年的 8.5% 下降至 4.97%。

从使用范围路径来看，日元通过开放金融市场，直接成为国际化货币，但由于存在国际货币职能不平衡，受经济增长长期停滞影响等问题，开始退回亚洲，谋求成为区域化货币。从货币职能路径来看，日元同样基本遵循“国际结算货币—国际投资货币—国际储备货币”的路径，但由于在国际结算货币职能上的发展停滞，令其国际储备货币职能出现了地位下滑。

三、人民币国际化路径选择

中国作为一个发展中国家，发展货币国际化没有先例可循。中国的人民币国际化具有自身的特殊性，不可简单照搬历史经验。美元、欧元和日元作为当今主流世界货币，其国际化路径具有较大的借鉴和参考价值。

（一）美元经验

美元国际化的历史契机在当今世界难以重现，目前世界的主流思想是和平发展，这决定了国际政治经济大格局和国际货币制度在短期内不会有大的变化，人民币难以通过制度变迁实现国际化。但其国际化路径表明，强大的经济实力是一国货币成为国际化货币的经济基础和先决条件。

（二）欧元经验

欧元是“最优货币区理论”[①] 的一次有益尝试，为一些国际经济同盟区的建立和人民币国际化发展提供了参考。但一方面，欧洲债务危机的爆发说明欧元体系仍存在需要进一步完善的空间；另一方面，从亚洲国家之间的历史渊源、政治现状和经济差异来看，人民币国际化并不适合走直接构建“亚元区”的区域化货币发展道路。

（三）日元经验

日元的国际化建立在其强大的经济贸易实力和开放的金融系统基础上，但由于日本经济极度依赖美国，同时缺乏独立自主的汇率政策，最终导致了日元国际化的失败。当前中国经济发展状况和市场结构与日元国际化初期的日本存在相似之处，此外，中国与日本同处亚洲，人民币与日元面临直接竞争关系。因此，日元国际化过程中因丧失独立货币政策带来的惨痛教训，对当前人民币国际化发展具有重要的参考意义。

此外，从美元、欧元、日元的历史经验来看，在其货币国际化发展过程中，货币使用范围并不存在明显的逐步扩大的变化过程，往往存在较大的跳跃性，而且使用范围的大小与货币国际化程度并没有表现出显著的直接联系。相比之下，货币职能的逐步演进路线较为明显，通常都是首先通过跨境贸易往来取得一定范围内的初步认可，进而进入国际金融市场取得定价交易地位，最终逐步获得国际储备货币的地位。因此，相较使用范围路径的“三步走”，货币国际化更应注重货币职能路径的“三步走”。

四、人民币国际化的实践现状

人民币国际化始于2004年。当时中国香港的本地银行获准向香港居民推出个人人民币业务，成为第一个开展人民币离岸业务的地区，并已逐步成为人民币离岸中心。

---

① 蒙代尔（Mundell，1961）率先提出了最优货币区（optimum currency area）的理论框架。最优货币区理论是指在一定的最优地理使用区域，对区域内多种货币实行稳定的固定汇率制度，相互盯住且可自由兑换，对区域外实行浮动汇率制度，联合对外浮动，最终同时实现内部均衡和外部均衡。

近年来，人民币在跨境贸易、跨境投资的使用规模上稳步上升。2016 年 10 月 1 日，人民币加入国际货币基金组织的特别提款权，极大地提升了人民币的国际地位，为人民币国际化迈出了战略性的关键一步。人民币国际化发展进程中，“结算货币—投资货币—储备货币”三项货币职能前后承接，互为支持，协同推进。

（一）国际结算货币职能

人民币贸易结算是当前中国推进人民币国际化的首要方向。2009—2012 年，中国逐步开放人民币跨境贸易。2017 年，我国跨境贸易人民币结算量达到 4.36 万亿元，占我国对外贸易总量的 16%，全球贸易结算份额接近 2%。

人民币跨境贸易结算的大幅增长直接带来了境外人民币存款的大幅增加。截至 2017 年年末，中国香港、中国台湾地区，以及韩国、新加坡、英国的人民币存款余额合计超过 1.1 万亿元。

（二）国际投资货币职能

人民币跨境投融资是我国促进人民币参与国际金融市场的主要措施，包括海外人民币债券发行、人民币跨境直接投资和人民币合格境外机构投资等。2007 年，中国国家开发银行在香港发行首只 50 亿元人民币债券。2012 年，中国开放国内非金融机构在香港发行人民币债券。截至 2017 年年末，人民币国际债券和票据存量为 1 033.47 亿美元，国际债券市场份额为 0.43%。

2011 年，中国陆续开放境外直接投资人民币结算业务，以及人民币合格境外机构投资者（RQFII）业务。2017 年，中国以人民币结算的对外币直接投资 4 569 亿元。截至 2017 年年末，境外机构 RQFII 累计获批 196 家，总额度 6 050.62 亿元。非居民持有境内人民币金融资产余额增至 4.28 万亿元。

（三）国际储备货币职能

货币互换协议具有部分储备货币的属性。自 2009 年起，我国陆续与多个国家或地区签署了货币互换协议。2018 年 10 月 26 日，中国人民银行与日本银行签署中日双边本币互换协议，协议金额 2 000 亿元人民币。截至目前，中国已与境外 37 个国家或地区签署了双边互换协议，总额度超过 3.5 万亿元。

2016 年 10 月 1 日，人民币正式加入国际货币基金组织的特别提款权（SDR），权重为 10.92%，仅排在美元和欧元之后。目前，全球已有 60 多个国家将人民币纳入官方储备。截至 2018 年第二季度，人民币在全球外汇储备中占 19 933.8 亿美元，排名第 6 位，占比 1.84%。

五、政策建议

（一）调整对外贸易结构，提升国际贸易整体竞争力

中国的对外贸易模式在国际贸易分工中处于底层，缺乏国际贸易定价权，制约了人民币发挥国际结算货币职能。中国在对外贸易中依然处于弱势地位。在进口方面，中国的重要能源、原材料自给不足，石油、铁矿石大半需要依靠进口；在出口方面，中国主要出口劳动密集型加工产品，产品附加值低。中国应加快转变外贸增长方式，提升国际分工地位，重点发展高端制造业、节能环保产业和现代服务业，多元化调整外贸进出口市场布局，提升出口产品科技含量，争夺贸易规则制定话语权。

（二）深化金融体制改革，拓展金融市场的广度和深度

人民币金融产品单一，缺乏价格弹性和投资回流渠道，限制了人民币发挥国际投资货币的职能。中国金融市场体系仍不完善，人民币尚未完全开放资本项目，人民币汇率也尚未实现完全自由浮动，人民币计价的金融产品仍相对匮乏。中国需要继续推动利率市场化和汇率市场化改革，建立多元化的金融产品市场，加快离岸人民币金融市场建设，推进金融市场对外开放，稳步有序地开放资本项目，完善人民币跨境流通循环机制。

（三）转变经济发展模式，提升经济实力内在质量

中国较低的人均 GDP 水平制约了人民币发挥国际储备货币职能。人均 GDP 反映了一国经济发展的内在质量，直接影响世界其他国家对该国货币的信心。中国人均 GDP 水平依然较低，2017 年中国人均 GDP 仅为 9 481.88 美元，在世界排名第 70 位。中国要推进市场经济转型，深化供给侧改革，加快产业结构调整，通过科技创新和效率进一步提升经济增长的质量，优化国民收入分配格局，建立完善的劳动就业和社会保障体系。

中国央行货币政策逻辑研究

青岛市分行　王　嵩

美联储加息后，中国货币当局将会如何应对显得尤为引人关注。这里面实际上蕴含两个问题：一是美联储加息过后，中国央行是否会选择跟进；二是放长期限来看，美联储持续加息，会对国内利率政策造成多大的约束？本文将从中国货币当局的政策脉络及运筹机制入手，对央行货币政策逻辑进行初步分析与探讨。

一、前期央行利率调整思路

每次届临美联储加息，对加息与否的猜测总是层出不穷，大家所切入的角度也各有差异。通过对比人民银行公开市场业务负责人在媒体的表态不难发现，前两次上调政策利率央行的逻辑基本一致，操作目的主要包括以下几点：

- 市场供求的反应，既货币市场利率显著高于公开市场操作利率，适度收窄二者价差。
- 引导市场主体形成合理的利率预期，即避免金融机构过度加杠杆和扩张广义信贷，控制宏观杠杆率。
- 应对美联储加息。

二、政策利率调整对应需求分析

我们逐一考虑在当前背景下，上述 3 个目的是否需要跟随上调政策利率予以配合。

（一）货币市场利率和政策利率之差

这里所说的货币市场利率和政策利率之差涵盖两层意思：

- 市场供求的反应：如果政策利率调整是“随行就市”的结果，则目前显现的是流动性供给充裕，因而从供需关系上讲并不支持流动性“涨价”。

- 价差收敛的需求：无论是逆回购还是回购系列的资金利率，在充足的供给背景下，利率大幅下跌，甚至一度跌破公开市场操作利率。目前市场利率与政策利率基本贴合运行，不存在央行担忧的“套利”空间。

（二）引导预期，控制宏观杠杆率

在分析宏观杠杆率时需要特别注意两个变化：一是去杠杆取得了初步效果，2018年第一季度的货币政策执行报告首提“稳杠杆”；二是目前货币政策的关键是疏通传导，从“宽货币”努力实现“宽信用”。

在目前的信用环境下，非政府机构的加杠杆行为得到明显控制；而广义信贷扩张目前也无须过度担忧——整个广义信贷已经呈现下行趋势，增速已非常之低。

也就是说，在目前的背景下，再去通过上调公开市场利率，影响预期，控制宏观杠杆率和广义信贷扩张的必要性相当有限。

（三）应对美联储加息

实际上这才是市场的真正关注点。随着美联储持续加息，中美短端利差只有约 50 个 bp，本次加息过后，如果央行未进行跟随，这一利差会进一步收敛到 30 个 bp 以下。如果出于稳定利差的考虑，那么加息 5 个 bp 或者 10 个 bp 意义不大，这需要央行对应采取同等幅度的跟随，目前尚未看到政策有这样跟随的迹象。

原因在于央行对于应对美联储加息本质的认知。2017 年下半年以来，央行“放任”中美短端利差的收敛，关注利差的核心目的不在于利差本身，而是利差背后反映的“资本流失”/汇率贬值压力。

对于是否跟随加息这个问题，作为一个短期行为，我们没必要纠结于人民币究竟存不存在长期的贬值压力，只需关注短期的人民币贬值压力是否已经得到充分释放，有以下几个数据可供参考：

- 2018 年 4 月以来，美元指数上行幅度在 5.1% 左右，但人民币已显著贬值 8.6%，从跟随的角度基本上已补贬到位，如果国内外宏观环境没有显著变化，短期其实并无一个显著的贬值压力。
- 2018 年 7 月过后，作为比较指标，美元指数实际上已经有所下行，目前的美元走势在反映完加息预期后短期大幅上行的概率不大，从比价角度而言，人民币贬值压力也有限。

- 2018 年以来，掌控人民币贬值节奏和幅度的一个关键是“贸易摩擦”引发的预期，2 000 亿美元商品新增关税已经落地，人民币当日走低后又有所反弹，这实际上意味着“贸易摩擦”升级这一变量的短期风险已被市场充分接纳和反映。

很明显，从目前“汇率—资本流失”压力的角度来看，央行跟随美联储加息的必要性也不是很显著。

（四）总结：央行跟随加息并非板上钉钉

综上所述，无论从随行就市、引导预期还是应对美联储加息的角度来看，当前时点，跟随加息的必要性都较低。

三、“加息 + 降准”组合模式可行性分析

在这种背景下，我们再探讨一下当前市场上的一种普遍预期——上调政策利率以缓冲美联储加息带来的本币贬值压力，降低准备金率支持国内“宽货币”到“宽信用”的传导，也就是“加息 + 降准”的组合模式。

我们不妨先看一下这个组合模式对央行上述目标达成的影响：

- 就随行就市而言，现在的流动性是充裕的；而从货币市场和政策利率利差角度而言，由于目前二者贴合运行，则加息抬升政策利率之后，降准可能使得短端低价资金供给充裕，压低市场利率。
- 就引导市场预期、稳定宏观杠杆率而言，目前央行货币政策的重点在于引导“宽信用”向“宽信贷”转化，疏导传导机制才是当务之急。
- 就应对美联储加息而言，一个关键问题在于中美利差不是政策利率之差，而是目标市场利率之差。上调政策利率，再进行同步降准，如果上调的幅度不大，总体效果上将压低货币市场利率（降准释放的资金成本显著低于公开市场投放），从这个机制出发，“加息 + 降准”反而会恶化中美短端利差。

也就是说，“加息 + 降准”并不符合目前的政策逻辑。在当前经济增速回落、部分企业融资受限的大背景下，定向精准扶持“融资贵、融资难”的民营、小微企业就显得尤为重要。不排除在特定情境下，出于对维稳经济发展、化解金融风险的考虑，央行会在总量可控、投向明确的前提下通过公开市场操作、再贴现利率，甚至“降准”的方式进一步提供流动性支持。

四、中长期货币政策约束

除了短期政策选择以外，实际上更值得我们担忧的是如果美联储持续加息，在中长期对国内货币政策限制的影响。

央行行长易纲在博鳌亚洲论坛2018年年会分论坛“货币政策正常化”的问答实录中谈道：“目前中国10年期国债收益率约为3.7%，美国10年期国债收益率约为2.8%，中美利差处于比较适中的区间。包括货币市场的隔夜利率和7天利率，中美利差也在舒适的范围内。简短地说，面对主要经济体货币政策正常化，我们已经做好了准备。”

通过易纲行长的讲话不难发现，央行层面既关注长端利差，也关注短端利差。长端利差目前有60个bp，仅考虑加息跟随问题，2018年12月的加息预期概率已超过70%（大部分在美债收益率中反映），那么即使2019年的加息完全反映到长端，基于目前的中债收益率，至少也能容纳4次以上的加息冲击（2018年9月、12月及2019年两次），然后才有倒挂压力。

但短端压力就不这么乐观了。美联储2018年9月、12月加息落地后，如果央行完全未跟随，那么中美利差就已经处于倒挂边缘，如果2019年美联储仍继续加息，中美之间就将进入负利差状态。

由于压力集中在短端，在此以短端利差展开分析。

（一）利差的舒服区间在哪里

需要明确的一点是：利差只是镜像，从汇率或者更深一点来说，外储的稳定才是核心。因而利差本身的波动不重要，只要汇率或者说外储能维持稳定，则利差本身就是处于舒服的区间。因此判断短端利差能否持续下行，关键点在于判断人民币有没有持续贬值压力：由于目前外储的稳定性除了长变量——经常项目平衡以外，关键点还在于人民币到底有没有持续贬值的预期。

从人民币汇率压力角度出发来分析，从内部来看，人民币汇率首先需要考虑新兴市场国家汇率的贬值压力如何衡量：人民币汇率适用的框架是“资产组合分析法”，核心是对比本币资产（M2）和外币资产（F，外储）的供给增速之差；新兴市场国家货币（M2）的基石是外储，外储和M2的相对变化可以衡量货币的贬值压力。据此构建“M2—外储：同比增速之差”在绝大部分新兴市场国家都与汇率变动高度拟合，从这一指标来看，经历了2018年年初压力的充分释放后，这个时点，人民币确实尚无持续大幅贬值基础。

从外部来看，在人民币中间价定价机制中，美元指数是核心，因而要对美元的走势重点关注。在美元指数中主导占比的货币是欧元，因而美欧之间的经济形势对比是决定美元指数的关键指标。从目前的情况来看，美元指数虽有小幅上行压力，但持续上行的动力并不存在，从牵引角度而言，美元指数难以对人民币造成持续贬值压力。

也就是说，现在的人民币汇率情况并不存在持续贬值的基础，因而利差的收缩并不必然使得外部环境变得“不舒服”。不过这种对人民币贬值压力，乃至于美元指数的判断仍然是一个趋势外推的结果，如若美元保持持续加息，国内进一步面临宽松困境，那么人民币仍有贬值压力重来的趋势，这种情况下该如何抉择呢？

（二）贬值压力回归时的政策选择

首先，通过跟随“上调政策利率”收敛利差应该是杯水车薪。美联储每次加息幅度高达25bp，如果央行每次跟随5～10bp，那么随着加息的持续，到2019年仍然避免不了倒挂（未来加息4次，即使每次跟进10bp，利差仍然会收窄60bp）。也就是说要通过收敛利差平衡内外压力，至少需要政策利率每次上调20个bp左右的幅度，这对于货币政策而言就不是技术性调整，而是实质性的“转向”了。

故而要讨论在面临外部压力的时候，央行是否会选择放弃国内目标，而基于外围压力“转向”，这就涉及对于“蒙代尔不可能三角”中固定汇率、资本流动和货币政策独立的选择问题了。央行给的答案是比较明确的，大国状态下优选国内货币政策独立。典型的例子如2014—2015年，在汇率贬值压力之下，并未停止宽松。在“三元悖论”体系下，选择货币政策独立、平衡外部压力的思路比较简单：放弃固定汇率，释放贬值压力。

但是央行的研究表明：在新兴市场，由于不存在自然汇率，贬值预期会自我叠加，使得汇率自由流动，加大资本流失压力——蒙代尔的“三元悖论”不成立，往往成立的是“二元悖论”（货币政策独立和资本自由流动只能二者取其一）。也就是说，汇率贬值不是压力宣泄的渠道，反而会加大资本流失压力，在这种背景下，稳定资本流动的第一个思路是稳定汇率。

在稳定汇率的过程中，如果采用直接的外汇市场干预，则会显著消耗外储，在这种背景下，央行往往会率先使用行政手段去稳定汇率。2018年的汇率干预过程典型地体现了这一特征。如果通过干预手段逆转市场贬值预期，则由于汇率被“逆周期调控”，那么利率可以获得一定的空间，利差约束相对“偏软”，甚至在强干预下，利差完全可以不成为约束。例如在2008年8月确定“以市场供求为基础的、有管理的浮动汇率”制度之前，汇率的行政化管控程度较高，可以看出，无论是“SHIBOR－LIBOR”还是“R001—联邦基金利率”之差都处于负利差状态；2010年，央行公告增加汇率弹性以后，利差继续大幅上行。这充分表明一点：在汇率管控背景下，由于利差和汇率脱钩，则“利差”本身并不重要，可以处于负利差状态。

不过在现行汇率制度下，如果汇率贬值的压力是长期的，则汇率的单边干预是比较难以扭转其走势的，典型的就是2014—2015年，在调控过程中汇率持续贬值。在这种背景下，由于贬值预期不能逆转，因而宏观调控的着力点不在汇率而在管控资本项目流动。这时，由于资本项目被人为管死，则利差是一个“弱约束”，压力不会直接反映在资本流动上，利率会释放出明显的空间。近期国家相关部门对境内个人资本项下跨境资本流动的一系列调控措施充分证明了这一点。

总结来看，如果美联储持续加息，国内经济又偏向下行，由于“二元悖论”下的调控思路问题，无论是“汇率管控”还是“资本管控”，都意味着利差不会作为主要的调控项而改变国内货币政策走向，因而“利差”是个弱约束，央行并不会亦步亦趋地跟随。

五、特殊情况分析：汇率升值预期

2018年人民币贬值的节奏和幅度，充分体现了贸易摩擦“谈”与“战”对汇率截然不同的影响。如果在加息的中途中美重新回到谈判桌上，从市场预期和双方谈判的筹码来讲，汇率升值都是一个重要的走向。

由于存在持续的升值压力，则市场投资本币资产会有一个汇兑收益，由于汇兑收益存在，只要总体上资本都是净流入的，理论上利差可以持续收敛为负。在实践上，日本和德国的经验为我们呈现了这一点：在日美、德美贸易摩擦下，日元和德国马克进入持续升值预期，长短端利率都持续走低，低于美国，直到1992年贸易摩擦缓和，日元和德国马克升值预期被打散后，日美、德美利差才再度正向收敛。也就是说，理论和实践都表明，在本币汇率存在持续升值预期背景下，本币和外币资产之间的利差可以不断收敛，而典型的汇率先行的例子就是贸易摩擦（为了压缩顺差，逆差国通常要求顺差国货币升值）。

六、总结

从短期而言，2018年9月的加息中国货币当局大概率不会跟随，另外市场预期的“加息”配比“降准”政策也并不利于央行政策逻辑的实现，因而大概率也不会配比落地。

从中长期来看，如果美联储持续加息，在人民币无中长期贬值压力的情况下，利差本身不重要，其持续收敛也并不意味着不在“舒服的”区间。但是如果国内宽松需求升级，美联储加息节奏依然较快，人民币汇率重新进入贬值渠道，则可能出现下列情形：

- 单纯 5 ~ 10bp 的技术性跟随，无法避免利差大幅走低乃至倒挂，也就无法缓解贬值压力，在这种情况下，央行如果为了平衡压力进行跟随，所需要做的是货币政策的大幅转向。
- 央行在优选货币政策独立的背景下，主要通过汇率的行政调控或资本项目的强制管控来平衡外围压力，在这种背景下利差并不对国内货币政策造成硬约束，负利差状态也在同样历史情况下出现过。
- 如果贸易摩擦重新进入谈判状态，参照德日经验，持续的中美利差收敛，乃至大幅为负也符合逻辑。

从总体上而言，美联储的持续加息难以改变我国货币政策的独立走势，货币政策的松紧取向仍要基于国内基本面，目前来看，尚不存在转向基础。

普惠金融篇

大型商业银行反哺小微企业的路径与实践

江苏省分行　周长富

小微企业是现代经济体系不可或缺的组成部分，是新时代美好生活需要的主要提供者，是吸纳就业的主力军和主渠道。但是，“融资难、融资贵”一直是制约小微企业发展的世界性难题，传统的观点认为由于信息透明度不高、抵押担保条件不足、经营稳定性较差等原因，导致大型商业银行更倾向于为大型企业提供融资服务，而不愿意为资金需求规模小的小微企业提供融资服务，进而认为中小金融机构为小微企业服务更具优势。略显不足的是，已有的讨论只是停留在理论层面分析小微企业融资困境，并没有与我国经济发展阶段、科学技术进步、大型商业银行社会责任等联系在一起，这样提出的政策建议难免会出现一些偏差，政策的可操作性不强。实际上，随着互联网技术的发展，大数据技术的运用有效解决了信息不对称问题，大型商业银行推进普惠金融更具有技术优势、规模优势和资源优势。本文首先分析了小微企业在我国现代经济体系中的重要作用；其次从小微企业经营情况、商业银行内部管理制度、金融体系的建设等角度分析小微企业融资困境的主要原因；最后结合建设银行的普惠金融实践，提出新时代背景下大型商业银行支持小微企业融资的比较优势和实践新模式。

一、小微企业在现代经济体系中的重要作用

改革开放以来，我国个体、私营等非公有制经济不断发展壮大，已经成为社会主义市场经济的重要组成部分和促进社会生产力发展的重要力量。个体、私营等非公有制经济发展，有利于繁荣城乡经济、增加财政收入，有利于扩大社会就业、改善人民生活，有利于优化经济结构、促进经济发展，对全面建设小康社会和加快社会主义现代化进程具有重大的战略意义。

（一）小微企业是高质量发展的重要推动者

当前，我国经济已由高速增长阶段转向高质量发展阶段，这是十九大做出的重大判断。高质量发展的一大内涵就是高效率增长，高效率增长是指以较少的投入获得最

大的收益，而决定高效率增长的一个重要因素是技术创新。因此，为了实现高效率增长和高质量发展，就必须有效推动技术创新，尤其是要获得颠覆性技术与原创性技术。

小微企业一直是技术创新的主要推动者。研究发现，许多革命性的创新成果往往在中小企业中首先被创造出来，中小企业在技术进步中发挥着十分积极的作用。很多富可敌国的超级跨国公司都是从一家名不见经传的小企业逐步发展起来的，比如福特、丰田、微软等，这样的案例在美国硅谷更是比比皆是。阿克斯和奥德斯（Acs and Audretsch，1990）分析了20世纪80年代初期美国各个行业的技术创新情况，发现在技术进步较快、产品个性化程度较强的行业（如计算机、程控仪器、塑料制品）中，中小企业的优势较为明显。林毅夫和李永军（2001）指出，我国资本密集型行业中的企业主要是一些国有大型企业，往往赢利能力较差，甚至在竞争的市场中缺乏“自生能力”。近几年，在我国创新驱动发展中，民营企业完成了我国65%的专利、75%以上的技术创新、80%以上的新产品开发[①]。因此，在高质量发展阶段，必须充分调动小微企业的积极性，充分发挥其主观能动性，实现以较少的消耗获得更大的利益，提高我国自主创新能力。

（二）小微企业是美好生活需要的主要提供者

十九大报告指出，中国特色社会主义进入新时代，我国社会主要矛盾已经转化为人民日益增长的美好生活需要和不平衡不充分的发展之间的矛盾，人民美好生活需要日益广泛，对物质文化生活提出了更高要求。近年来，随着我国居民收入水平的不断提高，居民的消费观念和消费结构出现了明显的更新升级。1978—2017年，我国城镇居民和农村居民的恩格尔系数分别从57.5%、67.7%下降到28.6%和31.2%，表明日常消费支出占收入比重呈现不断下降的趋势。通过细分城乡居民的消费内容和消费结构可发现，随着居民收入的增加，“吃、穿、用”消费性支出占居民消费的比重呈下降趋势，而“住、行、学”所占比重呈上升趋势[②]（王国刚，2010），并且从2013年开始“住、行、学”方面的支出超越了“吃、穿、用”的支出。其中，城镇居民的“吃、穿、用”占居民消费性支出的比重，从1995年的72%下降到2017年的42%；城镇居民“住、行、学”占居民消费性支出的比重，从1995年的24%上升到2017年的63%（见图2.1）。从生活质量的角度看，“住、行、学”代表了居民美好生活的物质需要。

美好生活的物质需要更多的是依托小微企业提供的服务，也催生了很多的新兴业态。随着新产业、新业态、新商业模式的蓬勃发展，小微企业投资快速增长，2017年

---

① 资料来源：邹伟、安蓓、胡浩．坚定不移将改革进行到底——当前中国改革发展述评之二［P］．人民日报，2018.10（10）．

② 本文所指“吃、穿、用”分别是统计指标中的食品、衣着和家庭设备及服务支出；“住、学、行”支出是统计指标中的居住、交通和通信、文教娱乐用品及服务、医疗保健。

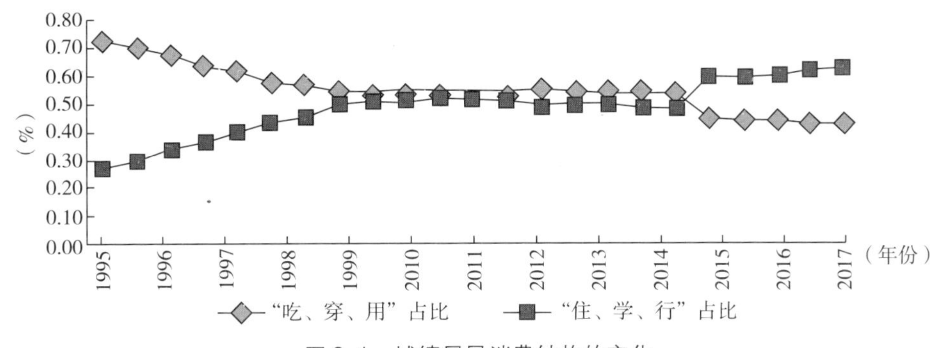

图 2.1 城镇居民消费结构的变化

资料来源：万得资讯。

小微企业投资同比增长 11.2%，增速高于同期全社会投资 4.2 个百分点，新注册小微企业平均投资规模高于存量小微企业，为新时代居民生活水平的提高提供了物质保障和服务保障。

（三）小微企业是解决劳动者就业的主要载体

劳动力资源丰富是我国融入全球经济分工的重要比较优势，正是依托劳动资源禀赋，我国的劳动密集型企业在过去几十年的经济发展过程中做出了非常重要的贡献。由于大企业在进行大规模生产的过程中，通常会用更多的资本密集型的设备代替劳动力，属于资本密集型行业，就业增长相对比较缓慢。而中小企业多数是劳动密集型企业，是吸收新增劳动力就业的重要渠道。古德金（Gudgin，1979）的研究表明，在英国很多地区，就业的增长主要依靠新成立的中小企业，而非当地的大企业。同时，中小企业的地区化倾向较强，在中小企业较多的地区，人们更倾向于建立自己的小企业，而不是受雇于大企业。根据《中国经济普查年鉴 2013》的数据显示，2013 年我国共有小微企业法人数 784.98 万家，从业人员数达到 1.47 亿人。2013 年总从业人员数为 3.48 亿人，小微企业就业人数占比达 42%。如果考虑中小企业对就业的贡献，比例可能更高，2004 年中小企业就业量在整个企业部门总就业量中的比例达到 79.7%①（见表 2.1）。

表 2.1 2013 年我国中小企业就业人数统计 （万家/万人）

从业人员组距	1～7	8～19	20～49	50～99	100～299	300～499	500～999	1 000～4 999
企业法人数	562.98	267.2	144.15	55.63	37.87	7	4.54	2.85
从业人员总数	2 047.48	3 161.56	4 330.94	3 800.31	6 215.77	2 651.05	3 123.27	5 413.84

资料来源：根据《中国经济普查年鉴 2013》的数据整理获得。

① 资料来源：田大洲，曲涛，田娜．我国中小企业发展及其就业贡献［J］．人口与经济，2011（2）．

二、小微企业融资困境的主要原因

小微企业融资困境是一个世界性的难题，国际国内学者做了大量分析和研究，将中小企业融资面临的困难归为筹集资本金的困难（简称资本缺口）和筹集债务资金的困难（简称债务融资缺口）。具体来看，既有抵押不足、财务制度落后等企业内部问题，也有我国金融体系发展、商业银行授信审批等宏观制度问题。

（一）小微企业自身存在的不足

国际上最早开始关注小企业融资困难这一世界性难题是麦克米伦（Macmillan, 1931）在《麦克米伦报告》中阐述了企业规模是影响企业融资难易程度以及融资方式选择的重要因素。一方面，小企业的经营不确定性较大。中小企业由于企业家管理能力、企业抵御宏观经济风险的能力等方面的不足，导致出现较高的倒闭和歇业概率，作为经营风险的商业银行，肯定不愿意向经营不稳定的中小企业贷款。根据美国小企业管理局统计，2 年内倒闭的小企业比率达 23.7%，4 年内因为经营失败、倒闭和其他原因退出市场的比率达 52.7%。根据我国的数据估计，30% 的中小企业在 2 年内消失，在 4 ~ 5 年内消失的企业比率达 60%。由于小微企业较高比率的经营不善，所以如果银行向企业贷款，出现不良的比率较高，这就导致很多商业银行将小微企业排除在客户名单之外。乌代和贝尔热（Udell and Berger, 1998）指出，由于小微企业的规模较小、管理不规范、信息不健全，导致商业银行难以收集到企业的实际经营情况信息，从而难以从商业银行获得融资支持。保拉·萨皮恩扎（Paola Sapienza, 2002）指出小微企业的借贷成本比大企业高，主要是由于企业规模、企业的偿贷能力和抗风险能力存在较大的差异。

另一方面，中小企业的抵押和担保不足。企业的财务报表是商业银行信贷审批的重要材料之一，但是很多中小企业难以向银行提供经过审计的合格财务报表，导致商业银行难以判断企业的经营情况。在此背景下，银行为了控制信贷风险，必须要求企业提供相应的抵押或担保措施。乌代（1998）研究发现，美国小企业从金融机构获得的信贷中，91.94% 是有抵押或担保的债务。从我国的实际情况来看，银行在抵押品的选择上，主要接受价值易评估、易变现的资产，如房地产和土地。但是小微企业厂房和土地的价值相对较少，这也导致这些企业通过抵押获得银行贷款的难度较大。

（二）商业银行内部管理体制的缺陷

商业银行作为企业间接融资资金来源的主要渠道，在融资的过程中，银行在贷款前会对企业进行筛选并约定企业信贷资金的使用，贷后还要对企业的资金使用进行监督。由于小微企业自身经营管理的问题以及商业银行的战略定位、考核体系和信贷文化等，银行更愿意为大型企业提供融资服务。

一是商业银行的信贷资源配置导向。施蒂格利茨和韦斯（Stiglitz and Weiss，1981）经典信贷配给理论指出，在金融市场存在信息不对称和逆向选择的情况下，银行在高利率水平上拒绝给小微企业发放贷款有两个原因：一是企业愿意支付高利率的行为向银行发出它们是更高风险成本借款者的信号，从而使银行望而却步；二是因为在更高利率水平发放贷款会使企业选择更高风险的行为，从而进一步增加银行的风险成本。所以，银行利润最大化的选择是对大中型企业和小微企业实行差别待遇。威廉森（Williamson，1988）的层级控制理论指出，当银行规模扩大和组织机构复杂到一定程度时，它们可能会减少对小微企业的贷款，而集中为大企业提供金融服务。林毅夫和李永军（2001）从金融制度和银行结构角度指出，信贷市场规模结构对小微企业融资有重要影响，特别是在大型银行处于寡头垄断的国家，小微企业的信贷约束状况较严重。图2.2较好地解释了银行对不同客户采取的差别待遇。其中D_1代表大企业的需求曲线，D_2代表存在信息不对称的小企业的需求曲线，银行为了避免逆向选择，将对大企业制定竞争性均衡利率R，而对存在信息不对称的小企业制定信贷配给均衡利率R^*。

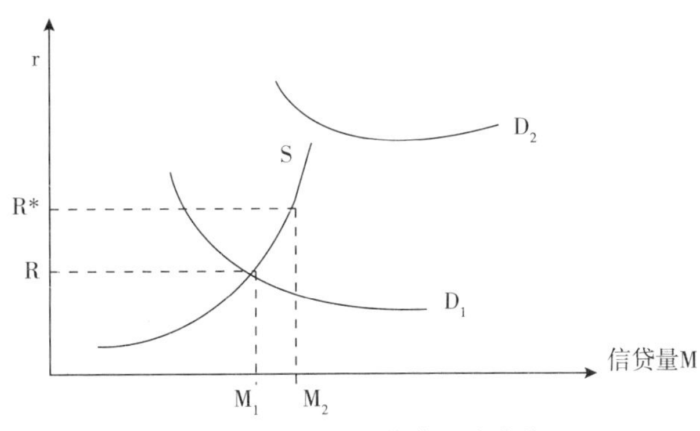

图2.2　商业银行信贷配给曲线

二是商业银行的内部考核体系导向。商业银行受指标考核体系等因素的影响，一直以大企业、大业务为主要战略导向，以存款、贷款、利润、不良率等作为核心指标，缺乏对小微企业贷款的激励机制，未制定小微企业信贷差别化的考核体系。在此背景下，由于小微企业单笔业务的贡献率低，不良贷款的可能性高，所以即便总行以战略为导向推动小微企业信贷业务发展，在业务规模和利润指标为主要考核指标的体系下，分支行必然会选择少做或者不做小微信贷业务，导致总行小微企业信贷发展战略难以执行到位。

三是商业银行的信贷风险导向。随着我国商业银行管理制度的不断完善，很多银行都建立了非常规范的信贷管理流程，企业授信需要经过客户评级、授信审批、放款审批、风险管理等环节，而小微企业的经营情况难以满足商业银行的授信管理制度要求。首先，在信用评级环节，小微企业由于往往处于创业起步期或者成立时间较短，企业的财务报表等书面资料不健全，银行难以获得企业的资产负债率等指标，无法用传统的手段对企业进行客户评级。其次，在授信审批环节，由于小微企业的资金使用具有“短、小、频、急”等特征，而银行的贷款发放需要从支行、二级分行、省分行等环节层层上报、审批，流程长、效率低，难以解决小微企业的资金使用需求。再次，在风险定价环节，随着利率市场化进程的推进，商业银行存贷款价格的浮动幅度越来越大。对小微企业而言，由于小微企业的风险较大、违约率相对较高，导致商业银行在对小微企业贷款定价环节往往上浮较多，提高了小微企业的贷款成本。

（三）金融体系建设滞后

赵鹏程（2016）指出金融体系是为实体经济服务的，金融体系与实体经济的关系本质上是一种供给与需求的关系，金融体系必须与实体经济决定的金融需求相适应，恰当的金融体系能够满足社会经济活动中实体经济提出的金融需求，从而起到提高资源配置效率等功能，促进经济发展，反之，则会阻碍经济发展。近年来，虽然我国不断加大金融市场体系的建设，推进金融市场化进程，但是金融制度变迁滞后于产业部门的改革，垄断的金融体系仍难以满足市场经济发展的内在需要。一是金融市场体系发展不充分。由于我国资本市场尚不发达，我国金融体系中缺少一个多层次的，可以为中小民营企业融资问题服务的资本市场，小微企业融资仍然主要依托于商业银行的间接融资。但是商业银行是以盈利为目标的企业，小微企业难以满足银行的贷款要求，所以在以国有银行为主导的金融体系中，小微企业难以获得资金支持。二是商业银行市场化程度仍然较低。虽然近年来商业银行的数量越来越多，但四大国有商业银行仍然具有很大的规模优势和资源优势。与大银行相比，中小银行由于存在服务定位和管理方面的差距，中小金融机构在盈利动机的驱动下，与大型商业银行争抢风险相对较低的优质大企业，导致中小金融机构对小微企业融资支持的不足。三是配套信贷服务体系建设滞后。由于小微企业经营风险大且抵押品不足等原因，小微企业贷款迫切需要引入融资性担保公司进行增信。肖兰华、金雪军（2010）认为解决信息不对称问题的关键是建立信贷担保机制，有效分担银行信贷风险。但是我国融资性担保公司普遍存在规模小、融资担保能力有限、经营管理不规范等问题，对小微企业信贷担保支持有限。

三、大型商业银行的普惠金融优势和实践——以建行为例

前文的分析表明，小微企业是经济新动能培育的重要源泉，是大众创业、万众创新的重要载体。但是小微企业融资问题具有综合性、复杂性特征，特别是在当前经济

结构深度调整和新旧动能加速转换的背景下，小微企业依附的宏观产业链条和大中型企业面临转型升级阵痛，加上金融机构避险偏好回升，商业银行激励机制不到位等原因，小微企业融资压力有所上升。在此背景下，大型商业银行寻找、培育有潜力的小微企业，加强小微企业信贷风险管理，既是商业银行履行社会责任的职责所在，也是商业银行推进业务转型发展的需要，更是商业银行提高竞争力的重要内容。

（一）践行普惠金融是大型商业银行履行社会责任的有效方式

大力推动普惠金融、加大薄弱领域金融支持力度，既是新时代背景下提高经济发展平衡性、包容性、可持续性的关键因素，也是决胜全面建成小康社会的内在要求。国有商业银行作为金融市场服务的主要提供者，作为资金资源调配中心，在现代经济体系建设中发挥着重要的造血输血功能和宏观调控作用。自 2005 年普惠金融概念被引入国内，我国的普惠金融实践取得了巨大进步。国家高度重视普惠金融的发展，2015 年国务院专门印发《推进普惠金融发展规划（2016—2020 年）》，将普惠金融列为国家战略；2017 年全国金融工作会议强调，要建设普惠金融体系，加强对小微企业的金融服务。但是经过多年的发展，我国的普惠金融发展仍没有切实解决小微企业的融资困境，主要原因是商业银行在贯彻执行普惠金融战略的动力不足，监管机制不到位。因此，普惠金融的发展必须结合中国经济发展的特色，充分发挥大型国有商业银行的社会责任和使命担当。

近年来，建设银行全面推动普惠金融战略实施，将普惠金融业务打造为新时代背景下建设银行应对市场新形势、新变化的战略支点。一是明确普惠金融战略。2018 年，建设银行率先宣布将普惠金融确定为全行发展战略，随后推出大数据产品“建行惠懂你”App（手机应用程序），实现“小微快贷”线上一站式办理，为小微企业发展提供更加便捷、及时、有效的金融服务。二是创新服务模式。通过借力“新一代”金融科技优势，完善“小微快贷”全流程在线融资模式，为广大小微企业提供速度快、费用省的金融服务，助力解决小微企业“融资难、融资贵”问题。创新“裕农通”与农村地区基层机构合作模式，为涉农小微商户及农户提供集“存贷汇缴投”于一体的综合金融服务。立足数字化管理思维，以科技应用和系统工具为手段，持续优化风险控制模式，实现覆盖信贷全流程、穿透式的风险管控，保障普惠金融业务持续健康发展。三是丰富的产品体系。自 2016 年起，建设银行积极运用金融科技，突破传统业务模式，推出线上融资服务“小微快贷”，成为大银行服务小微企业，解决社会痛点的典型范例。同时，根据多维度数据的整合分析，小微快贷针对不同客户类型及需求场景，已形成“云税贷”“账户云贷”“医保云贷”等丰富的产品体系。四是丰硕的服务成果。2017 年建设银行普惠金融贷款新增位居同业首位，成为唯一达到中国人民银行普惠金融最高激励目标的国有大行。2018年上半年，建设银行普惠金融贷款余额4 912.89亿元，比上年末新增727.87亿元，同比增速44.33%；普惠金融贷款客户数86.85万户，同比新增38.34万户。

（二）推进普惠金融是大型商业银行促进业务转型的有效手段

改革开放40年来，我国经济的高速发展主要是依靠投资驱动，推动我国工业化进程。既有金融体系主要适用于传统工业发展模式，商业银行主导的金融体系在功能设计上难以为服务业、高附加值工业行业融资，主要以工业大项目、大企业的“双大”为服务对象。但是，当经济增长模式由传统的投资驱动转向消费驱动时，小企业、小行业成为满足人民美好生活需要的主要服务提供者。在城镇化进程中，商业银行应针对中小企业的金融需求，创新产品与服务，向小微企业集中的区域延伸服务网点，根据小微企业不同发展阶段的金融需求特点，支持金融机构向小微企业提供融资、结算、理财、咨询等综合性金融服务。商业银行服务小微企业的市场空间和潜力巨大，是商业银行推进业务转型的重要方向。

在此背景下，建设银行提出了普惠金融的“双小”战略，用“双小”连接和承接“双大”。一方面，传统的业务发展空间受限。随着我国经济的转型升级，服务业对经济的贡献已经超越工业，从投资驱动向消费驱动转变，大型固定资产投资项目明显减少，地方政府也在化解高企的债务融资；同时房地产行业经过多年的非理性繁荣，在国家宏观调控的背景下，房地产行业发展的空间有限，这对商业银行传统的经营模式提出了挑战，难以依靠大企业、大行业作为利润的主要增长点。另一方面，小微企业金融服务潜力巨大。由于信息不对称的原因，中小商业银行一直是小微企业服务的主力军，但是在互联网技术等的带动下，大型商业银行的优势不断凸显。同时，海量的小微企业和个体工商户等市场主体与大众生活息息相关，这些目前相对弱势的企业没有被金融满足，却是关系国计民生、关系未来发展的方向性领域，有广阔的市场空间。

（三）实施普惠金融是大型商业银行发挥比较优势的有效途径

传统观点认为，中小金融机构在为中小企业提供服务方面具有信息优势、区位优势和成本优势（林毅夫，李永军；Berger，Udell），斯特拉恩和韦斯顿（Strahan and Weston，1996）提出小银行优势假说，进一步论证了银行规模与中小企业贷款规模之间的负相关关系。但是随着科技的进步，大型商业银行在推进普惠金融方面更具有科技、网点、资源等方面的比较优势。

一是金融科技优势。近年来，商业银行对金融科技的重视程度显著提高。通过金融科技助力普惠金融，大型商业银行服务小微企业的信息劣势逐步破解，信息不对称的问题在大数据时代迎刃而解，将大数据和平台作为突破口，开创了小微金融服务的新模式。比如建设银行历经6年建设的新一代系统，为传统银行业务的发展插上了科技的翅膀。2018年，建设银行在国有大行中率先成立了金融科技公司。借力金融科技，实现小微企业贷款全流程网络化、自助化操作，运用大数据互联网技术，减少了客户信息采集、调查、验证等人工操作，又保证了信息的真实性、有效性。二是网点资源优势。小微企业往往植根于县域经济中，具有非常明显的长尾特征，过去更多的是依托于当地的中小农商行。实际上，大型商业银行可以充分发挥网点数量多、信贷资金规模足的优势，解决普惠金融中的县域地区和长尾客户的有效金融需求。从小微企业的贷款投放来看，截至2018年6月末，国有商业银行占比为30.17%，股份制银行占比为18.15%，城市商业银行占比为23.61%，农村商业银行占比为27.04%。其中，建行普惠金融贷款余额4 912.89亿元，是支持小微金融服务的主力军。根据万得统计数据显示，网点数量最高的是邮储银行，达40 000个网点；其次是农业银行，网点数量超过20 000个；工行、建行和中行的网点数量均超过10 000个。而股份制银行和中小银行的数量都要远低于国有大行。因此，国有大行仍有非常大的空间可以挖掘，更应充分发挥网点资源优势，推动普惠金融战略的落地。三是信贷资源优势。近年来，在国家去杠杆政策的导向下，货币市场的流动性大幅收缩。受流动性收缩的影响，企业的融资面临非常大的困境，债券市场违约事件频发，其中受到冲击和影响最大的就是民营企业、中小企业以及中小金融机构。在金融去杠杆的背景下，大型商业银行的信贷资源优势将更加凸显。根据万得数据统计，大型商业银行的资产占银行业金融机构的比重达35.96%。同时，近年来伴随着去杠杆进程的推进，央行采取了MLF（中期借贷便利）、SLF（常备借贷便利）等货币政策工具释放市场流动性，这些工具对大型商业银行而言更具有身份优势，而部分中小金融机构难以直接获得央行的流动性，只能通过银行间市场拆借获得资金。因此，大型商业银行更应该主要承担为小微企业输血的职责，提高对小微企业的融资支持。

重返县域

——普惠金融战略背景下建行县域支行发展新机遇与新路径

湖北省分行　毛　磊

作为我国最古老、最基本的行政单元，县域近年利好不断，乡村振兴战略、新型城镇化建设等政策联翩而至，使县域经济焕发了蓬勃生机，成为各家商业银行寸土必争的新“蓝海”，更成为普惠金融的“主战场”。因此，在战略性撤退十余载后，重新聚焦县域，对我行深入拓展县域市场、助力普惠金融战略落地具有非常重要的意义。

一、当前我行县域支行面临的发展困局

经过对县域的长期耕耘，建行县域支行成绩显著，市场地位突出，但随着经济形势、市场环境的改变，难免面临着一些困局，影响县域支行发展。

（一）定位之困：心无所向

随着各家金融机构纷纷抢滩县域，县域市场逐渐步入舞台中央，各县域金融机构也形成了针对性的市场定位。比如：全国性银行中，农行和邮储银行根据其总体发展战略，均进行了“三农”金融事业部改革，将县域支行定位为“服务‘三农’”，助力县域经济发展；地方性银行中，各地农商行也都明确了“支农支小”的市场定位。

建行县域支行历经抢滩设点、战略收缩、结构优化等几次大的转型调整，县域金融业务发展方向并不是太清晰。虽然建行分条线成立了主管县域支行相关业务的对应机构，并面向县域支行制定了针对性的考核办法，但将县域支行进行统筹管理的机制尚不健全，“部门银行”的管理弊端在县域表现得尤为明显，导致县域支行，尤其是所辖各网点，一直缺乏针对县域市场实际的明确的市场定位，总是疲于完成上级行下达的各项指标任务。另外，县域市场和大中城市差别较大，有其根深蒂固的特殊性，是否可以利用同一套盈亏标准进行业务取舍，是否可采取同样的价值取向评价县域市场，都有待商榷。

（二）市场之困：外患内忧

在近几年市场环境急剧变化的背景下，建行经营“三大一高”的传统优势正在被蚕食甚至消失，特别是在县域市场尤为显著，县域支行正面临着外患内忧的市场困境下。

1. 外患同业竞争

随着股份制商业银行的触角延伸至县域，目前县域市场已实现了各类银行机构的全覆盖，县域市场竞争日趋惨烈，前有农行、邮储、当地农商行等老牌县域强行的阻击，后有股份制商业银行甚至外资银行等县域新秀的追赶。甚至，还有不少互联网企业跨界参与县域金融竞争，如蚂蚁金服的千县万亿计划。而作为一级法人体制下的县域支行，在业务审批、人力与财务资源配置等方面的权限较少，自主性和灵活性方面也有一定的差距，与同业短兵相接时不占优势。

2. 内忧业务拓展

目前国内银行业务模式相对简单，特别在县域市场，主要利润来源仍是存贷息差，容易受到冲击。如，利率市场化对县域业务的影响较大，特别是存款业务，由于定价策略分化使得当地农商行等中小银行机构优势明显。此外，县域市场产品同质化严重，建行面向县域市场的创新较为滞后，适合县域经济特色且有针对性的产品和服务较少，和县域市场日趋多样丰富的金融需求反差较大。

（三）信用之困：如履薄冰

受制于产业特征、社会环境以及个人观念等因素，县域支行所面临的信用环境不理想，承受的风险压力较大，开展业务如履薄冰。

1. 县域产业自身局限

县域大多数产业具有先天的弱质性，且以小微企业为主，核心竞争力不强，受经济周期影响较大，容易出现业务量滑坡、资金链紧张等问题，进而导致信用风险。同时，大量借款主体缺乏优质土地、厂房等有效抵押物，而担保公司普遍规模不大，融资担保能力弱。

2. 社会信用基础薄弱

我国信用体系建设比较落后，特别是县域地区，信用基础异常薄弱，信用风险防范与化解困难较大。一方面，征信体系不健全，不少企业没有严格执行财务制度，会计信息准确性较差，而县域居民、农户相关信用数据更是寥寥无几；另一方面，失信惩戒机制不健全，失信人违法成本低，容易形成不良示范。

3. 个人信用观念淡薄

县域小微企业主及老百姓法律金融知识普及不够，信用观念淡薄，风险意识、诚信意识较差，导致一些客户容易卷入非法集资，要么因正规资金渠道有限而借助高利贷，要么受高息诱惑参与集资。另外，也容易出现逃废债现象，须诉诸法律，但即便胜诉也难执行。

（四）人力之困：力不从心

近些年建行高度重视基层网点人力资源配置，特别是向县域支行倾斜力度较大，所以县域支行员工总量方面的劣势并不显著，但在员工结构、活力及工作强度等方面问题较为突出，导致经营管理过程中力不从心。

1. 员工结构

总体上呈现出“上老下小中间少”的结构。自县域战略性收缩以来，近 10 年，县域支行人员“只出不进”，导致员工老龄化明显，直到近些年，才陆续有应届大学生被分配到县域，补充了新鲜血液。但县域青年员工离职率较高，无法有效沉淀为中生代力量，人员断层严重。

2. 员工活力

县域支行里中老年员工较多，实现自身价值的渠道有限，导致部分员工心生倦怠，且生活水平经多年积累在当地有优势，正向、负向的物质激励效果不明显。对青年员工而言，除晋升不易，还存在业务单一等问题，很难获得知识积累和技能提升，容易失去工作热情和目标。

3. 工作强度

县域客户文化程度等方面较城市略有差距，且老年人较多，高度依赖员工的“保姆式”服务，使员工要耗费大量精力去完成简单、重复的劳动。比如，容易出现单据填写不规范、密码记错输错等问题，需反复沟通、改正；对自助智能设备接受程度低，即便使用也需手把手帮助，甚至要求代操作。

二、普惠金融战略背景下建行县域支行发展新机遇

作为有大格局、大担当的国有大行，建行顺势而为，将发展普惠金融提高到全行战略高度，提出了面向蓝海、面向大众、面向草根的普惠金融战略。县域正是“蓝海、大众和草根”的典型代表，是普惠金融落地的“主战场”，普惠金融战略给县域支行带来了发展新机遇，为破解定位、市场、信用、人力等发展困局提供了新方向。

（一）政策机遇：县域推进普惠金融的“天时”

自 2013 年“普惠金融”一词第一次正式出现在十八届三中全会的文件中以来，政府对其重视程度与日俱增，两年后又发布《推进普惠金融发展规划（2016—2020

年)》，进一步将其提升到国家战略的高度。近几年，在各类利好政策的支持下，普惠金融发展速度突飞猛进，而银行一直走在普惠金融的最前沿，是普惠金融坚定的践行者，也得到了更多的政策倾斜。

安永事务所近期发布的有关普惠金融创新的研究成果指出，将世界上60个新兴市场受到金融排斥的中小微企业、个人实施普惠金融全覆盖，银行机构预估收入增幅将达到2 000亿美元/年，而我国银行业增幅居首，到2020年能达到634亿美元。县域正是大量普惠金融需求者的聚集地，存在大量尚未享受正规金融服务的小微企业和消费者，县域市场在推进普惠金融进程中理应站在更加主动、更加重要的位置，积极把握时代赋予的政策机遇。因此，县域支行全面推进普惠金融恰逢其时，时不我待。

（二）市场机遇：县域推进普惠金融的“地利”

十八大明确了涵盖“新型工业化、信息化、城镇化和农业现代化”的新“四化”之路，县域作为统筹城乡协调发展的重要平台，追求新“四化”之路责无旁贷，更是城镇化和农业现代化的绝对主力，正面临着前所未有的重大市场机遇，而这也是历史使命。

一方面，近几年我国陆续启动了农、林、水利、供销等一系列重大改革举措，十九大更是明确提出实施乡村振兴战略，最新发布的《乡村振兴战略规划》明确农村地区要加强基础设施投入，未来4年投资规模预计有4.52万亿元。另一方面，新型城镇化建设规划要求进一步激发新型城镇化的潜在内需，国家也将在城镇基础设施建设、城乡公路开发、城乡居民生活配套设施建设等一系列领域加大投入。此外，打好三大攻坚战也是县域发展的重要任务，尤其涉及精准脱贫，县域更是重中之重。

总之，无论是乡村振兴战略、新型城镇化建设，还是三大攻坚战，需要众多普惠金融需求主体参与其中，存在非常多潜在的普惠金融需求，为县域支行推进普惠金融提供了难得的市场机遇，也是县域支行必须承担的历史责任。

（三）客户机遇：县域推进普惠金融的“人和”

普惠金融是指一系列产品和服务，所服务的客户不仅包括小微企业，也涉及双创、扶贫、涉农等各领域的企业或个人，上述客户群体与县域有较高的重合度，给县域业务拓展提供了大量潜在客户。

比如，小微企业是县域市场的主力军，承担着大量与县域发展息息相关的任务，且不少是建行存量客户供应链上下游的客户；在双创方面，既有回乡创业潮下的本籍能人、务工人员、本地大学生回乡创业，也有一些资金雄厚、经验丰富的城市创业者创业下沉；还有符合扶贫产业准入的企业以及建档立卡户。此外，随着土地经营权流转的逐步落实，以及集体林地经营权、水滩养殖权、集体建设用地使用权、房屋所有权的确权，涉农业务抵押担保机制将会进一步创新，涉农业务发展空间较大。

上述客户在负债端、资产端或中间业务端都蕴含着巨大的需求，为县域支行发展奠定了良好的客户基础。在负债端，投资渠道较少且有更强的储蓄偏好，能提供稳定和低成本的资金来源；在资产端，“短小频急”的资金需求较多，相比成本而言更关注可得性，此外基础设施建设也会带来更多的中长期贷款需求；在中间业务端，县域市场尚未有效开发，潜力较大。

（四）科技机遇：县域推进普惠金融的“长技”

随着互联网、移动互联网、社交网络、大数据等技术的日趋成熟，给银行业带来不小冲击的同时，也帮助传统商业银行完成了蜕变。一方面，在各种先进技术的武装下，越来越多的传统银行业务实现了不同程度的自主、自助、智能化办理，甚至开发了基于互联网平台的新业务、新产品，提高了业务处理效率及客户体验；另一方面，通过借鉴学习互联网金融企业的运作机制，商业银行充分利用自身海量的数据资源以及强大的服务网络不断创新服务模式，提升了核心竞争力和价值创造力。

金融科技的不断进步，给县域金融机构带来了实实在在的好处，也给普惠金融业务的推进提供了便利条件。比如：拓展了县域服务边界，在银行网点、ATM（自动取款机）难以布放的偏远区域，银行可以利用电脑、手机以及通信网络提供交易服务，甚至办理现金业务，使远离城市中心的人们也能享受金融服务；提高了服务效率，面向县域海量长尾客户，通过互联网技术、大数据技术等可以降低边际成本，实现针对性、差异化的服务，满足普罗大众的金融需求。

三、普惠金融战略背景下建行县域支行发展新路径

沉沉浮浮几十载之后，县域支行要抓牢当前出现的政策、市场、客户及科技方面的战略机遇，借普惠金融的东风“重返县域”。“重返”并不是指任何形式的跑马圈地，而是重新审视县域市场，提高重视程度，形成战略聚焦，从市场定位、渠道体系、产品体系、营销服务模式、风险管控机制等方面探索县域支行发展新路径。

（一）确立“普惠＋可持续”的市场定位，统一县域市场经营机制

作为普惠金融的“主战场”，县域银行推动落实普惠金融责无旁贷，同时必须统筹兼顾市场原则和社会责任的辩证关系，走商业可持续的普惠金融之路。因此，要明确县域支行“普惠＋可持续”的市场定位，通过普惠金融形成差异化的竞争策略，并进

一步优化县域市场经营机制，推动县域支行统一协调发展，形成商业可持续性，打造县域支行新的竞争优势。

在明确市场定位的基础上，采取“两步走”的思路统一县域市场经营机制。首先，建立县域支行业务管理联席会议制度，成立县域业务部际协同小组，涉及县域发展的各项规章制度统一提交部际联席会议讨论，协同小组负责推进落实县域业务的开展。后期，在条件成熟的前提下，可在一级行层面固化协同管理平台，将分散在各部门涉及县域业务发展的各项职责进行整合，专门成立县域金融事务部，统一协调管理县域业务的推进和发展。要把县域作为一个整体板块进行经营和管理，赋予相应权限，形成独立的综合服务、统计核算、风险管理、资源配置以及考核激励机制，持续激发县域支行的发展活力。

（二）构建“网点 + 金融服务站 + 线上”的渠道体系，打造县域综合经营生态圈

县域普遍存在金融机构数量少和金融服务需求者遍布区域广而散的矛盾，存在金融服务覆盖程度不足与传统渠道覆盖难度大、成本高的矛盾。因此，要对现有产品营销渠道、客户服务渠道进行重构，构建“1 + 1 + N”的营销服务渠道体系，即网点 + 金融服务站 + 各类线上产品或渠道（App），将所有渠道利用资金流、物流、信息流、商流进行联结，打造客户、银行以及第三方之间“三位一体”的互融互通的县域综合经营生态圈。

物理网点是县城及富裕乡镇的金融服务主阵地，更是推动县域普惠金融服务的主阵地，能发挥网点“一对一、面对面”的普惠金融服务优势。对客户资源丰富、功能齐全、人力资源配置充足的网点，全面拓展普惠金融业务，形成普惠金融的排头兵；加快探索县域普惠金融特色网点建设，根据普惠金融客户群体特征和自身经营优势成立县域特色支行。

打造普惠金融服务站，作为一般乡镇及农村的金融服务主阵地，充分利用“龙易行”“裕农通”等载体，从空间和功能两个方面加快服务点拓展。在空间上扩大覆盖面，向偏远地区、贫困地区延伸，向金融机构覆盖不足的村庄、工厂、学校和大型社区延伸；在功能上扩大业务范围，创新合作模式，积极与当地卫生系统、社保局、通信公司等第三方机构合作，增加便民缴费、结算等解决民生痛点的功能。

基于物理网点和金融服务站，按照客户群体、客户需求，结合政府民生、文化教育、车主消费、日常缴费等生产生活场景，搭配相应的线上产品和渠道，打造综合经营生态圈，并根据客户生产、生活的场景提供相应的金融或非金融全场景服务，有效解决县域社会的金融需求和民生痛点。

（三）优化“普适性+个性化”的产品体系，提高县域客户体验和黏性

随着金融创新的不断下沉，各类金融产品纷纷进入县域市场，县域面临的已不再是金融产品不多，而是不精的问题。因为县域市场上大多数产品均不是针对县域实际开发的，而是面向某个区域、某项业务或者某类群体，县域往往是“搭便车”；为数不多面向县域需求开发的产品，容易因适用范围不广、准入条件严格等原因而得不到广泛应用，甚至有的异化为“形象工程”或者变成“烂尾楼”。因此，必须切实做到以客户为中心，按照实事求是的原则，从县域客户的实际需求出发进行产品布局与设计，建立“普适性+个性化”的产品体系。

一方面，优化现有产品结构，结合县域实际对存量产品进行调整，以客户需求为视角理清现有产品内在逻辑，对功能相近的产品进行整合，对内各部门协同支持与管理，对外统一推广，避免分散销售精力、模糊客户焦点，有效提高产品认知度。另一方面，加强针对性的产品创新，对目标客户群进行深入调研，因地制宜地深入细分市场，针对现实“痛点”提出产品解决方案。总的来说，就是要重点推广几款满足县域广大需求的“普适性”拳头产品，集中优势兵力打造“爆款”；同时提供部分“个性化”产品作为补充，满足县域特殊群体、典型代表的需求。

（四）打造“大数据型+关系型”的营销服务模式，增强核心竞争力

县域市场的客户群体与大中城市相比有一定的“二元性”，既有涉足新材料、新技术、新制造等战略新兴产业的“高大上”企业，也有技术含量低、家店一体的夫妻店、小作坊；既有对智能、自助、线上等高科技手段的好奇，也有对人员面对面手工操作、现场交流特有的依赖；既有按照现代经济特点运行的市场原则，也有传统熟人社会固有的行为模式。因此，对县域客户的营销服务既要讲速度，更要讲温度，要打造“大数据型+关系型”的营销服务模式，即基于个人信息、财务信息等硬数据对客户进行精确画像，进而细化客户分类、开展精准营销；同时，通过与客户之间长期、密切的商业交往与接触收集软信息，基于软信息的支撑给客户提供针对性、个性化的金融服务。

通过“数据+关系”的营销服务，做好获客、活客、留客等关键环节，提高知名度、美誉度和忠诚度，增强核心竞争力。获客方面，通过“软、硬”数据的结合优化客户选择，充分利用政府或第三方机构的相关信息，深入市场调研，掌握客户群分布特征，分类批量拓展目标客户。活客方面，对小微企业、商户、小微企业主、个体经营户、农户等县域典型客户群进行信息挖掘，结合资金需求情况、日常活动信息等开展名单制营销，组织有针对性的活动。留客方面，加强与客户的沟通联系，在满足日

常需求的基础上进一步提供超值服务，如利用建行大学等资源提供培训教育服务，使员工与客户共同成长，巩固银企关系。

（五）强化“疏导+堵截”的风险管控机制，助推县域业务高质量发展

县域属于典型的熟人社会，人与人之间交流更加频繁、关系更加密切，既容易信任对方，也容易放任对方，人情大于制度的氛围比较浓厚，给孳生风险提供了有利土壤；同时，县域地区接受法律金融等相关教育的资源和渠道有限，无论是员工还是客户，对相关规则敬畏不够，对后果严重性认知不足，导致风险防范意识较差，往往在无知或无畏的情况下卷入风险事件。县域的员工和客户更需要有效地疏导，通过持续的教育培训引导他们不断增强风险意识，学会防范应对风险。因此，必须强化“疏导+堵截”的风险管控机制，采取疏堵结合、以疏为主的方式进行风险防控，有效降低信贷风险、操作风险、道德风险以及各类案防安防事件的发生，助推县域业务高质量发展。

疏堵结合、以疏为主的风险防控重点要从明确责任、强化教育、加强管理三方面着手，让县域员工和客户知规则、懂规则、守规则。明确责任方面，要落实风险防控主体责任制度，将风险防控责任明确到每名员工、每个岗位、每道流程。强化教育方面，采取集中培训、专题讲座、案例分享等多种形式对员工进行教育，同时结合金融知识普及等宣传活动强化对客户的法律金融知识宣贯。加强管理方面，做好过程管控，关心关爱员工，关注员工异常行为，同时多维度动态监测客户相关数据信息，完善风险预警及处理机制。

普惠金融现状、前景与建行业务重点建议

总行战略与政策协调部　李丹红　刘兴赛

在全球范围，普惠金融是一项说易行难的事业，其根本难点在于要实现商业绩效与社会绩效双重目标。长期以来，我国金字塔型社会结构与“倒金字塔”型金融供给结构形成非对称结构性矛盾，导致越往金字塔底层金融供求矛盾越突出，制约了经济转型和社会发展。2015 年国务院发布《推动普惠金融发展规划（2016—2020）》，明确农民、小微企业、城镇低收入人群和残疾人、老年人、贫困人口等特殊群体为普惠金融重点服务对象。2017 年，人民银行发布《关于对普惠金融实施定向降准的通知》，将普惠金融贷款界定为：单户授信 500 万元以下小型企业贷款、微型企业贷款、个体工商户和小微企业主经营性贷款、农户生产经营、创业担保、建档立卡贫困人口、助学等贷款，而中国银监会对小微企业贷款的定义为单户授信 1 000 万元以下的贷款。目前，国内普惠金融业务以小微企业贷款为核心，但从概念上说，普惠金融不是仅局限于贷款，而是涵盖多种金融产品和服务；不应限于小微企业，还应涵盖广大个人客户。因此，本文从小微企业金融、农村金融和个人普惠金融 3 方面出发，探索和研究普惠金融的发展现状、市场前景和我行业务重点。

一、我国普惠金融发展现状和问题

近年来，我国普惠金融呈现快速发展态势。商业银行尤其是大型商业银行是供给主体，供给方呈多元化趋势，但业务发展不平衡、不充分问题依然突出，可持续的业务模式和盈利模式仍有待探索。

（一）小微金融：大型银行份额居首，“农商行＋城商行”是经营主体，对接互联网成为主要创新方向

截至 2017 年年末，我国银行业金融机构小微贷款余额 30. 74 万亿元，占银行业金融机构各项贷款总额 24. 6% 。

一是商业银行占据主导地位，“农商行+城商行”是经营主体。截至2017年年末，商业银行小微贷款余额23.34万亿元，占全部银行业金融机构小微贷款余额的75.9%，其中，大型银行①占31.8%，居首位；农商行占25.7%，居第二；城商行占23.1%，居第三。“农商行+城商行”的市场占比达48.8%，且其小微贷款占自身资产比重分别高达18.3%、17.0%，“农商行+城商行”是名副其实的小微金融经营主体。股份制银行②无论是市场份额还是小微贷款在自身贷款中的占比，都低于城商行和农商行。外资银行市场份额低于1%（见表2.2）。

表2.2　2017年年末，各类银行小微贷款市场占比及在自身资产中占比

项目	大型银行		股份制银行		城商行		农商行		外资银行		互联网银行及其他	
	余额（亿元）	市场占比（%）	余额（亿元）	市场占比（%）	余额（亿元）	市场占比（%）	余额（亿元）	市场占比（%）	余额（亿元）	市场占比（%）	余额（亿元）	市场占比（%）
小微贷款	74 225	31.80	42 864	18.40	53 935	23.10	59 971	25.70	2 214	0.90	218	0.10
资产总额	928 145	47.20	449 620	22.80	317 217	16.10	328 208	16.70	—	—	—	—
小微贷款占资产比重	8.00%		9.50%		17.00%		18.30%		—		—	

资料来源：各家银行年报。

二是银行基于传统逻辑，对小微金融业务模式进行了积极探索。2008年，民生银行等银行就开始对小微金融业务模式进行探索。第一，基于大数定律，推进小微贷款的小额化、零售化；第二，通过小微企业综合金融服务，提高服务能力和收益水平；第三，将商圈和供应链作为目标市场；第四，专业化经营以及事业部制改革。

三是互联网和金融科技为小微金融创新提供了新思路。2016年以来，银行与互联网结合更加紧密：一是带来授信等业务流程线上化；二是通过电商平台或银税直连等获取客户；三是以大数据风控破解长尾客户征信不足；四是基于供应链体系开展供应链融资；五是切入具体行业和场景。其中，涌现出建行“云税贷”、网商银行“网商贷”等典型产品。

① 大型银行包括工、农、中、建、交五大行。

② 股份制银行包括招商银行、中信银行、光大银行、华夏银行、广东发展银行、平安银行、浦东发展银行、兴业银行、民生银行、恒丰银行、浙商银行和渤海银行。

（二）农村金融：大型银行市场份额最大，“农商行+农信社”占据较大份额，电商企业积极展开战略布局

截至 2017 年年末，我国涉农贷款余额 30.95 万亿元，同比增长 9.6%，银行业金融机构涉农贷款合计占比 67%。目前，我国农村金融服务主体包括大型银行（工、农、中、建、交和邮储银行）、农商行、农信社、村镇银行和小贷公司等机构。

我国农村金融发展主要有以下特点。一是大型银行在县域市场占主导地位。截至 2016 年年末，大型银行涉农贷款 10.39 万亿元，占全部涉农贷款 37%。农行是县域金融传统强者，2017 年年末涉农贷款余额超 3 万亿元，占全部涉农贷款 9.6%。目前，水利、县域城镇化和专业大户等仍是大型银行县域金融的主要着力点，对普通农户贷款涉及较少。农行和邮储银行正积极推进“三农事业部”改革，试图通过差别化组织框架和政策体系，推动农村金融专注、专营和下沉。

二是农商行、农信社、村镇银行是县以下金融服务主体。截至 2016 年年末，我国有 1 114 家农商行、1 125 家农信社以及 1 443 家村镇银行。三者涉农贷款合计占全部涉农贷款 30%。农信社网点下沉、合作化、深耕本地、产品适应性强，在县以下区域具有竞争优势。当前，农信社向农商行转制成为主要改革方向，但也带来经营脱农化问题。与之相似，村镇银行也面临着经营向县城集中、脱农的问题。

三是电商等互联网巨头积极介入农村金融。2014 年，阿里巴巴启动“千县万村计划”，计划建立 1 000 个县级服务中心，10 万个村级服务站，实现网货下乡，农产品进城。依托“村淘”计划，蚂蚁金服积极拓展农村金融市场。截至 2017 年 3 月，支付宝“三农”用户已达 1.63 亿户。2015 年 9 月，京东金融发布农村金融战略，通过京农贷、乡村白条等产品为农村提供多元化金融服务。2016 年，苏宁金融成立农村金融部，借助 O2O（线上到线下）金融优势探索农村金融发展模式。

（三）个人普惠金融：大中型商业银行是经营主体，互联网消费金融快速成长

截至 2017 年年末，我国消费信贷余额 31.53 万亿元，同比增长 25%。其中，住户短期消费贷款余额 6.81 万亿元，相当于 2012 年余额的 3.5 倍。

一是商业银行是消费金融主要提供者。截至 2017 年年末，商业银行个人消费贷款余额 30.99 万亿元，占金融机构消费贷款余额 98.3%。其中，大中型商业银行是经营主体，截至 2017 年年末，5 家大型银行个人消费贷款余额 18.89 万亿元，占比 60.96%，并且其主要通过三项业务展开：第一，个人住房贷款，截至 2017 年年末，银行个人住房贷款余额 21.9 万亿元，占消费贷款余额 70.6%；第二，信用卡融资，截至

2017 年年末，全国信用卡贷款余额 5.56 万亿元，占金融机构短期消费贷款余额 81.6%；第三，个人消费贷款，近年，互联网消费贷款成为重要增长点，2017 年，建行新增个人消费贷款 1 176.13 亿元，增幅 156.74%，其中主要是“建行快贷”快速发展。

二是持牌消费金融公司行业规模有限。目前，我国共批准了 25 家消费金融公司，开业 22 家。主要有中银消费金融、捷信消费金融、招联消费金融等，大部分为银行持牌公司。2017 年，招联消费金融、捷信消费金融净利润超 10 亿元，超过无锡银行等上市银行。2017 年年末，行业贷款余额为 1 500 亿～2 000 亿元，占我国短期消费贷款余额 2% 左右（见表 2.3）。

表 2.3　截至 2017 年年末，主要持牌消费金融公司经营规模　（亿元）

消费金融公司	成立时间	注册资本	营业收入	净利润（%）	贷款余额
招联消费金融	2015 年 3 月	28.6	14.63	11.89	468.29
捷信消费金融	2010 年 11 月	80	132.36	10.22	
马上消费金融	2015 年 6 月	13	46.68	5.78	298.45
中银消费金融	2010 年 6 月	5	40	13.75	
兴业消费金融	2014 年 12 月	3	10.36	2.09	98.7

三是互联网消费金融爆发增长。2013—2016 年，我国互联网消费金融业务从 60 亿元增长至 4 367 亿元，年均复合增速 317.5%[①]。主要为三类机构。第一，电商或网络社交平台。腾讯金融、蚂蚁金服充分利用自身平台优势，通过平台获客、大数据风控拓展客户边界。截至 2017 年 8 月，成立两年的微众银行消费贷款余额已突破 1 000 亿元。第二，分期购物平台。主要为创业公司，通过与校园商户及购物网站合作开展分期业务。分期乐与趣分期是领导者，贷款规模已超过部分消费金融公司。第三，其他互联网金融机构。2017 年以来，很多现金贷以及 P2P 平台开始转战消费金融领域。

但是，我国普惠金融发展仍面临诸多挑战。第一，服务体系发展不充分、不平衡。民营银行、互联网银行等新兴主体刚刚起步，广大中西部金融供给严重不足，农村金融仍是最薄弱环节，传统银行业务仍是绝对主体。第二，业务模式、风控技术、盈利模式、组织架构尚不成熟。“圈链”模式无法有效应对行业性、地区性风险冲击，互联网获客、大数据风控尚处于初级应用阶段，普惠金融体制机制尚没有真正建立。第三，发展环境、基础设施有待完善。财政支持力度不足，政府配套政策少，仍有大量农村

① 资料来源：艾瑞咨询数据。

人群没有被纳入央行征信体系，同时缺乏土地经营权、林权有效流转的要素市场，城乡互联网普及率差距仍然较大。

二、我国普惠金融市场前景和重点领域

（一）普惠金融发展的市场前景广阔

1. 小微金融市场空间巨大

根据国家工商总局统计，截至2017年年末，我国实有市场主体9 815万户，其中，企业3 034万户（小微企业2 000多万户），个体工商户6 580万户，农民专业合作社201万户。据此测算，属于普惠金融范畴的小微企业、个体工商户和农民专业合作社等注册市场主体共计约8 800万户，而有关银行调研数据显示，我国平均每家小微企业资金缺口约70.5万元①，据此估算，2017年，我国仅这一块资金需求就达到62万亿元，扣除当年金融机构小微企业贷款余额30.74万亿元，则2017年我国注册市场主体普惠金融资金缺口为30万亿元左右。由此粗略推测，2018—2020年，我国累计小微企业普惠金融资金缺口将达90万亿元。

2. 农村金融市场空间广阔

2017年年末，我国本外币农村（县及县以下）贷款余额25.1万亿元，占全部金融机构本外币各项贷款余额的20.76%，而城镇贷款余额占比接近80%。同期，我国农村人口占比为41.48%，县及县以下经济在全国GDP中的占比约为45%。据社科院“三农”互联网金融蓝皮书显示，早在2014年，我国农户资金缺口就达到3.05万亿元，而当年农户贷款占农村贷款的比重仅25%左右，而《中国普惠金融发展报告（2016）》② 显示，目前农户贷款中由银行机构提供的占75%以上。据此保守测算，2018—2020年，我国广大农村地区资金缺口至少约36万亿元，其中需要由银行机构填补的资金缺口超过27万亿元。

3. 个人普惠金融供求缺口巨大

从个人客户角度看，中国拥有广阔的个人普惠信贷市场。2017年度《中国工薪阶层信贷发展报告》③ 显示，当前，我国就业人口中有26%属于工薪阶层，多分布在80后、90后及受过高等教育的人群中。近年来，这一群体的家庭信贷需求持续增长，平均每个家庭信贷需求额为26.5万元，而非工薪家庭平均总信贷需求额为13.3万元。据

---

① 2018年6月末，建行小微快贷户均贷款余额73.79万元。

② 《中国普惠金融发展报告》由中国人民大学国家战略与发展研究院联合有关机构于2015年第一次发布，为年度报告。

③ 由中腾信金融信息服务（上海）有限公司和西南财经大学下属的中国家庭金融调查与研究中心联合发布。

此测算，2017 年，我国约有 2.02 亿工薪阶层人口，按每个家庭 2 个从业人员计算，约有 1 亿工薪家庭，因此，2017 年我国工薪阶层家庭信贷总需求为 26.5 万亿元；2017 年，我国非工薪家庭约 2.87 亿户，信贷总需求为 38 万亿元，两者加总，2017 年我国家庭信贷总需求约 64.5 万亿元。而人民银行数据显示，2017 年，我国住户贷款总额仅 40.52 万亿元，个人信贷缺口约 24 万亿元。按此预测，2018—2020 年，我国个人普惠信贷缺口将达到 72 万亿元。

此外，中国拥有最广阔的个人普惠财富管理市场。截至 2017 年年末，金融资产在美国居民资产配置中占比 70%，在中国居民资产配置中占比仅 40%。而在金融资产中，美国居民的通货与存款占比为 12.85%，而股票、债券、基金、养老及保险担保计划等金融资产占比为 84%；我国居民的通货与存款占比为 55%，股票、债券、基金、信托、理财等金融资产占比为 35% 左右。中美居民资产配置的巨大差异主要体现在我国居民通货与存款配置比例大大高于美国，而股票、债券、基金、理财产品的配置比例远远低于美国。这意味着我国居民有巨大的财富管理需求，未来，普惠财富管理市场必将有极其广阔的发展空间。

（二）普惠金融发展的重点领域

1. 从地域看，普惠金融在中部地区和三四线城市具有尤其广阔的发展前景

从区域分布看，我国中部地区普惠金融供求缺口最大。2016 年年末，我国金融机构本外币各项存款在东部、中部、西部和东北地区①占比分别为 58.30%、16.40%、19% 和 6.3%，本外币各项贷款在东部、中部、西部和东北地区的占比分别为 55.90%、16.40%、20.70% 和 7%，而 2016 年我国东部、中部、西部和东北地区 GDP 占比分别为 52.22%、20.67%、20.32% 和 6.79%，人口占比分别为 38.39%、26.55%、27.24% 和 7.82%。无论从与 GDP 贡献的匹配度，还是与人口的匹配度看，我国金融资源明显向东部地区倾斜，并且近 10 年来改善幅度较小，其中，中部地区普惠金融供给不足问题最为突出，其次是西部地区（见图 2.3）。

从城市间分布看，一二线城市聚集了我国 50% 以上的存贷款资源，而数量众多的三四线城市占比仅 30% 左右，五六线城市②占比更低。截至 2016 年年末，按照城市等级划分，我国 5 个一线城市（北、上、广、深、津）、28 个二线城市，以 6.33% 和

---

① 东部：北京、天津、河北、上海、江苏、浙江、福建、山东、广东和海南；中部：山西、安徽、江西、河南、湖北和湖南；西部：内蒙古、广西、重庆、四川、贵州、云南、西藏、陕西、甘肃、青海、宁夏、新疆；东北部：黑龙江、吉林和辽宁。

② 我国城市分级排名根据计算公式加权评定，城市分级综合排名指标 = 城市规模（人口、面积）×0.5 + 经济发展水平（GDP、财政收入）×0.2 + 商业繁荣度 ×0.1 + 区域首位度 ×0.1 + 城市发展潜力 ×0.1。

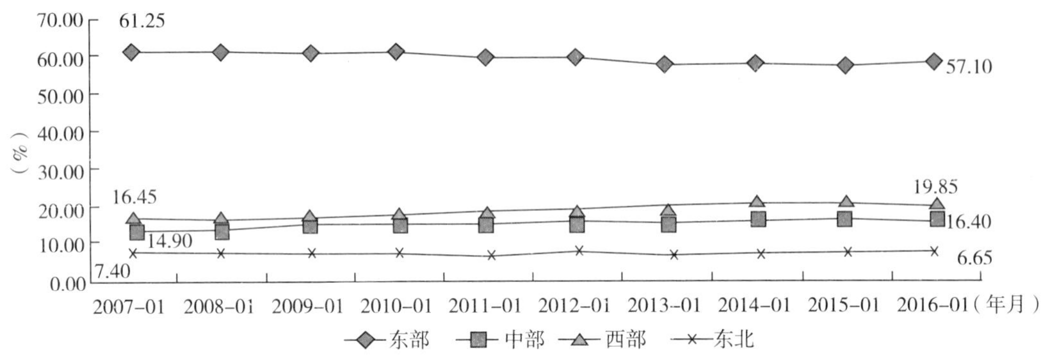

图 2.3　我国金融资源在四大经济区聚集情况

资料来源：万得资讯。

16.57%的人口占比，分别拥有全国金融机构本外币存款资源的24.72%和28.90%，贷款资源的19.32%和34.27%，而166个三四线城市以49.76%的人口占比，仅享有我国存款资源的29.02%，贷款资源的28.82%。作为我国城镇化建设的主阵地，三四线城市普惠金融供需矛盾非常突出。

2. 从产业看，普惠金融在第二、第三产业有非常巨大的供求缺口

近年来，我国第一产业GDP增加值占比不断下降，而第二、第三产业GDP增加值占比持续提升。2017年年末，我国第一、第二、第三产业GDP增加值分别为6.55万亿元、33.46万亿元和42.70万亿元，GDP增加值占比分别为7.92%、40.46%和51.62%，第二、第三产业合计GDP增加值占比超过90%。但在第二、第三产业快速发展的同时，相应金融支持却明显不足，尤其是一些新兴产业普惠金融供求缺口巨大。仅以绿色产业①为例，根据央行测算，2015—2020年，我国绿色产业每年需投入资金约占GDP 3%，按照2017年GDP测算约2.5万亿元，而在绿色产业投资中，社会投资比重占85%~90%，即绿色产业每年社会资金需求超过2万亿元，而2015年以来我国每年绿色信贷新增约0.6万亿~1万亿元，即仅绿色产业我国每年资金供求缺口就超过1万亿元。除此以外，我国第二产业中的先进制造业，第三产业中的教育、医疗、卫生、健康养老、旅游、信息技术等行业普惠金融供求缺口都非常大。

3. 从行业看，普惠金融在小行业有旺盛的需求

根据国家质量监督检验检疫总局和国家标准化管理委员会联合发布的2017年行业划分标准，我国国民经济行业划分为20个门类、95个大类、396个中类和913个小类，在各小类行业下又划分出众多小行业。近年来，随着我国产业集群化发展，围绕主导

① 包括环保、节能、清洁能源和交通等。

产业和核心企业的产业链纵向与横向拓展愈演愈烈，形成了专业化分工越来越精细、数量越来越多的小行业和细分行业。而无论是在高科技产业集群下的小行业，还是在传统产业集群下的小行业，无论是在以中小企业为主的产业集群下的小行业，还是在以大企业为核心的产业集群下的小行业，其企业基本上都以小微企业为主。数以千计的小行业汇聚了数以千万计的小企业，普惠金融需求旺盛。

三、建行发展普惠金融的优劣势

（一）发展小微金融的优劣势

与城商行、农商行等其他小微金融服务主体相比，建行在科技、平台、客户基础、资金成本、行业地位等诸多方面具有竞争优势。

一是技术实力占优。“新一代”成功投产为建行业务智能化发展奠定了系统基础。同时，建信科技子公司成立，又为建行科技发展注入体制活力。这些可以使建行更好地适应小微金融业务线上化、风控大数据化的创新趋势。

二是平台基础良好。善融商务、银税直连系统、E 商贸通等系统和平台，为小微金融线上获客、活客以及大数据收集奠定了基础。

三是客户群体庞大。截至 2017 年年末，建行小微贷款客户数 60. 5 万户，客户总量居四行之首。

四是资金成本较低。数量众多的网点以及支付结算业务发展，使建行得以汇集大量低成本存款，在资金成本上可以适应小微金融低成本定价需要。

五是行业地位重要。作为市场份额第二的大型银行，建行通过与政府机构、第三方平台、征信企业、科技公司广泛合作，可以构筑小微金融生态体系，破解小微金融难题。

但是，建行经营体系长期对接“双大”，存在风险偏好、组织架构、营运体系、人员配置、考核激励机制等不适应小微金融发展等问题。

（二）发展农村金融的优劣势

相对于农商行和农信社等农村金融经营主体，建行发展农村金融具有独特优势。

一是资金实力雄厚。2017 年年末，建行存款 16. 36 万亿元，占金融机构存款总额近 1/10（9. 67%）。而截至 2016 年年末，我国全部 1 114 家农商行负债总额仅 18. 75 万亿元，1 125 家农信社仅为 7. 48 万亿元，平均每家农商行和农信社负债额分别为 168 亿元和 66 亿元，与建行资金实力相距甚远。

二是业务品种丰富。除了在传统存贷汇领域拥有丰富产品线和服务链之外，建行在几乎所有新兴业务领域都拥有国内银行中最丰富的业务品种。在农村金融领域，建行推出“乾元—惠民系列”理财产品、惠农还款易等产品、“裕农通”服务、“村口银行”，为广大农村客户提供基础金融服务。

三是电子渠道发达。截至2017年年末，建行手机银行用户数2.66亿户，短信金融用户数3.81亿户，微信银行用户数7 212万，个人网上银行用户数2.71亿户，企业网银用户数603万户。与此同时，善融商务互联网交易平台服务范围覆盖27个省市、545个贫困县。发达的电子渠道有效弥补了建行农村地区网点不足的劣势。

四是风险管控能力强。凭借业已形成的稳健风险管理文化、健全的风险管理体系、完善的操作流程和机制、优秀风险管理人才队伍，加之“新一代核心系统”上线后，建行运用互联网、大数据等新技术，对风险精准预警和主动管控能力显著提高，为在农村金融领域精细化控险提供有力保障。

但由于历史上专业分工等原因，建行发展农村金融存在不容忽视的劣势。一是本地化不足。目前，建行在全国21%的县域（500多个县域）网点空白。而截至2016年年末，我国农村地区网点共计12.67万个，其中，农信社网点4万余个，排名第一，农商行网点3万余个，排名第二，数量远高于建行。二是灵活性不足。相对于农商行和农信社，建行规模庞大、业务链条长、信贷审批手续烦琐，流程复杂，较难适应农村金融决策快速多变的特点。

（三）发展个人普惠金融的优劣势

无论是在传统业务还是在新兴业务拓展上，建行发展个人普惠金融都具有优势。

一是传统业务优势。截至2017年年末，建行个人住房贷款余额4.21万亿元，居同业首位；信用卡累计发卡1.07亿张，服务客户总量达到8 163万户，贷款余额达到5 635亿元，占全国个人短期消费信贷比重达到8.2%。客户总量、贷款余额、活动商户数和资产质量等核心指标保持同业领先。

二是新兴业务战略先行优势。2017年，建行依托住房金融传统优势，紧抓租购并举住房制度建设历史机遇，在同业率先推出住房租赁综合解决方案，基本实现住房租赁平台覆盖全国主要大中城市，打响“要租房，到建行”品牌。在互联网消费金融领域，“快贷”带动个人消费金融快速增长。2017年，建行个人消费贷款新增同业第一，其中“快贷”电子渠道个人自助贷款余额1 563.3亿元，新增1 274.6亿元。

但是，相对于互联网科技巨头，建行在个人普惠金融领域仍存在不足。一是场景嵌入能力弱。与阿里巴巴、腾讯和京东等科技巨头比较，建行在移动支付金融入口之争方面处于劣势，建行电商平台获客、活客能力与上述巨头相比明显不足。二是生态构建不足。阿里巴巴和腾讯金融科技输出成为两者构建金融生态的有力工具和手段。另外，两者都有个人征信公司参与试点，这些征信公司广泛嵌入居民租房、旅店、租车等诸多领域。三是产品创新迭代慢。以客户体验为导向的产品迭代创新是互联网金融产品成功的关键，但囿于机制、文化、系统束缚，建行产品创新迭代存在明显差距。

四、对建行发展普惠金融业务重点的建议

2018 年 5 月 2 日，建行召开普惠金融战略启动大会，将普惠金融上升为全行战略，这是建行在新时期顺应时代发展要求的战略选择。综合我国普惠金融发展的市场前景、重点领域和建行优劣势，我们认为推进普惠金融战略，建行需在进一步巩固对“双大”客户、东部发达地区、中心城市和重点城市竞争优势的基础上，对区域战略、产业战略、行业战略、客户战略和经营模式进行调整。

（一）从区域看，除了传统经济发达地区外，建行应抓住中部地区、广大农村和三四线城市开拓普惠金融业务市场

针对中部地区普惠金融供给不足、分布不均问题，聚焦“一带一路”、长江经济带沿线经济活跃省市以及“中国制造 2025 国家示范区”城市群，加大对小微、“三农”、“扶贫”、个人金融支持力度。从实际情况看，2017 年，建行中部地区普惠金融贷款新增额位列全行第二，仅次于珠三角地区，高于长三角地区，这从一个侧面说明了在中部地区拓展普惠金融潜力巨大。

针对农村重点县域，加大对优势产业、现代农业、扶贫开发、农村产业融合、重大涉农工程和新型城镇化建设服务力度。采取“抓两头带中间”策略，一方面聚焦强县富镇，选择经济竞争力强县和综合实力强镇作为普惠金融重点；另一方面向贫困县倾斜资源、延伸网络，聚焦建行定点扶贫县域，带动整体县域普惠金融服务提升。

针对三四线城市消费持续升级趋势，适时转移消费金融服务重心，尽快完善对三四线城市业务布局、渠道下沉和深度渗透，加大对个人消费者服务力度。

（二）从产业看，我国第二、第三产业，尤其是其中的战略新兴产业，应是建行拓展普惠金融业务的重点产业

一要适应产业转型升级趋势，拓展先进制造业领域普惠金融业务。重点围绕新一代信息技术、高端装备制造、新能源汽车、生物医药和医疗器械、新材料新能源五大产业领域，深入挖掘小微企业信贷、理财、投行、信用卡、代发工资、代缴税签约、科技金融服务方案等金融需求，及时提供服务。

二要积极寻找新经济增长点，大力支持战略新兴产业普惠金融需求。围绕国家产

业政策和经济转型方向，针对小行业、细分行业普惠金融需求旺盛的特点，精耕、深挖普惠金融商机。大力拓展新能源、节能环保、电动汽车、新医药、新材料、生物育种和信息产业等战略新兴领域的普惠金融业务。

三要顺应第三产业成为支柱产业的趋势，积极拓展现代服务业普惠金融业务。加大对教育、卫生、健康养老、文化、体育、旅游、信息技术等基本公共服务领域普惠金融拓展力度。重点支持高校、医疗卫生机构、文化产业示范基地建设、城市商业区和旅游景区，以及物联网、云计算、大数据等现代信息技术领域小微企业金融需求。

（三）从客户看，小微企业和80后、90后个人客户应是建行普惠金融重点客户

一要对接“双大”客户，深入挖掘央企及全球客户上下游客群资源。根据我们的分析，小微企业和个人客户平均每年分别有30万亿元和24万亿元资金供求缺口，建行要牢牢把握这一“蓝海”市场。及时将客户战略侧重点转向“双小”和个人，对接“双大”客户，依托大数据优势、供应链平台、客户经销网络及大客户电子平台等，围绕资质优良、成长性好的下游小微企业，以及80后、90后个人客户发展普惠金融。

二要响应国家政策，加大对“双创”类小微企业支持力度。在高端科研成果密集区域和经济发达区域，加大对国家新兴产业、先进制造业、现代农业、现代服务业中的科技企业，尤其是获得国家和地方政府认定的高新技术企业以及获得科技专项资金支持、进入科技计划项目库的优质科技小微企业的支持力度。

三要拓展农村市场，大力支持涉农小微企业。项目上，优先选择国家“三区、三园、一体”[①] 规划项目；客户上，积极支持第一、第二、第三产业融合发展的新型农业经营主体，包括家庭农场、专业合作社和农业产业化龙头企业及其上下游企业等；产业上，重点支持“种养加”一体化、优势特色农业、生物育种、规模高效养殖、生态修复、乡村休闲旅游产业等。

四要立足建行扶贫地区，重点支持贫困地区小微企业。依托贫困地区资源禀赋，支持和培育特色产业，优先给予具有地方特色、经营状况良好、具备特殊工艺且市场口碑良好、带动建档立卡户就业较多的小微企业金融支持。

五要着力满足80后、90后客户群体居住和消费金融需求。一方面支持其自住购房、住房租赁等信贷和非信贷金融需求，另一方面持续满足其购车、装修、育儿、教育、旅游、健康、通信、娱乐等信贷和非信贷消费金融服务需求。

---

① 粮食生产功能区、重要农产品保护区、特色农产品优势区，现代农业产业园、科技园、创业园，田园综合体。

（四）从业务看，普惠信贷和普惠财富管理应是建行发展普惠金融的重点业务

一要扩大资源配置规模，有效增加普惠信贷资金供给。要进一步加大对普惠信贷专项资金配置，并建立专门体系加强内部激励，包括强化内部资金成本、业绩和利润考核，加大对分支机构和业务人员的奖励力度等。

二要加大产品和服务创新，满足不同客户群体普惠信贷需求。普惠金融不仅涉及建行传统“双大”客户产业链上下游企业，也涉及众多非建行传统优势领域客户，如一些新兴主体、新产业和新业态，还涉及很多传统个贷产品难以覆盖的个人普惠金融客户新需求，建行亟须针对新客户群体特点和需求，研发、丰富小微和个贷产品及服务体系。

三要提高定价能力和风控能力，保持普惠信贷商业可持续性。要提高普惠贷款风险定价能力，对于小微企业，要按照保本、微利原则，在有效覆盖资金成本的同时，最大程度降低附加成本；对于个贷客户，要提高根据客户信用等级差别化定价能力。还要提高普惠金融客户筛选能力，基于“新一代”平台技术和能力支撑，筛选和锁定业绩优良、成长性好的小微企业，以及个人信用记录良好、有实际信贷需求和偿付能力优质的个人客户，有效降低风险、提高收益。

与此同时，随着我国广大城镇中低收入居民财富积累和理财意识的增强，普惠财富管理必将成为银行普惠金融业务的另一个重要增长点。鉴于普惠财富管理客户大多是长尾客户，数量庞大、单笔理财金额不高，建行要尽快实现从传统的为高端客户理财向为广大普惠客户理财的业务模式转变。目前，广发智投、招行摩羯智投、工行AI（人工智能）投都是智能投顾在财富管理上的应用。建行要以智能投顾系统建设为突破点，打造一套以金融科技为核心生产力的普惠财富管理业务体系，推动建行理财业务从一对一、个性化高端客户模式到以金融科技为中心的普惠财富管理模式的转型。

（五）从经营模式看，应着力打造以金融科技为支撑的普惠金融综合服务平台

一要加快普惠金融综合服务平台开发。加快联合研发步伐，聚合客户、接入场景、集成数据，尽快打造完成面向市场和客户的普惠金融交易平台，并要从单一场景向多场景切入，发挥银行信用和数据优势，从收入、支出、生产、消费以及投资理财等多维度交叉认证，打造综合服务平台。

二要不断丰富平台场景功能。围绕小微、涉农、双创、扶贫和个人领域金融服务痛点和市场契机，综合考虑不同类型客户，针对小微企业生命周期和经营管理过程，

紧贴个人客户衣、食、住、行、娱需求，完善普惠金融场景功能设计，加快子平台和业务模块的设计开发。

三要持续创新互联网 + 大数据经营模式和产品。进一步整合对公对私客户信息，接入税务、工商、法院、人行征信等政府公共数据，提高客户信息真实可靠性；不断优化“小微快贷”“云税贷”模型；健全产品体系，建立面向成长型与创业型客户、线下与线上、抵质押与信用互补的小微企业产品体系。

四要不断延伸平台服务领域。拓展“双小”离不开“双大”，要在“承接”和创新上下功夫。总分行要深耕双大客户下游的优质小企业和客户；子公司要契合集团战略，功能上补充、战略上策应；主要业务和技术保障部门要加大创新，在夯实“双小”客户基础上，围绕涉农、双创、扶贫、个人等普惠金融客户群体下功夫，针对消费升级、绿色低碳、共享经济、现代服务业等领域，拓展平台服务客群和服务领域。

从信贷供求视角探索普惠金融助力乡村振兴

——以福建省为例

福建省分行　李彩燕

实施乡村振兴战略，是党的十九大做出的重大部署，是新时代“三农”工作的总抓手，受到全党全社会的广泛关注和高度重视。作为习近平总书记探索与实践“三农”思想的重要发源地，福建省高度重视乡村振兴工作，努力开创新时代福建“三农”工作新局面。普惠金融关键在乡村，如何有效发挥金融支持乡村振兴是当前迫切需要研究的问题。

一、福建省农村普惠金融的需求现状

福建省共有 287 个乡、640 个镇、15 363 个村；全省乡村人口为 1 377 万人，占总人口比重 35.2%；耕地面积 2 004.46 万亩，实际经营的林地面积（不含生态防护林）11 369.36 万亩。2017 年，全省农林牧渔业完成总产值 4 302.44 亿元，比上年增长 3.7%；2017 年全省乡村人均可支配收入 16 335 元，比上年增长 8.9%；人均生活消费支出 14 003 元，比上年增长 8.5%。

根据第三次全国农业普查数据，2016 年，全省共有 6.98 万个农业经营单位，其中在工商部门注册的农民合作社总数 3.42 万个，有 570.69 万农业生产经营人员。这些农户、农村企业构成了农村金融需求主体。他们的金融需求主要包括两个方面：一是满足日常生活的需要，包括日常消费、临时性消费及婚丧嫁娶、建房、教育、医疗等大额消费；二是满足生产经营之需，包括农业生产资料采购、人工费用、仓储运输、农村承包土地经营权的租金支付等。在金融服务需求类型上，主要是信贷需求，其他如支付结算、票据承兑、理财、贵金属、农业保险等需求快速增加。

二、福建省农村普惠金融的供给现状

近年来，福建省为更好地支持全省农业供给侧结构性改革，进一步强化农村金融服务，加大农业发展信贷投入。在农村金融渠道服务上，根据福建省银监局 2017 年年报显示，福建辖区有乡镇银行网点 2 131 个，行政村金融便民服务点 1.5 万个，其中 1 843个已升级为具有综合功能的金融服务站。此外，福建省全面推广“垄上行”金融服务队“背包银行”“党员信贷快车”等经验做法，通过走村串户把银行服务柜台搬到村民家中，实现乡村基础金融服务不出村。在贷款投放上，福建省银监局建立涉农贷款考核方法等多维度统计评价体系，引导金融机构围绕农业供给侧结构性改革方向，加大对新型农业经营主体的信贷投入。至 2017 年年末，辖区农户贷款余额同比增长 17.8%，高于辖区贷款增速 7.6 个百分点。

三、福建省农村普惠金融存在的问题

近年来，福建省农村普惠金融服务体系相对于之前取得了很大的成就，但与城市相比，农村普惠金融服务在实际情况中仍然存在一些问题。

（一）农村普惠金融需求端存在的问题

一是季节性和复杂性。农业主要是露天生产，容易受自然环境的影响。以福建省为例，该省是受台风影响较大的区域，每次台风登陆都会导致大面积农田被淹，粮食减产。虽然现代科学技术可以有效应对农业自然灾害，提高农业防灾减灾水平，降低自然因素对农业生产的影响，但农业生产仍呈现出明显的季节性，仍要遵循“春夏秋冬”四季的时节轮转。与此相对应的是，涉农金融需求也呈现明显的季节性特点，沿袭“春贷秋还”的周期性交替。此外，涉农企业大多是小微型企业，它们在管理体制、生产技术、资信水平、担保能力等方面存在较大的个体差异，金融需求呈“短、小、频、急”的典型特征，而且它们量多面广，分散在农村的各个角落，这导致了农村金融需求的分散性和复杂性。

二是低收益和高风险。目前福建省农产品精深加工比例很低，仍然以简单的重复再生产以主，农业生产附加值低，农业企业利润率也相对较低。因此农业经营主体较难承受高利率水平，金融服务的收益也相应降低。另外，农业生产容易受到客观自然环境因素的影响，且农村企业由于自身规模小的局限性，进一步限制了其抵御自然风险的能力，因而还贷能力也面临较大的自然风险。此外，农业担保、保险体系均不健全，难以为农户和农村企业在融资时提供有效的风险缓释措施，最终导致涉农贷款的高风险性。

三是缺乏有效的担保。目前涉农贷款产品大多是抵押类或保证类贷款。农户和农村企业所拥有的房产大多为自建房，没有取得房产证，无法提供抵押登记，难以提供符合金融机构要求的抵押品或第三方保证。在农村，土地是农民最大的资产，但是农民只有土地经营权而没有土地所有权，且现阶段农村土地承包经营权抵押仍存在一定的法律障碍。以福建省为例，该省是最早开展农村土地承包经营权抵押贷款的，但一直存在“假抵押”或“变相抵押”的情况，当地金融机构普遍采取“组合担保”或“反担保”的模式，而不是将土地承包经营权单独作为合格抵押品。

（二）农村普惠金融供给端存在的问题

一是涉农贷款供给规模在贷款余额总量上不均衡。农林牧渔业贷款余额占各项贷款余额的比重和第一产业产值占地区生产总值的比重不相称。以福建省2017年的信贷结构为例，当年第一产业产值占地区生产总值的比重为7.56%，而农林牧渔业贷款余额占各项贷款余额的比重却只有2.2%。涉农贷款供给规模在贷款余额总量上不均衡，说明福建省农业的发展没有得到足够有效的金融支持，这既不利于农业生产的发展壮大，也不利于乡村经济的持续发展。

二是涉农贷款投放对象结构不均衡。金融机构在选择客户对象时，一般优先支持自身经营好、企业主素质好、社会口碑好、风险缓释好、合作意愿好的“五好”农业龙头企业，因此这些龙头企业较容易获得充足的信贷支持。但对于农户和农村企业，农业产业发展中的不确定因素较多，较之其他产业客户受自然环境、政策因素影响较大，大部分客户自身抗风险能力较弱，农业客群一般也缺乏变现能力较强的抵质押物，影响了金融机构对农业客户的准入政策和产品创新，制约了信贷投放。

三是涉农贷款投放用途结构不均衡。一号文件指出，要大力开发农业多种功能，以农产品加工业和农村“双创”为重点促进第一、第二、第三产业融合发展，延长产业链、提升价值链、完善利益链。要因地制宜地形成“龙头企业+基地+合作社+农户”“订单收购+分红”“农民入股+保底收益+按股分红”等多种产业化经营体系。因此，农村在信贷需求结构上也正在发生变化。但金融机构往往不能及时调整信贷政策，创新适合农村经营主体需求的产品，此外，随着农业产业结构的转型升级，农业生产投入产出周期变长，但各金融机构对于农业结构调整的跟进较为滞后，仍按照农村传统产业的周期发放贷款，不能提供与市场需求周期相匹配的贷款期限。

四、关于建设银行发展普惠金融助力乡村振兴的对策和建议

面对新时代、新机遇、新挑战，建设银行要深刻领会加大金融支农是促进农业全面升级、农村全面进步、农民全面发展的迫切需要，要将金融资源配置到“三农”发展的重点领域和薄弱环节，满足“三农”多元化、多样性的金融需求，助力乡村振兴。

（一）强化金融科技引领

发展农村普惠金融就要把握其科技属性，借助互联网思维、大数据应用、平台经

营模式等科技手段，将金融和科技充分融合，把金融科技渗透到服务乡村振兴战略的方方面面、延展到乡村的角角落落。

一是加大网络融资服务在涉农领域的拓展应用。建设银行可基于农业大数据信息，以“互联网 + 大数据 + 全产业链”模式，创新线上、线下相结合的涉农信贷产品，推进农业全产业链整体金融服务。以福建省为例，该省农业厅正在开发“131 农业云”平台，建设银行福建省分行已与之签署战略合作协议，未来将通过系统对接获取涉农交易、资金及物流等“三流合一”数据信息，为涉农小微企业、农户提供“小微快贷”“个人快贷”等全线上融资产品。

二是搭建“智慧乡村”平台。“智慧乡村”是“互联网 +”在农村的应用，包括智慧农业、智慧村务、智慧医疗、智慧家居、智慧安防、智慧电子商务和智慧旅游七大模块。建设银行应结合农民地域特点及金融科技普及的前沿趋势，运用新一代技术，为各级政府搭建全事项、全流程、全覆盖、全场景的政务便民综合性服务平台，打造以农村土地、农业生产为核心（包括上下游），为农业农村经济参与方提供的全生态覆盖的综合服务平台，扩大农村金融服务的广度与深度。

三是延展普惠金融渠道。借助“信息进村入户工程”，挑选符合条件的“益农信息社”建设成为农村普惠金融服务点，充分发挥“裕农通 +”即“产品叠加、场景叠加、平台叠加”优势，解决偏远农民金融服务需求。通过合作赋能、服务出海、数据经营，推动建行普惠金融服务网络深入乡村腹地，解决乡村地区金融产品服务供给不充分等痛点，增进县域乡村客户关系，提升县域普惠金融服务能力，构建服务三农、乡村振兴、金融扶贫三位一体，内部充分整合、外部交互开放，助力农户美好生活的县域普惠金融共享综合服务平台。

（二）创新服务产品

当前，金融机构要顺应农业供给侧改革新形势，紧抓智能化、规模化、现代化农业领域中的业务发展机遇，深入研究新型农业主体的金融需求，打造适合他们的涉农金融产品，满足农民日益增长的美好生活需要。

一是聚焦优势特色产业客群。依托福建省的资源禀赋和地域特色，针对茶叶、水产、花卉苗木、林竹、水果、畜禽、蔬菜、食用菌、乡村旅游、乡村物流十大全产业链产值超千亿元的优势特色产业，创新契合农产品全周期的信贷产品。推广农业设施抵押、大型农机设备租赁、订单质押等产品，发展农业综合开发贷、农业科技贷等业务，进一步增强服务的针对性和有效性。根据乡村各产业生产周期、资金周转频次和贷款用途，合理确定贷款额度和期限，支持乡村发展。

二是丰富涉农信贷方式和手段。跟随国家政策制度转变，抓住第二轮土地承包到期后再延长30年的政策机遇，创新风险缓释方式。积极稳妥地推广接受以林权、农村土地承包经营权、农村集体经营性建设用地使用权、农民住房财产权等为标的的新型抵押担保方式。积极探索与财政涉农资金、风险补偿基金、政府背景农业信贷担保机构、保险机构等的合作，充分发挥政策性担保公司和保险机构对“三农”群体的增信作用，有效分散银行涉农信贷业务风险。

三是立足客群服务，推动金融支持“集群推进”。按照中央深入推进农业供给侧结构性改革、培育农业农村发展新动能的要求，大量涉农小微企业通过各类产业集群实现集聚发展，规模快速增长，专业化程度不断提高。构建全涉农客群、全产业链金融服务产品体系，抓好产业集群类客户群批量化服务工作，对拓展和培育优质小企业客户具有重要意义。

（三）完善风险管控机制

发展普惠金融是实施乡村振兴的迫切需要。建设银行要针对“三农”金融风险综合施策，加强涉农信贷风险全面风险管理，实现农村普惠金融持续健康发展。

一要关注宏观政策，做好市场规划。应对国家及当地政府出台的涉及或影响农业生产、消费的政策进行全面梳理，了解国家政策导向，并积极关注后续出台的新政策，及时调整行业及客户政策，防控因政策变化引发的风险向信贷业务的传递。在业务模式及产品创新和推广中，应牢固把握风险控制与合规理念，确保风险管控跟得上产品创新步伐，踏得准新技术创新应用节拍。

二要完善全流程主动管控。由于农业产业链各环节的风险点差异化明显，如种植、加工环节主要关注种植、采购、厂房建设等风险点，流通、消费环节主要关注企业库存及农产品价格波动等风险点，因此要实现对客群、内容、流量和数据等各关键节点的风险识别，针对不同环节的企业重点关注不同的风险点，加强风险控制能力，消除风险隐患。

三要强化风控科技属性。在建设银行现有风险管控基础上，依托大数据、人工智能等新技术的应用，实现对客户聚合、场景接入、数据集成、输出产品等各关键环节的风险梳理，探索机控、数控、智控、技控等新方式。要积极与农管部门、司法、不动产中心等第三方平台系统直连，共享数据信息，缓解“三农”信贷业务信息不对称问题，提升风险管理能力，全面强化普惠金融识险、防险、控险、化险工作。

小微快贷业务可持续发展相关建议

——从一起小微快贷案例谈起

福建省分行　潘秋香

小微快贷业务[①]是建行落实国家普惠金融的一项重大经营政策，也是目前建行小企业业务的一项重大主营业务。目前各级机构都在大力推广小微快贷业务，其能否可持续发展对建行而言意义重大。我拟结合一起小微快贷案例，透视目前该业务中存在的若干问题，并提出若干可能的意见和建议，以助力建行小微快贷业务实现可持续发展。

一、案件情况简介

借款人A公司开户行为B银行辖内某支行，A公司于2017年9月~2018年3月通过电子银行平台申请办理支用了5笔小微快贷信用贷款，金额合计30万元，但其自2018年6月开始无法履行按月付息义务，B银行辖内某支行遂将A公司及其共同借款人C、C的配偶D一并诉至法院，要求判令A公司还款，C与D承担共同还款责任。在诉讼过程中，A公司及C、D均提交答辩状，称本案借款仅仅是A公司的债务，C未在借款合同上签字，D也未签字，因此C与D均无须对A公司借款承担共同还款责任。主审法官提出：（1）电子借款合同上并无签字盖章，特别是没有C的签字，无法证明C需对A的借款承担共同还款责任，遂要求B银行辖内某支行对小微快贷业务办理进行公证；（2）D是C的配偶，并未在借款合同上签字，因此要求D承担共同还款责任的请求不能得到支持。鉴于该案有示范性效应，如果要公证，则涉及以后的小微快贷诉讼都要进行公证，因此B银行辖内某支行与主审法官进行大力沟通，终取得主审法官对其小微快贷业务的理解，无须进行公证，并于最近收到判决书，支持其要求A公司及共同借款人C还款的诉讼请求，但驳回其要求配偶D承担共同还款责任的诉讼请求。

---

① 本文所述小微快贷业务，若无特别指明，均指小微快贷信用贷业务。

二、问题的提出

在案件办理过程中，B 银行遭遇了一系列的举证困境，具体包括以下内容。

（一）在证明 C 是共同借款人方面遭遇的举证困境

主审法官提出，共同借款人 C 未签字，但根据《合同法》规定，当事人发出要求或具有要约含义的要约邀请后，受要约人以实际行动接受的，则合同成立，当事人应受合同及要约条件的约束。因此，如果能证明 C 明知小微快贷业务公告的借款条件就是实际控制人要作为共同借款人，C 仍予以接受该条件并去申请办理贷款的话，则其以实际行动证明了其愿意作为共同借款人。为此，B 银行展开了证据收集工作。

1. B 银行人员首先打开总行网站，查询所公告的小微快贷业务，但上面的办理条件仅写着“小微企业主；信用状况良好；中国内地居民（不含港澳台）；个人网银网银盾客户；持有建行个人金融资产（包括存款、理财等）或诚信纳税企业”，并无案件所涉最关键的“实际控制人应作为共同借款人”这一条件。

2. 在公告条件无路径时，B 银行人员想到登录网上银行申请办理小微快贷的签约界面上，应该会提示要求实际控制人需接受作为共同借款人才能完成签约，于是让业务部门提供了小微快贷办理的操作流程截屏图，但界面上并无相关要求实际控制人作为共同借款人的提示。

3. 在签约界面也无路径时，B 银行人员想到在办理小微快贷过程中需要企业向实际控制人进行授权办理贷款，如果授权的条款中有明确需要实际控制人作为共同借款人才能办理贷款，也是一个有力的证据。但是业务人员反馈，该协议内容无从打印，而从授权界面看，仅表明企业授权实际控制人办理小微快贷业务，并无显示要求实际控制人作为共同借款人，因此该举证努力也被阻断。

（二）在证明 D 应承担共同还款责任方面遭遇的举证困境

D 作为 C 的配偶，要求其承担共同还款责任的依据在于 B 银行辖内某支行主张案涉借款是 C、D 夫妻共同债务。《最高人民法院关于审理涉及夫妻债务纠纷案件适用法律有关问题的解释》规定，夫妻一方以个人名义所负债务虽未经另一方签字或追认且超出家庭日常生活所需的债务，如果能证明该债务被用于共同生产经营的，则认定为夫妻共同债务。本案中，被告 D 虽未签字，也拒绝追认，但若能证明案涉借款用于家庭共同生产经营的，那么案涉借款则为夫妻共同债务，D 就应承担共同还款责任。欲证明 A 公司为 C、D 共同生产经营的企业，则需收集 D 是否有无独立的职业、D 是否在 A 公司任职共同经营等证据，但小微快贷业务除了线上录入的企业信息外，并无任何线下尽职调查资料，而从B银行系统中记载的企业的相关信息中，并无任何关于实际控制人C之配偶相关信息，因此，B银行在证明实际控制人C之配偶D应对案涉借款承担共同还款责任方面也遭遇了举证困境。

三、问题的引申

该笔案件发生后，案件承办人在与经办行交流过程中，得知A公司所办理的小微快贷并不多，每月利息很少，却不能按期支付利息的主要原因在于实际控制人C在民间大量融资，民间债务至少500万元以上，其在支用B银行小微快贷之前，其实已欠了大量民间债务。而B银行的小微快贷简易、方便、快捷，特别容易办理，C遂利用电子银行平台前后支用了合计30万元贷款，之后便失联了。在与其他主体交流的过程中，还获知因小微快贷贷款额度的获取主要取决于企业结算交易量，交易量大的额度就高，因此有人创办中介公司专门为具有借款需求之人成立的企业刷交易量，以此套取小微快贷贷款，还有人一人实际控制成立好几家关联公司，然后以每家公司为主体套取小微快贷贷款。所以，目前的小微快贷业务除了在案件诉讼举证上存在问题之外，至少可能还存在以下三大基本问题。

（一）无法有效识别过度负债，容易引发不良

如本文所述案例，A公司实际控制人C实已超额负债，已无还款能力，但是不论是在贷前客户筛查还是在系统中补录客户信息时，均未能配套对应措施有效识别其过度负债情况，不能将其有效排除在贷款办理对象之外，致使贷款成为不良。

（二）无法有效识别关联关系，容易造成过度授信风险

为确保企业贷款金额与其还款能力相匹配，在平常信贷业务办理时，要求贷款企业应披露关联关系，要求客户经理加强贷前调查，对于存在关联关系的应进行集团授信，防范过度授信风险。但是对于小微快贷，就目前所了解，各支行在营销过程中并未去调查企业是否存在关联公司，在系统需要录入的信息要素中也无是否存在关联公司或者实际控制人所控制的其他企业等有助于识别关联关系的栏位，因此，也就可能出现如上所述的一人实际控制成立多家企业成功套取小微快贷贷款的现象，形成过度授信的风险。

（三）无法有效识别真实交易，容易成为投机者套取贷款资金的手段，从而引发不良

根据小微快贷管理办法，系统是根据小微企业及企业主金融资产、房贷、账户结

算、POS（销售终端）交易、纳税金额等数据，分别测算贷款额度，然后取其中最大值作为小微企业信用贷款额度，即系统仅仅依据的是一系列数字来测算贷款额度，那么谁能做大交易量，谁就能取得更大的贷款额度。而这交易量并不都是真实的企业业务发展完成的交易，完全可以靠专业公司刷单完成，明显与企业的实际经营能力不匹配，所获取的贷款需要的对应偿还能力自然也与企业的实际还款能力不匹配，如此，贷款也极可能会成为不良。

四、关于小微快贷业务的可持续发展建议

"可持续发展"是一个宏观的概念，最早出现于1980年国际自然保护同盟的《世界自然资源保护大纲》中，根据世界环境与发展委员会发布的布兰特报告定义，其含义大致为在实现经济发展的同时，应当保护好自然环境和资源，使得子孙后代能够永续发展。应用到小微快贷业务上，本文认为"可持续发展"主要是指小微快贷业务能够得到健康、有序的发展，能够获得持续性的发展，而不是一个风险越来越多的业务，也不是一个生命力短暂的业务。之所以提出小微快贷业务的可持续发展，主要基于对所获知的个人快贷业务有关现状的担忧而提出。就我个人目前的了解，某地区个人快贷业务频频出现不良，其中某支行至今为止拟起诉的快贷已60多笔，还有许多行因业务本身的问题无法完成举证责任而不敢诉至法院。

金融科技是当下一个非常热门的话题，如何充分运用科技的力量创新业务品种是各家金融机构都在绞尽脑汁、苦心钻研的事情，但产品创新后，如何仍旧充分运用科技的力量去完善产品、防范产品运行中产生的风险，也是十分重要的，而这之于小微快贷也一样。为使小微快贷业务不至于像个人快贷业务那样发展到后期频频发生风险，且还无法实现有效的救济（至少目前是如此现状——许多行因担心败诉而不敢起诉），能够实现健康的、具有可持续性的发展，我结合上述分析存在的问题及金融科技的运用，提出以下几点建议供参考。

（一）建议采取措施固化有关实际控制人作为共同借款人的证据，以顺利实现对其追索

1. 建议修订小微快贷信用贷业务对外公告的办理条件

从案件诉讼来看，小微快贷案件并不担心来自企业本身的抗辩，称其未办理过小微快贷，因为企业支用的快贷最终是转存到企业的银行账户中，通过企业实际收到款项这一点即可完成借贷关系成立的论证。需要担心的是如上所述的来自共同借款人的抗辩，称其未签字，不是共同借款人。而从业务办理实质而言，这个共同借款人并不是任何人都可以担当的，它必须是企业的实际控制人（通俗而言即为企业主）。从小微

快贷信用贷的办理条件而言，对客户影响最大也即客户最关注的应当是实际控制人需承担共同还款责任这一点，因为这一点关系到个人责任的承担，对个人而言利害关系最大。可能有人会提出小微快贷信用贷管理办法中已明确“信用快贷实行共同借款人，即由借款企业和企业主作为共同借款人”，但该办法是内部文件，且在内部文件中规定实际控制人须作为共同借款人，而在对外公告的贷款条件中却未体现，会给人造成内外有别、存在隐瞒的错觉，无法作为有效证据。而《合同法》第十五条规定：“商业广告的内容符合要约规定的，视为要约。”即商业广告的内容具体确定，且希望他人与自己订立合同关系、自己将受要约内容约束即视为一种要约。总行网站发布的小微快贷业务公告虽为一种商业广告，但实际明示了贷款办理条件、额度等，本质上可视为一种要约，若在公告的办理条件特别明示企业实际控制人应作为共同借款人的情况下，那么在实际控制人看到这一条件后，还同意接受并进行下一步的贷款办理签约的，则实际控制人通过其办理贷款这一实际行动证明其认可同意了本人愿意作为其企业办理小微快贷的共同借款人。由此，建议对建行发布的小微快贷公告内容进行修订，特别增加“企业实际控制人作为共同借款人”。

2. 建议优化系统操作界面

在实际控制人接受授权的界面增加“本人同意接受企业授权办理贷款并作为贷款的共同借款人”之类的描述，以增加证明实际控制人已同意本人作为其企业所办理的小微快贷贷款之共同借款人的证据。

3. 建议将智慧柜员机小微快贷业务办理签字模式推广到电脑端的网上银行及手机端的手机银行

目前，小微快贷业务客户可通过网上银行、手机银行及智慧柜员机办理，经向客户经理调查，其中智慧柜员机办理的小微快贷业务在最后签订电子借款合同时，需要共同借款人通过智慧柜员机在电子借款合同上签字才能完成。该模式落实了客户签字，可以较大程度地避免争议，因此，建议充分运用科技手段，优化电脑端网上银行办理小微快贷的界面以及手机端手机银行办理小微快贷的界面，移植智慧柜员机办理模式，在电子借款合同签订的最后环节均增加一个共同借款人签字环节。

（二）建议优化系统小微客户信息补录界面，增加有关企业是否夫妻共同生产经营的相关信息调查栏位，以固化认定借款为夫妻共同债务的相关证据

即便顺利主张共同借款人应承担共同还款责任，但对于夫妻共有财产，依法仅能申请执行其中归属于共同借款人的那部分财产，不能实现对实际控制人含其配偶在内

的全面追索。欲实现对配偶的追索，前提是需认定借款为夫妻共同债务、判定其应负共同还款责任。而在认定夫妻共同债务上，《最高人民法院关于审理涉及夫妻债务纠纷案件适用法律有关问题的解释》规定了比较明确的4个标准：（1）债务经配偶签字同意；（2）配偶追认债务；（3）债务用于家庭日常生活；（4）债务用于夫妻共同生产经营。如果经办行能取得配偶签字同意借款或追认借款的书面文件，便解决了配偶应承担共同还款责任的举证责任；若无法取得配偶签字同意借款或追认借款的书面文件，则需要依赖于借款是否用于家庭日常生活及夫妻共同生产经营之证据的固化。在这些证据的固化上，建议优化小微客户信息补录界面，增加有关企业是否夫妻共同生产经营的相关信息栏位且设置为必填项，包括但不限于：（1）公司经营收入是否为用于家庭日常开支；（2）公司经营收入是否为家庭日常生活的主要经济来源；（3）除公司经营收入，家庭是否有其他经济来源；（4）配偶名字及身份证号；（5）配偶是否有独立的职业；（6）配偶是否也在本公司工作，担任何职务等。

（三）建议优化系统小微客户信息补录界面，增加借款企业及实际控制人相关债务信息栏位，防范过度负债致贷款不良

为防范借款企业及实际控制人在过度负债、已无还款能力的情况下，仍套取小微快贷的风险，建议优化系统小微客户信息补录界面，增加借款企业及实际控制人相关债务信息栏位，包括但不限于：（1）公司是否参与民间借贷，民间债务金额多少；（2）公司是否在其他非银行机构融资，融资金融多少；（3）实际控制人是否参与民间借贷，民间债务多少；（4）实际控制人是否在其他非银行机构融资，融资金额多少等。

（四）建议优化系统小微客户信息补录界面，增加实际控制人控制的关联公司相关信息栏位，并设计相应程序，防范过度授信风险

为防范小微快贷业务中某一实际控制人利用自己的关联公司套取小微快贷造成过度授信风险，建议优化系统小微客户信息补录界面，增加实际控制人控制的关联公司相关信息栏位，包括但不限于：（1）实际控制人是否有其他控制的企业；（2）实际控制人控制的企业个数；（3）实际控制人控制的企业名称及营业执照号；（4）实际控制人是否在其他企业任职，任何职务；（5）实际控制人是否为其他企业股东，以及企业名称及营业执照号，持股比例是多少等。在增加上述信息栏位后，充分运用科技的手段设计相应程序，待实际控制人企图利用自己的关联公司办理小微快贷时，系统会自动识别，合并测算其贷款额度，对于超过贷款额度的贷款申请自动拒绝办理。

（五）建议借鉴反洗钱可疑预警机制，优化系统参数，有效识别非真实交易量，防范投机者刷单套取小微快贷

为有效履行人民银行可疑交易报告义务，在极少量的人工识别可疑交易之外，建行建立了一系列可疑交易模型，并设立了相应的执行参数，对于触发模型的交易，反洗钱系统将自动抓取筛选出来，排查确认后报告人民银行。为防范投机者通过专业公司刷单或者相互之间串通起来刷单，制造虚假交易量来套取小微快贷，建议充分运用科技的手段，借鉴反洗钱可疑预警机制，抽象出相关虚假交易特征，建立相应的可疑交易模型，并设立相应的执行参数，对于触发虚假交易模型的，自动拒绝其贷款申请。

（六）建议增加客户信息承诺，警示客户应保证所填信息的真实性

优化系统后，能够借助该等信息有效甄别客户的前提条件是客户信息应当真实、准确。为满足这一前提条件，建议应当注意落实客户信息真实承诺：一方面，在业务办理界面增加客户信息真实准确的相关承诺；另一方面，对于客户前来我行，由客户经理进行补录信息的，则可要求客户出具书面信息真实准确承诺函。

关于普惠金融助力脱贫攻坚跨越2020的探讨与研究

总行办公室　范蔚然

精准扶贫、精准脱贫离不开普惠金融的支持。普惠金融，是指立足机会平等要求和商业可持续原则，以可负担的成本为有金融服务需求的社会各阶层和群体提供适当、有效的金融服务，涉及小微、双创、扶贫、涉农等领域。普惠金融扶贫特别强调为贫困地区、少数民族地区、革命老区、偏远地区以及农民、贫困群众提供金融服务。大力发展普惠金融扶贫，不仅对于建行助力打好打赢脱贫攻坚战有重要意义，更是新时代实现建行业务可持续发展的必然选择。

一、发展普惠金融助力脱贫攻坚的重要意义

（一）发展普惠金融助力脱贫攻坚是落实党中央、国务院决策部署的重要举措

普惠金融扶贫是金融扶贫的重要组成部分。党中央、国务院高度重视发展金融扶贫工作，一直将金融扶贫作为政策“组合拳”的“重头戏”来安排部署。习近平总书记多次强调，要做好金融扶贫这篇文章。在全国金融工作会议上，习近平总书记强调，要建设普惠金融体系，加强对小微企业、“三农”和偏远地区的金融服务。

2015年，国务院印发《推进普惠金融发展规划（2016—2020年）》，提出“（要对小微企业和贫困群众）提高金融服务覆盖率、提高金融服务可能性、提高金融服务满意度”。

2017年，中国人民银行、银监会、证监会、保监会印发《关于金融支持深度贫困地区脱贫攻坚的意见》，提出“做好金融助推深度贫困地区脱贫攻坚工作，是金融系统义不容辞的责任。金融部门要坚持新增金融资金优先满足深度贫困地区、新增金融服务优先布设深度贫困地区，加大对建档立卡贫困户和扶贫产业项目、贫困村提升工程、基础设施建设、基本公共服务等重点领域的支持力度，着力增强深度贫困地区自我发展能力，为深度贫困地区打赢脱贫攻坚战提供重要支撑”。

2017 年，国务院扶贫办印发《中央单位定点扶贫工作考核实施方案》，并从帮扶成效、组织领导、选派干部、督促检查、基层满意情况、工作创新 6 个方面对建行定点扶贫工作进行了考核。其中工作创新部分的考核明确要求“中央单位要发挥自身优势，开展精准帮扶”。对建行来讲，发展普惠金融就是国有大行助力脱贫攻坚的最大优势，也是增加扶贫投入，按要求完成国务院扶贫办对建行定点扶贫考核的重要举措。

（二）发展普惠金融助力脱贫攻坚是实现乡村可持续发展的长期模式

普惠金融的有偿性与激发贫困群众脱贫内生动力的要求相一致，可以助推形成精准扶贫长效机制。普惠金融扶贫既不是政策性扶贫，也不是无偿扶贫，商业银行是经营单位，不是慈善机构，贷款也不是善款，不仅要放得出去，还要收得回来，需要有一套可持续的普惠金融支持脱贫攻坚模式。

扶贫对象将从建行获得的贷款资金，与劳动力、土地等生产要素结合，投入生产过程，创造价值，提高生产能力，提升生活水平，实现脱贫目标。在这一环节中，普惠金融扶贫以“造血”的形式改变了以往财政扶贫“输血”的形式，体现了“授之以渔”的理念，确保了扶贫的长期效用，将给扶贫带来质的改变，让脱贫攻坚跨越 2020 年，成为“后扶贫时代”实现乡村可持续发展的长期模式。

（三）发展普惠金融助力脱贫攻坚是银行未来赢得农村潜力市场的必然选择

当前，我国城镇化率已接近 60%，但作为有着 960 万平方公里土地、13 多亿人口的大国，不管城镇化发展到什么程度，农村人口还会是一个相当大的规模，还会有几亿人生活在农村。进入新时代，我国社会主要矛盾已经转化为人民日益增长的美好生活需要和不平衡不充分发展之间的矛盾，这其中不平衡不充分最突出的短板就在农村，发展和增长潜力最大的也在农村。

到 2020 年全面建成小康社会、到 2035 年基本实现社会主义现代化、到 2050 年把我国建成富强民主文明和谐美丽的社会主义现代化国家，必须让农民在共同富裕的道路上赶上来，必须让农村跟上国家发展的步伐。随着脱贫攻坚和乡村振兴战略的实施，未来农村的快速发展，势必让乡镇农村和贫困群众收入水平不断提升，其相应的金融服务需求也将不断增多。并且在新兴金融科技支持下，传统的“二八”定律正在被颠覆，未来的金融，必将是“得草根者得天下”。

发展普惠金融助力脱贫攻坚，不仅是建行落实中央决策部署、服务国家发展战略的政治担当，更是建行赢得未来农村潜力市场的重要战略安排。

二、当前在贫困地区发展普惠金融面临的挑战

（一）发展普惠金融的配套制度尚不完善，基层推动业务发展的动力较弱

目前，全行发展普惠金融的配套制度尚不完善，缺乏完整有效的资源配置和考核激励机制。由于利润最大化的内在要求，基层行和客户经理缺少推动业务发展的动力，而各级管理机构也缺少创新农村金融产品和服务的动力，导致总行的战略部署难以有效落实。

（二）农村普惠金融服务对象抵御市场风险能力差，业务发展风险较大

贫困地区欠发达，经济体制机制相对落后，地理、气候条件相对恶劣，自然灾害频发多发，贫困地区产业化发展尚在初级阶段，企业生产规模小，多处于产业下游，承受市场风险能力较差，淘汰率较高，建行如管控不力，资产质量难以保证。防范化解重大风险和精准脱贫都是党的十九大明确要坚决打好的攻坚战，不能因为扶贫而增加了金融风险，两者不可顾此失彼，要始终将商业可持续发展作为金融扶贫的核心。

（三）信贷产品和审批流程的设计不够接地气，无法充分满足客户差异化需求

一方面，普惠金融扶贫服务的对象是贫困地区小微企业和贫困群众，建行对这类客户群体的金融需求、风险缓释措施、现金流特点等了解有限、研究不深，专门针对“三农”的产品较少，无法充分满足客户的差异化需求。

另一方面，当前，建行信贷管理愈加注重风险控制，基层行的贷款审批权限被不断上收，基层行自主能力受限，管理越来越严格。虽然建行已推出了“小微快贷”业务，但部分不满足“小微快贷”业务要求的客户在建行办理信贷业务手续多、时间长、放款慢，无法有效满足企业的流动性需求。

（四）普惠金融的发展依托地方政府的重视程度，缺乏与地方政府的联动长效机制

普惠金融的发展依托地方政府的重视程度，目前建行各级机构与各级政府相关部门之间缺乏全链条的合作，特别与扶贫部门之间缺少配合，与建档立卡贫困户还缺少对接机制。在推进普惠金融助力脱贫攻坚工作中，没有与扶贫部门进行资源共享，缺乏与地方政府的联动长效机制。

（五）普惠金融服务客户数量大，分布范围广，批量获客与贷后管理难度大

普惠金融在扶贫领域服务的客户数量众多，分布范围广。一方面，客户经理在营销时很难顾过来，很难对贷款对象有深入全面的了解，要靠传统的增加网点、增加客户经理，通过“扫街”的方式来获客的成本高，效率低；另一方面，大量的客户涌入，会导致贷后管理跟不上，甚至没有贷后管理，进一步增大了普惠金融业务发展的风险。

（六）贫困地区设置物理网点成本较高，金融服务覆盖能力不足

建行的传统优势在城市地区，对于贫困地区和乡镇农村，建行的金融服务覆盖能力明显不足。但在贫困地区和乡镇农村新设物理网点的成本较高，未来，有相当比例的乡镇农村和贫困地区依然无法设置建行的物理网点，仅能依靠“裕农通”开展基本的金融存、取款业务。

（七）贫困地区对金融的认识有限，金融生态环境建设有待提升

在贫困地区和乡镇农村，金融支付服务、综合金融服务、金融知识普及等农村综合金融生态环境建设方面还有很多不足或缺失。贫困地区小微企业的结算渠道通常公私不分，企业财务规范不够，透明度也较差。大多数贫困群众不懂基本的金融知识，不知道基本的金融产品，不会用金融渠道获得基本的服务。

（八）贫困地区是银行新的业务领域，缺少既懂金融又懂扶贫的综合型员工

总行的顶层设计再完善、制度再健全，也要依靠具体负责业务的员工来落实执行。建行员工虽金融业务素质过硬，但缺少对农村、农民、贫困地区和扶贫工作的深入了解。可以说，贫困地区和贫困群众是建行新的业务领域和客户群体，建行尚缺少既懂金融又懂扶贫的综合型员工。

三、做好普惠金融助力脱贫攻坚的意见和建议

新时代的银行竞争，早已不是单兵作战，而是战略、管理、机制、创新、科技以及人才的全方位比拼。我对于做好普惠金融助力脱贫攻坚有如下意见和建议。

（一）完善普惠金融助力脱贫攻坚政策制度配套

2018 年 3 月，总行针对贷款资金用于安康市一区三县①产业发展和项目建设，并

① 指总行定点帮扶的陕西省安康市汉滨区、汉阴县、紫阳县、岚皋县。

能够对当地建档立卡贫困群众有服务、带动作用的陕西省分行对公客户，从信贷政策、担保政策、授信审批政策、风险管控政策、规模安排、绩效考核政策6个方面制定差别化的管理政策，在政策层面给予一区三县最大限度倾斜。针对扶贫领域的差别化信贷管理政策，可根据实际情况在全行范围进行推广。除此之外，还应考虑一是加大对普惠金融扶贫的考核力度，在将普惠金融纳入一级分行KPI（关键绩效指标）主指标的基础上，细化出普惠金融服务、带动建档立卡贫困群众脱贫增收数量和质量的考核分项指标；二是加强财务资源配置，设置专项普惠金融扶贫营销费用，根据对小微企业授信客户、普惠金融贷款新增、普惠金融服务、带动建档立卡贫困群众脱贫增收等条件配置员工费用；三是进一步完善信贷审批制度，加强对贫困地区小微企业和贫困群众的研究，制定专门的信贷政策和审批指引，合理确定和动态调整审批权限，缩短信贷审批时间；四是完善责任认定和责任追究机制，一方面要在现有规章制度基础上，结合实际，进一步完善普惠金融扶贫责任认定和责任追究办法，明确尽职免责标准，保护肯干事有作为敢担当的员工，另一方面也要加强对普惠金融扶贫领域的执纪问责，整治以贷谋私、内外勾结、利益输送等问题。

（二）丰富非金融服务手段，将融资、融智、融商相结合，降低金融风险

解决好贫困地区市场信息缺失、销售渠道不畅、产业升级滞后等问题，将有效降低建行普惠金融扶贫贷款的风险。发展普惠金融扶贫，需要标本兼治，丰富非金融服务手段，做到融资、融智、融商相结合，增强扶贫的有效性和可持续性。一是要大力发展农村电子商务，在有条件的贫困地区设立“善融商务”电商扶贫工作站，为贫困地区小微企业和贫困群众生产的产品扩宽销售渠道。二是要发挥建行客户资源广的优势，帮助贫困地区小微企业和贫困群众推广其产品，为其寻找合作伙伴，帮助其撮合交易，增强其市场竞争力。三是要通过建行的帮扶，为贫困群众提供国家“三农”政策、种植养殖技术和基础金融知识培训，解决其少信息、缺技能等问题。

（三）创新丰富更适合贫困地区的普惠金融产品

目前，总行已经创新了针对安康市移民搬迁安置工程的“新社区工厂贷”和以安康市茶叶为押品的“富硒茶叶贷”等产品。还要进一步创新丰富基于贫困地区各类产权的金融产品和抵押担保服务，拓宽贫困地区小微企业和贫困群众的融资渠道，盘活贫困地区的资源、资金、资产。可由各级分支机构根据地域特色，定向精准支持贫困地区特色优势产业发展。

（四）进一步加强与地方政府合作，建立金融扶贫长效机制

普惠金融扶贫要遵循市场经济和金融市场运行规律，风险与收益要相匹配。这就要求将政府“有形的手”和市场“无形的手”紧密结合起来，由建行和政府共同建立普惠金融扶贫担保补贴和风险共担机制。因此，要积极和各级政府衔接，争取共同设立扶贫产业发展基金和扶贫贷款担保基金，实现金融资源与政府扶贫资源的有机结合，在控制风险敞口的前提下，发挥金融杠杆的放大效应。

（五）构建“智慧城市”大数据信息网络，打造批量获客平台

如果没有充分的信息，普惠金融扶贫将无法实现。应通过构建“智慧城市”大数据信息网络，打通建行与扶贫、税务、海关、征信、工商、行业协会以及其他第三方机构的信息对接渠道。一是要全面掌握小微企业的盈利情况、纳税情况、交易情况、带动贫困群众脱贫情况和企业主的个人素质，以及周围人对贫困群众的道德评议等方方面面的信息，在实现批量化获客的同时，做到第一时间全方位识客。二是要通过大数据强化贷后管理，及时优化客群。小微企业淘汰率高，资金使用不尽规范，要通过大数据专门分析跟踪小微企业的贷后表现，及时发现并化解潜在风险。

（六）在贫困地区大力发展互联网金融

越贫困的地区越需要高科技的滋润，越困难的问题越要用互联网的思路来破解。要在贫困地区大力发展线上电子银行，延伸金融服务触角，解决贫困农户分散、贫困地域偏远、物理网点不足等问题，增加贫困群众对金融服务的可获得性。大力推广“龙支付”业务，促进贫困地区建立无现金交易社会。

（七）加大对贫困地区金融知识普及力度

加大宣传推广力度，打响建行普惠金融扶贫品牌。一是可以通过贫困地区网点宣传普惠金融扶贫产品，使建行普惠金融助力脱贫攻坚的理念深入人心，扩大社会影响力。二是可以在贫困地区产业园区建立普惠金融工作站，每周固定时间安排专人到园区办理业务并接受业务咨询。三是可以与贫困地区扶贫部门和金融监管部门合作，针对脱贫带动能力强的小微企业和贫困群众，开展普惠金融大讲堂，介绍相关业务知识和办理流程。

（八）建设一支懂金融懂农村的干部队伍

干事创业，关键在人。一是要加强对基层员工的培训力度，在 2018 年已办两期扶

贫培训班的基础上，将普惠金融助力扶贫的服务流程进一步标准化、模板化，统一规范工作流程，让基层可操作性强。二是要发挥脱贫攻坚主战场对培养、锻炼干部的重要作用，有计划地选派优秀干部到贫困地区挂职参与扶贫，担任县区党政副职或到村担任第一书记，挂职结束后安排到普惠金融岗位上工作，有计划地建设一支既懂金融又懂农村的干部队伍。

数字普惠金融视角下小微企业融资领域的创新研究

——基于宁波市小微企业融资情况的调查研究分析

宁波市分行　施立可

一、宁波市小微企业融资变化情况

宁波是我国的制造业大市，小微企业众多、民营经济发达、产业集群优势明显是其区域经济发展的显著特征。除个体户外，宁波市有30多万家企业，其中95%以上是小微企业，为宁波贡献了70%以上的生产总值、80%左右的外贸出口额、60%左右的税收和90%以上的社会就业岗位，而发展“数字普惠金融”将对它们的惠及程度更高，也可以为宁波经济持续发展奠定扎实的基础。本文以数字普惠金融服务为主题，开展了小微企业融资需求变化情况的问卷调查，通过电子渠道调研了815家中小企业客户融资现状，实际发放问卷815份，回收588份，回收率72.1%。

（一）受调研企业行业分布符合宁波区域行业结构特点

从受调研企业行业分布情况看，制造业为分布最为密集的行业，占比高达76.19%；批发和零售业占比达11.9%，排名第二；其他行业分布较为分散。上述调研情况也基本符合宁波市小微企业行业结构特点。因此，本次调研能基本反映宁波市小微企业融资现状，具有一定的参考代表性。

（二）受调研企业经营较为稳定

从数据统计情况看，受调研企业经营时间在10年以上的占比最高，为40.48%；成立3~5年以上的占比19.05%，5~10年以上的占比16.67%。从企业生命周期分析，一般成立3年以上、且稳健经营的企业处于成长期，本次受调研企业成立3年以上的占比高达76.2%，具有一定的代表性。

（三）企业经营呈现多元化

受调研企业生产的产品主要以国内销售为主，占比为66.67%，内销外销结合方式的占26.19%，而单一出口的企业为7.14%。从2017年销售情况看，主要为销售收入2 000万元以下规模的小微企业，占比80.96%，其中销售收入500万元以下的为38.1%。

（四）影响企业生产经营的主要因素分析

通过对问卷的数据统计分析，发现成本上升是影响企业生产经营的主要因素，包括原材料成本、劳动力成本、资金成本，其中有78.57%的受调研企业认为原材料成本上升影响较大，69.05%的受调研企业认为劳动成本上升影响较大。

（五）企业资金周转和融资需求状况

统计结果显示，有57.14%的受调研企业表示有融资需求，但不急需；有融资需求的，较为急需的占比为14.29%；而暂无融资需求的企业占比为28.57%。从调研情况看，企业普遍处于稳健经营状态，但受限于各项成本上升，对资金的需求正逐步增加。

但是，受调研企业普遍反映缺乏抵质押物，占比为54.76%；26.19%的企业认为担保公司、保险公司的担保费用较高，无法负担资金成本，融资难现象依然存在。同时，多数企业融资的目的是维持正常生产经营和更新设备、技术，占比分别为66.67%、59.52%，也有部分企业是为了增加新的经营项目、引进人才、工资开支等。

（六）银行依然是小微企业的主要融资渠道

在融资渠道方面，银行依然为企业主要的融资渠道，占比高达66.67%，也有部分企业通过小贷公司、担保公司等机构进行融资，占比为9.52%。通过民间借贷融资的企业占7.14%，通过其他渠道融资的占比38.1%，例如股东借款、关联企业出借资金等。

（七）企业从银行贷款难的原因分析

对于企业融资难的问题，受调研企业认为主要在于贷款手续烦琐、贷款利息过高、找担保难等原因，其中57.14%的企业认为贷款手续过于烦琐，42.86%的企业认为银行的贷款利息过高，企业无法负担。无法落实抵押等担保措施的受调研企业占比为23.81%。

（八）企业融资方式调查分析

为了解企业认为的最佳融资方式以及最关心的内容，本次调研设计了“最佳的融资方式”和“企业融资时最关注的内容”两个问题。从调研情况看（可多选），54.76%受调研企业偏向于选择银行互联网自助办理的融资产品，也有50%的受调研企业偏向于银行传统融资产品，部分企业选择互联网小贷、小额贷款公司。

在融资时，贷款价格优惠是企业最关心的内容，占比高达78.57%；64.29%的受调研企业认为审批速度快、放款速度快较为重要；59.52%的受调研企业认为最好贷款使用能实现随借随还，以降低融资成本；42.86%的受调研企业认为手续简便很重要，甚至无须提供任何材料。

（九）企业融资时效性调研

从问卷反映情况看，当企业在需要资金时对融资的时效性要求较高，也符合小微企业“短、频、快、急”的融资需求特点。28.57%的企业认为应在3天内将资金到位，26.19%的企业认为1周较为合理，要求融资时间在1天之内的企业占比为42.86%，而能承受2周时间的企业占比仅为2.38%。

（十）大数据产品市场接受度与满意度调查

一般情况下，大数据产品具有纯信用、通过互联网渠道自助申请和办理、随借随还等特点。为了解市场对数字普惠金融项下大数据产品的市场接受度，本次调研设计了两个相关题目。假设银行推出具有大数据产品特性的金融产品，97.62%的受调研小微企业会选择使用。同时，在服务满意度方面，52.38%的受调研企业对当前金融机构提供的融资服务表示基本满意，11.9%的企业表示不满意，没有达到融资目的，而比较满意、非常满意的占比仅为23.8%。

综合上述调研问卷分析，受企业经营成本上升、技术更新换代、转型升级等诸多因素影响，宁波市小微企业融资需求依然旺盛，“短、频、快、急”的特点突出。同时，由于缺乏抵押物、融资成本高等原因，融资难问题也较为突出；在融资渠道方面，相对其他非银行金融机构，小微企业偏向于传统的银行，在融资时更加关注贷款价格、手续便捷、审批快、使用方便等内容，而这些企业需求正好就是数字普惠金融的特性。

在此背景下，随着“互联网+”、大数据等概念的加快推广，现代数字科技的普及应用与金融服务的普惠提供具有了耦合性。数字普惠金融顺应时代发展，金融机构不断加强产品和服务创新，不断推出具有数字普惠特性的金融产品，例如京东金融的白条贷款、网商银行的小贷，工行的“融 e 借”、中行的“中银 E 贷”、建行的“快贷”等产品。这类产品最大的亮点是运用手机银行、网上银行等移动终端，可使贷款申请人足不出户就可在线自助办理，依托大数据技术、数字技术进行贷款审核与风险监控，由“人控”变为“机控”，实现“秒申秒审秒签”，而通过确定贷款额度、使用“随借随还”功能，也使贷款成本进一步下降。对于金融机构来说，相较于传统小微金融服务获客和信息处理方式的效率低、成本高的困局，运用数字技术能获得更广泛的客户群体，以及更加低廉的渠道成本、更加精准的风险定价，解决了银企信息不对称、成本与收益不对称的问题，促使普惠金融发展实现商业可持续性。

二、宁波地区发展数字普惠金融存在的问题及挑战

（一）风险管理方面的挑战

小微企业具有信息披露不完整、财务制度不健全的特点，其融资难的重要原因就是银企信息不对称，以及社会征信体系不健全导致的。而运用数字化技术，依托金融机构内部交易数据、外部税务和征信等大数据，能基本解决信息不对称问题。但由于数字技术正处于起步阶段，且在应用过程中并不会改变金融的实质性风险，也无法改变小微企业金融风险的隐蔽性、突发性等特性。同时，由于各类大数据普惠金融产品依托于系统技术、互联网终端，因此数字普惠金融也具有技术风险和网络风险。

（二）“数字鸿沟”客观存在

由于社会发展存在很大的不平衡性，如教育、年龄、区域等各种因素在不同社会群体之间存在差异，从而导致这类群体在使用现代信息技术方面产生差距，进而使得不同群体从银行的金融服务中产生的收益出现分化，这就是“数字鸿沟”，在普惠金融推广过程中客观存在。宁波作为准一线城市，城市化发展较快，但不同群体之间“数字鸿沟”依然较大，尤其是在小微企业主及其配偶，例如部分年龄相对较大的群体在操作使用互联网移动终端上存在困难，从而无法获得数字技术带来的便捷金融服务。

（三）移动终端覆盖面有待提高

互联网移动终端是数字普惠金融产品推广的基础，宁波各家金融机构推出的互联网大数据产品均需使用网上银行、手机银行，但从目前情况看，宁波市小微企业的电子渠道覆盖度依然不高，还有很大一部分企业不会使用电子渠道。同时，数字普惠金融也对移动终端的信息通信技术、信用信息体系等基础性工作提出了更高的要求。

（四）社会征信体系有待完善

数字普惠金融推广依赖于大数据分析，结合各方面的信息数据，为小微企业“描像”，从而解决金融机构现场调查成本高、评价分析速度慢的问题。而“画像”的质量好与坏，取决于数据的有效性与全面性。目前金融机构可通过人行征信、信用网等查询企业信息，宁波市税务部门在企业授权、保证信息安全的前提下，逐步放开了纳税信息，为推广数字普惠金融提供了便利，但工商、海关、水电等信息仍未实现共享，社会征信体系有待进一步完善。

（五）金融监管存在一定难度

数字普惠金融具有创新快、模式多、产品多的特点，尤其是在小微企业融资产品方面，贷款使用随借随还，资金使用监管难度大，给金融监管机构提出了更高的要求。从监管制度方面来看，数字普惠金融兴起较快，各项监管制度有待完善。在监管手段上，由于小微企业客户数量众多，推进数字普惠金融后，信贷覆盖率大幅提升，也给金融监管带来一定压力，监管流程、系统等有待优化。同时，随着政银双方共享信息逐步扩大，信息泄露问题也需高度关注，严防不法分子运用保密信息进行犯罪活动。

三、应对措施及政策建议

（一）金融机构应对措施

1. 加大数字普惠金融的科技投入

数字技术为普惠金融大规模发展提供了技术可行性和商业可持续性。在此大背景下，金融机构应加大人力、物力、财力的投入，加快数字化技术的研发，以“互联网＋大数据＋金融”为中心，构建客户筛选、大数据征信、评分卡风控模型、贷后管理行为预警等全流程系统化的互联网金融生态场景，降低业务运营成本。

2. 加大产品创新优化力度

建议金融机构进一步加大数字普惠金融产品创新力度，研发成本低廉、流程简便和准入门槛低的标准化产品；进一步拓展和挖掘税务、海关等第三方机构拥有的相关数据信息，针对不同的客户群体开发个性化的融资产品。优化现有大数据信贷产品设计，统一大数据信贷产品客户基本条件、贷后管理等共性办理条件，减少效果弱的差异化管理要求，统一前后台风险偏好，提高产品普惠适用度。对于已完成大数据征信和评分卡风控模型的金融机构，要将线下业务搬至线上自助办理，简化办理手续，由“人控”变成“机控”；开发随借随还功能，在核定授信循环额度项下，灵活使用贷款。

3. 完善风险监测与管理体系

随着数字普惠金融的深入推进，金融机构可以基于存量历史数据进行综合化分析，运用大数据技术提取风险控制模型关键变量，进行交叉验证，不断完善数字普惠金融推进过程中的评分卡审批模型与贷后管理监测模型。在贷后预警监测过程中，不仅要关注金融机构内部的监测数据，更要关注税务、涉诉以及互联网负面信息等，并将个人信用与企业信用联系起来，通过综合分析企业及企业主行为，及时进行系统预警。对于发生的预警行为，可直接推送至贷后管理人员、客户经理，提升预警处理时效。

（二）政府及监管部门政策建议

1. 创造良好的政策推广环境

建议政府能为数字普惠金融业务发展营造良好的金融生态环境，降低和分散数字普惠金融推广、普及的运营成本和风险成本。加大对失信行为的惩罚和执法力度，严厉打击逃废银行债务的行为，为大规模推进企业和企业主信用为基础的标准化、自动化审批的小微企业信贷产品营造诚信环境氛围。同时，建议政府应出台相关政策，鼓励和引导数字普惠金融发展，推进小微企业融资普及化。

2. 完善数字普惠金融监管机制

建议监管机构完善数字普惠金融监管机制，加强对数字普惠金融的行为监管、审慎监管以及市场准入，在贷款服务、信息安全、隐私保护、网络安全、合同等方面进行管控。加快推进数字普惠金融统计和监测评估体系的建设，利用数字化技术来改进监管流程，实施动态监测与跟踪分析，防止数字化技术信贷产品发生系统性风险。

3. 推进公共信息共享与信用体系建设

发展数字普惠金融，关键在于各类大数据的积累和数字化的技术，数据越多越健全，对小微企业的“描像”越准确，贷款可获得性越高。建议政府部门在条件成熟的前提下，适时将工商、税务、征信、海关、水电等信息与金融机构进行共享，通过搭建互联互通的专线模式，促使金融机构能实时获取小微企业最新信息，持续完善针对数字普惠金融的信用评价体系和征信系统。

商业银行普惠金融风险管理策略研究

业务处理中心成都分中心　王夏珊

一、引言

2005 年，联合国在推广“小额信贷年”时率先提出普惠金融的概念。普惠金融现已成为衡量一个国家金融发展程度和金融服务深度的重要指标。2015 年，国务院在《推进普惠金融发展规划（2016—2020 年）》中将普惠金融定义为：立足机会平等要求和商业可持续原则，以可负担的成本为有金融服务需求的社会各阶层和群体提供适当、有效的金融服务。普惠金融的服务对象包括小微企业、农民、城镇低收入人群、贫困人群、残疾人、老年人等特殊群体。

普惠金融并非传统观念中的金融扶贫，而是具有可持续性的商业发展模式，是支持实体经济发展、发挥社会责任的金融服务模式。在新的时代背景下，中国建设银行积极顺应国家经济形势的变化，于 2018 年 5 月 2 日全面启动普惠金融战略，即在巩固“大行业、大企业”传统经营战略优势的同时实施“小行业、小企业”战略。

2018 年 6 月末，建设银行普惠金融贷款余额为 4 912. 89 亿元，同比增长 44. 33%；普惠金融贷款客户 86. 85 万户，同比新增 38. 84 万户[①]。建设银行普惠金融业务发展虽然已取得突破性进展，但普惠金融的服务群体存在规模小且数量庞大等特点，使银行面临着较大市场风险、操作风险、信用风险甚至声誉风险的考验，因此，提升风险管理水平是确保普惠金融业务高质量发展和普惠金融战略顺利实施的关键。

二、普惠金融风险管理难点

普惠金融的本质仍是金融，金融的实质则是经营风险，风险控制是商业银行的生命线。与银行传统信贷业务相比，普惠金融业务的广度和深度更为复杂，容易成为信贷不良的高发领域，风险管控的难度更高。因此，风险管理问题一直是阻碍普惠金融

① 资料来源：《中国建设银行 2018 年半年度报告》。

业务可持续发展的难点，梳理和剖析普惠金融风险管理的难点可为制定风险管理策略提供科学依据。

（一）风险承受能力弱

小微企业、个体工商户等普惠金融服务群体具有天然高风险性，资产实力不足，管理手段简单，股权相对集中，财务机制不健全，经营业务种类单一，风险分散性较差，易受行业周期性或行业政策的影响，因此抵御市场风险、宏观经济风险等各类风险的能力都较弱。

（二）信息不对称

普惠金融服务群体不具备像大中型企业一样的信息披露机制，银行人员充分了解和收集客户真实信息的成本高，风险识别、计量、监测、分析的工作量大且难度高，这导致银行很难对客户的真实还款能力做出准确的判断。此外，长尾群体的信用意识和信用基础普遍非常薄弱，不利于银行进行风险评估和预测。因此，严重的信息不对称问题导致商业银行在向普惠金融服务群体发放贷款时存在较高的风险。

（三）传统风险管理机制失灵

商业银行现有的风险管理流程主要针对大中型企业，依托于对借款主体的资产、抵押物等进行信用等级评估，授信结果在一定程度上取决于银行人员的工作经验和主观判断。普惠金融服务群体的风险特点与大中型企业完全不同，具有“短、小、频、急”的贷款特征，且普遍缺少足额的信贷抵押物，因此，依据财务信息的评估结果进行授信的传统风险管理理念和技术失灵。此外，普惠金融业务的客户数量庞大，银行人员难以对逐个客户进行贷前、贷中和贷后管理，商业银行传统的线下风险管理流程不能适用于普惠金融业务。

三、普惠金融风险管理策略

在充分了解普惠金融风险管理难点的基础上，制定有效的风险管理对策，才可确保普惠金融业务的可持续发展。以大数据、人工智能为代表的新一轮科技革命和产业变革的集中爆发为解决风险管理领域相关痛点提供了很好的契机。

风险管控的灵魂是数据，所有风险管理的决策均以数据为驱动。建设银行须充分运用“新一代”的成果和金融科技的力量，构建智能“风控大脑”，实现风险管理的标准化、智能化和模型化，实施贷前、贷中、贷后“线下 + 大数据”一体化风险管理流程，提升风险识别的敏感性和准确性，确保风险看得见、理得清、控得住，塑造建设银行在普惠金融业务领域的核心竞争力。

（一）建立大数据风险管理模型

大数据风险管理模型是指充分利用商业银行的海量和多维度数据，借助数据挖掘技术，将行为数据和交易数据转化为信用数据，全方位分析客户的风险特征，最终形成客户的风险“画像”。

建设银行积累的海量金融交易数据为建立大数据风险管理模型提供了良好的条件。整合普惠金融服务群体的交易流水、存贷款、信用卡等各类金融信息，对接政府相关数据平台，如人行征信、税务、工商、海关、公安、司法等公共信息，同时可积极引入第三方征信公司的信用评分，如芝麻信用、前海征信等。通过大数据挖掘技术对海量数据进行综合分析，实现对客户精准“画像”，完整呈现客户的身份特质、信用属性、履约能力、行为偏好、消费属性、人脉关系等。银行根据客户的风险“画像”决定是否对该客户进行贷款授信，以及根据客户风险等级为贷款产品定价。

大数据风险管理模型将烦冗的数据标准化、结构化，并转化为有效的风险维度指标，同时可根据最新的数据实时动态调整。客户的“画像”可有效甄别客户风险，进行客户等级划分和风险预测，将普惠金融的风险管理流程不断前移，从而有效提升风险管理能力。大数据风险管理模型是客户授信准入和风险定价的重要依据，直接形成对客户的风险管理策略，实现贷款产品规模、定价与客户风险等级的精准匹配。此外，大数据风险管理模型不是基于银行人员的经验判断，而是基于算法和规则，比传统的风险管理技术更具有客观性，使银行的风险管理机制从主观的信用模式转变为客观的信用模式，使传统的线下风险管控转变为标准化、批量化的线上风险管理流程。

（二）搭建物联网抵押监管平台

在物联网的环境下，任何物品都有唯一的身份条形码。普惠金融服务群体在申请贷款时，可以将具有唯一身份条形码的原材料、半成品或产品等抵押给银行，银行则根据条形码，运用先进的无线射频识别等物联网技术，实时追踪抵押物的状态和变化，实现智能化的抵押监管流程。

例如，一家食品公司经营的业务是销售巧克力给下游分销商，因分销商无法立即全额付款给食品公司，于是向银行提出贷款需求。银行可通过物联网传感设备对这批巧克力进行追踪、监控和管理，实时掌握下游分销商的销售收入数据。物联网技术还可应用于收集餐饮行业收银小票的数据信息。银行可通过收银小票了解餐厅的收入状况、消费客流数据、菜品消费数据、消费时段分布等信息，进一步还原餐厅的真实营业数据。此外，通过无线上网探针技术检测客户手机的 MAC 地址（局域网地址），可以测算餐厅的客流分布。将收银小票的金额、时间等信息与探针技术的测算结果相结合，可在一定程度上相互验证获取的餐厅数据是否真实可信。使用物联网技术实现对客户经营状况的智能监管和金融信息流的实时监控，可提升银行预估客户还款能力的准确性和客户获得银行贷款的可能性，降低客户的贷款成本。

物联网数据具有实时性、多维度、真实性高等特点，因此采集和分析物联网数据可全面降低风险，这在普惠金融业务的风险管理中具有独特的优势。普惠金融服务群体通常缺少足额且有效的不动产抵押物，只能提供动产抵押物予以补充。由于动产抵押物的监控成本高且难度大，银行难以甄别还款来源，这导致银行传统信贷业务很少接受动产作为抵押物。物联网先进的质押系统及数据支持则可赋予动产以不动产的属性，实现银行对动产的主动监管，有效解决重复抵押、虚假抵押等问题，从技术角度降低动产抵押的风险，解决银行和客户之间在动产抵押贷款中的信息不对称问题。银行可根据客户的实际需求分批放款，提高普惠金融服务群体的抵押能力和贷款获得能力。

（三）研发区块链+供应链模式

区块链是一种加密的分布式同步更新的记账技术，充分利用其公开、透明、去中介化、不可篡改等优势，可重建银行与普惠金融服务群体之间的信任关系，提升建设银行普惠金融业务的风险管理水平。

区块链技术适用于需要信任和公开透明的场景。将区块链技术应用于建设银行供应链金融业务中，可解决银行与小微企业之间的信息不对称问题，提高银行为小微企业提供贷款的积极性。供应链金融业务是指金融机构围绕核心企业，将上下游小微企业的资金流和物流看作一个整体，进行批量管理并提供金融产品和服务的融资模式，其实质为小微企业借助核心企业和整条供应链的信用申请融资。

在银行供应链金融业务中，区块链技术可实现从原材料采购、产品生产、包装、运输、销售整个流程中信息流、物流以及资金流信息的分布式记录、公开共享和追踪查验。积极引入区块链技术，银行可绕过核心企业获取供应链中的各项数据信息。同时，区块链技术使小微企业的信用历史公开透明，这使得小微企业具有诚实经营、保持较高征信的动力，减少因违约成本低而骗贷和不诚实使用贷款等的可能性。此外，区块链技术大幅度减少人工介入，可有效降低操作风险，免去了传统供应链中第三方监管的部分，不仅提高了供应链金融的效率，而且降低了交易成本。

运用区块链技术，促进传统贸易融资向依托供应链的“交易金融”模式跨越，实现资金流、信息流和物流“三流闭环”，使核心企业的信用真实完整流转到上下游的小微企业，解决银行与供应链上小微企业之间的信息不对称问题，降低银行开展供应链金融业务的风险，提高银行为链上小微企业融资的积极性，提升资金在供应链中流动的效率，从而支持小微企业的发展。

（四）构建普惠金融风险产品体系

建设银行现有的普惠金融产品包括小微快贷、助保贷、云税贷等，但各类产品相对独立，未构成产品体系。构建普惠金融风险产品体系，形成能有效覆盖所有普惠金融服务群体的金融产品超市，银行可根据客户的个性特征定制风险产品组合，实现风险对冲功能，降低为普惠金融服务群体提供贷款的风险。研发普惠金融风险体系需满足各类客户个性化、多元化、多层次的风险偏好需求，引入场景思维设计普惠金融服务群体的金融产品需求，增强客户黏性，同时应以客户为中心研发风险产品。

四、总结

在新的时代背景下，建设银行面向蓝海、面向大众、面向草根，全面推进普惠金融战略，而发展普惠金融业务的核心是风险管理问题。普惠金融服务群体由于自身风险承受能力较弱，与银行之间存在严重的信息不对称问题，导致传统的风险管理机制失灵。为解决普惠金融业务风险管理的难点，本文提出应实施积极主动的智能化风险管理，通过科学运用大数据、物联网、区块链等新技术，建立大数据风控模型，搭建物联网抵押监管平台，研发“区块链 + 供应链”模式，提升风险防控的科技力量，促进普惠金融业务的可持续发展，助力建设银行普惠金融战略。

县域普惠金融发展策略研究

——基于重庆市县域经济特征及区域发展战略

重庆市分行　张小勇　李祖兵　肖　敏　刘明东

发展普惠金融，目的就是要提升金融服务的覆盖率、可得性、满意度，满足人民群众日益增长的金融需求，特别是要让农民、小微企业、城镇低收入人群、贫困人群和残疾人、老年人等及时获取价格合理、便捷安全的金融服务。普惠金融具有参与主体广泛、服务方便快捷、业务种类全面、发展可持续等特点，可获得性是其核心内容，其服务客体主要集中在县城及以下区域。

一、发展县域普惠金融的重要意义

（一）县域经济转型升级需要普惠金融

“郡县治则天下安，郡县富则天下足。”党的十八大报告已明确提出要“壮大县域经济”。作为国民经济的重要组成部分，县域经济是城乡统筹的主战场、区域崛起的关键点、经济发展的新引擎，对于全面建成小康社会具有重要意义。然而，当前县域金融服务不足，资源匮乏，资金外流，“融资难、融资贵”等金融排斥顽疾长期存在，县域经济转型升级亟须金融服务支持。

（二）普惠金融是解决县域社会痛点的有效举措

金融是现代经济的核心和血脉。田国立董事长多次强调，金融是解决社会问题最温柔的“手术刀”。县域是社会痛点多、金融资源少、服务支持弱的重点区域。普惠金融契合了全面建成小康社会决胜阶段形势与任务的根本需要，贯彻了以人民为中心的发展理念，为解决县域社会痛点提供有力支撑。

（三）普惠金融发展的重点和未来在县域

普惠金融服务对象集中在县域，决定其发展重点在县域。伴随各类金融机构全面发力普惠金融，城市区域市场竞争逐渐白热化，普惠金融的市场竞争已经“从城市走向农村”。“得草根者得天下”，县域成为保障普惠金融持续发展的战略关键。

二、重庆县域经济社会发展主要特征①

重庆市是西部大开发的重要战略支点，处在“一带一路”和长江经济带的连接点上，产业结构日趋优化，就业、物价形势稳定，经济运行稳中向好。

根据《重庆统计年鉴——2018》的统计结果，重庆市 38 个区县分为主城、渝西、渝东北及渝东南四大片区，其中渝西、渝东北及渝东南均归属于县域，共计 29 个行政区域。截至 2017 年年末，重庆全辖户籍人口 3 389 万人，其中县域人口 2 718 万人，占比 80%；全辖国土面积 8.24 万平方公里，其中县域 7.62 万平方公里，占比超过 90%。全市地区生产总值 1.95 亿元，其中县域 GDP 总值 1.03 亿元，占比 52%（见图 2.4 和表 2.4）。

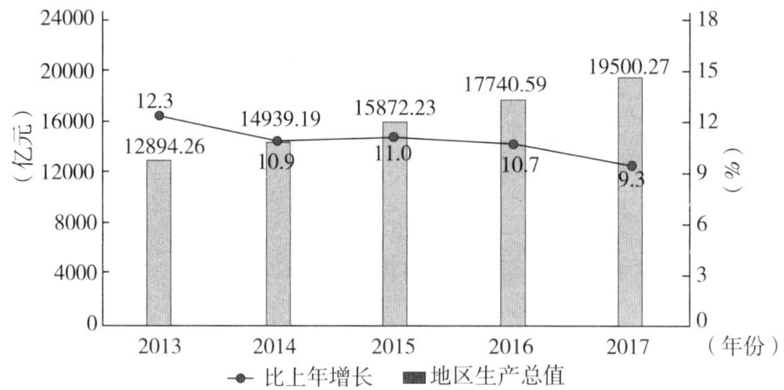

图 2.4　2013—2017 年重庆地区生产总值及增长速度

表 2.4　2017 年重庆市主要经济指标

区、县	国土面积（平方公里）	户籍人口（万人）	城镇化率（%）	农林牧渔生产总值（亿元）	工业生产总值（亿元）	年度财政收入（亿元）	金融机构人民币存款（亿元）	金融机构人民币贷款（亿元）	区域人民币存贷比（%）
主城区	5 467	671	90	174	9 703	619	21 477	20 396	94.97
渝中	22	51	100	0	13	50	4 744	3 963	83.54
江北	221	61	96	2	823	77	6 132	6 346	103.49
大渡口	103	26	97	2	183	19	423	475	112.29
沙坪坝	383	83	95	10	1 864	67	1 594	1 213	76.10

① 资料来源：除国土面积、旅游业收入外，本节采集和使用的经济指标数据均来自重庆市统计局、国家统计局重庆调查总队编撰的《重庆统计年鉴——2018》（中国统计出版社 2018 年 8 月第 1 版）。

（续表）

区、县	国土面积（平方公里）	户籍人口（万人）	城镇化率（%）	农林牧渔生产总值（亿元）	工业生产总值（亿元）	年度财政收入（亿元）	金融机构人民币存款（亿元）	金融机构人民币贷款（亿元）	区域人民币存贷比（%）
九龙坡	432	93	93	14	1 233	60	1 766	1 562	88. 45
南岸	274	71	95	6	857	70	1 239	1 093	88. 22
北碚	755	63	82	23	730	29	633	475	75. 04
渝北	1 452	130	81	43	3 384	62	4 181	4 647	111. 15
巴南	1 825	92	80	74	615	38	765	622	81. 31
渝西	22 585	1247	62	956	9 552	491	6 185	4 059	65. 63
涪陵	2 946	116	67	90	1 415	63	737	537	72. 86
长寿	1 415	89	64	67	1 049	37	507	295	58. 19
江津	3 200	150	67	126	1 384	70	833	488	58. 58
合川	2 356	153	67	107	778	42	695	331	47. 63
永川	1 576	113	68	84	906	48	580	468	80. 69
南川	2 602	69	59	67	227	23	334	243	72. 75
綦江	2 182	120	61	87	659	38	603	402	66. 67
大足	1 390	107	57	67	555	38	352	277	78. 69
璧山	912	65	56	42	953	56	446	312	69. 96
铜梁	1 342	85	55	66	476	30	426	310	72. 77
潼南	1 585	95	52	79	466	21	329	179	54. 41
荣昌	1 079	85	55	74	684	26	343	217	63. 27
渝东北	33 899	1 098	48	648	1 437	227	4 277	2 177	50. 91
万州	3 457	174	65	103	413	69	1 095	621	56. 71
开州	3 959	168	46	93	176	25	579	226	39. 03
梁平	1 890	93	45	64	173	21	379	156	41. 16
城口	3 286	25	35	14	10	4	105	59	56. 19
丰都	2 896	82	45	50	103	19	302	148	49. 01
垫江	1 518	97	45	64	180	19	333	193	57. 96
忠县	2 184	100	43	60	129	17	414	183	44. 20
云阳	3 634	134	42	71	187	17	415	163	39. 28
奉节	4 087	106	42	66	46	17	301	195	64. 78
巫山	2 958	64	40	36	11	11	196	159	81. 12
巫溪	4 030	54	35	28	9	8	159	74	46. 54
渝东南	19 808	373	40	231	480	90	1 288	1 050	81. 53

（续表）

区、县	国土面积（平方公里）	户籍人口（万人）	城镇化率（%）	农林牧渔生产总值（亿元）	工业生产总值（亿元）	年度财政收入（亿元）	金融机构人民币存款（亿元）	金融机构人民币贷款（亿元）	区域人民币存贷比（%）
黔江	2 397	55	49	35	136	23	226	238	105. 31
武隆	2 872	41	43	34	36	15	215	191	88. 84
石柱	3013	55	42	39	115	13	217	129	59. 45
秀山	2 450	67	40	35	101	13	207	172	83. 09
酉阳	5 173	85	34	45	47	12	236	140	59. 32
彭水	3 903	70	35	42	45	14	187	180	96. 26

注：两江新区的数据为计入相应的区县数据里，但包含在全市（主城）数据中。
资料来源：《重庆统计年鉴——2018》。

从经济结构看，重庆市经济呈现出人口及资源分布不均衡，城乡差距大，具有“大城市、大农村、大山区、大库区”的区域特点和典型的城乡二元经济结构特征。从主要经济指标看，重庆经济有以下特点。

（一）农业和农村经济——县域片区区间差距较大，渝西占比接近全市的一半

渝西片区产值是渝东北的1. 47倍、是渝东南的4. 14倍。渝东北、渝东南片区生产总值与其面积占比较大的情况不相匹配，但特色农业发展情况和趋势较好，如石柱的辣椒、莼菜、黄连，江津的花椒，南川的方竹笋等特色农产品品质及数量均在全国领先（见表2. 5）。

表2. 5　2017年重庆农业和农村经济

区域	农林牧渔总产值		
	金额（亿元）	比上年增长（%）	占比（%）
全市	2 009	3. 7	100
主城	174	-1. 8	8. 66
渝西	956	4. 2	47. 59
渝东北	648	4. 6	32. 25
渝东南	231	4. 7	11. 50

（二）工业——渝西与主城产值相当，县域片区增速均远高于主城

县域中，渝西片区增速最快（19. 4%），利润占比最高（51. 86%）。渝东北、渝东南工业相对较弱，合计产值不足2 000亿元，利润贡献仅约8%（见表2. 6）。

表 2.6　2017 年重庆工业经济指标

项目	金额（亿元）	比上年增长（%）	占比（%）	全员劳动生产率（元/人年）	利润总额（亿元）	利润占比（%）
全市	21 173.21	14.4	100.00	318 885	1 501.87	100.00
主城	9 702.89	10.7	45.83	324 035	602.17	40.09
渝西	9 552.37	19.4	45.12	313 583	778.85	51.86
渝东北	1 437.55	16.3	6.79	243 248	88.78	5.91
渝东南	480.39	14.2	2.27	449 478	32.06	2.13

（三）建筑业——主城、渝西和渝东北三大片区齐头并进，渝东南严重滞后

渝西片区从业人数最多、产值最大，施工面积约为渝东北的 2 倍、渝东南的 23 倍；渝东南建筑业从业人员不足 5 万，产值占比仅为 3.1%（见表 2.7）。

表 2.7　2017 年重庆四大片区建筑业经济指标

项目	从业人数（万人）	总产值（亿元）	占比（%）	房屋建筑施工面积（万平方米）	房屋建筑竣工面积（万平方米）	其中：住宅（万平方米）	占比（%）
全市	187.28	7 608	100.00	33 210.82	13 448.18	9 593.89	71.34
主城	59.93	2 528.81	33.24	14 029.43	3 593.43	2 497.03	69.49
渝西	75.99	2 872.06	37.75	12 051.6	5 987.82	4 387.91	73.28
渝东北	46.52	1 971.49	25.91	6 557.65	3 622.72	2 520.33	69.57
渝东南	4.85	235.63	3.10	527.14	334.21	188.6!	56.43

（四）旅游业——乡村旅游富民工程及“巴渝人家”品牌建设成效显著，全域旅游竞相发展、协调发展

2017 年年末重庆有国家 A 级及以上旅游景区 223 个，全国特色景观旅游名镇 14 个，全国特色景观旅游名村 7 个；市级特色景观旅游名镇 38 个，市级特色景观旅游名村 18 个。全市乡村旅游接待游客 1.7 亿人次，实现乡村旅游综合收入 510 亿元（见表 2.8）。

表 2.8　2017 年重庆旅游接待及收入情况

区域	接待人数		旅游收入	
	人数（万人次）	比上年增长（%）	金额（亿元）	比上年增长（%）
全市	54 230.21	20.3	3 308.04	25.1
主城	24 298.99	18.1	1 522.24	21.1
渝西	12 213.62	19.6	593.12	24.5
渝东北	9 188.74	23.1	607.27	29.7
渝东南	8 528.86	25.0	585.41	32.0

资料来源：2017 年重庆市旅游业统计公报。

渝东南、渝东北旅游收入产值高、增速快，分别高出全市平均增速6.9个百分点、4.6个百分点，旅游业已经成为渝东南、渝东北的核心支柱产业。

（五）固定资产投资——全市快速增长，县域片区增幅均高于主城，投资结构区域差异显著

渝西固定资产投资额占比最高、增速最快，是主城增速的2倍。渝东南固定资产投资严重不足，投资额仅为1 035亿元，占比不到6%，但增速高于渝东北和主城。

从投资结构看，主城片区投资均衡发展。县域建设与改造投资占比是房地产开发投资的7倍多。

表2.9　2017年重庆固定资产投资经济指标

项目	固定资产投资额			其中：建设与改造投资（亿元）		其中：房地产开发（亿元）		商品房竣工面积（万平方米）	商品房销售面积（万平方米）	商品房销售金额（亿元）	
	金额（亿元）	比上年增长（%）	占比（%）	金额	其中：工业	金额	其中：住宅			金额	其中：住宅
全市	17 441	9.5	100	13 460	5 881	3 980	2 633	5 056	6 711	4 558	3 602
主城	5 169	6.0	29.64	2 558	996	2 611	171	2 896	3 407	3 049	2 391
渝西	7 502	12.1	43.01	6 607	3 815	895	599	1 584	2 274	1 012	808
渝东北	3 106	8.2	17.81	2 739	798	367	253	416	7 725	375	315
渝东南	1 035	11.2	5.93	929	197	106	76	160	257	122	87

（六）社会消费品零售总额、居民收支——县域消费均衡快速增长，但人均消费额仍处于较低水平，消费升级潜力较大

主城片区人均消费6.08万元，是渝东南片区的5倍多。县域片区合计消费总额不足全市的一半。伴随国家消费提质升级，引导消费新模式加快成长，推动农村居民消费梯次升级，县域消费市场潜力较大（见表2.10和表2.11）。

表2.10　2017年重庆社会消费品零售总额

项目	金额（亿元）	比上年增长（%）	占比（%）	人口总数（万人）	人均消费额（万元）
全市	8 067.66	10	100.00	3 389.82	2.38
主城	4 079.52	8.8	50.57	671.4	6.08
渝西	2 322.98	13.3	28.79	1 247.19	1.86
渝东北	1 231.36	13.2	15.26	1 097.87	1.12
渝东南	433.82	13.1	5.38	373.36	1.16

表 2.11　2017 年重庆城乡居民人均收支情况　（元）

全体居民人均可支配收入	城镇常住居民可支配收入	农村常住居民可支配收入	全体居民人均生活消费支出	城镇常住居民人均生活消费支出	农村常住居民人均生活消费支出
24 153	32 193	12 638	17 898	22 759	10 936

（七）区县金融机构存贷款——金融机构及存贷款分布极不均衡，县域金融资产未能有效服务本地经济社会发展

县域片区存款、贷款占比均较低，存贷比低于全市平均水平，处于存差行状态。县域存款外流，信贷不足。

表 2.12　2017 年重庆区县金融机构存贷款

区域	金融机构人民币存款余额（亿元）	区域占比（%）	其中住户存款（亿元）	人口总数（万人）	金融机构人民币贷款余额（亿元）	区域占比（%）	存贷比（%）	人均储蓄存款（万元）
全市	33 718.98	100	14 367.38	3 389.82	27 871.89	100	82.66	4.24
主城	21 477.22	63.69	6 227.13	671.40	20 395.89	73.18	94.97	9.27
渝西	6 184.71	18.34	4 292.48	1 247.19	4 058.66	14.56	65.63	3.44
渝东北	4 276.99	12.68	3 040.64	1 097.87	2 177.31	7.81	50.91	2.77
渝东南	1 288.36	3.82	805.24	373.36	1 050.37	3.77	81.53	2.16

三、重庆县域普惠金融发展痛点与业务机遇

（一）发展痛点

1. 金融生态环境方面

（1）县域金融机构供给不足。从金融机构总量看，2017 年年末重庆县域金融机构 1 347 家，占比 42.77%，低于县域经济总量占比高达 14.56 个百分点。从金融机构结构看，国有商业银行大多仅在县城设立机构网点，服务范围仅到达乡镇层面，多元化竞争格局尚未形成。信托、证券、金融租赁等非银金融机构在县域的业务范围和规模极为有限，甚至在一些县域处于空白状态。

（2）县域金融服务基础设施不健全。重庆县域人口 2 718 万、面积占比超过 90%，县域金融服务对象众多，但县域特别是农村地区结算渠道不畅、融资担保不足、信用体系建设滞后。受制于通信网络基础设施建设滞后以及金融需求主体金融理念落后、金融知识匮乏等因素，网上银行、手机银行等现代金融产品和服务在县域地区普及率较低。

（3）县域金融产品供给不足。县域经济主体多元，金融服务需求在数量、频度、层次上呈现出多元化、多层次、多种类，但银行金融产品供给仍然主要为传统的“存、贷、汇”服务。信托、租赁、保险、证券等非银金融机构在县域提供金融服务较少，尤其是在农村几乎尚未开展业务。

（4）信用环境建设亟待加强。普惠金融服务对象中小微企业大部分是私营性质，存在信息披露少、财务管理不规范、抵御风险能力差等问题；农户真实信息收集较为困难，一些农户信用意识也较为淡薄，加之地方政策性担保公司较少，实力不强，增信手段较为单一。

2. 建设银行方面

（1）县域市场拓展难度大。一是在渠道覆盖上，县域行与农行、农商行、邮储银行等定位为服务三农的金融同业之间存在差距，县域客户拓展难度相对较大。二是在金融科技运用上，与蚂蚁金服、腾讯、京东等互联网巨头相比，线上产品数据采集单薄、风险监测较弱、精准获客能力不足。

（2）商业可持续压力大。普惠金融主要服务对象收入水平不稳定、风险承担能力较差、单笔业务金额较小，导致普惠金融业务具有成本高、风险大、盈利低的特点，加之县域金融服务风险分担和化解缺乏政策支持，发展普惠金融面临较大的可持续发展压力。

（二）业务机遇

伴随重庆市政府及相关部门不断增强普惠金融政策支持，持续改善县域金融生态环境，普惠金融业务机会不断增多。

一是县域特色农业及旅游金融服务。渝西片区农业农村产值大、占比高，但金融服务明显不足；县域特色农业、旅游及文化产业链尚未开展针对性的金融服务，可作为空间较大。

二是县域工业及供应链金融支持。渝西片区工业产值与主城相当，但区域内优质客户、项目及上下游供应链的金融支持力度远低于主城，可主动增强服务。

三是建筑施工及民工金融服务。县域片区建筑业产值超过 5 000 亿元，从业人员超过 120 万人，金融服务涵盖结算、消费、融资、工资代发、金融咨询等方面，需求巨大。

四是固定资产投资金融服务。2017 年县域片区固定资产投资进入高速增长期且投资金额较大，仅渝西片区就高达 7 502 亿元（比主城多出 2 333 亿元），固定资产投资及其配套的金融需求快速增长。

五是消费升级金融服务。尽管当前县域片区合计消费总额不足全市的一半，但伴随消费提质升级，县域人口多、潜力大，消费信贷及相关衍生金融服务将迎来潜力释放。

六是县域金融资源的撬动和归集。2017 年县域片区储蓄存款总额 11 749 亿元，基数大且稳定性强、资金成本低，通过增强普惠金融服务，资源撬动和资金归集的空间较大。

七是推进国家及地方战略新增的县域金融服务需求。如长江经济带建设战略带来的环境保护、防护林种植等绿色信贷需求；重庆“8 +3”行动计划、“乡村振兴”等战略带来的县域交通、城乡环保、乡村治理、棚户区改造等基础设施建设金融需求，及配套衍生的拆迁代发、消费信贷、移动支付、文化旅游等金融需求。

四、重庆建行县域普惠金融发展策略建议

（一）总体策略

全面把握长江经济带建设、农业供给侧改革、精准扶贫、城镇化等战略规划，紧扣《重庆市推进普惠金融发展工作方案》和重庆“8 +3”行动计划，加强市场研究和客群分析，构建县域普惠金融支持体系。

1. 构建县域普惠金融发展机制

一是增设县域普惠金融研究发展中心，负责县域普惠金融业务的政策研究、制度制定、产品研发、市场拓展等职责，为县域行提供市场辅导、创新支持、科技支撑和服务响应。二是完善制度安排，适当扩大县域机构经营授权，调整现行信贷政策、授权制度、定价政策等不满足县域普惠金融发展需求的制度设计，扩大县域机构业务自主权和灵活性，增强市场竞争力。

2. 增强县域机构资源配置

一是科学设置业务考核机制，适当倾斜财务资源，增强正向激励，激发县域机构普惠金融发展动力。二是加强县域机构队伍建设，适当倾斜人力资源，选强配齐领导班子，及时补足人员，加快队伍结构优化。三是配置专项信贷规模，适当倾斜信贷资源，优先投放县域客户和项目，增强信贷资源的市场撬动和业务带动作用。

3. 加快县域普惠金融服务与产品创新

一是要用科技的思维、创新的力量加强普惠金融产品自主创新能力建设，搭建自下而上的创新渠道。二是要加强县域市场研究和客户需求分析，遵循“地域差异化、产业特色化”的思路，“一县一策、一行一品”地开发适合县域普惠金融客户群体的服务和产品。

（二）模式策略

以金融科技为支撑，以平台经营为落脚点和核心，运用互联网思维，探索搭建契合县域实际的“普惠＋赋能机构”发展模式。

1. 普惠＋政府机构

一是加强与财政、税务、工商、社保等政府机构合作，推动信息系统互联和数据资源共享。二是主动对接乡镇、街道、社区服务中心等掌握区域数据、了解区域需求的管理部门，提高获客质效。三是引入政府增信机制，与国家及地方担保机构合作，着力解决“担保难”。

2. 普惠＋金融同业

加强与渠道布局完善、客户群体庞大的县域农商行、保险、担保等金融同业的合作，依托金融科技和“新一代”系统功能推进系统连接和科技输出，实现客户、数据、场景、服务等全方位合作。

3. 普惠＋核心企业

围绕机械制造、建筑、笔电代工、医药、材料制造等领域的优质核心企业，依托资金流、信息流和物流信息，加强与核心企业的供应链金融合作，积极推动 e 贷款、供应贷、票据池融资等供应链融资产品。

4. 普惠＋互联网金融

加强与阿里巴巴、京东、腾讯、马上金融等布局县域金融市场的互联网金融公司合作，精准链入客户、数据、场景，依托我行资金、客户和风控优势，整合互联网公司的技术优势、渠道优势，实现批量获客、精准获客。

5. 普惠＋基层组织

一是加强与县域工商联、供销社、行业协会、商会等行业性组织的合作，搭建契合行业特点的普惠金融服务渠道。二是加强与县域医院、学校、公交、燃气、电力、水利等事业性组织的合作，创新供给基于数据、流量、行为习惯的金融服务。三是加强与乡镇干部、党员、劳动模范、经济标兵、养殖大户等致富“领头雁”的合作，试点聘请乡镇金融业务顾问，构建基于能人带动、口碑传播的县域普惠金融生态圈。

（三）渠道策略

结合县域网点较少，普惠金融服务半径不足的实际情况，加强新型服务渠道建设，增强普惠金融服务覆盖。

1. 完善物理渠道布局

结合建行物理渠道布局规划，通过新设、搬迁等措施，适当加强物理网点在强县及富裕乡镇空白区域的渗透力度。发挥离行式自助银行覆盖作用。

2. 大力推广线上和移动金融渠道

加强手机银行、网上银行、“善融商务”、微信银行等线上渠道和移动渠道的推广和使用引导。依托金融科技，加强“E 动终端”“龙易行”“在线金融”等电子设备应用。

3. 依托“县域机构 + 第三方”延伸渠道

广泛开展与保险、供销社、农机、中国移动、中国电信、卫生系统、教育系统等相关行业的合作，利用其在县域乡镇及农村地区的渠道，为县域客户提供金融服务，实现跨界合作和“金融下乡”，大力推广“裕农通”村口银行。

（四）区域策略

依循县域经济特点、资源禀赋、区位条件、金融需求，契合“宜农则农”“宜工则工”“宜商则商”“宜游则游”的发展实际，创新供给差异化的普惠金融服务（见表 2.13）。

表 2.13　县域普惠金融发展区域策略建议

区域	行业	客户	普惠金融服务
渝西	1. 重点行业：具有集群效应、产值较大的农业、工业、建筑业、旅游业、制造业 2. 延伸行业：商务服务业、旅游观光业、建筑施工产业链上下游配套行业	1. 小微企业、小微企业主、个体工商户、农户、商户 2. 机械制造、建筑、笔电代工、医药、材料制造等领域优质核心企业及上下游产业链客群 3. 现代农业产业园、科技园、创业园、产业融合发展示范园等新园区、新主体	1. 全面推广总分行开发的普惠金融基础产品，重点发展小微企业“信用快贷”及个人“快贷” 2. 加快发展网络银行 e 贷款、政府采购贷、供应贷、商保通、票据池融资等供应链融资产品 3. 围绕购房、购车、装修等消费场景，重点发展个人住房按揭、信用卡分期、消费贷款 4. 主动收集客户线上线下行为数据，加大“特色产品”“定制产品”创新
渝东北	1. 重点行业：旅游业及旅游产业链、建筑业及建筑产业链金融服务 2. 延伸行业：商务服务业、旅游观光业、“医、食、住、行、养、休”行业	1. 小微企业、小微企业主、个体工商户、农户、商户 2. 农户、农场、专业合作社、民宿、餐饮等涉农客群 3. 提供家政服务、维修、社区照料等生活性服务业的小微企业，以及信息技术、物流等生产性服务业的小微企业 4. “村官、村医、村教”“木匠、泥水匠”等特色县域群体	1. 重点拓展“云税贷”“善融贷”“账户云贷”“结算云贷”等基于数据模型开发的普惠金融产品 2. 积极拓展农民进城购房、自建房、汽车消费和生活消费信贷业务 3. 推广惠农保险、理财等县域特色金融产品，拓展企业及个人存款 4. 围绕国家乡村及县域扶持政策及区域特色产业，加强产品和服务创新

（续表）

区域	行业	客户	普惠金融服务
渝东南	1. 重点行业：县域特色农业、旅游业 2. 延伸行业：农副食品加工、旅游设施建设、旅行社、餐饮、酒店、民宿等农业、旅游业相关行业	1. 公务员及村“两委”干部、供销产业链商户、农村种养殖经营户、外出务工人员、农村留守居民等客群 2. 家庭农场、种养大户、农民合作社等新型农业主体 3. 乡村旅游优质项目和“农家乐”优质经营户	1. 运用“助农富通”涉农金融综合服务方案，重点发展“扶贫供应贷”“助农贷”“富民合作贷”等产品 2. 探索农村“两权”抵押和林权抵押 3. 加大农户贷款、农村个人生产经营贷款以及农民工、科技人员等返乡下乡人员开展“双创”的信贷支持 4. 定制特色理财产品，拓宽富裕客户投资渠道 5. 加强裕农通金融服务点、手机银行推广等渠道建设 6. 运用金智惠民工程、渝微聚惠沙龙等增强金融知识宣传培训，推动县域信用体系建设

住房租赁篇

稳健推进中国住房租赁市场发展的思考

河北省分行　曲隽煜　赵亚旗

一、中国住房租赁市场发展现状

（一）租赁规模持续扩大

伴随城镇化和城市化进程中的人口流动、高房价的限制，以及限购限贷政策对部分买房需求人群的挤出，近年来中国住房租赁市场迎来了快速发展。根据智研咨询发布的数据，2016 年我国住房租赁面积为 60.21 亿平方米，2017 年这一数据增长至 64.15 亿平方米，同比增长 6.5%。从市场规模看，2016 年我国住房租赁市场规模为 13 800亿元，2017 年我国住房租赁市场规模增长至 15 088 亿元，同比增长 9.3%。

（二）房源供给结构改善

房源供给一般来自居民自有住房、专业性机构、政府保障房以及城中村改造房等。其中，居民自有住房是最主要的来源，目前在住房租赁市场上占比近 90%①；保障性租赁房，也称"廉租房"，主要针对中低收入城市居民，目前中国存量保障房约为 1 300 万套，虽然较以往有了一定增长，但整体覆盖人群较少；中介房源方面，中国专业化的住房租赁机构从 2009 年开始出现，目前整体房源市场占有率为 5% 左右，与发达国家相比差距较大。整体而言，保障房和专业化租赁机构房源占比在持续增加，但仍有很大发展空间。

（三）市场发展潜力巨大

受近年房价持续攀升的影响，开发商倾向于售房，居民倾向于买房，对于提供更多租赁房源和租房居住的意愿较低。根据链家研究院的数据，中国当前租赁住房占比

① 见《2018 年中国住房租赁白皮书》对全国 10 个重点城市的测算。

仅为16%。此外，当前中国城镇化率水平还不到60%，在未来城镇化的过程中，人口从农村向乡镇、从乡镇到城市、从中小城市向大城市的不断流动，也增加了大量租房需求。根据中国房地产业协会商业和旅游地产专业委员会秘书长蔡云在“2018亚太房地产租赁峰会”上的发言，预计2025年中国住房租赁市场规模将超过3万亿元、一二线核心城市长租公寓市场规模将超3 000亿元。

二、中国住房租赁市场存在的问题及原因分析

受中国多年来“居者有其屋”传统观念的影响，中国人的住房自有率较高。近年来，住房租赁市场虽然取得一定发展，但与房地产市场相比，住房租赁发展相对较为缓慢，存在房地产市场和住房租赁市场“一条腿长，一条腿短”的现象。且在住房租赁市场内部，存在“短租多、长租少”的现象。

（一）“居者有其屋”的传统观念影响租房行为

受中国几千年延续的“安居乐业”观念影响，中国人将有稳定的自有住所作为安家立命、事业有成的重要衡量指标和提升安全感的重要保障。近年来，虽然随着住房租赁市场的发展，这种传统观念正在中国年轻人中逐渐淡化，但根深蒂固的观念的消失仍需要漫长的时间，住房租赁市场发展需要一个长期的过程。

（二）租房买房性价比差距较大

在利率整体维持稳定的情况下，受中国近年来持续上涨的房价影响，购买住房的增值率较高，持有住房的成本相对较低，使得消费者在买房和租房两者之中更倾向于购买住房，不仅可以解决个人住房需求，获得稳定的、长期的居住场所；同时持续上涨的房价使得购买住房后能够获得较大的投资收益，买房所需付出的成本支出与房价持续上涨能够获得的收益相比，很多人更倾向于购买住房，也就是说，买房的性价比远远高于租房。

（三）租购不同权抑制部分租房需求

当前，中国大中型城市中普遍存在租购不同权的问题，这种现象在教育方面更为突出。教育作为公共产品，在当前存在基础教育资源短缺、区域间分配不均的突出问题，能否接受好的教育，剔除其他不公平的渠道外，唯一有效的渠道就是购买学区房、落户片区内。虽然政策规定部分学区内的租房家庭也能享受与区域内的自住家庭同等的入学权利，但一般鲜少有人能满足条件规定。如，仅租住家庭的父母双方就业单位均在学区房片区内这一项，就将很多租房人群拒之门外。

(四)租赁服务水平较低

一是房源供给层次较低。针对租房市场上具备不同承租能力、租住时限和租住需求的群体，目前市场上存量出租房在房源、价格、装修状况等方面为租客提供的选择较少，除部分房源被中介集中收储之外，大部分房源分散在个人出租者手中，房源分散、零碎化，且条件不一，缺乏品牌式供给。出租房源中，商品房占比偏低，老式公房、农村自建房、城中村搭建房、回迁房和小产权房等占了很大比例，配套不完善，居住环境破旧脏乱等问题突出。中介机构仅根据出租方和租客需求，在现有房源内进行匹配，未充分实现将合适的房源推荐给合适的客户，比如，同一地段、同一类型房源装修为精装修、一般装修和简装的差别化，同等价格上无法有效提供更多地段、更多户型的房源供其参考。

二是专业化租赁机构不发达。目前，租赁市场逐渐出现了一些品牌租赁机构，如自如、蛋壳、魔方、新派等，但部分长租公寓资金链条破裂而爆仓，以及部分中介不顾环保标准用劣质板材、追求工期造成装修不达标而导致租客患病，引发了社会上对这些机构的服务的诟病。

三是服务水平低，承租体验差。由于专业化机构不发达，以及住房法律制度不健全，房屋中介机构一般只以促成交易、赚取中介费为目的，部分中介存在重复发布房源、刻意隐瞒房屋真实状况的问题，对于出租房屋不提供任何售后保障。房东作为交易的强势方，不仅具有较强的议价能力，而且一般对于所出租房屋存在问题的维修采取拖延、消极、不配合的态度，部分房东还存在随意涨价、退房时无理扣押租房押金等行为，使整体服务水平较低。而租客也大多只能通过租房满足租住需求，但在融入租住社区方面程度较低。

(五)租赁结构失衡，长租少，短租多

目前，市场上的租房群体根据租房用途和承租能力，大致可分为初入职场5年以内的年轻人、因孩子入学需就近租住的群体、进城务工的低收入群体、异地交流或任职的较高收入人群。其中，初入职场5年以内的年轻人，有一定的承租能力，对于所租房屋有一定的品质和安全需求，但租房地点可能随工作而不断变迁，且一般在毕业5年内考虑买房成家。因孩子入学需就近租住的家庭，一般有一定经济能力，对于租住的地段和租住户型有一定要求，且租住期限倾向于与孩子上学的期限相匹配，一般在3~6年，可将其归纳为长租群体。进城务工的低收入人群，从事的一般是体力行业，对居住环境要求较低，倾向于小户型、低租金，也是短租群体。因工作需要异地交流或任职的干部，收入较高，对租住要求较高，租住时间一般在1~2年或者2~3年，可

划分为中租群体。根据前面分析的几个方面的问题及原因，中国人很多还倾向于凑钱买房或者短期内租房攒钱后买房，因此市场上的短租群体相对长租群体来说较多，即便是长租的人在其他地段大部分也已有房产。

（六）住房租赁法规和管理制度不健全

相较于国外住房租赁市场发达的国家而言，中国在住房租赁市场上的管理制度相对不健全。目前现行的涉及住房租赁市场的专门性法规主要有两部，一是《商品房屋租赁管理办法》（2011 年 2 月 1 日开始施行），二是《公共租赁住房管理办法》（2012 年 7 月 15 日开始生效），但仅适用于公共租赁住房的管理，且仅仅针对住房保障对象。相比于目前蓬勃发展的中国住房租赁市场而言，这些法规明显滞后且与市场发展脱节，缺少重要内容，且在公平性、完整性、科学性等方面有待改进提升。

（七）缺乏统一的住房租赁管理平台

除各地的公租房具有各自的管理平台且各家不一外，目前国内市场上最缺少的就是统一的住房租赁管理平台，供各类交易主体去使用，去为所有出租的房源备案，实行透明交易，确保房源真实性和同类房源的价格参照。仅有的几个网站比如安居客，仅提供各类房源信息，且不能确保所有房源的真实性、有效性。

（八）住房公积金在促进住房租赁市场发展中的作用发挥不充分

当前，公积金提取的用途规定为购买、建造、翻建、大修自住住房及偿还住房贷款本息等情况。虽然对职工房租超出家庭工资收入的规定比例的，可提取职工住房公积金账户内的存储余额来支付房租，但是各地规定的住房公积金提取限额与职工半年缴存额挂钩，而且需提供经房管部门登记备案的房屋租赁合同、房租发票、家庭收入证明。当前，低收入人群普遍未缴存公积金或缴存比例较低，而且由于提取手续复杂且公积金提取与近半年的缴存额度有关，对部分缴存金额较少且急需解决租房需求的职工帮助不大。此外，获取租房发票对于很多个人出租房源来说也较为困难。因此，目前提取公积金用于支付租房费用的占比较低。

三、对规范发展中国住房租赁市场的建议

（一）转变理念

1. 政府

一是改变土地出让金模式。政府应逐渐减少当前对土地出让获取收入的依赖，积

极改变当前传统的一次性获取土地出让金模式，在低价出让专门用于住房租赁开发建设的地块基础上，允许受让企业分多次或者按年缴纳租赁建设用地的土地出让金，减轻房地产开发企业的土地获取成本。通过低成本获取地价，鼓励和引导房地产开发企业加大住房租赁开发建设力度。

二是积极推进租购同权。针对当前租房买房在性价比上的差距，积极推进租赁住房与购买住房的权利相同，通过赋予租赁住房住户与购买住房住户同等的教育、医疗等权利，推进租房和买房行为的性价比逐渐趋于一致，引导人们结合自身实际，理性地选择租房或购买住房。

2. 房地产开发企业

房地产开发企业作为住房市场的主要参与者，也应积极履行企业的社会责任，坚持让利于民。一是主动转变当前传统的靠实现房屋销售一次性获取销售现金流的方式，将部分存量未出售房源转为租凭房源和在新开发房源中加大租赁住房建设比例，从单一出售房屋向出售房屋和出售持有房源并重转型，获得长期稳定的现金流，并以此引导社会的租房理念。

二是以服务社会和微利运营为目标，与政府和其他社会资本合作，组建房屋租赁公司，针对社会上不同租房群体的需求，通过改造和提供相应房源，提高房源供给层次，满足不同群体的租房需求，推进住房租赁市场结构更加合理。

（二）创新模式

1. 区分客户群体，提供合适房源

针对上述分析中不同租房群体在租赁期限和租赁房屋结构质量方面的要求，加大存量房源改造和增量房源供给力度，满足不同群体的个性化租房需求。比如，对于初入职场的年轻人，将市中心地段的大型房屋进行改造，集中打造具有厅、厨、卫的小户型公寓式住宅，满足这类群体的一定品质租房需求。对于在学校周边租住、解决孩子上学问题的租房群体以及因工作需要租赁住房的工作群体，可将房源供给放在提升房屋装修质量方面、解决好租房的品质问题方面。对于进城务工等群体，由于其对房租价格敏感，对租住地段和品质没有较高要求，可将房源供给放在满足必要的居住需求、确保安全方面。

2. 建设开放统一的住房租赁服务平台

如可借鉴建设银行目前推广的 CCB 建融家园，开发或引进类似的住房租赁服务平台，平台功能应集合政府监管、房源发布、线上签约交易、租赁贷款全流程线上办理以及租房价格趋势等各种功能，使得各个层面的人群都可以使用。这样，不论短租长租，出租方和承租方都能提前找到合适的目标，可减少出租方空置成本和承租方的房源寻找成本。此外，服务平台应设计为开放式，允许部分地区和机构在平台基础上进行各类特色开发，不断提升平台的实用性。

3. 积极推进租购同权

鼓励和推进住房租赁市场发展，就要让社会公众感受到买房和租房在性价比上的基本一致性，我认为首要的就是推进租购同权。如果租住住房能够享受到与买房一致的落户、入学、社保等待遇，则买房的性价比将逐渐趋近于租房，相信租房将成为更多人的选择。

4. 畅通公积金提取用于支付租房贷款和租金的制度流程

一是建议进一步完善住房公积金提取各项规定，允许公积金提取后用于支付租房支出。二是赋予各地公积金中心更大的自主权，使其结合实际出台适用于本区域的公积金提取支付房租的比例。三是配套住房租赁服务平台建设，在有效防控风险的前提下最大限度地简化公积金提取的流程和相关手续，或者推行网上备案、网上获取发票等方式，便利公积金提取。四是比照公积金住房贷款，尽快创新推出公积金租赁住房贷款产品，将公积金取之于民用之于民，更多地用于支持百姓安居。

（三）完善管理

1. 完善住房租赁相关法律法规

政府应尽快完善住房租赁相关法律规定，明确规定租赁双方的责权利和纠纷处理，以法律的手段约束租赁双方行为，使得租赁管理法规条例跟得上住房租赁市场的发展。特别是应加强对房屋中介机构的监管，重点优先保护租客的居住权、租赁权。出台鼓励金融机构创新住房租赁相关产品服务的政策文件，鼓励在风险可控的前提下积极研发推出更多符合监管要求、满足群众需求的住房租赁相关产品。研究积极推动住房租赁贷款资产证券化以及允许住房租赁专业机构债券发行的政策框架，为住房租赁市场发展创造良好的法律环境和政策空间。建立涵盖租赁双方的信用体系，对失信人和失信企业建立黑名单，以信用约束规范住房租赁行为。

2. 增加租赁住房建设用地供应

当前，社会上的租赁房源除了个人商品房源外，公租房多为棚改房和廉租房，能够直接推向社会，满足更多人群由于就业、上学等流动性需求和差别化需求的房源占比较低。建议政府在加大保障房建设力度的同时，充分利用掌握的各类资源，特别是土地资源，增加用于租赁住房用途的地块供应，鼓励更多主体和房产开发商积极参与租赁住房建设。

3. 施行税收优惠

结合房产税和个人所得税调整等，适当考虑将租金抵消个人纳税所得和出租租金收入部分抵消房产税，以减轻租房者负担，鼓励更多房源出租。

4. 施行租金补贴

加大财政支出力度，针对社会上不同人群给予不同的租金补贴。比如对于新毕业大学生、低收入人群、市场亟须以及引进人才等，根据其学习、收入、就业等情况，提供不同层次的租金补贴。必要时可将补贴标准与社保缴纳、工作情况等挂钩，通过租金补贴机制，帮助这类人群应对房租较快上涨带来的压力。

5. 建立租金涨幅指导价

在尽快推出住房租赁服务平台的基础上，对于各区域的房源给出一定的租金指导价和涨幅指导价，引导市场规范定价。

6. 严格管控租赁中介金融化

加强对房屋中介机构的监管，强调其房源中介属性的发挥，避免租赁中介演变为对租客和出租方的单向金融中介，通过强化监管促进中介合规履职。

四、大型商业银行参与住房租赁市场的发展建议

目前，中国的租赁房源主要为存量房源，今后加快推进住房租赁市场既要鼓励更多闲置房源进入市场，又要从增加特色、差别化房源入手，丰富房源供给，满足租赁需求。在此方面，考虑到大型商业银行的巨大资金实力、众多存量客户群体，以及丰富的房地产开发贷款和按揭贷款经验，我认为金融机构特别是大型商业银行应该在推进住房租赁市场发展中发挥更大作用，而且参与住房租赁业务对于银行主动规避风险集聚的房地产开发贷款也是一种主动选择和结构变革。

1. 积极参与租赁市场建设

在租赁市场建设方面，商业银行可以说拥有资金实力、客户基础、技术支持，在推进租赁市场建设方面集“天时、地利、人和”等多种要素于一身，理应发挥优势，积极参与。特别是大型商业银行，作为金融市场上的主力军，面对当前房价居高不下对居民消费、住房以及青年人婚恋观、创新精神等多方面的不利影响，也应主动担当，大行带头新气象，可通过参与组建住房租赁专业公司的方式，从金融的视角，用金融的触角，推动租赁市场建设，助力百姓安居工程。

2. 从供需两端发展，开发租赁住房建设贷款和个人住房租赁贷款

大型商业银行应积极发挥自身连接供给端和需求端的优势。在供给端，积极支持住房租赁用地开发建设，以信贷资金助推租赁住房建设，丰富房源供给；在需求端，加快创新针对不同类型、不同需求的个人住房租赁贷款产品，满足居民住房租赁贷款需求。

3. 积极推动政府保持按揭贷款政策的连续性和稳定性

中国住房市场需要租房和买房两条腿走路，针对当前由于限贷政策造成的部分买

房需求被转移到租房市场的情况，大型商业银行应主动与政府沟通，建言献策，保持住房抵押贷款政策的连续性和稳定性。比如，针对房贷发放认房认贷的情况，建议以客户拥有的存量房产数量为主要依据，可探索对到贷款申请日止只拥有一套或两套房产的客户发放贷款，而不是以客户办理过抵押贷款的次数为准，这样，可以充分保障刚需性客户和改善性客户的需求，也有利于住房市场的稳健发展。

4. 规范操作，防范信贷风险和金融风险

做实贷款调查，严格按照客户标准选择贷款企业和客户，优选客户，优选企业，严禁向打着住房租赁开发名义而实质上开发商品房的企业发放住房租赁开发贷款，严禁向炒房以及其他高风险人群发放住房租赁贷款。强化贷中审查，严格贷款受托支付管理，严格贷款资金用途管理，严防信贷资金违规流入股市和民间借贷等其他领域。加强贷后管理，定期走访、回访客户，多角度、多方位了解借款企业和客户的真实状况，确保资金安全。

“存房养老”和“租房养老”模式研究与实践

建信养老金　冯丽英

自2000年起进入老龄社会后，我国的老龄化速度一直居高不下。截至2017年，60岁及以上人口已达2.41亿，占比超17.3%，预计2050年占比将达35%，约占届时全球老年人口的25%。中国正在经历前所未有的社会结构变革，“未富先老”和“人口断层”及其连带的系列连锁反应，给我国养老保障制度建设和医疗保健事业造成了巨大压力。如何让国民住有所居、老有所养，是政府和全社会都关心的重要问题。

国家在十一五期间提出“9073”养老格局，但家庭规模逐渐缩小、子女流动性增强等都造成传统反哺式家庭关系正在瓦解。同时，养老也不再是简单的对“衣食住行”的保障，现代老年人更注重退休后的个人价值实现，强调物质和精神双方面的优质生活。这无疑对我国的养老服务和养老资产管理提出了更高、更迫切的要求。而当前的养老服务供给，无论是机构数量、结构分布及服务质量都与养老需求存在较大差距，一方面，高端养老服务价格昂贵，普通民众无力负担；另一方面，低端养老服务质量难以保证。供需错位造成了我国养老服务市场的扭曲，“一床难求”与高空置率现象并存。

“以房养老”正是在这一背景下引入国内开始试水，但房屋反向抵押保险市场反应冷淡。行业迫切需要借模式创新撬动以房养老市场，打通产业链，重塑供需关系。本文的研究重点正是如何通过引入养老资产管理和养老服务，将住房租赁与养老金融、养老服务整合，探索以房养老模式在中国的实践路径。

一、以房养老市场现状及困境

在人口加速老龄化的背景下，我国现有养老金体系也面临巨大压力。以基本养老保险替代率为例，从最高的77.30%逐年下滑，2016年年末仅为45.70%，平均年降幅达8.35%。而依照国际劳工组织（ILO）《社会保障最低标准公约》的标准，养老金最低替代率为55%，经合组织（OECD）则认为替代率达到70%才可维持退休前的生活水准。当前我国基本养老保险替代率已严重低于警戒线。从长期来说，需要优化三支柱结构，大力发展第二、第三支柱企业和个人养老金。但当前也需要通过金融、服务模式创新来多元化养老金来源，提高养老金替代率，提升老人的生活品质。而以房养老就是在这一背景下出现的。

从国家政策角度来看，2017 年 7 月国务院印发《关于加快商业养老保险的若干意见》，要求大力发展反向抵押保险等适老性强的商业保险。但从以房养老落地至今，开展业务的仅幸福人寿一家，且完成承保手续不足百户。房屋反向抵押保险在国内市场“遇冷”，有着多方面原因。一方面受传统观念影响，房产作为特殊的家庭财产，难以单纯用出售或抵押的方式处置以满足养老需求。另一方面，保险产品本身的设计存在缺陷，抵押意味着所有权转移，而市场中对房屋估值、房产处置机制缺乏统一标准，产品办理流程复杂、风险分散机制不足，再加上相关保障法律的缺失等问题，严重制约了消费者的参与热情。

从行业角度看，我国保险业很早就开始探索将保险产品与养老服务结合，通过养老服务全周期产业链的整合实现保险产品与养老资源供给的对接，推进医疗、健康和社区护理相融合的服务模式。但值得注意的是，保险公司投资的养老社区主要是为其中的高端客户提供“一站式”的养老服务，如高端的泰康人寿“泰康之家”养老社区，采用“保险产品挂钩 + 社区入住”的形式，养老年金分红险产品购买门槛为 200 万元（视被保险人年龄、性别不同），即可获得入住养老社区的权益和享受投保每年的分红收益。此模式虽极大促进了保险、医疗、养老服务的融合发展，但由于定位高端，其在全国的可复制性和对解决普通民众的养老需求作用有限。

不可否认，由于家庭代际关系变化、空巢老人数量持续增加、自有房比重增加、房产价值上升等因素，未来我国以房养老市场具有极大的发展潜力，甚至可能成为第三支柱的重要补充，但目前仍缺少颠覆性的“爆款”产品来加速消费者养老理念的转变和完成市场的破冰。

二、租房养老和存房养老模式研究

如何通过产品服务的创新，解决房产反向抵押产品的消费者痛点问题，激发参与积极性，是未来以房养老模式发展的首要问题。建信养老金管理公司在建行蓝海战略下，将租房、存房和养老三者结合，针对社区养老和机构养老，创新性地提出了“租房养老”和“存房养老”模式。其本质是通过金融创新和跨业务领域的资源整合，疏通房地产和养老服务市场循环不畅的梗阻，激发市场的潜力。下面本文将对两种模式进行介绍。

（一）“租房养老”的概念

“租房养老”是指建信养老金与政府、开发商合作规划并建设附带养老设施的城市综合体，或与养老机构合作提供成熟运营、可供租赁的房源，为租房消费者（本人或亲属）提供专业养老服务的模式。消费者在实现“租住”功能的同时也解决了自身或家人的养老服务需求，从而实现“长租即长住，长住即安家”的目的。在具体产品上涵盖“租房+社区养老”和“租房+养老公寓”两类。前者通过整合具备条件的房地产开发商、养老运营商，增加社区的养老服务功能，主要针对家中有老年人需要赡养的中青年客户群体。该群体在选择通过建行租房的同时，可单独或捆绑为其家里老人选择相应的养老服务。后者则是建信养老金与运营成熟的养老社区机构合作，在平台展示养老公寓出租房源。该方案中的房源既针对自身有养老需求的老年客户，也可覆盖为家中老年人选择机构养老的中青年客户。

（二）“存房养老”的概念

“存房养老”模式，简单地说即消费者通过将存量房屋纳入建行可供租赁的房屋池，将租金收益用于购买金融产品或享受配套养老服务的模式。“存房养老”与房屋反向抵押不同，房屋资产所有权不变而只是使用权转移，规避了消费者最关注的产权痛点。“存房养老”模式一方面扩大了社会可租赁的房源，促进租房市场多主体多渠道供给；另一方面，通过建信养老金平台实现养老需求与高质量养老服务供给的有效匹配，形成了租房、养老金融全产业链闭环运作。

（三）“租房养老”与“存房养老”的商业实践

若按产业链的结构来说，在养老保障产品端，建信养老金利用个人养老保障产品牌照，将“租房养老”和“存房养老”模式具化为建养“安心”“省心”“放心”系列产品体系。其中，“建养安心”为附加权益型个人养老保障产品，其特点为消费者不仅可获取正常的养老保障产品收益，而且可选择与平台合作的养老机构提供的养老服务优惠权益。“建养省心”是在附加权益的基础上增加支付功能，消费者可使用个人养老保障产品的本金和收益支付入住养老机构所发生的费用。“建养放心”为长期限周期性产品，消费者可以使用养老产品完成其养老理财规划，平衡养老投资和养老支出的需求。此类系列产品认购起点低，购买和行权方式灵活，具有较强的普惠金融属性。目前共发行建养“安心”系列产品6期，规模1.3亿元。

在产品的设计与服务体验上，借助平台遴选优质养老机构，制定准入标准，以满足客户多层次、候鸟式的养老需求。截至目前，已与29家养老机构签署合作协议，1 500多套养老房源在集团建融家园App上线，5 500多张养老床位在建颐人生App进行展示，其中不乏万科、复星、绿地等知名康养机构和江西麓林湖等入选工信部《智慧健康养老产品及服务推广目录》的养老机构。同时已与福建省民政厅和天津滨海新区、安徽滁州、重庆涪陵、重庆南川民政局，以及45家养老机构达成平台使用意向。

在后端养老服务供给能力建设上，建信养老金从养老金资产管理这一本职业务出发，全周期介入养老房源开发与服务提供，为养老项目建设提供融资支持。目前已储备优质项目80多个，累计为养老项目提供资金13亿元，并成功投资国内首单长租公寓储架式权益类REITs（房地产信托投资基金，高和晨曦—中信证券—领昱1号）。目前由建信养老金公司、建行上海市分行、上海建信住房服务公司和上海申养公司联手打造的首个“CCB建融家园—建养安心养老基地”已在上海长者公寓“滨江澜悦”正式挂牌，“存房养老”模式已正式落地。

三、以房养老创新模式下的总行三大战略融合

“租房养老”和“存房养老”是将养老服务、养老金融纳入住房租赁，“一站式”的服务体验在丰富“蓝海战略”落地产品的同时，强化了蓝海战略项目的差异化属性，有力支持了长租即长住目标的实现。从消费者角度来看，租房和存房模式都将租房消费与养老消费结合，并行解决了租房、养老两大社会痛点难题。从养老金三支柱结构优化角度来看，将存房租金对接养老金资产管理，初期能起到扩充个人养老金收入和强化消费者养老教育的作用，而在未来伴随着存房养老规模的增加，还可能起到补充第三支柱的重要作用。从养老商业生态角度来看，借助“安心养老综合服务”等平台，总行与建信养老金得以打通住房租赁、养老金融、养老服务的上下游产业链条，通过闭环式的产品服务机制设计，增强了蓝海战略的服务生态延伸性与商业壁垒。

依托“安心养老综合服务平台”，建信养老金公司将建行普惠金融理念融入养老产业，提出“普惠养老”理念。一方面，通过对服务商资质审核和服务能力分类，形成惠及不同养老群体的多层次养老服务体系。另一方面，也通过制定面向养老服务商的轻享、乐享、安享、尊享四类平台模式，为不同的服务商提供差异化套餐服务。此外，在服务实体经济、支持产业转型升级、助力民生发展等方面，租房养老和存房养老模式也同样爆发出极大的潜力。在解决社会养老服务照护、亲情陪伴等民生痛点问题的基础上，将短期房屋资产出租收入通过养老保障产品转化为长线资金，有力支持了实体经济的发展。

需要强调的是，借助建行的金融科技基础，建信养老金具备了快速将产品服务创新概念转变成市场潜力和营销战斗力的能力，实现了金融科技、蓝海战略和普惠金融的互动融合。“安心养老综合服务”平台已借助大数据、物联网、人工智能等科技手段，为个人养老客户、养老机构、政府部门、第三方养老服务商等提供多场景、全线上的互联网服务，实现了客群—内容—流量—数据—客群的良性循环。在此基础上，

打通后端数据链路，企业年金客户也可通过建颐人生 App 登录系统，完成日常年金业务办理，未来将形成“全一站式”的便捷服务体验。

四、政策建议

我国以房养老市场整体仍处于初级阶段，存在消费者教育滞后、市场机制不完善、相关领域保障法律缺失等问题，故结合本文的研究，提出以下建议。

（一）拓展顶层设计思路

以房养老制度建设需要金融和服务创新的支持，国家应着眼长远，加强顶层设计。当前研究和商业实践大多关注养老房地产硬件建设，而对养老服务软件，特别是不同情境软硬件对接问题，尚无明确的顶层规划。建议国家相关部门进一步拓展思路，创新模式，制定更加清晰和有包容性的国家战略。建信养老金公司也应在此背景下充分发挥试点的作用，先试先行，探索一条符合我国国情的以房养老发展路径。

（二）关注风险防范

加强风险防范制度建设，明确风险分担机制，确保以房养老全流程居民房屋资产和养老金融产品的安全。建议国家建立健全风险管控政策，完善有关法律和监管体系，做好税收优惠安排、信息披露机制和政府监管等保障措施等。同时，建议国家出台养老服务体系建设方案和服务供应商标准，避免因养老服务供应商质量的参差不齐而对参与以房养老的消费者造成损失。建立以房养老服务全流程监管机制，确保资产与服务配套衔接，严防以房养老相关金融诈骗案件的发生。

（三）搭建“一站式”管理服务平台

面对多元化、多层次的养老需求，需要专业化的服务内容和多元化供给主体来支撑。针对老年人的特点，建议在现有信息平台的基础上，将金融产品购买、养老机构选择、适老用品介绍等功能融于一体，实现养老资产管理与养老服务提供的“一站购齐”。专业机构应充分发挥在养老金融领域的专业优势，在精算、生命周期、产品品质等方面深入研究，优化“金融 + 养老服务”类产品的服务体验水平。

（四）加大支持力度

将个人房屋资产与养老金、养老服务对接，需要客户端、资金端、资产端、服务端的联动，既有养老金投资的轻资产运营，也有养老服务提供的重资产运营。一方面要加强对消费者养老观念的教育，引导个人未来的养老服务预期。另一方面，建议国家出台相关政策，对于开展此类运营模式的机构在税收等方面给予相应支持；对于选择此类产品的个人，可采取提供风险保证等措施，引导和吸引其参与。通过调动社会各方能动主体积极参与，吸引更多社会资本加入，从而形成养老、金融、服务三者的有机结合。

房地产企业进军住房租赁市场的机遇与挑战

总行战略客户部　张　犇

一、住房租赁的含义

房屋租赁指由房屋的所有者或经营者将其所有或经营的房屋交给房屋的消费者使用，房屋消费者通过定期交付一定数额的租金，取得房屋的占有和使用权利的行为。房屋租赁是房屋使用价值零星出售的一种商品流通方式，用于居住用途的房屋租赁行为，称为住房租赁。

二、发达国家住房租赁市场情况

（一）美国住房租赁市场情况

美国是世界上住房租赁市场化程度最高的国家，相比欧洲国家，美国的自有住房持有率较高。截至 2017 年年底，美国住房租赁市场的承租户达到 4 300 万户，占在用住宅的 35. 6%。

1. 供给端

美国核心城市租赁房屋占居住用房比例超过 60%，空置率约 7%。从租赁房的分布来看，集中于大都会地区。在各类租赁住房的供给主体中，专业化的公寓出租企业占据大多数。按营业收入占比计算，公寓出租企业占出租机构总体收入的 70% 以上。以公寓出租业为主体的住宅出租业是美国各地区房地产业中一个非常重要的行业。租房者入住专业化公寓，可以享受到良好的居住环境和齐全的公寓设施，也有专业的物业公司提供服务。

2. 需求端

美国租房者多是优先从工作和生活方便的角度出发，租房选择的区域多是大型城市的核心地段，或是商圈附近。从年龄结构上看，美国租房群体中 40 岁以上承租户占一半以上，其中单身群体占比最大。因为在美国持有房产本身也有不低的成本，所以退休群体更希望住进设施齐备、服务便捷的专业养老公寓中，对于单身群体来说，租房更加方便。

3. 承租参与方

美国住房租赁市场的承租方中，规模最大的是一家 REITs。EQR（公平住房信托）是美国最大的公寓租赁投资经营企业。这家 1969 年成立、1993 年上市的公寓类 REITs，在美国 18 个州持有 800 多处物业、17 000 多套公寓，是住房租赁企业中的龙头老大。在美国，如果自己持有物业，房屋出租后每年需缴纳房产税，且租后维护成本较高。因此，市场上的投资者更多的是机构而不是个人。

（二）欧洲住房租赁市场情况

欧洲住房租赁市场最成熟的国家是德国。以德国为例，德国住房自有率仅为 51%，接近一半的家庭选择租房居住，较高租房率的主要原因是政策和市场需求。

1. 供给端

按照德国的住房政策，不管开发新房或经营租赁，企业要获得土地、信贷，房子要在一定期限内先让渡政府出租，或按接受补贴后的低租金出租，一定时间后才能按市场租金出租，这就保证了市场有足够的租赁房源。德国住房租赁市场中，政府公租房占比 25%，私人机构房源占比 23%。此外，德国大型城市较低的人口集中度也让房源变得更加充足。得益于政府严格的监管与检查制度，这些租赁住房普遍居住环境良好，设施齐全，物业服务周到，让租房者感觉舒适。

2. 需求端

较高的租售比让德国住房租赁市场拥有充足的客源。租客租赁住房时除了看中工作、生活的便捷性外，还更多地关注居住质量、物业服务水平等。租客年龄段分布较广，不局限于学生和年轻白领，中老年人也较多。从房价水平来看，自 20 世纪 90 年代以来的近 30 年间，德国的实际房价累计增幅仅为 2%，因为房价增速缓慢，投资房地产收益较低，民众购房热情不高，这也为租赁住房提供了市场空间。

3. 承租参与方

根据德国住房和房地产公司联邦协会统计数据，36% 的租赁房源由专业化机构提供，其中私人机构供给占比 38%，政府公司占比 28%，住房合作社占比 26%，供给主体比较多元化。特别要说明的是住房合作社，这是一种为社员提供租赁房屋的股份制公司。就租房成本而言，由于前期缴纳的股份费用可以获得股息收益，退社时可以退还，所以相比直接购/租房均较低。运作模式上，会员申请入社后一次性缴纳会员费（获得对应股份），合作社利用会员费以及银行贷款进行住房建设（依需定量），按合同分配社员入住，而社员除享受永久租赁权之外，也按照持股比例获得定期股息分红。

（三）发达国家住房租赁市场的共性

发达国家住房租赁市场具有共同的特点，既通过政府指导和市场化运作相结合的方式，尽可能保障租房者的利益，最大程度给予租房者良好的居住条件，实现民众“居者有其屋”的基本需求。

三、我国住房租赁市场情况

我国住房租赁市场的出现始于20世纪90年代，当时以个人投资者为主，机构投资者较少。近年来，随着房地产市场基本面的变化，国家开始对现有住房体制进行调整和改革，将住房制度的重心转为关注低收入人群的住房保障需求。特别是在十九大提出“房子是用来住的、不是用来炒的”“加快建立多主体供给、多渠道保障、租购并举的住房制度，让全体人民住有所居”的口号后，中国的住房租赁市场加快了发展速度，出现了增长趋势，投资者结构也逐渐发生了变化。

（一）供给端

国家在“十二五”期间新增公租房1 000万套，廉租房400万套，发放租赁补贴150万户。目前市场上可供出租的房源中，商品房占比40%、公寓占比20%、农民自建房占比8%、回迁房占比8%、小产权房占比2%、其他类型占比22%。“十三五”规划提出，继续加大租赁住房的供给，提高租售比例，进一步规范完善住房租赁市场。以北京为例，未来5年计划供应租赁住房50万套，年均10万套，2017年以来北京成交的自持地块带来的租赁住房套数占比在20%左右。以上海为例，“十三五”期间将新增租赁住房70万套；同时，将对存量房源进行盘活，新增代理租赁房源30万套，并通过政策引导扶持住房租赁企业扩大规模。

（二）需求端

中国的城镇化发展速度加快，2016年年底我国城镇化率达到55%，而这个比率还在不断增加。城镇化的进程为人口流入城市带来了大量流动人口，这些流动人口成为租赁住房的主力军。根据中投顾问发布的《2017—2021年中国住房租赁市场投资分析及前景预测报告》，我国采用租房方式解决居住问题的人口数目约为1.6亿人，是通过购买住房解决居住问题人数的4倍。有租房需求的人群年龄段集中在20～35岁，且收入水平偏低，区域分布上主要在北京、上海、广州、深圳等一二线城市。

（三）承租参与方

我国住房租赁市场的主要承租方目前为中介机构、个人。在国内房地产市场高位运行、利润率较高的大环境下，传统房地产企业多以开发销售为主，对住房租赁市场无更多涉足，进入市场较晚，持有或租赁供出租的房源较少。但是，其中也不乏部分房地产龙头企业对市场先行判断，在住房租赁市场已经开始布局，并取得了一定的成效。以万科为例，其于2016年创建“泊寓”长租公寓品牌，以青年群体为服务对象，以提供优质租住空间及一体化社区服务为服务目标。目前，“泊寓”已在北京、上海、广州、深圳等20多个城市成功运营，项目超过50个，房源逾2万套，平均出租率达80%以上。

四、发展机遇与面临挑战

中国的住房租赁市场刚刚起步，方兴未艾。对于习惯了“拿地—开发—销售”传统运营模式的房地产企业来说，住房租赁市场这片蓝海充满了机遇与挑战，如何能在这一新兴领域找准定位、抓住机会、拓展市场，对房地产企业未来的发展至关重要。

（一）发展机遇

1. 政策预期利好

住房租赁市场的发展“生逢其时”，在国内房地产政策“回归房屋基本居住属性”，让“居者有其屋”思想的指导下，“租售并举”已经成为新时期国家房地产政策的核心之一。为了更好地平衡供需关系，满足人民群众基本的居住需求，国家将大力推广租赁住房，适时出台相关政策，配套机制建设，规范市场秩序。住房租赁市场将成为住房销售市场的有益补充和调剂，二者相互促进，会使我国房地产市场的发展更加稳健。利好的政策预期，为住房租赁市场的发展奠定了坚实的基础，提供了有力的保障。

2. 市场空间巨大

我国人口流动性强，农村外出务工人员多，各城市房价与收入比普遍较高，居民购买能力有限，许多人通过租赁住房解决居住问题。据统计，50%以上的农民工在所在的打工城市租房居住，城镇租赁住房家庭户数占城镇家庭总户数的20%以上，我国城镇居民每年居住消费性支出市场规模超过3.6万亿元。另外，相较于国外来看，发达国家租赁住房在房地产市场的占比达50%以上，而我国租赁住房占比较高的北京、上海等城市也不过35%，全国整体只有约20%，国内住房租赁市场还有广阔的发展空间。

3. 自身房源有保障

传统的房地产企业擅长的是房地产项目的开发和销售，其对所开发项目的市场价值、定位、受众群都有自己的分析和判断，具有较强的专业性。转战住房租赁市场，房地产企业最大的优势之一就是房源，其可以直接开发租赁住房项目，也可以将过往的销售项目转化为租赁项目。无论选择哪种方式，房子都是开发商自己的，相较链家、我爱我家这些房屋中介机构，房地产企业不用寻找房源，也省去了与房源持有者的谈判和沟通，避免了作为“二房东”的麻烦。

4. 提升市场地位

越来越多的房地产企业已经意识到，在“租售并举”的大环境下，必须要在住房租赁市场有所动作。一方面，是对国家政策的积极响应；另一方面，也是调整自身经营模式以适应未来市场发展的需要。房地产企业可依托其在开发销售市场上积累的经验和品牌优势，在住房租赁市场继续“开疆拓土”“有所作为”，通过良好的运营，形成品牌效应和标准化体系，建立一定的市场口碑和租客群体，从而巩固提升市场地位。事实上，像万科、绿地、龙湖这样的知名房企已经取得了显著的成效，他们倾力打造的“泊寓”“铂骊”“冠寓”品牌获得了市场的广泛认可。

5. 培育潜在客户群

就房地产企业而言，“租”不是目的，而是一种手段，是为了适应市场变化的需要。在“边租边售”的同时，结合市场情况和自身发展，找到一个合适的“租售平衡点”，对于房地产企业至关重要。在中国人的传统观念中，如果经济条件允许，还是要拥有一套属于自己的住房。很多租房者未来还是要买房的，租房只是他们一段时期内的选择。房地产企业可以借助在住房租赁市场的经营运作，获取租客的认可，提高租客满意度，提升品牌在租客心目中的地位形象，从而培育更多的潜在购房人群，为争取这些购房者购买自己品牌的住房打下良好的基础，在日后住房销售市场的争夺中占得先机。

（二）面临挑战

1. 外部政策不够完善

长期以来，国内的住房租赁市场一直处于“自由生长”状态，不管是政府主导的公租房、廉租房，还是中介机构主导的商租房，都缺乏有力的政策指导和制度规范。“资格审核不透明”“一房多租”“价格不合理”“中介骗取租金”等各种乱象层出不穷，市场中各种角色“鱼龙混杂”。在这样的情况下，房地产企业作为住房租赁市场的“新学生”，缺乏经验又没有政策指引，在现阶段只能摸索前行，边学边做。另外，外部政策的时效性和连贯性也十分重要，这将对住房租赁市场的健康发展带来深远的影响。未来，随着国家层面对住房租赁市场的日益重视，相关的政策文件、制度办法将陆续出台，市场势必会更加规范。

2. 投资回报受到限制

租赁住房的收益来源是租金，销售住房的收益来源是售房款。两者比较来看，销售比出租有更多优势，比如资金数额大、回款周期短等。房地产行业注重资金的运转效率，只要有足够的资金流动性，房地产企业就能够开发运作更多的项目，为自身带来更大的利润。从某种程度上讲，一个新开盘项目的销售周期越短、回款越快，就越成功。而如果将开发的房子用于出租，投资回报的期限会拉长，投资回报的利润会降低，这将导致资金周转速度的下降和资金量的缩减，影响项目的收益水平，也不利于后续其他项目的开发。这显然是房地产企业所不愿看到的。

3. 租金收益测算难

租金受外部政策、城市区域、房屋属性、租住对象等许多因素的影响。根据具体项目情况，选择一种合适的测算方法，综合考虑各种因素，对租金进行测算，并在未来的出租周期内根据市场变化适时调整租金，对于房地产企业绝非易事。另外，租金测算具有一定的不可复制性，不同的住房租赁项目之间不能简单地套用同一种测算方式，同一个住房租赁项目在不同的时期也要调整租金测算方法，很难想象一次性的租金测算可以一劳永逸地贯穿整个出租周期。对租金的测算出现问题，带来的后果不言而喻，房屋的出租收益将直接受到影响，如果综合考虑对房屋维护管理的成本投入，甚至会出现亏损。

4. 未来资产如何处置

房地产企业可以通过自建自持、购买自持、租赁转租 3 种模式实现对租赁住房项目的经营运作。前两种模式下，房地产企业对项目资产具有所有权；租赁转租模式下，房地产企业通过租赁其他企业房屋、承租政府公租房或整合个人房源用于出租，进行品牌化运作。如果采用前两种模式，房地产企业会持有大量的固定资产和应收账款，开发从轻资产转向重资产，这将导致资金回流速度降低，影响流动性。此外，房地产企业还要考虑对项目资产如何管理，出租的周期如何确定，未来是否要“转租为售”或是“有租有售”等。

5. 融资渠道较少

房地产开发贷款是“拿地—开发—销售”传统运营模式下一种常见的融资方式。除贷款外，债券、信托、基金、REITs、ABS（资产证券化）、CMBS（商业房地产抵押货款支持证券）等也是房地产企业融资的重要手段。在住房租赁市场中，房地产企业持有住房或租赁住房一样需要资金支持，但目前这类融资产品较少，渠道有限。

在银行贷款方面，现只有建行推出了住房租赁贷款产品，未来人民银行或将出台住房租赁贷款相关政策。在其他融资渠道方面，现已有保利、碧桂园等大型房地产企业获批 REITs，但标的物均为混合资产，而且 REITs 的相关税收政策尚不完善，市场也缺乏发行经验。有限的融资渠道一定程度上也制约了房地产企业在住房租赁市场的经营和发展。

关于大连地区利用住房储蓄创新惠民的模式探析

中德住房储蓄银行　雷　明

2017 年，在大连市政府的积极推动下，成功地将住房储蓄业务体系引入大连，使得大连成为全国为数不多的，通过最为多样化的住房金融工具，为居民安居、宜居、乐居提供市场化与政策化住房融资手段共同支持的地区，进一步地普惠大连市居民。

为积极落实执行市政府引入住房储蓄业务体系的政策意图，进一步完善大连市多层次住房政策体系，促进大连市住房金融市场的健康发展，鼓励大连市居民参与住房储蓄，帮助更多的居民利用住房储蓄等住房融资方式实现住有所居、改善居住条件，在传统的住房储蓄业务体系的基础上，我们结合大连地区的政策、经济、金融、民生特点，对住房储蓄创新惠民的模式进行了以下研究。

一、住房储蓄的原理与特点

（一）住房储蓄的基本原理

住房储蓄业务是指住房储蓄银行通过与住房储蓄客户签订住房储蓄合同，吸收住房储蓄存款，达到约定的期限和金额等条件后，向住房储蓄客户发放住房储蓄类贷款的业务。[①] 这是一套在欧洲较为普遍的互助性住房融资体系，与商业按揭体系、住房公积金体系共同成为国际三大主流住房贷款方式。

居民参与住房储蓄业务体系，是为了获得住房消费贷款而进行有目的、有计划的专项储蓄，通过专项储蓄锁定远期贷款利率及额度，可获得低至 3.3% 年利率的固定低息贷款，从而在未来大幅降低购房成本，增强其住房消费能力。

（二）住房储蓄的特点

住房储蓄是一套封闭运行、专款专用的互助性住房融资体系，具有“民众自愿参

---

① 引自《中德住房储蓄银行管理暂行办法》，中国银行业监督管理委员会 2016 年 12 月 21 日颁布。

加、银行商业运作、政府政策支持”的普惠特点。住房储蓄产品还具有存贷一体化、金融杠杆率低、投融资计划性强、定价体系独立等特点。

住房储蓄贷款，除利率（3.3%）低于商业抵押贷款并保持固定不变外，其贷款用途也与商业按揭贷款有一定差异，可购买、建造、维护、租赁及装修用于居住目的的住房及建筑物，以及清偿上述行为产生的债务。

（三）住房储蓄的发展

住房储蓄起源于中国汉代，成熟于现代欧洲，在欧洲已有约150年的发展历史。住房储蓄体系及经营住房储蓄的银行在德国、英国、法国、美国、意大利、奥地利、克罗地亚、捷克、匈牙利、哈萨克斯坦等国家和地区广泛分布。在德国，住房储蓄体系为其战后重建和两德统一后解决居民住房问题发挥了极为重要的作用，对其房地产市场，特别是房价长期保持稳定也功不可没。

20世纪后期，中国进行的住房制度改革为住房消费金融的发展提供了丰沃的土壤。中国政府陆续将商业性住房按揭融资体系、政策性住房公积金管理体系、专业性住房储蓄业务体系引入中国，服务于社会、经济和民生的发展。这其中，2004年，在中德两国政府时任总理朱镕基和施罗德的倡导和推动下，中国建设银行与德国施威比豪尔住房储蓄银行共同出资，成立了专业经营住房储蓄业务的中德住房储蓄银行。随着住房储蓄银行逐渐试点成熟，经国务院和银监会①批准，住房储蓄被纳入国家多层次住房政策体系，并获准在全国更多地区开展业务。住房储蓄作为一种独特的住房金融工具，为中国百姓住房金融消费提供了更多的选择。

二、引入住房储蓄对区域金融体系和政策体系的意义

2012年，大连市政府积极推动将住房储蓄业务体系引入大连，几经周折，2017年12月，最终成功瓜熟蒂落。住房储蓄业务体系的引入，对大连地区社会、经济、产业、民生的发展都具有重要价值。

（一）丰富政策体系和手段，提高政府的社会保障能力

第一，在政策的引导下，住房储蓄作为金融工具，成为政府支持并保障居民通过市场化的手段解决住房问题的一个基本的住房消费融资渠道。第二，利用住房储蓄体系，在解决中低收入群体、住房保障群体等的住房消费和居住条件改善的方面，政府也能够更有效地着力提供帮助和保障，以弥补商业抵押贷款和公积金体系在民众惠及

① 即现银保监会。

面上的缺口。第三，大连市政府给予住房储蓄客户政府补贴，也成为进一步完善多层次住房政策体系的内容，引导居民参与住房储蓄，更为理性地规划住房消费。第四，按照大连市政府出台的政策意见，未来在制度设计、政策制定、行政资源配置、住房保障类资金归集与托管等方面，住房储蓄的引入，也将形成更大的政策创新空间。

（二）引导住房消费更趋理性，促进房地产行业稳定发展

一方面，住房储蓄具有较强的投融资计划性，能够引导居民对住房消费有所规划，提早安排，住房消费行为因而更具可预见性；另一方面，住房储蓄是一种杠杆率较低的金融工具，能够更为有效地规避投机型的住房消费，回归“房住不炒”的本源。与此同时，住房储蓄作为一个新的购房融资工具，引入后对区域房地产行业去库存、调产能、优化结构、稳定发展也能起到积极的作用。

（三）完善金融体系，稳定金融市场，防范和化解金融风险

住房储蓄引入金融市场，使得大连成为全国又一个齐聚三大住房金融工具的地区，区域金融体系进一步完善升级。低杠杆住房融资工具对市场的补充，对金融客群的分层引导，对住房融资需求的多样化解决，对高杠杆、高利率房贷的接替，对区域金融市场的有序竞争和稳健发展，对打好防范和化解金融风险的攻坚战也有积极帮助。

（四）降低住房消费融资成本，帮助居民安居乐业

住房储蓄融资工具的介入，将在一定幅度上降低居民住房消费融资的成本。对符合条件的客户群体，还能够实现以低利率的住房储蓄贷款替换高利率的商业抵押贷款。这对于当下数量可观的“房奴”一族，以及即将步入“房奴”队列的居民来说，无疑是一个有力的帮助。特别是对于中低收入群体，在装修、租赁和偿还私人因住房消费产生的债务等方面，住房储蓄也有很大的价值空间。还贷压力的降低，不仅能够帮助居民适当改善生活品质，促进居民消费，也会进一步提升居民幸福指数，增强社会的稳定性。

三、住房储蓄创新惠民模式的探析

在传统的居民互助参与的基本模式之外，针对大连当地实际情况和住房消费市场的特点，住房储蓄在以下几个方面也能够积极创新，有所作为。

（一）政策保障惠民模式

这是一种以政府职能机构为主导的创新惠民模式。在这种模式下，政府将一定的

公共资金以住房储蓄方式存管，资金的权属、使用和收益都基本不发生变化。但基于住房储蓄的原理，将会由此产生额外的固定利率低息贷款权利。这部分低息贷款权利，可以由政府制定合理的惠民政策规则，提供给指定的住房保障群体使用，比如就业落户的大学生、政府引进人才、转业退役军人、中低收入住房保障群体等。而这部分定向群体则不需要自行存款（这也符合政策保障的特点），即可享受由政府提供的包括低息贷款权利在内的配套住房保障政策，构建起“政府主导、金融助力、市场运作、百姓受益”的全新政策保障模式。

政策保障体系引入住房储蓄的这种运作模式，既不增加政府的负担，公共资金还可获得额外的固定低息贷款权益，进而创新政策保障模式，突显政策惠民的效应；由银行协助管理的资金不仅能够自主可控，还能够保障资金运作的规范透明，同时通过住房储蓄封闭管理体系的自平衡，保障资金的流动性和政策的公平性。

（二）企业/组织主导惠民模式

这是一种以企业或组织为主导的创新模式，基本运行原理与“政策性资金惠民模式”相近，其管理主体为企业或组织。企业在资金正常使用的情况下，会额外累积固定低息贷款权利。低息贷款权利的受益群体为企业或组织的内部成员。这种模式在不违反财经规定的情况下，还能够合理合法地为职工创造一定的政策福利。

（三）租赁市场惠民模式

十九大明确“房住不炒”的基本要求，提出“加快建立多主体供给、多渠道保障、租购并举的住房制度”，在十九大之后也进一步引发了一系列关于“租购并举、租购同权”的理论探讨与实践探索，使得住房租赁市场的发展提升到了国家基本发展策略和民生保障战略的高度，进一步多元化、多模式地进行提速。

住房储蓄的功能和特性，在很多方面也能够契合住房租赁市场和交易的特点。以下几个方面的创新发展值得尝试。

一是对于住房租赁平台或项目，通过专项基金、房屋租金或闲置资金的存管，产生固定低息贷款权利，由平台或项目管理方控管，由租房客户申请使用。公租房、廉租房项目非常适用这种方式。

二是对于中长期租户，可以对住房储蓄进行基于同一交易事项的存、贷主体分离的创新。由承租方将租金按期存入住房储蓄账户，直至租约满期。住房储蓄体系一次性将全额租金以住房储蓄贷款的方式发放给出租人，这样，交易双方基本权益都未减少，而出租方可提前获得现金流。

三是对于将来可以进行租转购的项目，承租人通过有计划地加入住房储蓄，可以帮助其提前进行购房融资规划，在未来行使购房权利时，较大幅度地减少购房融资成本。

四、在创新进程中还需要解决的问题

（一）外部政策的引导和支持

一方面，住房储蓄作为新引入大连地区的金融工具，在其发展和创新中，还需要政府给予积极有力的政策支持和引导，以利于促进发展，尽早发挥其积极效用；另一方面，对于这一新事物在新环境中的发展，也期待监管政策给予更多的支持，鼓励和指导其创新发展，并且对创新与试错给予合理范围内的包容。

（二）基础产品的改造和创新

对住房储蓄产品本身，需要用发展和变革的眼光，由传统一对一的模式，向着一对多、多对一等模式进行创新。同时，围绕产品管理，也需要对价格体系、流动性管理方法、准入和退出机制、客户与产品生命周期衔接等方面进行改造和优化。

（三）产品理念的传播与深耕

住房储蓄引入的时间还比较短，现阶段还是“藏在闺中人不识”，政府、企业和广大居民还都不了解，更谈不上利用其业务特点解决实际问题了。大力进行宣传推广，加快住房储蓄产品理念的传播，适应本地政策特点，扎扎实实地深耕市场，树立起品牌、口碑和美誉，是需要一步一步向前迈进的。

（四）服务体系的完善与支撑

一方面，住房储蓄银行刚刚成立不久，自身的服务体系还需要抓紧建立完善，更需要努力突破物理机构对业务创新和发展的制约。另一方面，住房储蓄更有效地发挥对区域金融体系补充的功效，更好地发挥稳定金融体系、防范和化解金融风险的效能，进而更好地获得自身与外部经济金融体系的协调同步发展，也还需要本地政策性机构、商业性金融机构等方面的理解与帮助。

深挖存量房贷客户资源，夯实住房租赁基础

陕西省分行　李　楠

一、建行住房租赁业务发展情况

（一）业务发展背景

党的十九大报告中明确提出“坚持房子是用来住的，不是用来炒的定位，加快建立多主体供给、多渠道保障、租购并举”的住房政策。报告中提出的“租购并举”“多渠道保障”进一步明确了加快推进租赁住房建设、培育和发展住房租赁市场是贯彻落实“房子是用来住的，不是用来炒的”这一定位的重要举措，是保障人民住有所居的重要内容，是实现全面建成小康社会住有所居目标的重大民生工程。

建设银行住房租赁战略就是聚焦解决社会痛点问题，培育支持住房租赁市场发展，落实“房子是用来住的，不是用来炒的”的战略举措，也是建设银行积极响应以习近平同志为核心的党中央的号召，学习贯彻十九大精神，为国分忧，为民谋福，找准社会痛点，契合人民居住需求，用金融力量改变社会中不平衡和不充分问题的实际担当。

（二）住房租赁主要内容

十九大明确了租购并举的政策发展方向。建设银行先行一步，领先于同业布局住房租赁市场这片新蓝海，提出住房租赁战略。住房租赁战略主要包括三部分内容：第一是依托“新一代”核心系统技术，在国内率先搭建能够精准匹配地方政府和市场监管运营需求的住房租赁综合服务平台，为政府、租赁企业、租客、房东、中介机构、金融机构等所有市场参与方提供一站式、全流程线上综合服务；第二是配套推出一系列金融和非金融服务产品，满足租赁企业和居民的融资需求；第三是组建专业化公司，作为市场主体，深度参与住房租赁市场，动员组织房源供给，支持改善住房市场租售结构，努力提高百姓租住品质。

（三）业务发展优势

住房租赁战略是建行的新兴业务，对于全行未来业务转型至关重要。目前建行发展住房租赁业务的主要思路是通过打造平台来规范市场、活客获客，树立住房租赁行业标杆。这里面存在一个问题：建行的住房租赁综合服务平台和市场上已存在的服务平台相比，胜在功能全面，特别是对于政府管理层监管角度来说意义重大；但是在市场化房源拓展方面，建行的系统从零开始起步，就系统功能和客户储备方面来说，建行平台与那些深耕多年的住房租赁服务平台相比并无优势。发展住房租赁业务，我们的优势在哪里？

随着我国房地产业的迅猛发展，银行房地产金融类业务蒸蒸日上，其中以建行的业务基础最牢，发展势头最猛。从全国范围来看，建行的存量房贷客户超过 1 000 万，个人贷款余额更是突破 4.5 万亿元。经市场调研发现，存量房贷客户中大多数客群存在房屋租赁的需求。

这些存量房贷客户是建行宝贵的资源财富，而这个财富是建行独有而其他企业或机构无法复制的。能否盘活存量房贷客户，将其引导转化为住房租赁客户，推动住房租赁业务快速发展呢？

二、方案设计思路及意义

（一）整体思路

住房租赁战略整体发展思路不变，在住房租赁综合服务平台原有基础上，开发第 6 个子平台：存量房贷客户服务平台（以下简称“平台”）。平台围绕盘活存量房贷客户的这一理念，基于 PLPM 系统及公积金管理系统中的存量房贷客户，以为房贷客户提供商业贷款、维修资金、物业管理等业务线上办理渠道为抓手，依托大数据系统，从用户信息、用户行为、用户偏好等多个维度分析用户需求。通过深度挖掘存量房贷客户潜力，盘活个人存量闲置房源，探索“存房”新模式，促进房主、租赁企业和租客达成住房长租交易，增加稳定的长租房源，联动促进其他传统业务的发展，为建行带来更多综合效益。

（二）目标客户及需求分析

平台服务主要面向以下两类客户：

（1）商贷新增、存量客户。

（2）公积金贷款新增、存量客户。

个贷客户的统一特征是有房可居，客户经理已核实了借款人员的身份、家庭收入、个人征信等信息，保证了客户的还款能力，因此，个贷客户属于建行优质客户群体。根据所属行业的不同，可以将存量房贷客户划分为公务员、小微企业主、企事业单位人员、个体工商户等多类客群。

（三）方案实施意义

1. 促进住房租赁业务快速发展

相较于普通客户来说，房贷存量客户经过建行审核，在信用、收入、房源拥有情况等方面具备成为住房租赁客户的条件。建设银行拥有超过 1 000 万的存量房贷客户，如果充分挖掘这部分客户资源，将会带动建行住房租赁业务飞速发展。

2. 提升个贷客户服务体验

目前建行个贷相关业务办理渠道主要在线下，如果存量房贷客户服务平台能够为房贷客户提供线上办理贷款试算、贷款申请、贷款进度跟踪，以及贷后信息查询、提前还款等业务，将会大大提升建行个贷客户的服务体验。

3. 为建行带来更多综合效益

存量房贷客户是建行优质客户，这些已经带给建行大量利润的客户群体，通常也有其他潜在金融需求。

（1）个金。针对这部分客户可以联动营销信用卡业务、分期贷款、银保理财、贵金属交易等传统个金业务。

（2）个贷。房贷客户往往也同时存在个人快贷、家装贷、汽车分期等消费信贷需求，因此个人住房贷款客户亦是消费类信贷的主力军。

（3）普惠金融。如果房贷客户符合建行普惠金融政策，普惠金融相关服务也是进一步提升客户黏性和贡献度的有益途径，例如助业贷款、小微企业贷款等融资产品，此外还存在 POS 商户的商机。

（4）其他服务。通过引进后续电商服务、家政服务、托管服务等一系列合作商户，并为客户提供基于位置、兴趣等方面的社交服务，逐步把平台产生的流量转化为建行的业务成果，在支付结算、存款、信贷融资等方面获取综合收益。

三、方案设计具体内容

（一）总体架构

1. 总体目标

盘活、挖掘建行存量房贷客户资源，推动建行住房租赁业务前进，同时也能带动建行各项业务共同发展。

2. 内涵

该平台联动建行各业务管理系统，利用大数据技术等，分析用户金融需求，实施精准营销。

3. 主要思路

围绕盘活存量房贷客户理念，发挥金融和科技优势，建立存量房贷客户服务平台。一是通过提供现有个人商业贷款相关业务、公积金贷款自助查询、维修资金的线上办理渠道，吸引存量房贷客户转化为平台客户；二是利用大数据技术等，结合建行客户信息，分析客户金融需求，利用平台实现精准营销；三是引导存量房贷客户成为存房客户，以及传统业务客户，深挖存量房贷客户潜力，让房贷客户为建行贡献出更大的价值。

（二）平台功能

平台主要包括以下五大功能。

1. 贷款业务线上办理功能

主要包括建行贷款试算、线上贷款申请、现有贷后业务办理（如提前还款、变更还款账户等业务的线上预约及办理）等。

2. 不动产盘活功能（“存房中心”）

针对家庭多套房的持有客户，平台可为客户提供房屋交易撮合功能，实现存房到建行，盘活不动产。具体功能包括房屋出租信息发布、租金评估、交易撮合、资金收付、租务管理等，为房主、租赁企业和租客搭建房屋租赁交易桥梁。

3. 精准营销功能

平台将对接公积金管理系统、建行新一代 PLPM 系统、楼盘大数据系统、个人业务系统以及对公业务系统等相关系统，通过系统存量数据以及本平台用户使用行为来分析用户需求，定向地为不同需求的用户推送适合他的金融产品信息，并联动行内业务办理提示，实现对目标用户的精准营销。

4. 金融资产增值服务功能

提供个人理财、银保产品、黄金、基金等金融产品的购买服务。

5. 便捷城市生活服务功能

为用户提供公积金、维修基金查询、缴存、提取等功能，同时结合建行智慧社区平台，为用户提供物业管理、家政服务等一系列的智能生活配套服务。

（三）平台渠道

平台包括个人电脑端网站、手机 App、微信平台公众号 3 个渠道，为后台管理员提供个人电脑端管理系统。各个渠道之间数据实时同步。

（四）客户盘活思路

1. “来客”

以建行PLPM系统数据库中的存量信贷客户为目标、引导存量房贷客户关注存量房贷客户服务平台，为平台“来客”提供基础。

2. “留客”

提供一揽子线上金融综合服务，为“留客”提供抓手。

3. “转化”

通过“信息大数据分析”“客户行为分析模型”筛选目标客户，实行精准营销，为客户“转化”提供技术支持。

4. “落地”

通过信息匹配、资金支付、小秘书服务等手段的配置，为存房交易全流程线上办理提供技术支撑，为客户提供其他条线的金融产品和服务。

（五）业务流程

平台所有功能模块从用途分类，可分为“信息查询”及“业务办理”两大类。对于“业务办理”类功能，从业务流转路径来分，可分为“建行行内业务”及“与外部机构及系统对接”两类。

针对“与外部机构及系统对接”类业务，例如公积金、维修资金、物业管理、家政服务等功能，主要将外部机构相关业务网站嵌入本系统，以链接外部网站的形式进行数据交换及业务办理；针对个贷相关业务，将其业务办理渠道由线下迁移至线上，通过存量房贷客户服务平台实现；针对住房租赁类业务，与建融家园、建融公寓等平台打通关联，实现客户引流；针对建行特色业务“存房”，单独开发“存房中心”模块。“存房中心”具体交易流程如下所示。

1. 存房交易撮合

房主提出存房业务申请以及对于租金的预期，系统结合房东与住房租赁企业双方提交的需求，精准匹配房东与住房租赁企业。同时对房源进行在线验真和收益在线评估，并将评估结果推送至长租企业，长租企业与房主通过本平台线上即时通信，沟通达成合作意向后，双方完成线下看房、签订存房协议、支付租金等业务流程。

2. 房租试算

利用建行楼盘大数据系统，为客户提供房屋信息租金试算，分片区租金价格查询、信息发布等功能，使用该部分功能的客户自动进入建行存房业务的目标客户储备数据库。

3. 线上交易

线上交易流程为：存房客户线上业务申请—系统长租权价值评估—租赁企业匹配—租赁企业抢单（二级支行系统通知）—线下看房—租赁协议签订—线上租金支付—房源同步上线“CCB 建融公寓”—租赁企业租赁运作及租后管理。

若未达成协议，则信息重新匹配，继续上述流程，至交易成功/申请人撤单/三次匹配失败为止。

4. 业务咨询与投诉

为建行“存房”业务提供服务及后台保障支持。

（六）盈利模式

通过该平台深度挖掘存量房贷客户，主要可以促进建行以下类型的业务发展。

1. 住房租赁类

主要包括租房客户的引导和存房交易撮合及租金沉淀。

2. 个人金融类业务

包括账户开立、信用卡业务、理财产品、商业保险、贵金属等产品销售。

3. 个人贷款类业务

包括快贷、装修贷、车贷等个人类贷款发放。

4. 小微企业贷款类业务

主要包括助业贷款投放。

5. 其他业务类

包括电商服务、家政服务、托管服务等。

通过平台的搭建最终带动全行综合效益提升。

浅析 CCB 建融家园服务优化对住房租赁的影响

贵州省分行　龙勤雯

一、CCB 建融家园概述

（一）建融家园的有关概念

为突破自身发展，实现全行改革创新和经济转型升级，建设银行通过制定并实施“三大战略”为未来发展指明方向。“三大战略”是指金融科技、住房租赁、普惠金融。其中“住房租赁”是建行为响应十九大报告中指出的“加快建立多主体供给、多渠道保障、租购并举的住房制度”的有关精神而启动的发展项目。该项目提出“长租即长住，长住即安家”的现代住房概念，并打出“要租房，到建行”“房子是用来住的，租挺好”的新口号。蓝海项目的实施是致力于实现住房“共享”，减少甚至于杜绝炒房现象。为助力蓝海项目的开展，加快落实住房租赁的战略决策，CCB 建融家园应运而生。它是建行打造的共享云租赁平台，旨在依托建行作为国有大行的丰富资源，为广大租房群体提供真实、高品质的居住空间和一系列租房金融服务。

（二）建融家园平台搭建的原因

一方面，要想将住房租赁从理论化为实践，真真切切地成为造福民众的实际工作，需要依托实质性的平台空间达到真正意义上的资源共享。建设银行以“建设”起家，在多年发展中多次成功转型，近年来随着住房压力的不断上升，拓展了住房贷款相关的银行业务。而作为国有银行之一，建设银行成为广大居民的选择，并深受群众信任。在群众看来，由建行牵头打造的住房租赁平台更具安全性，这是在建融家园宣传过程中建行所占据的天然优势。

另一方面，市面上五花八门的租房 App 层出不穷，不少租房 App 披着房屋租赁平台的外壳，以“信用租房”为诱饵，让租客在不知不觉中踏入其精心布置的网贷陷阱；部分租客反映在某些 App 上租房并提出看房请求后，遇到线下实际房源与发布房源不符，更有出租方存在发布虚假房源的情况；住房租赁至今仍缺乏有效监管措施，长租业务存在监管盲区。

因此，为解决国内当下买房难、租房贵、房源不可靠等问题，建设银行联合多家房地产公司及政府房屋住建部门，为房屋真实性提供保障，扮演资源整合者的角色，搭建“建融家园”作为房屋租赁平台，旨在为租房民众提供一个拥有放心、安心、可靠的房源的云平台。而在整个过程中也将保证租房条款的公开透明，维护出租方、租客的个人隐私安全，让租客不再担心信息泄露和在不知情的情况下“被网贷”。

二、建融家园手机端服务优化的必要性

随着网络的飞速发展，各行各业已经踏入互联网时代，而智能手机的普及更助推了互联网对居民日常生活的渗透。“低头一族”不仅是对当下社会普遍现象的侧写，更强调了当今科技发展下手机的重要地位。手机作为每日陪伴每个人时间最长的电子设备，一款好用的手机软件就是对产品或项目最快、最高效的推广宣传手段。建设银行要推动“三大战略”的实施，将蓝海项目的开展落到实处，通过对建融家园手机 App 的开发及优化能够带来的好处是可以想象的。

相对于较为笨重且价格较高的电脑，智能手机可以说是各个经济阶层群众的日常用品。无论是初入社会的年轻人，还是事业有成的中年人，都离不开对智能手机的使用。这也代表着，相较于电视、网页、报纸杂志，手机 App 的使用频率将会更高，受众也更广。因此，为了让更多人了解建行的“住房租赁”，让蓝海项目走入家家户户，让人人培养出使用“建融家园”这一云租赁平台的习惯，手机软件的开发势在必行。

此外，一个好用的手机 App 本身即是一种宣传。要想让民众形成依赖，首先 App 本身提供的服务必须能够满足用户要求。对“建融家园”手机 App 的不断优化，不但能够令用户看到建设银行在致力为民众提供便捷化服务的诚意，也能让建行在同业住房租赁项目上置于行业领先的地位，因为在租房业务发展之初，能够抢占市场的必定是服务内容随着用户需求及未来发展情况不断更新优化的平台。

三、问题归纳及案例分析

“建融家园”App 使用过程中存在的问题也不容忽视，与应用市场中已趋成熟的房屋租赁平台相比，“建融家园”的开发尚且处于起步阶段，因此，先人一步的各类优秀租房软件为建融家园的服务优化指明了方向。

（一）建融家园 App 存在的问题

1. 作为租房方能够获取的与房屋相关的信息过少

在通过审核已发布的房源信息中，大多数出租房源仅有一张房屋内部照片，且发布信息的中介没有完善发布过程中对房屋配套设施的选择，房源介绍也多为一句话的简单介绍，租客无法获取更详细的房屋信息。

2. 中介信息录入不完善

打开租房中介评价能够发现，无论是中介还是经纪人，都缺乏个人或公司照片，若租客想要上门看房，无法凭借手头信息核实中介身份，也就无法保证中介经纪人及中介公司的真实可靠。

3. App 使用缺乏智能客服及人工服务端口

在 App 使用过程中如遇到问题，暂无途径能够通过 App 自身获得解答或答复。

4. 出租方与租客缺乏有效的沟通渠道

租客在查看完 App 内出租页面提供的房屋信息后，只能直接申请预约看房，被动等待出租方的联络，无法就获得信息的困惑与出租方进行沟通；而中介一方仅能通过拨打电话与租客进行交流，部分租客不愿意在尚未决定是否签约的情况下将联系方式透露给中介，平台缺乏保护租客个人隐私的渠道。

（二）贝壳找房的优质服务

贝壳找房是当前市场上使用人数较多的一款房屋租赁软件，各个手机系统均可下载使用。除去与建融家园提供的租赁平台的基本使用内容外，它提供的租客与出租方的在线交流功能，是当前的建融家园所不具备且极具参考价值的。

在贝壳找房中，租客可以首先通过 App 与出租方在线联系。这一功能可令双方无须通过额外的联络方式进行沟通，保障了交易双方的隐私，使得双方能够自由选择联络、回复的时间，并在未来双方可能产生纠纷时，平台能够有查验的依据。其次，在线交流的过程中可以发送图片及语音，便于租客就自身疑惑对出租方进行提问并获得答复。

四、对策及建议

通过手机软件的推广，能够令更多的群众了解建行的“三大战略”，切身体会到建设银行在此过程中承担的企业责任，感受到建行的企业文化。“建融家园”的服务优化能够使百姓享受到建行提供的优质服务，将建行的服务从线下延伸至线上，从金融机构的基本服务逐步延伸至生活中的方方面面。根据前文的案例分析，我总结出以下一些“建融家园”可以采取的服务优化方向。

（一）针对个人出租方及中介

第一，应当根据发布方所选择的户型，强制要求发布方针对户型中包括的每一个房间，提供至少一张对应实拍图，发布方也可选择拍摄一段房屋相关视频供租房客户观看；针对房屋配套设施，要求发布方如实选择房屋内配套设施，不可不选。

其二，要求发布房源的中介经纪人及中介公司上传本人或公司照片，帮助上门看房的租客核实，减少实际见面看房过程中可能产生的风险。

（二）针对 App 自身服务优化

其一，参考建设银行手机银行中的智能助手小微，首先设置智能客服解答客户在软件使用过程中遇到的基本、常见问题，避免客户无处下手、求解无门。而人工服务端口可在 App 后期推广较为成功后，视该阶段发展状况再逐步接入，这样既能满足客户基本使用功能的需求，也能暂时缓解所需配备的人工方面的压力。

其二，参考贝壳找房加入在线联系功能，让租客与出租方能够及时沟通，这样不仅使得租客与出租方的交流更高效，也能够通过平台保护双方个人隐私，还能在产生纠纷时有可以参考的依据。

五、总结

根据上文分析可以得出，CCB“建融家园”的优化对推动建设银行住房租赁的实施有着重要作用。在进行上述优化整改后，首先可以为租房客户提供更加真实可查的房源信息，从“建融家园”平台即可就自身需求对房源进行初步筛选，这满足了租房者的需求，同时也使出租方发布的房源真实性更为可控，避免图文不符的情况。其次，对中介信息的补全，也进一步控制了“建融家园”平台的房屋交易过程中可能产生的风险，侧面来说更是对客户与中介间线下看房接触的安全保障。再次，智能助手的接入使得客户在使用 App 遇见常见问题时，能够得到及时、全天 24 小时在线待机的答复，这有助于客户了解“建融家园”的使用及 App 的推广。最后，对发布房源信息功能的完善，也为出租方带来了更为良好的服务体验，保障出租方应当享有的自身权益，有利于打造租客及出租方双方满意的租赁平台。

金融科技篇

金融科技平台应用推广模式的探讨

广西区分行　杨　蕾

中国建设银行总行党委通过对建行传统业务优势和未来发展趋势的分析，于2018年提出了“三大战略”，其中金融科技战略作为重要支撑，承担了提供服务手段、拓展业务领域、重塑业务流程的重任。金融科技战略在行内的主要表现形式为“新一代”重要产品的推广深耕，让本行员工通过产品组合为客户提供精准服务；在行外主要是多个金融科技平台的推广应用，客户通过自主使用建行提供的平台或渠道获得建行服务。两者的有机结合，通过大数据分析将提高建行客户的黏性，拓展建行的获客渠道，使建行更好地为客户提供服务，提高建行的创新经营能力和精细化管理水平。总行的这一战略决策不仅高瞻远瞩，执行的好坏也是关系到未来建行业务发展走向的重要一环。下面将着重针对金融科技平台的应用推广模式进行探讨。

一、金融科技平台概述

目前建行推出了14个金融科技平台。

（一）平台名称、主要涉及业务领域和客群

平台名称、主要涉及业务领域和客群见表4.1。

表4.1　平台名称、主要涉及业务领域和客群

平台名称	平台的目标	客群	接入渠道
住房租赁综合服务平台	利用建行住房服务领域领先优势，为政府、企业以及个人提供住房租赁服务，落实租购并举、改变住房消费观念、促进住房租赁市场健康发展	政府部门、拥有房源的企业、中介，以及个人用户	PC（个人计算机）网站、手机App、微信公众号等
智慧社区云平台	通过人工智能和物联网技术实现智慧社区服务，提升社区服务和居民生活品质，打造社区金融生态圈	单个物业公司、集团公司（地产商/物业公司）、对小区统一运营的指定运营商或运营公司	PC网站、手机App、微信公众号等

（续表）

平台名称	平台的目标	客群	接入渠道
安心养老综合服务平台	打造建行、政府、养老机构、养老者四位一体的良性生态环境，全面支撑机构养老、社区养老、居家养老三种养老模式的实际运作	地方政府、养老机构及养老服务商、老人及其子女	PC 网站、手机 App
公益教育综合服务平台	打造“科技 + 教育 + 公益”三位一体的智慧教育综合服务模式，利用科技力量推进教育公平和提高教育质量	各地市教育局、学校、教育机构、教师、学生、家长	PC 网站和手机 App 等
党群综合服务平台	提供党建、工会、团建为一体的综合解决方案，建设标准合规、全覆盖、全流程的党群综合服务平台，创造线上线下相互融合、相互促进的党群工作新格局	各级党委组织部、大系统客户、地方工委等	手机 App、PC 网站、微信公众号
智慧政务综合服务平台	构建“互联网 + 政务 + 金融”新业态，打造智慧政务新模式	政府部门	手机 App、PC 网站、微信公众号
善行宗教事务服务平台	针对宗教事务提供一站式、整体综合解决方案	宗教管理部门、宗教团体、宗教院校、宗教场所、信教群众	PC 网站、手机 App
企业采购服务平台	搭建社会化商业平台，实现互联网 + 采购	提供采购业务的企业	PC 网站
企业共享服务平台	采用人工智能及大数据技术的工具和方法，为资金或资源需求双方提供信息发布、需求撮合、商机推荐等综合服务	企业客户	PC 网站、手机 App
商户共享服务平台	提供“聚合支付 + 行业应用”的商户综合服务，成为连接商户、银行、消费者的纽带	大中型商户、商盟商圈、服务类商户，以及个人商户、小微商户	PC 网站、手机 App、微信公众号
同业合作平台	整合建设银行在科技、业务、管理、渠道等多方优势，提供科技服务，实现建行与合作机构之间的共建、共享、共赢，以产品化的方式共同创造商业价值，助力合作伙伴降低成本、防控风险、提高效率、优化体验	中小银行和非银行金融机构（比如证券、保险、基金、财务公司等）	
区块链应用平台	贸易融资区块链平台具备联盟链的性质，在“中国贸易金融区块链联盟”主导下，协助建立、建设具体的规范和标准，开发实施相关国内信用证、福费廷、国际保理、保函等业务应用	各大银行	
公有云服务平台	提供云服务器、云存储、网络等信息技术基础设施资源和行业应用、金融服务在内的多项技术对接服务	对公有云资源有需求的合作客户	
开放银行管理平台	将建行有优势的产品功能嵌入第三方场景，为第三方提供标准化的便捷接入服务	政府部门、企事业单位、个体工商户等	

（二）平台特点

1. 各平台的客群不同

按使用平台的客户不同类型划分，有对公对私客户、政府或企业客户、大中小企业客户、老中青客户。不同客群的服务需求和行为习惯很不一样。

2. 各平台的功能差异大

平台涉及的领域有住房租赁、商业、物业、企业、教育、养老、党群团务和宗教事务管理等。各领域的差别很大，平台的功能和使用场景各不相同。

3. 各平台的使用频度不同

平台功能和服务对象的差别，造成用户使用平台的频度差别很大，同一个平台的用户使用频度也可能存在较大差异。例如党群平台，党员党费每月一般只交 1 次，党务工作者使用系统的频度则要高得多。又如智慧社区平台，物业费有可能每季度或者半年才交一次，但停车费每个月交甚至按次交都有可能。

4. 各平台的客群之间有交叉

平台以功能领域划分，对应客户的多重社会身份和应用场景，必然会产生客群的交集。例如某公务员是党员，有孩子，住在商业小区，其年老的父母住在养老社区，则该客户同时可能会是建行党群、公益教育、智慧社区、安心养老平台的使用客户。平台大数据分析正是通过各方面的数据汇总，生成客户数据画像，准确反映客户的经济和信用状况。

（三）平台延伸的商机和发展趋势

由于 14 个平台涉及的领域广，所起的作用和面临的商机各不相同，所以有些能带来更多的经济效益，有些更能体现社会效益。同时 14 个平台提供的功能或服务并非都为建行所独有，不少平台社会上已有同类产品，甚至已有品牌效应。但即使是同类平台，建行与其他平台之间并不是简单的竞争关系。建行不是靠平台运营盈利，而是希望通过搭建平台为客户提供增值服务，形成资金流在建行的体内循环，结果还是回归金融服务。确实也应该看到，目前 14 个平台还处于起步期，发展前景并不明朗，各平台的营销难易程度也不一样，最终肯定是有的平台会发展得很好，成为建行的核心品牌，而有的平台可能在推广过程中被淘汰，后续还有可能推出新的平台。

二、移动互联网时代的网民喜好和获客渠道

当前社会早已进入移动互联网时代，主要表现形式为以智能手机为代表的移动端广泛使用和 App 对用户的争夺已经进入红海时期，流量入口的头部效应明显。再好的

平台，如果没有好的引流入口，就算投入巨资拉来了新用户，也将很快在信息洪流中被淹没。下面将从网民上网的主要设备和应用情况进行分析。

（一）个人电脑的客户使用情况

根据艾瑞咨询《2017 年 PC 指数排名解析》分析报告，中国网民整体由 PC 端向移动端迁移，但 PC 端网站流量整体上持续维持稳定。根据艾瑞 iUserTracker 监测数据显示，2017 年 PC 端网站月度覆盖人数最高为 5.30 亿人，最低为 5.04 亿人，两者差距整体不大。在具体月度覆盖人数头部网站方面，搜索、社交、购物仍是人们生活的主旋律，以 BAT（百度、阿里巴巴、腾讯的简称）为代表的网站常年雄踞头部位置，吸引庞大的用户群体。用户对 PC 端及移动端的应用行为呈现交互趋势，移动端与 PC 端是相互辅助，而不是相互替代。

（二）手机 App 分析

网民移动端使用以手机 App 为代表。

1. 手机操作系统情况

PChome 网站 2018 年 5 月 4 日发布的《手机系统市场份额出炉：安卓占有绝对优势》指出，市场调研机构 Kantar 发布了 2018 年第一季度移动操作系统市场份额数据，其中中国市面上安卓系统占比为 77.4%，苹果 IOS 系统占比为 22.1%，其他手机操作系统占比可忽略不计，这一趋势在近几年不会有大的变动。

2. App 的用户行为习惯

品途网 2018 年 1 月 16 日极光大数据发表的《2017 年 App 榜单大盘点：谁昙花一现，谁领跑全年》显示，2017 年度 App 市场渗透率前 1 000 名榜单中有 78% 是去年的老面孔。第四季度每个移动网民手机中平均装有 40 个 App。12 个月里人均下载 4.13 款 App，卸载 3.42 款 App。

网民 App 使用习惯如图 4.17 所示。

排名前 10 名的 App 榜单如表 4.2 所示。

显而易见，娱乐休闲类 App 占据优势，微信和 QQ 由于其社交属性，流量入口的霸主地位近几年内不可能被撼动。

在银行类 App 中，中国建设银行 App、中国工商银行 App 和农行掌上银行 App 名列网上银行 App 市场渗透率前三。建行手机银行具有一定的市场优势和知名度。

建行这几年也陆续推出了与业务相关的 App，表 4.3 为在苹果应用商店搜索到的建行原有 App，不包含与 14 个平台相关的或与业务无关的 App。除“中国建设银行”App 外，其余 App 的影响力都较弱。

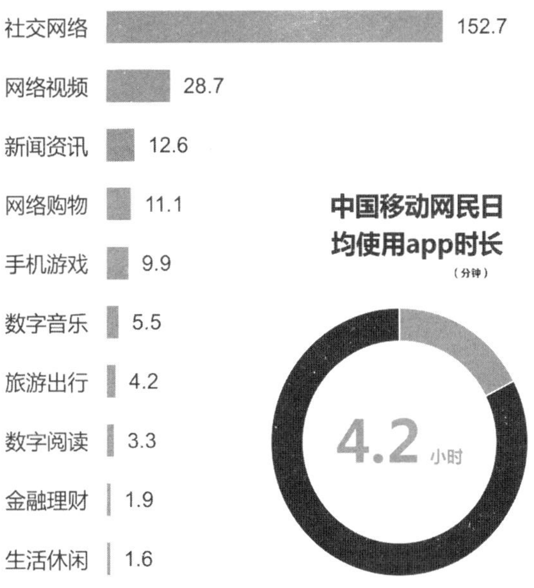

图 4.1　2017 年 12 月移动网民日均使用时长前 10 名的 App 类型

资料来源：极光大数据。

表 4.2　2017 年 12 月市场透率排名前 10 名的 App

2017 年 12 月排名	较去年变化	应用名称	市场渗透率（%）	同比（去年 12 月）（%）
1	—	微信	84. 72	-1. 4
2	—	QQ	71. 06	-6. 0
3	—	手机淘宝	53. 39	7. 7
4	—	支付宝	53. 37	11. 9
5	+2	WiFi 万能钥匙	44. 74	11. 7
6	+3	腾讯视频	43. 12	18. 3
7	-2	搜狗输入法	41. 26	-1. 1
8	—	爱奇艺	40. 38	3. 1
9	+4	高德地图	38. 92	30. 7
10	-4	手机百度	36. 25	-11. 9

表 4.3　建行推出的 App 列表

App 名称	业务或功能	最后更新日期
建行惠懂你	解决小微企业“小、频、急”的融资需求	2018
中国建设银行	建行个人用手机银行	2018
建行企业银行	建行企业用手机银行	2018
建行善融商城	善融商务	2018
建行云商通	为商户提供“互联网 + 收单”支付产品	2016
建行短信银行	为短信金融用户打造	2014

（三）微信和“小程序”

微信小程序作为腾讯公司的一款产品，于 2017 年 1 月 9 日正式上线。虽然推出的时间不长，但由于其独特的设计理念和依托微信强大的导流效应，而越来越显示出生命力。“小程序在朋友圈、公众号、微信群、个人号之间成了一个连接器，把这个封闭的圈子生态造活了。微信通过守住用户的时间，让微信从简单的社交产品转向成为链接人的一个全功能性的超级 App，成为腾讯的增量杀器。”①

小程序非常适合低频长尾的应用服务。“2017 年 5 月，第一个爆款小程序‘匿名聊聊’一夜之间病毒式传播，上线短短 5 个小时，创造 1 700 万访问量。在没有任何广告费、纯粹靠社交裂变的情况下，礼物说小程序实现了 3 天 10 万单的小小里程碑。拼多多通过在微信中利用小程序拼团、抢红包、零元购、助力购等关系链裂变模式，两年多做到 3 亿用户、千亿元年成交总量。”② “林清玄读书会”用小程序实现公众号低成本半年涨粉数百万③。小程序给企业带来的新用户增量，是小程序增量价值的一个缩影。而以小程序链接更多生活场景的用户再造活，是企业活跃用户和服务用户的一种新的衍生形态，让企业有了一种全新的触角来触达更多的用户。

三、各金融平台的应用推广模式分析和存在的问题

从目前已陆续上线的平台看，除嵌入式 API（应用程序接口）应用外，主要采用 PC 网站和 App 相结合的模式进行应用推广，各平台的发展也很不平衡。这除了与各地的客群资源不同和建行在当地的影响力密切相关外，平台的应用推广模式对其也有较大影响。其中最为突出的是多个 App 的下载与安装使用，已经成为必须面对和亟待解决的问题。

从前面的分析可知，14 个平台几乎不可能成为大多数客户的高频使用场景，主要为低频分散应用。PC 端主要提供给企业和个人的深度应用，个人使用场景偏重于移动端。而存量客户一般已安装有建行的常用 App，再增加 App 的难度不小。对新客户而言，反复下载、注册多个 App，不仅费时，还占用客户手机资源，容易引发客户不满，影响平台的推广效果。

四、解决方案

从建行推出平台的目的分析，对建行而言，客户选择哪个渠道不是关键，客户使

① 资料来源：June，苑晶．小程度：腾讯的增量杀手．http：//www. pintu360. com/a55398. html. 2018－06－28。

② 资料来源：June，苑晶．小程序：腾讯的增量杀手．https：//www. pintu360. com/a55398. html. 2018－06－28。

③ 资料来源：序多多．半年涨粉数百万！“林清玄读书会”如何用小程序实现公众号低成本快速增粉？http：//www. xudoodoo. com/detail/446. html. 2018－05－14。

用 PC 端或移动端登录也不是关键，客户真正的与平台发生关系才是核心问题。要实现快速获客活客，必须通过技术手段降低客户的使用门槛，借助头部流量入口引流，依托客户口碑实现裂变式传播。因此我提出如下建议。

（1）整合各平台入口。加快进行平台间客户注册信息自动共享授权机制的开发，减少客户在不同平台间反复注册和需要记忆多个注册信息的麻烦。可通过建行门户网站或统一注册平台进行统管。

（2）依托建行手机银行的市场优势开展营销活动，实现平台导流。

（3）加强与互联网头部流量公司的合作。基于微信流量入口的霸主地位和社交属性，有必要仔细研究，借助其影响力助力金融科技平台获客。加快小程序开发，利用小程序易传播、易使用、低占用的特点，引发客户裂变式传播，加快平台的推广和应用。

（4）不同的平台应用采用不同接入模式，对于高频场景和涉及高价值客户的平台要考核 App 端活客数，有利于全行集中资源进行拓展，提高平台获客和活客效率。

目前其他银行也正在做金融科技转型，在移动互联网时代，面对同样的市场和客户，只有抢先一步才能有立足之处，决策层的战略意图只有通过具体的实施方案和激励措施才能落地。

基于微信小程序的客户服务新模式探索

远程智能银行中心　张旺遥

当前，商业银行主要依托网银网站、手机银行、微信公众号等渠道开展客户服务工作，部署咨询入口向客户提供智能服务。但随着互联网金融及其他行业的服务多样化、客户行为习惯简单化，商业银行受其渠道性质、关系、功能的影响，可提供一次问题解决方案的业务范围较少且服务模式劣势逐渐显现，亟须探索新模式。

一、商业银行客户服务模式发展现状

（一）传统商业银行客户服务模式的劣势

在移动互联网时代，客户倾向于利用碎片化的时间得到简单快速的服务，促使在线服务覆盖面不断扩大。但目前在银行内，线上客户服务渠道普遍存在以下问题。

1. 服务功能不丰富

提供的功能支持较弱，不便于客户一次咨询即可解决问题，容易造成客户重复咨询。

2. 服务使用不简单

银行服务渠道查询入口不易寻找，操作步骤烦琐，不便于客户简单操作，容易造成简单问题大量咨询。

3. 服务体验不新颖

金融科技发展态势强，客户对不新颖的服务操作不感兴趣，一定程度上降低了客户自主操作的积极性。

（二）建行客户服务模式现状分析

随着客户习惯的变化，仅提供简单业务咨询的在线服务已难以满足客户需求，客户对服务功能、服务速度、服务体验都提出了更高的要求，同时也对建行的服务价值带来了挑战。

1. 以微信服务为例，2018 年以来建行微信公众号的粉丝数量增长速率逐步下降。

研究表明，使用过程中需进行关注的操作已不满足用户“用完即走”的行为习惯，且微信公众号入口寻找操作步骤较多、推送功能易被用户习惯性忽视，用户重复使用情况不够理想。微信公众号服务效果递减，较难带来更多流量，从长期运营角度看存在弊端（见图 4.2 和图 4.3）。

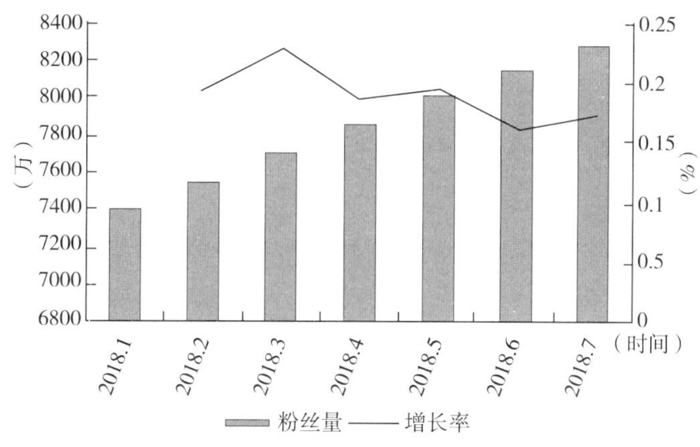

图 4.2 “中国建设银行”粉丝数情况（月）

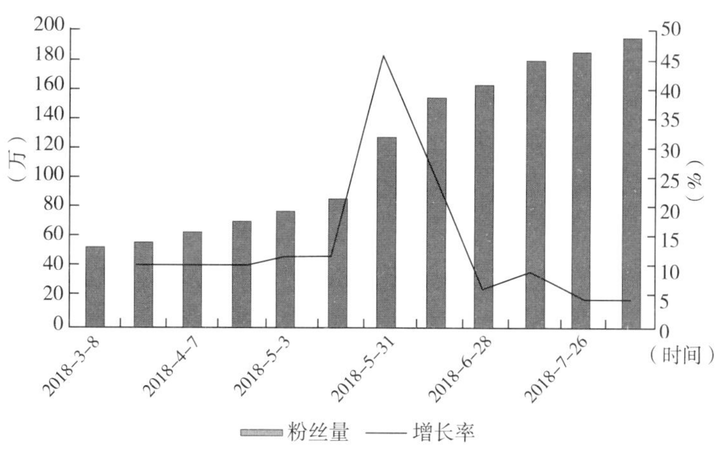

图 4.3 “建行客服”粉丝数情况（半月）

2. 客户体验无法实现较大提升

目前商业银行的客户服务模式基本都是提供咨询服务或较少的功能辅助，客户通过在线渠道体验的服务功能相对较弱。随着新科技手段对操作方式及风险控制的不断突破，客户亟须体验新鲜简便的科技提供的功能支持。

3. 维护成本高

微信公众号自主操作性不强，受限多、要求高、传播慢。如因功能受限，在满足合理设置菜单的前提下，为了适应业务发展则需要定期修改菜单，这不仅对用户使用习惯造成影响，无法积累成熟用户，而且增加了维护成本。

4. 价值创造低

大数据和信息技术已经使银行具备了批量获客的能力，但商业银行在价值创造的过程中还存在客户信息利用程度较低和营销困难等问题，主要原因有成熟用户辨认及信息收集不足、辅助验证手段缺乏、风险无法控制等，从而无法创造更多价值。

二、基于微信小程序的客户服务新模式——建行“轻客服”

随着时代的发展与客户习惯的变化，客户希望体验不被打扰、更轻松、更新颖、更简单的服务。

（一）微信小程序的概念及特点

微信小程序，简称小程序，是一种不需要下载安装即可使用的应用，它实现了应用“触手可及”的梦想，用户扫一扫或搜一下即可打开应用，与订阅号、服务号、企业号是并行的体系，其明显优势主要体现在以下方面。

（1）小程序不需要下载安装且无须关注即可使用，用完不会仍显示在交流页面或订阅号内，满足了用户“免打扰”的心理需求，有利于积累稳定客户。

（2）小程序具有多个入口，如线下扫码、公众号关联、搜索查找、历史记录列表、附近的小程序、群小程序等，易推广、传播快，且自带9亿的月活量，有利于获取客户资源。

（3）小程序可以引入拍照、地图、GPS（全球定位系统）、指纹验证等功能，扩大客服功能范围，增强客户场景化体验，有利于向客户提供更简便、更准确、价值更高的服务。

（二）建行“轻客服”

利用微信小程序关联公众号，通过程序开发，打造建行“轻客服”应用，构建包括基本业务咨询服务、简单操作业务附加服务、身份验证业务增值服务等在内的综合服务平台。

1. 基本业务咨询服务

通过公众号关联，可以实现公众号与小程序之间相互跳转，结合小程序的辅助功能提高基本业务咨询服务的客户体验。举例来说，在目前的客户服务工作中，有关网点服务类的工单占比较大，究其原因，主要是网点服务与客户期望存在差距，且没有更好的反馈渠道，只能通过线上渠道生成工单处理。打造小程序建行“轻客服”，可以更顺畅地连接线下网点和线上服务，快速处理客户在网点办理业务时产生的问题或不满情绪，大幅提升服务效率。

场景一：客户前往网点办理业务前，打开建行“轻客服”，轻松查询实时更新的网点当前服务窗口数、排队人数、等待时间、固定电话等信息，通过比较选择 A 网点办理业务（见图 4.4）。

图 4.4　轻松查看网点信息，适合需要选择出行

场景二：客户在某网点办理业务时，柜台某工作人员态度良好，想对其提出表扬。客户通过扫一扫网点贴示的“轻客服”应用二维码，进入该网点线上客户留言评价区进行评价，客户对网点的所有评价由该网点专人负责并及时回复（见图 4.5）。

2. 简单操作业务附加服务

电话与在线服务均存在高频问题，处理方式虽然简单，但由于进线量大，仍占用了不少服务资源。比如“查询开户行”问题，虽然建行已为客户提供多种方式查询开户行信息，但客户咨询量仍居高不下。通过“轻客服”提供更新颖的自助查询开户行方式，以及其他高频问题解决方案，可以有效减少客户进线咨询，并提升客户黏性。

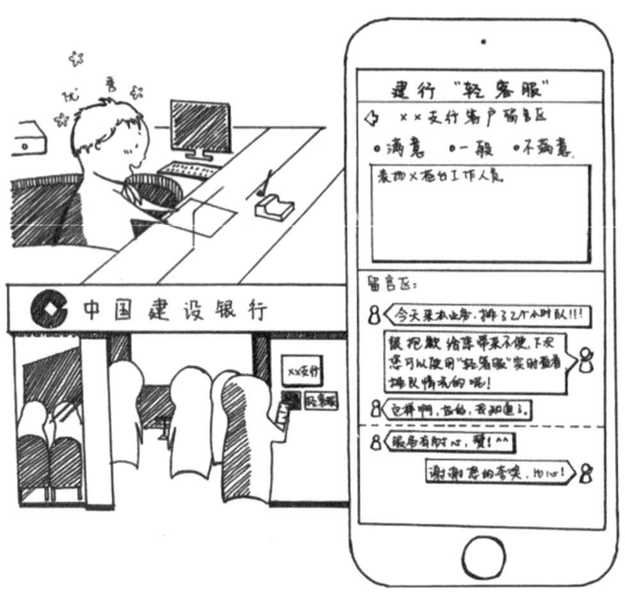

图 4.5　轻松表达情绪，及时得到响应

场景三：客户需要知道其储蓄卡的开户行信息，且其微信已绑定建行账户。客户打开建行“轻客服”，通过“一键拍照”拍摄储蓄卡，获取开户行、联行号等信息；通过拍摄信用卡，获取卡种、账单日、还款日等信息（见图 4.6）。

图 4.6　“一键拍照”识别获取信息，告别“艰难”核实对话

场景四：客户与友人聊天时，获知建行正在开展××信用卡加油特惠活动，于是打开建行“轻客服”，在地图页面搜索“××信用卡加油”，显示附近可参与该活动的加油站点（同时显示各站点是否仍有参与名额），前往参与活动（见图4.7）。

图4.7 情谊“轻客服”，轻松“薅羊毛”

3. 身份验证业务增值服务

除了与线下网点联动、提供高频问题自助解决方案之外，“轻客服”还可以利用生物识别技术，增加身份验证功能，做深客户服务内容，增加服务附加价值。

场景五：客户想修改手机银行绑定的手机号码（根据后台的客户信用数据库，该客户是低风险客户，在绑定其账户微信小程序中显示修改手机号码菜单），打开建行“轻客服”，通过指纹、人脸识别、虹膜识别等具唯一性的生物特征验证，完成修改（见图4.8）。

场景六：客户想给妈妈送一份保险作为生日礼物，打开建行“轻客服”，进入理财/保险产品板块后，选择合适的产品付款购买成功，并分享给妈妈，妈妈领取验证其身份证信息后即可生效（见图4.9）。

三、建行“轻客服”的发展前景

通过互联网技术实现的在线服务，尤其是移动端在线客服，更符合移动互联网时代的客户行为习惯。小程序的特点与优势，使其提供的服务迎合了客户使用习惯，满

图 4.8　生物验证修改信息，轻松操作解决问题

图 4.9　无论身在何方，心意轻松传达

足了客户使用期望，结合其发展趋势打造建行“轻客服”，有利于获客、黏客、活客。

（一）建行“轻客服”的综合效益

1. 获客

通过“轻客服”打造的各种场景化服务吸引客户，与无法接触的客户建立联系，成为银行获取新客户的有力抓手，带动各项业务指标。

2. 黏客

“轻客服”作为集业务咨询、简单操作、身份增值验证为一体的服务平台，且适应客户使用习惯，易积累成熟客户；同时通过与行内各种金融产品的组合，构建服务网络，可提高存量客户的忠诚度。

3. 活客

通过“轻客服”服务客户，获取有价值的数据、挖掘有价值的客户，对客户进行精准画像，提供营销机会的多种场景化服务，提高营销转化率。

（二）建行“轻客服”的发展趋势

1. 推广简单

小程序基于 LBS（基于移动位置服务）推广和附近的小程序功能，而且通过关键字搜索、小程序码等方式均可进入小程序，容易推广给客户。

2. 用户体验流畅

在微信生态中，小程序的功能和体验都相较于其他更加流畅，有利于提供优质服务，同时打通线上线下，通过链接融合快速解决用户问题。

3. 成本较低

小程序适合各类应用场景，在开发、推广、维护等环节均操作简单、接入容易，极大地降低了运营成本。

4. 增强建行在商业银行中的综合竞争力

结合建行业务特色，运用小程序功能优势，降低客户咨询，不断完善产品、流程、系统及服务，提升客户体验，实现价值创造。同时建立客户数据库，通过数据互通传递信息和服务，挖掘市场商机。

5. 赋予金融行业更亲民的科技属性

推动商业银行突破业务发展壁垒，结合市场上多种手段强化自身风险控制，带动行业发展。

金融科技助力银行实现客户360度全景分析的模型研究

——“三层嵌套+六维框架”打造客户管理的精准时钟

山东省分行　杨　颖

一、浅析美林的投资时钟理论

美林（Merrill Lynch）在2008年爆发金融海啸之前，是世界著名的投资银行，虽然今天已成为次贷危机中的典型案例，但公司提出的投资时钟理论依然具有深远意义。简言之，投资时钟是将资产、行业、债券收益率曲线和经济周期等进行关联分析的实用工具。

（一）投资时钟结构及内涵简介

根据经济增长和通货膨胀情况，投资时钟将经济周期分为4个不同的阶段——衰退、复苏、过热和滞胀（见图4.10）。为了便于理解，投资时钟以循环的形式绘制了经济周期。经济增长和通货膨胀是时钟的驱动力，经济增长率指向南北方向，通货膨胀率指向东西方向。在经济衰退和复苏的经济周期，经济过热和滞胀，如不同阶段，沿顺时针方向循环，不同种类的金融资产将显示显著差异，每个阶段都有一个特定的资产可以得到市场的超额收益（当然，投资时钟有时会逆时针运动或跳过一个阶段，主要是因为海外影响或异常事件的影响，见图4.11）。

1. 衰退阶段

GDP增长疲软、产能过剩和商品价格下跌导致通货膨胀率下降。公司的收入很少，实际利润也在下降。央行试图将经济推回到一条可持续的增长道路上来降低利率，而债券收益率曲线则会下降。在这个阶段，债券是最好的资产选择。

2. 复苏阶段

拥有宽松的政策，经济在接近长期增长趋势的情况下加速增长。然而剩余产能尚未消耗完，因此通货膨胀率继续下降，周期性生产增长强劲。企业利润大幅反弹，但央行仍然保持宽松的货币政策，债券收益率曲线仍然很低。这个阶段是股票投资者的

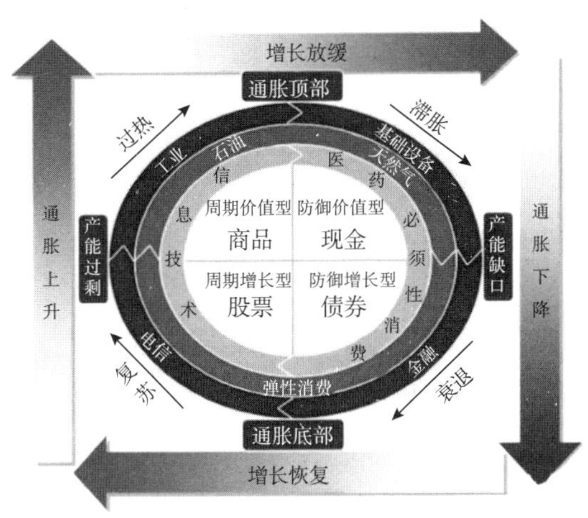

图 4.10　投资时钟将经济周期分为 4 个阶段

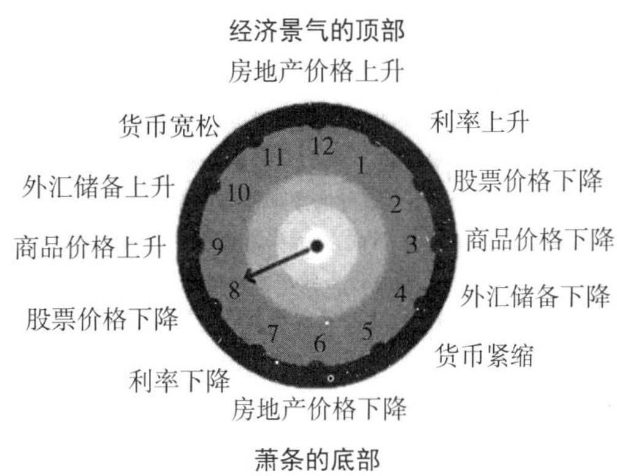

图 4.11　投资时钟绘制的经济周期

黄金时期，股票是最好的资产选择。

3. 过热阶段

企业生产增长放缓，生产能力接近极限，通货膨胀率上升。央行提高利率，推动经济回到可持续增长的轨道，但 GDP 增长率仍高走。债券表现不好，股票投资回报取决于强劲的利润增长和价值重估之间的权衡，通常伴随着债券的销售。在这个阶段，大宗商品是最好的资产选择。

4. 滞胀阶段

GDP 增长下降，通货膨胀率继续上升，由于经济衰退，以及公司利润的恶化，股票市场表现不佳。在这一阶段，现金是最好的资产选择。

在经济周期的不同阶段，通过识别一个转折点，及时调整资产配置，可以获得超额收益。

投资时钟反映了实体经济和投资战略之间的基本关系。由于不同国家的经济发展阶段和经济政策不同，上述 4 个阶段的持续时间不一样，甚至跳过了某一阶段，然而，投资时钟仍可以为我们提供资产配置的总体方向。

（二）历史验证

1. 在美国的验证

在美国近 70 年的历史中（除了第二次世界大战），经验表明投资时钟在经济周期的每一次变化中都大致匹配。美林公司用 1973 年 4 月至 2004 年 7 月美国完整的数据（30 多年的资产回报率和行业数据），证明了时钟理论的有效性。

2. 在中国的历史验证

中国的市场经济起始时间较晚，我们可以粗略地把 2006—2007 年划为“复苏期”、

2007 年年末至 2008 年前期划分为“过热期”、2008 年下半年开始进入“滞涨”和“衰退”期、2009 年在政府 4 万亿元的刺激下，经济快速复苏。

（三）美林时钟“失效”的原因

2008 年金融危机后，全球大类资产走势已经摒弃了美林投资时钟的资产轮动模式，在新一轮经济周期中，债市—股市—大宗商品市场的轮动彻底被打乱，一度出现股债双牛、大宗商品逆向发展等趋势，学术界出现了诸多“美林时钟失效了”“美林时钟不适用于中国”的说法。如果撇开事物的现象探索潜在的本质，我们会发现，美林时钟的理论基础一直是有效的，而其失效的主要原因在以下 3 个方面。

1. 经济周期的本质与金融周期的映射关系被打破

传统的投资时钟理论建立在经济领先金融的基础上，然而全球央行前所未有的货币宽松政策破坏了经济和金融的传导机制。经济复苏的势头尚未恢复，宽松的货币政策无法传递到实体经济的信贷方面，导致大量流动性直接流入金融市场，推动各类金融资产的价格上涨，从而使美林投资时钟理论失效。

2. 政府的干预必然会在一定程度上干扰周期性规律

就一个完整的市场经济周期而论，美林时钟将总是沿顺时针方向转动，即顺序永远是复苏—过热—滞胀—衰退—复苏，但是政府干预可能导致时钟颠倒或跳跃。中国在 30 年内走完了国外 100 年的发展轨迹，如此强大的外部力量将不可避免地导致时钟运行的偏差。

3. 银行资产配置的方向决定了整个金融配置的方向

中国金融体系最重要的权重是银行，在 2009 年 7 月之前，银行投资的主要目标是房地产、地方融资平台和各种类型的公共基金会。2009 年 7 月后，国家开始整顿 4 万亿元人民币的偏差，控制贷款发放率（这引发了 2009 年 8 月股市的大幅调整）。然而，银行有继续放贷的冲动，已经开始的各种房地产和基础设施项目需要继续放贷，尽管银行已经收缩了表外业务和控制信贷，但仍然大量扩大了表外业务。近两年，由于信贷管制，银行的净利润增长和利润率没有下降，房地产和投资的增长率也没有大幅下降，经济没有像许多人预测的那样出现硬着陆。然而，由于资本配置实体、财务管理回报率和无风险利率的上升，最终在 2011—2014 年的熊市之后，股票市场面临着持续的资金撤出和股票博弈。因此，大规模资产调整是银行资产的重新分配。

二、“时钟理论”的现实指导意义

美林投资时钟诞生于成熟市场，也是成熟市场中的知名品牌。其核心前提是经济周期性和市场化程度高。发展中的新兴市场如中国，周期性、规律性和市场化程度与成熟市场非常不同，导致差异化的存在，但其发展规律仍源于美林的时钟理论。

第一个启示是学习其理论分析的缜密逻辑原则。整合传统的经济、金融分析指标与我国经济领域的特色指标，从“宏观、中观、微观”3个层面入手，找到经济拐点，分析我们所处的经济周期、金融周期，判断具体的行业周期、产业链及客户的发展周期和盈利空间，通过建立分析模型，挖掘出资产配置的优先领域和行业，提出银行信贷资产的配置策略和方向，提高风险控制的整体水平。

第二个启示是建立一个动态的资产配置和风险控制模型。“投资时钟”是利用其“报时功能”适时调整投资方向和比例，暗示了动态配置的概念。

（1）银行的信贷运作与此类似，在不同的经济周期、金融周期，优先配置的行业、客户具有动态特性，随着行业和客户生命周期的发展，客户群体具有明显的更新特征。资产收益率的波动是风险的表现方式，由于难以做到甚至是根本无法始终保持资产的高收益，所以需要在不同经济周期将资产配置到不同的领域。

（2）资产分配是选择资产类别并确定其比例的过程。资产配置的好处在于可以分散非系统性风险，在一个相对固定时期，要选择资产具有相对收益优势的领域，调整资产组合中各类不同风险水平的资产比例，当某种类型的金融资产正在上升时，它将被分配更高的比率，而当某类金融资产呈下降趋势时，就降低此类资产的配置比例。

第三个启发是精选参数，建立立体分析体系。我们所处的经济/金融环境变得更复杂了，所以我们应用的模型必然要“源于美林而繁于美林、差异于美林”。一是适当加大“维度”选择总量。在秉承美林“从简”的原则下，结合我们的实际需要，将美林时钟的“四大方面”（资产、行业轮动、债券收益率曲线、经济周期）拓展为包含“经济、金融、行业、产业、客户”等在内的立体多维模型。二是提高与行业板块的契合配对率。美林模型侧重金融资产，以板块和大类金融资产作为投资标的进行研究。在银行领域，信贷资产配置需要与行业板块配对，当经济在低谷出现拐点，刚刚开始复苏时，石化、建筑施工、水泥、造纸等基础行业会最先受益。在随后的复苏增长阶段，机械设备、周期性电子产品等资本密集型行业和相关的零部件行业会表现优异，所以对行业板块的资金配置方案可以在不同时期进行倾斜。

第四个启发是定量与定性结合，建立“动态”的模型调整管理机制。第一，采取定量与定性结合的方式，注重落地实施与操作。资产配置如同投资者拿钱去投资，不同之处是银行对实体经济或企业的支撑度会更加直接地体现在其对大类资产/大量资金的配置上。采取定量与定性结合的方式，对配置的资产领域进行风险和收益判断，既要考虑宏观经济数据，也要考虑地域差别，同时还要将行业、客户进行纵横对比分析，与实际工作相结合，易于落地实施。第二，模型仅是一种快捷的分析工具，并无固定的模式化。我们所处的经济环境会越来越复杂，其间可能出现多种变量，所以要“因地制宜、因时制宜”，模型本身也需要紧跟形势的变动及时进行修正和调整。

三、银行版“美林时钟”的拓展模型

2015 年下半年以来，全球资产呈现出三大特征：高估值、高波动、高联动。所以，我们立足于全球（国）资产以及国内外宏观与行业中微观的相互传导钩稽，重构“美林时钟”，帮助我们找到经济发展的拐点、信贷投放时机/回收时机，尽快确定不同时期投放或回收的行业大致方向，有效管理所辖客户的银行资产配置比例、控制投放速度，实现利润的平稳过渡。

（一）总体框架——针对所处经济周期确定大资产配置的基础方向

首先，确定经济周期。对应美林时钟，我们将经济周期分为四大部分，即复苏—发展、高速发展—过热、过热—滞胀、滞胀—衰退（实践证明：任一经济周期不可能完全做到泾渭分明，不同周期的某些特点甚至会存在重叠性，如果能够有 70% ~80% 的特征与之重合，就可以判断某个时点处于某个经济周期内，见图 4. 12）。

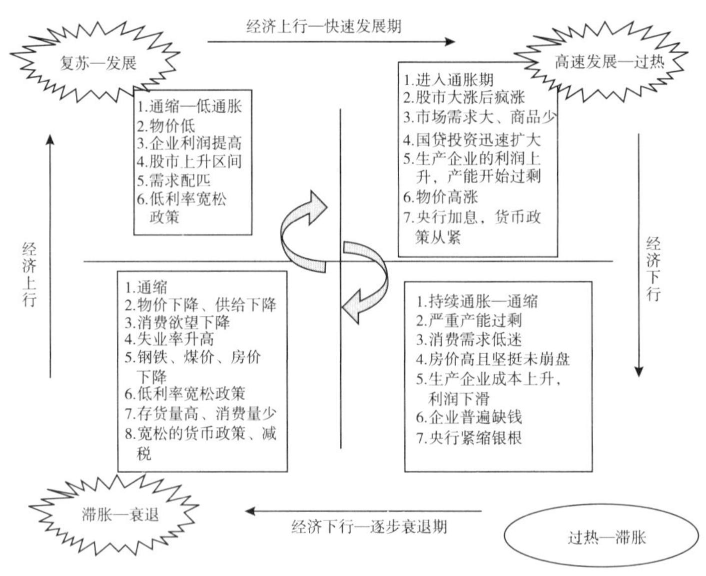

图 4. 12　经济周期现状分析模型

复苏—发展期的特点：通缩收窄，向低通胀发展，物价仍普遍较低，需求开始旺盛，企业利润在低成本、高需求的带动下逐步提高，股市步入上升空间，国家在此阶段依然采取较为宽松的货币金融政策。

高速发展—过热期的特点：伴随生产的扩大、需求的旺盛，物价开始升高，进入通胀期，由于市场需求大，使得流通的商品短缺，又带动了企业再投资，固定资产投资提高迅猛。而伴随企业利润的提高，产能开始过剩，国家开始加息，实施从紧的货币政策。

过热—滞胀期的特点：持续通胀，产能严重过剩，伴随企业成本上升、需求端低迷，利润开始下滑，房价依然坚挺未崩盘，企业普遍缺钱，央行紧缩银根。

滞胀—衰退期的特点：钢价、煤价、房价下降，物价普遍下降，供给下降，消费需求下降，失业率提高、企业破产率升高，库存高企，进入通缩期，国家开始执行宽松的货币政策，刺激消费。

其次是确定资产配置的方向。经济周期简单地分为两个动态区间：上行和下行。根据经济周期和周期性行业之间的相关性，大型资产的分配要提前做好准备。一般来说，循环产业的周期通常按一定的顺序进行，复苏始于下游产业，如汽车、房地产、基础设施建设、机械和设备制造；然后是中游加工和制造产业，如化学纤维、非金属矿产品、有色金属冶炼和黑色金属冶炼；最后是上游产业，如有色金属、石油、煤炭和石化产业。衰退也是从下游开始的，然后蔓延到中上游。因此在上游部分，我们应该依次做好周期性行业项目储备，可以最大限度地增加贷款投资，如大型基础设施项目；在下游部分，应提前做好周期性行业信贷控制或退出计划的安排，结构调整和创新发展成为该时期的主题，利用同业业务、金融市场业务、投行业务来增加中间业务收入，腾挪信贷空间（见图 4. 13）。

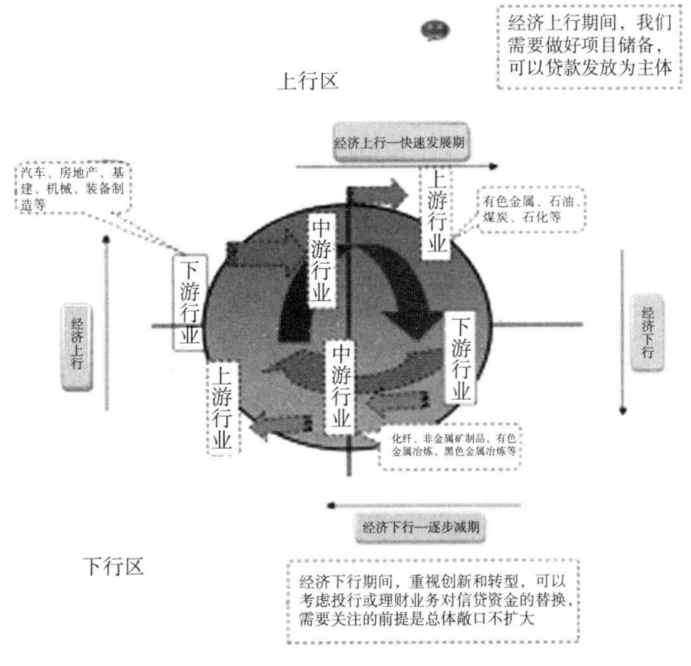

图 4. 13　资产配置趋势模型

（二）建立360度分析模型——三层嵌套+六维框架

“三层嵌套+六维框架”模型的理论内涵为，我们确定了“宏观、中观、微观”三大层面，宏观相当于一个生存环境，主要有经济周期、金融周期；中观有大量竞争对手组成的行业，主要有行业周期、产业链；微观是从企业端分析其资产结构、盈利能力，由此形成六维框架，实现“从宏观到微观、从行业到客户、有投放有控制”的银行大资产配置的预期及风险预警。

其主要逻辑关系为，宏观是生存环境，主要有经济周期、金融周期；中观是行业集群，由大量的竞争对手组成，主要有行业周期、产业链；微观是具体企业，从企业端可以分析其资产结构、盈利能力（见图4.14）。

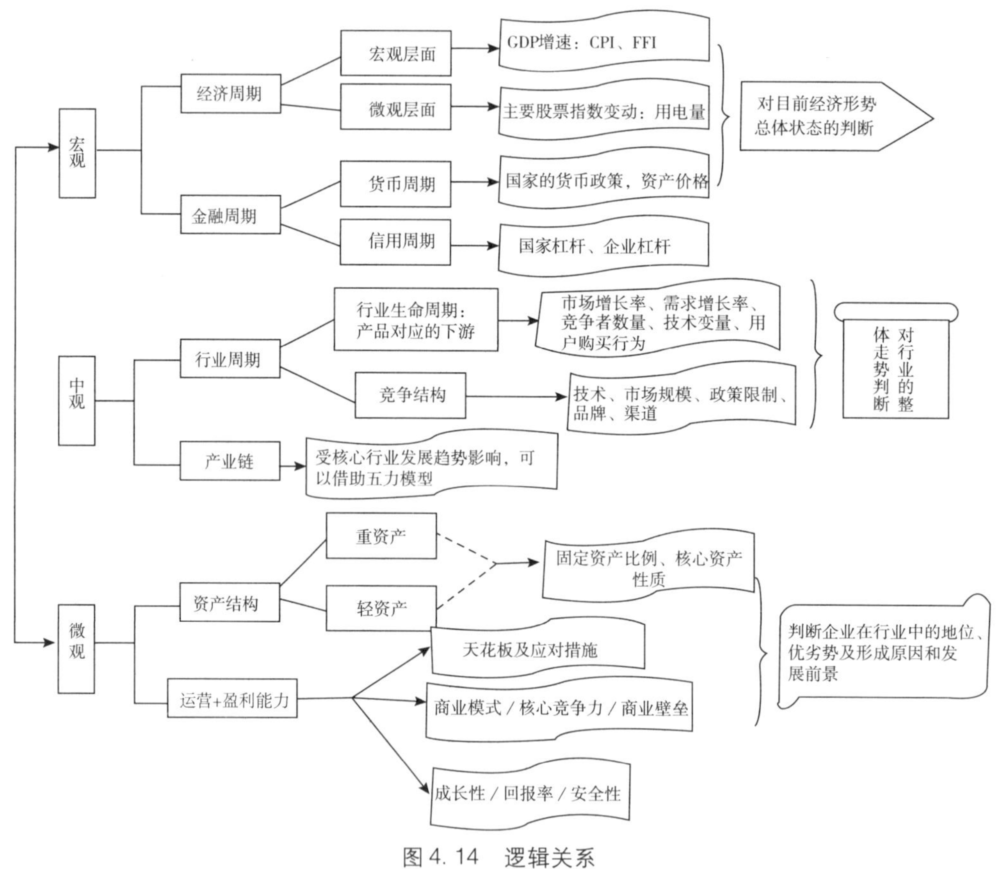

图4.14　逻辑关系

1. 第一层：宏观层面分析，主要包括对经济和金融两大周期的分析

经济周期。经济周期是分析资产配置的起点同时也是最终的落脚点，它决定了大类资产的长期收益率中枢。在宏观层面，我们可以跟踪GDP增速、CPI（居民消费价格指数）、PPI（生产价格指数）的上下波动幅度及持续时间来预判处于具体哪个周期

中，还可以利用社会用电量等大数据的变动来辅助判断周期所在的区间。

金融周期。一是货币周期，可以选取央行资产的基准利率与央行资产负债表的规模增速作为衡量大类资产货币周期关键性指标。二是信用周期，它反映一个实体的杠杆水平的变化。杠杆既能成为助力商业周期扩张的因素，也会成为制约实体增长的约束与风险因素，跟踪的核心指标为宏观与微观层面的杠杆率。

2. 第二层：中观层面分析，主要包括对行业周期和产业链的分析

产业周期。一是一个产业的生命周期是指一个产业从出现到完全退出所经历的时间。主要指标有市场增长率、需求增长率、产品品种、竞争对手数量、技术变化、消费者购买行为等。产业发展生命周期包括 4 个主要阶段：初始阶段、成长阶段、成熟阶段、衰退阶段。此外，对于行业生命周期的判断必须与产品规格相结合。二是产业周期性分类，其中周期性产业分为产业周期性产业和消费周期性产业。周期性产业与宏观经济周期的关系最为密切。上游产品（原材料）的波动越大，中间资本产品的波动越小，消费品的波动就越小。非周期性产业，如公用事业和食品等行业基本上不受经济周期的影响。三是行业的竞争结构，可分为完全竞争和完全垄断市场、寡头垄断市场和垄断竞争市场。技术、市场、政策限制、品牌、渠道等都可以成为垄断的原因。理解了技术垄断、市场垄断、政策垄断、品牌垄断、渠道垄断等行业企业，可以帮助我们判断其规模的风险。

产业链。它包括上游和下游的关系，以及彼此之间的交易行为，本质上是一个劳动分工所带来的工业细分，大规模专业生产可以大大提高工业效率的操作。产业链向上游延伸使得核心企业进入原材料环节和研发环节，向下游延伸则进入营销环节。我们可以整合上游和下游企业投资组合的主线产业链，将单个企业的不可控风险转变为可控风险供应链的一个企业整体。

3. 第三层：微观层面分析，主要包括企业资产结构、运营和盈利能力等方面的具体分析

资产结构。一般来讲，轻资产行业可变成本高，固定资产投资少，边际投资收益率较高，企业核心资源是一些不可计入资产负债表的东西，如技术、品牌、渠道等。相反，重型资产行业拥有大量资本投资、较少的流动资产和较多的固定资产。了解重资产还是轻资产结构可以帮助我们建立客户的融资产品配置模型，不同类型的企业必然对应不同的需求。

盈利能力。对一个企业盈利能力的判断可以采用杜邦分析法，挖掘企业盈利背后的原理，可以选取“利润率、周转率和杠杆比例”等指标，找到每个行业的平均水平，然后对照目标企业进行分析，判断出企业在行业中所处的位置，判断其是领先还是落后。

（三）分析结论及输出形式

分析结论主要包含三大部分内容：一是对当下所处经济周期及环境的总体判断，二是对行业的现状及走势判断，三是对具体客户的优劣势分析及发展前景预判。

输出模式有两大类：第一类是对银行大类资产的投向趋势判断，即现阶段银行的资产配置到哪几个领域，或以何种资产形式（如信贷类或债券承销类等）投放，或对哪几个领域需要提前实施退出策略；第二类是在第一类分析的基础上，进一步计入客户的信息，形成完整的客户现状及发展趋势预判。

四、金融科技在模型建设中的应用及重要作用

模型中涉及的宏观、微观数据需要嫁接外部系统进行数据提取并按照权重比例进行测算，客户财务指标和对比数据可以通过行内新一代系统获取并进行加工获得。

首先，是对宏观环境形成判断。虽然我们对应美林时钟将经济周期分为“复苏—发展、高速发展—过热、过热—滞涨、滞涨—衰退”4 个阶段，并定义了不同的发展特点，但任何一个经济周期不可能完全做到泾渭分明，如果能够有 70% ~80% 的特征与之重合，就可以判断处于某一经济周期内。

其次，是用链式思维整合行业/产业信息。我们将经济周期简单划分为上行和下行两大动态区间，银行资产投放对应着行业资产的布局。

最后，根据角色不同可以形成不同的分析版本。比如：针对客户经理，要具体到每一个客户，逐户形成完整的分析报告，并定期予以数据更新；针对管理层，一是可以利于把握当前一段时期内的资产投放方向和产品搭配技巧，二是利用精简的报告或表单了解所管理客户及行业的综合情况。

综上所述，我们在今后要结合山东区域经济环境、经营实际及发展预判，围绕“三大战略”“五个第一”和总行、省分行提出的工作要求，利用大数据分析，结合金融科技的创新应用，在对公客户营销和管理中建立起 360 度全景分析模型，实现“有效投放、高质量投放、智慧投放”的管理及营销目标。

基于“区块链”架构的供应链应收账款质押融资

天津市分行　武　鹏

一、区块链技术基础

区块链技术目前已被应用于多个领域，其本质是通过密码学的原理，建立一个不依赖任何中心的、完全分布式的数据库。区块链技术作为一种在虚拟空间记录数据的方法，该记录能被所有节点分享，同时不被任何节点所控制，任何参与者都不能随意删除和修改。

具体来说，区块链是一串使用密码学方法产生的数据块，每个区块都包含一个时间戳和前一个区块的链接，是一种将数据区块以时间顺序相连的方式组合成的链式数据结构。区块链技术是利用链式数据结构来验证和存储数据，利用分布式节点共识算法来生成和更新数据，利用密码学的方式，保证数据传输和访问的安全利用，由自动化脚本代码组成的智能合约来编程和操作数据的一种全新的分布式基础架构与计算范式。

区块链技术的特征包括分布存储、时间序列、全链共识、智能合约，从区块链发明者创造的“比特币”实验来看，区块链技术可以追溯数字资产的最初来源，证明其真实性，同时所有交易经过全网验证，确保了交易的唯一性。区块链可以不需要第三方信用中介的参与，由数字资产的所有交易历史参与者的共同监督来形成信用，在主体多为理性人的假设下，这种机制使得主体按规则行事，形成了一种互不信任的节点之间的交易记账规则。

由此我们可以看到，在本质上，区块链就是一种创造信用的机制，在互不信任的节点的博弈之下，大家至少认可已经共同确认的交易。区块链技术的陆续应用，开始从根本上改变人们对交易信用资源配置的理解，直至改变政府监管信用中介和商业主体参与经济的方式。在区块链架构下，让参与主体在公开透明的机制中各自对行为负责，对自己的信用负责，基于参与者共享一部不可更改，只能持续增加的交易总账。

二、供应链金融现状

供应链金融旨在服务中小企业，该业务围绕供应链条中的核心企业展开，通过整合供应链的物流、资金流、信息流，将核心企业的优势信用注入供应链的节点中的中小企业。

回顾银行业在供应链金融领域的发展，最初是以人工授信审批为主的“1+N”模式。在获得核心企业承诺支持与参与的情况下，核心企业为债项提供信用背书，使得与核心企业交易的中小微企业容易获得授信。这种线下模式依赖于业务人员对行业和核心企业的经验判断，属于被动的授信审批一项一审规模效应与技术的应用效果不明显，客户缺少黏性。

此后，银行创新与核心企业的 ERP（企业资源计划）系统互联，客户对 ERP 系统的黏性转化为对融资服务的黏性。在核心企业的配合与参与下，银行可以低成本的获得批量客户线上化，实现了融资服务的规模效应和操作成本的大幅下降。如今已有银行实现了在平台商业模式中构建金融服务平台，以独特的双边效应结合互联网+的长尾效应，成为整合商流、物流、资金流三流合一的信息平台，银行在平台模式下，可获得与交易相关的丰富信息，这为银行提供了极大的创新空间，打破了传统的二八定律和重点客户思维，银行获得大量的潜在客户操作成本与风险管控成本，可进行持续优化。

总体来看，目前供应链金融的应用场景多、应用行业多、平台类型多，但其核心的信用机制和风险控制逻辑仍然较少有人涉及，因此是研究与应用创新的重点。

三、区块链与供应链金融的匹配

供应链的结构是一组企业的集合，而供应链金融是对供应链整体进行结构化融资，其基本逻辑为：虽然节点信用难以达到授信标准，但依托于供应链结构，动产（如应收账款）具有可质押、可评估、流动性较好的特点，以质押或保理形成可预期的未来现金流，从而偿还本息。

供应链整体的信用是由核心企业信用与所有节点企业信用之和构成，但又并不是简单的加和关系，供应链节点之间的信用关系，相比一般性交易关系的企业关系更为牢固、可信，同时其内部存在相互制约、相互协调的复杂关系。

供应链中的采购与供应关系具有结构化的关联性，体现为在核心企业的订单驱动下，根据产品结构、生产计划、销售计划等逐步推进，而非随意性、临时性的采购与供应关系。结构化的交易链具有高度的严密性，上一级节点的采购，被下一级节点的订单所驱动，上一级节点的交易输出，为下一级节点的交易输入，所有交易来自核心企业订单的驱动，环环相扣，形成高速运转的供应链系统。

链式关系的重要价值在于交易本身可以证明交易的真实性，真实性的价值体现为债项的真实性，从而可以大大减少第三方机构来参与交易真实性的证明或增信。在核心企业不参与虚假交易的情况下，虚假交易链的形成难度极高，3个节点以上的虚假交易的难度远高于2个节点的合谋作假，所以依据交易链的内在联系，以相互验证的方式形成可信度极高的真实交易、真实债项。

区块链依据参与节点的结构来布置分布式账本，数据无须单一的中心化结构来统一维护，共识达成的协议具有不可篡改性节点，不可能按照有利于自己的原则来操控数据，因此区块链建立点对点的关系，将简化供应链金融越来越复杂的业务模式，为供应链金融的高级化提供强信任关系的保证。

在区块链数据的高信用下，数据具有重复使用可追溯性和实现供应链透明化的优势，有助于构建高效率融资处理的服务平台。在传统的中心化模式下，需要很多中介发挥作用，才能保护交易的正常进行，区块链的去中心化架构，可发挥全局互信机制，以组织链本身来形成互信，参与方越多，实现的互信成本越低，同时区块链作为分布式总账，需要多方参与才能确保分部持续及不可篡改的特性，所以区块链技术应用于供应链资产交易是较为理想的应用场景。借助区块链技术，以加密的方式来形成不可篡改的单证，以共识机制及参与者共同确认的方式来杜绝参与者作假行为，基于计算的信用自证，是依据交易内在逻辑关系的自我证明。

四、应收账款质押的区块链应用

下面，以供应链金融业务中的应收账款质押业务为例，探析应用区块链技术的可行性。

应收账款融资的主要风险来自真实性问题，如果交易为虚假，则应收账款质权不成立。在实践中应收账款的真实性、合规性审核，以及价值确定等，是该类业务的关键操作要点。

应收账款质押融资交易结构包括质权人（以下简称为银行）、出质人（一般为核心企业的供应商，以下简称为供应商）、次债务人（以下简称为核心企业）3个主体。流程大致如下所示：

（1）依据基础合同发生交易，形成应收账款债项，符合可质押条件。

（2）经银行审查合格后，签订质押协议，转让应收账款。

（3）供应商书面通知核心企业的出质事项。

（4）银行向系统“登记公示”与“确认”，供应商线上确认，质权确立。

（5）银行向供应商放款。

（6）核心企业向银行支付回款。

以区块链作为业务平台构架，将登记公示、银行、供应商及核心企业等纳入业务平台，实现登记公示、单证、交互与确认四大环节的协作，形成全过程的文档记录，减少风险管理的复杂度，降低操作难度与操作成本。

具体而言，单证及过程文件加密、记账，包括基础合同、订货单、入库单、增值税发票、应收账款账龄清单等总账及明细账、银行权力清单等。同时，当事人的流程化确认，履约过程产生的交互记录、文件，经确认后存档。将原来手工处理单证，线下签章单证集中保存的形式，更改为线上确认，每一个节点都保存相同的账本机制，所有规则与约定都公开透明，所有涉及权益及合同执行的环节，如合同瑕疵付款条件登记确认，同时确认等都在交互式处理下达成共识并存证，不可更改，不可抵赖，以作为日后争议的处理依据。所有节点都参与互动与见证监督账本上的所有数据，由每个人共同维护，参与维护的每个人都保存一份完整的数据库备份。

应用区块链技术后，其流程优化为：

（1）供应商与核心企业的应收账款形成后，供应商向银行提交基础合同、相关单证（扫描上传），向银行申请质押借款。

（2）银行对供应商的债项进行交易真实性调查，对核心企业进行还款能力调查，对相关单证进行真实性验证，对债项的可质押性进行评估。

（3）银行与供应商签订在线合同，登记公示节点确认并生效，供应商确认所有单证和回答银行的质问，相关文件加密保存后不可更改。

（4）银行、供应商、核心企业在线签订三方协议，规定支付事件和账户管控。

（5）履约过程中处理各种争议，达成共识，形成文件并加密保存，不可更改。

（6）账本公开，各方无须对历史单证进行反复查验，降低操作成本，形成信用机制。

各方操作时，确认无误后，使用私钥签名，具有法律效力。在过程中合同可以查询，大量支持性文件、证据以不可被篡改的方式保存在系统中。

应用区块链技术后，银行将极大缩短应收账款质押融资业务的真实性审核的操作时间，提高业务整体办理效率。同时，区块链技术应用的基础在于银行与客户共享平台的搭建，这也是该技术应用的实现前提。

人工智能在投资银行领域中的应用

建信理财　谢银霜　青海省分行　何　勤　浙江省分行　胡诗超

一、人工智能简介

AI（人工智能）自 20 世纪 50 年代诞生后，历经了 3 次大发展。第一次是从 20 世纪 50 年代到 80 年代。在此阶段，虽然可编程数字电脑的出现使得符号主义发展迅速，但由于很多元素不能量化表达，所构建的模型存在一定的局限性。此外，随着计算任务日益复杂，人工智能的开发应用遇到瓶颈。第二次是从 20 世纪 80 年代到 90 年代末。由于专家系统缺乏知识获取和推理能力，以及高昂的开发成本，人工智能的发展再次陷入低谷。第三次是从 21 世纪初开始，随着大数据的积聚、理论算法的创新和计算能力的提高，AI 拓宽了应用领域，开启繁荣新时期。

二、人工智能在金融领域的应用

目前，AI 已在国内外金融领域内得到广泛的应用，包括智能投顾、交易预测、量化投资和风险管理等方面。

（一）人工智能在投资顾问领域的应用

智能投资是指根据投资者的风险偏好，通过模型算法追求相同风险下的最大收益或相同收益下的最低风险。智能投资使用 AI 中的多层神经网络技术，实时采集经济数据指标，通过不断学习，多元化的资产投资策略可以实现大规模的个性化定制投资计划，以不追求短期的波动，而是期望长期、稳健的回报为目标，进一步践行长期服务客户的理念。智能投资服务降低了普通家庭的财富管理门槛。

1. 国外人工智能在投资顾问领域的应用

花旗集团利用 IBM（国际商业机器公司）的 AI 电脑沃森（Watson），向客户提供产品需求分析、未来经济形势分析等服务，还可以结合投资者的投资概况制订个性化投资计划。日本创业公司（Alpaca）交易平台采用基于图像识别的深度学习技术，帮助用户从档案中查找和分析外汇交易图表。科技金融公司 Fincite 与德意志银行合作开发机器人投资顾问“Anlage Finder”，通过问卷调查和算法帮助特定的客户群以低成本建立投资组合，提升投资风险抵御能力。

2. 我国人工智能在投资顾问领域的应用

从产品开发主体看，我国智能投顾系统研发主体主要分三大类型。

（1）互联网金融信息服务公司。同花顺 iFinD 智能投顾可进行舆情监控和数据提醒，天弘爱理财可实现量化择时智能调仓等。

（2）互联网巨头。京东金融推出的智投工具可定制客户组合投资方案；蚂蚁金服则在许多领域进行创新和应用，如互联网小额贷款、保险、信用报告、智能投资和客户服务。

（3）传统证券公司、基金公司、银行和理财平台。招商银行的“摩羯智投”可进行公募基金组合定制投资；平安银行的“平安一账通”推出智投产品业务；申万宏源证券公司联合股利多和天音通信推出“股神 +”，可提供智能理财解决方案；广发证券的“贝塔牛”，提供 A 股及大类资产配置智能投顾服务；兴业银行、广发银行、光大银行、江苏银行、工商银行等银行机构也积极加入了“智能投资”的行列。

（二）人工智能在交易领域的应用

国内外 AI 技术在交易预测方面的应用比比皆是。世界首个以纯 AI 驱动的基金 Rebellion 成功预警了 2008 年金融危机。日本三菱公司研发出 Senoguchi，历经 4 年，模型正确率高达 68%。AI 对冲基金 CommEq 结合了定量模型与自然语言处理的技术，可以处理各类信息。Palantir 推出基于知识图谱的金融数据分析平台 Palantir Metropolis，可以整合多元的量化资料，并提供一套方便易用的分析工具来满足复杂的研究需求。

（三）人工智能在风险管理领域的应用

金融业的发展将产生无数有用或无用的数据，包括金融交易、客户信息、市场分析等。随着存储技术的发展，一些将被清除的数据有机会被存储。通过对这些数据的深入分析，可以进一步整合金融活动的复杂信息，实现风险管理的作用。通过 AI 的深度学习系统分析大量数据，将大大降低劳动力成本并提高财务风险控制能力。

（四）人工智能在报告自动生成领域的应用

Narrative Science 是一家领先的美国自然语言生成企业服务公司，Quill 是其 NLG（自然语言生成）平台。它可以像人一样读写，自动将数据转换为智能且富有洞察力的自然语言，并完全显示、聚合与主题相关的其他信息，为分析决策提供完整透明的依据。Narrative Science 目前服务的客户包括银行、会计师事务所和政府部门等，如瑞士信贷和德勤。FactSet 则是一家美国金融信息服务提供商，它将 Narrative Science 的 NLG 功能集成到其分析和客户报告平台中。与 Narrative Science 集成的工具将使 FactSet 的客户能够自动生成投资组合评估，从而大幅增加投资管理公司所涵盖的报告范围。在季度报告的第一天，可以自动生成报告，并在满足合规性要求的同时满足内容要求。

（五）人工智能在建行的应用现状

在建行，AI 也已在总分行对公和对私条线中实现了业务上的应用。总行个人金融部构建了个人产品智能投顾系统，基于客户生命周期分析，根据客户历史交易行为，构建客观风险评价，结合客户收支流水交易，分析流动性自由度，并基于客户群体数据建模，建立预测标签体系。北京分行创新研发了“辞海数心”智能产品，利用文本挖掘技术分析建行经营过程中产生的非机构化文本数据，并从中挖掘关键信息。厦门实验室将从信用厦门上收集的近 70 个部门 2 亿条信用信息作为数据基础仓库，进一步丰富信用数据，导入全国 133 亿条社会信用数据，实现信息共享共用，鼓励金融机构基于信用信息开展金融创新，同时也在行内积累信用数据，打造大数据产业链、全方位服务链和全面治理链。总行投资银行部的债券承分销系统和财务顾问系统充分利用了 AI 技术，目前已完成系统开发和上线，为业务带来极大便利。

三、人工智能在投行领域的技术应用探讨

为进一步挖掘和了解 AI 在投行业务的具体需求和业务应用场景，课题小组对全行投行兼职研究分析员进行问卷调查和深度访谈，发现目前 AI 在投行业务领域的应用需求可分为格式化文档自动生成、商机发现和甄别、客户需求挖掘与方案设计和智能风险内控管理这四大类。

（一）问卷调查反馈

1. 格式化文档自动生成

在投资银行的相关业务中涉及大量的固定格式的报告撰写工作，如招股说明书中的部分章节、研究报告，以及投资意向书等。这些报告的撰写需要大量的投行初级员工进行长时间枯燥烦琐的数据罗列、整理、重复操作等。使用 AI 技术，可以从各类公开信息渠道抓取信息导入标准化模板，减少重复性劳动，提升劳动效率，解放劳动资本。如债务融资工具发行募集说明书自动生成、财务顾问智能咨询报告的生成，以及标准化的尽调模板设计。

2. 商机发现和甄别

将庞大的宏观、中观和微观数据汇聚梳理，同时收集历史数据并加以比对，进行预测，可以对潜在客户和商机进行遴选和甄别。具体应用场景可分为：

（1）债券承销业务精准营销。通过对接万得等资讯平台，获取发行人债券到期信息，到期前提早介入营销；分析发行人以往债券的发行周期和频率预测发行概率，并通过分析债券发行价格走势，帮助发行人选择发行窗口。

（2）IPO 客户的自动筛选。提前锁定未来一两年内符合条件的客户进行提前维护和布局，这对于投行抢抓客户和市场的先机意义重大。

（3）挖掘并购重组机遇。对不同上市板块、行业和发展阶段的已上市企业并购重组数据进行分析，预估这些公司或者新上市公司后续进行并购重组交易的可能性。

3. 高效撮合机制的搭建

分析前期成功撮合的交易数据，总结出不同投资者（子公司、金融同业机构、民营企业、政府引导基金和私募机构等）的投资偏好、风控要求和执行效率，并通过联动全行和各分支机构，广泛收集资产或者项目信息，使得资产和资金的匹配能够在大范围内高效进行，解决客户融资难题。

4. 智能风险和内控管理

在业务开展的过程中，利用 AI 技术识别企业在实际经营中可能存在的交叉担保、重复担保等情况，分析客户的还款能力，并在某些指标出现较大变化时提示经办行及时采取相应措施，还可通过网络媒体收集客户相关舆情，以便及时把握客户的动态经营情况，做好风险防控（见图 4.15）。

格式化文档自动生成	商机发现与甄别	高效撮合机制的搭建	智能风控和内控管理
· 发债业务中募集说明书的撰写 · 并购理财业务中尽调报告的撰写 · 财务顾问咨询报告的撰写	· 债券业务的到期再营销 · 上市和并购重组业务机会的发现	· 撮合债权类融资需求，如海外债发行 · 撮合股权类融资需求，如并购重组财务顾问业务中买卖双方的匹配	·提升理财业务投后管理水平 ·排除多层嵌套、交叉担保、重复担保等情况 ·反欺诈 ·内控管理

图 4.15　AI 在投行业务中的应用场景

通过对问卷内容的提炼，结合后续投行业务的发展方向，我们筛选出如下 4 个需求做进一步的技术可行性探讨，分别是：格式化文档的自动生成，应用场景为债券发行募集书的撰写；商机的发现与甄别，用于发债客户的业务预判和时机指导；高效撮合机制的搭建，用于财务顾问业务中资产端与资金端的匹配；咨询报告的生成，用于企业的财务顾问咨询服务。

（二）债券发行募集说明书的自动生成

1. 需求描述与应用场景

在投行业务中，债券发行中的募集说明书的撰写工作，是一项十分烦琐和高人工占用的工作。目前，在全行的投资银行业务条线中，大多数一级分行、二级分支行都面临着人员不足这个共性问题，由于人力资源的缺失，导致投行业务开展单一、业务发展不均衡、被同业抢占业务先机等例子比比皆是。以 AI 技术自动生成债券发行中的募集说明书等初步模板报告来代替投行人员手动撰写大量的模板和格式报告，可以节省投行人员大量的精力和时间。

2. 技术实现

（1）算法目标。使用 AI 解决高度模板化的文档人工撰写的低技术含量的高工作量问题，分为针对模板化内容和非模板化内容的两大技术模块。

（2）需要准备的数据。任意公司募集说明书 100 份、该公司以往募集说明书 1 份、该公司所聘请中介机构（评级公司、会计师事务所与法律事务所）所审定的材料文件 3 份，以及该公司起草注册上报的文件 1 份。

（3）对文档进行数据处理，特征提取。根据实际需求，对该公司以往募集说明书进行数据预处理，进行章节定位、段落定位和图表定位，并按照段落进行特征提取与分类识别（如内容是否变更、是否为年份数据等）。

（4）模型搭建与实现。募集说明书的单个文本量较大，所以技术手段将采用复合技术模型，具体包括两个技术模型：TD-IDF 词频向量文本相似度检测技术与 Simple RNN 文本生成技术。

3. 预期效果

表格数据更新效果示例如下所示。某公司 2014 年至 2016 年 9 月末货币资金明细情况如表 4.4 所示，结合评级公司文件描述数据得到截至 2017 年 9 月的公司项目情况，可以生成表 4.5。

表 4.4　发行人 2014 年至 2016 年 9 月末货币资金明细　（万元）

项目	2016 年 9 月	2015 年年末	2014 年年末
现金	1.93	0.31	6.62
银行存款	6 134.50	311.11	5 740.47
其他货币基金	6 076.58	0.00	0.00
合计	12 213.01	311.42	5 749.09

表 4.5 发行人 2015 年至 2017 年 9 月末货币资金明细 （万元）

项目	2017 年 9 月	2016 年年末	2015 年年末
现金	8.32	7.80	0.31
银行存款	4 731.67	6 792.20	311.11
其他货币基金	1 111.68	2 276.37	0.00
合计	5 851.67	9 076.37	311.42

通过现有技术可实现，数据定位提取准确率为 97%，进行数据匹配并重组成功准确率为 88%。

主观性文本分析段落数据更新示例如下所示：

2014 年年末，发行人货币资金余额 5 747.09 万元，其中现金 6.62 万元，银行存款 5 740.47 万元。2015 年年末，发行人货币资金余额 311.42 万元，其中现金 0.31 万元，银行存款 311.11 万元。2015 年货币资金较 2014 年减少 5 429.05 万元，主要原因是 2015 年支付了大量工程款。2016 年 9 月末，发行人货币资金余额 12 213.01 万元，其中现金 1.93 万元，银行存款 6 134.50 万元，其他货币资金 6 076.58 万元。2016 年 9 月末货币资金较 2015 年增加 11 901.59 万元，主要原因是新增向银行申请开具应付票据所存入的 6 076.58 万元保证金存款，其中因抵押、质押或冻结等对使用有限的其他货币资金全部是银行承兑汇票保证金。

根据新的表格，更新后的文本如下：

2015 年年末，发行人货币资金余额 311.42 万元，其中现金 0.31 万元，银行存款 311.11 万元。2015 年货币资金较少，主要原因是 2015 年支付了大量工程款。2016 年年末，发行人货币资金余额 9 076.37 万元，其中现金 7.80 万元，银行存款 6 792.20 万元，其他货币资金 2 276.37 万元。2016 年年末货币资金较 2015 年增加 8 764.95 万元，主要原因是新增向银行申请开具应付票据所存入的 6 076.58 万元保证金存款。其中因抵押、质押或冻结等对使用有限制的其他货币资金全部是银行承兑汇票保证金。2017 年 9 月末，发行人货币奖金余额 6 851.67 万元，其中现金 8.32 万元，银行存款4 731.67万元，其他货币资金 1 111.68 万元。2017 年 9 月末货币资金较 2015 年减少3 224.7万元。

通过现有技术，主观文本自动生成部分可实现 70% 的准确率。

（三）债券承销业务商机的发现与甄别

1. 需求描述与应用场景

通过获取某一段时间内债券发行较为频繁的企业数据，总结这些企业的共性因素，如企业类型、所属行业、评级、财务指标和外部宏观经济因子，来预测此类企业在未来某一段时间内发债的可能性，为银行开展发债业务和为客户建议发债时机提供参考。

2. 技术实现

（1）算法目标。对所收集到的历史数据加以比对和分析，来预测未来一段时间内将会开展发债业务的潜在客户。

（2）需要准备的数据。近5年内某一地区（如杭州）发行的企业债信息，包括发行主体、发行时债项评级和主体评级、债券期限、发行日期、到期日期和发行人财务信息等。

（3）数据预处理，特征提取。根据实际需求，对企业数据信息进行文字转成可识别数据的预处理，并提取该企业所有特征项，删除不必要的数据，填充空数据，将部分文本数据进行数字编码以进行数据运算等。

（4）模型搭建与实现。该模型为使准确率更高，采用随机森林与深度学习网络模型共同搭建而成的复合模型来预测结果，即将随机森林与深度学习网络模块预测结果再加权输出最终预测结果。

3. 预期效果

以债券承销深度学习网络模型为例，预期效果如下所示。

输入数据表，部分数据如表4.6所示。

由此预测出未来3个月内极可能有发债需求的企业有财通证券、富春环保、浙商银行、广厦控股集团、富阳农商银行、杭州银行、杭州市城市建设投资集团有限公司、巨化集团有限公司、杭州汽轮动力集团有限公司华融金融租赁股份有限公司、浙江省交通投资集团有限公司、杭州王才控股集团有限公司、浙江创联信息技术股份有限公司、浙江省兴合集团有限责任公司。

（四）财务顾问高效撮合机制的搭建

1. 需求描述与业务场景

撮合型财务顾问业务是指建设银行发挥自身的专业优势和信息优势，为融资主体或资产出让方（简称“资产端”）撮合对接投资者（简称“资金端”），并收取财务顾问收入的业务。根据资产端类型，撮合型财务顾问业务分为债权类撮合业务和股权类撮合业务。

债权类撮合对象的筛选标准为：客户主营业务为非限制性行业，可以提供合法合规、无权利瑕疵的项目/资产，且可以承受高于银行融资的价格；如果客户属于小企业客户，则财务顾问收入需从其他合作机构方来收取。股权类撮合对象的筛选标准为：符合国家产业政策和建行行业政策的企业，关注节能环保、新一代信息技术、大健康、高端装备制造、新能源等战略性新兴产业。就企业本身而言，应更多关注当前的发展阶段、创始团队和核心竞争力等。

表 4.6 债券承销部分数据表

证券代码	证券简称	到期日期	发行总额（亿元）	债券期限（天）	所属 Wind 行业名称（行业级别）一级行业	发行起始日期	发行价格（元）	营业总收入（报告期）去年年报（报表类型）合并报表
1282536. IB	12 浙交投 MTN3	2002 - 12 - 13	25	3 625	工业	2012 - 12 - 12	100	110 813 874 263. 9000
q14010604. ZJE	13 创联信息债			1 096	信息技术		100	
101359018. IB	13 盾安集 MTN002	2018 - 11 - 20	16	1 826	工业	2013 - 11 - 19	100	58 614 982 085. 8800
122308. SH	13 杭齿债	2019 - 07 - 11	4	1 826	工业	2013 - 11 - 19	100	1 658 490 746. 9300
1380043. IB	13 杭高新债	2020 - 01 - 28	5	2 556	工业	2013 - 01 - 28	100	663 554 105. 1600
101359008. IB	13 杭金投 MTN001	2018 - 09 - 16	7	1 826	工业	2013 - 09 - 12	100	8 945 099 653. 990
1380147. IB	13 杭运河债	2020 - 04 - 02	10	2 557	工业	2013 - 04 - 02	100	3 645 121 792. 0200
1322008. IB	13 华融租赁 02	2018 - 09 - 12	4	1 826	金融	2013 - 09 - 11	100	2 970 718 040. 1100
1380033. IB	13 吉利债	2020 - 01 - 24	12	2 556	可选消费	2013 - 01 - 24	100	278 264 593 706. 9800
106022. ZJE	13 临江债 1	2018 - 12 - 21	3	1 826	工业	2013 - 12 - 20	100	
101360014. IB	13 钱江水利 MTN	2018 - 10 - 16	1	1 826	公用事业	2013 - 10 - 15	100	981 292 457. 3200
q13102804. ZJE	13 天马债			730	信息技术		100	188 701 620. 8700
1380122. IB	13 余创债	2020 - 03 - 18	12	2 557	工业	2013 - 03 - 18	100	3 698 043 760. 7900
124141. SH	13 浙吉利	2020 - 01 - 24	12	2 556	可选消费	2013 - 01 - 24	100	278 264 593 706. 9800
101354013. IB	13 浙能源 MTN002	2020 - 09 - 04	30	2 557	公用事业	2013 - 09 - 03	100	81 343 729 272. 8100
1320028. IB	13 浙商银行债	2018 - 09 - 12	15	1 826	金融	2013 - 09 - 10	100	34 221 741 000. 0000
101359013. IB	13 浙兴合 MTN001	2018 - 11 - 11	4	1 826	工业	2013 - 11 - 07	100	84 849 715 784. 8800
123322. SH	14 财通 01	2019 - 10 - 28	10	1 826	金融	2014 - 10 - 28	100	4 001 533 664. 0400
123306. SH	14 财通 02	2019 - 11 - 17	10	1 826	金融	2014 - 11 - 17	100	4 011 533 664. 0400

我们认为可以采用人工智能算法在以往成功撮合的基础上建立撮合交易模型，使资产端与资金端能够更高效、更智能化地进行撮合匹配。

2. 技术实现

（1）算法目标。在建设银行财务顾问业务中为资产端与资金端之间搭建高效的撮合机制。

（2）所需数据集。主要为大量的资产端与资金端的历史撮合数据集，部分资金方数据集如表4.7所示。（3）数据预处理。通过历史撮合数据集构建语料库（资金端语料库与资产端语料库），每个语料库均包含资产端数据与资金端数据。接下来生成单词映射表，进行语料库处理，并对资产端数据与资金端数据一同进行 one-hot 编码（文本数据到向量数据的一种转换编码）。

（4）模型搭建与实现。在资产端模型中输入一方融资主体（或称资产端），输出与该资产端匹配度由高到低的排行前10位投资者（或称资金端）。在资金端模型中输入一方投资者（或称资金端），输出与该资金端匹配度由高到低的排行前10位的融资主体资产端。已进行撮合过的公司，若双方再次进入备选状态，将优先进入排行榜。

3. 预期效果

输入为“沈南鹏”和“熊晓鸽”资金端时，输出预测数据如下所示。

可为沈南鹏资金方所选择的资产方有：

大众汽车集团、御车神匠汽车服务科技有限公司、航铄工业股份有限公司、红能科技制造股份有限公司、赛恩智能科技有限公司、诺比侃机械制造有限公司、诺比侃科技有限公司、宏能科技有限公司、卡西威尔科技有限公司、瑞铂尔生物科技有限公司。

可为熊晓鸽资金方所选择的资产方有：

瑞克医疗产业有限公司、叮泉医药有限公司、福山生物科技有限公司、不器医疗器械有限公司、瑞铂尔生物科技有限公司、贯众健康管理有限公司、行为科技心理健康有限公司、上海仁学健康管理有限公司、修缘健康管理有限公司、诺比侃科技有限公司。

（五）财务顾问咨询报告的生成

1. 需求描述与应用场景

企业智能咨询服务，是在充分了解企业需求和经营现状的基础上，结合企业所属行业特征以及运用各种智能模型，得到：（1）企业纵向发展分析以及经营现状；（2）行业中企业所属地位和份额；（3）利用多维模型，构建可比企业筛选模型，为服务企业提供对标企业盈利能力、偿债能力、营运能力、公司结构和管理层、资源整合能力等比较信息；（4）锁定同赛道企业，为企业在发展中遇到的问题瓶颈、进一步发展方向、产业链整合发展等提供参考思路。

表 4.7 撮合数据集

资金方	投资行业偏好	黄金规模（亿元）	投资次数	跟投次数	资产方	行业类别	主营	盈利（千万元/年）	增长	方式	地域类型
沈南鹏	制造业	6	7	2	金安制造业公司	机械制造业	汽车、摩托车毛坯	1～2	连续 3 年	出让股权	境内并购
沈南鹏	制造业	6	7	2	大众汽车集团	汽车制造业	汽车及零部件	50～70	连续 5 年	出让股权	境内并购
沈南鹏	制造业	6	7	2	昊锐电气	制造业	桥梁、母线槽的制造	3～4	连续 2 年	出让股权	境内并购
沈南鹏	制造业	6	7	2	丽水船舶有限公司	制造业	船舶以及各种零件制造	5～7	连续 2 年	出让股权	跨境并购
沈南鹏	制造业	6	7	2	森泰高新技术公司	高新技术业	有色金属合金棒等	3～5	连续 4 年	出让股权	境内并购
熊晓鸽	生物医疗	4	7	1	金城生物有限公司	生物工程类	现代生物工程	1～2	连续 3 年	出让股权	境内并购
熊晓鸽	生物医疗	4	7	1	瑞克医疗产业基金	生物医疗产业	生物、医药医疗	2～4	连续 2 年	出让股权	跨境并购
熊晓鸽	生物医疗	4	7	1	沼泽医疗有限公司	医疗器械	康复护理、家庭护理	3～4	连续 1 年	出让股权	跨境并购
熊晓鸽	生物医疗	4	7	1	爱泰浦生物医药	生物医药	靶向生物多肽药物研发	20～25	连续 4 年	出让股权	境内并购
熊晓鸽	生物医疗	4	7	1	医帝生物科技	生物医疗器械生产	生物医疗器械研制	5～6	连续 4 年	出让股权	跨境并购
熊晓鸽	生物医疗	4	7	1	翼羽康复科技有限公司	医疗器械	生物医疗器械	3～5	连续 2 年	出让股权	境内并购
薛蛮子	汽车、财经、互联网	7	10	3	汽车之家	汽车销售	汽车销售	5～6	连续 5 年	出让股权	待定
薛蛮子	汽车、财经、互联网	7	10	3	雪球财经	财经新闻	财经新闻	3～4	连续 3 年	出让股权	境内并购
薛蛮子	汽车、财经、互联网	7	10	3	华艺百创	互联网新媒体	互联网新媒体	7～9	连续 2 年	出让股权	境内并购
薛蛮子	汽车、财经、互联网	7	10	3	中华学习网	互联网教育	互联网教育	6～8	连续 2 年	出让股权	境内并购
薛蛮子	汽车、财经、互联网	7	10	3	上海唔车网络科技有限公司	汽车媒体	汽车	5～6	连续 2 年	出让股权	境内并购
薛蛮子	汽车、财经、互联网	7	10	3	投呗传媒	互联网、新媒体	互联网、共享信息	4～6	连续 4 年	出让股权	境内并购
薛蛮子	汽车、财经、互联网	7	10	3	北京点线网络	互联网、游戏	游戏美术	10～12	连续 3 年	出让股权	待定
何劲松	电商	4	12	6	广州邦耀信息科技有限公司	电商	服装	3～4	连续 2 年	出让股权	境内并购
何劲松	电商	4	12	6	怡凡鲜果有限公司	电商	水果	4～5	连续 4 年	出让股权	境内并购
何劲松	电商	4	12	6	一六五进口商城有限公司	电商	进口服装	4～6	连续 3 年	出让股权	待定
何劲松	电商	4	12	6	购家装商城有限公司	电商	家装	9～11	连续 2 年	出让股权	境内并购
何劲松	电商	4	12	6	笨牛电子商务公司	电商	农资供应链	10～11	连续 4 年	出让股权	境内并购

企业智能咨询服务的意义是，除了可以帮助企业发现存在的“真正的问题”，也有利于银行做好行业研究，还能结合行业中龙头优质企业情况，向企业提出合理化发展建议。

2. 技术实现

（1）数据获取。人工智能建立在庞大数据量之上，目前数据来源一部分为企业提供，另一部分为网络大数据抓取。对于上市公司，可以在万得获取完整年报；而对于非上市公司，除了万得提供部分数据外，我们采用大数据聚焦爬虫技术进行网络抓取，并交叉验证，保证数据来源的可靠性。主要通过以下几个渠道进行抓取：政府网站、行业专业网站、媒体网站、咨询公司、海外以及其他。

上市公司：近 3 年公司年报或财务审计报告 1 份。

非上市公司：利用大数据技术获取近 3 年公司财务信息 3 份。

（2）模型搭建与实现。

①企业经营现状数据挖掘和评分模型。从数据预处理存储库中匹配抽取企业经营现状数据。包括财务效益状况、偿债能力状况、资产运营状况、经营效率状况、发展能力状况 5 个方面近 3 年的数据，得到 4 ×4 ×3 数据矩阵，生成企业近 3 年经营现状表格。使用如图 4. 16 所示的全连接神经网络评分模型，根据每种状况 4 个维度的数据对企业财务效益状况、偿债能力状况、资产运营状况、经营效率状况、发展能力状况 5 个方面进行评级，并根据 5 个方面对企业家进行评价，生成企业 3 年纵向发展动态变化曲线。

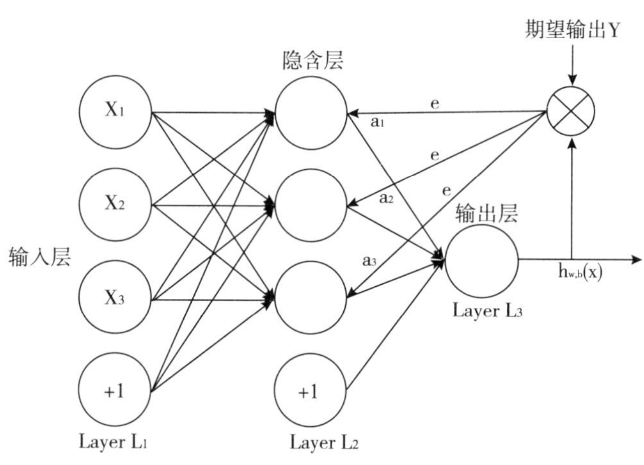

图 4. 16　全连接网络评级模型

②企业在行业中的地位和份额评价模型。根据每个行业的 18 个评价指标对行业进行评价，如表 4. 8 所示。

表 4.8　行业评价指标

公司数量	总市值（亿元）	本周涨跌幅（市值加权平均,%）
平均市盈率（TTM）	市值占比（%）	本月涨跌幅（市值加权平均,%）
平均市净率（LF）	市值平均（亿元）	本季涨跌幅（市值加权平均,%）
平均市销率（TTM）	市值中位数（亿元）	本年涨跌幅（市值加权平均,%）
营业总收入同比增长率	盈利能力最强的企业估值	最有核心竞争力的企业估值
发展最快的企业估值	最有潜力的企业估值	规模最大的企业估值

以 50 个行业为例，获取每一个行业上述表 4.8 中 18 类指标数据，组成 50×18 行业数据矩阵。

以同行业 50 个企业为例，获取每一个行业如表 4.9 所示的 20 类指标数据，组成 50×20 企业数据矩阵。通常在获取到的数据中会有数据缺失和奇异值的情况出现，首先采用众数和中位数对数据进行初步填充，避免个别数值较大的奇异数据的影响。中位数和数据排列相关，它是一组数据中间位置上的代表值，不受数据极端值的影响，能够表示数据的集中趋势。但是当数值没有明显次序时，可采用众数进行二次填充。

表 4.9　企业评价指标

净资产收益率	总资产报酬率	销售利润率	成本费用利润率
资产负债率	已获利息倍数	流动（速动）比率	现金流量负债率
总资产周转率	流动资产周转率	存货周转率	应收账款周转率
人均销售收入	人均利润率	人均利税率	全员劳动生产率
销售增长率	资本积累率	总（固定）资产成新率	3 年利润（资产）平均增长率

将行业矩阵数据和企业矩阵数据通过缺失值填充和去除噪音，最终得到完整企业信息数据。

从企业业务经营模式、企业规模、增长率、股权结构、资本结构、地域特点和营收来源 7 个维度进行可比企业筛选，从数据库中获取每个企业 7 个维度的信息，形成企业数量×企业筛选维度矩阵。将企业数量×企业筛选维度矩阵数据输入可比企业筛选模型，得到企业之间的相似度矩阵，同时将企业和企业自身相似度重置为 0，如表 4.10 所示。

表 4.10　企业相似度

	企业 1	企业 2	企业 3	企业 n
企业 1	0	r_{12}	r_{13}	r_{1n}
企业 2	r_{21}	0	r_{23}	r_{2n}
企业 3	r_{31}	r_{32}	0	r_{3n}
…	…	…	…	…
企业 n	r_{n1}	r_{n2}	r_{n3}	0

根据企业相似度矩阵，即可筛选出企业 n 个相似度最高的可比企业 k，并从数据库中匹配出可比企业 k 的盈利能力、偿债能力、营运能力、公司结构和管理层、资源整

合能力等比较信息。

③企业发展建议。根据基于因子分析的企业在行业中的地位和份额评价模型的结果，将同行业中企业按评分进行降序排序，取前10位的企业和所要服务的企业组成企业筛选维度矩阵 11×7，利用可比企业筛选模型得到所要服务的企业和前10位企业的相似度，筛选出前10位企业中和所要服务的企业相似度最高的企业。从数据库中匹配出相似度最高的企业的发展模式、融资渠道、并购重组、财务报表优化等信息，提供给所要服务的企业，生成企业的发展建议，为企业在发展中遇到的问题瓶颈、进一步发展方向和产业链整合发展等提供参考思路。

3. 预期结果

生成企业智能咨询服务报告，报告由4部分组成。

（1）企业纵向发展分析及经营现状。企业近3年经营现状数据表格（每年1份，共3份）；企业财务效益状况、偿债能力状况、资产运营状况、经营效率状况和发展能力状况评价结果1份；企业近3年纵向发展分析图1份。

（2）企业在行业中所属地位和份额。企业所属行业内所有企业排名表1份；企业在行业内综合得分数据分析1份；企业在行业内所占份额数据分析1份。

（3）可比企业信息。企业相似度矩阵表1份；可比企业盈利能力、偿债能力、营运能力、公司结构和管理层、资源整合能力等比较信息数据表1份。

（4）企业发展建议。所服务企业所属行业的前10位企业中与所服务企业相似度最高的企业信息一份；与所服务企业相似度最高的企业的发展模式、融资渠道、并购重组和财务报表等信息表一份。

四、总结

前文已对债券募集说明书自动生成、债券业务商机的发现进行了AI的技术应用探讨，并提出了财务顾问高效撮合机制的搭建和财务顾问咨询报告的需求分析。我们认为以上应用场景的落地对投行业务而言，无论是在业务获取数量、业务运作效率还是客户服务质量上，都将有很大的提振作用。

新的经济常态和监管环境对银行的业务发展提出了更高的要求，未来建行还必将加大在“智能投顾”和“量化交易”领域的AI技术投入。“智能投顾”通过向客户提供诸如产品需求分析、未来经济形势分析等内容，帮助客户进行资产配置，将财富管理的服务门槛降到普通个人。“量化交易”则以先进的数学模型替代人为的主观判断，有助于个人和机构做出理性的投资决策。两者结合，将有助于建行联动多方资源，打造“大投行、大资管、大财富”的发展战略。

论运用“金融科技”关爱视障人士的必要性及可行性

重庆市分行　杨　恩

科技在进步，给我们普通人的生活和工作带来了巨大便利，金融科技的运用更进一步提升了广大人民群众使用金融工具的便利性。而对于以视力障碍人群（包括视力有障碍的老年人群）为代表的残疾弱势群体的专门服务，却在一定程度上被我们忽视了。他们因为被忽视，导致失去了一些像正常人一样使用金融工具、购买金融产品、享受金融服务的权益。而作为国有大行，为广大群众提供全面、高效、便利的金融服务是我们义不容辞的责任，目前指纹识别、脸部识别、OCR 文本识别、语音合成技术等均已成熟，如果我们运用这些先进科技，在设计各项软硬件产品时充分考虑到视力障碍人士的需求，就可以实现对他们的专业服务。

一、为视力障碍人士提供金融服务的必要性

中国是世界上视力障碍人口最多的国家，仅盲人就占世界盲人人口的 18%，2016 年已超过 1 400 万，相当于每 100 个人中就有 1 人存在视力障碍。中国 60 周岁及以上的老年人有 2.5 亿，预计到 2050 年全世界患有中度至重度视力障碍人群（包括视力有障碍的老年人群）可能增长到超过 5 亿。中国的盲人数量比我们想象的多，却很难在银行网点柜台看到他们的身影，其主要原因是因为我们为他们提供的无障碍功能不够完善，在产品设计和使用上没有考虑他们的需求，如果没有人陪同，他们将很难独立在银行柜面办理业务，但如果要请专人或者亲人陪同，又会产生耗费金钱和时间成本大的问题。因此，帮助视力障碍人士到银行柜面办理业务，帮助其使用自助柜员机、智慧柜员机、手机银行、网上银行的无障碍功能，对他们来说就是刚需。

建行目前推进的“三大战略”之所以跟别人不一样，靠的是差异化的理念、差异化的服务和差异化的竞争手段。如果我们能够通过金融科技创新来切实为视力障碍人群提供服务，既能迅速打造差异化的竞争优势，又能体现社会工作者的责任和担当。现在所有网点都建立了“劳动者港湾”，视力障碍人士也是劳动者，他们也可以像其他

劳动者一样来网点歇歇脚、喝喝水，也有权利享受建设银行的金融服务，并且通过与他们的交流和为他们提供服务不仅能够增加与他们的联系，还可以带动他们的家人、朋友，从而带来更多的业务，另外还可以增进与民政局、特殊学校等的联系，进一步扩大客户群体。

二、为视力障碍人士提供金融服务的可行性

视力障碍人士的日常沟通和我们的不同之处在于，我们用眼睛选字，他们用耳朵听，用手指感觉。现代社会中，很多盲人喜欢使用苹果公司的产品，是因为苹果公司最早提供信息无障碍的产品，并且将功能做得很友好，例如通过读屏功能，帮助盲人顺畅地使用手机的各项功能。而反观国内不少安卓手机厂商，都把手机的读屏功能删掉了，导致视力障碍人士使用的不便。铁路 12306 网站还因为登录验证码为图片形式，没有提供可供盲人使用的语音验证方式，而被对方投诉了。中、农、工、交等商业银行目前也均未提供可供视力障碍人群使用的服务，如果建设银行能针对视力障碍人士优化各渠道产品，为他们的使用提供便利，就显得更难能可贵了。

（一）柜面业务实施的可行性及业务场景

1. 柜面需提供的软硬件设施

（1）在建行柜面提供视力障碍人群使用的专用耳机以及盲文专用键盘。

（2）对柜外清、自助柜员机、智慧柜员机等终端设备进行改造，在硬件上加入可外接耳机的功能。

（3）对新一代系统以及柜外清、自助柜员机、智慧柜员机等终端设备的软件进行优化，增加语音朗读功能，可将屏幕上显示的信息用语音的方式通过耳机进行播放，便于视力障碍人群辨识使用。

（4）对柜外清、自助柜员机、智慧柜员机等终端设备屏幕上显示的内容增加可全屏放大的功能，供视力障碍人群放大显示的内容，以方便其进行识别。

（5）在柜面业务交易凭证上的关键信息上增加盲文（如交易金额、交易方式、收付款人名称等），便于视力障碍人群辨识凭证上的内容。

（6）在柜面展示区提供盲文版的产品介绍资料，供视力障碍人群了解业务功能。

（7）在柜外清、自助柜员机、智慧柜员机等设备上增加指纹识别、人脸识别、录音录像功能，便于视力障碍人士进行业务确认。

（8）在柜面、自助柜员机、智慧柜员机等各种渠道增加“远程协助”功能，在视力障碍人士操作时可以通过远程协助的方式将操作界面的关键信息（如收付款人、账号、金额等）发送到其指定的人（如亲人）的手机，由指定的人员代其在远端电脑或

手机上进行操作确认。

2. 业务场景

(1) 当视力障碍人士初次到网点办理业务时，由网点大堂经理（或机器人、导盲犬）带领其到指定地点介绍业务，将盲文的产品介绍资料交予客户进行阅读，待客户确认需购买的产品后，由大堂经理带领至对应的柜台（高柜、低柜、自助柜员机、智慧柜员机）办理交易。柜台提供专用耳机及盲文键盘供视力障碍人士使用，通过指纹仪、脸部识别仪等留存其指纹、脸部信息，同时对整个流程进行录音录像，作为业务办理佐证留存。视力障碍人士通过盲文键盘完成确认信息的录入。

(2) 视力障碍人士再次到网点，可通过在柜外清、自助柜员机、智慧柜员机上的指纹仪、脸部识别仪等对其身份进行识别。柜外清、自助柜员机、智慧柜员机将屏幕上显示的内容放大显示，通过语音进行朗读，视力障碍人士通过专用耳机收听确认其办理相应的业务后，通过外接盲文键盘进行输入确认信息。待其业务办理完毕后，打印有盲文的交易凭证供视力障碍人士识别后加盖手印进行业务确认。对于相对复杂的业务，如汇款等，可选择通过“远程协助”的方式将屏幕信息发送至视力障碍人士指定的人员，由其指定的人员对屏幕的内容（如收款人姓名、账号、金额等信息）进行远程确认。整个业务办理过程通过录音录像设备进行全程录音或录像，作为以后业务办理的依据留存。

（二）其他渠道实施的可行性

(1) 在网上银行所有页面添加屏幕阅读器认可的标识，以利于操作系统内置的屏幕阅读器［Windows（视窗）系统］或 Voiceover（MacOS 系统）通过语音告知鼠标所在位置的内容。

(2) 对于网上银行、手机银行页面上以图片方式呈现的文字，由于无法通过屏幕阅读器进行识别，可采取 OCR 图文识别技术进行文字识别后，再通过语音合成技术进行朗读，便于视力障碍人士进行辨识。

(3) 在需要录入验证码的页面（包括图形验证、短信验证），增加语音验证方式，通过语音告知验证码内容，便于视力障碍人士使用。

(4) 在网上银行、手机银行中增加“远程协助”功能，在视力障碍人士操作时可以通过远程协助的方式将操作界面的关键信息（如收付款人、账号、金额等）发送到其指定的人（如亲人）的电脑或手机上，由指定的人员代其在远端电脑或手机上进行操作确认。

(5) 在商场 POS 机设备上增加盲文以及指纹识别、人脸识别、录音录像功能，便于视力障碍人士进行业务确认。

三、带来的社会效应和行业效益

（一）深化“劳动者港湾”成果

视力障碍人群的需求一直被金融机构长久地忽视，如果建行为其开辟专用功能，让其更多的感受到建行的关爱，能够体现出国有大行积极主动承担社会责任，进一步树立建设银行崭新的社会形象，赢得社会的尊重和支持，从而带来极大的社会效应。

（二）推动普惠金融发展

通过与特殊人群的密切联系，可以由此带来如特殊教育学校、残疾人社会保障机构等客户群体与建设银行的金融交往。

（三）提升行业形象

由于该客户群体自身的特点，其资金具有极强的稳定性，产品黏性极强，如果我们在设计产品的时候都能在金融同业中率先做好无障碍设计，那么将会形成事实行业标准。

（四）扩大社会效应

针对视力障碍人士优化的功能，也能为老年客户办理业务带来便利，使其感受到建设银行系统的优越性，从而进一步扩大客户群，带来更大的社会效应和经济效益。

建行金融科技促进重庆绿色金融发展

重庆市分行　李　睿

一、背景

（一）“绿色发展”已成为国家战略

绿色发展理念始终贯穿于我国治国理政的各核心环节，习近平总书记提出“绿水青山就是金山银山”，将生态优先、绿色发展提升到国家战略高度，全国上下积极践行“生态优先绿色发展”理念，各省市相继出台绿色金融发展规划、绿色金融发展指引等政策性文件，提出坚定不移走绿色发展道路，大力推动绿色金融发展，持续完善绿色金融体系相关要求。

央行重庆营管部在2017年10月9日印发《重庆市绿色金融发展规划（2017—2020）》和《加快推进重庆市绿色金融发展行动计划》，定义了绿色金融是指为支持环境的改善、应对气候的变化和资源节约高效利用的经济活动，即对环保、节能、绿色交通、绿色建筑、清洁能源、应对气候变化等领域的项目投融资、项目运营、风险管理等所提供的金融服务。重庆市由市金融办牵头，积极协调央行重庆营管部、重庆市发展和改革委员会、重庆市环境保护局、重庆市经济和信息化委员会等职能部门，加快构建绿色金融信息数据库，建立绿色项目标识和正面清单制，不定期向社会公开发布绿色项目信息，以促进绿色项目融资撮合。

（二）全行积极支持绿色金融业务发展

2018年6月6日，建总行在湖州召开绿色信贷工作推进会，王祖继行长提出“确保实现绿色贷款增速高于对公平均增速的战略目标”“绿色贷款由交通和能源领域，向绿色建筑、环境综合治理、节能环保服务业等新兴领域拓展”，首席风险官廖林提出“绿色信贷是调整对公信贷结构的重要的抓手”等支持绿色金融发展的观点。

二、重庆市绿色金融现状与问题

（一）现状

重庆市绿色信贷整体快步发展。2009 年，在全国率先试点将环保信息纳入企业和个人信用信息基础数据库，引导金融机构大力发展绿色信贷。截至 2016 年年末，全市绿色信贷余额 1 675.3 亿元，占全市贷款余额的 6.56%；2016 年，新增绿色信贷 254.76 亿元，占全市新增信贷的 9.92%。

（二）面临的问题

当前，我市绿色金融发展仍然面临很多问题和挑战。政策配套不够全面，针对绿色金融发展的评价、激励和风险控制等配套政策急需加快建立和完善。机制尚不健全，未形成“先行先试，整体推进”的运行机制，不利于绿色金融的长远健康发展。

（三）痛点分析

1. 针对政府机构

目前全市尚无统一绿色金融发布渠道，各职能部门发布项目信息方式多样，且发送对象不固定，缺乏专业化统一发布平台；项目融资撮合不足，项目发布后，对绿色项目的融资撮合、推介程度不够；数据统计分析不足，信息不及时，数据较单一，绿色金融整体情况难掌控。

2. 针对金融机构

传统信贷模式下绿色商机难获取，无法有针对性地吸引绿色企业融资，寻找绿色项目多数仅能靠“碰运气”；自身绿色融资金融产品难推介，无法更好地扩大推广面，且市场认可程度不高；对绿色项目认定标准难统一，项目甄别难度大，线下收集项目工作量大。

3. 针对企业

对政府政策了解不及时，不清楚绿色项目认定标准；对金融产品了解不深入，难以获取针对性的金融支持产品；无专门融资需求发布渠道，导致融资成本较大。

三、系统解决方案

（一）将“金融科技”与“绿色发展”“智能撮合”有机结合

为深入贯彻“以长江经济带发展推动经济高质量发展”的总体要求，积极践行

"生态优先绿色发展"理念，在广泛借鉴湖州市等先行先试模式的前提下，建行重庆市分行与重庆市金融工作办公室签订《绿色投融资项目库合作备忘录》，拟定基于建行智能撮合系统，开发搭建"绿色投融资项目库"，实现绿色项目信息发布、企业融资需求发布、金融机构产品发布及银企融资撮合等核心功能（见图4.17）。

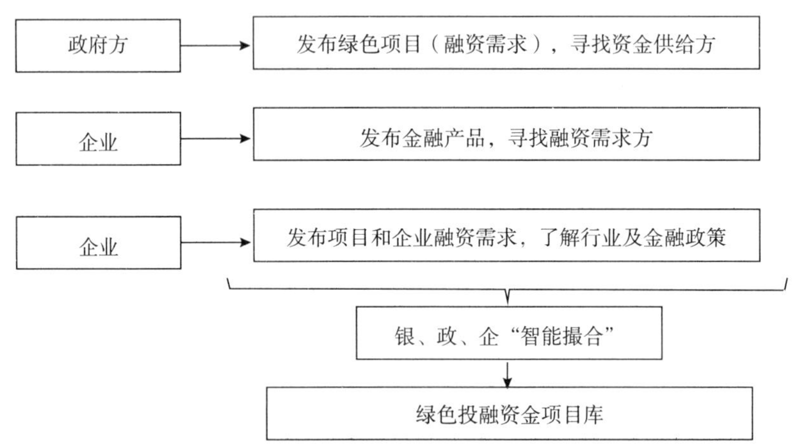

图4.17　绿色项目融资各方需求示意

一方面，该需求项目与建行现有"智能撮合系统"功能贴合，可共用客户架构，实现平台客户互联共享，客户资源向建行、向"智能撮合系统"引流。另一方面，通过政府部门主导推动，充分运用"智能撮合系统"现有功能，将该系统打造为重庆市唯一的集中化、电子化绿色项目发布平台，并积极开展平台推介，吸引绿色企业入驻及发布融资需求；同时，建行可在第一时间掌握项目信息，把握营销先机，并开放企业自主发布融资需求，将该系统打造为建行主动、高效的获客平台。

（二）与现有行内系统差异化分析

通过分析绿色投融资项目库与现有撮合平台主体功能，得出两者功能贴合，同时针对客户的具体场景和使用需求，可在撮合平台上提供部分差异化流程、角色、要素及定制化功能。

1. 改造优化点

在撮合平台基础上提供定制绿色金融专属界面、配套相应客户管理体系以及需求规则和推荐环节。通过"建融智合"撮合平台局部租户方式进行优化改造，定制绿色金融专属界面及运营参数管理，入库项目要素按照绿色项目认定标准进行个性化改造，同时提供独立域名登录。在客户管理方面，政府方作为制定项目认定标准方，也参与录入和发布需求，并给其单独分配机构操作号，金融机构包含银行等同业机构，向平台录入、提供金融类产品信息，也可浏览、反馈绿色项目信息，但要求与现有撮合平台上的其他客户和需求隔离。企业发布需求直接连接撮合平台寻求合作，并对绿色金融需求双方设计标签匹配进行推荐。

2. 新增功能

在撮合平台基础上新增专属需求主要体现在实现绿色子功能和客户专属定制服务两方面：需增加绿色项目、绿色企业融资和绿色金融产品子模块管理功能，为客户提供全方位绿色金融服务；向多方客户提供政策公告查询和多维度定制统计报表；并直联行内信贷系统，实现发起融资申请、自动反馈融资进展等自动化功能。

（三）“绿色投融资项目库”实施方案

1. 系统运作示意

系统运作示意如图 4. 18 所示。

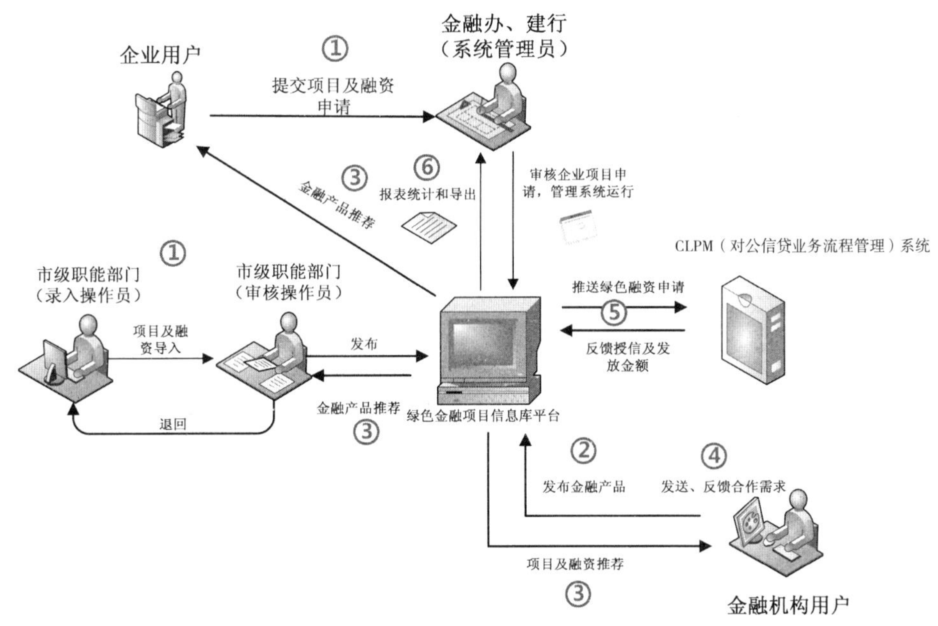

图 4. 18　系统运作示意

（1）由市金融办确定项目导入要素，政府和企业用户根据模板导入或手工录入并发布项目或融资需求。

（2）金融机构录入发布绿色金融产品。

（3）对新增需求或金融产品提取标签后进行消息推送。

（4）金融机构发送、反馈合作需求。

（5）与 CLPM 系统直连，实现建立信贷客户信息、发起信贷业务融资申请功能，并反馈授信金额和贷款发放金额至平台。

（6）对各方用户分权限提供实时和多维度的报表查询和导出。

2. 项目入库标准

“绿色项目”主要指满足《绿色债券支持项目目录（2015 年版）》标准的固定资产投资类项目，从行业分类来看主要包含节能、污染防治、资源节约与循环利用、清洁交通、清洁能源、生态保护和适应气候变化等类别。

项目库入库范围将综合考虑国家现行相关绿色标准要求以及重庆市绿色产业规划的相关要求。入库项目应具有显著的环境效益，同时应符合相关绿色标准的要求，包括《绿色债券支持项目目录（2015 年版）》《绿色债券发行指引》《绿色信贷指引》等相关文件的要求。入库项目除环境效益外，还应具有一定的社会效益，在同等条件下，优先支持在绿色扶贫、教育、医疗、社会保障、促进就业等方面具有示范作用和对区域绿色金融发展具有重大引领作用的项目。

3. 主要参与方

政府方：包括市金融办、人行重庆营管部、市发改委、市经信委、市环保局等重庆市涉及项目信息发布、管理的政府职能部门。

金融机构：银行等提供金融产品、满足融资需求的金融机构。

企业：具有独立法人资格的实体，绿色项目、企业融资的需求方。

系统管理员：市金融办、建设银行。

4. 金融机构操作流程

金融机构操作流程如图 4.19 所示。

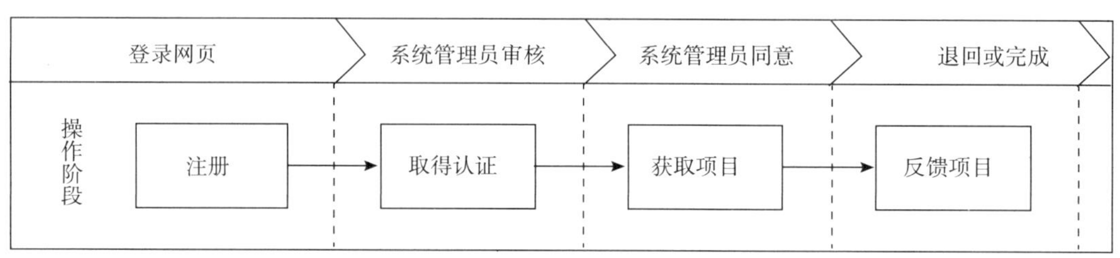

图 4.19　金融机构操作流程

（1）金融机构注册：市内各银行及金融机构注册完成后可浏览、查看所有项目信息。

（2）金融机构取得认证：对有项目撮合需求的银行及金融机构可向系统管理员发送实名认证申请，经管理员审核通过后开启获取及反馈项目权限。

（3）金融机构获取项目：为保护融资项目的单位隐私信息和提高撮合效率和质量，银行及金融机构需对目标项目发送获取意向，在征得系统管理员同意后才可获得项目联系人信息，此时项目详情中联系人信息由保密变为对其公开（后期可设置项目最多获取次数上限）。

（4）金融机构反馈项目：银行及金融机构在获取项目后开启反馈权限，并对项目实施情况及时进行反馈，对已经实施的项目反馈授信金额及融资投放金额，对未达成意向的项目及时反馈退回状态。

5. 项目状态实时更新流程

项目状态实时更新流程如图 4. 20 所示。

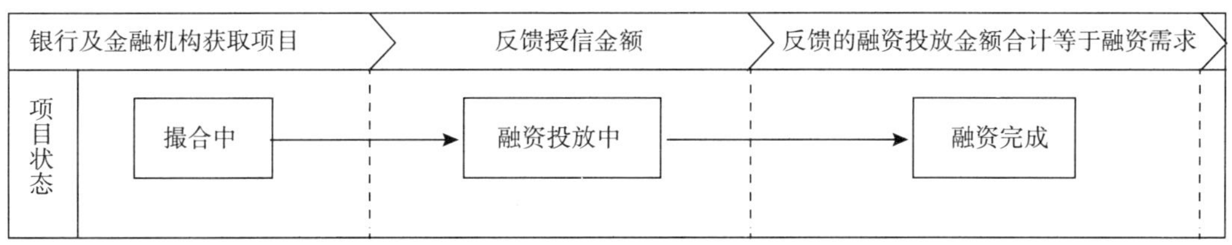

图 4. 20　项目状态实时更新流程

绿色项目库展示的项目，按金融机构反馈的情况，添加标签，划分为“撮合中”“融资投放中”“融资完成”3 种状态。

“撮合中”：绿色项目发布后，自动添加该标签。

“融资投放中”：金融机构反馈授信或融资信息后，自动更新标签。

“融资完成”：对于金融机构反馈融资投放金额已达到或超过录入融资需求的项目，自动更新标签，对于处于该状态的项目，企业、金融机构均不能再发送或反馈融资意向。

6. 公告新闻信息发布

向政府部门提供公告新闻发布模块功能，政府方可根据通知类型上传发布各类通知公告、政策意见、工作动态等消息；并对社会各方提供检索查询，可通过发布时间、发布机构、（标题、正文）关键字、发布机构等查看政策公告信息。

7. 数据统计

向政府、企业、金融机构分权限开放数据统计功能，包含数据查询、数据导出等功能。针对支持总量、结构分类、进度等多维度报表，选择对应要素后自动生成数据交叉统计表。在展示方面，可考虑加入动态热力图等功能以增强用户直观感受。

报表数据统计按时间点汇总入库，包括项目个数、入库项目总投资额、入库项目融资需求、平台金融机构数量、平台企业数量、授信总额、融资投放总额、融资余额及总额等数据。

四、实施效果预测

充分运用“智能撮合平台”进行定制开发，连接起政府、企业、金融机构，实现包括绿色项目信息发布、企业融资需求发布、金融产品发布、绿色项目融资撮合、融资合作情况监测、行业政策资讯、报表数据统计在内的全流程在线管理。

（一）解决当前问题

1. 政府

为政府打造专业化、统一化的绿色项目电子化信息平台，确保信息准确、共享、安全、及时。为绿色项目提供高效的融资撮合服务，提高金融支持效率。让政府及时掌握辖区内的绿色金融工作进度及成效，提供绿色项目信息统计依据。

2. 企业

企业及时获取绿色金融领域政策资讯、了解绿色项目认定标准和获取相关优惠政策信息，可以高效、快捷地对接绿色项目金融产品融资支持，并能自主发布融资需求，获得快速融资撮合及响应。

3. 金融机构

通过平台主动积极营销每年新增的绿色项目融资，拓展银行获客渠道，便于集中获客，获得精准商机。同时建行作为系统设计者，参与规则制定，有助于抢占业务先机，提升建行绿色项目市场份额。通过数据统计，实现金融机构排名，有助于树立建行绿色金融品牌形象。

（二）经济效益

目前重庆市绿色信贷余额超 1 800 亿元，存量企业和项目将陆续向平台迁移。重庆建行存量超 300 亿元绿色融资客户、项目全部迁移至平台，预计可累计实现向“智能撮合平台”年均 100 户以上的客户引流。

重庆市每年市级重点项目中绿色项目总投资超 3 000 亿元，客户和项目将全部向平台迁移，预计可直接联动建行每年新增项目授信 300 亿元以上，新增贷款投放 50 亿元以上，从而创造出巨大的经济效益。

（三）社会效益

若该系统顺利上线，将是重庆市范围内首个银政企合作的绿色项目信息发布和融资撮合平台，具有极强的示范效应和品牌价值。待项目稳定运营后，拟通过重庆市金融办将相关成果报送政府部门，逐步打破地域限制，扩充项目来源，实现“一点对全国”。这对树立建行绿色金融、科技金融的形象，推广建行“三大战略”有极大助益。

基于“波特五力”的企业手机银行建设构想

远程智能银行中心　沈楠楠　陈安琪

在中国经济转型发展的今天，小微企业有着大量金融服务需求，但由于分行客户经理队伍有限，只能优先服务于大型企业或集团客户，导致众多小微企业客户的金融服务需求无法得到充分挖掘与满足。企业手机银行作为企业客户电子渠道服务之一，是服务“双小”企业、落实普惠金融的具体措施，有着强大的经济效益和社会效益。

一、企业手机银行“波特五力”分析

企业手机银行是商业银行利用移动终端为企业客户提供查询、转账、理财、投融资等服务的产品。随着经济的快速发展，企业客户利用碎片化时间办公来达到提升效率、降低人力和时间成本的需求日益凸显，企业手机银行作为移动对公金融产品应运而生。

20 世纪 80 年代初，迈克尔・波特（Michael Porter）首度提出“波特五力”模型，包含 5 个因素，分别是行业内部现有竞争者、替代品威胁、潜在竞争者、供应商议价能力和购买者议价能力。“波特五力”将大量不同的因素汇集在一个简单的模型中，以此分析一个行业的基本竞争态势。利用这一工具来分析企业手机银行，有助于了解当前所处的竞争环境，从而采取有效的措施提高自身竞争力（见图 4.21）。

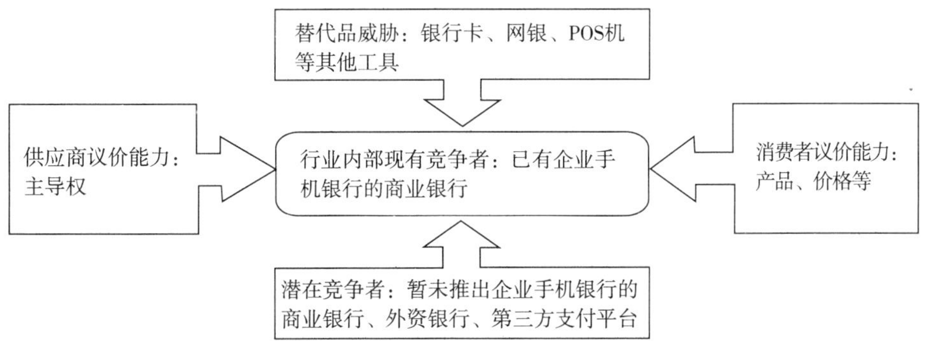

图 4.21　企业手机银行“波特五力”模型分析

（一）行业内部现有竞争者

企业手机银行作为各家商业银行竞相推出的对公移动金融服务产品之一，具有高收益、低成本的特点。目前，各家商业银行的企业手机银行发展情况不一，但大部分都是比照企业网银的现有功能，主要包括账务信息查询类、资金划转类、中间业务类（部分），同质化严重，竞争较激烈，具体情况见表4.11。

表4.11　部分商业银行企业手机银行功能概况

银行名称 （企业手机银行名称）	功能概况
工商银行 （工行企业手机银行）	财务信息查询类：账户管理 资金划转类：转账汇款、国际业务、支票扫码圈存、对公扫码支付 中间业务类：工行理财、网络融资、银企对账、工银小微金融、工银e商贸 辅助功能：回单验证、可视化分析、网点预约等
中国银行 （中行企业网银）	财务信息查询类：账户管理 资金划转类：转账汇款、跨行速汇、存款服务 中间业务类：电子商务 辅助功能：自助填单、回单验证等
农业银行 （农行企业掌银）	财务信息查询类：账户查询 资金划转类：转账支付、业务复核 中间业务类：理财基金 辅助功能：银企对账等
招商银行 （招行企业银行）	财务信息查询类：账户管理 资金划转类：支付结算、代发代扣、外汇买卖 中间业务类：电子商务、投融资 辅助功能：贴身金融助理等
交通银行 （交行企业银行）	财务信息查询类：账户查询、转账额度查询 资金划转类：转账 辅助功能：对账管理、利率查询、汇率查询等
浦发银行 （浦发企业版）	财务信息查询类：信息查询、集团查询 资金划转类：转账支付、三方存管、银期银商、手机号收款、ATM无卡取现、集团管理 中间业务类：理财产品、存款理财 辅助功能：银企对账、回单验证、电子印章、交易授权等

（二）替代品威胁

企业手机银行的替代品有银行卡、企业网银、POS机等其他工具。银行卡的特点是种类多样、功能丰富，所以它也是企业客户接受程度较高的一种工具。企业网银的特点是功能丰富，具备财务信息查询、资金划转、中间业务等各项功能，且流程灵活、方便快捷、成本低廉。目前，企业手机银行功能部署尚未完善，企业客户更认可网银渠道，这就要求在企业手机银行开发时，除了要覆盖企业网银各项功能外，还应提供契合移动办公需求的特色服务。POS 机虽具有操作简单、性能稳定等优点，但仅具备简单的查询和资金划转功能，使用场景较为有限。可见，对企业手机银行而言，企业网银和银行卡的替代威胁较大。

（三）潜在竞争者

企业手机银行面临的潜在竞争者包括暂未推出该产品的中小商业银行、外资银行和第三方支付平台。中小商业银行和外资银行在品牌影响力、客户资源、产品开发能力等方面虽与大型银行还有一定差距，但在企业手机银行市场尚未饱和的情况下，随着其公司业务的拓展，企业手机银行将逐渐成为这些银行新的发力点。另外，央行已向第三方支付平台市场颁发 218 块支付牌照，部分获得牌照的机构已推出企业支付产品，如用友的畅捷支付，是针对中小型公司的基于支付工具与企业财务软件的智能产品组合，目前部署在 POS 机支付终端，也将对当前企业手机银行市场产生一定威胁。

（四）消费者议价能力

消费者所处的谈判地位取决于其拥有的关于产品和价格的信息量。企业手机银行的替代品较多，资费基本相同，并且由于手机自身的物理条件限制使得屏幕显示信息有限，部分公司客户办理资金划转时较为不便，特别是对于业务规模较大、交易操作频繁的客户，使用手机办理查询转账等业务时信息展示的完整性大大降低。因此企业手机银行的消费者转换成本较低、议价能力较强。

（五）供应商议价能力

国内企业手机银行供应商是指各家商业银行、网络运营商、第三方平台运营商等。目前的合作模式是，商业银行向第三方平台运营商提供金融服务接口，网络运营商向第三方平台运营商提供通信接口，第三方平台运营商提供服务平台。在这三类供应商中，商业银行作为具有大额支付权限的主体，占据主导地位。

综上所述，企业手机银行目前在宣传方面存在认知少、推广难的问题；在体验方面存在功能需完善、资费无优势的困境。但作为一种结合移动通信技术的对公业务新模式，企业手机银行给公司客户带来了高效率、低成本、现代化的移动办公新体验，具备银行卡、企业网银等其他产品无法替代的优势。商业银行应该紧跟金融科技创新节奏，加大产品研发力度，进一步提高企业手机银行的实用性。下面以建行为例，具体分析企业手机银行发展面临的问题。

二、中国建设银行企业手机银行发展现状

2015 年 6 月，中国建设银行正式推出了企业手机银行服务，功能涵盖账户查询、转账业务、代发业务、电子支付、缴费业务、服务管理等，涉及账务信息查询类、资金划转类和辅助功能三大板块，其中资金划转类仅部署复核和审批功能。2017 年 10 月，建行企业手机银行客户端全面升级改版，推出交易制单、对公预开户、二维码收付、税务登记等功能，实现了移动端资金划转全流程交易。截至 2018 年 9 月，建行企业手机银行用户达 95 万户，约为企业网银用户的 13%，仍有较大发展空间。

（一）客户活跃度方面

截至 2018 年 9 月，建行企业手机银行存量活跃客户占比约为企业网银的 1/4，企业手机银行活跃度较低。究其原因主要有以下三个方面：一是建行企业手机银行的客户拓展主要依靠网点柜面人员营销，客户被动开通，主动使用意愿较差；二是在 2017 年 10 月改版前，客户必须通过企业网银制单后才可在企业手机银行上完成复核、审核等后续操作，无法实现业务全流程办理，进一步降低了客户使用意愿；三是使用建行企业手机银行需同时开立对公账户和高级版企业网银，两者均会产生一定费用，对于仅有账务信息查询类操作需求的客户来说门槛较高。而在开通方面，平安银行已推出查询版的企业手机银行，客户只需拥有企业结算账户即可查询相关信息，对于推广普及企业手机银行有较好的促进作用。

（二）功能部署方面

建行企业手机银行具有账务信息查询类、资金划转类部分功能及辅助功能，但中间业务类，比如投资理财、电子商业汇票、投融资等仍无法通过企业手机银行办理，功能单一，只能满足客户基本需求。2017 年 10 月，建行创新推出对公扫码收款，面对面一键扫码即可获取收款人信息，同时与华为强强联合推出手机内置盾，实现科技金融重大突破。但上述功能仍存在一定局限，如对公扫码收款仅支持建行账户，创新安全工具手机内置盾只适用于华为手机用户。而在二维码收款方面，工行企业手机银行已实现针对企业结算账户及公司一卡通生成标准银联收付款二维码的功能，扫码他行账户也可完成付款。

（三）客户服务方面

企业客户咨询具有业务种类多、操作复杂等特点，对客户服务的需求更大。但目

前，建行企业手机银行客户的线上咨询渠道较少，只有 95533 客服电话和官网在线客服，客户在使用企业手机银行过程中遇到问题，无法一键咨询。在客户服务渠道方面，中行、农行、招行等已在企业手机银行上部署在线客服，其中招行还提供了人工客服 + 智能机器人的服务方式，给企业客户提供了新的咨询途径和体验。

三、关于建设企业手机银行的几点构想

根据企业手机银行普遍面临的现状及问题，在开展企业手机银行建设时可参考以下几点构想。

（一）完善功能部署，开发特色服务

为了降低银行卡和企业网银等替代品威胁，提高企业手机银行竞争力，商业银行需完善企业手机银行各项功能，增加投资理财、票据业务、国际业务、信贷融资等中间业务类功能，实现企业手机银行替代企业网银交易操作；同时利用多屏互动，即在不同多媒体终端上（如手机、平板电脑、电视等之间）实现图片、文字等内容的传输、解析、展示、控制等一系列操作，降低手机屏幕尺寸的局限性，体现对公移动金融的特点。

此外，商业银行可通过大数据分析，精准用户画像，在细分用户的基础上，针对集团客户、军队武警类客户、中央财政和地方财政客户、小微企业开发专属企业手机银行。具体来说，针对集团客户开发中间业务丰富的手机银行，让客户掌控集团资金整体情况和成员单位的各类信息，同时充分利用闲散资金进行投资理财。针对小微企业则可开发功能较少、适用性更强的小微企业专属手机银行，让客户通过简单的账务信息查询和资金划转等操作即可完成日常业务运营。

（二）建立开放式平台，挖掘潜在客户

为挖掘更多潜在客户，做大客户规模，实现规模效益，商业银行可采取以下措施：一是在合理评估的基础上尝试取消开通企业网银的强制性要求，使开立对公账户的客户均可开通和使用企业手机所有功能；二是破除银行账户壁垒，吸收他行客户成为本行企业手机银行用户，实现部分信息查询功能；三是互联互通，实现柜面业务、微信银行、企业网银、企业手机银行等对公产品资源共享，让客户可以一站查询各渠道已办业务信息，进一步突显移动办公的便捷性。

（三）搭建海量场景，提高客户活跃度

企业支付结算与个人最大的不同在于，企业每笔收付款都必须对应清晰的收付依

据和做账凭证，以体现企业作为独立法人的授权意志。商业银行可基于企业手机银行的账户及产品服务体系，在金融产品、支付结算、身份验证等方面搭建海量公司运营场景，将线下金融需求转移到线上，在企业手机银行里融入更多互联网形态的线上金融需求，为不同行业客户群体提供定制化的商业场景服务。比如，商业银行可根据招投标场景，将线下招投标、投融资与客户财务情况结合起来，实现线上招投标资金审核、划转、退回等操作，让客户通过企业手机银行即可完成更多复杂的对公业务。

（四）打造立体智能服务，提高客户体验

一方面可部署统一客户服务专线、在线客服等服务渠道，增加企业客户服务路径；另一方面还可由被动服务向主动服务过渡，根据后台提取的客户数据，对有投资潜力的客户，在业务咨询服务后增加产品营销服务，打造“服务+营销”、实时互联的立体服务。此外，为增强企业手机银行核心竞争力，商业银行可引入智能语音交互、人脸识别、指纹等生物识别技术，将其应用到账户登录、转账汇款等业务场景中，缩短交易路径，降低操作难度，进一步提高客户体验。

业务研究篇

影子银行之同业非标对金融稳定的影响研究[①]

北京市分行 董瑾杰

一、引言

2018 年 4 月 27 日，大资管监管规定《关于规范金融机构资产管理业务的指导意见》正式实施。从 2017 年年末的数据看，资管新规将影响的业务余额达百万亿元之多。其中，同业非标[②]作为金融体系内影子银行的一部分已经浮出水面，成为大家共同关注的重点。我在 2017 年研究成果的基础上扩大了研究的样本，由原来的 13 家上市银行扩展到 A 股和港股两地上市共 41 家内资银行[③]，包括 6 家大型商业银行、9 家股份制商业银行、26 家城市商业银行和农村商业银行。这 41 家上市银行在 2017 年年末总资产达 169. 89 万亿元，占银保监会统计口径 2017 年年末商业银行 196. 78 万亿元总资产的 86. 33%；41 家上市银行 2017 年年末同业非标资产合计达 12. 63 万亿元，占股权及其他投资 22. 08 万亿元的 57. 2%，样本量足以代表整个银行业。本文新增加了监管效果分析部分，用于替换前作“发展情况”分析，除了统计同业非标资产的增减外，还运用面板数据分析同业负债（包括同业存单）与同业非标资产的关系、强监管年度影响等，得出大量新结论。同时，文章还继续深化了前作的“利益驱动、运作模式和

① 文章为精缩版，略去部分图表和内容，原文已发表于《投资研究》2018 年第 11 期。

② 本文所指的同业非标资产参考了银监发（2013）8 号文对非标资产的定义，是商业银行运用自营资金通过购买信托计划或资产管理计划等特殊目的载体投资于非标准化债权资产，包括但不限于信贷资产、信托贷款、委托债权、承兑汇票、信用证、应收账款、各类受（收）益权、带回购条款的股权性融资等不能在银行间市场或交易所流通的债权性资产，主要是资产负债表中三科目应收款项类投资、买入返售、可供出售项下的非标资产，部分银行包含权益类工具，暂未考虑以公允价值计量且其变动计入当期损益的金融资产科目下的非标资产。

③ 41 家上市银行为：工商银行、建设银行、农业银行、中国银行、交通银行、中国邮政储蓄银行、平安集团、兴业银行、招商银行、浦发银行、民生银行、中信银行、光大银行、华夏银行、北京银行、上海银行、江苏银行、浙商银行、南京银行、宁波银行、盛京银行、徽商银行、重庆农村商业银行、杭州银行、广州农商银行、锦州银行、天津银行、哈尔滨银行、中原银行、贵阳银行、郑州银行、成都银行、重庆银行、青岛银行、甘肃银行、九台农商银行、常熟农商银行、无锡农商银行、江阴农商银行、张家港农商银行、吴江农商银行。

资金流向分析”的研究内容，较前作选取的样本银行更有针对性，分析部分挖得更深，评估方法更合理，逻辑推理更完整。还有，在对金融稳定影响分析方面，不仅延续了前作的分析，还增加了格兰杰因果方法对金融稳定的实证研究，也得出了很多新结论。最后，我根据研究结论提出了有针对性的意见和建议，希望在防范系统性金融风险方面能够给读者以启发。

二、同业非标的监管效果分析

此部分与前作略有不同，前作分析的是同业非标绕过2013年、2014年票据非标强监管的实际发展情况，本文则是对近一年以来同业非标的强监管效果进行分析，既有进一步验证前作结论的内容，也有对新情况新发展的趋势分析。

（一）同业非标的宏观指标统计分析

如前作约定，截至2018年3月，金融机构同业资产的规模为56.52万亿元，增速在2017年大幅下降，占其他存款性总资产的比重从最高点25.27%下降到目前的22.32%，受强监管影响较大；金融机构同业负债的规模为29.16万亿元，占同期总负债的11.51%，2017年的趋势与2015年、2016年保持一致，受强监管的影响有限；M2（广义货币）的规模为173.99万亿元，增速在2016年、2017年大幅下降，从最高点14%下降到目前的8.2%，受强监管影响较大。

如图5.1所示，“其他存款性公司”（即商业银行）对其他金融机构债权和金融机构信贷收支表中的“股权及其他投资”从2015年开始增量几乎一致，股权及其他投资累计增量占同业资产累计增量的比重很高，并延续了之前的态势。同时，在图5.2中可以看出，随着股权及其他投资增速下降，广义信贷增速与M2增速差距迅速收窄。时隔一年，统计指标更加充分地证实了我前作的观点：“两科目累积增量一致，同业非标资产可代表股权及其他投资；同业非标资产通过股权及其他投资绕过了央行M2的监管，实现了广义信贷与M2的背离。”

（二）同业非标的微观指标统计分析

延续前作方法，如图5.3[①]所示，我统计了41家上市银行年报数据中三大科目（应收款项类投资、买入返售金融资产、可供出售金融资产）的同业非标资产，6家大型银行[②]2017年年末的数据为1.36万亿元，较2016年年底下降0.86万亿元，其中，

① 此处略去同业非标统计表。

② 2017年年末总资产大于9万亿元的6家大型银行。

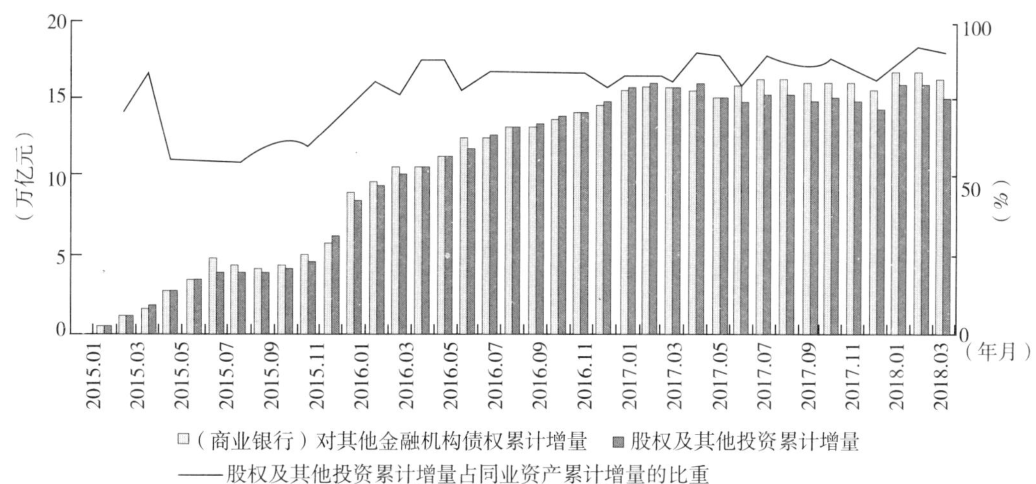

图 5.1 两科目累计增量比较

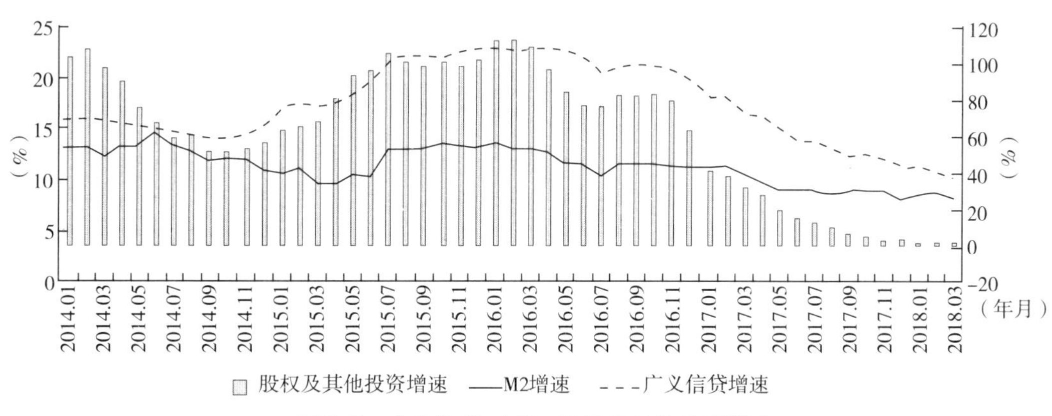

图 5.2 广义信贷、M2、股权及其他投资增速

资料来源：根据央行网站统计数据整理。

中国邮政储蓄银行 0.65 万亿元，占大型银行同业非标资产比重较大。15 家中型银行[①] 2017 年年末的数据为 8.9 万亿元，较 2016 年年底下降 1.11 万亿元，其中，平安集团、北京银行、江苏银行涨幅较为明显，兴业银行、中信银行、浦发银行、民生银行降幅较为明显。20 家小型银行[②] 2017 年年末的数据为 2.05 万亿元，较 2016 年增加 0.32 万亿元。41 家上市银行 2017 年年末的合计数为 12.63 万亿元，占股权及其他投资 22.08 万亿元的 57.2%，剩下未统计的主要是其他机构的股权及其他投资。由此，我们可以得出以下结论：第一，强监管控制了同业非标的增长速度，目前股权及其他投资已经

① 2017 年年末总资产大于 1 万亿元小于 9 万亿元的 15 家中型银行。

② 2017 年年末总资产小于 1 万亿元的 20 家小型银行。

开始下降；第二，6 家大型银行、15 家中型银行总量开始下降，20 家小型银行总量上升，同时，还可以判断其他机构的总量也在上升，说明整体的结构进行了调整，小型银行已成为同业非标资产发展的主力。

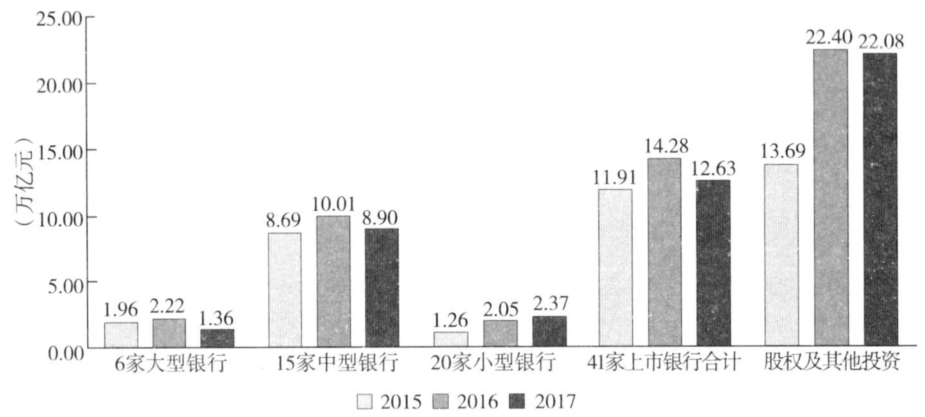

图 5.3　41 家上市银行同业非标数据统计表

资料来源：根据上市银行年报整理。

（三）同业存单规避监管情况分析

在同业非标监管效果评估中特别加入了前作没有的"同业存单面板分析"和"同业存单投资者结构分析"，主要是因为在 2017 年以前同业存单没有纳入央行宏观审慎评估体系（MPA）考核，使得同业负债约束条件中同业存放款项、同业拆借与同业存单不可比。对于发展比较突出的同业存单做面板分析可以评估未纳入 MPA 考核前和强监管下同业存单对影子银行的推动作用，找到症结后本文又进一步分析了同业存单的投资者结构，也是想看看支持影子银行发展的资金来源，为后续系列研究打下基础。

1. 同业存单面板分析①

根据面板数据分析结果显示，同业存单成为推动影子银行发展的新力量。第一，如果不考虑同业存单对同业负债的占比，同业负债占比系数只有 0.3 左右，低于考虑了同业存单的同业负债占比系数，应该说低估了同业非标的转化能力。从我的实务经验来看，0.63、0.69 的系数是比较合理的，而且与理财资金池中非标资产的转化能力也是接近的。通过同业负债支持同业非标资产发展模式并没有改变，只是同业负债成分中增加了同业存单。第二，在考虑了同业存单的 41 家银行和 28 家银行的转化模型中，28 家银行同业负债占比的转化能力为 0.69，高于 41 家银行的 0.63，

① 此处略去实证准备和检验结果。

这是符合逻辑的。国有大行相比于大中型银行同业非标资产占比低，通过提升同业负债占比提高同业非标占比的能力弱些，因而拉低了系数。另外，在考虑了时间固定效应的作用后，4 个模型在截距项都体现了相同的趋势，即 2015—2016 年，大做同业非标业务，截距项由负到正增长较多；2017 年强监管下，同业非标业务受到控制的比例下降，截距项也下降了。我们可以看到，考虑了同业存单的两个模型，大约都下降了 0.6，即考虑了时间效应，同业非标资产的占比下降了 0.6%。从监管效果上看，即使有同业存单的逆向推动，但强监管整体效果还是遏制了上升的势头，并拉低了 0.6%。

2. 同业存单投资者结构分析①

我统计了从 2014 年年底以来每半年的同业存单投资者结构时间序列数据，从数据中可以看出，非法人机构是同业存单的购买主力，根据我的经验，由于同业存单的回报率相对较高，银行违约的风险目前来看又不大，大、中、小型银行的理财资金肯定都会在非法人机构中，但是比较遗憾的是没有途径可以拿到非法人机构各家银行的份额。当然，从表内报表看，截至 2018 年 5 月，大银行同业购买同业存单的数据也不少，达到 7 861 亿元，农商行及农合行则更大，达到 1.26 万亿元。所以，同业存单投资份额方面非法人机构、金融机构表内各占一半左右。

三、同业非标的监管套利分析

本部分延续前作的“利益驱动、运作模式和资金流向分析”，实质就是监管套利分析。在利益驱动分析方面，重点选取了 2017 年同业非标占比高且增长迅速的银行作为研究对象，重点看它们的资产负债情况，同业负债方面则包括了同业存单。在运作模式分析方面，增加了同业存单和理财的部分，揭示了监管套利的本质。在资金流向分析方面即收益率成本率分析方面，我整理了 41 家银行年报中管理分析与讨论的重要内容，重在分析不同规模银行的监管套利方案。

（一）同业非标业务的利益驱动分析

1. 总资产与总负债规模增长驱动

本文选取的是强监管下同业非标资产占总资产比重高且 2017 年同业非标资产迅速增长的 13 家上市银行。

从图 5.4、图 5.5 可以看出，2016 年、2017 年 13 家上市银行通过同业负债②融资

① 此处略去同业存单投资者结构时间序列数据表。

② 同业负债口径：同业存放款项、同业拆借、同业存单。

同业非标投入模式还是比较明显的，其中，锦州银行同业非标资产占比达到 48.72%，同业负债占比达到 35.22%。同业负债占比超过 30% 以上的上市银行分别为天津银行、重庆银行、杭州银行、锦州银行、盛京银行。

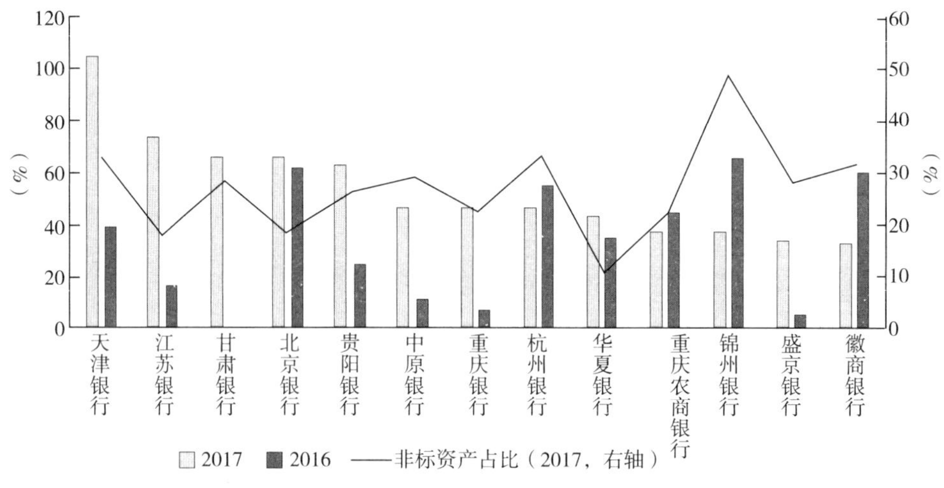

图 5.4　上市银行同业非标资产贡献及占比统计

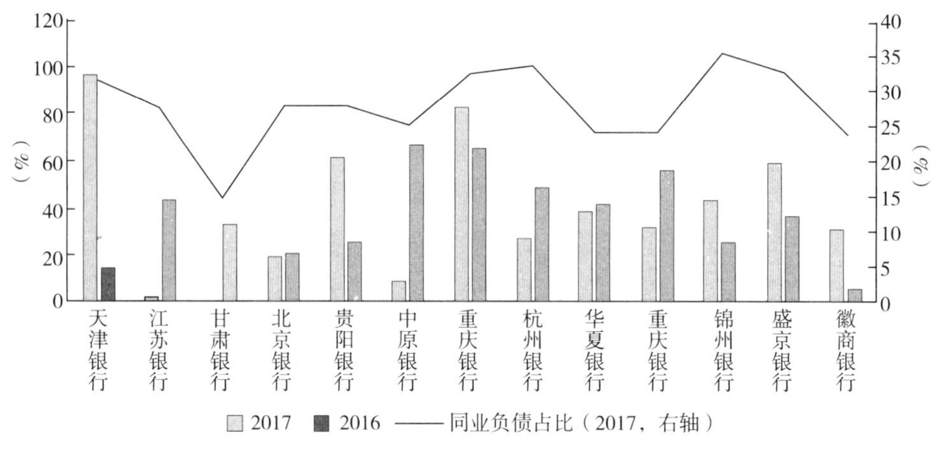

图 5.5　上市银行同业负债贡献及占比统计

资料来源：根据上市银行年报整理。

2. 收入贡献与减值贡献驱动

由于表内同业非标中实际情况为通道业务的规模不好估计，且不被提倡，故暂不考虑。我们假设所有表内同业非标均为自营资金主动管理的投资业务。此次，按照 2% 保守估计净收入，当然据我了解到的情况，实际的净收益率应该会更高。如图 5.6 所示，2016 年、2017 年同业非标逆势上涨的这些上市银行净收入相对其规模来说是非常可观的，同业非标净收入占营业收入的比重也比较高，很多银行都超过了 10%。由于图中的收入贡献只是预测，所以并不能十分准确。如天津银行[1]在2017年年报管理层分析与讨论中报告生息资产（信托受益权、理财产品及资产管理计划）平均余额的2 105.99亿元，与生息资产（客户贷款及垫款）的2 254.35亿元非常接近，按2%估算是42.12亿元（该行2017年实现净利润39.43亿元），比较合理。如果按前作的方法，以不同负债的成本率综合估计只有12.48亿元，明显偏低。而且还有一个问题，我们一直在说监管套利，其实同样数量的贷款与非标相比，非标的净收益率是要明显高于贷款的，我们没有将中间业务收入纳入考虑，当然也是因为计算的难度。

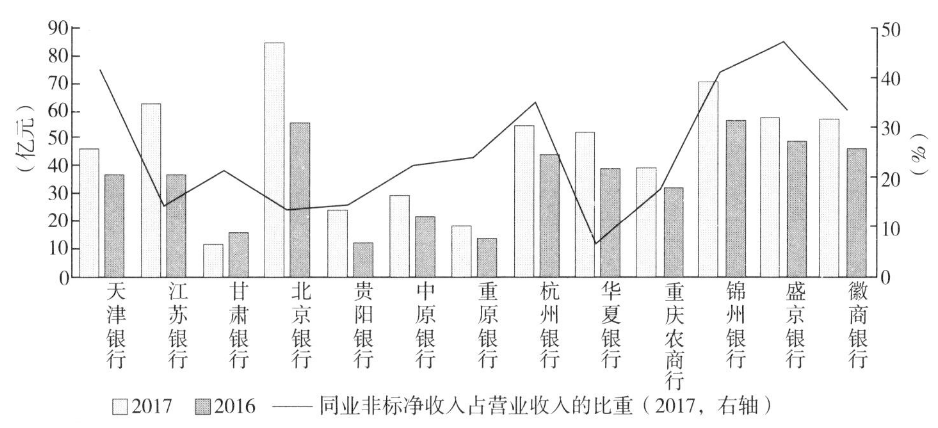

图5.6 上市银行收入贡献及占比统计

资料来源：根据上市银行年报整理。

与前作一致，因为没有直接数据可以计算，同业非标资产的减值比例按分子（三大科目的减值合计数，其中包括了标准资产）、分母（三大科目同业非标资产合计数）保守估计计算。这样，实际上同样的非标资产做分母还包含了三大科目中标准资产的减值，因而估计得到的比例比银行内部自己核算的比例要高。减值准备差额是通过将非标资产以同一银行贷款拨备率严格监管还原所需的数额。如图5.7，我们可以看出，部分上市银行差距不明显，部分上市银行差异较大，同业非标目前还是上市银行减值贡献的理想工具。

（二）同业非标业务的运作模式分析

如图5.8所示，在资管新规实施之前，银行业并没有被禁止资金池业务，也就是说无论表内表外，一部分资金购买非金融企业的标准资产，满足自身流动性和监管要

① 之所以拿天津银行做例子，并不是说它是最典型的同业非标银行，而是因为它在年度报告管理者分析与讨论中金融资产项下直接区分了标准与非标，让我拿到了该行全年平均的同业非标资产余额，大大降低了估计的难度。

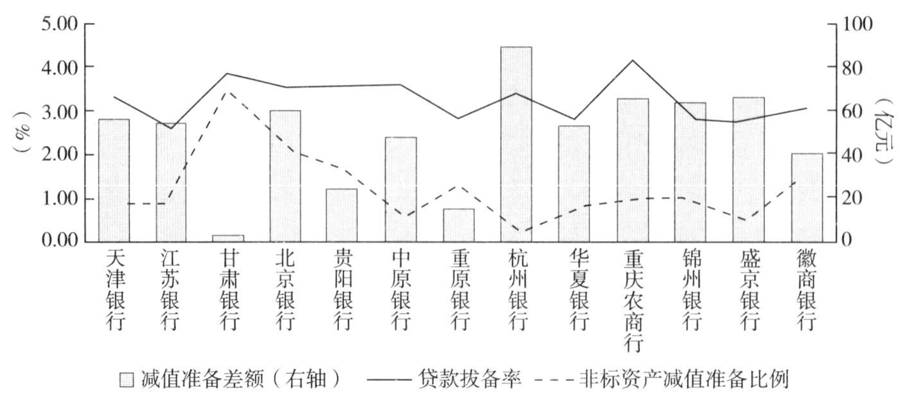

图5.7　上市银行减值贡献统计

资料来源：根据上市银行年报整理。

求；另一部分资金实施同业融资，存放同业或者购买同业存单，相互支持做大规模；还有一部分资金以非标类信贷的形式投向非公开市场。目前，银行业主要通过同业互做（同业存放、同业理财、同业存单），以无须或较少缴纳存款准备金、"以贷转存"的方式来放大杠杆做大规模。近期比较明显的是大量小银行在资产和负债两端都大幅增加同业存单，其他银行则通过表外理财投资中小银行同业存单，表内负债大量发行同业存单进行监管套利。

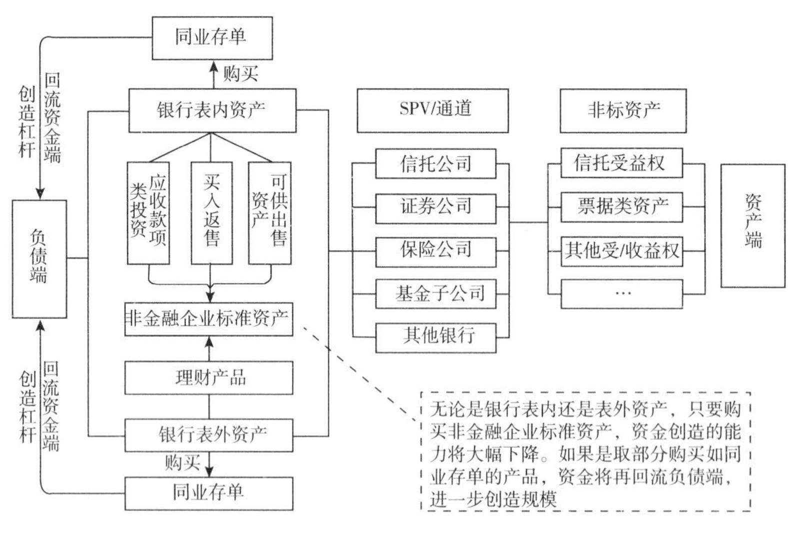

图5.8　银行非标资产的配置与运作图

如图5.9所示，在同业理财被监管大幅压缩以前，银行自营资金要投"理财可以投自营不能投"的产品时，挂一层理财就可以了。理财产品要投"机构投资者可以投理财不能投"的产品时，挂一层过桥企业就可以了。实际上，这种流程是针对监管对

“银行、非银行金融机构、机构投资者”的差异化限制要求的变通方法，在很多时候并没有那么复杂，最简单的路程可能就是银行 A – 信托公司 – 借款企业。当然，同业理财被大幅压缩后，银行通过同业理财的方式少了，但还可以通过 SPV（特殊目的载体）同业借款来投资。不过现在的这些企业都是要占授信的，同时它们也成为监管检查的重点，监管套利难度变得越来越大。在过去，如果过桥企业 N 是机构投资者，这个 M 的投资就可以很广泛，可以通过配资、场外高杠杆，以优先级或劣后级的身份投向房地产、股票、债券、外汇市场、两高一剩行业、地方政府融资平台。而且，各金融机构之间通过私下签订抽屉协议、回购条款，连内部审计也很难跨机构查出问题。还有，即使没有通过理财、企业、银行链条，银行自营资金也可直接投向地方政府融资平台。由于融资平台中涉及县市、街道办的也很多，这个资金监管也是问题，被挪用到限制领域也是可能的。此外，即使是银行自营资金投向租赁公司、财务公司、资产管理公司公开发行的标准资产债券，也不能确定其最后投向了实体经济，如租赁公司获得融资后将资金融出给学校、医院等事业单位，管理不规范就有可能从这些渠道部分进入限制领域。具体的方式可以是定期存单融资，获得融资的企业先将资金用于定期存款（不冻结），再将存款存单用于质押或者转成存单收益权，以获取使用范围宽松的资金。

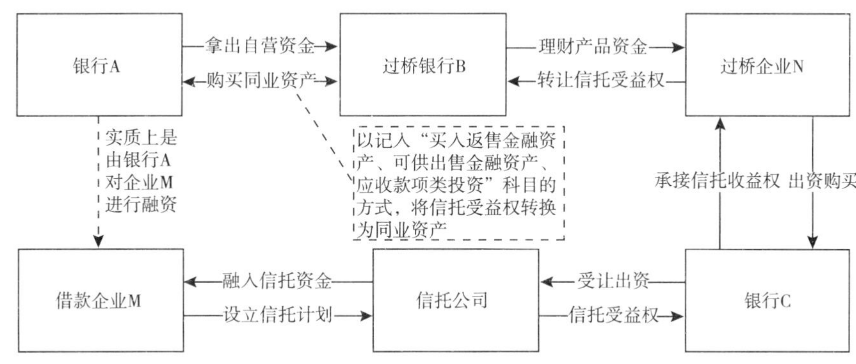

图 5.9　自营资金投资信托收益的业务流程

影子银行之同业非标业务的运作模式本质上是监管套利，是通过“卖合规”来赚钱的行为。这些违法违规行为在银监发（2018）4 号文中有所提及，但从实操的角度来看又不完全一样，具体表现在两个方面。第一，在具体融资流程中如申报、审批和放款环节进行差异化管理，以没有行内制度文件依据或系统支持为由，通过同业业务和理财业务等方式，违反宏观调控政策继续向股票市场、房地产和“两高一剩”行业等限制或禁止领域提供融资。如不是以“宏观调控政策”作为内控审批标准，而是以“优质融资客户的流动性支持文件”“担保文件”“大信托公司声誉风险”“信托固有资金刚兑、承接”作为风险防范措施，继续向“四证”不全、资本金未真正到位的房地产开发项目提供融资。又如，违反落实新《预算法》和国务院关于地方政府性债务管理的有关要求，通过产业基金、委托贷款等方式提供融资，放大政府性债务，通过产业基金等进行非标资产投资。第二，在同业、理财业务涉及的资产端，负债端进行差异化管理，以造假业务数据、篡改报监管定期监控指标、变更会计科目等方式，继续违规开展同业业务和理财业务。如关于同业融入资金余额占比负债总额不得超过1/3的规定，往往是通过扩大有利指标，压缩不利指标，在资产负债表日、季度末勉强达标，其他时点通过差异化管理变更会计科目，违规将同业存款变为一般性存款等手段进行监管套利。又如，通过将非标资产人为调整按照标准资产核算，影响流动性指标，变相突破理财资金投资非标债权资产总额不能超理财余额的35%和银行上一年度审计报告披露总资产的4%的上限进行监管套利。在监管套利问题上，当然不仅仅是中小银行有，国有大行、股份制商业银行也同样存在。根据2018年6月20日审计署发布的有关3家大型金融机构2016年度资产负债损益审计结果公告，审计署审计发现的经营合规性问题主要包括：违规向地方政府融资平台或实际承担融资平台功能的企业，向高污染、高耗能企业，以及向土地储备中心、“四证”不全的房地产企业提供新增融资等；违规向不符合条件的企业提供贷款、办理票据贴现、黄金租赁等业务；虚增存款规模、违规设立时点性存款规模考核指标等；违规同业发售、调节收益、向不符合条件的客户提供融资以及借助信托等通道将理财资金违规投资本行非公开发行优先股等；在未提供实质性服务的情况下，向企业收取顾问费等；小微、涉农等贷款统计不准确，部分业务未完成监管部门考核要求等。

一言以蔽之，各家银行本身或多或少会从事影子银行业务以获取违规经营超额收益，即使投向地方政府平台也有可能挪作他用，即使投向标准资产也有可能在第二层、第三层进入限制领域。同时，各家银行通过表内自营表外理财以存放同业、购买同业存单、购买同业理财的方式为其他银行提供流动性，通过互做放大系数、做大规模。

（三）同业非标业务的收益率成本率分析①

延续前作，我在此部分统计了41家上市银行2017年、2016年生息资产计息负债情况，其中包括生息资产的贷款和垫款、投资项下、存拆放同业、计息负债的存款、同业拆存放、应付债券的平均余额和收益率/成本率。通过不同年份、不同银行的数据比较方法，我发现了较前作更多更深的监管套利事实。

首先，2017年锦州银行、哈尔滨银行、贵阳银行、郑州银行、成都银行、重庆银行、甘肃银行及常熟农商银行这些在年报中的讨论与分析部分没有通过混合标准、非标资产拉低收益率的银行，明显体现了高收益资产的特征。如锦州银行2017年年末的

① 此处略去41家上市银行生息资产计息负债统计表。

同业非标资产与投资项下年平均值基本一致，也就是说可能这里面大部分就是同业非标资产，较少标准资产，收益率高达 6.9%，而该行的贷款和垫款的年平均值只有 1 756亿元，平均收益率为 6.33%。当然，应收款项类投资的英文是“the account loans and receivables”，其本身有很多在英文版年报中就是与贷款合并计量的，实际上就是贷款。

其次，投资项下的标准资产，如果主要是债券和票据，尤其是在正常的买入返售、可供出售科目下，基本上收益率都保持在 3.5% 左右，正常情况下大部分都是配置国债、金融债、地方债，小部分配置高信用等级企业债。这里的银行投资标准资产与私募基金还是有区别的，由于风险偏好的原因，它不会配置过多的低信用等级高收益债券。很明显，部分银行投资项下将同业非标和标准资产混合，以拉低收益率，隐藏监管套利事实。当然，这跟大小银行财务报表美化水平的高低也有关系，网上一直铺天盖地地在说理财非标表外回归表内，其实表内的同业非标资产数量也很惊人。

再次，虽然 2017 年许多银行贷款和投资项下收益率下降，应付债券、同业存拆放成本率上升，但只要边际成本低于边际收益，影子银行就会继续增加通过短期限同业负债（包括同业存单）长期限加杠杆配置同业非标资产。目前，我了解到的情况是各家银行开始积极进行同业转型，效仿贷款收益转中间业务收入的模式，加大了同业业务事业部和金融科技公司建设力度，不通过年度财务报表中讨论与分析体现，而以同业业务管理费、咨询费，金融科技同业业务服务费，低成本同业存款托管的方式来进行监管套利。所以，在统计表中，有些同业非标资产高，能提供流动性支持的银行如果同业非标的收益率偏低，除了混合了标准资产以拉低系数以外，可能还进行了收益转移，以表面上是通道、收费很低，其实综合收益很高，将真实收入计进非利息收入的方式欺骗监管。

通过收益率成本率分析，我发现对于监管套利来说，大、中、小银行各自有各自的方法。小银行由于规模小、服务少，报表调节空间有限，进行监管套利露馅儿的可能性就非常大。当然，验证监管套利的事实很容易，而其他隐藏的、复杂的就需要更多的数据和信息，不是通过年报等公开市场信息就可以获得的，不过根据从业经验，通过基本趋势和思路还是可以把握的。

四、同业非标对金融稳定的影响分析

此部分在前作脉冲响应分析的基础上增加了格兰杰因果关系分析，除了进一步验证前作的结论外，还发现了同业非标更多影响金融稳定的结论。①

① 此处直接给出结论，略去实证检验过程和结果。

（一）对股权及其他投资的脉冲响应分析有了新进展

第一，影子银行同业非标增速即股权及其他投资增速对于货币政策中介目标 M2 增速的影响随着其分量的不断变大而变强，从几乎毫无影响发展到产生 5 期正 5 期小负的影响，而 M2 增速对于股权及其他投资增速的影响则从剧烈波动变为快速下降，说明早期在宽松的货币政策下对股权及其他投资增速的影响是比较明显的，后期 M2 增速对股权及其他投资增速的影响有限而且快速减弱。第二，股权及其他投资增速变动一个标准差对贷款增速的脉冲在早年间几乎没有影响，总是小幅上下波动。后来贷款增速受到股权及其他投资增速的一个正向冲击后，从第 1 期到第 4 期会有一个从上到下的正值走势，然后是从下到上的负值走势，直到第 10 期结束。同时，通过贷款增速变动一个标准差对股权及其他投资增速的脉冲函数图，早先与后来还是产生了变化。第三，在 M2 与贷款的脉冲响应分析方面，第 1 期、第 2 期脉冲响应差异不大，说明股权及其他投资的发展还没有对贷款增速与 M2 增速的影响产生显著变化。

（二）在股权及其他投资与 M2、贷款、股市、房市的格兰杰因果关系分析方面有了新洞察

第一，股权及其他投资的增速与 M2 增速，无论是长期还是短期，双方互为格兰杰因果。即强监管下股权及其他投资增速大幅下降，M2 增速也大幅下降。第二，股权及其他投资的增速与贷款的增速，无论是长期还是短期，互为格兰杰因果。股权及其他投资作为自有资金，成为制度监管的漏洞，充当了资金掮客，实现了限制领域贷款发放的前提条件。第三，从实证的结论上看，强监管控制了股权及其他投资的增速，甚至是反向下降，那么股市应该也会有反应而跟着向下走。只要监管一直大幅压控股权及其他投资，如果市场上找不到其他影子银行渠道来输血股市，股市与股权及其他投资的这种相关关系必然会导致出现股市持续不断大跌的情况。第四，无论是短期限还是长期限，股票全量指数的增速变动能格兰杰引起贷款的增速变动，贷款的增速变动不能格兰杰引起股票全量指数的增速变动。第五，从实证的结论上看，股权及其他投资的增速变动能格兰杰引起一线住房均价增速变动，二、三线住房均价增速变动能格兰杰引起股权及其他投资的增速变动。

五、意见和建议

从我个人的理解来说，这些同业非标凡是嵌套的业务，哪怕只有一层，都是有违监管的因素在内，要不然何必多此一举呢？实质上是由于不同行业的管理、支持、限制不一样，银行的资金投表内贷款没有投同业非标好处多。因此，为了有针对性地解

决影子银行之同业非标的问题，我结合研究结论，提出以下三点建议。

一是建议国家加大对银行财务报表的跟踪压控。如果国家认识到同业非标的非法性，我建议以3年为限，每半年对银行财务报表评估一次，每次要求降低原始总量的1/6，争取在系统性风险攻坚战期限结束前完全压光同业非标资产。同时，对2017年强监管下仍然逆势上涨的银行加强非标资产的现场和非现场检查力度，对大量通过同业负债（包括同业存单）融资的银行应制定控制措施，鉴于同业存放的业务复杂性，可鼓励银行逐步以同业存单替换同业存放，并限制1个月及以上同业存放产品的发展。

二是建议国家加大对中间业务收入的检查力度，特别是涉及同业业务科技、服务平台（在检查时可以与通道业务收费进行关联分析，这样能够更快地定位到目标客户），并要求所有银行在年报披露中对所有同业非标资产必须单独披露，在讨论与分析中不能与标准资产混合来拉低收益率指标。同时，加大对银行理财、自营业务审批条件、放款条件、持续性条件、投后管理的检查力度，重新全面核查理财、自营报监管的系统开发逻辑，核查是否存在单笔业务数据造假、线上线下总分支机构有多套数据的情况。

三是建议国家更加深入地研究股权及其他投资增速对M2增速、贷款增速的影响，可在实施强监管“紧缩货币政策”的同时继续加大定向降准“宽松货币政策”，以对冲因为打击影子银行所带来的M2增速、贷款增速下降的影响。研究股权及其他投资与房地产、股市的内在关系变化，从实证上来看，股权及其他投资增速下降将带来一线住房均价增速下降，二、三线住房均价增速下降将带来股权及其他投资增速下降。国家可尝试通过多部门联合行动，通过控制二、三线住房均价增速或者直接控制股权及其他投资增速，进而控制一线住房均价增速。

发挥基石作用，打造建行“新零售”

——新时期零售业务定位与转型发展研究

建行大学普惠与零售研修院　杨绍萍　段玮珅

一、商业银行零售业务发展趋势

中国特色社会主义迈入了继往开来的新时代，我国商业银行零售业务也处在市场格局快速分化、金融科技催生重构的新阶段。主要体现在五个方面。

（一）人民的美好生活要求零售业务承担更大责任

我国社会的主要矛盾已经转化为人民日益增长的美好生活需要和不平衡不充分的发展之间的矛盾。零售业务是银行最贴近人民生活的服务领域，涵盖储蓄、信贷、支付结算和投资理财等金融服务，深入社保、交通、医疗和文教等民生性场景。2017 年年末，国内个人客户可投资资产已突破 188 万亿元，资产保值、增值和传承等需求十分旺盛。

（二）“消费时代”全面到来催生零售业务市场格局巨变

消费成为我国经济增长的主动力，2012—2017 年对经济增长的贡献率由 55% 升至 59%。客户“资产负债表”结构发生质变，住户贷款快速增长。2013—2017 年我国居民家庭债务占 GDP 比重由 33% 升至 49%。与此同时，客户代际更迭，80 后、90 后和 00 后正成为消费市场的主导力量，银行必须提供与之需求更适应的产品和服务。

（三）金融科技迅猛发展颠覆零售业务的传统经营模式

金融产品嵌入客户日常高频场景，实现了生活化、在线化和移动化。金融科技巨头以支付为入口，向投资理财、消费信贷领域渗透。客户行为正由线下全面向线上转移，金融脱媒加剧。2017 年，第三方支付在国内银行支付交易笔数占比 90%，建行第三方触发支付笔数占比 90% 。

（四）商业银行创新求变，力度之大、步伐之快前所未有

工行推出“工银小白”“AI投”智能投顾等服务。平安集团实施“金融+科技”的双轮驱动，打造金融、健康、汽车和房产生态圈。上海银行抓住个人账户管理新政，突破线上获客，二、三类账户交易规模已超过一类账户。

（五）监管进入新阶段，金融市场开放达到新程度

利率市场化向纵深推进，资管新规打破理财刚兑，理财大众化发展催生全民理财。国内投资市场震荡加剧，保险回归保障，外汇市场本币贬值，对综合化资产管理服务能力要求更高。央行重构账户体系、加强第三方支付监管、重塑移动支付规则、规范创新等多维度布局，带来金融机构和第三方支付机构的新一轮跑马圈地。

二、新时期建设银行零售业务经营定位分析

（一）特征属性定位：零售业务是全行经营的助推器和稳定器

在经济上升期，零售业务是商业银行经营的助推器；在经济波动期，零售业务是商业银行经营的稳定器。首先，零售业务呈“两低一高一稳”的特征。一是不良率低，2018年上半年零售贷款不良率为0.45%，全集团则为1.48%；二是经济资本消耗低，零售贷款余额占全行总量的45%，但经济资本消耗只占20%；三是经济资本回报率高，零售业务为63%，全行为28%；四是效益贡献稳定、持续提升，零售业务的净利润、经济增加值在全行占比分别为44%和68%，2008年以来的10年间没有出现过负增长。其次，零售业务与国有大行的客户口碑、品牌形象和社会影响密切相关，服务千家万户，延伸到社会末端细胞，国有大行有基础、有责任、更有优势做好零售业务。零售业务依托所有渠道，覆盖全行约六成员工，各级机构的士气、战斗力、执行力均主要源于零售业务。

以A分行和B分行两家省级分行为例，两省比邻，均处于东南沿海地区，经济社会发展水平较高。2017年，A省和B省的GDP分别为3.2亿元和5.2亿元，常住人口分别为3 900万人和5 700万人，B省的资源禀赋更优。2014年，两家分行都遭遇了严峻的外部经营压力，不良大幅攀升、经营陷入困境，两家分行的不良额一度达到系统前三，不良率大幅高于同期全行水平。从近几年发展情况看，A分行零售业务基础扎实，实现了快速回升，而B分行复苏相对缓慢。一是从等级行结果来看，2015年两家分行均为三类行，2017年A分行提升为一类行，B分行则提升为二类行。二是从不良来看，A分行实现了不良额和不良率快速缩降，B分行仍居高不下。三是从市场竞争力

来看，A 分行个人客户、存款和中间业务收入等核心指标继续保持四行第一，B 分行在零售业务等维度仍有较大历史短板。

在零售业务发展成效和零售思维理念运用维度的显著差异，是两家分行上述表现的重要原因之一。一是从资产负债结构来看，2017 年上半年末，A 分行个人存款在一般性存款余额占比超过六成，B 分行占比不足四成，A 分行零售贷款（含信用卡透支）在各项贷款余额占比六成、B 分行占比五成。二是从零售业务综合评价结果来看，A 分行连续多年保持系统前位，B 分行则一直较为落后，与其所在地区资源禀赋明显不符。三是从客户经营成效和基础来看，上半年末，A 分行个人有效客户在有资产客户中占比近五成，而 B 分行仅三成。

（二）经营贡献定位：零售业务贡献全行经营效益的半壁江山

第一，零售业务对全行效益贡献提升明显。2010—2017 年，利润贡献由 17.5% 升至 46.0%，营业收入占比由 29.3% 升至 38.0%，中间业务收入贡献由 36.2% 升至 52.0%，贷款占比由 24.2% 升至 40.3%，存款在客户存款中占比保持在 43% 以上，个人客户金融资产总量翻了一番（见表 5.1）。

表 5.1　2010 年以来建设银行核心经营指标零售业务占比情况　（%）

年份	税前利润	营业收入	中间业务	客户贷款	客户存款
2010	29.3	36.2	17.5	24.2	44.3
2017	38.0	52.0	46.0	40.3	43.4

资料来源：建行年报。

第二，2013—2017 年，国有四大银行零售业务合计税前利润的贡献由 27% 升至 43%，而建设银行零售税前利润四行占比由 24% 升至 29%，较工行差距明显缩小。零售营业收入、中间业务收入的四行占比也有所提升（见表 5.2）。

（三）发展方向定位：落实零售优先，打造建行新零售

十九大报告指出要建设现代化经济体系。现代化经济体系离不开现代化金融体系和现代商业银行，而零售业务是现代商业银行的主体业务。基于国家发展新的历史方位判断，董事长提出三大战略作为建设银行未来发展的战略调整，必将助力零售业务快速长期可持续发展，零售业务也必将成为“三大战略”的最佳实践地。新形势下，落实零售优先发展要运用新思维、锻造新能力、打造新零售；要主动协同，形成对公拉动零售、零售反哺对公的良性互动；要运用零售思维、零售理念和零售打法助力全行发展、提升经营水平。

表 5.2　2013 年以来四大行零售业务的全行贡献情况

年份	银行	税前利润		营业收入		中间业务收入	
		数值（亿元）	四行占比（%）	数值（亿元）	四行占比（%）	数值（亿元）	四行占比（%）
2013	建行	646	24	1 757	27	409	28
	工行	1 036	38	2 000	30	453	31
	农行	606	22	1 789	27	351	24
	中行	430	16	1 070	16	264	18
2017	建行	1 377	29	2 361	28	613	29
	工行	1 378	29	2 865	32	746	36
	农行	1 141	24	2 089	24	342	16
	中行	810	17	1 412	16	393	19

资料来源：各家银行年报。

三、新时期“新零售”转型发展思路建议

当前，新技术与金融的深度融合进入了新阶段，竞争主体发生了新变化，客户体验提出了新要求。零售业务要准确把握新时代历史方位，开放共享升级金融生态，价值共赢深化多维协同，数字互联强化科技引领，以客户为中心创造最佳体验，全力打造新零售。一是深化“以客户为中心”的理念，以消费者极致体验为中心、“客户关系为王”，遵循“人本原则”，把客户的需求作为一切经营服务活动的价值起点。二是加快线上线下深度融合，要在获客模式、双向引流和服务全触点统筹管理 3 个维度落地。三是科技引领，要把金融科技由“支撑力”升级为“原动力”，运用大数据、云计算、人工智能、区块链和移动互联等技术加快创新。四是从提供“综合服务方案”升级为“建行综合解决方案”，方案要实现综合化、个性化和场景化三要素深度融合，缺一不可。五是进一步巩固银行资源整合者地位，发挥集团优势，聚合优质第三方，实现合作共赢。

（一）开放共享，升级金融生态

加速账户出海，让金融服务走出去，延伸客户获得金融服务的边界和范围，而不是局限于人和物理渠道；突破民生领域，将生活场景圈进来，提供综合服务；拓展商户场景，整合形成企业级的商户管理；将蓝海项目升级为建行金融生态，将先发优势转化为建行基础客户牢固的经营优势，成为连接企业和个人的整个链条。要以住房租赁为切入点，把社区金融生态做活。

（二）价值共赢，强化多维协同

基于客户视角，推进集团一体化经营、资产和负债业务综合经营。加强与第三方的合作，实现双方价值共赢和共同成长。针对客户综合需求，提供一体化的建行解决方案，帮助客户在获取金融服务时实现更大价值、更低成本、更高效率，全面提升客户体验，深化建行与客户之间的关系。

（三）数字互联，科技赋能发展

强化全员数字创新意识，建立平台和机制，释放全员创新能力。依托科技连接对公对私，加强 B（企业）端和 C（客户）端之间信息共享，将对公业务传统源头优势转为零售业务终端资源，实现客户在建行价值的最大化。加快向数字银行转化，以线上为主推进线上线下协同，推进网点物理渠道功能开放和转型，手机上办银行，提升金融的便捷性和可获得性。加快打造“龙财富”平台，提供智能投顾家庭负债表管理，做客户的财富管家。

（四）以客户为中心，依托金融科技提高服务普惠金融能力，扩展金融服务的广度和深度

重点在裕农通县域普惠金融服务、金融扶贫、长尾客户、普惠信贷客户等领域实现突破。依托新一代平台，完善企业级客户统一经营管理体系，搭建个人客户分层服务和客户自激励服务体系，打造本部集约经营和客户经理差别化服务两大能力，全面理解客户行为，提供包含投资、融资、结算等在内的全方位金融服务。

乡村振兴战略背景下县域消费信贷发展影响因素解析模型与实证分析①

——基于某国有银行江苏省分行50家县域机构的样本数据

江苏省分行　孔德财

实施乡村振兴战略，不仅是支持供给侧结构性改革、释放乡村发展新动能的重大战略决策部署，也为商业银行开拓县域农村蓝海市场带来重要战略机遇。本文以商业银行消费金融业务为研究视角，基于当前县域地区消费经济特点，分析了县域市场中蕴藏的消费金融发展机遇及其发展的影响因素，有针对性地提出了若干对策、建议，以期为加快乡村县域地区消费信贷业务转型发展、助力实施乡村振兴战略提供参考。

一、消费信贷的国内外研究进展

从已有文献来看，国外对于消费信贷的探索与研究距今已有近百年的历史，最早起源于美国消费信贷市场的萌芽与发展。塞利格曼（Seligman，1928）研究认为分期付款销售已经成为事实，信贷必然会刺激消费，消费信贷对经济的影响是巨大而深远的。可以说，塞利格曼的研究结论为消费信贷提供了权威性的理论支撑。在此基础上，国外学者致力于消费信贷与消费、经济增长的量化关系研究，塞尔德斯（Zelds，1989）、卢德维格松和悉尼（Ludvigson and Sydney，1999）先后研究发现消费信贷增长与居民消费支出水平以及消费增长之间存在着显著的正相关关系，雅尼纳等人（Janine et al.，2012）基于现代 Ando-Modigliani 消费函数对比分析了英、美、日 3 个国家的住房信贷与消费之间的关系，研究结论为，英美两国由于房贷首付比例的降低、相关要求的放松以及信贷产品的持续创新与优化，极大促进了消费在总收入中的比重提升。从国内研究来看，边文霞（2002）通过对 GDP、投资和出口 3 个变量分别与消费间的函数关系的测定，研究了消费信贷需求受经济增长的影响作用；蔡浩、仪徐忠（2005）认为消费信贷与经济增长之间的关系是通过储蓄率的变化来传递的；赵霞、刘彦平（2006）

① 本文原载于《农村金融研究》2019 年第 3 期。

认为消费信贷业务在一定程度上缓解了消费者的流动性约束，对居民消费增长率的提高起到了一定的促进作用；阮小莉、仲泽丹（2013）运用 Probit 计量模型对城乡居民消费信贷影响因素的差异化进行了定性和定量分析，研究表明城乡居民在消费信贷观念、能力、层次和环境方面均存在较大差异。

总体而言，关于消费信贷的研究，国外主要聚焦其对缓解消费者信贷约束及促进消费增长的影响；而国内研究表明，总体而言当前我国消费信贷对拉动城乡居民消费增长的作用还不够明显。本文重点立足于商业银行的角度，以县域农村为分析视角，基于当前县域地区的消费现状与特点，从宏观、中观、微观层面构建了县域消费信贷业务发展的影响因素的解析模型，并进行了实证分析。

二、县域消费信贷发展：现状、机遇与挑战

（一）现状：消费信贷仍以中长期为主，短期消费信贷仍有较大拓展空间

从欧美发达国家来看，消费类用途的贷款在信贷总规模中的占比一般为 20% ~40%，美国这一比重甚至高达 60%。从国内来看，2017 年年底，全国金融机构信贷总额 124. 93 万亿元，其中消费贷款 30. 99 万亿元，占比 24. 8%（见图 5. 10），远低于美国等信贷发达国家。如果再在消费贷款中剔除以住房贷款为主的中长期消费贷款，真正意义上的短期消费贷款占比仅为 5. 44%。从重点消费信贷市场来看，2016 年全国汽车金融渗透率约 38. 6%（乘用车渗透率，不含二手车和商用车），而相比之下，2014 年全球汽车金融平均渗透率已达 70%，说明我国汽车金融产品渗透和创新都还有着较大的发展空间；而近 10 年来我国家装市场持续保持着 10% 左右的规模增速，显示出稳健的发展态势，据十三五规划，家装市场规模将由 2015 年的 1. 66 万亿元增长到 2. 4 万亿元，但目前对家装市场的消费信贷渗透仍然不高。从县域农村地区来看，2008 年国际金融危机之后，为了刺激经济增长，国家采取了家电下乡、农机直补等一系列政策来盘活农村消费市场，消费信贷业务也随之规模扩大，但从总量和结构占比来看，个人住房贷款占比高达 70% 以上，消费贷款仍然呈现长期化特点。随着居民收入水平的不断提升以及消费理念的不断更新，短期消费信贷如购车、住房装修、旅游购物等融资需求还有较大的提升空间。

（二）机遇：乡村社会消费品零售额增速超过城镇，消费结构优化升级加快

全国 2017 年社会消费品零售总额已达 36. 6 万亿元，最终消费支出对经济增长的贡献率达到 58. 8%，消费对经济发展的支撑作用持续加强。就地区而言，农村消费增长快于城镇。从江苏地区来看，近年来社会消费品零售总额增速开始企稳回升，其中 2015 年以后江苏农村地区消费品零售总额增速首次超过城镇（如图 5. 11 所示），增势明

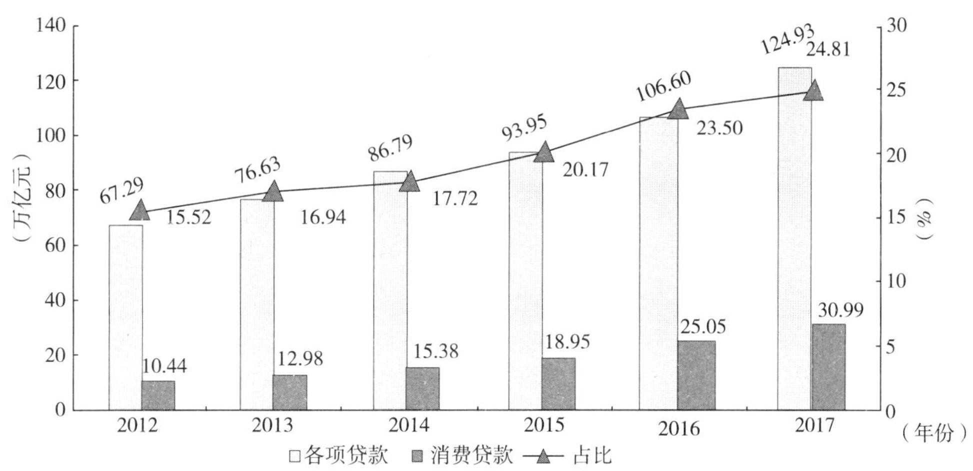

图 5. 10　全国消费贷款占信贷总规模比例情况

资料来源：国家统计局网站。

显，发展潜力较大，显现出近年来国家新型城镇化建设、供给侧结构性改革以及将农村消费列为消费升级方向之一等相关政策对加快农村消费经济增长起到的巨大推动作用。

图 5. 11　近年江苏社会消费品零售总额增速情况

资料来源：江苏省统计局网站。

在消费增速加快的同时，县域市场消费结构也在逐步优化。如表 5. 3 所示，以洗衣机、冰箱、电视机等家庭传统耐用品消费为例，总体上消费增速放缓，而以电脑、汽车为例的新兴消费则增速明显，显示出强劲的增长势头，且农村地区年均增长率高于城镇。因此，契合当前县域农村地区居民需求阶梯式发展层次的变化，深度开发居民从衣食住行到身心健康、从出生到终老各阶段各环节的生活性消费服务，积极对接与居民需求相匹配的循环透支或分期付款等消费信贷支持，在当前经济新环境中具有较为广阔的市场发展空间。

表5.3 江苏省居民家庭近年来平均每百户年末耐用消费品拥有量变化情况 （台，辆）

品名	类别	2005	2010	2011	2012	2013	2014	2015	2016	年均增长率（%）
洗衣机	城镇	99.38	102.08	101.04	101.90	97.71	98.81	99.4	100.4	0.09
	农村	67.9	91.5	90.6	92.4	88.69	90.43	91.94	96.2	3.22
电冰箱	城镇	96.47	99.36	100.70	101.92	98.73	99.52	101.12	103	0.60
	农村	36.0	59.3	66.9	71.4	89.40	89.55	95.2	101.5	9.88
彩色电视机	城镇	153.19	170.66	171.79	173.47	165.60	166.85	170.59	173.9	1.16
	农村	104.7	142.1	142.1	140.8	141.11	141.66	146.76	154.5	3.60
计算机	城镇	46.35	81.36	96.94	100.30	89.71	91.66	91.4	94.2	6.66
	农村	2.9	11.0	15.8	24.9	36.50	37.7	42.33	45.0	28.31
家用汽车	城镇	4.29	13.83	23.92	26.18	30.82	34.58	39.08	45.8	24.02
	农村	1.1	3	4	5.9	7.20	9.1	12.96	18.7	29.38

资料来源：江苏省统计局网站。

（三）挑战：商业银行一方面产品同质化现象突出，竞争激励，另一方面很多农村客户还难以符合信贷准入要求

从商业银行自身的产品体系来看，已从20世纪90年代单一的住房消费信贷逐步扩展到汽车、助学、装修以及个人综合消费贷款产品，产品体系基本覆盖了日常消费的各个领域。但目前各家银行产品同质化问题比较突出，在客户准入、利率、期限、申请方式等方面都大同小异，竞争激烈。出于风险防范的考虑，目前商业银行在客户选择上依然倾向于优质客户，以致农村客户还难以符合准入要求。目前县域农村客户拓展的主要障碍在于准入授信方面，其收入条件基本不符目前的政策准入，如无法提供公积金缴存、社保缴纳、代发工资或是个人所得税等证明材料，无专业执业（职业）资格，自有房产多为自建房（无房产证）等。受准入门槛限制，目前县域信用卡客户还是以城镇有稳定工作的居民为主，对真正意义上的农民还不能发行信用卡或办理分期业务。同时，县乡地区信用卡受理环境尚不够完善，消费信贷场景建设仍有待进一步加强。

三、县域地区消费信贷发展影响因素分析模型的构建

随着新型城镇化、新农村建设等国家战略的实施，农民收入增速持续高于城镇居民，且收入结构的稳定性不断提高，支撑县域地区金融消费力不断提升，使县域金融市场表现出巨大的发展潜力。

（一）某国有银行江苏分行县域机构经营发展能力总体情况

从某国有银行江苏地区的数据来看，辖内50家县行存贷款规模、中间业务收入占

全省的比重将近一半，尤其是16家经济富裕地区的强县行的占比近1/3，对全省整体业务转型发展贡献度极大。2017年，全省县域机构经营发展能力进一步增强，市场竞争力和价值创造力稳步提升，县域机构存款占全省系统的44.35%，贷款占比44.25%，中间业务收入占比47.51%，较年初均有所提升，且增速明显高于全省平均水平，表明县域机构的系统贡献度在不断提升（见表5.4）。

表5.4　2017年某国有银行江苏分行县域机构在全省系统内贡献度情况　（%）

项目	存款	贷款	中间业务收入
2017年占比	44.35	44.25	47.51
较上年提升	0.34	1.79	1.39
增速	7.92	13.34	4.50
全行平均增速	7.10	8.75	1.45

（二）某国有银行江苏分行县域机构历年消费信贷投放情况

从全省近年来分期信贷投放情况来看，由2015年的128.36亿元增长到2017年的188.15亿元，年均增长21.1%；县域地区从51.5亿元增长到72.62亿元，年均增长18.8%。但与传统存贷款业务相比，消费信贷业务作为县域地区的新兴业务，占比还不是很高，近年分期交易额在全省占比在40%左右徘徊，其中既有县域地区居民透支消费观念有待进一步转变，也有当前消费信贷产品在县域地区的创新适应性等诸多原因，但同时也说明，县域地区的消费信贷产品拓展潜力很大，是一片待挖掘的广阔蓝海（见表5.5）。

表5.5　某国有银行江苏分行及其县行近3年分期业务发展情况

年份	全省分期交易额（亿元）	县域分期交易额（亿元）	县域占比（%）
2015	128.36	51.50	40.1
2016	177.10	69.57	39.3
2017	188.15	72.62	38.6
年均增长率（%）	21.1	18.8	—

（三）县域地区消费信贷业务投放影响因素分析

从上述对比来看，县域机构存贷款占全省比重均在44%以上，但分期交易额占全省比重徘徊在40%左右，虽然总量规模在不断提升，但与当前宏观经济形势下整体业务发展不甚匹配，说明部分县域地区还存在消费金融服务供给不足或者消费金融服务不平衡不充分的问题。为了更加充分地解释县域地区消费信贷投放的差异化，从而有针对性地完善相关政策，更好地服务于县域地区消费转型升级以及乡村振兴战略的实施，本文选取了某国有银行江苏分行系统内50家县域机构作为样本数据进行相关分析，以期客观地解释县域地区消费信贷业务发展的影响因素。

1. 模型设计与数据准备

根据本文对50家样本机构分析需要，构建一个静态面板数据模型，其基本模型设计如下：

$$Y_{it} = a_{it} + X_{it}b_{it} + u_{it} \quad i = 1, 2, \cdots N; \ t = 1, 2, \cdots T$$

其中，a_{it}为常数向量，X_{it}为（$1 \times k$）维解释变量向量，b_{it}为（$k \times 1$）维系数向量，u_{it}为随机误差向量。

根据上述模型设计，本文从宏观环境到微观层面选取地区人口（P）等9项指标（见表5.6）建立指标体系，并建立消费信贷投放与上述指标体系的回归模型，解释其相关关系。

表5.6 投入产出指标选取

产出指标	投入指标		
	宏观	中观	微观
分期交易额（Y）	地区人口（P）	汽车保有量增量（A）	信用卡客户（C）
	地区生产总值（G）	住房成交面积（H）	合作商户数（M）
	社会消费品零售额（R）		营销员数量（S）
			营销费用（F）

依据该指标体系，选取江苏省某国有银行所辖50家县域机构所在地的社会经济发展数据及业务统计资料作为基础分析数据（受文章篇幅限制，数据表未在正文部分显示）。

2. 指标筛选与精简

从投入指标来看，指标体系尚不够简明，且部分指标之间可能存在共线性，因此需要对投入指标进一步简化。本课题应用相关分析法，通过计算各个指标之间的相关系数来剔除一些高度相关的指标，避免评价指标重复，确保指标体系简明，步骤如下所示：

（1）指标标准化处理。设Z_i为标准化值，X_i为指标原始数据，$\overline{X}$为指标原始数据均值，S_i为指标原始数据标准差，则：

$$Z_i = \frac{X_i - \overline{X}}{S_i}$$

（2）计算各评价指标之间的相关系数 R_{ij}。R_{ij} 的值范围在［-1，+1］之间，+1 表示完全正相关，-1 为完全负相关，0 为完全不相关。R_{ij} 计算公式为：

$$R_{ij} = \frac{\sum_{k=1}^{n}(Z_{ki} - \bar{Z}_i)(Z_{kj} - \bar{Z}_j)}{\sqrt{\sum_{k=1}^{n}(Z_{ki} - \bar{Z}_i)^2 (Z_{kj} - \bar{Z}_j)^2}}$$

（3）根据研究需求确定一个临界值 Q（$0 < Q < 1$）。如果 $R_{ij} > Q$，则认为指标 X_i 与 X_j 之间高度相关，可以删除其中之一；如果 $R_{ij} < Q$，则可以同时保留。本课题选择 0.9 作为临界值。经计算，初选的 9 个投入类指标相关系数如表 5.7 所示。

表 5.7　投入指标相关系数

Pearson 相关系数	P	R	H	C	M	S	F	G	A
P	1.000	0.578	0.451	0.431	0.436	0.226	-0.054	0.564	0.674
R	0.578	1.000	0.460	0.753	0.646	0.638	0.366	0.949	0.918
H	0.451	0.460	1.000	0.432	0.426	0.334	0.089	0.536	0.518
C	0.431	0.753	0.432	1.000	0.479	0.879	0.382	0.737	0.832
M	0.436	0.646	0.426	0.479	1.000	0.344	0.441	0.779	0.654
S	0.226	0.638	0.334	0.879	0.344	1.000	0.457	0.608	0.683
F	-0.054	0.366	0.089	0.382	0.441	0.457	1.000	0.472	0.347
G	0.564	0.949	0.536	0.737	0.779	0.608	0.472	1.000	0.907
A	0.674	0.918	0.518	0.832	0.654	0.683	0.347	0.907	1.000

从各指标相关系数来看，R（社会消费品零售总额）和 G（地区生产总值）的相关系数 0.949，R（社会消费品零售总额）和 A（私家车保有量）的相关系数 0.918，均大于设定的临界值 0.9，说明指标之间高度相关，为避免多重共线性且确保指标之间相互独立，可以删去指标 G（地区生产总值）和 A（私家车保有量）。

3. 建立投入产出关系模型

利用计量经济学软件 SPSS 16.0 对简化后的投入指标体系和产出指标建立线性回归模型，可得表 5.8 与表 5.9 所示的数据。

表 5.8　模型综述

模型	R	R^2	调整后的 R^2	标准差
1	0.923[a]	0.851	0.825	5 259.14598

表 5.9 模型系数

模型		非标准化系数		标准化系数	T 检验	显著性水平
		B	标准差	beta		
1	常量	-6 969.617	2 587.213		-2.694	0.010
	P	35.080	32.363	0.093	1.084	0.285
	R	4.899	9.901	0.057	0.495	0.623
	H	30.486	11.827	0.190	2.578	0.014
	C	1 096.023	599.099	0.289	1.829	0.075
	M	1.936E6	596 155.004	0.293	3.248	0.002
	S	3.878E6	2.094E6	0.266	1.852	0.071
	F	14.704	103.676	0.011	0.142	0.888

从模型运行结果来看，R^2 达到 0.851，拟合优度较好，指标参数检验整体显著性较强，模型整体呈高度相关性，故建立回归模型如下：

$$Y = 35.08 \times P + 4.9 \times R + 30.49 \times H + 1\ 096.02 \times C + 1.936E6 \times M + 3.878E6 \times S + 14.7 \times F - 6\ 969.62$$

从模型中各指标系数来看，首先指标 S 即营销员数量对消费信贷的影响系数最大，达到 3.878E6，即每增加 1 名客户经理，即可增加消费信贷投放 387.8 万元，因此，配备与业务发展规模相匹配的客户经理（营销员）数量是保持消费信贷稳定增长的前提。其次是签约合作商户对消费信贷的影响，系数达到 1.936E6，即每签约 1 个分期合作商户（如汽车经销商、装修公司等），即可增加消费信贷投放 193.6 万元，表明了场景化外部渠道获客对消费信贷业务发展的至关重要的作用。再次是信用卡客户对消费信贷的影响，每新增 1 名信用卡客户，即可增加消费信贷投放 1 096 元，表明了信用卡客户拓展对消费信贷投放的基础性作用。地区人口、社会消费品零售总额、商品房销售面积对消费信贷投放也呈明显正相关关系，这些指标作为宏观或中观层面的影响因素，在一定程度上解释了资源禀赋对各地区消费信贷投放差异化的客观原因。最后是营销费用投入对消费信贷的影响，每增加 1 万元费用投入，即可增加消费信贷投放 14.7 万元，表明了营销费用投入对业务发展的有效促进作用。需要说明的是，地区人口（P）、社会消费品零售额（R）的参数检验显著性水平不是很强，前两个与指标数据选取的是特定的金融机构而不是所有商业银行的全量数据，营销费用（F）参数检验的显著性水平与被调研机构费用核算统计口径有关，但都同时反映了对因变量的正向影响作用。同时，该模型所解释的自变量与因变量的关系系数，是基于特定指标体系和数据的相对影响作用，如果指标选取范围不同或数据时间段不同，相关系数还会有所变化。

四、进一步拓展县域地区消费信贷发展的建议

从分析来看，县域消费信贷仍有较大发展潜力与提升空间，但一定程度上也存在客户授信准入难、同业竞争激烈等问题。助力乡村振兴战略的实施，商业银行还需在客户准入、产品创新、场景建设、组织架构等体制机制方面逐步完善。

（一）完善县域农村消费信贷抵质押模式，体现区域经济差别化优势

一是在农村承包土地经营权和农民住房财产权（简称“两权”）抵押贷款试点成功的基础上，运用试点成果扩大试点范围，进一步完善农村消费信贷抵质押模式。目前无锡惠山区已创新“经营权抵押＋村集体回购”“农业公司（合作社）＋农户租赁经营权”贷款模式，有效满足了各层次农业经营主体的融资需求，可以参考借鉴；未来还可进一步试点扩大农村客户准入类型，研究通过农机具、鱼塘、大棚等资产抵押贷款作为准入与授信依据，填补县域农村地区经营消费类信贷授信准入方面的空白。二是以社区、村镇为基础，依托区域内有相关资质的资信评级中介机构或村镇组织对辖区居民个人信用等级的客观评估，作为银行授信准入依据。以江阴地区为例，多家银行以及部分汽车金融公司等已将“村委出具的自建房产证明”作为购车分期业务的准入条件和授信依据。三是把握中心城市增量换购及县域市场普及需求旺盛的契机，体现地区经济发展差异化水平，进一步优化中高端车型的授信政策，满足优质客户改善型购车需求，加快二手车、摩托车等汽车细分领域分期产品的市场拓展。

（二）契合县域市场需求，创新推出具有县域特点的消费信贷品种

首先要以住房贷款为突破口，积极与有信誉、有实力的装修公司合作，充分发挥房贷、公积金等客户资源优势，多渠道做大装修分期业务规模；围绕住房衍生的消费信贷需求，大力开展消费贷款新产品新业务的组合营销，并运用数据库营销挖掘存量房贷客户需求，从客户端、区域端、消费场景端、产品营销策略端深化经营。其次，适应富裕农村地区消费结构转型升级的需求，积极尝试推出市场潜力较大的医疗、教育培训、境内外旅游、车生活、居家住房消费需求及生活保障等方面的分期信贷产品，丰富产品线，实现各类消费应用场景、各类目标客群的产品分类全覆盖。三是完善县域地区信用卡服务功能，依托行业应用提升信用卡在农村的覆盖度。将信用卡产品与国家粮食补贴与农机购置补贴发放、新型农村合作医疗等行业应用相结合，推进信用资源共享，实现“一卡多用”。四是针对农民收入存在较强的季节周期性特点，开发反收入周期的消费信贷产品，有效解决农民在购置农机家电、助学就医时的暂时性资金短缺，以平衡其在一年内各期的消费。

（三）完善支付场景建设，扩大县域消费金融生态圈覆盖面

县域地区信用卡受理环境尚不够完善，收单、特惠等商户延伸较少，尤其是受支付宝、微信等第三方支付影响，传统小额消费应用场景受到巨大冲击，信用卡消费交易额增长缓慢。因此，加大软硬件投入力度、强化营销资源配置、完善信用卡产品受理环境是发展县域地区信用卡业务的基础性条件，当前应主动适应移动互联网金融快速发展的趋势，加大聚合支付产品在县域地区的投放力度，通过高效整合商户资源，完善场景建设，加大营销宣传力度，扩大外部渠道获客来源，既使客户消费需求目标与消费场景结合，又有通过商户让利促销创新分期信贷模式，实现银行、商户、消费客户同场景多方共赢，打造良好口碑效应。再者，依托农村地方特色，选择优质农家乐类型的餐饮、娱乐商户，开展刷卡优惠营销活动，着力构建农村特色消费金融生态圈，进一步打开县域信用卡消费市场。

（四）加强专业化营销队伍建设，完善县域消费信贷业务组织架构

从本文建立的分析模型来看，充实与业务发展规模相匹配的营销员数量是消费信贷业务稳步快速发展的基础，但从目前来看，受机构设置所限，绝大多数县行缺乏专职的消费信贷营销团队，从业人员数量及质量和业务规模不匹配，专业化支持能力较弱，直接影响了县域地区消费信贷业务的发展。因此，为提升县域机构专业专注水平，建议参照个贷经营中心的成功运作模式，以强县区域为试点，探索组建分期和个贷集中经营的消费金融中心，进一步内化联动营销机制，明确专职客户经理、明确业务发展目标、明确考核激励机制，组建“专业专注”的装修、汽车等分期团队，实现集约化经营，提升作业效率。

邻居选择法揭示银行产品间的内在关系

北京市分行　罗昊京

一、引言

银行产品种类繁多，有些是客户熟知的主要产品，而有些则非常罕见，虽然大多数客户可能对此感兴趣，但从未听说过。因此，要求银行的营销人员向客户推荐合适的产品。然而，简单地列出所有的产品不仅会耗费大量的时间，而且会引起客户的反感。

本文旨在发现银行产品之间的内在联系，从而指导这些产品的进一步销售推荐，进而有助于提高产品的销售业绩。

有几种成熟的技术可以帮助发现产品之间的内在关系。例如，在电影推荐中，诸如协同过滤、矩阵因式分解的方法已经显示出成功的经验性结果，因此这些方法成为建立产品营销推荐系统的主要方法。然而，这些方法的局限性也很明显。一方面，它们需要每个单独客户的详细历史消费记录，这很难获得；另一方面，它们通常仅在新客户具有相对充足的历史行为之后才能向客户推荐新产品。由于我们每天都会遇到大量的新客户，所以目前这些方法不适用于银行的产品营销推荐。

因此，本文感兴趣的不是为每个新客户推荐产品，而是基于历史累积的销售信息来估计这些产品之间的内部关系。这些过往的信息可以很容易地获得，并且很好地理解这些产品的内部关系，从而可以帮助银行营销人员在客户消息有限的情况下仍然做出最有效的产品营销。

为了满足估计这些网络内部关系的需要，本文采用邻居选择方法，在高维数据的高斯网络估计中取得了令人满意的经验性能。尽管邻居选择（及其后续改进，例如 Graphical Lasso）已经被用于包括金融场景在内的很多不同的应用程序，但我们注意到驱动邻域选择的基本方法（及其后续的各种改进方法）识别稀疏变量的组件（即 Lasso）有几个问题。其中一个问题是无法区分相关度较高的变量。因此在本文中，我们建议使用一个最近开发的方法，即 Precision Lasso，来取代这个组件，以帮助我们更可靠地识别产品之间的内部关系。本文进一步应用此技术来揭示这些产品的内部关系，并且这些内部关系大部分都是通过以往的销售经验来验证的。因此，我们相信本文所确定的新关系能够进一步指导银行今后的销售推荐。

本文的其余部分组织如下：首先在第二部分中介绍使用的方法——Precision Lasso；然后报告将这种新技术应用于大数据集时的结果，并讨论它们之间的内在联系；最后，详细讨论此方法的优缺点，得出结论，并对今后的工作进行了展望。

二、方法介绍

首先，我们将介绍本文使用的变量。本文用 $X \in R^{n \times p}$ 来表示所拥有的数据，其中 n 是汇总销售记录的数量，p 是产品的数量。本文使用 Ω 来表示协方差矩阵的逆，也叫作精度矩阵（Precision Matrix）。$\beta \in R^{n \times (p-1)}$ 表示回归系数。众所周知，精度矩阵的稀疏模式与数据的网络结构存在一一对应的关系。因此，我们可以利用 β 的稀疏模式来估计 Ω 的稀疏模式。

（一）邻居选择法

邻居选择法是一种方便的迭代方法，可以估计一个节点的网络的边缘。对于节点 S，邻域选择是解决下列 Lasso 问题：

$$\beta_s = arg \min_{\beta_s} \| X_s - X_{-s}^T \beta_s \|_2^2 + \lambda \| \beta_s \|_1^1 \quad (1)$$

更进一步地，我们可以将完整的 Ω 填充上：

$$\Omega_{s,i} = 1 \quad \forall i = 1, \cdots p \qquad \beta_{s,i} \neq 0$$

此外，我们需要通过采用简单的启发式规则来确保精度矩阵是对称的，即只要从节点 A 到节点 B 有边，那么从节点 B 到节点 A 也应该有边，换言之：

$$\Omega = \Omega \cup \Omega^T$$

（二）Precision Lasso

然而，公式（1）中所引入的必要步骤有各种各样的已知的问题 。例如，如果若干个相互关联的变量都与结果变量有相互联系，则 Lasso 将只选择其中一个变量。Lasso 的这种局限性自然地承继到邻居选择，并进一步导致邻居选择的结果不可靠。为了解决这个问题，本文建议使用一种最近开发的技术，称为 Precision Lasso，它可以在相关变量上进行有效的工作。基本上，Precision Lasso 解出了下列函数的解：

$$arg\min_{\beta}\frac{1}{2}\|y-X_{-s}\beta_{-s}\|_2^2+\lambda\|[\gamma(X_{-s}^TX_{-s})^{\frac{1}{2}}+(1-\gamma)(X_{-s}^TX_{-s}+\mu I)^{-\frac{1}{2}}]\mathrm{diag}(\beta_s)\|_* \tag{2}$$

其中 γ 是模型的一个参数，μ 只是一个确保矩阵可逆的参数，$\|\cdot\|_*$代表核范数。

因此，通过用更新的技术公式（2）替换基本构建块公式（1），本文提出了能够更可靠地估计网络的方法。在第三部分中，本文将把这个方法应用于真实世界的银行大数据中，并报告我们的发现。

三、银行大数据的应用

本文将此方法应用到银行产品销售的大数据集合。对于超参数，自动将 γ 作为相关变量与线性相关变量的比值计算，并调整 λ 以选择每个节点的 3 个边缘。结果如图 5.12 所示。图 5.12 左边示出了网络估计的结果，其中每个节点的半径代表它的边缘。因此，节点的半径也可以被解释为节点的重要性。每个节点的含义如图 5.12 右边所示，这些节点的不同颜色代表了这些产品的不同群。

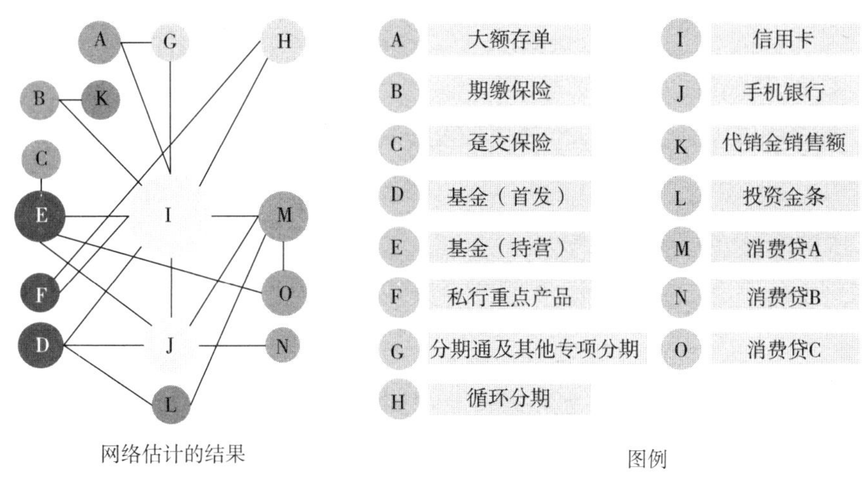

图 5.12 用本文方法估计的产品

基于以上大数据分析结果，结合实际工作中银行产品销售的经验，我们可以看到：银行中绝大部分产品的销售量都与信用卡和手机银行的销售量有着紧密的联系，信用卡和手机银行作为银行的两大重要产品，可以提高现有客户的活跃度与黏度。当客户对信用卡和手机银行产生青睐，并逐渐依赖于使用它们的时候，银行就在无形中获得了这个客户的信赖。在这种信赖的基础上，客户更容易接受该银行的其他产品，从而带动其他产品的营销。另外，该客户的频繁使用会影响身边的亲朋好友，创造品牌效应，在潜移默化中提高潜在客户对该银行其他产品的认可度。

四、结论

本文提出用 Precision Lasso 代替普通的 Lasso 来提高网络估计的邻居选择方法的性能，并将该技术应用于银行产品相关度的估计。然而，我们应该注意到，Precision Lasso 具有极高的计算复杂度这个缺陷，但这是它达到更稳定的变量选择性能的前提。

本文用更新的方法从这些产品中估算出一个网络。估计网络的许多边缘与我们实际工作中对这些产品的普遍认知是一致的，表明本文所提出的技术是有效的。此外，网络中有几个边缘是出乎意料的。本文的结果表明，虽然这些关系并不是直观的，但我们预计这些联系将有助于促进未来的销售业绩提升。

我国上市银行经营效率与产权结构的相关性研究

陕西省分行　曹　鹏

一、引言

我国银行业在现代金融体系中始终处于主体地位，尤其在我国目前金融市场发展不成熟以及信贷市场以间接融资为主导的情况下，更加体现出了商业的重要性。因此如何通过改革来保证银行业又好又快地发展，成为我国金融业的一个长期课题。上市商业银行是我国银行业的主体，其经营效率反映了投入与产出的对比关系，是自身经营业绩的一种集中体现，因而能够体现出整个银行业对资源有效配置或优化的情况以及市场竞争力。如此，研究银行经营效率的影响因素或者说能否准确把握银行的效率值就显得尤为重要。虽然我国上市银行经营效率在近些年来提升较快，但依然存在继续提高的空间，影响效率提高的因素仍然普遍存在。因此，深入揭示我国上市商业银行经营效率的具体影响因素，以及进一步确认和量化其影响方式和影响程度，然后以此为基础提出有效提高经营效率和防范金融风险的具体应对措施，就可以为上市商业银行的进一步改革提供相应的决策依据。另外，对于目前我国上市商业银行来说，自身的产权与治理结构普遍都存在着一些问题，如国有上市商业银行的产权结构中，国有股一股独大与产权界定不明所导致的所有者虚置问题依然存在，而股份制上市商业银行和城市上市商业银行自身的员工持股计划与利益相关方共同治理等改革创新也都陷入了瓶颈。这些产权结构改革所存在的问题会严重影响我国上市商业银行的竞争力的持续提高，因此研究产权与治理结构进一步的深化改革对于保证我国上市商业银行的平稳高效运行，保证其市场竞争力的稳步提高，就具有十分重要的现实意义。

二、上市银行经营效率与产权结构研究的理论基础

（一）上市银行经营效率研究的理论基础

1. 上市银行经营效率的概念与界定

效率是经济学中的重要概念，围绕着效率的相关问题一直是学术界的研究重点。

关于效率的定义目前并没有一个确切的界定，从不同的研究角度出发便有相应的效率定义。上市银行的经营效率不仅体现了银行在整个经营过程中的盈利性与竞争力，而且也是自身赖以生存和发展的基础。① 考虑到上市商业银行是以货币商品作为其经营业务，其自身经营状况必然会与金融市场的发展息息相关，从而其经营效率对我国金融及资本市场的建设有着很重要的影响。② 因此在对上市银行经营效率进行界定时，不仅需要从微观影响方面入手，而且也需要结合相应的中观和宏观影响因素进行研究。

2. 上市银行经营效率的影响因素分析

通过对以往相关文献的归纳梳理，可以将影响上市银行经营效率的因素归纳为宏观影响因素、中观影响因素和微观影响因素这 3 个方面。首先从宏观影响因素来看，若宏观经济发展呈现出稳健上升的状态，社会信贷资金的需求也会相应增大，那么银行就会制定比较积极的经营目标。这相当于为银行的发展提供了强有力的经济基础，进而会促进其经营效率持续稳定的提高。相反，如果宏观经济发展呈现出萎靡不振的态势，银行便会对未来产生悲观的预期，那么会对自身业务进行强制性收缩，进而会使得经营效率不断下降，并且随着经济萎靡的态势愈演愈烈。其次从中观影响因素来看，一般来说，市场竞争结构对上市商业银行经营效率有着很重要的影响，银行业市场竞争程度越高、市场机制越完善，那么其经营效率便会越高。最后从影响上市商业银行经营效率的微观因素来看，其产权结构与公司治理机制是使得银行个体间经营效率产生差异的两大影响因素。③ 通常来说，明晰的产权结构能够产生很好的激励效果和约束作用，通过自身的公司治理结构来对银行的资源配置和经营模式产生影响，从而有助于提高商业银行的经营效率。

三、上市银行经营效率的测度与分析

（一）我国上市银行生产过程特征分析

上市企业的经营目标是建立在以最少的投入生产最多的产品的基础上的，进而实现自身收益的最大化。上市银行作为特殊企业的原因是在于自身的经营对象的特殊性，其经营对象是以各种金融负债和金融资产等货币业务为主。具体来说，商业银行是社

① 资料来源：姚树杰，蒋春霞，冯根福．中国银行业的改革与效率：1995—2008［J］．北京：经济研究，2011，(8)．

② 资料来源：梁夏．产权结构对我国商业银行效率的影响分析［D］．山东大学，2014.

③ 资料来源：李琦光．影响我国上市银行盈利能力的微观因素研究［D］．西南财经大学，2013.

会间接融资的主体，其主要是借助各种金融工具把社会上闲散的资金集中到银行，然后再通过放款业务把资金借贷给社会各经济实体和消费者。这种行为相当于是一种信用中介，将吸收来的资金一部分用来发放贷款，另一部分用于相关投资，以其差额来赚取中间收益，进而实现资本的融通。从银行的经营过程来看，明显体现出阶段性的特点，大体可以将其概括为两个阶段。第一阶段银行凭借自身的现有优势，如人力、物力和财力资源，进而吸收社会上各个经济实体的闲散资金，为自身的后续经营奠定基础，这一阶段可以称为资金筹集阶段。然后在第二阶段，银行利用第一阶段所吸收的资金一方面将其放贷给需要资金的个人、企业和金融机构来赚取利差，另一方面也利用这部分资金来从事各类证券投资来赚取相应的收入，这一阶段可以称为资金获利阶段。

（二）基于两阶段网络 DEA 的我国上市银行经营效率的测度

1. 模型与样本的选取

（1）两阶段网络 DEA 模型。网络 DEA 方法不仅包含决策单元整体的投入产出项，而且也考虑到了中间阶段的各项投入产出以及与整体阶段的相关性。网络 DEA 评价方法从本质上来说是属于打开黑箱评价的分析方法，即能够测度出决策单元整体及各个阶段的效率，并且能够分析出决策单元具体是在哪一阶段出现了问题。① 就此而言，打开黑箱的网络 DEA 的优点不单单是能够决策单元的相关效率，而且更能够对评价的结果进行分析，这才是模型的真正优势所在。定义的 WYP 模型如下，即是一个由多元线性规划所构成的综合网络 DEA 模型。假设决策单元 DMU_j 为（z_j^1，z_j^2，…，z_j^l），$j=1$，2，…n，其中 $z_j^l>0$，$k=1$，2，…n，则称 $T=\{(z^l, z^{l+1}) \mid z^l>0, z^{l+1}>0\}$ 为综合网络 *DEA* 模型的生产可能集②。另外假定 θ_l、λ_j^l $l=1$，2，…n，$j=1$，2，…n 为模型的最优解，则必有 $\theta_l>0$，$(\lambda_1^l, \lambda_2^l, \cdots \lambda_n^l) \neq 0$，并且 $\sum_{l=1}^{n}\theta_l \leq n$。若 $\sum_{l=1}^{n}\theta_l = n$，则称决策单元 DMU_j 为序贯意义下的网络 *DEA* 有效。

$$
(P)\begin{cases} MIN\sum_{l=1}^{k}\theta_l \\ (\theta_l Z_0^l, \theta_{l+1} Z_0^l) \in T^l, \quad l=1,2,\cdots k-1 \\ (\theta_k Z_0^k, Z_0^{k-1}) \in T^k \end{cases}
$$

---

① 资料来源：Fare R, Grosskopf S. “Network DEA”［J］. Socio-economic Planning Sciences, 2000.

② 资料来源：C. Kao, S. N. Hwang. “Efficiency Decomposition in two - stage Data Envelopment Analysis; An Application to Non-life insurance Companies in Taiwan”［J］. European Journal of Operational Research, 2008.

$$
(P)\begin{cases}
MIN\sum_{l=1}^{k}\theta_l \\
\sum_{j=1}^{n} Z_j^l\lambda_j^l \leqslant \theta_l Z_0^l, \quad j=1,2,\cdots n, \quad l=1,2,\cdots k-1 \\
\sum_{j=1}^{n} Z_j^l\lambda_j^l \geqslant \theta_{l+1} Z_0^{l+1}, \quad j=1,2,\cdots n, \quad l=1,2,\cdots k-1 \\
\lambda_j^l \geqslant 0, \quad j=1,2,\cdots n \\
\sum_{j=1}^{n} Z_j^k\lambda_j^k \leqslant \theta_k Z_0^k, \quad j=1,2,\cdots n \\
\sum_{j=1}^{n} Z_j^{k+1}\lambda_j^{k+1} \geqslant Z_0^{k+1}, \quad j=1,2,\cdots n \\
\lambda_j^{k+1} \geqslant 0, \quad j=1,2,\cdots n
\end{cases}
$$

对于我国上市银行来说，其内部的经营过程可以简化为如图 5. 13 所示的两阶段网络结构。为了方便描述，假定 *K*1 代表上市商业银行的资金筹集阶段，*K*2 代表上市商业银行的资金获利阶段，Z^1代表资金筹集阶段的各项投入，Z^2代表资金筹集阶段的各项产出同时也是资金获利阶段的各项投入，Z^3代表资金获利阶段的各项产出，其中 Z^1、Z^2、Z^3均大于 0。假设有 *n* 个部门具有此图所示的网络结构，则称这些部门为决策单元 DMU_j。

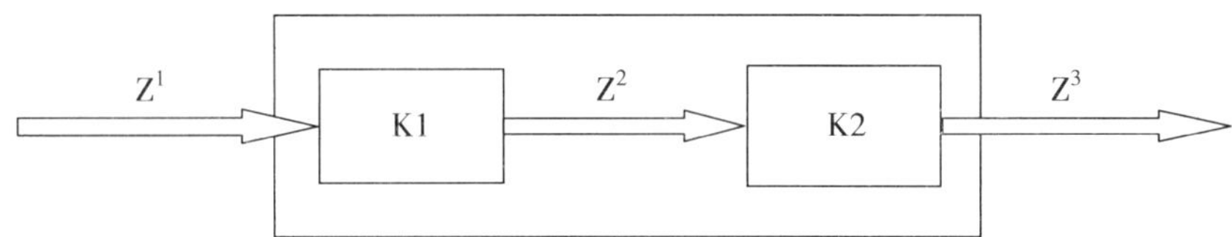

图 5. 13　商业银行两阶段网络结构

根据我国上市商业银行两阶段的网络结构图，可以将上述模型简化为两个阶段来进行测度，其模型结构如 *P'* 所示。模型在评价决策单元 DMU_j 的有效性时，将由最终产出的资金获利阶段开始直到资金筹集阶段由后向前进行逆向检，具体来说，若第一阶段最初的投入 Z^1经过 *K*1、*K*2 两个阶段之后所得到的最终产出 Z^3时，最初的投入 Z^1不能够减少，或者说当产出为 Z^{k+1}时，$K=1$，2 时，投入由 Z^k 可以减小为 $\theta_k Z^k$，其中 θ_k 为模型在第 *K* 阶段的效率最优值。通过上述两阶段综合 *DEA* 模型进行评价时，一方面可以对决策单元整体及内部各个阶段的子效率进行测度，另一方面也可以对其测度结果进行相应的评价分析，因而可以实现真正意义上的打开黑箱评价。

$$
(P)\begin{cases} MIN\sum_{k=1}^{2}\theta_k \\ (\theta_1 Z^1,\theta_2 Z^2)\in T \\ (\theta_2 Z^2, Z^3)\in T \end{cases}
\begin{cases} MIN\sum_{k=1}^{2}\theta_k \\ \sum_{j=1}^{n} Z_j^1\lambda_j^1 \leqslant \theta_1 Z_0^1,\quad j=1,2,\cdots n,\quad \lambda_j^1\geqslant 0 \\ \sum_{j=1}^{n} Z_j^2\lambda_j^1 \geqslant \theta_2 Z_0^2,\quad j=1,2,\cdots n,\quad \lambda_j^1\geqslant 0 \\ \sum_{j=1}^{n} Z_j^2\lambda_j^1 \leqslant \theta_2 Z_0^2,\quad j=1,2,\cdots n,\quad \lambda_j^2\geqslant 0 \\ \sum_{j=1}^{n} Z_j^3\lambda_j^3 \geqslant Z_0^3,\quad j=1,2,\cdots n,\quad \lambda_j^3\geqslant 0 \end{cases}
$$

（2）样本数据的选取。本文以上述研究为基础，使指标选取方式与所用的综合网络 *DEA* 模型相符合。首先在资金筹集阶段选择营业支出与固定资产值作为此阶段的投入项；其次在资金获利阶段选择利息收入和投资收益为此阶段的产出项。在两阶段的生产过程中，选取客户存款总额和银行同业拆入资金来作为中间变量。我国目前共有 26 家上市商业银行，但基于数据的可获得性和口径一致性，本文选取 2011—2016 年 6 年间 16 家上市银行作为样本，其中包括五大国有上市商业银行、8 家股份制上市商业银行和 3 家城市上市商业银行。这 16 家上市商业银行的资产规模占到我国银行的 90% 以上，因此具有很好的代表性，其中各项数据来源于《中国金融年鉴》和各银行公开的年报。

2. 上市银行各个阶段效率实证结果分析

为解决文中综合网络 *DEA* 模型所涉及的线性规划问题，运用 *lingo*11 软件进行编程计算，进而得到 2011—2016 年我国上市商业银行的总体经营效率以及资金筹集和资金获利两个阶段的子效率（见表 5. 10 和表 5. 11）。

表 5. 10 和表 5. 11 分别给出了基于综合网络 *DEA* 模型所测度出的上市银行整体及各个阶段的效率值及其均值。首先从整体效率来看，在 2011—2016 年这 6 年间，国有上市银行整体阶段效率在上市银行中处于一个相对较好的水平，尤其是在后面 3 年中其效率值普遍超过了股份制和城市上市商业银行，这说明国有上市商业银行经过股份制改革后，其在经营效率上取得了显著的成效。① 但五大国有上市商业银行的效率值都普遍小于 2，并未达到整体有效，由此可以看出国有银行效率水平还有很大的提高空间，需要进一步深化改革。在股份制上市商业银行中，浦发银行、兴业银行、华夏银行和平安银行这 4 家银行的整体阶段效率值较高，其中兴业银行和平安银行在某些年份也

① 资料来源：李南成，王蒙．中国商业银行效率差异动因的实证研究［J］．西南金融，2014（08）：39 –42.

表 5.10 基于复合序贯 DEA 模型的银行效率评价

2011 年	θ_1	θ_2	θ	2012 年	θ_1	θ_2	θ	2013 年	θ_1	θ_2	θ
工商银行	0.99	0.87	1.86	工商银行	0.70	0.92	1.62	工商银行	0.43	0.93	1.36
建设银行	0.91	0.89	1.80	建设银行	0.47	1.00	1.47	建设银行	0.29	1.00	1.29
中国银行	0.70	0.66	1.36	中国银行	0.50	0.71	1.21	中国银行	0.40	0.78	1.18
农业银行	0.71	1.00	1.71	农业银行	0.34	1.00	1.34	农业银行	0.26	0.99	1.25
交通银行	0.90	0.79	1.69	交通银行	0.50	0.78	1.28	交通银行	0.42	0.83	1.25
招商银行	0.75	1.00	1.75	招商银行	0.60	1.00	1.60	招商银行	0.47	0.95	1.42
民生银行	0.61	1.00	1.61	民生银行	0.64	1.00	1.64	民生银行	0.45	0.99	1.44
浦发银行	1.00	0.84	1.84	浦发银行	0.91	0.81	1.72	浦发银行	0.86	0.85	1.71
华夏银行	1.00	0.86	1.86	华夏银行	0.56	0.79	1.35	华夏银行	0.52	0.84	1.36
平安银行	1.00	0.75	1.61	平安银行	1.00	0.74	1.74	平安银行	1.00	0.77	1.77
中信银行	0.96	0.84	1.80	中信银行	0.86	0.80	1.66	中信银行	0.61	0.86	1.47
光大银行	0.92	0.85	1.77	光大银行	0.53	0.79	1.32	光大银行	0.52	0.78	1.30
南京银行	0.83	0.99	1.82	南京银行	0.43	1.00	1.43	南京银行	0.55	1.00	1.55
北京银行	0.96	0.76	1.72	北京银行	1.00	0.79	1.79	北京银行	1.00	0.71	1.71
宁波银行	0.71	1.00	1.71	宁波银行	0.38	1.00	1.38	宁波银行	0.50	1.00	1.50
2014 年	θ_1	θ_2	θ	2015 年	θ_1	θ_2	θ	2016 年	θ_1	θ_2	θ
工商银行	0.98	0.92	1.90	工商银行	1.00	0.91	1.91	工商银行	1.00	0.71	1.71
建设银行	0.87	1.00	1.87	建设银行	0.92	1.00	1.92	建设银行	0.88	0.65	1.53
中国银行	0.89	0.78	1.67	中国银行	1.00	0.75	1.75	中国银行	0.88	1.00	1.88
农业银行	0.79	1.00	1.79	农业银行	0.93	1.00	1.93	农业银行	0.95	0.83	1.78
交通银行	0.80	0.79	1.59	交通银行	0.91	0.72	1.63	交通银行	0.97	0.68	1.65
招商银行	0.69	1.00	1.69	招商银行	0.61	0.96	1.57	招商银行	0.76	0.95	1.71
民生银行	0.65	0.89	1.54	民生银行	0.68	0.83	1.51	民生银行	0.86	0.73	1.59
浦发银行	0.96	0.83	1.79	浦发银行	0.94	0.85	1.79	浦发银行	0.94	0.86	1.80
兴业银行	1.00	1.00	2.00	兴业银行	1.00	1.00	2.00	兴业银行	1.00	1.00	2.00
华夏银行	0.80	0.88	1.68	华夏银行	0.85	0.78	1.63	华夏银行	0.74	0.85	1.59
平安银行	1.00	1.00	2.00	平安银行	1.00	1.00	2.00	平安银行	0.92	1.00	1.92
中信银行	0.81	0.87	1.68	中信银行	0.86	0.74	1.60	中信银行	0.95	0.69	1.64
光大银行	0.83	0.76	1.59	光大银行	0.81	0.75	1.56	光大银行	1.00	0.73	1.73
南京银行	0.76	1.00	1.76	南京银行	0.77	0.96	1.73	南京银行	0.72	1.00	1.72
北京银行	1.00	0.78	1.78	北京银行	1.00	0.77	1.77	北京银行	1.00	0.77	1.77
宁波银行	0.68	1.00	1.68	宁波银行	0.66	1.00	1.66	宁波银行	0.71	0.79	1.50

表 5.11　银行效率评价结果均值分析

项目	均值	2011 年	2012 年	2013 年	2014 年	2015 年	2016 年
资金筹集	国有上市银行	0.83	0.50	0.35	0.88	0.96	0.93
	股份制上市银行	0.89	0.70	0.66	0.83	0.84	0.88
	城市上市银行	0.83	0.60	0.68	0.81	0.81	0.81
资金获利	国有上市银行	0.86	0.91	0.93	0.93	0.92	0.80
	股份制上市银行	0.89	0.87	0.87	0.90	0.86	0.84
	城市上市银行	0.92	0.92	0.90	0.93	0.91	0.85
整体阶段	国有上市银行	1.68	1.41	1.27	1.81	1.88	1.73
	股份制上市银行	1.77	1.57	1.53	1.73	1.70	1.72
	城市上市银行	1.75	1.53	1.59	1.74	1.72	1.66

都达到了整体有效，说明这些银行的治理和内控机制相对成熟，因而有利于促进自身效率的提高。但除这些银行之外，其余股份制上市银行整体阶段的效率水平都不是很理想，由此可以看出对于股份制银行来说同样有着很大的提高空间。

四、我国上市银行产权结构与经营效率相关性实证研究

（一）实证研究方法设计

1. 指标变量的选取

首先描述我国上市银行经营效率的变量分别为上述所测度出的资金筹集阶段效率（CE）、资金获利阶段效率（HE）。其次描述我国上市商业银行产权结构的变量，在借鉴相同类型研究文献的经验与做法的基础上，将从产权结构性质和产权结构集中度两个方面来进行相应的指标选取。① 其中产权结构性质分别由上市商业银行国有股比例（GO）、境内法人股比例（NO）和外资股比例（FO）3 部分进行描述。② 而产权结构集中度分别是由第一大股东持股比例（O1）以及第五大股东持股比例（O5）进行表示。最后关于控制变量的选取分别从影响银行经营效率的微观、中观和宏观影响因素中来进行选取，即资本充足率（CAR）、不良贷款率（NPL）、市场份额（MS）和国内生产总值增速（GDP）。③ 以上各变量的详细说明见表 5.12。

① 资料来源：李丹．基于因子分析的我国商业银行经营绩效评价研究［D］．东华大学，2013（60）．李南成，王蒙．中国商业银行效率差异动因的实证研究［J］．西南金融，2014（08）：39－42.

② 资料来源：王梅励．产权结构对我国商业银行经营效率的影响［D］．山东大学，2016.

③ 资料来源：刘瑞翔，吕大雪，骆依．不良贷款约束下我国商业银行效率的测评——基于两阶段 DEA 模型的分析［J］．南京审计大学学报，2016，13（06）：41－50.

表5.12 我国上市商业银行产权结构与经营效率实证分析的变量选择

变量类型	变量名称	变量符号	变量定义
被解释变量	资金筹集阶段效率	CE	上市商业银行资金筹集能力
	资金获利阶段效率	HE	上市商业银行资金获利能力
解释变量	国有股比例	GO	国有股与总股本的比值
	境内法人股比例	NO	境内法人股与总股本的比值
	外资股比例	FO	外资股与总股本的比值
	第一大股东持股比例	O1	第一大股东股份与总股本比值
	第五大股东持股比例	O5	第五大股东股份与总股本比值
控制变量	资本充足率	CAR	资本总额与加权风险资产总额比值
	不良贷款率	NPL	不良贷款占总贷款余额的比值
	市场份额	MS	各银行资产对银行业金融机构资产比值
	国内生产总值增速	GDP	国内生产总值增长率

2. Tobit 模型的构建

由于本文用综合网络 DEA 方法所测度出来的上市银行整体及阶段子效率值存在截断的现象，因此普通的 OLS 回归模型不再适用于相应的研究。如果使用 OLS 回归模型进行分析，便会导致由于无法呈现完整的因变量数据，进而导致回归结果出现较大的偏差。因而本文将采用 Tobit 回归模型来对我国上市商业银行产权结构对经营效率的影响进行相应的研究，模型的形式如下所示，其中 Yi 为被解释变量，Xi 为解释变量，β 为待估参数，δ 为随机干扰项。

$$\begin{cases} Y^* = \beta^T X_i + \delta_i, \\ Y_i^* = Y_i, if \quad Y^* > 0 \\ Y_i^* = 0, if \quad Y^* \leqslant 0 \end{cases} \tag{1}$$

针对上述 Tobit 模型的一般表达式，将产权结构对我国上市商业银行经营效率的相关变量带入，得到如下（2）的回归模型表达式。其中被解释变量 E 代表上市商业银行整体及阶段子效率，解释变量 OWNSTRUC 代表相应产权结构因素，控制变量 MICFAC、MESOFAC 和 MACFAC 则分别代表相应的微观控制因素、中观控制因素和宏观控制因素。

$$E = C + \beta_i \mathrm{OWNSTRUC} + \gamma_j \mathrm{MICFAC} + \mu_t \mathrm{MESOFAC} + \eta_k \mathrm{MACFAC} + \delta \tag{2}$$

（二）产权结构对我国上市银行经营效率影响实证结果与分析

根据（2）的模型构建思路，分别将上市商业银行 CE、HE 作为被解释变量带入，然后分别将国有股比例（GO）、境内法人股比例（NO）和外资股比例（FO）以及产权集中度作为解释变量带入，最后将相应的控制变量带入可以得到如下模型一（3）、模型二（4）……模型六（8）。其中 i = 1，2，…16，t = 2011，2012，…2016，CE、HE 为选取的效率变量，GO、NO、FO、O1 和 O5 为所选取的产权结构变量，CAR 和 NPL 为所选取的微观因素控制变量，MS 为所选取的中观因素控制变量，GDP 为所选取的宏观因素控制变量，δ 为误差项。运用 Eviews 8.0 软件分别对其进行相应的 Tobit 回归，具体回归结果见表 5.13 ~ 表 5.18。

$$CE_{it} = C + \beta_1 GO_{it} + \beta_2 O1_{it} + \beta_3 O5_{it} + \gamma_1 CAR_{it} + \gamma_2 NPL_{it} + \mu_1 MS_{it} + \eta_1 GDP_{it} + \delta_{it} \quad (3)$$

$$CE_{it} = C + \beta_1 NO_{it} + \beta_2 O1_{it} + \beta_3 O5_{it} + \gamma_1 CAR_{it} + \gamma_2 NPL_{it} + \mu_1 MS_{it} + \eta_1 GDP_{it} + \delta_{it} \quad (4)$$

$$CE_{it} = C + \beta_1 FO_{it} + \beta_2 O1_{it} + \beta_3 O5_{it} + \gamma_1 CAR_{it} + \gamma_2 NPL_{it} + \mu_1 MS_{it} + \eta_1 GDP_{it} + \delta_{it} \quad (5)$$

$$HE_{it} = C + \beta_1 GO_{it} + \beta_2 O1_{it} + \beta_3 O5_{it} + \gamma_1 CAR_{it} + \gamma_2 NPL_{it} + \mu_1 MS_{it} + \eta_1 GDP_{it} + \delta_{it} \quad (6)$$

$$HE_{it} = C + \beta_1 NO_{it} + \beta_2 O1_{it} + \beta_3 O5_{it} + \gamma_1 CAR_{it} + \gamma_2 NPL_{it} + \mu_1 MS_{it} + \eta_1 GDP_{it} + \delta_{it} \quad (7)$$

$$HE_{it} = C + \beta_1 FO_{it} + \beta_2 O1_{it} + \beta_3 O5_{it} + \gamma_1 CAR_{it} + \gamma_2 NPL_{it} + \mu_1 MS_{it} + \eta_1 GDP_{it} + \delta_{it} \quad (8)$$

表 5.13　国有上市银行产权结构对资金筹集阶段效率的实证结果

	模型一			模型二			模型三		
变量	系数	z 检验	P 值	系数	z 检验	P 值	系数	z 检验	P 值
GO	-1.5941***	-3.3849	0.0007	—	—	—	—	—	—
NO	—	—	—	0.1469	0.0451	0.9640	—	—	—
FO	—	—	—	——	—	—	1.3998***	3.0951	0.0020
O1	-0.4874*	-1.7501	0.0800	-0.6525	-0.8613	0.3891	-0.8061***	-2.8633	0.0042
O5	-25.2280***	-2.9117	0.0036	-23.8350**	-2.1767	0.0295	-26.8170***	-3.0111	0.0026
CAR	0.0195	0.5738	0.5661	0.0802**	2.0802	0.0375	0.0192	0.5396	0.5895
NPL	0.7709***	5.5216	0.0000	0.4309***	3.4394	0.0006	0.7060***	5.3001	0.0000
MS	4.8157**	1.9718	0.0486	-1.9992	-0.4591	0.6462	2.2113	1.1366	0.2557
GDP	2.2550	0.7068	0.4797	2.1628	0.5720	0.5673	2.0337	0.6229	0.5334

注：*** 表示在 1% 的水平上显著，** 表示在 5% 的水平上显著，* 表示在 10% 的水平上显著。

表 5.14　股份制上市银行产权结构对资金筹集阶段效率的实证结果

	模型一			模型二			模型三		
变量	系数	z 检验	P 值	系数	z 检验	P 值	系数	z 检验	P 值
GO	-0.0656	-0.6117	0.5407	—	—	—	—	—	—
NO	—	—	—	0.1343	1.5505	0.1210	—	—	—
FO	—	—	—	—	—	—	-0.6910***	-3.0667	0.0022
O1	-0.4107*	-1.8561	0.0622	-0.3097	-1.3723	0.1699	-0.1285	-0.5830	0.5590
O5	-9.2010***	-3.459	0.0005	-8.4250***	-3.1651	0.0016	-6.0493**	-2.2754	0.0229
CAR	0.0040	0.1117	0.9110	0.0062	0.1746	0.8613	0.0088	0.2639	0.7918
NPL	0.1497**	2.3772	0.0174	0.1379**	2.2156	0.0267	0.1025*	1.7110	0.0000
MS	3.5517	0.8635	0.3878	2.5755	0.6306	0.5282	0.5033	0.1289	0.8974
GDP	0.1601	0.0634	0.9494	0.2038**	2.0639	0.0390	0.3190*	0.1407	0.0130

注：*** 表示在 1% 的水平上显著，** 表示在 5% 的水平上显著，* 表示在 10% 的水平上显著。

表 5.15　城市上市银行产权结构对资金筹集阶段效率的实证结果

	模型一			模型二			模型三		
变量	系数	z 检验	P 值	系数	z 检验	P 值	系数	z 检验	P 值
GO	-1.4858	-0.5450	0.5857	—	—	—	—	—	—
NO	—	—	—	1.6729	1.1615	0.2724	—	—	—
FO	—	—	—	—	—	—	-2.9035*	-1.8850	0.0594
O1	2.7904	0.9086	0.3636	4.2465	1.4164	0.1870	3.5694**	2.1553	0.0311
O5	-1.2940	-0.9298	0.3524	-1.3029	-0.7640	0.4621	-1.2204	-0.9918	0.3213
CAR	0.0041	0.1147	0.9086	-0.0080	-0.2320	0.8206	-0.0277	-1.0254	0.3052
NPL	0.0317	0.1678	0.8667	-0.0534	-0.3260	0.7505	-0.1852	-1.3209	0.1865
MS	68.0990***	4.0487	0.0001	64.1540***	3.7989	0.0035	54.4440***	4.2120	0.0000
GDP	4.4899	1.3637	0.1727	4.9402	1.2841	0.2280	4.0209	1.5013	0.1333

注：*** 表示在 1% 的水平上显著，** 表示在 5% 的水平上显著，* 表示在 10% 的水平上显著。

表 5.16　国有上市银行产权结构对资金获利阶段效率的实证结果

	模型一			模型二			模型三		
变量	系数	z 检验	P 值	系数	z 检验	P 值	V 系数	z 检验	P 值
GO	0.2924	0.9769	0.3286	—	—	—	—	—	—
NO	—	—	—	3.3618**	1.9993	0.0456	—	—	—
FO	—	—	—	—	—	—	-0.3428	- 1.2318	0.2180
O1	0.0758	0.4285	0.0800	0.8198	2.0980	0.0359	0.1418	0.8186	0.4130

（续表）

	模型一			模型二			模型三		
变量	系数	z 检验	P 值	系数	z 检验	P 值	V 系数	z 检验	P 值
O5	10.8980**	1.9793	0.0478	14.8460***	2.6282	0.0086	11.3620**	2.0731	0.0382
CAR	-0.0099	-0.4612	0.6446	-0.0026	-0.1312	0.8956	-0.0062	-0.2839	0.7764
NPL	-0.0923	-1.0411	0.2978	0.0259	0.4018	0.6878	-0.0975	-1.1900	0.2340
MS	1.7859	1.1506	0.2499	7.2757***	3.2387	0.0012	1.9934*	1.6649	0.0959
GDP	2.0739	1.0228	0.3064	1.5548	0.7971	0.4253	2.0267	1.0086	0.3131

注：*** 表示在 1% 的水平上显著；** 表示在 5% 的水平上显著；* 表示在 10% 的水平上显著。

表 5.17　股份制上市银行产权结构对资金获利阶段效率的实证结果

	模型一			模型二			模型三		
变量	系数	z 检验	P 值	系数	z 检验	P 值	系数	z 检验	P 值
GO	-0.1023*	-1.7720	0.0764	—	—	—	—	—	—
NO	—	—	—	0.0877*	1.8480	0.0646	—	—	—
FO	—	—	—	—	—	—	-0.1399	-1.0381	0.2992
O1	-0.1477	-1.2465	0.2126	-0.1154	-0.9334	0.3506	-0.1409	-1.0681	0.2854
O5	-0.5057	-0.3534	0.7238	-0.1180	-0.0809	0.9355	-0.0452	-0.0284	0.9773
CAR	-0.0234	-1.2004	0.2299	-0.0229	-1.1769	0.2392	-0.0238	-1.1948	0.2321
NPL	-0.1284	-0.3789	0.7047	-0.0186	-0.5464	0.5848	-0.0195	-0.5452	0.5856
MS	5.2702*	2.3810	0.0173	5.6279**	2.2372	0.0119	5.4690**	2.3411	0.0192
GDP	1.2250	0.9024	0.3668	1.1747	0.8723	0.3830	0.7616	0.5615	0.5744

注：*** 表示在 1% 的水平上显著，** 表示在 5% 的水平上显著，* 表示在 10% 的水平上显著。

表 5.18　城市上市银行产权结构对资金获利阶段效率的实证结果

	模型一			模型二			模型三		
变量	系数	z 检验	P 值	系数	z 检验	P 值	系数	z 检验	P 值
GO	0.9422	0.7933	0.4274	—	—	—	—	—	—
NO	—	—	—	-0.7900*	-1.6925	0.0905	—	—	—
FO	—	—	—	—	—	—	1.6013**	2.5125	0.0120
O1	-1.8450	-1.3794	0.1678	-2.2834**	-2.3499	0.0188	-2.1474***	-3.1338	0.0017
O5	0.5481	0.9043	0.3658	0.5170	0.9363	0.3491	0.4895	0.9614	0.3363
CAR	-0.0020	-0.1287	0.8976	0.0058	0.5221	0.6015	0.0166	1.4870	0.1370
NPL	0.0139	0.1694	0.8654	0.0664	1.2544	0.2097	0.1399**	2.4115	0.0159
MS	39.2500***	5.3580	0.0000	36.4730***	6.6635	0.0000	31.2520***	5.8433	0.0000
GDP	0.0193	0.0134	0.9892	0.0942	0.0755	0.9398	0.3096	0.2794	0.7799

注：*** 表示在 1% 的水平上显著，** 表示在 5% 的水平上显著，* 表示在 10% 的水平上显著。

如表5.13～表5.15所示，分别是对我国国有上市银行、股份制上市银行和城市上市商业银行三者产权结构与其资金筹集阶段效率之间相关性的实证研究。从实证结果上来看，主要可以从以下这些方面来进行分析。从产权结构性质上来进行分析，可以发现国有股对国有上市商业银行、股份制上市商业银行和城市上市商业银行的资金筹集阶段呈负向关系。[①] 其中国有上市商业银行中国有股对资金筹集效率的影响更为显著，其系数达到了在1%水平下的显著。从境内法人股对资金筹集阶段效率的影响来进行分析，其对我国上市商业银行整体来说都是呈正向影响关系，但是其影响程度并不显著。再从外资股角度进行分析，其对国有上市商业银行资金筹集阶段呈现出显著的正向影响关系，这说明适当地引入外资股对其自身资金筹集效率的提高具有显著的影响。但是对于股份制上市商业银行和城市上市商业银行来说，外资股对其资金筹集阶段呈现出显著负向影响，这是近年来股份制和城市上市商业银行自身经营管理及内控制度不断完善的结果，即上市银行外资股所带来的管理技术经验已渐渐不适于银行的发展。

表5.16～表5.18是分别对国有上市商业银行、股份制上市商业银行和城市上市商业银行各自产权结构与其资金获利阶段之间相应的实证研究。从产权性质上来看，国有股对股份制上市商业银行的资金获利阶段呈负向关系，但是影响程度并不是十分显著，即只在10%的水平下显著。但是在国有上市商业银行和城市上市商业银行中国有股对其资金获利效率都起到正向的影响，不过影响程度都不显著。从境内法人股来看，国有上市商业银行和股份制上市商业银行中境内法人股对资金获利效率呈正向的影响关系，并且其分别在5%和10%的水平下显著。在城市上市商业银行中境内法人股对其资金获利效率呈负向的影响，但这种影响并不显著。从外资股角度来看，在国有上市商业银行和股份制上市商业银行中外资股对资金获利阶段呈负向影响，但其影响的相应程度并不显著。而在城市上市商业银行中外资股则对其有着显著的正向影响。之所以会出现这种情况，说明外资股所带来的先进管理经验和盈利模式是有助于资金获利效率提高的，但这种促进作用在逐渐减弱。

五、政策建议

（一）有关国有上市银行经营效率进一步提高的政策建议

1. 推动产权主体进一步多元化

从我国国有上市商业银行目前的产权结构来看，除交通银行外，都是属于国家绝

---

① 资料来源：王梅励．产权结构对我国商业银行经营效率的影响［D］．山东大学，2016.

对控股的，这符合我国在保持金融稳定的前提下逐步改革的理念。但是随着我国市场机制的不断完善以及资本市场的逐渐成熟，国有上市商业银行自身的竞争力和盈利模式的持续性都会面临很大的挑战。鉴于这种情况，应考虑适当降低国有股的占比，建立起更加合理的相对集中、多股制衡的多元化持股结构。具体来说，国有上市商业银行可以通过引进不同类型的持股主体来达到优化产权结构的目的。在引入持股主体的选择方面，可邀请民营企业资本加入以及适度提高机构投资者和优秀外资银行股份的占比。

2. 推动产权主体进一步多元化

国有上市商业银行都是具有国有性质的股份处于控股地位，因而可能会产生来自政府的过度行政干预，或由于产权定位不明晰而造成所有者缺位，从而造成经营效率的低下。鉴于这种情况，需要对国有性质股东的股东行为进行规范，一方面需要完善汇金公司的内部结构与体制，即可以明确定义为专门的金融控股公司，进而使其切实履行国有股东出资人的责任①；另一方面可以通过对国有上市商业银行现有的股权管理模式进行进一步改革，即让国有股权按照优先股或金股的方式进入国有商业银行，从而在保有国有股东重大决策权的前提下限制其自身的事前表决权，并相应增强其他性质的股东权利，进而增强银行经营效率。

3. 大力发展普惠金融

对于上市商业银行来说，要保持盈利和效率提高的持续性，就得要求不断扩大自身的产品服务以及潜在客户人群。这也就是要求寻找一种有效的经营模式，即通过扩大自身的金融产品服务的潜在需求客户人群，刺激提升这部分人的消费购买力，从而提升自身的经营效率。具体而言，国有上市商业银行可以向中国银行最早建设的中银消费公司一样，积极参与各自的面向中低收入客户群的消费金融公司，设立满足客户短期、平稳和快速资金需求的产品，进而有效推进普惠金融的发展。

（二）有关股份制与城市上市银行经营效率进一步提高的政策建议

1. 实施员工持股的股权激励计划

从产权的角度来看，股份制上市银行基本是要优于国有上市银行的，但其自身仍然存在着相应的问题，若要将自身经营效率进一步提高，就需要着手对产权结构进行再次优化。对于股份制上市银行目前的状况而言，招商银行和民生银行都已经启动了各自核心员工的持股计划，并且其余股份制上市商业银行也都在陆续地筹备中。这是因为实施员工持股计划可以形成一种股权的长期激励机制，对银行自身激励约束机制

① 资料来源：黄菁. 产权结构对商业银行效率的影响研究［D］. 南京：南京师范大学，2013.

的建设是一项十分重要的举措，并且也将极大提升银行的公司治理能力和管理水平，最终实现银行股东、经营管理者和银行员工之间的多方共赢。① 另外，员工持股计划有助于股份制上市商业银行资本金的进一步补充，能有效提高自身的资本充足率及抵御风险的能力，从而提高银行的经营效率。

2. 积极开展金融科技创新

随着近年来金融科技的不断崛起，新兴电子渠道对银行传统的物理渠道的冲击越来越大，银行在客户服务和产品设计等方面也随之发生了很大的变化。由于股份制上市商业银行自身规模的限制，长期而言，在其资金筹集阶段都会与国有大型上市商业银行之间具有一定的差距，并且目前经营模式相对粗放，且业务模式相对单一，无法满足客户多样化业务需求。因而其迫切需要在金融科技创新方面取得一定的成果，这样才能够保证自身经营效率的不断提高。具体而言，上市商业银行将利用区块链、大数据和云计算、物联网和人工智能等新兴科技来为自身经营环境提供良好技术支持，以构建新一代银行业务及服务模式，从而适应未来市场竞争及金融发展新形势。

3. 加快实施轻型银行战略转型

由于我国经济已呈现出新常态的特征，说明粗放式的经济增长模式已基本结束，因而商业银行的经营战略也必须进行相应的调整，即从重资产向轻资产转变，从而建立起资本消耗少、风险权重低、风险可控的资产与业务体系。因此股份制上市商业银行一方面应该主动调整自身的信贷结构，大幅度压缩相关领域的风险资产，以加快自身资产的轻型化；另一方面也应优化自身存款定价和相应信用授信机制，并且大幅压缩银行内具有高成本的结构性存款，以加快自身成本的轻型化，进而双管齐下地加快自身的战略转型，保证自身经营和管理效率的稳步提高。

① 资料来源：吴成颂，郭开春. 资本缓冲、产权结构与银行风险和绩效——来自城市商业银行的经验证据［J］. 商业研究，2016（12）：56－64.

国际一流银行交易业务之16年历程

总行金融市场交易中心　陈　浩　袁　培　任　静

一、研究对象：外资行FICC业务

按标的不同，建行金融市场交易业务可分为汇率、利率、债券、贵金属及大宗商品四大类。对应外资银行，可比业务多数集中在“全球市场”条线，一般可称为FICC①业务。但主要由于我国资本项下未完全开放等机制问题，使国内银行交易业务在内涵上与外资银行有所区别。从业务收入上看，建行体量明显小于摩根大通、汇丰等外资大行，长短板较明显，利率弱、商品强（见表5.19和图5.14）。

表5.19　中外银行金融市场交易业务内涵区别

项目	外资行区别于中资行的特点
利率	产品基本类似，外资行拥有较强定价能力
信用	1. 现券交易以国际市场为主，与我国基本割裂 2. 衍生品应用较发达
汇率	收入结构上以G10货币为主，而非人民币
商品	1. 在期货交易所做市对冲 2. 经营现货业务 3. 收入结构上以大宗商品为主，而非黄金

二、切入视点：金融危机后交易业务的集团收入贡献度

以2008年为分水岭，全球金融危机后，外资银行交易业务基本维持较高水平，鲜有变化。2017年，摩根大通和花旗交易业务收入分别是128亿美元和121亿美元，这也是危机后的平均水平，交易业务对全集团的贡献度维持在15%～20%（见图5.15）。

① 即固定收益、货币及大宗商品（Fixed Income，Currencies & Commodities）。

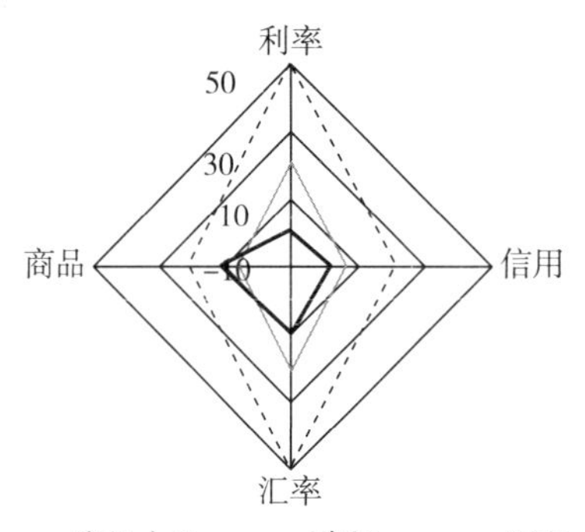

图 5.14　2017 年建行交易业务和外资行结构对比

资料来源：相关银行财报、建行金融市场交易中心。

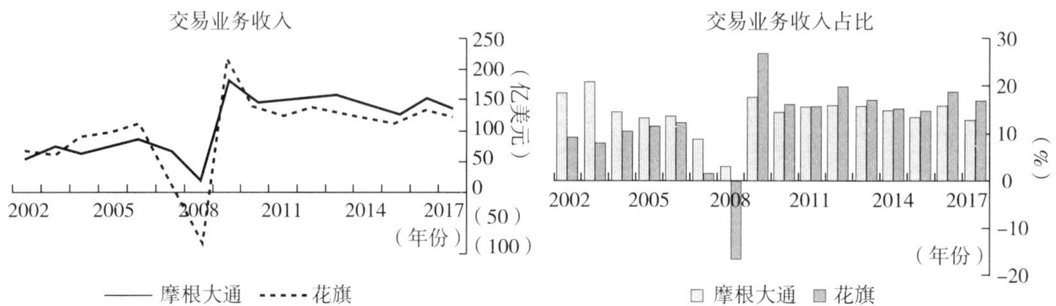

图 5.15　摩根大通和花旗交易业务收入及占比情况

资料来源：相关银行财报、彭博资讯、建行金融市场交易中心。

（1）业务规模跨越式提升主要来自并购。以摩根大通为例，收入伴随并购事件，呈阶梯式上升趋势。1996 年，大通曼哈顿银行并入化学银行，收入翻倍至 20 亿美元以上；2000 年，JP 摩根集团与大通曼哈顿银行合并成为摩根大通银行，合并后交易收入增至 50 亿美元；2009 年收购贝尔斯登后，收入更是跨越 150 亿美元，并保持至今。

（2）得益于“资产荒”和债务衍生品创新，2001—2006 年是交易业务内生高速发展的黄金期。6 年间，美国利率周期明显缩短，前 3 年降息、后 3 年升息，经济和货币政策环境的巨大变化带来大量债务衍生品创新。2001 年，在“资产荒”背景下市场对交易产品需求强烈，摩根大通抓住机会推出 CDO（担保债务凭证）及系列衍生品，此后几年收入增长约 60%。

（3）危机中，花旗亏损 87 亿美元，摩根大通略有盈利，截然不同的业绩表现源自杠杆率。危机前 6 年，摩根大通杠杆率稳步下降至 16 倍，花旗则持续加杠杆至 25 倍。其间，花旗将经营重心放在 CDO 业务上，不仅占据承销市场份额的 1/10，位列商业银行第一，而且成立了结构性投资实体（SIV），买进千亿美元次级 CDO，虽当年因次贷亏损超 200 亿美元，减计后 CDO 净敞口仍达 120 亿美元。

（4）危机后，摩根大通持续降低衍生品交易规模，收入领跑市场。2008 年市场因次贷危机恐慌情绪导致价格混乱，摩根大通敢于大量购买资产，2009—2010 年金融市场业务的业绩的较好表现，大多源于2008 年留下的头寸盈利。更重要的是，此后危机蔓延至欧洲，经济二次探底，摩根大通逐年顺周期降低衍生品交易，花旗则与之相反。

三、做强关键：依赖刚需较强的做市收入，有逆周期特征

做市收入包括点差以及价差收入，是纯粹的中收。其占交易收入的比重，往往跟业务结构关系紧密，生息资产尤其是信用产品会降低该比例；其占非利息收入的比重，反映中收对做市收入的依赖性。

除了危机和“伦敦鲸”等特殊事件影响，两家银行做市占交易收入比重基本在 50%左右，并体现出两个特点：一是以危机为分界线，前高后低，这与 CDO 等信用产品的荣枯周期相关；二是危机后花旗基本保持领先，主要是因为其迅速削减信用产品头寸。

做市业务刚性需求较强，与其他中间业务关联性趋弱。做市占非利息收入比重差异较大，摩根大通维持在 15%，花旗在危机后整体收入下降，因此占比上升很快，侧面反映出交易业务的刚性需求较强（见图 5. 16）。

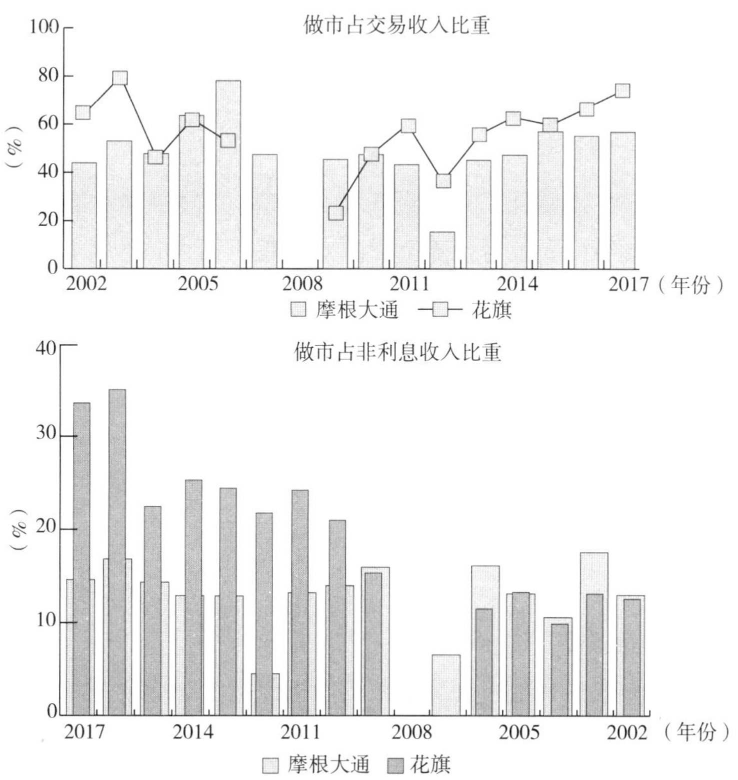

图 5. 16　摩根大通和花旗做市收入占交易收入和非利息收入比重情况

资料来源：相关银行财报、彭博资讯、建行金融市场交易中心。

四、主要抓手：汇率业务是稳定器，商品业务收入取决于现货

近5年内，两家银行做市收入不同品种间分布较为稳定，利率和信用占比六成，汇率占比为20%～30%，商品不超过15%。摩根大通以汇率产品为主，花旗以利率为主（见图5.17）。

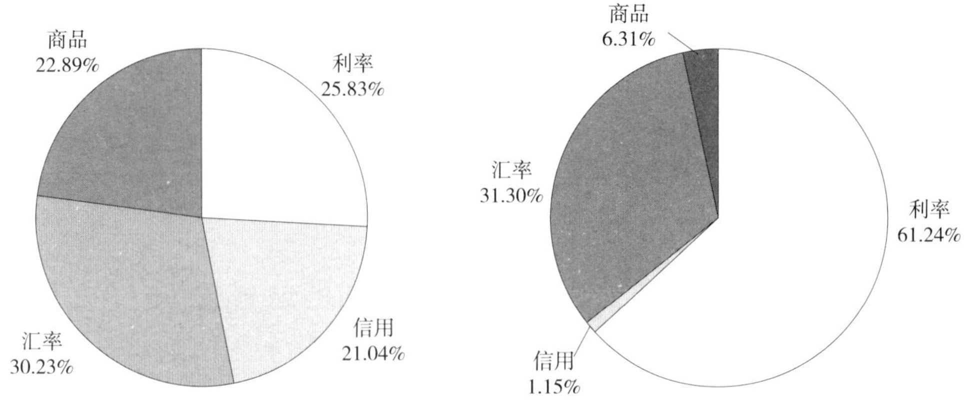

图5.17　摩根大通（左）和花旗做市收入结构

资料来源：相关银行财报、建行金融市场交易中心。

（1）利率和信用产品收入的波动非常大，和金融体系的信用扩展关联较大。如前所述，危机后，信用收入快速收缩，花旗把经营重心放在利率业务上。

（2）汇率业务有实需托底，是交易业务的稳定器。从统计上看，巧合的是，以汇率业务为重点的银行，整体交易收入领先于同业。危机前数十年，花旗汇率业务始终占比最大，也是同业最好；危机后，汇率产品对摩根大通做市收入的贡献度上升到首位，整体交易收入也超过花旗。此外，高盛逐步将重心转移到汇率产品，近两年其贡献度超过80%。

（3）商品业务收入主要取决于现货业务。普遍而言，商品在交易业务中占比最小，品种以能源和金属为主。花旗和摩根大通以开展现货业务为契机，曾领跑商品领域。

从2003年起，中国加大商品消耗，格林斯潘放松监管，同意金融机构涉足大宗商品现货领域，商品进入繁荣周期，花旗商品做市收入从不到2亿美元做到最高近10亿美元，直至2009年出售现货贸易子公司。

摩根大通商品收入的盛衰也来自现货业务。2010年，收购苏格兰皇家银行旗下商品现货商RBS Sempra，2014年卖出，其间年均收入24亿美元，是平常的两倍，对做市收入贡献达到1/3以上（见图5.18）。

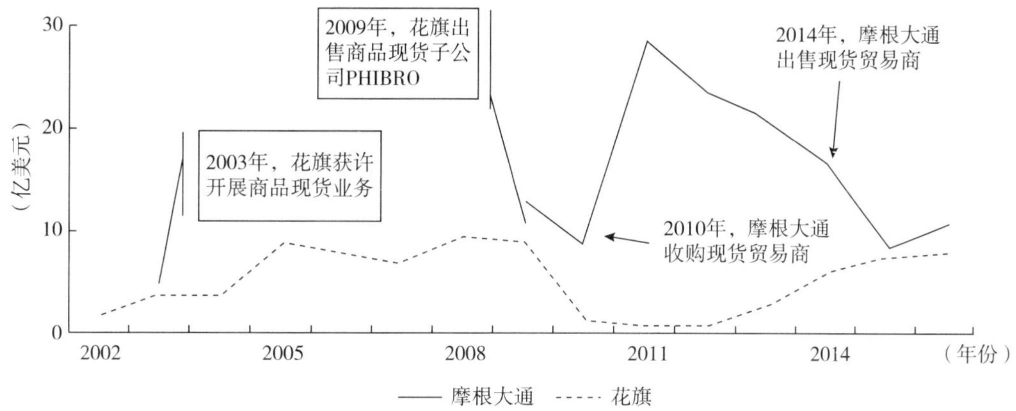

图5.18　摩根大通和花旗的商品做市收入（2002—2016）

资料来源：彭博资讯、建行金融市场交易中心。

五、对建行策略的建议

（一）从周期角度看待各项业务及收入结构

根据外资行经验，静态看业务占比顺序是利率、信用、汇率、商品，动态看各时期业务结构差异较大，其根源在于周期性。

其中，汇率业务关乎贸易周期，期限较长，曲线平滑，有较强实需背景，通常是顶梁柱；商品业务受经济和监管周期影响，前者带来持续稳定收入，后者并不连续，带来杠杆和不确定性；利率、信用业务与银行其他资产业务类似，关乎金融周期，期限最短，波动最剧烈，信用扩张和收缩造就了金融繁荣和危机。

我们从周期变化角度看待业务，既要按照不同周期特点确定优先级，大体保持汇率和商品业务的主导地位，将交易业务发展为全行中收的稳定器；又要追踪明确当前所处的周期位置，寻找不同级别周期共振带来的业务机遇，规避周期下行风险（见图5.19）。

（二）提升做市定价能力需考虑的三大原则

区别于外资行的做市，我们需强调三个关键词。

一是本源性。金融服务实体经济，我们的价格要更多反映客户意愿和实体的基本面情况，而非由金融机构操纵。因此我们作为服务商，最重要的是缩短客户和市场之间的距离，包括信息、价格等。

二是货币性。金融资产定价来源于货币定价，这是美国的银行做市能力最强的根本原因。给我们的启示是，紧紧跟随人民币定价的衍生品市场，全面参与，一旦有新

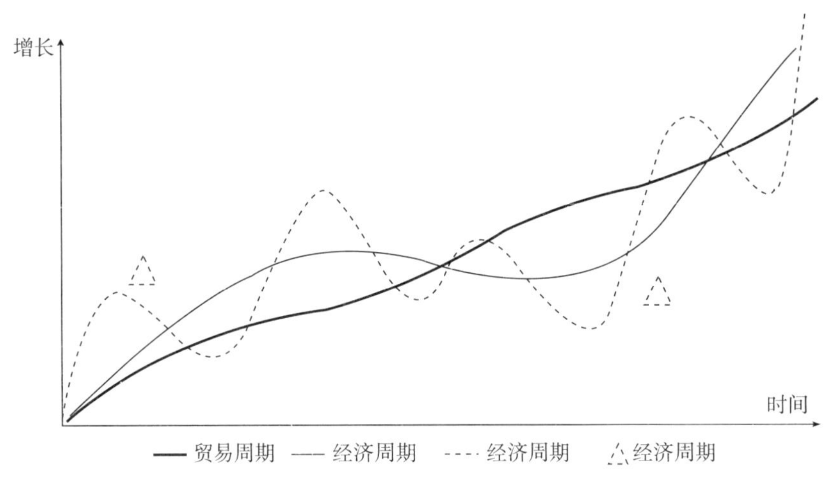

图 5.19　四类周期示意

资料来源：建行金融市场交易中心。

品种或新市场开放，需第一时间进去做市。比如近年港交所收购 LME（伦敦金属交易所）后推出了较多人民币计价的期货。

三是结构性。由于在现货和衍生品组合程度上的差异，每一类业务的定价要求都是不一样的。比如，汇率业务重点在于市场放开后，需避免出现日本银行的情况，日元交易由欧美银行定价；黄金业务既要依托于境内外的成本、需求差异，注重境内的定价能力，又要力争交易链条的上游，成为国内银行的批发商；大宗商品业务只有衍生品交易，短时间内尚谈不上做市能力。

（三）集中力量办大事，理性看待自营交易

过去欧美银行的自营交易很多时候都是脱离实体经济的，过度追求财富和创新。在顺周期经营中，追求自营交易，杠杆的扩大和操作风险几乎是必然结果，每一次危机都会让一些自营太多的银行一蹶不振，花旗和德意志银行是前车之鉴，在国内外，境外危机的传导和监管趋严都会达到类似效果。建行现阶段的核心是覆盖全面市场和产品，锻炼产品组合和分拆定价，提升做市能力，可暂时搁置自营交易。

（四）内生和外延两个维度并重，推进交易业务的国际化布局

常年以来，大型外资行的利润主要集中在发达市场，比例变动极小，交易业务客户以金融机构和跨国集团为主，利润有 70% 来自客盘。中资银行如要在交易业务的全球市场中占有一席之地，直接收购外资机构、从零售商向批发商过渡，是较为理想的选择。当前，港交所和工行在这方面的步伐相对较快。未来，建行在设置海外交易平台的基础上，可根据集团战略部署，适时建议收购外资金融机构，获取交易团队和客户资源。

商业银行贷款利率的决定因素

——基于贝叶斯模型平均方法的实证研究

江苏省分行　黄　磊

一、引言

近年来，我国利率市场化改革按照“放得开、形得成、调得了”的原则稳步推进，存贷款利率管制有序放开，金融市场基准利率体系逐步形成，金融抑制进一步解除。在此过程中，商业银行贷款利率定价的自主权进一步扩大。作为一个中间变量，商业银行贷款利率不仅间接反映了货币政策和金融监管导向，也会对社会融资行为产生直接影响。因此，理解贷款利率的决定因素，对于考察货币政策传导和金融监管的有效性，解决企业“融资难、融资贵”的问题具有重要的现实意义。

目前，国内学术界对于贷款利率定价机制的研究成果较多，但直接针对贷款利率影响因素的实证分析较少，且主要局限于单一线性模型，解释变量选择不够全面，存在模型不确定的问题。本文利用贝叶斯模型平均法（Bayesian Model Averaging，简写为BMA）建立回归模型，兼顾宏观和微观、短期和长期两大维度，选取10个解释变量，综合考察2^{10}个单一线性模型，对商业银行贷款利率的决定因素开展定量分析。一方面针对盛松成和潘曾云（2013）、金中夏（2014）、刘春航等（2015）的定性研究结论开展实证检验，另一方面为深入理解商业银行贷款定价机制、制定科学合理的金融政策提供理论支持。

二、文献综述

目前，国内对于商业银行贷款利率定价的研究主要分为定性和定量两大类。定性研究主要侧重于描述各类宏、微观因素对我国商业银行贷款利率的可能影响，着力于厘清利率的传导机制，提出完善市场化利率体系的相关建议。定量研究则主要从风险调整资本收益（RAROC）的角度分析贷款利率的决定因素。

在定性研究方面，近年来国内学者对于利率市场化问题较为关注，针对商业银行贷款利率的形成机制已经形成较为全面的分析框架。盛松成和潘曾云（2013）指出，我国商业银行的贷款利率主要是在筹资成本基础上，运用成本加成定价来确定，银行成本主要包括营业费用、利息支出等经营成本和闲置资金的机会成本两方面，二者与贷款价格正相关。刘珺（2013）分析了影响贷款利率的结构性因素，指出筹资成本/基准利率（期限）、流动性溢价、信用风险溢价、运营成本以及利润目标这几个要素对贷款价格影响较大。金中夏（2014）、张方波（2015）对货币市场和信贷市场的传导机制开展研究，认为央行能够通过数量型和价格型工具调节市场流动性，引导政策利率水平，进而通过货币市场和信贷市场的传导机制影响商业银行贷款利率。刘春航等（2015）考察了主要发达国家的利率水平后指出，影响商业银行贷款利率的因素主要包括宏观和微观两方面。从宏观影响来看，央行货币政策调控将引导利率短期变化，经济增长速度和居民储蓄率则会决定利率中长期走势。从微观实践来看，商业银行运营成本、资本回报目标、经济资本成本以及企业的经营风险等因素都会对银行贷款利率定价水平产生约束力。刘春航等（2015）提供了一个较为完整的分析框架，从宏观与微观、长期和短期两个维度讨论了贷款利率的关键影响因素，并给出了降低商业银行贷款利率和企业融资成本的可行措施。

在定量研究方面，随着 RAROC 模型在我国商业银行系统内的广泛应用，基于 RAROC 的贷款定价方法已逐渐成为主流。商业银行通过设定相应的风险收益目标，将风险的预期损失转化为当期成本并反推出合理的贷款价格，促进贷款价格与信贷风险相匹配，有效提高了经济资本配置效率。国外学者对基于 RAROC 方法的贷款定价研究起步较早，扎伊克等人（Zaik et al.，1996）详细阐述了美国银行（Bank of America）建立 RAROC 定价管理体系的过程；克里斯托弗（Christopher，1997）系统论述了 RAROC 方法的经济学原理，并以美国银行为例，进一步研究了 RAROC 方法在资本预算、限制管理寻租、资金定价等方面的作用；古特霍夫和吕特尔（Guthoff and Rüter，2001）研究了 RAROC 模型对商业银行投资决策机制的影响，提出了在商业银行管理过程中优化 RAROC 模型的相关措施；斯托顿等人（Stoughton et al.，2007）讨论了基于 RAROC 和 EVA 方法的定价机制的合理性，研究了如何形成最优资本结构，认为外部投资机会的增加可能导致银行增加经济资本的使用并过度投资风险项目。随着利率市场化的深入，国内学者逐渐重视基于 RAROC 模型的贷款定价方法。边俊杰等（2008）分析了商业银行使用 RAROC 方法进行贷款定价的必要性，提供了国有银行的运用案例，同时指出 RAROC 方法存在局限性，未能充分考虑宏观经济形势、企业微观经营状况等因素；周朝阳、王皓白（2012）对样本银行运用 RAROC 方法开展贷款定价测算，并与实际情况相对照，发现样本银行现行的定价方法对非预期损失的风险补偿不足，而 RAROC 定价方法有利于纠正这一倾向，提高风险控制能力和资金使用效率；黄纪宪、顾柳柳

(2014）构建了基于客户关系的 RAROC 定价模型，与样本银行实际定价情况开展实证比较，发现 RAROC 定价模型能够充分反映银行的资金成本、风险成本、经营成本等，提高贷款业务的市场竞争能力；熊正德等（2017）引入《巴塞尔协议Ⅱ》行业风险标准构建 RAROC 定价模型，对网络贷款进行定价，发现 RAROC 定价模型同样适用于网络贷款，能够提高网贷利率的定价质量。

对以上文献的分析可以发现，现有的研究存在以下三点不足。一是针对贷款利率定价的定性研究结论实证检验不够充分。金融危机后我国金融领域改革不断深化，随着利率市场化的加速和互联网金融的兴起，银行业的经营环境已经发生深刻改变，传统定性研究结论需要辅以实证研究做进一步审慎分析。二是考察盛松成和潘曾云(2013)、刘珺（2013)、刘春航等（2015）的研究可以发现，自变量选择在商业银行贷款利率决定因素研究领域方面存在很大的不确定性。哪些宏微观因素对于贷款利率具有更加显著的影响？哪些政策组合具有更高的实践价值？这些问题亟待解答。三是正如边俊杰等（2008）指出，基于 RAROC 方法的贷款利率定价模型具有局限性。影响贷款利率定价的因素既包括企业财务等微观因素，也包括央行货币投放、政策利率等宏观因素，甚至从长期来看，利率的最终决定因素是一国的经济增速和居民储蓄率。而基于 RAROC 方法的贷款定价模型更多考虑了银行和企业的微观层面，对于宏观和长期因素考虑相对不足。四是单个线性模型的定量研究方法存在模型不确定问题。在存在较多潜在解释变量的情况下，解释变量选择的自由度越大，模型的不确定问题就越明显，在一定程度上会影响到结论的可靠性和稳健性。

三、模型设定及变量描述

（一）模型设定

贝叶斯模型平均方法（BMA）是模型平均方法的一个重要分支，该方法以贝叶斯理论为基础，将可能具有解释力的自变量纳入备选模型，通过赋予先验概率和后验概率度量模型以不确定性，并通过后验概率对自变量的解释力进行加权平均，最终挑选出最优模型。BMA 方法相对于传统单一线性模型的优势主要体现在三个方面。一是对于数据信息的挖掘和使用更为充分。由于纳入了更多的潜在解释变量，且通过模型平均进行严格的统计筛选，能够最大限度降低由于人为确定解释变量导致的信息损失。二是模型选择更为科学。传统的单一线性模型往往会面临模型选择问题，即建模者由于观测到部分自变量不显著而进行自主挑选。由于数据样本的随机性，不同的建模者针对同一问题的实证检验所选择的自变量往往不同。而 BMA 方法基于后验概率设置权重，科学判断出不同模型及其变量的解释力度，避免了建模者对于模型变量的自主挑选。三是 BMA 方法能够通过解释变量的后验包含概率及后验均值判断其在模型中的重要程度，即分辨出哪些自变量包含在正确模型中的可能性更高，哪些自变量对于因变量的影响作用更为明显。

由于 BMA 方法具有良好的建模灵活性和解释力，近年来国内外应用该方法研究经济金融问题的文献逐渐增多。多佩尔胡弗和米勒（Doppelhofer and Miller，2004）、艾歇尔等人（Eicher et al.，2009）、埃里斯和乌拉尚（Eriș and Ulașan，2013）、冈萨雷斯和维纳亚加塔桑（González and Vinayagathasan，2015）运用 BMA 模型研究经济增长的宏观决定因素；赖特（Wright，2008）、萨尔穆特（Salmutter，2011）、费尔德基歇尔（Feldkircher，2014）运用 BMA 模型预测汇率波动；纳塔芬（Nathaphan，2014）、艾哈迈德和切瓦帕特拉库（Ahmed and Chevapatrakul，2015）建立了 BMA 模型预测股票市场收益水平。从国内文献来看，杨爱军、周影辉（2012）利用 BMA 方法分析 SHIBOR（上海银行间同业拆放利率）的影响因素，发现 1 年期银行贷款利率、回购利率、上一日 SHIBOR 报价和资金成本对 SHIBOR 存在长期正向影响；陈伟、牛霖琳（2013）运用 BMA 方法建立模型，筛选通胀预测模型的关键影响因子并对样本外通胀率进行预测，实证结果表明，BMA 方法样本内拟合优于单一模型，样本外预测能力优于传统的 AR 模型、主成分分析模型等；李洁、张天顶（2014）基于 52 个国家的面板数据，建立 BMA 模型考察跨境资本流动的影响因素，发现结构性因素、周期性因素以及资本管制政策等对于资本跨境流动产生了显著影响。但我目前尚未见到该模型在贷款利率定价领域的应用。接下来对 BMA 方法的基本原理及参数先验分布做相关说明。

首先，构建如下 BMA 线性模型：

$$y = \alpha_k + X_k \beta_k + \varepsilon \varepsilon \sim N(0,\sigma^2 I) \tag{1}$$

其中 y 是因变量项，α_k 为截距项，β_k 为系数项，X_k 为自变量项，ε 为服从正态分布的误差项。若自变量 X 包含 n 项，则共存在2^n个不同的自变量组合，也就存在2^n个可能的备选模型。根据贝叶斯公式，各个备选模型的后验概率为：

$$p(M_k \mid y,X) = \frac{p(y \mid M_k,X)p(M_k)}{\sum_{m=1}^{2^n} p(y \mid M_t,X)p(M_t)} \tag{2}$$

（2）式中 p（M_k）为备选模型M_k的先验概率，得出备选模型后验概率 p（$M_k \mid y$，X）后，可进而计算出系数项的后验概率为：

$$p(\beta \mid y,X) = \sum_{k=1}^{2^n} p(\beta \mid M_k,y,X)p(M_k \mid y,X) \tag{3}$$

（2）式中，对于先验形式的选择会直接影响到备选模型边际似然的估计。本文采用 BMA 建模中一个常用的先验形式——Zellner's g 先验，该先验形式由策尔纳（Zellner，1986）提出，形式较为简洁，计算效率较高，且便于进行模型间的比较，设置方法是令β_k服从如下多元正态分布：

$$p(\beta_k \mid \sigma^2) = N[\beta^0, g\sigma^2 (X_k' X_k)^{-1}] \tag{4}$$

同时，将方差σ^2设置为无信息先验分布：

$$p(\sigma^2) \propto \frac{1}{\sigma^2} \tag{5}$$

（4）式和（5）式是 Zellner's g 先验的核心假设，通常令 $\beta^0=0$，指定超参数 g 的情况下，可得β_k和σ^2的联合后验密度：

$$p(\beta_k, \sigma^2 \mid y, X) \propto p(\beta_k \mid y, X, \sigma^2) p(\sigma^2 \mid y, X) \tag{6}$$

其中，$p(\beta_k \mid y, X, \sigma^2)$ 服从多元正态分布，$p(\sigma^2 \mid y, X)$ 服从逆伽马分布，均为常见的分布形态，便于进行参数估计。

（二）变量选择

综合考虑国内外现有的定性研究和定量研究成果，本文从宏观与微观、长期和短期两个维度选取 10 个解释变量，建立 BMA 模型讨论其对贷款利率的影响。与 RAROC 定价模型相比，BMA 模型设定中不仅包含银行和企业层面的微观变量，也兼顾了中央银行、宏观经济、人口结构等变量，对贷款利率决定因素的考察更为全面。主要解释变量设置如下。

1. M2 增长率

M2 供应量属于央行执行货币政策的数量型工具。一般来讲，M2 增长越快，通过商业银行渠道流入市场的资金就越多，市场资金面就越宽裕，企业对于贷款利率的议价能力就越强，贷款利率趋于下降。因此，预期 M2 增长率与贷款利率之间存在负相关关系。

2. 银行间债券 7 天回购利率（R007 利率）

近年来，我国利率走廊逐渐成形，央行运用价格型工具执行货币政策的有效性明显提高。考察趋势可以发现，央行常备借贷便利操作（SLF）7 天利率和超额存款准备金率构成了利率走廊的上下限，而 R007 利率则在其间波动，能够反映出央行的价格型工具引导轨迹。央行货币政策趋于收紧，则 R007 利率上升，市场资金价格上升，商业银行贷款利率将提高。因此，预期 R007 利率与贷款利率之间存在正相关关系。

3. 商业银行成本收入比

成本收入比是商业银行成本控制和经营效率的综合体现。盛松成和潘曾云（2013）指出，商业银行的贷款利率定价主要基于成本加成法，商业银行控制营业成本支出的能力越强，经营效率越高，则成本收入比就越低，也就越能提供具有市场竞争力的贷款价格。因此，预期商业银行成本收入比与贷款利率之间存在正相关关系。

4. 商业银行净息差

净息差是指商业银行净利息收入与平均生息资产的比率，用以衡量商业银行生息资产获取净利息收入的能力。该指标是评价商业银行生息资产收益能力和风险定价能力的关键指标。由于我国商业银行的主要生息资产为各项贷款，净息差越高，一定程度上反映出生息资产，尤其是贷款利率的定价水平越高。因此，预期商业银行净息差与贷款利率之间存在正相关关系。

5. 流动性比例

流动性比例是指商业银行一个月内到期的流动性资产与流动性负债的比率，是衡量商业银行短期流动性状况的主要监管指标之一。流动性比例从剩余期限的角度反映了银行短期流动性风险状况，一般来说该指标数值越高，银行持有的短期流动性资产也就越多，短期（一个月内）流动性也就越好。该指标并非越高越好，实际操作中，商业银行往往会根据市场流动性风险状况，权衡安全性、流动性、盈利性三者之间的关系，设定一个合理的目标流动性比例。当市场流动性风险提高时，商业银行出于审慎经营考虑，持有的短期流动性资产增加，流动性比例提高，可用于贷款投放的资金量相对减少，贷款利率将上升。因此，预期商业银行流动性比例与贷款利率之间存在正相关关系。

6. 资本利润率

资本利润率指商业银行在一个会计年度内获得的税后利润与资本平均余额的比率，主要衡量商业银行所有者投入资本所形成权益的获利水平。从股东或者投资者的角度看，资本利润率反映了商业银行资本的增值能力。商业银行实际经营过程中，年初的综合经营计划会根据股东要求匡算全年净利润目标，进而形成大致的资本利润率目标。刘春航等（2015）指出，商业银行股东适当调低资本利润率目标要求，有利于降低商业银行经营过程中的利润压力，进而降低贷款利率。因此，预期资本利润率与贷款利率之间存在正相关关系。

7. 企业资产负债率

该指标反映了企业负债总额与资产总额的比例关系，主要度量企业的负债水平。一般来说，企业资产负债率越高，其债权违约风险就越大，相应的贷款风险溢价就越高。值得注意的是，实践经验表明，商业银行对大中型企业的信贷投放往往存在“垒大户”现象，即信贷资金往往向一些大项目、大企业过度集中，虽然企业的资产负债率已经很高，但由于银行间竞争激烈，多头授信反而可能降低其贷款价格。因此，企业资产负债率与贷款价格之间的关系并不确定，需要做进一步的实证研究。出于数据可得性，本文选用工业企业资产负债率作为解释变量。

8. CPI 和 GDP 增速

泰勒（Taylor，1993）指出，货币当局对短期名义利率的调控主要依据实际产出与潜在产出的偏离及通货膨胀率与目标通货膨胀率的偏离开展。在潜在产出和目标通货膨胀率给定的情况下，实际产出水平和通货膨胀率越高，则短期名义利率水平相应越高，商业银行贷款利率也随之提高。因此，预期 CPI 和 GDP 增速与贷款利率之间存在正相关关系。

9. 居民储蓄率

弗里和梅森（Fry and Mason，1982）、希金斯（Higgins，1998）、蔡昉和陆旸（2014）指出，人口年龄结构和居民储蓄水平会对长期利率水平产生深远影响。人口年龄结构趋于老龄化，居民储蓄率越高，则市场上的可贷资金供给量就会越多，贷款利率水平将降低。因此，预期居民储蓄率与贷款利率之间存在负相关关系（见表 5.20）。

表 5.20　主要变量列表

变量类型	影响主体	变量	变量名称	预期相关关系
被解释变量	—	DK	人民币贷款加权平均利率	—
解释变量	中央银行	M2	M2 增速	负相关
		R007	银行间债券 7 天回购利率	正相关
	银行业金融机构	CIR	商业银行成本收入比	正相关
		NIM	商业银行净息差	正相关
		LR	流动性比例	正相关
		ROE	资本利润率	正相关
	企业	ALR	企业资产负债率	待检验
	宏观经济	CPI	CPI 增速	正相关
		GDP	GDP 增速	正相关
	人口结构	SR	居民储蓄率	负相关

四、实证结果

（一）数据描述

本文数据根据万得中国宏观数据库及银监会年报等资料整理，频率为季度，样本区间为2010年12月~2018年3月。如前文所述，因变量为人民币贷款加权平均利率（DK），自变量共10个，包括M2增速（M2）、银行间债券7天回购利率（R007）、商业银行成本收入比（CIR）、商业银行净息差（NIM）、流动性比例（LR）、资本利润率（ROE）、企业资产负债率（ALR）、消费品物价增速（CPI）、GDP增速（GDP）、居民储蓄率（SR）。主要变量的描述性统计见表5.21。

表5.21　主要变量的描述性统计

	样本数	均值	中位数	标准差	最小值	最大值
DK	30	0.0646	0.0671	0.0085	0.0522	0.0806
M2	30	0.1334	0.1323	0.0319	0.0817	0.1985
R007	30	0.0401	0.0399	0.0122	0.0239	0.0656
CIR	30	0.2951	0.2945	0.0231	0.2530	0.3530
NIM	30	0.0249	0.0258	0.0024	0.0203	0.0277
LR	30	0.4623	0.4637	0.0258	0.4130	0.5139
ROE	30	0.1830	0.1919	0.0323	0.1256	0.2260
ALR	30	0.5751	0.5780	0.0117	0.5550	0.5910
CPI	30	0.0256	0.0209	0.0140	0.0090	0.0636
GDP	30	0.0762	0.0730	0.0104	0.0670	0.1020
SR	30	0.4826	0.4899	0.0205	0.4541	0.5139

观察表5.21中的数据，可以发现以下两个值得关注的现象：

1. 样本期内，人民币贷款加权平均利率（DK）和商业银行净息差（NIM）的波动程度明显小于M2增速（M2）、GDP增速（GDP）等指标

这一现象既反映出2010年以来，我国商业银行在银行业监管机构的政策引导下，贷款利率定价管理能力有所提高，有效避免了资金价格的大起大落；又从侧面反映出商业银行贷款利率具有一定的内生性，并非完全由市场环境和宏观经济等外部因素决定，尤其是近年来国家大力号召商业银行对小微企业开展定向价格优惠，一定程度上熨平了信贷资金价格的周期波动。

2. 样本期内，M2增速（M2）的波动程度大于银行间债券7天回购利率（R007）的波动程度

这一现象与马文涛（2011）的结论相符，即与数量型调控工具相比，价格型工具对宏观结构性参数的变化并不敏感，相对而言较为稳定。而数量型工具受限于不断变动的货币乘数和流动速度（范从来，2004），以及巨额外汇储备导致的被动基础货币投放、国企投资冲动和财政政策导致的贷款倒逼机制等因素（张杰、晓鸥，2006），导致央行投放基础货币的独立性、稳定性受到考验（周小川，2016），波动性高于价格型工具。

（二）解释变量的后验包含概率

在 BMA 模型中，解释变量的后验包含概率主要表示该变量包含于正确模型的概率。后验包含概率值越大，其包含在正确模型中的可能性就越高，解释力就越强。根据多佩尔胡弗和米勒（2004）、马桑贾拉和帕帕耶奥尔尤（Masanjala and Papageorgiou，2008）等人的研究，解释变量后验包含概率大于 50% 即可被视为有效解释变量，大于 90% 则可被视为最有效解释变量。表 5.22 展示了 10 个主要解释变量的 BMA 实证检验结果。分析结果表明，资本利润率（ROE）、M2 增速（M2）、商业银行成本收入比（CIR）、银行间债券 7 天回购利率（R007）4 个解释变量后验包含概率大于 50%，对于贷款定价水平具有较强的解释力。其中资本利润率（ROE）包含概率大于 99%，意味着该变量对于贷款定价水平具有最强的解释力。

表 5.22　解释变量的 BMA 实证检验结果

变量	后验包含概率	后验均值	后验标准差	后验相关关系
ROE	0.9960	0.3319	0.0967	正相关
M2	0.7355	-0.0752	0.0586	负相关
CIR	0.6634	0.0759	0.0706	正相关
R007	0.6546	0.1083	0.1006	正相关
SR	0.3880	-0.0420	0.0715	负相关
ALR	0.3387	-0.1350	0.2673	负相关
LR	0.2996	0.0179	0.0386	正相关
GDP	0.2759	-0.0462	0.1249	负相关
CPI	0.2274	0.0179	0.0678	正相关
NIM	0.2025	0.0553	0.3597	正相关

表 5.22 中各解释变量的后验包含概率能够用更加直观的方式展现。图 5.20 中横坐标为各单一模型的累积概率，纵坐标为 10 个解释变量，图中对应各解释变量的着色部分面积越大，说明该解释变量包含在正确模型中的后验概率越高。观察图 5.20 容易发现，资本利润率（ROE）、M2 增速（M2）、商业银行成本收入比（CIR）、银行间债券 7 天回购利率（R007）4 个解释变量所对应的着色面积相对于其他变量更大，即包含在正确模型中的可能性较高，对自变量的解释力较强。

以上实证结果有利于深化对我国商业银行贷款利率定价机制的认识。首先，影响商业银行贷款定价水平的因素主要来源于央行和银行业金融机构本身，GDP 增速、CPI 增速、居民储蓄率等宏观因素解释力相对较弱；其次，从央行角度来看，数量型政策

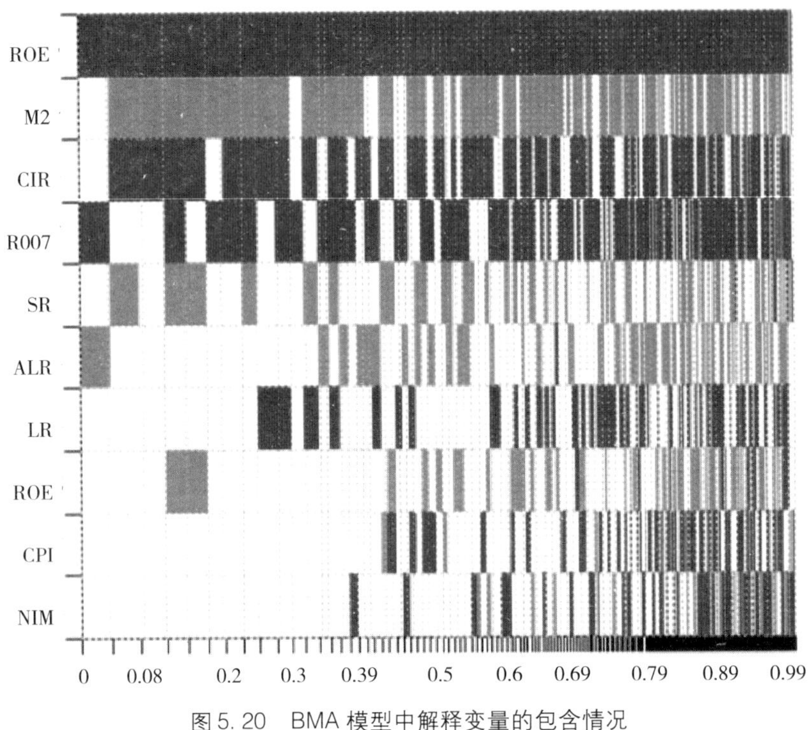

图 5. 20　BMA 模型中解释变量的包含情况

和价格型政策对于商业银行贷款定价的解释力均较强，且后验包含概率相差不大，一定程度上反映出 2010 年以来，央行着力提高价格型工具的运用能力，数量型工具为主、价格型工具为辅（唐齐、熊洁敏，2009）的传统操作思路正逐步改善；再次，从商业银行角度来看，资本利润率（ROE）、商业银行成本收入比（CIR）对于贷款价格的解释力明显高于流动性比例（LR）和商业银行净息差（NIM），说明银行资本回报目标设定、经营管理水平对于贷款利率的影响更为显著。

（三）解释变量的后验相关关系

BMA 模型中，自变量的后验相关关系表示该变量对于因变量的影响方向。事实上，后验相关关系与后验均值的正负相一致，后验均值为正，则后验相关关系为正相关，后验均值为负，则后验相关关系为负相关。考察表 5. 22 中的实证检验结果，并与表 5. 20 中的预期相关关系比较，可以发现，M2 增速（M2）、银行间债券 7 天回购利率（R007）、商业银行成本收入比（CIR）、商业银行净息差（NIM）、流动性比例（LR）、资本利润率（ROE）、CPI 增速（CPI）、居民储蓄率（SR）8 个解释变量在 BMA 模型中得出了符合预期的后验相关关系，这为盛松成和潘曾云（2013）、刘春航等（2015）、泰勒（1993）、弗里和梅森（1982）、希金斯（1998）、蔡昉和陆旸（2014）等学者的研究结论提供了实证支撑。其他两个解释变量的后验相关关系需要进一步说明：首先，

表5.20中企业资产负债率（ALR）与贷款价格之间的预期相关关系未能确定，经实证检验，其后验相关关系为负相关，这一结果为探究商业银行授信投放“垒大户”、多头授信导致过度竞争提供了研究线索；其次，GDP增速（GDP）与贷款价格之间的后验相关关系为负相关，与泰勒规则推论的预期不符，对这一现象的可能解释是，我国央行事实上实行了多元目标制，导致决策独立性相对不足，未能完全实现泰勒规则的独立运用（卞志村，2006；周小川，2016）。

（四）解释变量的后验均值

BMA模型中，解释变量的后验均值为每个单一模型的包含概率与该模型内自变量系数乘积之和，即经过模型平均后的解释变量系数。一般来说，解释变量的后验包含概率越高，其后验均值也越高，对被解释变量的影响力就越大。观察表5.22可以发现，4个后验包含概率大于50%的解释变量中，资本利润率（ROE）对于商业银行贷款利率的正向影响最大，其次为银行间债券7天回购利率（R007），M2增速（M2）、商业银行成本收入比（CIR）对于贷款价格的影响基本相当，但方向相反。这一结果为盛松成和潘曾云（2013）、金中夏（2014）、刘春航等（2015）提出的关于如何适当降低贷款价格的政策建议提供了优先顺序：从商业银行角度来看，资本利润率（ROE）对于贷款价格具有最为显著的影响，成本收入比（CIR）次之；从央行角度来看，银行间债券7天回购利率（R007）对于贷款价格的影响大于M2增速（M2），从侧面反映出价格型工具对于贷款利率的引导作用大于数量型工具。

五、结论与监管建议

本文选取M2增速、银行间债券7天回购利率、商业银行成本收入比、商业银行净息差、流动性比例、资本利润率、企业资产负债率、CPI增速、GDP增速、居民储蓄率10个解释变量，运用贝叶斯模型平均方法建立模型，探讨了各解释变量对贷款利率的解释力和影响程度，主要结论有以下三点。

第一，我国商业银行贷款定价受股东资本回报目标设定、自身经营管理水平以及央行政策影响更为显著，其他如企业资产负债水平、宏观经济环境、人口结构等因素虽然也可能对贷款价格存在一定程度的影响，但实证来看后验包含概率偏低，解释能力相对较弱。

第二，通过与预期相关关系对比，本文考察了各解释变量与贷款价格之间的后验相关关系，一方面为盛松成和潘曾云（2013）、刘春航等（2015）的定性研究结论提供实证支撑；另一方面绝大多数变量的后验相关关系符合预期，体现了BMA建模方法的有效性和灵活性。同时，实证结果发现，企业资产负债率、GDP增速与贷款利率之间存在后验负相关关系，为进一步探讨商业银行“垒大户”多头授信、央行决策独立性等问题提供了线索。

第三，通过考察解释变量的后验均值绝对值大小，本文发现资本利润率对于贷款利率具有最为显著的影响，而价格型工具对于贷款利率的影响大于数量型工具。这一实证结论为盛松成和潘曾云（2013）、金中夏（2014）、刘春航等（2015）提出的政策建议提供了政策优先顺序。

值得指出的是，本文运用BMA方法着重研究了商业银行贷款利率的决定因素，侧重于厘清哪些宏观、微观因素对于贷款利率具有更加显著的影响，而在精准测度每一个自变量对贷款利率的影响力度以及贷款利率预测方面（Vosseler and Weber，2018）仍有较大的进一步研究空间。

基于此前构建的BMA模型和相关结论，本文对我国货币及金融监管政策提出如下建议。

一是加快探索数量型工具和价格型工具协同发力的货币政策机制，尤其要加强价格型工具的应用，细化利率工具，推动货币政策由数量型为主向价格型为主转变，促进对商业银行贷款定价的市场化引导。

二是加强对商业银行资本利润率目标的监管政策引导，推进绩效考核体系深化改革，严禁层层加码，引导商业银行多从自身经营优化，以及盘活存量资金与资产、提高中间业务收入入手，减轻商业银行资产端的经营压力，进而促进降低贷款利率，扩大企业服务边界，增强服务实体经济能力。

三是深化推进商业银行经营转型改革，积极发展金融科技，加快高质量发展步伐，充分借鉴国内外商业银行的先进经验，努力提高精细化管理水平，着力压降成本收入比，进而提高贷款利率定价能力，为更广泛的融资主体提供更具竞争力的贷款利率。

利率市场化对银行信贷结构的影响

湖北省分行　程　波

一、引言

我国金融市场利率市场化进程经历了四个阶段。初始阶段（1986—1990），银行间资金可以相互拆借，拆借资金期限和利率由借贷双方共同商定。发展阶段（1996—2003），银行业同业拆借市场成立，拆借双方根据货币市场供求决定利率水平；银行间债券市场成立，以公开招标方式发行金融债券，同时放开债券市场回购和交易利率。攻坚阶段（2004—2008），人民银行对于金融机构人民币贷款利率逐步放开上限阈值管理，实行下限阈值管理；上海银行间同业拆借利率（SHIBOR）开始运行。全面放开阶段（2012—2018），人民银行放开金融机构贷款利率管制，商业银行和农村金融机构不再设置存款利率浮动上限；逐步推进存贷款基准利率和货币市场利率“两轨合一”。

利率市场化是指存贷款利率水平由金融市场供给需求关系决定，金融市场根据现有资金状况和货币市场流向来自主调节利率水平，让市场机制在利率决定过程中起主导作用，从而形成以人民银行基准利率为参考数值，金融市场供求关系决定存贷款利率的形成机制。商业银行作为推动利率市场化工作的主要载体，其业务调整、盈利水平、发展规模等必定受到利率市场化的影响。随着我国利率市场化工作的逐步推进，商业银行市场竞争加剧，单位资本贷款收益率发生变化，银行传统盈利点发生改变，从而迫使银行积极调整信贷资源配置结构。同时，在金融市场监管趋严的背景下，单纯依靠资产规模增长，难以实现银行盈利水平持续稳定的增长，优化信贷资源结构的任务迫在眉睫。

因此，在金融市场利率市场化的大背景下，研究商业银行市场价格竞争如何影响信贷结构调整，对于保持银行持续稳健的发展具有重要意义。另外，分析利率市场化对银行信贷资源配置结构的影响，疏通银企间信贷资源传导渠道，对于扶持和振兴我国实体经济发展也具有重要的现实意义。

二、文献综述

在我国的利率市场化进程中，关于商业银行利率放开对于信贷资源配置和企业经营行为的影响存在不同的观点。一些学者认为利率市场化能够促进信贷资源配置更为合理，企业更容易获得银行信贷扶持。希门尼斯（Jimenez，2013）研究发现市场竞争能够打破原有的银行对于信贷资源配置的垄断，对于经营管理优良或具有市场发展潜力的企业，更容易获得银行信贷。帕拉维西尼（Paravisini，2008）认为市场竞争能够减少银行与大型企业之间传统的关系型贷款，银行能够将更多的信贷资源投放给中小企业，扶持中小企业发展。然而，还有一些学者认为利率市场化也存在一些负面影响。赫尔曼（Hellman，2000）认为市场竞争会导致银行单位资本信贷收益率降低，经营利润下降，为了追逐更高收益率，会转向偏好高风险投资。孙国峰和蔡春春（2014）发现在我国利率管制时期，当市场利率向上突破合理阈值时，人民银行会加大货币投放力度，市场利率出现回落，增加企业货币市场融资可得性，但在利率市场化条件下，企业货币市场融资缺少政策扶持，融资存在不确定性。另外，还有些学者从其他角度分析利率市场化对于银行信贷资源配置的影响。谭之博和赵岳（2013）进行反向试验发现，通过增加市场中中小企业数量，使得银行同业之间出现信贷竞争，市场利率下降，在此种情况下中小企业更容易获得银行信贷。战明华等（2018）认为当前积极推进互联网金融发展，借贷双方信息不对称情况得到缓解，利率市场化工作推进更加容易，银行信贷资源配置更为合理。饶品贵和姜国华（2013）发现，虽然我国利率市场化已经推行较长时间，但在货币政策紧缩环境下，国有企业相对于非国有企业更容易获得信贷扶持。

既有文献对于在当前国内产业结构转型环境下，从利率市场化角度分析商业银行信贷结构调整的研究相对较少。因此，本文构建商业银行贷款决策理论模型，分析市场竞争对商业银行信贷结构调整的作用机制。

三、理论框架

为了分析在我国利率市场化背景下，市场竞争对商业银行信贷结构调整的影响，本文基于德扬（De Young，2015）提出的信贷供给模型，构建商业银行信贷决策理论模型。同时，在银行垄断竞争条件下，建立市场竞争与商业银行单位资本贷款收益率的关系函数，探讨市场竞争对银行信贷资源配置的传导机制。

在垄断竞争条件下，商业银行通过制定最优经营策略来实现目标函数效用最大化。商业银行从事信贷行为，t 期末银行 i 的贷款存量为：

$$L_{t,i} = L_{t-1,i} + NL_{t,i} \tag{1}$$

其中，$L_{t-1,i}$是 $t-1$ 期末银行 i 的贷款余额，$NL_{t,i}$是 t 期末银行 i 的新增贷款。由于商业银行属于负债经营，银行自有资本较少，所以假定 t 期末银行 i 的可贷资金 $L_{t,i}$ 等于银行客户存款量 $F_{t,i}$。

t 期末商业银行 i 的贷款总收益包括两个部分：$t-1$ 期贷款余额收益和 t 期新增贷款收益。因此，单位资本贷款收益率分为两部分：一是 $t-1$ 期的 t 期银行 i 的单位资本贷款收益率，为 $\tilde{R}_{t,i/t-1}=1+r_t+\kappa_{t-1,i}-\tilde{\eta}_{t,i}$；二是 t 期的 t 期银行 i 的单位资本贷款收益率，为 $\tilde{R}_{t,i/t}=1+r_t+\kappa_{t,i}-\tilde{\eta}_{t,i}$。其中，$1+r_t$ 表示银行外部融资成本，$r_t=r_t(h_{t,i})$ 表示银行外部融资成本是市场竞争度 $h_{t,i}$的函数，即银行融资成本受到市场竞争度的直接影响。$\kappa_{t,i}$表示 t 期银行 i 的信用利差，即商业银行 i 自身要求的超出成本之外的风险补偿收益率，$\kappa_{t,i}=\kappa_{t,i}(h_{t,i})$ 表示银行贷款风险补偿收益率也是由市场竞争度 $h_{t,i}$决定。银行 i 在 t 期的单位资本贷款收益率决定了银行 t 期新增贷款量，即 $NL_{t,i}=NL_{t,i}(\tilde{R}_{t,i/t})$。$t$ 期银行 i 的新增贷款产生的经营管理成本为 $C_{t,i}=C_{t,i}(NL_{t,i})$。进一步，假设 t 期商业银行 i 共有 n 个部门，那么 t 期末银行 i 的经营利润函数如下：

$$W_t=\sum_{i=1}^{n}(\tilde{R}_{t,i/t-1}\cdot L_{t-1,i}+\tilde{R}_{t,i/t}\cdot NL_{t,i})-(1+r_t)\cdot F_t-\sum_{i=1}^{n}C_{t,i}(NL_{t,i}) \tag{2}$$

其中，W_t 表示银行经营利润，$\tilde{R}_{t,i/t-1}\cdot L_{t-1,i}$表示 $t-1$ 期银行贷款存量在 t 期的本息总和，$\tilde{R}_{t,i/t}\cdot NL_{t,i}$表示 t 期银行新增贷款在 t 期的本息总和，$(1+r_t)\cdot F_t$ 表示银行贷款融资成本，$C_{t,i}(NL_{t,i})$ 表示银行新增贷款的经营管理成本。商业银行为了追求期望效用最大化，t 期银行期望效用函数为 $E[U(W_t)]$，因为效用函数为凹函数，即满足 $U_w>0$ 且 $U_{ww}<0$。

为了实现期望效用 $E[U(W_t)]$ 最大化，银行通过调整 t 期新增贷款量 $NL_{t,i}$，即 $\max\limits_{NL_{t,i}}E[U(W_t)]$。因此，根据银行贷款约束函数［公式（1）］和效用函数［公式（2）］，计算出 t 期银行最优新增贷款量公式：

$$NL_{t,i}=-L_{t-1,i}-\sum_{j\neq i}\frac{\sigma_{i,j}}{\sigma_{i,i}}\cdot L_{t-1,j}-\sum_{j\neq i}\frac{\sigma_{i,j}}{\sigma_{i,i}}\cdot NL_{t,j}+\frac{1}{r}\cdot\frac{\kappa_{t,i}(h_{t,i})-\mu_{t,i}-\partial C_{t,i}/\partial NL_{t,i}}{\sigma_{i,i}}-\frac{1}{A\gamma}\cdot\frac{\kappa_{t,i}(h_{t,i})}{h_{t,i}\cdot\sigma_{i,i}} \tag{3}$$

其中，$L_{t-1,i}$表示 $t-1$ 期银行 i 的贷款存量，$\sigma_{i,i}$表示银行 i 的贷款损失方差，$\sigma_{i,j}$表示银行不同部门间的贷款损失协方差。$\gamma=-E[V_{WW}]/E[V_W]$ 表示银行风险规避参数。$(\kappa_{t,i}-\mu_{t,i}-\partial C_{t,i}/\partial NL_{t,i})/\sigma_{i,i}$表示银行期望贷款收益率。

从公式（3）可知：一是商业银行当期信贷投放量受到众多因素的影响；二是 $t-1$ 期银行信贷投放量较大时，t 期银行会选择减少市场信贷投放量；三是银行当期新增贷款量与市场竞争度相关；四是市场竞争对银行不同类别贷款风险补偿收益的影响不同，进而不同类别单位资本贷款资本收益率存在差异，最终导致银行不同类别贷款资源配置调整。

四、实证分析

（一）样本描述

本文实证样本数据来自万得数据库，选取时间段为 2007—2016 年股份制改造后的银行样本。经过数据清洗，样本银行数量为 54 家，其中大型国有银行 4 家，股份制银行 9 家，城市商业银行 29 家，农村商业银行 12 家。

（二）计量模型

根据第三部分的理论模型，构建新增贷款增长率模型方程，具体方程式如下：

$$Ratio_{\frac{NL_{t,i,j}}{L_{t-1,i,j}}} = \alpha + \Sigma_m(L_{t-1,i,m})\beta_m + \Sigma_{m\neq j}(Ratio_{\frac{NL_{t,i,m}}{L_{t-1,i,m}}})\varphi_m + \frac{\kappa_{t,i,j} - MC_{t,i,j}}{\sigma_{i,jj}} \cdot \delta + c_{t,i} \cdot \pi + z_{t,i} \cdot \rho + x_t \cdot \vartheta + \varepsilon_{t,i,j} \tag{4}$$

其中，$i=1$，$2\cdots$，N 表示银行个体，$m=1$，$2\cdots$，n 表示银行内部不同贷款部门，t 表示时间长度。新增贷款增长率 $Ratio_{NL_{t,i,j}/L_{t-1,i,j}} = NL_{t,i,j}/L_{t-1,i,j}$，$NL_{t,i,j}$表示银行 i 第 t 年部门 j 的新增贷款额，$L_{t-1,i,j}$表示银行 i 第 $t-1$ 年部门 j 的存量贷款余额。在模型方程式中，新增贷款增长率 $Ratio_{NL_{t,i,j}/L_{t-1,i,j}}$作为被解释变量，反映了当期银行信贷资源配置结构的变化。（$\kappa_{t,i,j}-MC_{t,i,j}$）/$\sigma_{i,jj}$表示经过风险调整后的资本收益率，其中 $MC_{t,i,j}$表示银行资本边际成本，$c_{t,i}$表示银行贷款市场价格竞争度。$z_{t,i}$和 x_t 作为控制变量，分别表示银行和宏观经济特征变量。从公式（4）可知，因为模型方程式中的被解释变量 $Ratio_{NL_{t,i,j}/L_{t-1,i,j}} = NL_{t,i,j}/L_{t-1,i,j}$中包含上一期的贷款余额 $L_{t-1,i,j}$，公式（4）的解释变量中也包含 $L_{t-1,i,m}$，因此该方程回归测算时可能存在内生性问题，所以实证回归采用广义矩估计方法（GMM）对模型进行测算。

（三）变量选取

模型方程式中，被解释变量为商业银行信贷分类：一是按信贷类别分类（公司业务、住房抵押、消费零售）；二是按信贷期限结构分类（短期贷款、长期贷款）；三是按抵押物分类（信用贷款、担保贷款）。被解释变量包括市场竞争度、贷款收益率、不良贷款率、银行规模、消费价格指数以及 GDP 增长率。市场竞争度利用勒纳指数测算，银行风险利用不良贷款率指标进行衡量。

表 5.23 中的指标数值显示：一是贷款增长率，消费零售贷款增长率大于公司商业和住房抵押贷款增长率，长期贷款增长率大于短期贷款，信用贷款增长率大于担保贷款；二是贷款存量，公司商业贷款、长期贷款和担保贷款存量均高于同类型其他贷款存量。从上面的描述可知，商业银行仍属于传统金融服务业，我国商业银行为了资产安全和稳健经营，目前还是以公司贷款、长期贷款、担保抵押贷款为主。但是，当前国内经济受到内外环境影响（中美贸易摩擦、产业结构调整等），下行趋势明显，实体企业扩大再生产动力不足，贷款需求不强烈，银行为了保持业务持续增长态势，积极调整信贷资源配置结构，将更多的信贷资源投放在消费零售、长期贷款、信用贷款等方面。

表 5.23　变量的描述性统计

变量	均值	方差	中位数	最小值	最大值
公司商业贷款增长率	0.27	0.381	0.15	−0.17	6.82
住房抵押贷款增长率	0.29	0.604	0.13	−0.79	5.19
消费零售贷款增长率	0.82	2.553	0.29	−0.83	31.55
短期贷款增长率	0.19	0.237	0.16	−0.29	1.42
长期贷款增长率	0.34	0.791	0.19	−0.65	7.38
担保贷款增长率	0.22	0.372	0.18	−0.77	7.19
信用贷款增长率	0.69	4.594	0.13	−0.84	69.48
公司商业贷款存量	483.6	1 139	58	0.31	7 251
住房抵押贷款存量	127.3	335.7	5.32	0.01	2 081
消费零售贷款存量	59.74	128.3	7.48	0.01	1 025
短期贷款存量	562.8	893.5	116.2	2.35	4 375
长期贷款存量	695.4	1 196	79.38	0.12	6 249
担保贷款存量	499.2	1 153	56.41	3.27	7 331
信用贷款存量	135.5	428.9	7.19	0.01	3 385
贷款收益率	0.07	0.03	0.05	0.02	0.13
资产规模	6.13	1.82	4.62	0.57	9.54
不良贷款率	1.19	1.51	0.89	0	20.85
通货膨胀	104.1	1.84	101.55	97.4	101.6
GDP 平减指数	9.33	1.95	9.14	6.9	12.7

注：贷款存量单位为 10 亿元。

（四）实证结果

本文分析市场竞争对银行信贷结构的影响，分别构建3组模型方程式，被解释变量根据银行贷款类别进行划分，实证回归结果如表5.24所示。

表5.24 市场竞争对银行信贷结构的影响

模型	模型1			模型2		模型3	
变量	（1）公司商业贷款增长率	（2）住房抵押贷款增长率	（3）消费零售贷款增长率	（1）短期贷款增长率	（2）长期贷款增长率	（1）担保贷款增长率	（2）信用贷款增长率
竞争	-0.228**	-0.473***	6.123**	-0.129**	0.672**	-0.272**	3.853*
公司商业贷款	-0.000**	-0.000**	0.000***	—	—	—	—
消费零售贷款	0.000**	-0.000*	-0.000***	—	—	—	—
住房抵押贷款	0.000***	-0.000***	-0.000**	—	—	—	—
短期贷款	—	—	—	-0.000*	0.000**	—	—
长期贷款	—	—	—	0.000**	-0.000**	—	—
信用贷款	—	—	—	—	—	-0.000**	0.000***
担保贷款	—	—	—	—	—	0.000**	0.000**
单位资本贷款收益率	0.243**	-14.544**	-35.865*	-3.247**	-11.938**	-4.225***	-26.151***
不良贷款率	0.024**	0.073**	-0.483**	-0.005**	0.181**	-0.042*	-0.095*
资产规模	-0.023*	-0.056**	-0.223**	-0.006**	-0.139**	-0.0068***	-0.374*
通胀率	-0.023*	-0.086**	0.071*	0.016***	-0.025*	-0.015**	-0.124***
GDP平减指数	0.015**	-0.034**	-0.046*	-0.048**	0.068***	0.013***	0.146**
样本数	138	96	125	89	112	105	99
修正拟合优度	0.24	0.36	0.29	0.15	0.29	0.41	0.23

注：*、**、***分别表示在10%、5%和1%水平上显著。

从表5.24的实证结果可知，模型1、模型2和模型3中竞争变量参数值有正有负，即说明市场竞争能够改变银行信贷资源配置。进一步分析，模型1将银行信贷资源按类型拆分发现：竞争能够促进消费零售贷款增加（6.123），但是竞争会减少银行公司商业贷款（-0.228）和住房抵押贷款（-0.473），说明随着国内产业结构转型，银行积极调整自身信贷资源配置，将信贷资源从传统的公司、住房业务向新兴消费零售行业转型。模型2将信贷资源拆分为长期和短期贷款，结果发现竞争会促使银行进行更多的长期贷款投放（0.672），而短期贷款投放减少（-0.129），说明在利率市场化背景下，银行为了减少自身经营风险和降低贷款管理成本，更愿意与企业保持长期贷款合作关系。从模型3可知，竞争会促进信用贷款量增加（3.853），但会抑制担保贷款投放量（-0.272），为了响应国家扶持中小企业的号召，银行积极与工商、税务等部门合作，国家信用评价体系不断完善，除了传统抵押担保贷款外，还可以根据企业缴税、实际控制人征信信息等给予企业一定的信用授信，企业能够获得更多银行信贷。在3组模型中，资产规模系数值均为负数，说明资产规模越小的银行信贷增速越快。单位资本贷款收益率数值大部分均为负，说明贷款利率越高，风险越大，银行基于风险考虑选择减缓信贷发放增速。3组模型中的不良贷款率回归系数值为负，说明银行不良贷款率上升，银行信贷投放增速会减弱。

表5.24从整体上分析了市场竞争对银行信贷结构的影响，发现市场竞争对于不同类别银行信贷的作用效应存在差异。因此，下面进一步分析市场竞争对银行信贷结构的作用机制。实证分析结果如表5.25所示。

表5.25　市场竞争对银行信贷结构影响的机制分析

模型	模型1			模型2		模型3	
变量	（1）公司商业贷款增长率	（2）住房抵押贷款增长率	（3）消费零售贷款增长率	（1）短期贷款增长率	（2）长期贷款增长率	（1）担保贷款增长率	（2）信用贷款增长率
竞争	-0.336	-1.875**	38.766*	5.326**	16.196**	-0.446	21.246*
单位资本贷款收益率	-1.776*	-14.478**	-72.562*	-4.239**	-9.282*	-3.474*	-36.142**
交互项	0.231	3.194*	-522.636**	-68.122*	-268.578**	-4.378**	-357.232**
样本数	114	106	117	93	96	126	132
修正拟合优度	0.13	0.17	0.38	0.25	0.26	0.18	0.22

注：（1）交互项=竞争变量数值与单位资本贷款收益率数值的乘积。
（2）*、**、***分别表示在10%、5%和1%水平上显著。

从表5.25回归结果可知，模型1中单位资本贷款收益率对于消费零售贷款增速（-72.562）的影响大于公司商业贷款（-1.776）和住房抵押贷款（-14.478）。模型2中单位资本贷款收益率对于长期贷款增速（-9.282）的影响大于短期贷款增速（-4.239）。模型3中单位资本贷款收益率对于信用贷款增速（-36.142）大于担保贷款增速（-3.474）。同样，在模型1、2、3中，交互项对于消费零售贷款增速（-522.636）、长期贷款增速（-268.578）以及信用贷款增速（-357.232）的影响大于其他被解释变量。在利率市场化背景下，银行对于利率具有一定的自主定价权，在面对市场竞争时，银行为了占领市场份额会选择下调贷款利率，银行借贷利差收窄，银行盈利减少，银行需要积极拓展新的利润来源。又因为我国金融市场的发展，企业工商税务信息获取更加容易，征信信息系统建设不断完善，从而银行调整信贷资源配置，将信贷资源投放到消费零售、信用贷款等方面。

五、结论与建议

利率市场化是发挥市场配置社会资源的重要前提条件，也是为了让金融机构在货币市场拥有自主定价权。本文分析得出如下结论：一是在利率市场化背景下，市场竞争促使银行存贷款利率降低，银行为了寻找新的利润来源，积极调整信贷资源配置结构；二是资本规模越小的银行在面对市场竞争时，对于信贷资源配置结构调整越积极；三是随着金融监管趋严，单位资本贷款收益率越高，市场风险越高，银行信贷投放越谨慎；四是不良贷款率越高，银行信贷投放力度越弱。

为了使银行信贷业务在利率市场化背景下能够继续稳定健康地发展，需要政府政策以及其他改革措施相互配合。一是政府监管机构积极利用市场竞争实现银行积极转型。二是政府监管机构对于大中小型银行实施差异化政策。传统大型银行与中小企业信贷合作意愿不强，扶持力度不够；而资本规模较小的银行转型积极性较高，追逐高收益信贷投资，但也带来了高风险。三是对于偏好高风险的小规模银行实施更为严格的风险管控机制，减少银行业系统性风险发生的概率。

结构性理财产品市场风险控制研究

陕西省分行　周笑微

一、当前我国结构性理财产品风险控制现状及问题

在普通的非结构性银行理财产品走上收益率的下坡路时，结构性理财产品也经历了发行缩量，最终兑付收益达标率低的窘境。从当前的表现看，购买结构性理财产品并不合算，对于普通投资者来说，如果对相关挂钩产品的行情走势没有很好的把握，只是盯着预期最高收益率而盲目购买结构性产品，基本就成了赌博式的投资，最终遭遇承担的风险较大、获得的平均预期收益较低的情况。

（一）当前我国结构性理财产品市场现状

如图 5.21 所示，2015 年 32 家商业银行共发行 3 754 款结构性理财产品，相比于 2014 年减少了 21.73%。

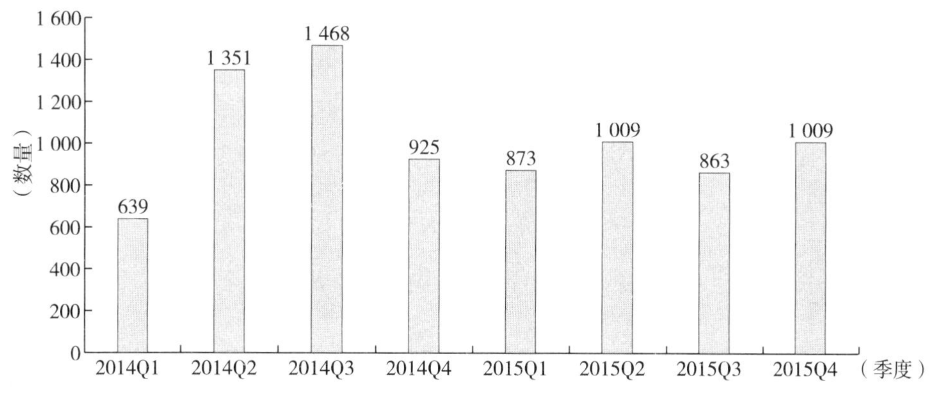

图 5.21　2014—2015 年商业银行结构性理财产品数量

资料来源：银率网。

据统计，2015 年共有近 3 500 款结构性理财产品到期，其中披露了到期数据的产品有 2 100 款左右，这部分数量占到总量的 60%，并不算很多。仍有将近 40% 的产品

在到期后没有进行结果披露。在已披露的产品中，有 1 255 款产品达到预期最高收益率，占披露结果的60%，有836 款产品未达预期最高收益率，占披露总量的40%，也就意味着仅有刚超过一半的理财产品数量能达到预期的最高收益率，若考虑到未披露的产品数量中未达到标准的产品数量，则这一合格率还将下降。在披露的产品当中，挂钩股票指数型产品比重较大，有 450 款左右，占比过半；接下来是挂钩黄金型产品，有 253 款，占总体比重的 30.26%；以及挂钩汇率型的产品，有 67 款，占总量的 8%。

2015 年结构性理财产品短期投资，即期限在 1 个月以内的结构性理财产品总计发行 66 款，占总发行量不到 2%，跟上一年相比，同比减少 83.54%，由此可见，银行将减少对一个月以下的理财产品的发行。投资期限为 1 ~3 个月的产品共计发行 2 000 款左右，是一个月以下的理财产品的 30 多倍，占总发行量的 52%，同比减少 20%；投资期限在 3 ~6 个月的结构性理财产品总计发行 827 款，是一个月以下投资产品的 12 倍，是 1 ~3 个月的理财产品数量的 41%，占总发行量的 22%，跟去年同期相比增长了不到 2%。中长期产品，即投资期限为 6 ~12 个月的结构性理财产品总计发行 611 款，同比增长 34%，逐渐占到发行总量的 1/3。投资期限超过 1 年的结构性理财产品共发行 300 款左右，是一个月以下产品数量的 3 倍多，同比小幅增长。因此我们可以看出，当前结构性理财产品市场上，中短期产品发行量大幅减少，而中长期产品发行量逆势增长（见图 5.22）。

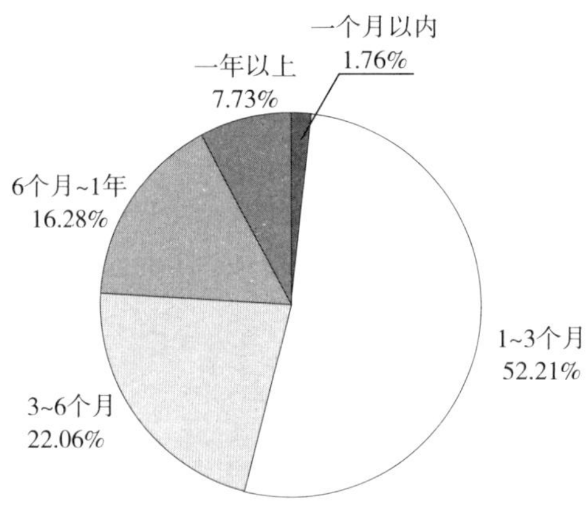

图 5.22　结构性理财产品各发行期限占比

资料来源：由银率网发布数据总结。

另外，我国当前结构性理财产品的币种包括人民币、港币、美元、欧元和澳元等，虽然币种丰富，但仅有极少数的外币产品。从币种上看，在结构性理财产品市场上，人民币产品依旧是一家独大。同时我们还要看到，2015 年理财产品收益率形势并不乐观，收益率下降成为威胁整个行业的大问题，而 2016 年 1 月，各类人民币理财产品不分收益类型、期限，延续 2015 年下降的趋势，收益率继续下滑。在外币理财产品中，只有欧元产品幸免于难，其他产品泥沙俱下，形势也不容乐观。

从分收益类型来看，以保本浮动收益类为主，但占比大幅下降。非保本浮动收益类和保证收益类产品占比上升，2015 年保本浮动收益类共发行 2 479 款，占比 66. 04%；非保本浮动收益类产品发行 726 款，占比 19. 34%；保证收益类产品发行 549 款，占比 14. 62%。

从挂钩标的来看，除挂钩股票型之外，其他挂钩标的如挂钩指数型、挂钩汇率型以及挂钩黄金等贵金属型的数量不分伯仲，平分秋色，挂钩股票型数量稍多，占 24. 91%，挂钩利率的结构性理财产品最少，发行 526 款，占整体的 14. 01%，这些类型的产品数量总计超过 75%（见图 5. 23）。

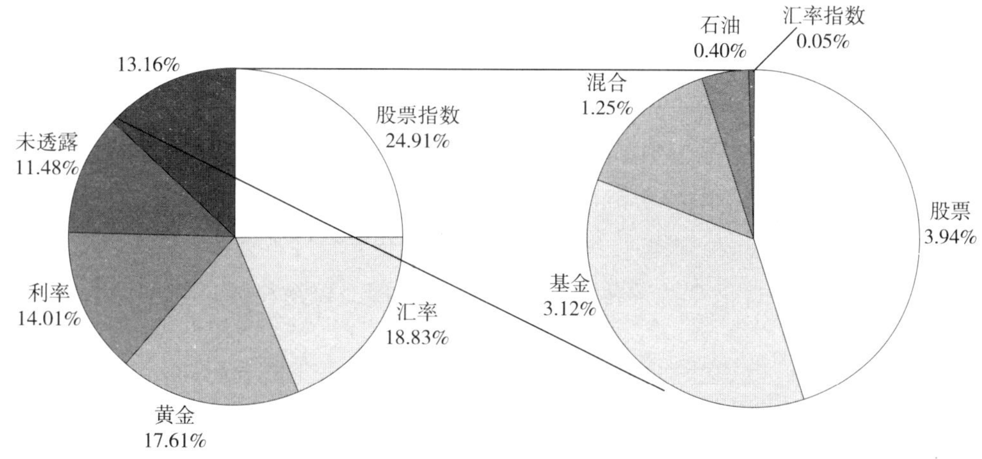

图 5. 23　结构性理财产品各挂钩标的占比

资料来源：由银率网发布数据总结。

从平均预期最高收益率来看，挂钩基金和股票的结构性理财产品的平均预期最高收益率较高，分别为 11. 72%、8. 67%，而挂钩利率和 SHIBOR 的结构性理财产品的平均最高预期收益率较低，分别为 4. 43% 和 4. 09%。

（二）当前我国结构性理财产品市场风险控制存在的问题

我国的商业银行长期以来一直对市场风险比较漠视，管理非常薄弱，这都是由于我国金融市场化水平不高，同时商业银行对于市场风险控制管理空间较小所导致的。然而，近年来，明显加快的利率市场化速度、显著提升的金融自由化程度、发展迅速的金融衍生品以及不断加深的汇率市场化程度等因素的变化，极大地加大了我国商业银行所要面临的市场风险，因此，不断提升管理手段，加强对市场风险控制已经迫在眉睫。

1. 市场风险度量工具与技术的滞后性

当前，我国商业银行没有将现有的风险度量方法充分运用，而且还主要采用的是简单的缺口分析法来计量利率风险，跟国外相比较为落后。比如衍生品的市场风险管理还未应用到久期分析法，对国外运用的风险计量方法，如 VaR（风险价值模型），还未投入国内的风险度量的实践中，仍处于探索阶段。

想对市场风险进行合理的控制，必须要先对市场风险进行度量，否则将影响风险控制的有效性，加大风险。所以，我国商业银行对结构性理财产品的市场风险的度量工具与技术亟待加强。

2. 信息系统管理不完善

我国人口众多、数据繁杂，银行在信息管理方面的滞后性使得自己没能把握住客户需求，不能更好地提供合适客户的理财产品，在客户选择理财产品时也不能设身处地地为客户提供针对性建议，这些都加剧了不稳定因素。因此，信息管理系统的更新完善是银行下一步要进行重点建设的方面。

3. 缺少市场风险控制部门

我国商业银行在风险评估与预警方面比较薄弱，缺乏专门的结构性理财产品市场风险管理部门。当前，我国商业银行的风险管理部门和业务部门联系甚少，缺乏风险信息的传递机制，管理效率较低；风险管理部门的上下对接不充分，存在滞后性，执行效率不高；基层银行仍注重于传统的信贷风险管理，对结构性理财产品缺乏重视，没有前瞻性。

4. 相关人才缺失

由于我国结构性理财产品起步较晚，相关的专业风险控制人员数量有限，专业队伍的建设没有跟上产品和市场的变化。同时，结构性理财产品种类较多，复杂性强，对其市场风险进行控制必须要对市场变化、挂钩标的的变化有良好的把握。这两个原因使得我们在产品研发设计方面和风险控制方面都处于较被动的局面，因此，在之后的发展中，必须将人才招募、培养以及专业队伍的建立作为第一要务。

二、基于 VaR 模型的结构性理财产品市场风险度量研究

（一）结构性理财产品市场风险度量方法选择及基本步骤

我国的金融市场是一个新兴的市场，随着改革开放的深入，以及国家简政放权的不断推进，市场将代替政府，发挥越来越重要的主导作用。证券市场与货币市场的发展活跃、释放的外汇市场、处于新兴阶段的衍生品市场，随着这些市场的高速发展，金融工具不断发展的同时也会带来各种前所未有的难题需要我们去克服，例如，史无前例的市场风险。在经历了度量证券组合价值的变化量、方差—协方差度量之后，VaR 模型的应运而生使得对风险的控制更为清晰直观。VaR 模型以其更具有科学性、适用

性，以及严谨的特点将风险控制的途径变得更全面、更便捷、更能有效地运用。

目前，大多数关于 VaR 的文献都是研究市场风险的，测量市场风险的 VaR 模型已比较成熟。其中若里翁（Jorion，1997，2001）和王春峰等（2000，2001）分别对用 VaR 模型进行金融市场风险度量做了详细的阐述。

本文面对结构性理财产品的市场风险，采用 VaR 模型并计算的方法，对市场风险进行度量，进一步予以控制。

第一步，先选取样本，通过 Eviews 软件对样本序列分别进行平稳性、自相关性以及正态检验，检验其是否满足使用 VaR 模型进行风险度量的前提假设。

第二步，使用蒙特卡洛模拟法，用蒙特卡洛模拟法对观察日内的未来的美元兑日元汇率进行模拟，模拟了 10 000 次来防止特殊性。

第三步，求出产品的期望收益率、零值 VaR 以及均值 VaR。

（二）结构性理财产品市场风险度量模型运用

1. 产品介绍

选取中国农业银行的“金钥匙如意”2016 年第 11 期看跌日元汇率人民币理财产品，其产品说明书如表 5.26 所示。

表 5.26　“金钥匙如意”2016 年第 11 期看跌日元汇率人民币理财产品说明书

产品名称	“金钥匙如意”2016 年第 11 期看跌日元汇率人民币理财产品
产品类型	非保本汇率挂钩型
发行银行	中国农业银行
投资收益起止日期	2016 年 1 月 19 日～2016 年 4 月 18 日
投资期限	90 日
认购资金/认购资金返还/投资收益币种	人民币/人民币/人民币
投资起点金额	5 万元
期末观察日	产品到期前两个交易日
挂钩标的	美元/日元汇率
产品收益说明	（1）如在期末观察日，美元/日元汇率大于或等于 113.8，则到期时投资者收取 4.5% 的年化收益 （2）如在期末观察日，美元/日元汇率大于或等于 87.8，但小于 113.8，则到期时投资者收取 3.1% 的年化收益 （3）如在期末观察日，美元/日元汇率小于 87.8，则到期时投资者收取 3.0% 的年化收益。理财收益 = 理财资金 × 到期年化收益率 × 实际理财天数 ÷ 365

这款产品期限为90天，较短，风险较小，观察日那两天内的美元兑日元汇率的观察水平决定了到期收益率，若大于等于113.8，则收益率最高，为4.5%；若大于等于87.8，小于113.8，则收益率为3.1%；若小于87.8，则收益率为3.0%。因此，该产品所面临的主要市场风险是汇率风险。

2. 样本选取

选取2015年3月5日至2016年1月18日的日汇率，共217个样本数据。样本来源于国家外汇局网站，我们对此期间美元兑日元汇率的走势进行一定的分析。

由图5.24可以看到，美元兑日元汇率在2015年3月5日后一直高于触发汇率，因此其在观察日高于出发汇率的概率较大。

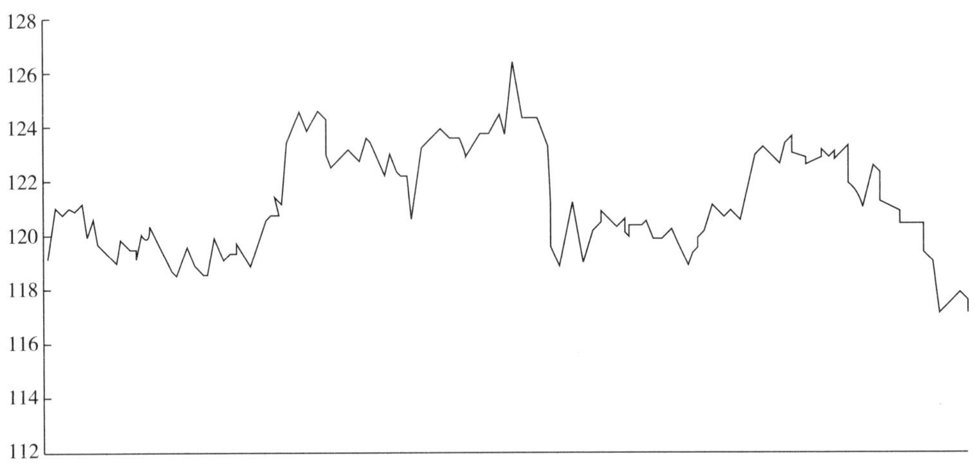

图5.24　2015年3月5日至2016年1月18日美元兑日元汇率

以2016年1月19日的汇率价格为期初价格，在中国农业银行网站上查得P0 = 117.72。假设市场有效、波动随机，利用Eviews 8.0对模型的假设进行检验。

3. 序列平稳性检验

下面开始进行ADF检验。

表5.27　ADF统计变量

虚假设：D数值有一个单元根

外因：连续

滞后除数：0（自动默认SIC信息准则，最大滞后阶数 = 14）

		t统计量	伴随概率
ADF测试检验：		-12.88876	0.0000
测试重要数值：	1%水平	-3.460739	
	5%水平	-2.874804	
	10%水平	-2.573917	

从表 5. 27 可看到 ADF 统计变量 -12. 88876 远小于 1%、5% 和 10% 显著性水平下的临界值 -3. 460739、 -2. 874804 和 -2. 573917，以此，我们完全可以判定，该序列为平稳序列。

4. 序列相关性检验

序列相关性在计量经济学中指对于不同的样本值，随机干扰之间不再是完全相互独立的，而是存在某种相关性，又称自相关，反之，则服从随机游走。序列要服从随机游走的特征是能否运用 VaR 模型的前提条件，而检验时间序列分布是否服从随机游走特征，实际上则是检验随机扰动项的相关性。

我们通过使用 Eviews 中相关图 Q-统计量的方法，检验序列相关性。由表 5. 28 可以看出，Q-统计量和 P 值都比较大，因此不存在序列相关，即样本汇率序列符合随机游走特征，可以进行下一步检验。

表 5. 28　序列相关性

自相关	偏相关		自相关系数	偏相关系数	Q-统计量	P值
	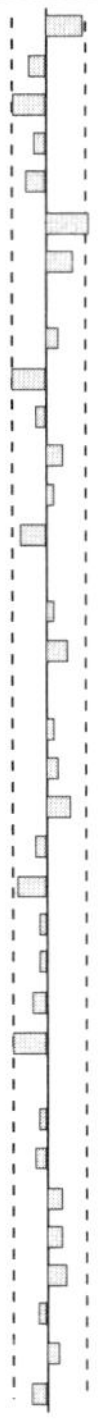	1	0.117	0.117	3.0004	0.083
		2	−0.039	−0.053	3.3285	0.189
		3	−0.132	−0.123	7.1903	0.066
		4	−0.060	−0.032	7.9849	0.092
		5	−0.080	−0.082	9.4049	0.094
		6	0.153	0.158	14.681	0.023
		7	0.142	0.095	19.217	0.008
		8	0.033	−0.004	19.461	0.013
		9	−0.010	0.026	19.484	0.021
		10	−0.154	−0.135	24.920	0.005
		11	−0.095	−0.031	27.001	0.005
		12	0.033	0.042	27.254	0.007
		13	0.092	0.021	29.198	0.006
		14	−0.044	−0.093	29.660	0.008
		15	−0.002	−0.010	29.661	0.013
		16	−0.013	0.024	29.701	0.020
		17	0.023	0.070	29.824	0.028
		18	−0.003	0.002	29.827	0.039
		19	0.050	0.022	30.418	0.047
		20	0.047	0.040	30.947	0.056
		21	0.082	0.083	32.565	0.051
		22	−0.049	−0.047	33.145	0.060
		23	−0.121	−0.103	36.704	0.035
		24	−0.036	−0.022	37.026	0.043
		25	0.007	−0.020	37.040	0.057
		26	−0.035	−0.065	37.344	0.070
		27	−0.097	−0.128	39.674	0.055
		28	0.014	0.007	39.725	0.070
		29	−0.042	−0.023	40.160	0.081
		30	−0.055	−0.036	40.937	0.088
		31	0.007	0.054	40.951	0.109
		32	0.053	0.042	41.675	0.118
		33	0.075	0.081	43.134	0.111
		34	−0.004	−0.018	43.139	0.135
		35	−0.005	0.035	43.145	0.162
		36	−0.075	−0.053	44.628	0.153

5. 正态检验

VaR 模型的蒙特卡罗模拟是参数确定情况下，假设汇率差分布满足某一随机分布，然后结合假定的随机分布形式来模拟实际分布[①]。本案例中假设汇率的一阶差分的随机分布为正态分布，因为服从正态分布形式更具有可确定性：均值和方差均为已知的，因此便可求得分布形式。

第一步：先将序列的统计特征求出。通过 Eviews 软件，序列 Rt 的统计特征如图 5.25 所示。

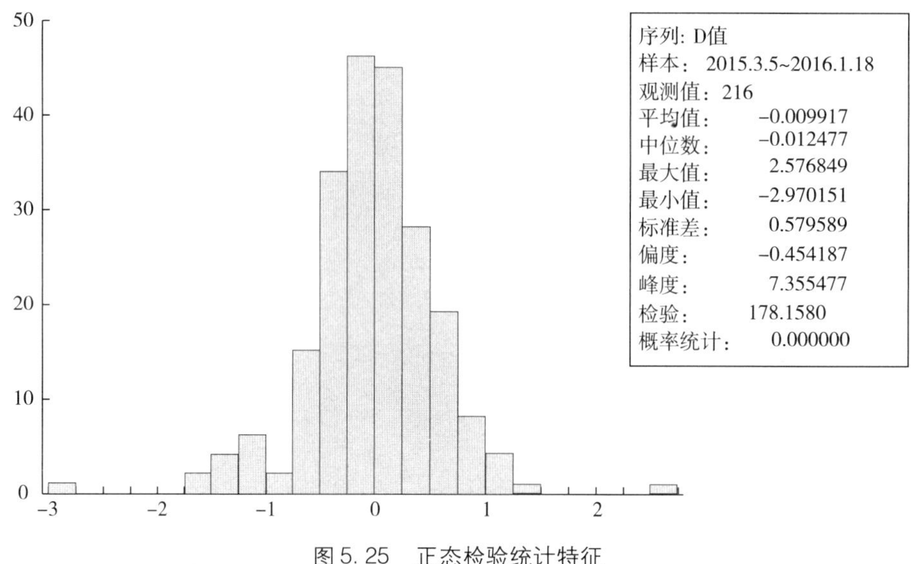

图 5.25　正态检验统计特征

从图 5.25 可以看出，序列的均值为 -0.009917，方差为 0.579589，方差值较大，说明收益波动较大，风险相对高；峰度 K 为 7.35，偏度 S 为 -0.45，说明该序列偏度接近标准正态分布偏度为 0 的标准，因此该序列较接近正态分布，且呈现尖峰后尾的分布特征。

第二步：根据正态 Q-Q 图可以直观地判断序列的正态分布情况。序列的正态 Q-Q 图如图 5.26 所示。

由图 5.26 可看出，汇率序列基本符合正态分布。因为该汇率序列的分位数图像与图中直线差不多完全重合，基本符合标准正态分布的图像是一条直线的要求。虽然图像中有些部分稍有偏差，但与 $s<0$ 基本符合。因此，根据以上可知，汇率序列虽然不严格服从标准正态分布，但是服从尖峰后尾的正态分布，所以可以将它作为正态分布，使用在 VaR 模型的未来汇率的模拟过程中。

6. VaR 计算

此产品为一种期限为 90 天的汇率挂钩型结构性理财产品。虽然其期限为 90 天，但

① 资料来源：彭湘军．我国结构性理财产品的市场风险管理研究［D］．安徽大学，2012.

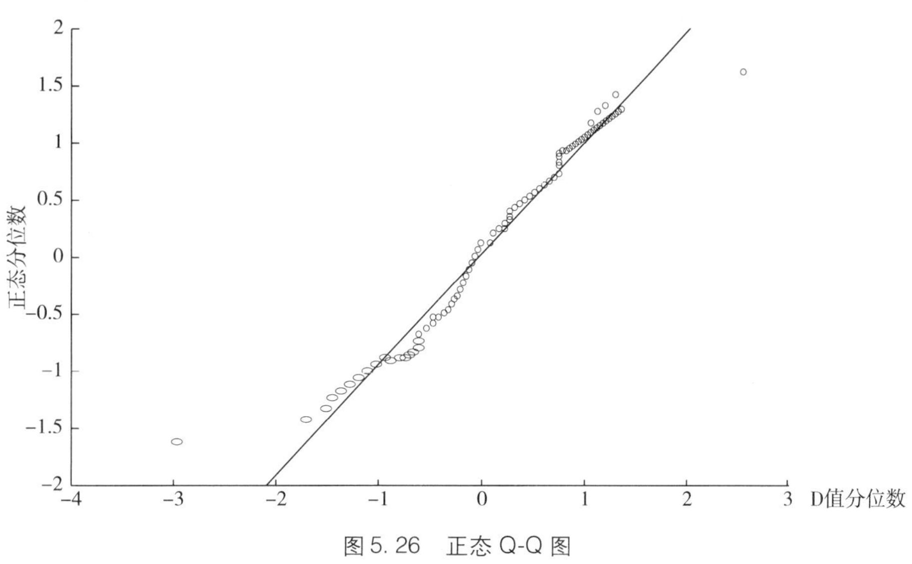

图 5.26　正态 Q-Q 图

该产品的到期收益率仅与观察期内的汇率情况有关，观察期为 2 个交易日，由前面的 Eviews 图像我们可以看出，该汇率序列平稳、随机、基本符合正态分布。我们可以用蒙特卡罗法对 2016 年 1 月 19 日 ~2016 年 4 月 15 日的 58 个交易日的汇率收益分布进行模拟。根据前面所求的序列的统计变量，均值为 -0.009917，方差为 0.579589，可得出模拟汇率的式子：

$$h = u \times 0.579589 - 0.009917$$

其中 u 为随机干扰项。分别对第 57 天与第 58 天进行 10 000 次蒙特卡罗模拟法来模拟汇率变动，通过特定均值和方差模拟出未来观察日的汇率分布，如表 5.29 和表 5.30 所示。

表 5.29　第 57 天汇率分布

121.03	114.64	121.96	115.42	126.83	119.48	121.24	115.32
120.59	118.23	126.90	124.79	116.84	114.50	119.90	117.98
132.54	116.42	117.84	117.09	122.78	124.03	124.26	115.18
122.03	119.88	123.67	130.00	123.88	122.33	112.19	123.03
123.67	122.65	115.70	124.01	129.81	118.48	118.27	115.68
113.01	116.59	127.27	120.68	118.79	118.79	125.03	125.28
118.51	117.92	124.78	124.71	124.35	121.67	116.89	119.00
121.00	123.22	115.47	114.10	125.11	120.02	119.98	111.68
…	…	…	…	…	…	…	…
127.55	117.61	130.74	117.72	114.78	118.93	117.52	112.29

表 5.30　第 58 天汇率分布

123.60	122.29	119.60	121.18	120.64	120.19	116.13	129.21
113.30	116.82	123.35	119.64	125.56	112.11	123.50	117.24
118.21	126.06	120.88	121.27	128.00	124.78	131.32	129.77
130.48	122.56	117.67	121.11	126.90	122.41	117.99	123.46
123.61	127.53	121.51	128.37	119.16	128.66	118.53	122.47
116.60	129.91	128.29	118.25	118.69	130.38	119.04	112.57
121.91	119.69	118.75	113.46	122.82	124.11	118.54	127.02
123.80	117.89	118.46	122.88	123.79	116.54	113.21	120.77
…	…	…	…	…	…	…	…
115.56	112.52	129.71	123.44	114.35	119.81	112.03	127.08

对两个交易日内 20 000 个数据样本进行统计，得到汇率分布如表 5.31 所示。

表 5.31　汇率分布及收益率

汇率	P≥113.8	87.8≤P<113.8
分布	90.8%	9.2%
收益率	4.5%	3.1%

由表 5.31 可得，期望收益率为：

$$90.8\% \times 4.5\% + 9.2\% \times 3.1\% = 4.3712\%$$

已知投资期限为 90 天，假定投资金额为最少投资金额 5 万元，则期望价值为：

$$E = 5 \times (1 + 4.3712\% \times 90/365) = 5.0539 \text{ 万元}$$

投资收获的最小收益为：

$$E_{min} = 5 \times (1 + 3.1\% \times 90/365) = 5.0382 \text{ 万元}$$

最大收益为：

$$E_{max} = 5 \times (1 + 4.5\% \times 90/365) = 5.0554 \text{ 元}$$

将本金的时间价值考虑在内，中国农业银行同期城乡居民及单位存款活期存款利率为 0.3%，5 万元在 2016 年 4 月 1 日的价值为：

$$5 \times (1 + 0.3\% \times 90/365) = 5.0037 \text{ 万元}$$

$$VaR\text{（零值）} = 5.0037 - 5.0382 = -0.0345 \text{ 万元}$$

$$VaR\text{（均值）} = 5.0539 - 5.0382 = 0.0157 \text{ 万元。}$$

（三）本章小结

对于“金钥匙如意”2016 年第 11 期看跌日元汇率人民币这款结构性理财产品来说，通过模拟发现，获得 4.5% 即最高收益率的可能性较大，最低不会低于 3.1%，因此，此款产品对于投资者来说风险较小，可以购买。VaR 零值是负的表明如果同期选择活期存款作为保值手段的话会相对有损失。如果同期投资和该理财产品的期望收益率相同的产品则会损失 157 元，对于投资本金 5 万元来说损失较小。因此，该理财产品适于较多的投资者。

三、结构性理财产品市场风险控制途径

我们可以通过多种方式对市场风险进行控制，有效地减少甚至规避结构性理财产品所面临的市场风险。

（一）通过使用 VaR 模型加强对市场风险控制

首先，银行通过使用 VaR 模型，可以对结构性理财产品市场风险控制提出相关建议。以 VaR 模型所度量出的数据作为参考，对银行的资金进行有效的管理以及提出投资决策。即对商业银行卖出理财产品所获得的资金进行整合，以银行行为进行市场投资，为银行获取收益。待理财时间结束后银行支付给投资者相应的资金，同时还能得到在资本市场投资所获得的一部分收益。因此，银行不仅需要衡量自己所设计、发行的结构性理财产品所面临的市场风险，同时还需要衡量使用资金池中的资金进行投资时所面临的风险，并将前后两种 VaR 值进行比对，看是否平衡。若前 VaR 值大于后 VaR 值，则可以接受银行自身的投资决策，但在之后的产品设计中要更注重从设计开发时就对市场风险进行一定的规避；若前 VaR 值小于后 VaR 值，则银行方面应选择其他的投资方式，否则容易陷入赔本的情况。

其次，银行应更新风险评定等级方法。一直以来，银行都采用比较模糊的风险评定等级来让消费者忽略产品可能存在的相关风险，以达到刺激销售的目的。有些银行甚至为了效益，将产品说明书中的风险刻意写低或者以模糊的方式涵盖，与真实的风险并不一致。然而，这种行为并不利于银行的长久经营。随着投资者对理财产品知识的了解，以及互联网发展迅速所带来的大众反馈渠道透明，这种现象会越来越被投资者所诟病。这会减低投资者对银行的信任度，影响银行的公信力，从而不利于银行长期的发展。而 VaR 这种可以全面度量产品市场风险模型的出现和应用，可以在对消费者进行理财产品讲解时，简单、清晰、直观地让投资者明了购买该产品自己可能会面临的风险状况，了解损失数额，从而判定自己是否能承受风险，决定是否购买。这样

从长远的角度来看，促进了银行与投资者之间的信息对称，普及了相关的理财产品知识，也让银行受到了投资者的信赖，从而促进其长远的经营与发展。

再次，银行将 VaR 技术普及给产品经理等相关工作人员，可提高我们销售人员的整体水平，同时也能改善投资者与银行间信息不对称的现象。

（二）通过改进产品设计与发行加强对市场风险控制

对于发行结构性理财产品的银行来说，也可以通过对产品设计与发行方面进行改进，从而加强对市场风险的控制。产品设计的核心问题是产品定价，定价的合理性会对投资者对产品的需求产生直接影响。

以保本浮动收益的利率挂钩产品为例，先计算其固定收益债券价值，取当年定期存款利率为无风险利率；再取样本运用蒙特卡洛模拟法模拟路径，算出概率，得到平均收益，用无风险利率对平均收益进行贴现，即可得到期权部分的价值。

产品总价值 = 固定收益债券价值 + 期权部分价值。当产品总价值 > 最低购买资金时，该产品溢价发行；当产品总价值 < 最低购买资金时，该产品折价发行。由此，发行银行通过在定价环节就能控制住风险。

另外，银行也要根据发行的产品的投资期限来合理规划销售期，防止错过市场机会，将发行期间的市场风险控制住。

四、研究结论及展望

（一）研究结论

结构性理财产品作为一种新型的金融理财产品，利用金融工程技术将固定收益产品与金融衍生品结合，同时也是目前受广大客户青睐的一种个人理财方式。在商业银行竞争日趋激烈的今天，个人理财产品的收益率及安全性成为能否吸纳客户资金的重要参考指标。而结构性理财产品则高举着“高收益”的旗帜，一跃成为商业银行个人理财产品中最炙手可热的一类。于是，如何对结构性理财产品的市场风险进行有效控制已成为目前亟须解决的一个重要现实问题。国内外学者不遗余力的研究虽然成果斐然，但各方见解并不一致，本文借鉴国内外已有研究成果，结合我国当前的制度背景，利用 2014—2016 年数据样本，从结构性理财产品市场风险度量角度进行研究，最终得出的主要研究结论如下所述。

第一，目前，我国结构性理财产品市场存在以下问题。产品类型同质化严重、漠视风险、管理松散。投资者风险意识欠缺，知识储备薄弱。银行方面市场风险计量工具、模型和技术落后，产品开发与设计能力不强，风险管理信息系统建设相对落后，风险管理组织结构不完善，市场风险管理人才基础薄弱。同时，监管部门信息透明度低、法律法规不健全。因此，我国结构性理财产品市场当前仍面临重重挑战。

第二，VaR 模型可以为结构性理财产品市场风险的控制提供有力帮助。银行在卖出理财产品后会将销售的资金进行汇总并进行投资，此时银行可以将 VaR 模型作为参考，判断理财产品的 VaR 值与银行投资的 VaR 值是否平衡，进而保证银行不会遭受损失。同时，银行也可使用 VaR 模型更新风险等级标准，以值的形式正确体现产品风险。

第三，对产品的设计开发与发行进行改进，可以从源头减少或规避市场风险以及损失。发行银行通过计算以及多方面的考虑，可以在定价环节控制住风险。同时，银行也要根据发行的产品的投资期限来合理地规划销售期，防止错过市场机会，将发行期间的市场风险控制住。

区块链技术在银行一体化测试平台中的应用研究

建信金融科技　孙金金

一、测试管理的难点、痛点问题

软件测试是在规定的条件下对程序进行操作，以发现程序错误，衡量软件质量，并对其是否能满足设计要求进行评估的过程。通过软件测试的过程得到测试结果报告，根据测试结果来判定软件的质量，但是如何保证测试报告自身的质量，对于测试管理者而言是一个至关重要的问题。

就目前的测试现状而言，无论对测试管理人员还是测试实施人员的管理都是相对松散、不够严格的。首先，对测试实施人员的测试过程的执行是否规范、测试结果报告的正确性是否有保障、因测试不充分而造成的生产事件责任是否能追溯到个人、对测试过程的记录是否安全可信赖等的考虑都是欠缺的。其次，测试案例、测试过程记录、测试结果等数据的存储是否安全可靠，测试相关数据是否保密，数据的完整性、可用性、可靠性是否有保障等，这些都是值得关注的问题。除此之外，还有测试过程中存在的权限管理问题，如测试相关数据的可见范围、测试人员对测试任务的可见范围、测试案例的规范性审核、测试记录的可靠性审核等。

以上所说的问题，是目前测试管理中的盲区，依靠现有的存储技术难以保证数据的安全性、可靠性；依靠现有的管理模式，难以保证测试过程的可信度，难以保证测试结果真实有效，进而也给系统的安全生产带来潜在隐患。

二、区块链技术的发展和优势

图 5.27 中展示了区块链技术发展中的历史性事件，自 2008 年《比特币：点对点的电子现金系统》中首次出现区块链的概念以来，区块链技术先后经过了多个历史性节点。目前业界把区块链技术的发展分为 3 个阶段：（1）区块链 1.0 时代是指区块链概念出现以及以比特币为代表的去中心化数字货币的涌现；（2）以太坊等技术的出现，把区块链带入了 2.0 时代，智能合约的出现为区块链在金融领域的应用提供了更肥沃

的土壤；（3）目前行业对区块链 3.0 的概念尚存争议，借鉴《区块链：新经济蓝图》一书的观点，区块链 3.0 代表的是解决了关键性技术难题的全领域生态级别的底层系统出现以及区块链技术应用到各个垂直行业中去的时代。目前整个行业处于 2.0 时代的迭代阶段，大部分底层协议项目还是在以太坊的基础上进行的，距离 3.0 时代的标准还有一段距离。

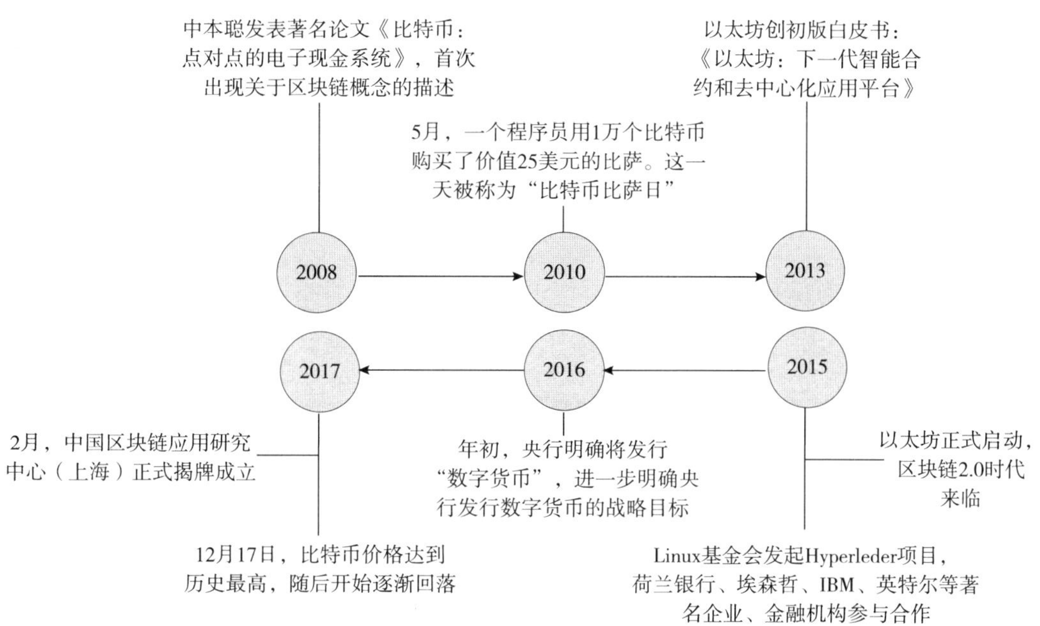

图 5.27　区块链发展的历史性事件

根据专家估计，随着底层协议的不断迭代更新，目前出现的项目 98% 以上将会随之淘汰。但即便如此，各行各业对区块链技术的追逐依然是保持着饱满的热情，根本原因在于区块链技术作为一种分布式存储技术，有传统存储技术不具备的特有优点。众所周知，数据的存储和管理，往往依赖于数据库的相关技术：包括关系型数据库［由埃德加·弗兰克·科德（E. F. Godd）博士提出］和 NoSQL 非关系型的数据库（解决大规模数据集合多重数据种类带来的挑战），但这两种传统的数据库都不能解决互联网中的信任问题。而区块链技术的去中心化、防篡改、可追溯等特点，恰恰能够解决在互联网背景下陌生人之间的信任问题，这又是互联网发展到今天所亟须解决的关键问题。

另外，根据区块链技术的核心——共识算法、密码学算法、分布式策略算法，能够保证所有记录在链数据的安全可靠性，这恰恰能够解决上述所说的测试管理中的痛点问题：通过把测试过程数据全部记录在链，从而保证测试流程中所有环节的真实性，进而保证测试结果的可靠性。接下来，我们将给出具体事例，详细阐述区块链技术如何解决测试痛点问题。

三、区块链技术解决测试管理问题的思路

作为全行的功能测试部门，我们站在了企业级的视角来管理全行的功能测试工作；未来，随着一体化测试平台的建设和推广，大量的测试执行过程中的数据将会沉淀下来，包括前面所说的测试人员信息、测试案例、测试脚本、测试报告等。用区块链技术来管理一体化测试平台的测试相关数据，能够对测试过程进行全流程、全生命周期的管理，进一步打造测试生态圈，保证测试的高质量，进而为全行系统的安全稳定运行保驾护航。

下面，我们来看看区块链技术在一体化测试平台中的应用实例。为了方便描述，我们以一个项目为背景：北京事业群某开发处室对系统代号为 A0781 的项目进行 4.0 版本更新，本次项目的项目经理是王一，测试经理是张一，李一是一名来自安阳分行的业务人员。周三的上午李一登录测试平台，发现该项目急缺多名有 A0781 系统测试经验的功能测试人员，李一考虑到自己 3 个月前参与过该项目的测试，故而申请报名参加，接下来我们将开启一波区块链之旅。

第一，依托区块链技术可追溯的特点，一体化测试平台中的所有数据都是有据可循且安全可靠的，据此可以展开对人员资质信息的审核。张一看到李一的信息后，对李一的历史测试记录进行查看，确认其是否确有 A0781 系统的测试经验。由于所有的测试过程数据都是记录在链的，张一在调取了李一的相关测试记录后发现，李一确实在 3 个月前参与了 A0781 测试，并且当时的测试经理对李一的打分为 90 分（由于链上的数据都是安全的，且不可修改，因此张一看到的信息均是真实存在、未经篡改的），确认了李一有能力胜任该项目。但由于测试任务紧张，张一并不确定李一是否有充足的时间参与任务，因此并未立即准许李一的加入，而是通知了李一的管理者李二，由李二确认李一是否符合条件（行内鼓励大家多多参与此种任务）。李二对李一的情况了解之后，同意李一参与该测试任务（多人管理模式下，保证任务的顺利开展）。然后，张一允许李一进入测试资源池，并为其分配测试任务。

第二，区块链技术的去中心化特点，保证了平台数据的完整性，该一体化测试平台保存了完整的、全量的全行测试案例资产（测试案例的编写、审核和验证等都是比较消耗人力成本的工作，案例资产的安全保存对测试任务而言是非常重要的）。李一根据任务情况，先从平台里搜索到了可以执行的测试案例 20 条（平台保存了全量的测试案例），在已有案例未充分覆盖业务需求的情况下，李一创建了一条新的测试案例，提交给张一审核。平台根据全量的案例库对李一创建的案例进行比对，确认其确实是一条新增案例，而非从已有案例库中复制而来，然后把案例推送给张一审核。张一对案

例进行阅读后，确认该案例为有效案例，准许案例进入测试案例库。

第三，区块链技术的多密钥管理机制，可以保证重要数据的私密性。对于一体化测试平台而言，全量的测试案例是一项重要的测试资产，考虑到后期测试平台和技术的行外推广，测试案例具有其自身的经济价值，并不是可以任意使用的。所以李一在准备执行从平台中搜索的 20 条案例时，需要申请这些案例的使用权限。申请提交后，由张一、张一的管理者王一、王一的管理者及其他相关领导中的 8 人，共 12 人中的 5 人同时确认后，李一才能读取到此 20 条案例。测试资产的多密钥管理，可以防止资产价值的损耗和流失。

第四，区块链技术的防篡改性，可以保证所有记录在链数据的真实性，防止任何人对数据进行作弊的行为。李一在准备好所有案例后，开始执行案例（该过程包括登录 A0781 系统，操作系统页面，输入必要信息，形成测试结果等），并形成最终的测试报告。执行完成后，由测试经理张一和项目经理王一对测试结果进行审核和评估，最后对李一的此次任务完成情况进行评分。区块链技术的防篡改性，可防止任何人对数据进行恶意修改。因此，对李一的评分一经做出，再也无法修改，防止了肆意修改评分的作弊行为。除了手动执行测试的情形外，防篡改的特性也保证了自动化测试的质量。假设上述过程后，李一还参与了对重要未变动的功能进行回归性测试，需要使用自动化测试工具。李一通过平台找到过去的测试脚本，在获取到脚本的读取权限后，开始运行脚本，形成测试报告。得到测试报告后，李一发现脚本的测试范围不全面，但由于其个人原因没时间修正脚本重新测试，因此他偷偷更改了测试报告，然后提交给张一。张一拿到测试报告后，立刻就看到了李一改动报告的痕迹，然后张一把任务进行了重新分配，进行再次验证，进而确保了测试的充分性。

以上，我们通过一个简单的例子描述了如何利用区块链技术保障测试流程的全生命周期安全可靠，包括如何挑选优秀的测试人员、怎样甄选出高质量的案例、如何保证测试案例的资产价值，还有最后测试结果的真实性认定。传统的依靠人和制度来管理测试人员、测试流程的模式是无法杜绝作弊、无法保证测试质量的，我们需要通过技术手段，用人为不可干预的方法来解决这一问题。

四、总结

根据行业评估，随着区块链底层技术的不断革新，约 98% 的项目将会被淘汰。即便如此，各行各业对区块链技术仍然趋之若鹜，原因在于，当前区块链技术及行业应用尚未成熟，这是它们在这个互联网时代发展的拐点处实现弯道超车的绝佳时机。图 5. 28 给出了当前区块链领域行业发展的三层产业：第一层是底层技术及基础设施层，主要是关注区块链的基础协议和相关硬件技术，目前基础协议的研究和突破关乎着区块链的发展前景；第二层是通用应用技术扩展层，主要是为第三层的行业垂直应用提供服务和接口的技术相关服务，是在第一层的基础协议的技术封装，比如类似智能合约的编码，为医疗行业或者金融行业等提供整套的解决方案等；第三层是垂直行业应用层，主要是各行业根据区块链技术的特点，对行业内的业务进行革新、探索业务新的发展模式。

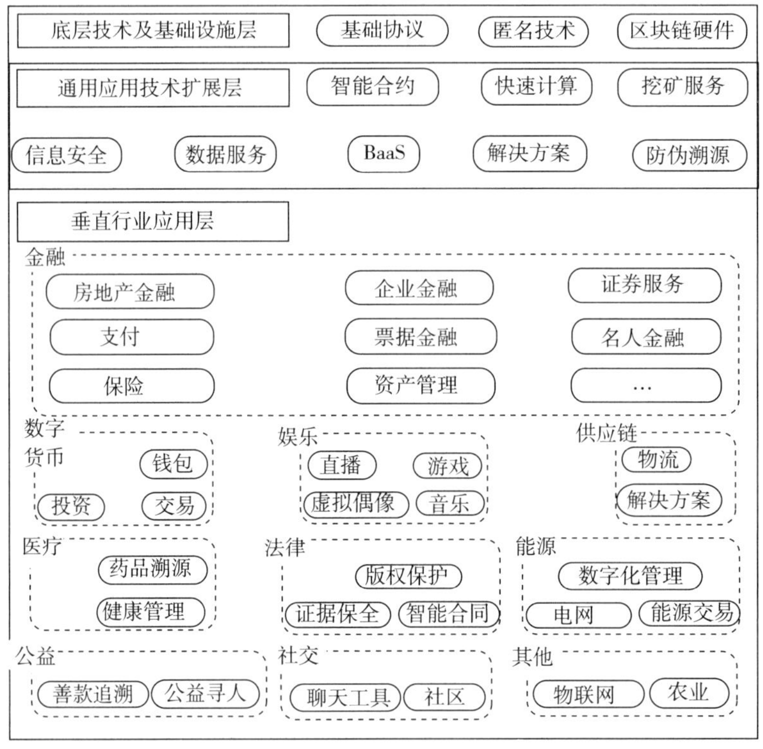

图 5.28　区块链技术的三层产业和垂直行业应用

对于企业而言，在区块链技术炙手可热的当下，可以结合自身优势，通过以下 3 种方式，在新技术背景下形成自己的核心竞争力：（1）解决区块链技术当前的难点（目前区块链底层协议尚未解决商业级别的高性能问题），形成新的核心竞争力，进而成为新兴行业的技术巨头；（2）形成专业技术输出团队，为业务领域提供技术服务；（3）打破传统业务场景，抢占市场，形成先发优势，进而成为行业领军者。而作为测试部门，我们是保证系统质量的关键一环，如何解决测试管理中存在的痛点、难点问题是我们的职责所在。我们通过对新技术的探索和应用创新，尝试打破传统的测试管理模式，结合区块链技术解决测试流程中的信任问题，进而形成专业的、先进的、成熟的测试管理技术和方案，打造新技术背景下的测试核心竞争力，进一步为建行的三大战略提供切实可行的落地方案。

我们可以看到，区块链技术不仅仅可以用在比较热门的领域，如保险、证券、医疗、物流等，在测试领域也有用武之地。随着全行测试系统和平台的不断推广，测试人员的庞杂和测试数据海量增长，给管理人员带来的挑战也越来越大，未来区块链技术在我们测试平台上的应用场景将会更加丰富。本篇文章只是给出了一个简单的场景描述，在未来我们还会给出详细的技术架构和落地方案。

基于 SEM 的信用卡客户中收影响因素分析研究

北京市分行　武　岩

一、引言

当前，我国经济发展正处于重要的战略机遇期，从以往的高速增长模式逐渐转为追求质量优化、结构优化的中高速增长新常态。在中美贸易摩擦的宏观经济形势下，拉动经济发展的“三驾马车”正逐步由新的经济增长要素替代，其中扩内需、促消费对经济增长的驱动力不容忽视。在此背景下，建行提出“三大战略”和“零售优先发展战略”，服务民生，拓展银行业务新的“蓝海”，而以打造客户家庭消费“第一钱包”为目标的信用卡业务就是其中重要一环。

作为商业银行，在践行大行责任、履行大行义务的同时，追求利润增长、回报股东权益也是建行重要的经营方向。无论国内外，信用卡业务都是商业银行实现中收的重要组件。影响信用卡业务中收的因素有很多，宏观经济发展、地区产业构成、人口特征分布、银行经营政策等都会对其造成影响。其中，客户的人口特征和资产水平是信用卡中收最直观的影响因子。本文以北京地区建行信用卡客户为主体，结合实际业务数据，利用 SEM 模型进行实证分析，为打造“1 个体系”“2 个引擎”，及全面提升客户服务质效提供新的发展思路。

二、SEM 的构建

（一）模型介绍

结构方程模型（Structural Equation Model，简写为 SEM）诞生于 20 世纪末，弥补了传统统计方法的不足，能够分析验证不可直接观测变量和目标之间的关系。它引入了“潜变量”技术作为不可观测变量的分析依据，能够通过对可观测变量的测度，结合研究者设计的路径图，将研究者想要研究的潜变量和目标变量的关系进行量化分析，揭示内生变量、潜变量与外生变量之间的关系。也正因此特性，SEM 被广泛应用于社会经济类学科的统计分析当中。

在 SEM 的构建里，较为常用的是由学者本特勒和威克斯（Bentler and Weeks）于 1980 年提出的线性结构形式（linear equations），此形式可进一步延伸为 Keesling-Wiley-Joreskog 结构关系模型，用来研究探讨结构方程之间的线性关系。模型可拆分成两部分，即结构模型（structural model）和测量模型（measurement model）。

结构模型为：

$$\eta = B\eta + \Gamma\xi + \zeta$$

测量模型为：

$$Y = \Lambda_y \eta + \varepsilon$$

$$X = \Lambda_x \xi + \delta$$

其中，η 为内生变量潜变量向量，ξ 为外生潜变量向量；X 和 Y 为观测变量组成的向量；ε 是对应 Y 的测量误差向量，δ 同理；Λ_y 是 Y 对 η 的因子载荷矩阵，Λ_x 同理。在结构模型中，B 为 η 对 η 的结构系数矩阵，用来说明内生潜变量之间的关系；而 Γ 为 ξ 对 η 的结构系数矩阵，体现外生潜变量对内生潜变量的影响；ζ 为结构方程残差向量。

本文的议题中，影响建行信用卡业务收入的因素主要由客户的资质水平和其资产状况来衡量，但这两个概念较为模糊、笼统，不能通过直接观测的方式进行量化分析，因此可以运用 SEM 技术，将它们视作模型中的潜变量进行推测。

（二）变量设计

如上述分析和建模要求，结合具体的数据要求，我们将需要分析研究的变量划为 3 个大类，即建行北京分行的信用卡业务收入、客户资质特征、客户资产水平，对应的潜变量设置为 $F3$、$F1$、$F2$。

在客户特征方面，选取可以观测的客户年龄、性别、婚姻状况、学历情况、年收入等观测变量作为对潜变量客户资质的具体测度，这些具有人口统计特征的因素都是对客户资质水平最常见的描述，具有较强的解释能力。

在资产水平方面，客户在建行的 AUM 值、信用卡额度、信用卡贷款余额、消费笔数、消费金额、专项分期金额等对客户资产的描述更为直观有效，可作为对潜变量客户信用卡资产的观测变量，构建与潜变量的关系。

建行信用卡收入潜变量对应建行信用卡收入这一指标。详细的变量设计及其具体的取值与解释见表 5. 32。

表 5.32　北京分行信用卡客户与信用卡收入的变量设计及解释

潜变量代码	潜变量含义	变量代码	变量含义	数据取值与解释
F1	客户资质水平	X1	年龄	客户实际年龄
		X2	性别	对指标进行赋值处理，男性为 1，女性为 2
		X3	婚姻状况	对指标进行赋值处理，未婚为 1，已婚为 2
		X4	学历情况	对指标进行赋值处理，从文盲到博士从 10 到 1 进行赋值
		X5	年收入	系统录入的客户年收入情况
F2	建行信用卡资产水平	X6	AUM 值	近 6 个月的客户月平均 AUM 值
		X7	信用卡额度	客户信用卡额度
		X8	现有信用卡贷款余额	客户信用卡贷款的时点余额
		X9	信用卡累计交易笔数	2018 年 1 月 1 日 ~8 月 31 日的累计交易笔数
		X10	信用卡累计交易金额	2018 年 1 月 1 日 ~8 月 31 日的累计交易总金额
		X11	信用卡专项分期额度	客户信用卡专项分期额度
F3	建行信用卡中收	Y1	信用卡业务收入金额	建行在 2018 年 1 月 1 日 ~8 月 31 日累计实现的信用卡业务收入金额

（三）模型构建及样本选取

如变量设计中陈述，客户的资质水平和资产水平能够通过年龄、性别、信用卡额度等反映出来，而客户的资质又能在一定程度上影响其在建行的资产情况，两类因素同时对建行的信用卡收入产生影响。这一逻辑关系可概括为图 5.29。

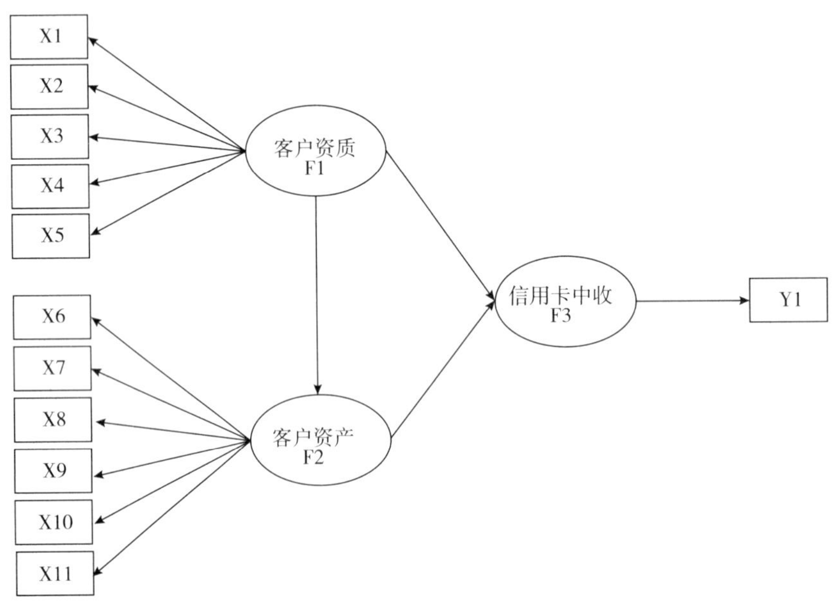

图 5.29　北京分行信用卡客户与信用卡收入的 SEM 路径

本文利用建设银行信用卡条线的实际录入数据，以北京地区建行客户 2018 年 1 月 1 日 ~2018 年 8 月 31 日的信用卡交易情况为研究基准，选取公共访问区《进件申请人信息》(T209_YS_APL_APLY_PSN_INF_H)、《信用卡客户统计事实》(T209_XXY_CCRDCST_STAT)、《信用卡账户收入成本统计事实》(T209_XXY_CRCRDACCIMCOST_STAT)、《信用卡交易统计事实》(T209_XXY_CRCRDTXN_STAT) 等数据集合中相关变量对应的数据信息。在所选数据中，删除该时间区间内没有交易记录、婚姻状况、学历记录、性别记录、年龄信息、年收入信息的客户资料，并在筛选后的数据中随机抽取 10 万条信用卡客户资料信息进行建模分析。

三、实证分析结果

（一）提出假设

结合信用卡业务实际情况，在客户资质上，一般而言，我们认为年龄较高的客户消费需求较高，所以使用信用卡的情况会很多，相应带来的信用卡收入也偏高；在消费的次数上，女性客户一般会比男性客户的消费频率高，进而影响信用卡收入；同理，已婚客户消费需求多，也会正向影响信用卡中收情况；而较高学历的客群可能存在更理性的消费规划，导致消费和信贷的情况不如较低学历客户，从而为建行产生较少的信用卡收入；另外，年收入较高的客户会产生更强的消费和信贷欲望，为建行带来更多信用卡收入。

因此提出如下假设以进行模型验证：

H1——客户年龄能够影响建行信用卡的收入。

H2——女性客户相比男性客户所产生的信用卡收入更高。

H3——已婚客户相比未婚客户所产生的信用卡收入更高。

H4——客户学历情况对建行的信用卡收入产生贡献。

H5——年收入越高的客户会带来更高的信用卡收入。

此外，在客户建行资产水平上，包括 AUM 值、信用卡额度、消费次数等指标，一般来讲都能够对建行信用卡收入和中收性产生正向的影响，即呈现正相关关系。

因此提出如下假设：

H6——客户 AUM 值越高产生的信用卡收入越高。

H7——信用卡额度对信用卡的收入有显著影响。

H8——已有信用卡贷款余额的客户产生的信用卡收入较高。

H9——使用信用卡消费笔数更频繁的客户产生的信用卡收入较高。

H10——使用信用卡消费总金额较高的客户产生的信用卡收入较高。

H11——拥有更高信用卡专项分期额度的客户能产生更多信用卡收入。

（二）结果分析

1. 假设验证

通过 SEM 建模分析，对上述假设进行了检验，结果如表 5.33 所示。

表 5.33 北京分行信用卡客户与信用卡收入的 SEM 假设检验结果

客户资质水平			客户资产情况		
原假设序号	检验结果	标准化参数	原假设序号	检验结果	标准化参数
H1	通过	0.00249	H6	通过	0.70710
H2	通过	0.00004	H7	通过	0.06400
H3	通过	0.00005	H8	通过	0.01280
H4	不通过	-0.00063	H9	不通过	0.00998
H5	通过	0.00984	H10	通过	0.07810
			H11	通过	0.01150

由表 5.33 可知，原假设 H4、H9 没有通过检验，其余均得到正确验证。在客户资质水平方面，年龄、年收入较高的客户能够为建行产生较高的信用卡收入，已婚和女性客户能够为建行带来更多信用卡收入，而学历的高低在建行信用卡收入方面并无明显差别。在客户资产情况上，客户的 AUM 值、信用卡额度、信用卡贷款额度、已使用信用卡的消费总金额、专项分期额度等都对信用卡收入造成正向影响，而已使用信用卡消费的次数并不能对收入造成明显影响。

此外，标准化参数显示出各假设中自变量对因变量信用卡收入的影响程度。其中 H6 参数数值最高，说明这一原因是影响建行信用卡收入的各个变量中最为关键的。诸如性别和婚姻等情况对信用卡收入影响的程度较轻。

2. 结构模型构建情况

根据 3 个潜变量的关系，通过模型的搭建，得到结构方程如下：

$$F3 = 0.01000 \times F2 + 0.00005 \times F1 + d$$

其中标准化参数均通过检验，参数数值较低，说明影响建行北京分行信用卡收入的因素还存在其他的原因，例如风险防范、宏观经济因素等。但本文旨在分析客户与信用卡收入之间的关系，因此通过结构方程也能反映出一些信息。在方程中，明显可以看出 F2，即客户资产情况要远远高于 F1（客户资质水平）对信用卡整体收入的影响。

四、展望

（一）重视客群特点，细分客户市场

在模型检验中，客户资质水平对信用卡中收具有一定的指导意义。首先，学历情况不能显著影响客户对建行的信用卡收入。从中收的角度讲，我们在发展信用卡业务时不应过分看重客户的学历水平，更应该关注客户自身的年收入情况、婚姻状况等。其次，正如模型检验结果所示，符合已婚、女性等特征的客户往往能够带来较高的信用卡收入。通常情况下，已婚客户因为家庭生活开支增加和子女的教育投入增多会提高自身的信用卡消费水平，进而增加信用卡收入；女性客群的消费频次和金额往往高于男性，从而影响建行信用卡收入。这些特点与模型检验结果相符。

（二）立足客户资产，丰富产品结构

通过数据分析，客户的资产情况相比客户本身资质来说对信用卡收入的影响更重要。最为重要的因素为客户的 AUM 值，这一资产衡量指标的变化能够对客户信用卡中收产生非常大的影响，因此在推广信用卡业务时，如果对客户资产情况有充分的理解，因人而异地进行产品个性化营销会产生不错的效果。此外，刺激信用卡大额消费和专项分期规模都是提升信用卡中收的行之有效的方法。近年来，北京分行不断践行“龙卡星期六”“玩转世界”境内外信用卡主题促销活动以及“分期有礼”等专项分期活动，以提升产品丰富程度，为信用卡业务“1 个体系”“2 个引擎”发展策略的落实贡献力量。

基层网点视角下银行网点对公业务发展问题分析与转型应对研究

——以昆明市分行下辖网点为例

云南省分行　曹　磊

随着中国经济的发展，金融科技应用渐广，加之外资银行逐步进入，使得我国商业银行的竞争日益激烈。基层网点作为商业银行的终端营销服务平台，是各项业务发展的重要依托。前期的零售网点转型，为银行个人业务的产品销售和服务提升打下了坚实的基础，提高了网点服务个人客户的能力。我作为基层网点负责人，深感近年来，在零售业务转型和零售优先战略下，昆明分行基层网点得到了跨越式的发展，同时个人业务保持了较高速度和质量的发展优势。

与此同时，基层网点如何继续保持高速度、高质量的发展势头，是一个值得令人深思的问题。对公条线和对私条线虽然服务于不同的客户群体，但其资源是可以相互利用、相互促进的。上级行已意识到网点发展对公业务的重要性，网点对公业务的转型也正在进行。然而公私业务的联动既是网点联动营销的重点，也是难点。[①] 如何破解该难点，已成为当下各家银行积极探索的重要工作之一。

本文在总行金融科技、普惠金融和住房租赁的战略下，从基层网点负责人的视角，以银行网点对公业务转型为背景，运用数据统计、资料分析等方法，结合我个人的工作实践，以某省分行省会城市下辖98个网点[②]、近3年对公主营指标为样本，拟对网点对公业务经营情况进行研究，分析其存在的问题及原因。试图探寻在银行网点转型过程和智慧银行逐步普及的背景趋势下，银行基层网点发展对公业务的重要性和提升网点价值创造水平的必要性，对完善网点对公职能、提升对公业务承载能力和价值创造能力提出一些粗浅的建议。

---

① 资料来源：陈中新．商业银行联动营销机制路径探析［J］．北京工商大学学报（社科版），2011（1）．

② 昆明分行下辖的114个网点，剔除单点行、县支行、营业部营业室、二级行营业室和轻型网点后为98个，但3年中由于有网点撤并情况，最终3年对比数据为97个网点。

从同业、系统内情况看，不少银行及相关研究人员已意识到网点对公业务发展对综合化经营的重要性。下文将先就银行网点对公业务发展现状和问题进行分析和梳理。

一、基层网点的业务发展现状

（一）昆明分行所辖基层网点发展简况

截至2018年6月，昆明分行下辖9个二级支行、119个营业网点。其中旗舰网点21家，综合网点84家，轻型网点14家。通过前期的零售网点转型及零售优先战略，提升了网点服务效能，促进了业务发展和产品销售，获得了更多客户认同，取得了较好的业绩及社会效益。并在金融科技的支撑下，加大渠道建设力度，如535台智慧柜员机遍布全市，业务办理速度较传统柜面业务平均提速5.48倍，切实提升了客户的满意度。

2015年~2018年6月，昆明分行个人日均存款实现稳步攀升。个人日均存款从2015年的419.82亿元，提升至2018年6月的513.95亿元（见图5.30）。

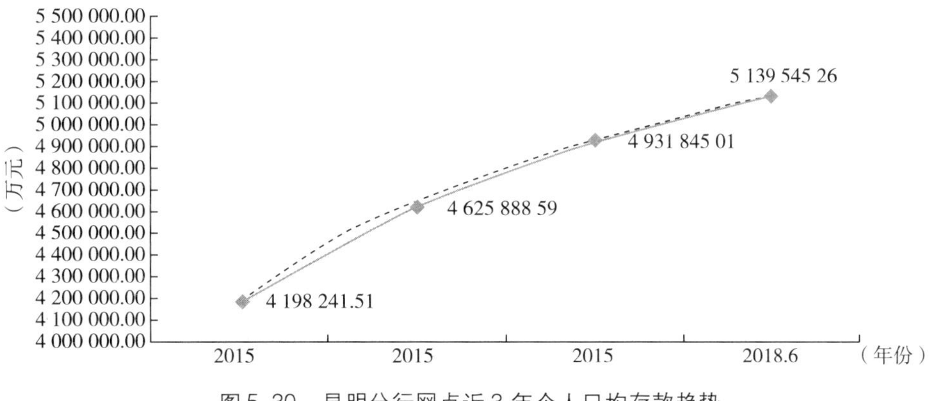

图5.30　昆明分行网点近3年个人日均存款趋势

（二）网点对公业务发展现状及问题

衡量网点对公业务发展的指标主要有：对公存贷业务、客户账户增量、中间业务收入等。故下文将对上述指标进行分析比对。

首先，2015年年末，昆明分行下辖114个网点支行的一般性日均存款为1 220.65亿元（不含房金业务）；其中，对公日均存款为701.11亿元，占比57.44%。截至2018年6月，一般性日均存款为1 725.98亿元；其中，对公日均存款为1 097.71亿元，占比63.59%。

由此可见，昆明分行日均存款中，以对公存款为主且近年来占比不断攀升。2015年对公日均存款占比57.44%，2016年占比58.09%，2017年占比63.87%，2018年6月占比63.59%。由于昆明分行对公日均存款余额占比较大，因此发展好对公业务对全行提升综合竞争力具有较为重要的意义。

其次，剔除主力网点后，以97家网点为样本进行分析。2015年年末，一般性日均存款为574.01亿元。其中对公日均存款为154.19亿元，占比26.86%。截至2018年6月，一般性日均存款为807.86亿元。其中，对公日均存款为293.91亿元，占比36.38%。

对比上述数据，剔除主力网点后，其余网点的对公占比较低，但占比却逐年提升。2015年对公日均存款占比26.86%，2016年占比30.66%，2017年占比35.85%，2018年6月占比36.38%。因此网点发展对公业务补齐短板，是网点综合发展的重要补充和助推器。

下文通过对昆明分行下辖97个网点、2015年1月至2018年6月主营业务指标的分析，发现其对公业务发展存在以下问题。

1. 网点对公存款规模占比较小、增长率下滑

（1）存款规模小，占比小。昆明分行下辖网点的对公日均存款规模中，10亿~50亿元规模的网点仅4个，占比4.08%；5亿~10亿元的网点13个，占比13.72%；1亿元以下网点44个，占比44.90%。可见近45%的样本网点对公存款规模较小，且2亿元以下规模的网点为70个，占比高达71%。二级行营业室下辖网点仅7个，对公日均存款规模50亿元以上的网点数就有4个，10亿~50亿元规模的网点有2个，5亿~10亿元规模的网点有1个。由此可见，样本网点的对公日均存款规模普遍远低于二级行营业室，且规模普遍偏小，详见表5.34。

表5.34 2017年样本网点对公日均存款规模占比情况

存款规模 / 网点	对公存款规模（亿元）	≥50	10~50	5~10	1~5	0.5~1	0.1~0.5	≤0.1
昆明分行网点	网点个数	0	4	13	37	15	23	6
	网点占比（%）	0	4.08	13.27	37.76	15.31	23.47	6.12
二级行营业室	网点个数	4	2	1	0	0	0	0
	网点占比（%）	57.14	28.57	14.3	0	0	0	0

从存款结构上看，2017年样本网点对公存款占比情况为：97个网点中69个网点的对公存款占比低于40%，占网点总数的70.40%；且对公存款占比低于20%的网点高达51个，占网点总数的52%（见表5.35）。可见，网点对公业务发展失衡，大部分网点仅用个人业务“一条腿”走路，综合发展能力不足。

表 5. 35　2017 年样本网点对公存款占比情况

占比 网点	项目	对公存款占比 40%以上	对公存款占比 40% ~20%	对公存款占 比 20%以下
昆明分行网点	网点个数	29	18	51
	网点占比（%）	29. 59	18. 37	52

（2）网点对公存款增长率下滑。对 2015 年 ~2018 年 6 月 97 家网点对公日均存款数据进行增长率分析，详见图 5. 31。

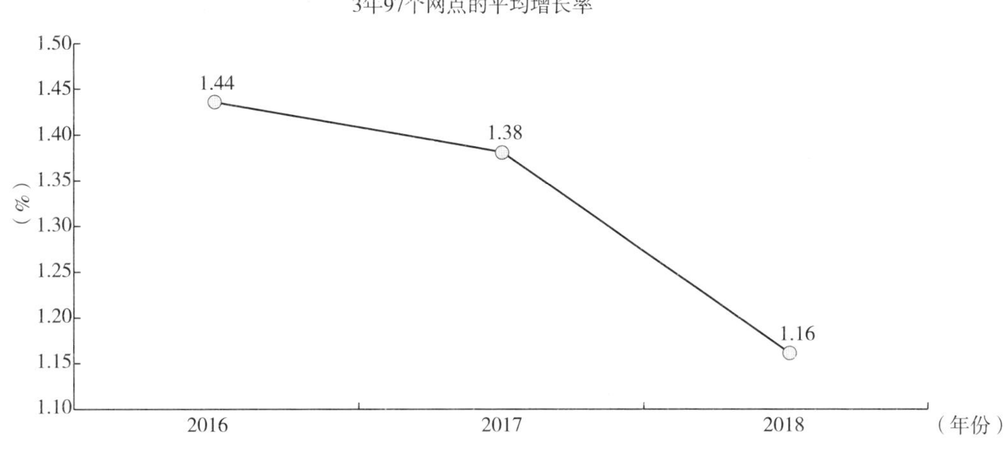

图 5. 31　2015 年 ~2018 年 6 月网点对公日均存款增长率分析

注：增长率 = 后一年度对公日均存款数/前一年度对公日均存款数。

由图 5. 31 可见，样本网点对公日均存款的增长率呈逐年下降趋势。2016 年较 2015 年，样本网点对公日均存款增长率为 1. 44；2017 较 2016 年，增长率下降至 1. 38；2018 年 1 至 6 月较 2017 年，增长率下降至 1. 16。

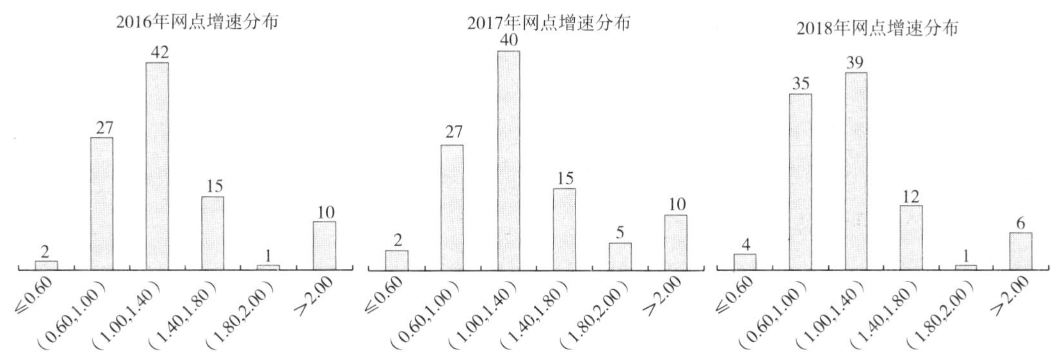

图 5. 32　2015 年至 2018 年 6 月样本网点对公日均存款增速分布

图 5. 32 展示了近 3 年样本网点对公日均存款的分布变化。根据数据分析，将网点

对公存款增长率分为6个等级。由图5.32所示趋势可见，近3年增速在1以下的负增速网点数量上升，增速在1.4以上的高增速网点数量减少。

2. 客户账户发展不理想且增速不足

从对公账户开立情况来看，近3年来除2017年各网点按照统一部署，开展账户专项活动后账户数量有所提升外，其余2年均为较低增长，全年网均账户增长40余户，平均6个工作日增长1户，如表5.36所示。

表5.36　2015—2017年网点对公账户增长情况

年份	新增有效账户	账户网均新增
2015	4 208	43
2016	4 011	40
2017	5 422	54

而从有效客户维度分析，如表5.37所示，网均有效客户在2015—2016年增长仅为个位数，全量客户增长也大幅小于账户增长。有效对公客户增长乏力。

表5.37　2015—2017年网点对公客户（有效户）增长情况

年份	新增有效客户	有效户网均新增	新增全量客户	客户网均新增
2015	676	7	2 726	28
2016	735	8	1 533	16
2017	1 304	14	2 846	30

3. 网点对公资产业务发展不足且业务单一

2015—2017年，半数网点对公贷款业务为空白。截至2017年5月末，在小微快贷上线前，昆明分行网点对公贷款日均451亿元。① 其中353亿元集中在7家二级支行营业室，占比78.27%；而有56个网点的对公信贷业务处于空白，占比超过57.77%。由此可见，对公业务的拓展基本依赖二级支行对公部门，网点作为银行对公业务前沿阵地的作用未能充分发挥。86.72%的网点开办业务为简单的低风险保证类业务及小微快贷，对公资产业务余额低于500万元的行多达73家，业务发展不足且品种单一。

4. 网点对公中间业务收入来源单一

一是中间业务收入集中在支行营业室。2017年年末，昆明分行中间业务收入87%集中在二级支行营业室，其余98个网点仅占13%，分布极度不均。二是产品局限于传统的结算、电子银行业务，除支行营业室外，其他网点在对公国际结算、财务顾问、

① 不含单点行、县支行、营业部营业室。

托管业务、国内贸易融资、国内保证及承诺业务等方面几乎为空白，开办的业务品种单一，对公中间业务收入渠道受限。

5. 网点对公业务同质化严重，具有较强的可替代性，客户黏性低

从目前网点的对公业务开办情况来看，主要集中在交易核算类业务、存款产品业务及部分标准化小微信贷业务。该类业务同业易模仿，相似程度高，客户随时可以在不同银行间轻易切换，替代成本低，网点与客户黏性较弱。

6. 网点对公资产业务人员配套不足

多数网点缺乏对公综合业务服务人员。在网点转型过程中，网点的“八岗位、一角色”里，没有设置对公客户经理和对公柜员岗位，甚至在系统设置中，存在对公客户经理岗位与网点其他岗位角色互斥的情况。不少网点已经习惯了以个人业务为主的经营模式，长期疏于对公业务综合经营的发展，从而导致客户对综合金融服务方面的满意度逐年下降。

二、网点对公业务存在问题的原因分析

结合我个人的工作实践及多网点调研情况，分析认为导致网点对公业务存在问题的主要原因如下所述。

（一）网点对公业务定位不清

网点对公业务发展定位是战略层面的指导，具有纲领性指导全局的作用。昆明分行对网点对公发展的定位需进一步细化。目前网点分类主要根据规模和发展前景对网点进行“三类五级”划分，即旗舰网点、综合网点和轻型网点。但由于网点目前还是以零售业务为主，故该标准主要是以个人存款和个贷规模为主要依据进行划分的，未来可加强针对对公业务发展的统筹考虑。如哪些网点适合主要发展对公业务、哪些网点适合主要发展综合业务、哪些网点适合主要发展零售业务等。又如从社区网点与商业网点、综合网点与专业市场网点的定位，考虑其对公业务的发展布局等。

从每年的任务指标分配上来看，由于定位不清，致使任务下达和考核针对性不足。目前的任务下达机制，主要是根据对公存款规模和基础账户数量，配以一定的增速比例进行下达，未充分考虑网点的定位、发展及实际经营情况。出现了一些老社区网点由于历史存量较大，承担了较重的任务指标；而一些新成立的网点，未充分挖掘其发展潜力，未起到新成立网点高速发展的引领作用。该类指标通过昆明分行的KPI排名、网点竞争力和片区发展情况排名、业务产品签约后进网点情况等指标就可以清晰地看出，老旧网点大多排名靠后。

（二）网点的综合化和特色化发展意识不足

网点对公业务转型是对网点经营提升的重要补充，但目前网点在业务发展中，多存在单一依靠个金业务发展“一条腿”走路的情况，缺少有效结合网点资源禀赋的统筹思考。第一，网点较少结合客群结构、周边业态情况开展特色化经营及综合化经营的发展意识；疲于应对业绩指标的完成，倾向于将精力投入见效快的项目中，缺少整体发展和长期发展的统筹考虑。第二，在转型实践中，一线员工还停留在网点对公业务的营销主要依靠网点负责人和客户经理，自己只要将柜台业务做好就行的思想认识上，在对公业务发展方面存在主动出击的营销意识、服务意识不足的情况，故而难以贴近市场、贴近客户。第三，对公、对私业务营销联动性不强。在公私联动、综合化经营方面还不够深入、高效，这会给客户带来不够专业的感受，影响客户对银行的总体评价。

（三）网点内部规划建设的科学性不够

网点转型后，网点高低柜做了一定程度的物理分割，但未充分考虑对公客户综合金融服务的需求，对公客户体验较差，网点对公业务和对公客户被“边缘化”。

1. 对公柜台设置不足

由于数据有限，无法全面统计样本网点共设置了多少封闭式和开方式柜台；所有柜台中，更难以统计有多少柜台是专职对公柜台或者优先对公柜台、多少是兼办对公与储蓄的柜台。但就我走访的样本网点来看，除各支行营业室外，其余网点很难单设对公业务柜台。

2. 对公客户服务提升不足

首先，银行网点转型后，个人优质客户服务质量提高明显，然而对公优质客户服务提升不足。零售转型后，对于高端个人客户，通过发放不同层级的 VIP（贵宾）卡等方式，使个人高端客户更易于识别和进行层级管理。通过客户经理、产品经理的专业服务、VIP 服务区的设置、优先办理业务等，使个人优质客户体验到了高效、优质、专业且彰显身份的服务。而对于对公客户，缺少有效的身份识别和层级管理，难以享受分层级的优质服务和优先办理业务的待遇。目前只能在办理业务时人为调整安排，易引发其他客户的投诉，同时也不能保证服务质量的统一。

其次，个人业务相对简单，单笔业务处理时间短；对公业务相对复杂，单笔业务处理时间较长。零售网点转型后，通过功能区的划分、排队叫号服务系统的使用、高低柜的设置、弹性排班制度及 STM 的分流使用，提高了个人业务服务效率。但对公业务由于受网点人员数量、渠道分流、对公业务数量、人员业务素质等因素制约，网点一般只能够设立半个或一个对公业务窗口，且对公客户的分层管理还未能如个人业务一样实现 VIP 层级化分类管理。当对公业务相对集中时，对公客户就会存在排队和等待时间较长的现象。

（四）网点对公业务人员数量和专业能力与业务发展不匹配

网点对公业务人员配备不齐和专业能力不足，已成为目前网点的普遍情况，具体表现如下所述。

第一，大部分网点缺乏专职对公柜员，而由开放式柜或 VIP 柜兼任，虽然昆明分行已推行综合柜员制多年，但在实际工作中，大部分网点的人力情况仅只能应对日常的个人业务，难以兼顾对公业务发展。另外网点人员因轮岗、辞职、生育、调动等情况，导致人员流动频繁，难以形成真正拥有专业技术且稳定在岗的“三综合柜员”。

第二，大部分网点无专职对公客户经理，有的由个人客户经理兼任，有的由产品经理或柜员主管兼任，无法做到专业专注，遇到商机难以把握，待相关信息与上级行对公业务团队联动时，往往已错失该业务的最佳介入机会。

第三，还有相当一部分网点对公业务、个人业务及网点管理均由负责人一肩挑。最终，网点对公业务难以全面顾忌，客户管理难以精细化。

对内，对公业务指标发展不理想。对公存款未实现全员营销，经营体现日常维护的日均存款增长乏力；对公贷款大多局限于二级行营业室和几个旗舰网点，其他网点仅实现小微快贷、云税贷等大数据产品投放，或者仅办理为数不多的几笔低风险业务；中间业务收入局限于传统业务和结算收入；新产品不会做，更无人做。

对外，客户营销维护能力不足，精力不够。从近两年优质客户减少、低质客户大幅增加的趋势可以看出，对于竞争激烈的优质新客户，网点对公营销拓展不够或者跟进不及时；对于存量客户，缺少分级维护和深度营销的精力和能力，客户贡献度低。

（五）绩效考核机制不完善

第一，在绩效考核上，对公考核机制不完善。目前，网点员工的绩效工资大部分有赖于产品营销挂价买单，诸多个人业务产品实行了买单制和“谁营销谁受益”的考核思路，在很大程度上调动了全员营销的积极性。由于个人客户数量多，产品相对简单，个人业务营销经验及营销话术易于掌握和学习，全员开口机会多、见效快。与之相比，对公客户数量较少，营销难度大，产品相对复杂，专业知识要求高，营销时间长、见效慢，且对公业务营销往往是多层级综合营销的结果，在绩效考核中难以立竿见影，所以营销人员更愿意将精力和时间投入见效较快的零售业务当中。

第二，网点对公柜员缺少绩效保证。特别是对公业务量较大的网点，对公柜员需从事大量的客户账务处理，如支票、汇款、账户资料变更、账户年检、反洗钱、零余额账户额度请领等工作，而这些工作缺少固定的绩效保障，更缺少合理的业务劳动量绩效。对公柜员只能通过账户开立、产品签约获得一次性的挂价，但账户开立后，不断增加的业务量又使对公柜员不敢多开户、不愿多开户，从而又导致存款新增乏力、账户新增不足。

三、网点提升对公职能的对策和建议

针对网点对公业务发展存在的问题，必须厘清思路、明确目标、增添得力的工作措施，通过对网点全方位、精细化的管理，形成一套行之有效、完整规范的对公业务经营机制，提升价值创造能力和市场竞争力。对策与建议具体如下所述。

（一）明确网点对公业务发展的功能定位及目标

商业银行网点的功能定位，是指银行营业机构在市场经济活动中所扮演的重要角色以及运作、发展的空间，具体体现在服务对象、业务范围、产品准入、服务方式、硬件建设、劳动组合、风险控制等方面。① 针对样本网点而言，我认为其对公功能定位具体如下所述。

第一，明晰网点对公业务转型定位。对网点的传统定位为核算交易型，我认为发展对公业务不是盲目的“一刀切”，而是要根据网点的资源禀赋、区域特点、客群结构、历史沉淀等因素综合考虑，网点对公业务转型的定位，是将网点打造为对公业务发展的触角、始端和承接器，使网点成为具有市场竞争力的价值创造终端。网点发展对公业务是在“零售优先”已获得优势的情况下的一种重要补充，同时也是公私联动，提升网点综合经营能力和满足客户综合金融服务需求的重要手段。

第二，明确网点业务发展目标。网点发展对公业务要与网点周边特色相结合，以外出拓展为辅助。所以需要结合各网点实际，立足于目前的经济形势，与其盲目外出拓展项目，不如深耕细作更具有可行性。

明确网点对公业务发展理念，突出“综合经营、梯次发展、特色定位”。以昆明分行为例，突出区域内“云花”“云药”“云茶”“云烟”“云游”的特色产业，有针对性地开展对公业务。提供对公结算、普惠金融信贷和对公产品销售等服务。立足网点人员、规模、资源、发展潜力等因素，分标杆网点、重点网点、推进网点和普及网点4个类别确定发展目标。具体如下所述。

一是发挥标杆网点的引领作用。体现“经营上规模、客户多层次、业务全品类、

---

① 资料来源：王海明. 商业银行营业网点对公业务转型研究［D］. 济南：山东大学，2012.

服务高品质、管理精细化”的特质，形成“基层行打造标杆网点、上级行挂钩指导”的模式。[①]

二是发挥重点网点的支撑作用。体现“经营求规模、客户分层次、业务多品种、服务优质化、管理规范化”，发挥主力军作用，打造综合性服务平台。

三是发挥推进网点的支持性作用。将对公业务资源丰富，但业务发展缓慢的网点列为推进网点。充分发挥传帮带的作用，挂钩的前台部门实施重点帮扶。

四是发挥普及网点的补充作用。重点做好对公客户拓展引荐、日常支付结算服务、对公产品销售等工作。

（二）网点对公业务发展的应对措施

1. 综合化、特色化经营，结合实际，充分发挥网点渠道功能

通过资源禀赋分析定位网点分类。根据昆明分行所有对公网点业务现状和考核导向，细分网点对公定位分类，因类施策，按类下达任务目标和特色导向，而不是简单地通过综合经营计划进行任务安排。通过资源禀赋分析，才能有效结合网点实际，挖掘网点业务潜力和业务特色，获得业务发展。以昆明分行为例，切实落实“圈、链、群”的打法，以互联网思维结合普惠金融理念，根据网点资源禀赋开展对公业务。如商业区部分网点可以拓展金融生态圈、商圈客户；大型集团企业及其上游企业附近网点，则可以大力开展链式营销，拓展核心企业的上下游企业。以供应链网络银行、e信通等为抓手，从向核心企业提供对公金融服务，逐步转变为向相关产业链条上的企业提供链式金融服务，以“双大”带动“双小”，以“双小”延伸和承接“双大”。

2. 发挥网点触角作用，切实承接普惠金融落地工作

物理网点、电子渠道、客户经理队伍是银行三大服务渠道。其中物理网点又是最具客户综合服务能力的渠道。特别是目前的物理网点，由于金融科技的支持，各项业务处理已经大幅度后台化，已经从交易核算型发展为营销服务型。普惠金融就是要以金融科技为支撑、普惠理念为抓手，让大众享受到更专业、更全面、更具深度的金融服务，帮助实体经济发展。网点要面向大众及与其相关的小微企业、个体工商户，通过网点专业服务、上门服务、远程服务等方式，以金融服务为切入点，全面融入客户的生活圈、商业圈、工作圈，提供多元化的金融服务；实现“线上线下一体化”服务，突出电子渠道、客户经理和物理网点服务的融合，线上线下联动，全面搭建全覆盖的服务网络。

线上服务重在以金融科技为支撑，利用“小微快贷”平台，基于资金结算、房产

① 资料来源：陆成之．多措推进网点对公业务转型［J］．现代金融，2017.

抵押、代缴税等内部数据，以及税务、工商等外部数据，加强线上主动服务，提高精准服务效率。以信贷业务为基础，通过大数据分析、商机推荐等手段，提供理财、企业年金、保险、税务咨询等各类非信贷服务，满足客户多层次、多样化的金融需求。

线下服务重在发挥网点服务的触角作用，通过营销拓展落地企业和客户账户，落实普惠金融落地工作，利用小企业中心、网点多渠道协同优势，不断提升网点办理小额化、标准化产品的能力，让更多实体企业就近享受普惠金融服务。

3. 建立网点对公客户的分层管理机制

要对客户实行分层管理，网点营销维护重点可分为三类：一是网点自主维护类的客户，金融服务需求单一或者日均存款余额较小的对公客户全面由网点自主负责营销和管理；二是存款余额大、金融服务需求复杂、专业知识要求较高的客户的营销与管理，由支行及以上专业团队负责，该类客户的结算业务由网点负责提供优质服务；三是符合潜在优质客户标准的前期营销和信息推荐上报工作由网点负责。

明确上述分类标准后，分层分级开展营销管理。对于网点管理的客户，网点要根据自身客户情况细化分层标准，落实网点负责人、客户经理、大堂经理和柜员的管护责任，分户到人，做好柜面的分层分级服务，制订拜访计划。

4. 落实对公业务服务软硬件条件

强化网点内部“柜面设置和大厅”的服务功能。一是网点应按业务实际情况增设专职对公柜台，明确对公柜台标识，叫号机对公业务专栏需要增加业务分类及客户分级，对于特殊情况或者业务量不饱和的对公柜台，可以兼办零售业务。二是在有条件的情况下，对公客业务区与大众客户进行合理区隔，使对公优质客户也可以享受贵宾服务。三是加强大厅内的广告和宣传，根据网点客户需求在大厅显眼位置张贴或放置对公产品宣传资料并定期更新，强化对公产品营销氛围。

5. 充实并稳定对公队伍，做好客户服务

（1）充实队伍，稳定网点对公条线人员，做好岗位配合，开展立体营销。根据网点业务实际情况，可设立专业对公业务人员，提升技能，保障绩效，保持人员的相对稳定。改革营销机制，各岗位明确职责分工：网点负责人全面负责网点对公业务的营销与管理，组织开展网点对公客户的关系维系与拓展；专职和兼职客户经理负责辖内存量客户的管理与维护及公私联动商机挖掘，协助网点负责人营销、拓展新客户和新业务，进行低风险业务受理和调查；大堂经理主要负责识别优质客户，将其推荐给对公客户经理；柜员主要负责办理柜面业务，收集客户信息，通过交易识别推荐优质客户，协助推介和销售对公产品等。① 不同岗位人员要密切配合，及时交流、传递、汇总

① 资料来源：贺雄田．商业银行基层客户经理队伍建设存在的问题及对策研究［J］．中国证券期货，2012（7）．

信息，制定工作计划和绩效激励机制。

（2）公私联动，加强培训，树立对公团队拓展营销服务意识。一是加强网点公私联动营销配合。网点大力开展公私联动，特别是网点高净值个人客户，其身后大多都有较为优质的企业，公私联动后，除了公私业务实现稳步提升外，还有利于后期个人客户的维护及提升工作。同时，对网点所有员工都要加强对公业务培训，要继续坚持利用晨会、夕会等时段组织学习对公营销话术和对公产品知识等，使网点所有员工都了解产品，树立网点全员参与对公业务商机的营销意识。二是加强网点和上级行业务部门的联动营销。公司业务部为网点提供智力支持，指导和协助网点共同营销，撰写对公金融服务方案或对公产品建议书等，通过团队营销提高营销的有效性。

6. 探索和完善网点对公业务人员的考核激励机制

（1）优化对公绩效考核分配体系。公平、合理的激励机制，是提高网点对公人员营销服务意识和能力，有效发挥对网点负责人、对公柜员的主动性和积极性的关键。上级行和网点要结合网点实际情况，逐步建立以产品销售业绩、结算产品业务收入、业务工作量、核算质量、风险控制为主要内容的绩效考核分配体系。对于网点的对公业务考核，我认为可以考虑从以下三个维度展开。一是根据网点对公客户结构特色，结合客户特点开展差别化的考核，如对集团客户的维护、业务的承接等，也可以按照“圈、链、群”的思路服务集团客户，认真分析不同集团客户的商业模式和客群结构，将建行金融产品和专业服务融合进去。二是结合网点对公产品，按照产品维度从易到难，匹配推荐给适合的客户，进行挂价奖励。三是要根据对公业务专业程度高、营销周期长的特点，有别于个人业务的挂价考核模式，可以根据项目营销进展分阶段匹配战略费用和奖励。在分层经营和管理的前提下，实现内部的分层考核，促使各层级机构各司其职，加大客户营销服务力度，改善我们现在经营客户不够深入、客户综合贡献度不高的情况。

（2）强化考核及产品竞赛，提升网点资源配置。全面梳理对公业务关键绩效考核指标，调动网点经营对公业务积极性。依据网点客户基础、业务量、对公存款、风险内控等指标为对公网点配置基础性绩效；[①] 新增普惠金融、住房租赁等作为重要考核指标，加大对公产品营销增量考核比重。KPI 考核体系是对公营业网点转型过程中的战略业务发展、公司金融产品下沉、对公销售人员队伍建设、风险内控等方面的综合性评价及考核。辅之以专项考核、穿透式激励，给予网点更多的资源配置。

（3）加大对公绩效保障，提升网点对公承载能力。结合网点对公情况和业务发展的可持续性，需要给予网点对公业务人员必要的绩效保证，让业务人员敢做、愿做、

---

① 资料来源：奚云鹏．商业银行对公营业网点转型研究［D］．昆明：昆明理工大学，2013.

多做对公业务。通过绩效保障条线人员的稳定性和积极性，最终才能帮助网点发展好对公业务。

四、总结

在保持零售转型已取得较大优势的情况下，对公业务发展是网点综合化持续发展的重要补充和助推器。本文通过分析昆明分行下辖各基层网点对公业务发展现状，结合基层一线工作实践，指出了网点对公业务存在的问题。针对存在的问题，提出了提升网点对公职能的对策和建议。然而客户和市场状况瞬息万变，网点对公业务的转型也应因时而变、因势而动，不断适应市场和客户的多元化金融服务需求。商业银行应始终坚持“以客户为中心”的经营理念，探究规律，敢于创新，推动转型工作更好、更快地发展，并最终实现效益增长、价值创造和核心竞争力的提升。

网点强，则全行强。商业银行网点对公业务转型及应对研究，是一种在基层一线实践中总结出来的、具有可操作性的理论方法，具有一定的现实意义。希望本文粗浅的分析和建议，能对商业银行在转型过程中找准基层网点的战略发展定位、加强公私综合经营发展能力、提升价值创造能力有所帮助。

互联网保险的思考与实践

建信财险　李　直　李树欣　杨　瑾

一、引言

互联网保险业务，是指保险机构依托互联网和移动通信等技术，通过自营网络平台、第三方网络平台等订立保险合同、提供保险服务的业务。

随着我国居民保险意识的增强以及互联网技术在各领域的应用普及，互联网成为保险公司宣传和获客的重要手段，互联网渠道成为传统保险公司实现渠道转型和升级的新机会。互联网保险在我国得到了快速发展，无疑成为当前保险行业的热点，也是众多资本的新风口，在一定程度上承担着保险行业创新的重任。

对于保险公司来说，互联网渠道费用低，受众面广，可以带来持续并具有一定消费能力的客户群体。根据中国互联网络信息中心（CNNIC）统计数据显示，我国互联网用户规模达到7.72亿人，互联网普及率达到55.8%。在互联网消费能力方面，截至2017年12月，我国网络购物用户规模达到5.33亿，相较2016年增长14.3%。保险公司通过选择互联网渠道可以降低渠道成本，提升服务质量，避免逆选择等信息不对称产生的道德风险。2017年，互联网保险保费收入1 835.29亿元，签单件数同比增长102.6%，达到124.91亿件，开展互联网保险的机构已超过130家。保险通过互联网的承载正在实现华丽的转身，在“互联网+”的政策下，可以看到保险在民生保障、社会稳定、金融风险控制方面起到了更为重要的作用。

目前建行集团正在实施普惠金融、住房租赁、金融科技“三大战略”，对于保险行业来说，保险科技也正从产品、渠道、流程、效率等对传统保险行业进行改造和提升，进而逐步重塑整个保险行业的商业价值生态链。而全球发展保险科技的普遍规律是要依托互联网开展业务，然后将大数据、人工智能、区块链、云计算等技术综合运用在公司运营形态和保险业务中，通过对保险业务流程的全面渗入，提高业务效率，改变产品形态，改进服务和交互方式，并进一步催生新的商业模式，建设保险生态。

二、当前互联网保险行业八大特征

（一）市场主体

根据保监会的统计，截至2017年，经营互联网保险的财险公司有70家，全国已有超过70%的保险公司通过自建网站、与第三方平台合作等不同形式开展互联网保险业务，互联网保险市场主体越来越多，市场竞争逐渐激烈，市场的集中度明显下降。另外，互联网保险经营主体也更具多元化，作为保险形式的创新，2017年保监会批准成立了3家相互制保险公司，其相互制的形式也为互联网保险经营主体形式上的一大创新。

表5.38　2017年互联网保险保费收入情况

序号	公司	2017年累计签单数量（单）	2017年累计保费收入（万元）	保费行业占比（%）	排名
1	平安产险	52 405 077	1 484 135.45	30.07	1
2	众安保险	5 371 998 962	595 735.37	12.07	2
3	人保财险	1 189 726 969	405 304.59	8.21	3
4	太保保险	739 654 511	280 547.10	5.69	4
5	大地保险	419 212 608	230 153.80	4.65	5
6	泰康在线	874 972 422	177 075.67	3.59	6
7	太平财险	880 207 518	175 785.24	3.56	7
8	中寿财险	6 558 549	167 912.10	3.40	8
9	永诚保险	2 254 336	165 688.56	3.36	9
10	华安保险	5 075 901	163 032.94	3.30	10
11	永安保险	2 015 413	143 011.64	2.90	11
12	阳光产险	11 672 357	112 845.00	2.29	12
13	国泰产险	2 368 643 483	97 315.46	1.97	13
14	中华财险	625 052	88 411.51	1.79	14
15	华泰财险	924 129 461	85 808.80	1.74	15
16	易安财险	21 827 305	83 876.85	1.70	16
17	天安财险	764 503	80 814.33	1.64	17
18	安心保险	8 871 201	79 443.20	1.61	18
19	亚太财险	435 646	37 638.00	0.76	19
20	安盛天平	83 495 972	32 837.83	0.67	20
21	建信财险	1 326 780	4 607.25	0.08	21

表 5.39　2017 年互联网保险保费占比情况　（%）

2017 年互联网保险		2017 年互联网车险		2017 年互联网非车险	
公司	保费行业占比	公司	保费行业占比	公司	保费行业占比
平安产险	30.07	平安产险	44.10	众安保险	31.56
众安保险	12.07	人保财险	9.81	泰康在线	9.08
人保财险	8.21	大地保险	6.62	平安产险	5.94
太保产险	5.69	太保产险	5.55	太保产险	5.91
大地保险	4.66	永诚保险	5.19	人保财险	5.58
泰康在线	3.59	华安保险	4.92	国寿财险	5.40
太平财险	3.56	永安保险	4.33	国泰产险	5.22
国寿财险	3.40	中华财险	2.86	太平财险	5.14
永诚保险	3.36	太平财险	2.61	易安财险	4.50
华安保险	3.30	阳光产险	2.59	安心财险	2.81
建信财险	0.08	建信财险	0.00	建信财险	0.22
其他	21.99	其他	11.43	其他	17.64

平安、众安、人保、太保、大地保险占据了互联网业务的前 5 名。在互联网车险业务中，平安、人保、大地 3 家占比超过 60%；在互联网非车险业务中，众安、泰康在线、易安、安心 4 家互联网财险公司占比为 47.95%（见表 5.38 和表 5.39）。

（二）渠道

2017 年互联网保险公司通过公司自营平台实现保费收入为 256.47 亿元，占比 51.97%，其中自营平台移动端占比 71.74%。从同期对比来看，保险公司自营网络渠道业务逐步下降，PC 端官网业务同期下降明显，但移动端业务增长较快。另外，第三方网络平台和专业中介机构的保费增长较快，达到了 217.59 亿元，占比 44.09%，但同时费用率也较高。渠道对于保险公司来说是产品与价值向外输出的必由途径，可谓“得渠道者得天下”。在“互联网 +”的浪潮下，产险公司传统的营销渠道也在亟待新的突破（见图 5.33）。

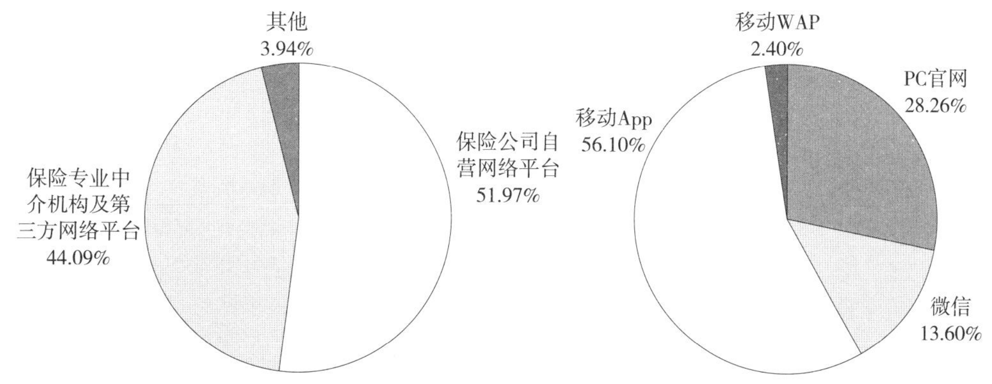

图 5.33　2017 年互联网保险渠道结构分析

(三)成本

表 5.40　2017 年第三方平台互联网保险情况分析

序号	主要合作中介机构名称	类型	2017 年累计保单数量(单)	2017 年累计保费收入(万元)
1	淘宝网	购物	9 691 495 724	424 445.60
2	支付宝	综合	1 293 598 47	232 642.62
3	携程网	出行	50 643 619	113 140.61
4	去哪儿网	出行	29 765 842	83 375.97
5	天猫	购物	1 176 843 865	74 088.24
6	永安保险销售	中介	625 339	61 019.44
7	优保万家	中介	254 291	59 799.00
8	大通保	中介	300 285	37 915.22
9	小赢理财	互联网金融	21 288 537	35 333.10
10	天地通保	中介	308 147	34 925.25
11	去啊/飞猪	出行	540 0821	25 585.79
12	平安普惠	互联网金融	383 932	25 181.92
13	明亚经纪	中介	7 847 006	24 674.53
14	北京十一贝科技有限公司	中介	716 119	20 286.69
15	网易	综合	82 890	19 852.62
16	宜信博诚保险	中介	488 138	17 903.15
17	慧择网	中介	4 779 705	16 600.66
18	江泰经纪	中介	7 803 500	16 355.38
19	同程网	出行	7 751 096	15 881.87
20	美团网	综合	49 172 737	15 139.07

表 5.41　2017 年财险公司利润情况分析

公司	原保险保费收入(万元)	业管费(万元)	手续费及佣金(万元)	费用率(%)	已产生赔款净额(万元)	综合赔付率(%)	综合成本率(%)
人保股份	34 929008.16	5 444 650.53	6 052 537.37	32.92	21 795 701.09	62.40	95.32
平安财产	21 598 387.43	3 973 681.85	3 921 201.77	36.55	12 224 687.29	56.60	93.15
太平洋财险	10 585 900.00	2 040 942.44	1 905 174.44	37.28	6 502 166.42	61.42	98.70
大地财产	3 712 319.15	892 328.54	577 322.35	39.59	2 075 186.40	55.90	95.49
太平保险	2 206 860.71	557 737.74	407 548.39	43.74	1 154 188.15	52.30	96.04
众安财产	595 735.37	301 644.21	62 390.97	61.11	356 249.75	59.80	120.91
家康在线	165 611.90	92 138.42	27 170.16	72.04	91 252.16	55.10	127.14
易安财产	83 909.28	41 925.27	4 212.59	54.99	40 192.55	47.90	102.99
安心财产	79 443.18	29 641.98	14 560.91	55.64	51 638.07	65.00	120.64
中银保险	555 860.19	110 239.33	121 975.41	41.78	325 734.07	58.60	100.38
华海财产	155 414.25	59 271.28	34 949.78	60.63	95 890.61	61.70	122.33

（续表）

公司	原保险保费收入（万元）	业管费（万元）	手续费及佣金（万元）	费用率（%）	已产生赔款净额（万元）	综合赔付率（%）	综合成本率（%）
珠峰财险	41 223.20	16 159.52	11 229.41	66.44	32 813.67	79.60	146.04
建信财险	24 457.36	21 734.62	3 348.28	102.56	3 241.07	13.25	115.81
4家互联网公司平均	231 174.93	116 337.47	27 083.66	60.94	134 833.13	56.95	117.89
行业平均	105 413	814.67		39.56	63 438 033.67	60.18	99.74

近年来财产保险行业手续费和佣金的平均涨幅均超过产品保费的平均涨幅，手续费及佣金的大幅提高缩减了公司的利润空间。目前4家互联网公司综合成本率为117%，远超过财产险行业平均值。而依靠代理或者第三方平台营销，则市场业务费用较高。场景化强且流量大的第三方平台，综合成本率高，且保险公司谈判话语权低。以非车险业务来看，市场集中度高，整个第三方平台非车险业务的62%集中在阿里系和携程系，其中阿里系平台占47.03%，携程系平台占15.04%。而保险商城和经代渠道平台对产品自身优势、产品价格、代理费用等要求高，同样造成保险公司利润较低（见表5.40和表5.41）。

（四）险种结构

车险业务保费收入307.19亿元，占比62.25%，比重持续下滑；非车险业务保费收入186.30亿元，占比37.75%，非车险业务持续保持较快增长。非车险热销产品以退运险、出行、健康为主，但目前非车险业务集中在第三方平台上，占比达到73.95%。而在财险公司自营平台业务中，车险占比超过95%。车险业务在自营平台占比约为八成，非车险业务在第三方平台占比接近九成（见图5.34和表5.42）。

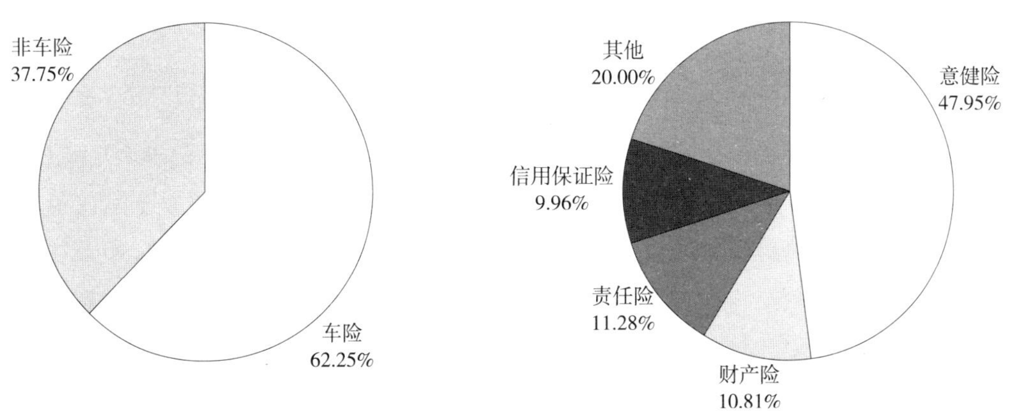

图5.34　2017年互联网保险险种结构分析

表 5.42 保险渠道与险种的综合分析

渠道细项	险种分类	2017 年累计保费收入（万元）	保费占比（%）
自营平台	车险	2 446 624.08	95.39
	非车险	118 132.27	4.61
	小计	2 564 756.35	
第三方网络平台	车险	566 903.92	26.05
	非车险	1 608 991.59	73.95
	小计	2 175 895.51	
其他	车险	58 337.86	30.04
	非车险	135 878.98	69.96
	小计	195 216.84	

年份	参与互联网业务的公司	互联网保险财产险保费收入（亿元）	同比增长（%）	车险占比（%）	非车险占比（%）
2015	49 家	768.36	51.94	93.20	6.80
2016	60 家	505.29	-34.63	79.42	20.58
2017	70 家	489.49	-1.75	62.25	37.75

险种分类	渠道细项	2017 年累计保费收入（万元）	保费占比（%）
车险	自营平台	2 446 624.08	75.65
	第三方网络平台	566.903.92	18.45
	其他	58 337.86	1.90
	小计	3 071 860.56	
非车险	自营平台	118 132.27	6.34
	第三方网络平台	1 608 991.59	86.37
	其他	135 878.98	7.29
	小计	1 863 003.42	

（五）业务条线

互联网车险业务条线自营平台占比大，并且主要依靠 O2O（线上到线下）。目前车险业务集中分布于东部地区，中西部地区也在快速发展。而从互联网非车险业务条线来看，目前非车险热销产品主要为退运险、航意险和航延险，集中于出行和购物两个场景。2016 年互联网非车险前 10 名的热销产品中运费险占据了六席，这表明高频、低价、场景化、标准化产品更加满足和适应市场及用户需求。而 2017 年热销产品与 2016 年相比，增加了健康险产品。通过分析可得，热销产品对股东资源和高流量场景平台的依赖性较强（见表 5.43 和表 5.44）。

表 5.43　2016 年互联网非车险热销产品分析

序号	产品名称	2016 年保费收入（万元）
1	退货运费险	250 165.19
2	航空意外险	201 036.27
3	航班延误险	61 568.20
4	公共交通意外险	46 793.37
5	个人意外伤害保险	25 730.21
6	账户安全险	26 840.35
7	酒店退订险	15 897.47
8	旅行意外险	13 702.16
9	旅程预定取消保险	11 947.39
11	接口合同信用保险	3 932.79
12	综合意外险	1 564.25
13	购票保障险	1 080.00
序号	产品名称	2016 年保单数量（单）
1	退货运费险	5 231 188 067
2	借款合同履行信用保险	171 343 680
3	账户安全险	101 786 675
4	航空意外险	73 247 541
5	航空旅行旅程延误险	40 586 252
6	公共交通意外险	33 309 969
7	个人意外伤害保险	8 073 534
8	食品质量保障险	6 194 761
9	购票保障险	6 054 039
10	酒店退订险	5 376 233
11	旅程预定取消保险	4 291 528
12	旅行意外险	3 742 327
13	国内货物运输保险	2 031 441
14	综合意外险	578 746
15	家财险	318 582
16	驾意险	48 717

表 5.44　2017 年互联网非车险热销产品分析

序号	公司名称	产品名称	2017 年累计保单数量（件）
1	众安保险	网络购物退货运费损失保险条款	1 986 085 345
2	人保财险	网络购物运费损失保险	1 156 489 163
3	国泰产险	个人意外伤害保险（单车专用）	1 049 258 461
4	国泰产险	网络购物退货运费损失保险（卖家版）	961 770 900
5	华泰财险	网络购物运费损失保险	912 289 814
6	太平财险	网络购物退货运费损失险	771 567 559

（续表）

序号	公司名称	产品名称	2017 年累计保单数量（件）
7	太保产险	网络购物运费损失保险	740 137 580
8	众安保险	网络交易平台卖家履约保证保险条款（B 款）	507 164 601
9	泰康在线	放心淘“网络财物计划”	495 505 998
10	众安保险	产品质量保证保险条款	490 771 999
11	大地保险	网络购物退货运费保险	417 521 759
12	众安保险	产品质量保证保险条款	270 632 370
13	泰康在线	网络购物退货运费损失保险（卖家投保版）	249 567 384
14	众安保险	国内水路、陆路货物运输保险条款	245 106 804
15	国泰产险	个人支付宝账户资金损失保险	162 414 763
16	人保财险	网络支付账户资金损失保险	109 527 086
17	太平财险	账户安全保险	92 962 453
18	安盛天平	网络购物退货运费保险	82 783 354
19	国泰产险	防骗险	68 697 206
20	浙商保险	网络购物退货运费保险	48 700 309
序号	公司名称	产品名称	2017 年累计保费收入（万元）
1	众安保险	网络购物退货运费损失保险条款	103 366. 80
2	国泰产险	网络购物退货运费损失保险（卖家版）	56 105. 38
3	人保财险	网络购物运费损失保险	50 199. 29
4	华泰财险	网络购物运费损失保险	46 430. 78
5	众安保险	航空意外伤害保险条款	40 761. 90
6	太平财险	网络购物退货运费损失险	39 835. 16
7	太保产险	网络购物运费损失保险	38 919. 91
8	泰康在线	交通工具意外人身伤害保险	35 799. 21
9	众安保险	营运交通工具乘客意外伤害保险条款	30 471. 63
10	众安保险	个人中高端医疗保险条款（2017 版）	26 567. 58
11	众安保险	个人中高端医疗保险条款	25 249. 29
12	泰康在线	综合意外险（含交通意外及住院费用）	23 492. 61
13	大地保险	网络购物退货运费保险	23 325. 40
14	太平财险	航空旅客意外伤害保险	20 908. 92
15	易安财险	个人航空意外伤害保险	19 477. 83
16	前海财险	航空人身意外伤害保险－060023	19 013. 15
17	泰康在线	人身意外综合保险	18 200. 77
18	安心保险	个人贷款保证保险（3 年期）	17 276. 50
19	国泰产险	个人支付宝账户资金损失保险	17 131. 49
20	安心保险	人身意外伤害保险	15 959. 30

（六）产品

互联网保险产品同质化严重，没有技术壁垒，因为新产品开发过程复杂，监管趋严，所以相对于创新产品，不少企业选择对现有的保险产品进行一定的改造。而同质产品容易形成恶性的价格竞争机制，不利于公司的发展也不利于产品的创新。另外互联网保险引流成本高，客户忠诚度弱，销售转化率较低。

从互联网保险客户群体分析来看，活跃的互联网保民集中在26～45岁，已婚，中高收入和高学历人群；90后人均持有4张保单，其中2.7张是健康险。

（七）监管

不当创新引发监管趋严。在场景化保险发展的初期，部分企业为了追求创新与噱头，推出了很多具有猎奇和博彩性质的保险产品，例如雾霾险、赏月险等，这类保险产品一味求“新”，背离了保险保障的本质，使得监管机构出台更加严苛的监管政策，不利于场景化保险产品的创新。

（八）互联网保险投保行为

目前保险需求与实际购买行为存在错位现象。调查显示，用户最常购买的产品中38.3%为汽车类保险，22.8%为电商类产品，13.1%为资金安全类。但用户自评最能影响生活的风险因素，依次是生病（44.4%）、电子账户被盗（15.2%）、手机丢失或损坏（13.2%）。用户在选择产品时，29.6%的人看重理赔渠道是否畅通，27.1%的人看重保险公司品牌美誉度，20.6%的人看重购买条款是否简明。

三、建信财险互联网保险SWOT分析

（一）优势（S，Strength）

一是依托建行优势资源，建行电子渠道客户基础好，业务结合点多，普惠金融、住房租赁、金融科技三大战略也为互联网保险提供了各种各样的业务场景，这是公司互联网保险业务发展的核心竞争力；二是借助建行的品牌效应，通过建行物理和互联网渠道，进行公司品牌宣传；三是具备信息化的后发优势，公司IT架构从一开始就考虑了互联网业务的特点；四是源自建行的管理团队，具备跨界经营能力，为公司走出一条差异化的发展道路奠定了基础条件。

（二）劣势（W，Weakness）

一是公司处于起步阶段，互联网基因有待培养，经验有待积累；二是作为一家新成立的市场主体，公司在品牌、产品等方面还没有影响力，被客户认可还需时日；三是公司注册资本金较低，费用支出受集团约束，落地服务机构较少，对部分业务开展造成一定影响；四是公司发展规划、基础设施建设与业务拓展、扩大保费规模等工作并行，争抢有限的人财物等资源。

（三）机会（O，Opportunity）

一是中国银行保险监督管理委员会成立，引导保险行业健康良性发展；二是互联网保险近几年兴起，老牌保险公司和互联网专业保险公司也是刚起步不久；三是国家制定了相关制度、政策来鼓励互联网保险的发展。

（四）挑战（T，Threat）

一是整个互联网保险行业刚刚起步，公司没有成功模式可供参考；二是监管政策趋严，公司要应对现代保险监管转型的挑战；三是保险产品绝大多数为非标准化产品，想要实现产品的互联网场景化，还有很多困难必须攻克；四是该如何有效融入建行集团资源，在为建行集团服务的同时，促进公司互联网保险业务的发展；五是公司自身能力建设的挑战，包括人才管理的挑战、产品创新、IT 技术系统的建设。

四、建信财险互联网保险应对策略

目前，建设银行正在实施普惠金融、住房租赁、金融科技三大战略，作为建行集团的成员，建信财险明确提出了服务建行集团战略、服务建行集团主业和服务建行集团客户的战略定位。在互联网保险业务方面，针对我们的优势与不足，提出了全方位、全渠道服务建行集团业务及集团客户，全面融入建行各个生态圈的工作思路，通过打造极致客户服务体验，凸显智慧型保险公司特点，实现在功能上有效补充、在战略上有力策应建行集团。

（一）客户策略

将核心目标客户锁定为建行员工、员工亲属以及建行客户；外部市场客户则集中于自媒体内容运营、活动运营带来的自然流量，不投入大量资源与费用广泛获客。另外基于互联网用户的客群特点，优先发展中青年客户，通过中青年客户延展到老年客户。利用大数据分析客户行为，实现客户分层；建立客户激励体系，提高活跃客户规模；适当激励刺激，提高活跃客户贡献度。

（二）渠道策略

建行渠道是优势。重点拓展、全方位渗透建行渠道和优质资源，全面渗透我司保险产品，实现服务、销售和引流。目标是将总行的渠道全部对接，持续跟进新增渠道对接；对建行各分行、子公司、海外分行的渠道，有条件的都实现对接。

自营网络平台是成为市场化的基础。作为公司互联网生态圈的核心，我们前期工作的重点在于搭建好具有黏性和影响力的体系，中期在于完成引流形成客户规模，长期在于拥有大规模稳定优质客群，为公司提供优质互联网业务并反哺建行业务。目标是通过自有互联网渠道打造极致客户服务体验，尽量汇聚公司所有客户，支持O2O业务，不花费大量资源引流，重点发展移动端渠道（建信财险App和微信），提供一站式服务，实现客户留存与激活、提升经营效率。

第三方渠道是补充。作为公司互联网业务效益和规模冲量的补充手段，追求效益和多点接入，在规模需求强时参与市场竞争。目标是第三方渠道以效益为中心，实现与60+第三方渠道多点接入；与主要第三方平台接入，不求流量；重点关注成长型、效益型第三方平台（见图5.35）。

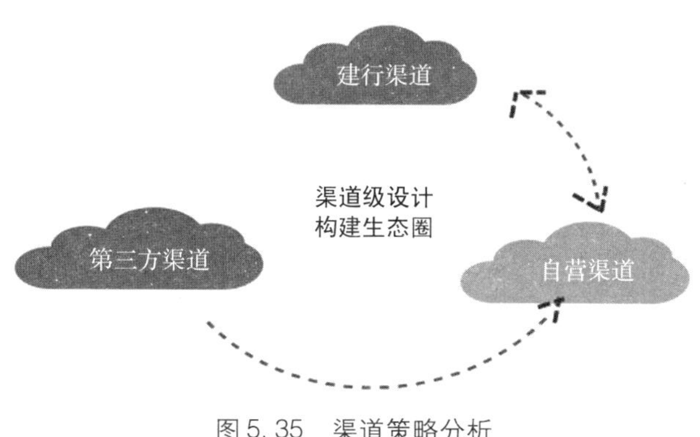

图5.35　渠道策略分析

（三）产品策略

丰富互联网产品。捕捉市场热点，探索场景化保险产品创新，以健康险、出行保险、车险、信用保证保险为重点，嵌入建行业务场景，嵌入各类互联网流程场景，上架互联网保险商城（见图5.36）。

（四）运营策略

以建信财险App为基础，聚合客户，提供一站式极致服务体验，在做好客户服务

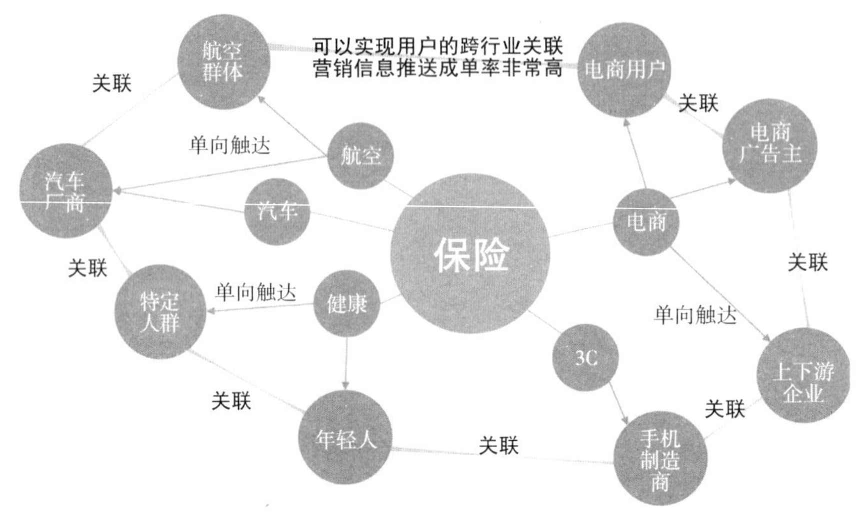

图 5.36　互联网保险场景关联

资料来源：艾瑞研究院。

的基础上，逐步做好内容运营、活动运营、客户运营和数据运营工作。通过自媒体内容运营、活动运营带来自然流量，不投入大量资源与费用广泛获客；利用大数据分析客户行为，实现客户分层；建立客户激励体系，扩大活跃用户规模。

五、建信财险互联网保险工作措施及初步成果

（一）以建行渠道为重点，构建立体化互联网渠道结构

一是全方位渗透、融合建行各个渠道。从机构维度、渠道维度、业务维度、建行云维度 4 个维度深入探索互联网保险应用场景。通过对接总行 44 个部门、39 家分行和培训中心、12 家子公司、28 家海外分行，梳理并分析建行手机银行、网上银行、STM、悦享生活、微信银行、慧兜圈、善融商务、员工 App、裕农通、建融家园、建融公寓、员工订票平台、金湘通等建行渠道，研究建行信用卡、房屋租赁、小微快贷、质押贷、房贷、车贷、消费贷、快贷、龙支付、电子支付、聚合支付等银行业务，寻找互联网保险合作切入点，融入互联网保险产品和服务。全面融合建行云平台建设，配合集团向外孵化包括财产保险产品在内的全面金融服务，为集团未来发展注入保险科技动能，提升集团金融科技竞争能力和服务水平（见图 5.37）。

二是发展自营渠道，特别是移动端自营渠道。官网主要作为我司官方信息披露及发布的主要渠道，同时配合开展产品宣传及保单服务。微信公众号作为我司主要的自媒体平台，定期推文、组织线上活动，利用微信自带流量吸引客户，销售公司的保险产品，为建信财险 App 导流。建信财险 App 作为公司客户的聚集平台，要秉承以客户

图 5.37　建行各业务产品

为中心的服务理念，通过提供极致客户服务体验，打造成公司移动端的门户和综合移动金融服务平台，为公司中长期发展目标奠定坚实的基础。在丰富建信财险 App、微信商城保险产品的同时，提供更全面、便捷、智能的保后服务、理赔服务，实现全渠道、全产品布放，快速响应市场。

三是稳步推进与第三方平台的合作。与第三方平台合作不以追求数量、流量为目标，重点营销创新型、效益型互联网公司，借力同时具有互联网基因和保险经验的公司，依靠“产品创新、场景创新”，合作造船驶向蓝海。寻找场景化互联网平台或专业保险代理及经纪机构，开展业务合作，实现共同成长。辅助营销具有客户流量大、知名度高的品牌型互联网公司，按照重点名单制，逐个梳理和寻求合作机会，实现与 60 多家第三方平台客户合作的目标，提升公司品牌效应和行业影响力。通过与渠道方合作第三方平台业务，一方面可以提升公司的整体能力，包括产品、渠道拓展、运营等能力，将成功的经验优化后服务行内客户；另一方面也可以积累客户，通过自助服务、运营活动等引流到自营平台，成为自营客户（见表 5.45）。

表 5.45　2017 年互联网保险创新企业 200 强

排名	企业	业务定位
1	从安保险	国内首家互联网保险公司
2	泰康在线	泰康人寿发起成立的互联网保险公司
3	易安保险	多家公司共同发起设立的互联网保险公司
4	安心保险	“互联网 +” 概念下的首批创新型保险公司
5	大特保	保险特卖平台

（续表）

排名	企业	业务定位
6	小雨伞保险	保险产品特卖销售平台
7	慧择网	一站式互联网保险服务平台
8	大象保险	智能保险顾问平台
9	意时网	保险产品 B2B 分销网络
10	悟空保	专注于 B2B 业务的互联网保险平台
11	灵犀金融—喂小保	车险聚合平台
12	国泰产险	主要经营业务包括车险、财产保险、货物运输险、责任险等
13	宜信博诚保险	提供风险管理、保险咨询、投保服务、查勘理赔等服务
14	盛世大联	保险代理服务平台
15	水滴互助	网络互助保障社群
16	和泰人寿	国内首个互联网寿险公司
17	信美相互	相互保险社
18	最惠保	移动车险比价平台
19	车车车险	一站式车险电商服务平台
20	保准牛	企业保险互联网平台

（二）以互联网场景为切入，丰富互联网保险产品

一是结合建行业务场景，丰富建行业务衍生保险产品，融入建行生态圈。结合建行普惠金融、住房租赁、金融科技三大战略，针对建行特定业务场景和渠道，推出退货运费险、账户保、租房保、抵押保等产品，后期根据公司情况，推出信用保险、保证保险等与建行信贷业务契合度高的保险产品。二是结合互联网保险市场热点，丰富市场需求旺盛的保险产品。在现有热销产品的基础上，推出旅行意外险、女性重大疾病保险、儿童重大疾病保险、老人防癌保险、百万住院医疗保险等在互联网上热度较高的保险产品。三是结合互联网场景特点，丰富互联网新生事物衍生保险产品，推出机动车驾驶培训费用补偿保险、手机碎屏险等产品，同时，结合互联网新生事物的业务机会，探索创新保险产品。

（三）以运营服务为基础，打造极致服务体验

公司的核心客户以建行集团员工及家属、建行集团客户为重点，逐步拓展外部市

场客户。依托保险科技，做好建行渠道客户引流，做好建行补医项目存量客户的促活、留存。建立内容运营、活动运营、用客运营、数据运营的全面运营体系。一是做好内容运营。打造自媒体与外部媒体原创内容，诉诸感性价值打造差异化区隔“引导教育”客户，触达痛点。二是做好活动运营。开展日常活动、新品推广活动、节假日热点活动、跨品牌营销活动等多样性活动形式，驱动客户增长，提升客户活跃度与品牌黏性。三是做好客户运营。搭建客户成长体系，不断优化产品/平台功能，满足客户核心需求与不断变化的新需求，为客户创造新价值，实现客户由“必须用”向“喜欢用”转变；提供适当激励刺激，提高活跃客户贡献度。四是做好数据运营。进行产品全生命周期数据监控和大数据应用。关注产品不同阶段数据和客户行为数据，通过数据分析指导运营决策、驱动业务增长。建立基于互联网大数据平台的精准营销模型，有效利用大数据分析客户行为和客户特点，实现客户分层和精准营销。五是集中精力和资源，将建信财险 App 打造成为一个零售客户的综合移动金融服务平台。为客户提供以风险保障为核心的家联网服务体验、高科技的智能服务体验、形式多样的线上活动体验、全面保险产品的快速投保体验、一体化的保单服务体验、极致的在线理赔服务体验、专业的智能投保顾问体验、丰富金融服务和保险衍生服务的增值体验，为客户提供售前、售中、售后的全流程一体化服务，塑造我司在建行集团内部的互联网品牌，体现我司的互联网基因，成为集团中子公司互联网业务发展的领跑者（见图 5. 38 和图 5. 39）。

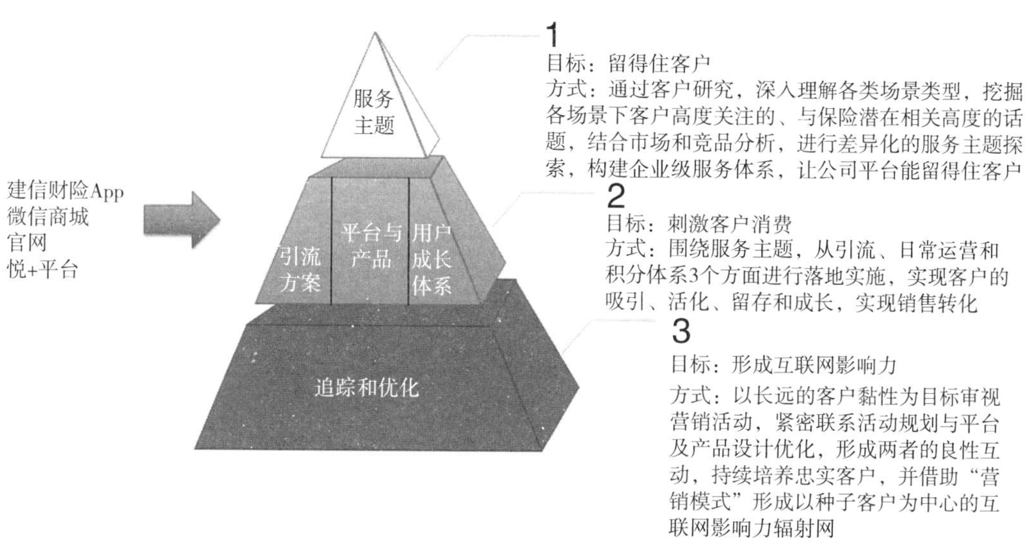

图 5. 38　自营平台运营服务模型

图5.39　建信财险 App 首页设计效果

六、结语

保险在近几年发展势头迅猛，资本争锋逐浪，技术推陈出新，这些因素都在促使保险进行创新。但是由于“保险姓保”的保障特性，使得保险创新如履薄冰，其速度势必不如其他行业。如何在推进“三大战略”落实的大潮中实现自身价值，运用互联网进行保险创新，以客户需求为导向，解决社会痛点，通过产品与价格优势抓住长尾客户，培养客户黏性，错开与传统型保险公司的直接竞争，实现“换道超车”，是目前仍然需要我们重点思考、继续探索的问题。

基于新发展背景的商业银行私人银行业务发展策略探讨

广西区分行　钟　雁

一、绪论

私人银行业务起源于16世纪的欧洲，繁盛于英国和美国，并逐渐扩展至亚洲地区。私人银行业务以高净值客户为服务对象，金融机构从客户多样化需求出发，以资产管理为核心，为其提供专业的财富管理服务。我国私人银行业务起步于2007年，近年来，我国居民财富总量与财富集中程度日渐提升，高净值资产人士数量与个人可投资资产总额也逐渐增多。2007—2017年，中资商业银行私人银行客户总量已经达到了50万，客户资产总量将近8万亿元[①]。我国商业银行私人银行业发展迅速。

如今，私人银行业务对于提高商业银行利润与银行综合竞争力等具有重要作用。格拉迪丝（D. B. Gladys，2000）认为私人银行业务可以迎合金融市场的发展趋势，银行利润未来将主要来源于私人银行业务[②]。20世纪初，意大利经济学家帕累托提出了“二八定律”，揭示了总体中20%的重要性，剩余的80%的次要性。二八定律具有普遍适用性，未来随着私人银行业务的逐渐发展，高净值客户虽然只是银行客户中的少数，但他们能给银行带来的利润会占银行收益的一大半。

然而，我国商业银行在发展私人银行业务过程中遇到瓶颈，难以满足日益增长的私人银行业务和多元化需求。尽管国内学者已经对我国私人银行业务的发展进行了较多问题与方法上的理论探讨，但在新时期下，私人银行客户特质有所变化、客户需求多元化发展的同时倾向性需求发生变化、金融科技化进程不断加快、境外投资规模增长、资管新规出台给私人银行业务带来新问题等，私人银行业务发展背景呈现新特点。

① 资料来源：正月．中国私人银行十年［J］．IT经理世界，2017（11）．

② 资料来源：D. B. Gladys. Successful organizational change-evolution and revolution in the organization［J］．Journal of bank Research，2000，13（1）：13 - 24.

因此，根据新时期私人银行业务的新背景，与时俱进地分析如何发展商业银行私人银行业务，具有重要的理论和现实意义。

二、商业银行私人银行业务发展现状分析——机遇与挑战并存

（一）高净值客户数量与可投资资产规模增长迅速

2006—2017 年，我国高净值人群数量与高净值人群个人可投资资产总量均增长迅速。2016 年，私人银行客户中可投资资产达到 1 000 万元人民币以上的为 158 万人。2016 年，高净值人群个人可投资资产规模已经达到 165 万亿元，2014—2016 年 3 年间，高净值客户年平均复合增长率已经达到 21%（见图 5. 40 和图 5. 41）。

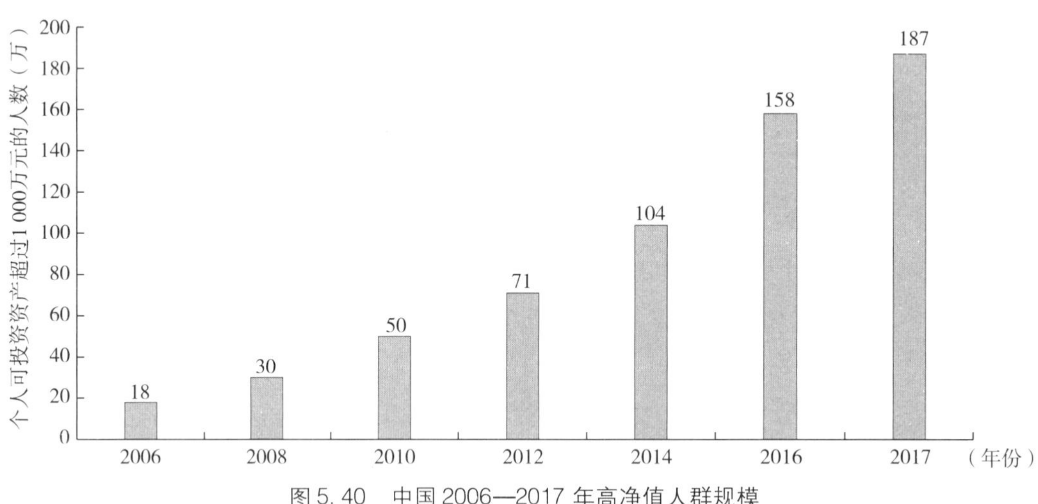

图 5. 40　中国 2006—2017 年高净值人群规模

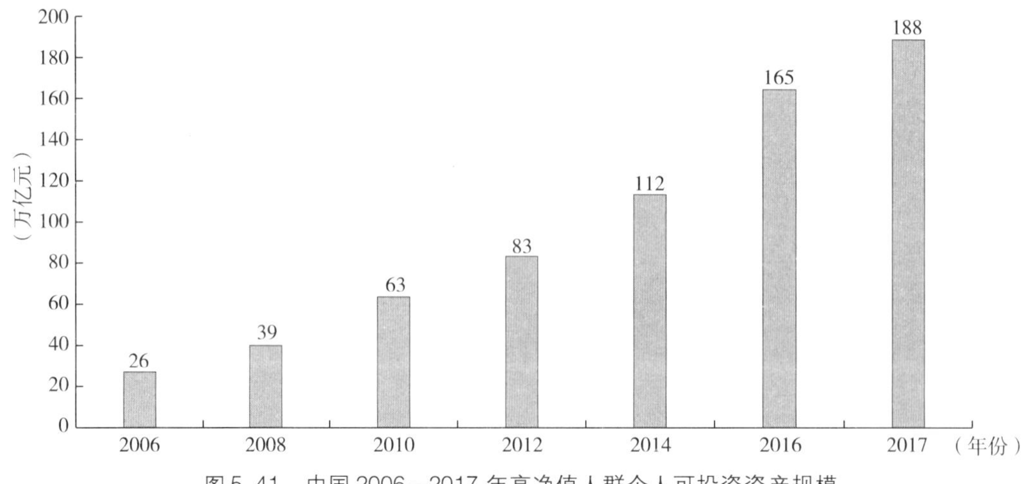

图 5. 41　中国 2006—2017 年高净值人群个人可投资资产规模

（二）高净值客户年龄结构变化引起风险偏好提高

2015—2017 年，兴业银行和波士顿咨询每年对相当数量的高净值客户进行采访调研，发现 21 ~ 39 岁客户的比重在上升，40 ~ 60 岁客户的比重有所下降。中国的高净值客户中，40 ~ 59 岁年龄阶段的客户仍占主体，但年轻客户慢慢成为重要组成部分，他们有较高的风险承受意愿，意味着高净值客户整体的风险偏好有所提高（见图 5.42）。

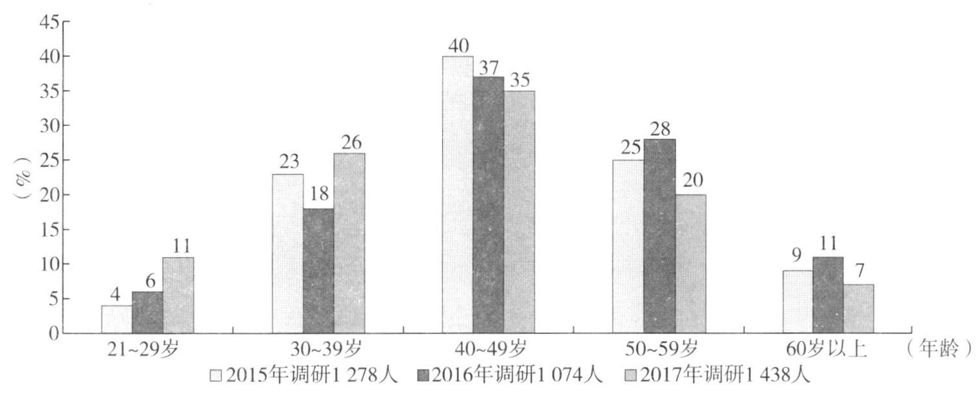

图 5.42　高净值受访者的年龄分布

（三）高净值客户需求多元化与需求倾向性

2009 年，创造更多财富与高品质生活是大部分高净值客户考虑的财富管理目标。但是 2011—2017 年以来，创造更多财富这一目标渐渐被淡化，高净值客户开始较多提及个人资产的安全性、延续性以及家庭子女的教育，这三者成为排名前 3 的目标，而“创造更多财富”的关注度则降低了（见图 5.43）。

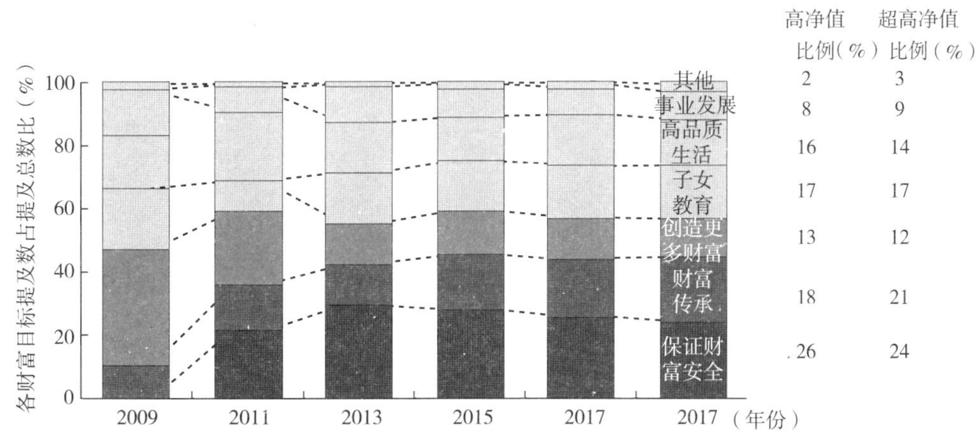

图 5.43　2009—2017 年中国高净值人群财富目标对比

资料来源：招商银行与贝恩公司《2017 中国私人财富报告》。

（四）高净值客户期待“金融科技”和数字化革新

随着科技的发展、大数据时代的到来，中国高净值客户对“金融科技”和数字化革新的期待值增加了。据《2017 中国私人财富报告》统计，高净值客户受访者期待出现数字化的私人银行，希望数字化的私人银行能提供个性化服务。也有受访者期望智能托管与投资策略实时跟踪服务能尽快到来。同时，较多受访者希望从各种创新渠道实时了解专家解读与投资建议，实时把控投资方向（见图 5.44）。

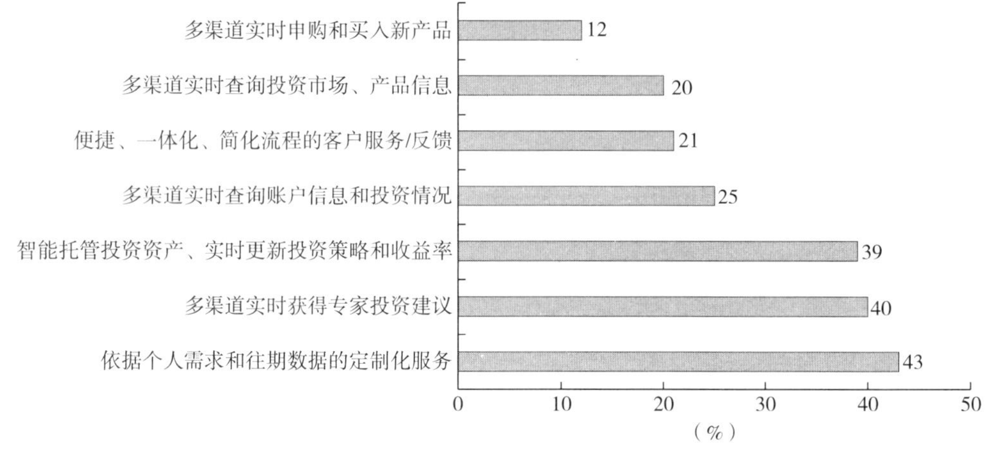

图 5.44　2017 年中国高净值人群对基于“金融科技”创新的各类业务模式的期待

（五）高净值客户海外资产配置意愿增强

招商银行与贝恩公司的调研数据表明，拥有境外配置资产的高净值人士比例上升较快。大多数客户的境外投资目的为分散风险，将近一半私人银行客户的目的在于寻求境外市场投资机会。但境外市场对于客户来说较为陌生，投资品种仅限于简单品种，复杂结构产品投资较少。数据说明，我国高净值客户境外资产配置的需求与意愿增强。

（六）非私人银行机构竞争

近年来，由于高净值客户市场的兴起，不仅商业银行开始重视私人银行业务的布局，而且金融市场中有越来越多的机构开始与商业银行抢夺高净值客户资源，不遗余力地发展私人银行业务。证券、保险、独立理财机构等第三方机构，开始组建专业的人才梯队，充分发挥自身优势吸引高净值客户，对商业银行私人银行业务形成极大威胁。

三、商业银行私人银行业务发展过程中存在的问题

（一）投资领域有限

调查显示，目前私人银行客户投资领域多样化，不仅局限于商业银行存款产品、理财产品等，还涉及其他非金融投资领域。但“分业经营、分业监管”的规定阻碍了我国商业银行的业务领域，不能实现多领域的金融业务种类的上线。投资领域的局限性，让商业银行难以实现高净值客户各式各样的投资目标，不利于商业银行全方位提供金融服务。

（二）产品与服务同质化

一直以来，我国商业银行缺乏金融创新意识与动力，产品与服务多为标准化，模式较为单一，存在严重的同质化问题。然而，不同高净值客户有着不同的投资风险偏好与不同的财富管理需求，导致单一的产品无法进行个性化的需求匹配。在服务方面，商业银行传统零售业务以销售产品为主，对客户信息的收集与需求的分析存在较严重的短板，而私人银行业务区别于一般业务之处在于，其是根据对客户的了解进行客户细化分类，再提供定制化服务。

（三）海外资产配置能力不足

我国银行业的全球化进程仍较为缓慢，商业银行跨境投资能力有限。然而，私人银行业务与普通财富管理的不同之处在于，前者能对客户资产做境外投资。但因为我国特殊的外汇管理体制，客户资产面临难以外出的局面。随着我国高净值客户境外投资意愿的增强，如果商业银行不能在海外资产配置上有所突破，将不能与时俱进地满足高净值客户需求。

（四）人才队伍参差不齐

目前，我国商业银行私人银行组织模式千篇一律，大多数采用层级管理模式。直接与客户接触的、最熟悉客户的网点零售业务客户经理学历较低，财富管理理论与实践经验不足；在管理层级的私人银行团队中，专业人才可能只局限于某个领域。但为客户提供综合金融服务需要涉及金融、法律等方方面面的学识与视野。

（五）私人银行金融科技化进程缓慢

在大数据时代背景下，越来越多的高净值客户期待金融科技化与数字化革命，但

我国商业银行私人银行金融科技化进程缓慢，客户拓展在很大程度上仍依赖于客户经理的上门拜访与柜台营销，这种传统的方式弊端明显，且无法迎合客户需求。即使目前各大商业银行手机银行、网上银行、电话银行等电子银行普及率越来越高，但针对私人银行进行专门开发的功能仍然稀缺。

四、关于商业银行私人银行业务发展的对策建议

面对目前我国商业银行私人银行发展面临的机遇与挑战，以及当前存在的问题，该如何解决发展困境，直面挑战，抓住机遇？我从以下几个方面提出了一些建议。

（一）加强与第三方机构合作，强强联合

针对展业约束问题，商业银行可以联合第三方机构，优势互补，共同合作，突破投资领域局限性。例如，针对逐渐凸显的财富传承需求，目前国内家族信托业务处于初探阶段，境内商业银行要借助第三方机构，以客户多样性需求为出发点，在产品设计、投资策略方面发挥商业银行和信托公司的自身优势，不断满足高净值客户在境内延续资产的目的。又如，针对家庭教育问题，除了为客户规划教育资金外，可以与海外留学机构、教育机构合作，为客户提供最专业的咨询服务。通过强强联合，扬长避短，商业银行可为客户提供最全面最优质的专属服务，在一定程度上解决展业约束问题。

（二）丰富产品体系与提供定制化服务

面对拥有不同风险偏好的客户，商业银行应建立丰富的产品体系，满足客户不同财富管理目的。除了银行自身要不断对私人银行存款产品、理财产品进行创新研发，增补产品种类外，还要通过科学的筛选，精选优质基金、保险、信托产品、增值类服务，为高净值客户提供一站式产品营销。同时，私人银行客户经理应注意收集客户信息，将需求信息有效传递到私人银行团队。通过细分客户群体，分析客户特征，私人银行团队方可为高净值客户制定专属综合财富规划书与提供专属增值服务。

（三）创建境外投资平台

面对高净值客户境外投资意愿的增强，商业银行可以选择在境内客户比较热衷的投资地区建立分支机构、并购当地公司或者与当地机构进行合作等，借助境外机构搭建境外投资平台，弥补自身在海外投资能力不足的弱点。

（四）人才队伍“术业有专攻”

术业有专攻，基层网点员工与私人银行客户距离最近、关系最亲密，是私人银行

客户最信赖的群体，掌握着客户的最真实情况与最核心诉求。而后台核心私人银行团队是最终私人银行产品与服务的制定者。为了加强队伍建设，一方面，商业银行要强化对一线私人银行客户经理的专业培训，从客户信息收集、客户关系维护等方面提升其专业能力；另一方面，引进不同领域的专业人才，如金融、法律、保险等领域的专家，构建后台核心私人银行团队，完善人才体系。如此，让一线客户经理与后台核心团队发挥各自专业特长，上下进行信息的有效传递，为私人银行客户提供最优质高效的服务。

（五）加快私人银行业务科技化进程

私人银行业务的发展离不开对科技的应用。面对高净值客户对金融科技与数字化革命的期待，商业银行应加大研发力度，借助科技的手段，利用互联网合作平台、电子银行等渠道，结合大数据分析，细化客户群体，分析客户特征，利用平台向客户传达和推送最符合需求的产品与服务信息，以提供高效专享服务。

建设银行服务经济高质量发展的六大战略方向

总行战略与政策协调部　许秋起　刘志勇

十九大后，依托质量变革、效率变革与动力变革，中国经济从高速增长阶段转向高质量发展阶段，其发展方式、经济结构、产业体系、空间布局等都将发生重大变化。高质量发展将为商业银行打开新一轮增长空间，同时也为其业务存量结构调整带来一定压力。新阶段实体经济结构调整，金融开启下行周期，金融风险结构演进也将呈现新的特点，商业银行把控风险底线面临一定挑战。在新阶段化解人民日益增长的美好生活需要和不平衡不充分发展之间的矛盾，实现经济社会和谐、均衡发展，作为大型营利性企业，建设银行社会责任更重，其传统企业目标需要适度调整。在新阶段科技进步成为创新驱动战略的主角，科技对金融业态、银行业务经营、管理模式影响日深，金融科技与相关人才将成为影响市场竞争力的核心因素之一。

鉴于高质量发展阶段的上述重大变化，同时紧紧围绕金融业“服务实体经济、防控金融风险、深化金融改革”三项任务，我们提出了未来几年建行发展的六大战略方向。

一、聚焦现代化产业体系建设，“调存量”与“保增量”均衡发展

经济转向高质量发展阶段，也是中国产业体系调整、转型、升级的现代化建设阶段。三次产业、产业内部行业产值、投资结构处于持续调整过程，动能转化、经济分化成为重要特征。第三产业尤其是高技术服务业、新型城镇化、基础设施建设、消费升级领域、民生短板领域投资将持续高增长；制造业2025发展战略加快推进，工业结构调整、优化、升级，工业战略性新兴产业、高技术制造业等新动能占比不断提升，传统工业领域将加大技改投资力度。这些将成为我国经济持续健康平稳发展的有力因素，也会持续创造新的金融服务需求，为商业银行带来新的业务拓展空间。同时，传统产能过剩、低技术含量与附加值、高耗能、高污染行业亦将面临阶段性压缩，对银行相关业务存量调整带来一定挑战（见图5.45、图5.46、图5.47）。

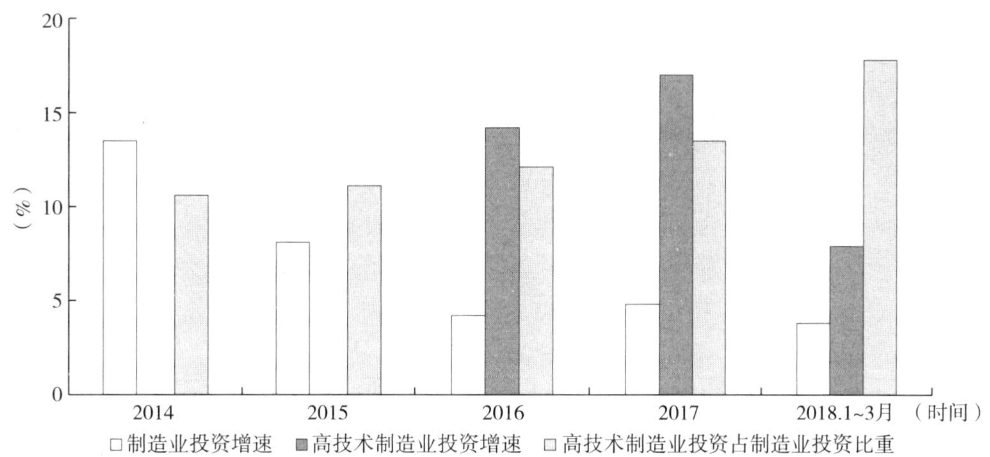

图 5.45　近年来制造业、高技术制造业投资增幅与占比走势

注：2017 年高技术制造业对制造业投资增长贡献率高达 43%，其中，通信设备制造业投资增长 46.4%，锂电池制造业投资增长 44.4%，工业自控系统装置制造业投资增长 29%，集成电路制造业投资增长 27.2%。

资料来源：万得资讯，据历年统计公报整理。

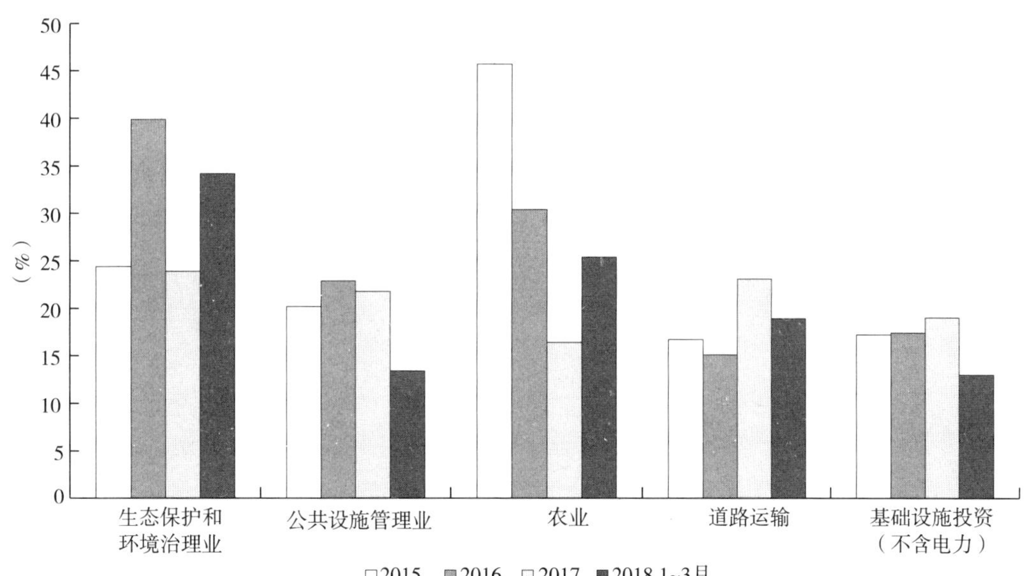

图 5.46　补短板领域近年来投资增长态势

注：2017 年社会领域投资增长 17.2%，比全部投资增速高 10 个百分点。

资料来源：国家统计局，据历年统计公报整理。

建议建行聚焦现代化产业体系建设，通盘考虑“调存量”与“保增量”，实现对公业务均衡一体化发展。一方面，加快升级金融服务，拓展新结构、新动能领域增长空间。稳步提升对战略性新兴产业、高技术制造业、先进技术服务业领域的融资比重，利用好基金、并购、投贷联动等多元化投融资手段，主动为客户提供创新产品和服务。

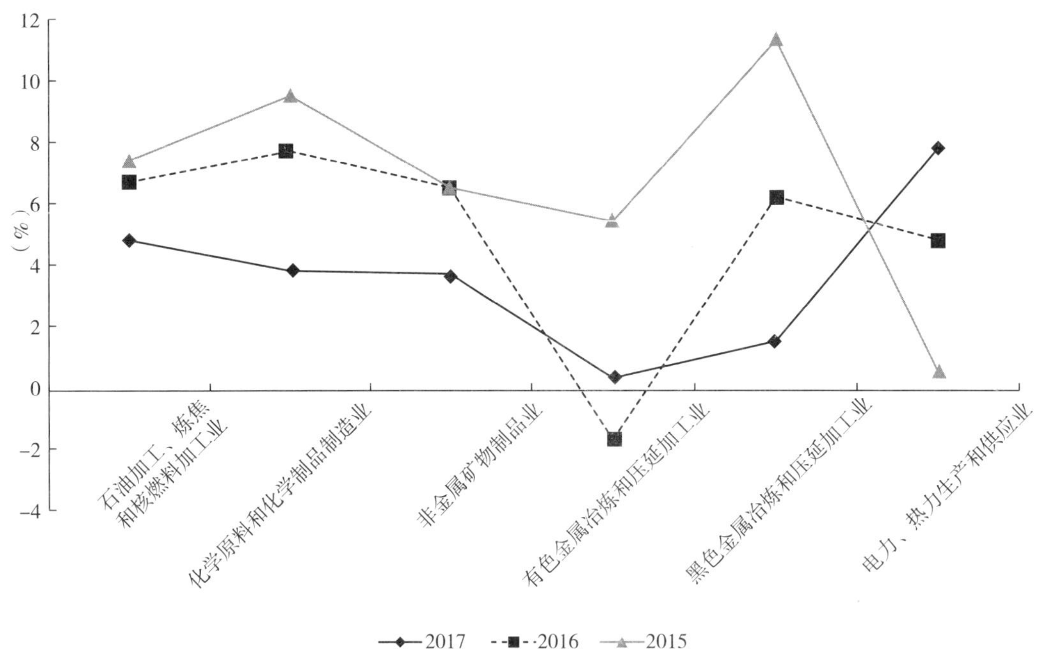

图5.47　六大高耗能、高污染行业近年来产值增速

注：2017年六大高耗能行业增加值增长3.0%，占规模以上工业增加值的比重为29.7%，投资下降1.8%，占固定资产投资（不含农户）的比重为10.2%。

资料来源：万得资讯。

聚焦绿色金融领域，加强对环境治理、绿色产业一体化等绿色新兴领域的研究和业务拓展。重点抓好重大基础设施区域一体化建设、城市地下管网、道路、通信、信息等网络联通工程项目。把握教育、医疗、旅游等消费升级领域对金融服务需求的最新态势。另一方面，严控高耗能、高污染行业，产能利用率较低、不良率较高的采矿业，黑色、有色金属冶炼，非金属矿物制品等行业融资额度，妥善处理相关行业僵尸企业的存量资产。

二、坚持优先发展零售业务战略

近年来，伴随中国经济增长动力转向更为贴近人民生活的消费、第三产业，居民收入水平、可投资金融资产持续提高，金融科技快速发展，零售业务不断取得新突破，成为商业银行稳健经营的主导力量。尽管当前商业银行零售负债市场竞争格局正在快速重构，传统营销模式正在被金融科技全面颠覆，但总体来看，零售业务发展机遇明显大于挑战。未来几年内，坚持优先发展零售业务仍是商业银行的主导发展战略之一。

从发展机遇来看，十九大后化解新的社会矛盾，满足人民群众快速增长的美好生活需求，消费和服务业成为拉动内需的主要动力。随着经济转向高质量发展，目前城乡居民可支配收入稳步提高，消费意愿良好，高净值人群数量、个人持有的可投资资产规模呈现持续上升态势，零售业务发展的宏观环境继续向好。从客户结构看，18～35 岁的新一代消费者成为国内市场的主导消费力量，其消费能力是 35 岁以上消费者的两倍多，网购增速快速增长与此密切相关，客户需求真正迈入了消费时代（见图 5.48 和图 5.49）。

从面临的挑战来看，客户需求正在由“储蓄时代”迈入“消费时代”，对零售负债业务发展形成强大压力。2010—2017 年，国内储蓄存款余额与同期个人贷款余额比值持续下降，由 2.8 逐步降至 1.6 以下，近期居民储蓄增长率转为负值。同时，商业银行的支付、投资、消费业务的传统盈利模式、获客能力、传统信用中介地位也面临着金融科技企业的强烈冲击。

从建行零售业务的发展态势来看，服务实体经济和民生的广度、深度不断提升，连续 3 年荣获“中国最佳大型零售银行奖”，成为同业竞争的领跑者。2017 年年末，建行服务个人客户已经超过 6 亿人，个人商户 300 万户左右，保有的个人客户金融资产超过 10 万亿元，零售贷款余额突破 5 万亿元，银行卡发行额近 10 亿张，个人人民币存款、零售贷款和零售中间业务收入全行占比分别达 47%、46% 和 50% 以上，零售业务的支柱性作用日益巩固。

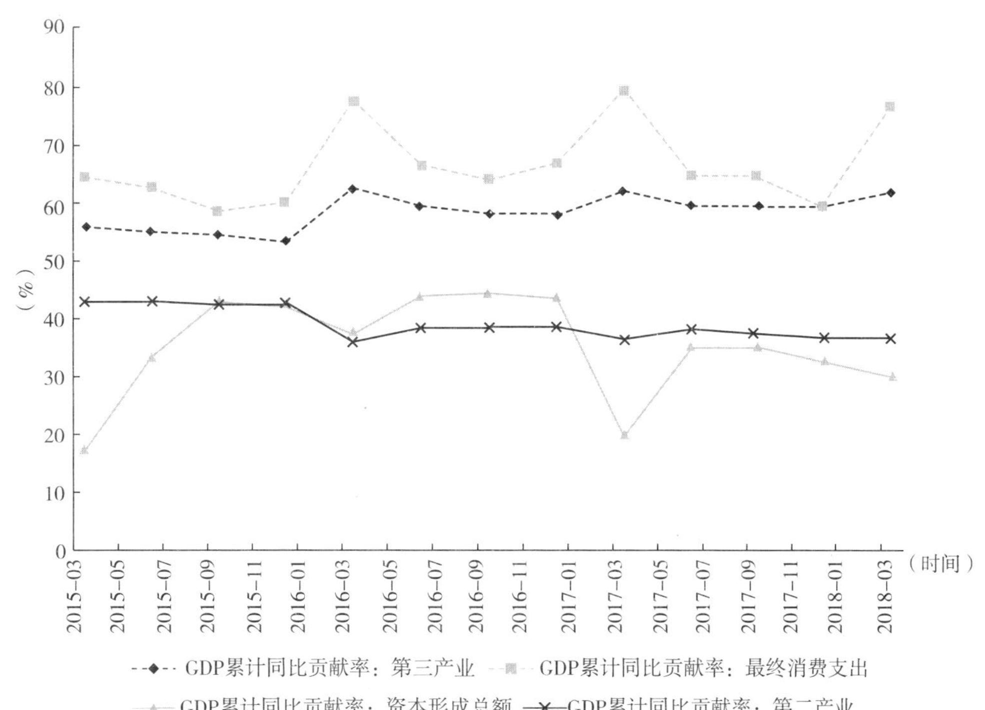

图 5.48　中国经济增长动力结构变动趋势

注：中国经济供需两侧结构持续调整，从需求侧来看，转向内生性需求大国，消费对经济增长的贡献稳中有升；从供给侧看，吸纳就业能力较强的服务业对经济增长的贡献持续上升。

资料来源：万得资讯。

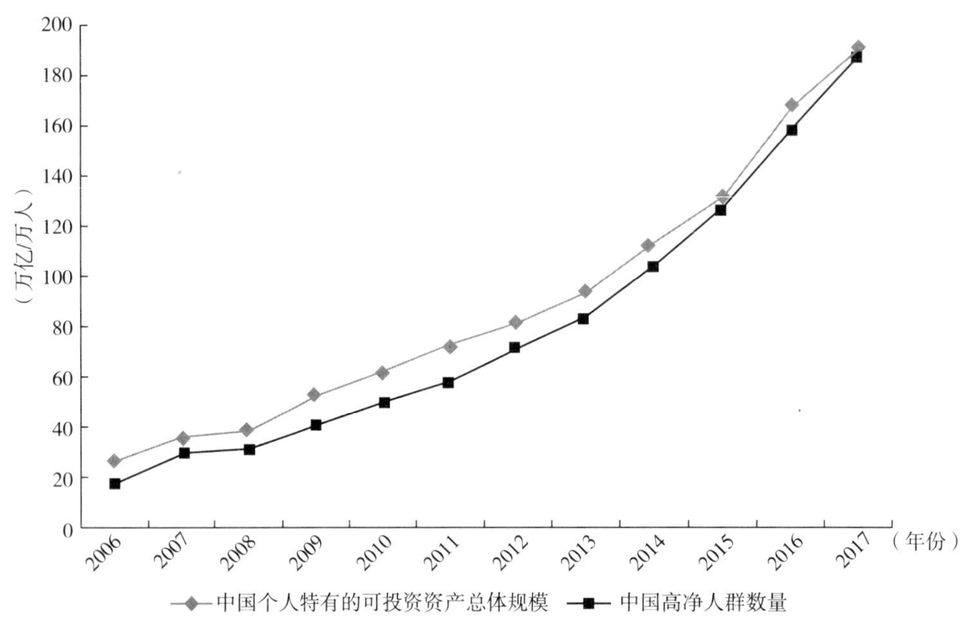

图 5.49　个人持有的可投资资产总体规模与高净值人群数量（2006—2017）

注：2017 年中国个人持有的可投资资产总体规模为 188 万亿元，高净值人群数量为 187 万人，分别是 2016 年的 7.34 倍与 10.33 倍。

资料来源：万得资讯。

当前和未来几年，零售优先战略既是保持建行竞争能力的重要支柱，又是全行改革和发展坚持的大方向。建议全面把握新时代零售业务发展机遇，突破投资理财、消费信贷和支付结算等零售业务基础性金融服务，快速拓展社保医疗、文化教育、社区服务、生活缴费和县域等民生领域金融需求热点，同时加快金融科技布局，加快产品创新，由“渠道为王”转向“客户关系为王”，重视零售业务发展的网点优势，创新体制机制，加大资源投入，切实落实零售优先战略。

三、适度调整目标定位，彰显大行社会责任担当

高质量发展不仅是经济的高质量发展，更是在五大发展理念指导下的全方位发展，其难处在于解决包括经济、社会、生态、城乡、区域等诸多领域发展的不平衡、不充分问题。而这些问题（包括精准扶贫、三农、小微企业融资、居民住房改善等）又多为社会痛点问题，单靠政府力量远远不够。营利性企业同时做公益，更多地承担社会责任不仅是时代担当，更有企业的“剩余风险”理论支撑：承担企业最后风险（合同外的风险）的并不仅仅是企业所有者、股东，还有所有的员工、社区，甚至整个社会，企业不能只向股东负责，也要向供应商、销售商甚至整个社会负责。作为大型营利性金融企业，建行理应适度调整经营目标定位，向营利性社会企业转型，彰显大行的社

会责任担当。

从现阶段来看，包括发展住房租赁业务、金融精准扶贫、小微企业融资、“三农”融资、社会短板领域项目融资等在内的普惠金融服务，成为金融企业承担社会责任的重要内容。建议建行稳妥处理好企业盈利与金融普惠业务之间的关系，在提升担当社会责任能力的同时，实现自身健康可持续发展。

一是全力推进住房租赁服务创新，推动租购并举住房制度建设。依托已构建的住房服务生态圈，不断创新产品和服务，以租赁住房管理和监测平台为切入点，不断拓展服务智慧城市建设的新领域。

二是探索符合小微客户成长规律、信贷金额期限特点、信用和风险特征的普惠金融模式。

三是支持善融商务电商扶贫系列活动，鼓励分行用好善融商务平台，衔接好供需两端，积极支持贫困地区发展。

四是调整 KPI 考核内容和考核机制，落实党的十九大精神和总行党委要求，设置“社会责任”指标，突出对普惠金融业务指标的考核。

五是加快创新覆盖普惠金融客户群体的产品体系，搭建包括普惠金融特色网点、电子渠道、移动渠道在内的立体渠道网络。

四、主动实施全方位风险管理模式

十九大以来，随着宏观环境稳中向好以及经济结构调整效果进一步显现，近期商业银行资产质量呈现企稳向好态势，但现阶段我国经济正处在转变发展方式、优化经济结构、转换增长动力的攻关期，随着经济转向高质量发展、金融转入下行周期，未来几年以信用风险为焦点的各类风险仍较为复杂，预计会在局部行业、企业、区域等特定领域暴露出来（见图 5.50 和表 5.46）。

经济转向高质量发展过程中，经济调整分化导致的信用风险压力并未减弱。深化供给侧结构性改革促使僵尸企业、信贷过于集中的一些快速发展的跨行业大中型企业信用风险加快释放。部分产能过剩的高污染、高耗能行业的信贷存量大额风险还将继续释放，一些批发零售、制造业等周期性更强的行业的信用风险也会持续爆发一段时间。房地产市场缩量调整对商业银行资产质量平稳运行也存在一定影响。产业结构老化、升级缓慢、经济增速不振的东北和中西部内陆地区信贷风险尚在释放中。

监管新规落地对商业银行经营风险的影响相当复杂。严禁资产期限错配、实行净值管理、打破刚兑、大量的表外资产业务接回家等新变化不单是资产结构调整问题，商业银行还会面临资金的衔接、客户融资转换风险、中小金融机构的风险导入等系列风险管理问题。

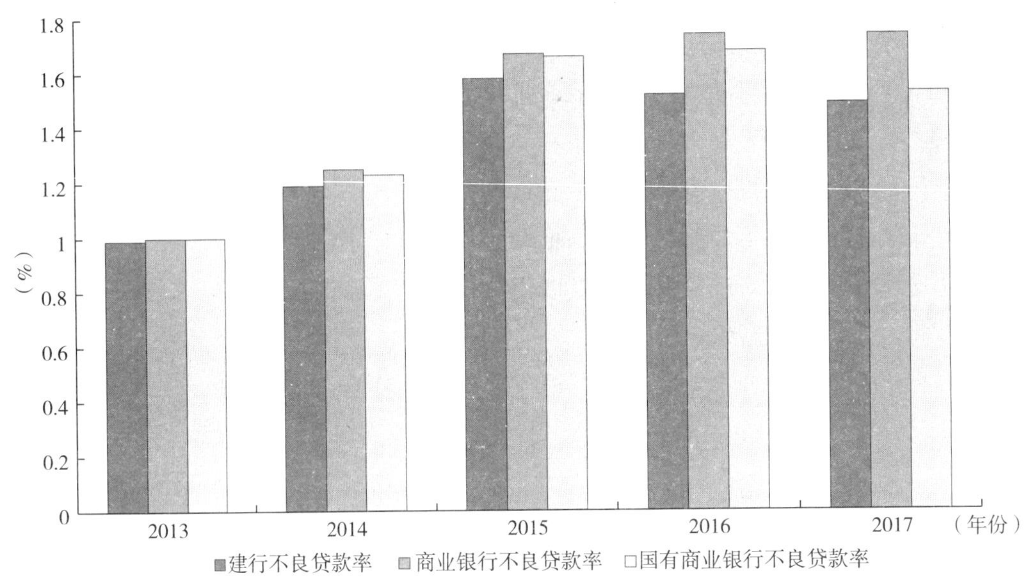

图5.50　近年来商业银行不良贷款率变动情况

资料来源：万得资讯，银监会网站。

表5.46　近两年建行不良较高领域分布情况

领域	2017年12月31日		2016年12月31日	
	不良率（%）	不良额（百万元）	不良率（%）	不良额（百万元）
公司类贷款和垫款	2.58	166 044	2.6	152 323
短期贷款	3.93	80 638	5.18	92 547
中长期贷款	1.94	85 406	1.47	59 776
个人助业贷款	4.45	1 620	4.54	2 106
制造业	6.36	75 000	5.92	69 764
批发和零售业	7.69	33 564	9.01	37 016
房地产业	2.23	9 236	2.53	8 652
建筑业	2.59	6 549	3.13	7 402
采矿业	5.22	11 625	5.1	11 040

资料来源：中国建设银行年报。

境内外合规、反洗钱风险处于上升期。当前违规经营案件从柜面延伸到了信贷、资管和同业领域，基层机构负责人案件多发。境外合规风险也开始暴露，洗钱风险正成为国际国内高度关注的热点问题。随着金融新业态、新产品、新业务的不断涌现，非法集资、走私诈骗等违法活动借助新渠道卷土重来，未来一段时间反洗钱工作面临的挑战越来越大。

建议建行主动推动风险管理模式转型，建立以战略为导向、以精细化管理工具为手段的全面风险管理体系。

一是未来一段时间内把信用风险防范作为全行主抓重点工作。针对上述特定风险领域，把好出口和入口，持续优化信贷投放结构。持续完善信贷常态化和长效化管理机制，力争押品、放款、贷后“三项专业化建设”取得新成效。

二是持续强化审慎的流动性风险管理。进一步强化集团流动性集中统一管理，明确海外机构、子公司、资管中心对自身流动性管理负主体责任，在集团统一风险偏好和管理架构下，切实健全流动性管理的制度和流程。

三是重点加强对跨市场、跨行业、跨境交叉传染和导入风险的研判和预控。

四是加快构建清晰、统一的合规管理框架与案防体系，高度重视反洗钱风险管理。

五、实施金融科技战略，确保竞争优势

颠覆式金融科技已成为全球领先银行的重大战略性布局。麦肯锡对全球100家领先银行的调研显示：52%的银行与金融科技公司有合作关系，37%的银行采用风投或私募的形式布局金融科技。例如，花旗银行于2010年设立了花旗风投（Citi Venture），密切关注并投资大数据、电商与支付、金融服务、安全与IT这四大金融科技领域（见表5.47）。

表5.47　多种形式的金融科技布局

金融科技布局形式	银行
开展跨机构和行业合作，探索改造商业银行服务模式	摩根大通、渣打银行
与初创公司联合，针对从无到有的颠覆式创新概念进行孵化，加速全新业务的成果转化	巴克莱银行、西太平洋银行、渣打银行
购买金融科技公司服务，改善内部业务和流程的“痛点”	花旗银行、富国银行、桑坦德银行
投资或并购具有领先技术、创新理念的初创公司，快速提升科技创新能力	摩根大通、西班牙对外银行

近年来，国内银行也纷纷拥抱金融科技。大型银行与互联网金融巨头相继牵手（见表5.48），2017年工商银行、招商银行、建设银行、中信银行、浦发银行、华夏银行分别与腾讯达成了战略合作，工商银行、中国银行、中信银行、交通银行、民生银行和兴业银行则分别与阿里巴巴展开合作。

除跨界合作外，国内银行还通过组建金融公司的方式拥抱金融科技。兴业银行的“数金云”能提供人工智能云服务、区块链云服务、备份云服务、容灾云服务、专属云服务和金融组件云服务6个品类的基础云服务；平安集团的平安科技，多年来服务集团及各子公司，后向外输出；招商银行也着手打造金融云，其“招银云创”走定制化

表 5.48　四大行与互联网金融巨头合作的主要内容

银行	合作对象	合作的主要内容
建设银行	蚂蚁金服	支付
工商银行	京东	金融科技、消费金融、企业信贷、校园生态等领域
农业银行	百度	金融科技
中国银行	腾讯	在云计算、大数据、区块链和人工智能的合作基础上搭建金融科技云平台

路线，金融云不局限于 IT 服务，还包括金融业务。正式亮相的建设银行旗下的建信金融科技有限责任公司，则是从战略层面主动拥抱金融科技。

未来几年内，把握新技术快速改变金融服务方式与格局的大趋势，加快金融科技与业务融合发展，不仅是保持同业竞争优势的重大战略，也是其他发展战略得以实施的根本保障。建议建行一是把握金融科技发展方向，持续抢占金融科技发展的制高点，继续加大信息技术的投入，加强科技人才队伍的建设，确保建行在云计算、大数据、物联网、人工智能、区块链等新技术创新应用领域始终居于行业前列。

二是加强业务与技术的融合。优化金融科技与银行业务的互相渗透、互相促进、螺旋上升的良性机制，推动建行运用新技术、新工具创新金融产品，开发业务新模式。借助金融科技，在客户服务、产品设计、运营模式等多个领域，为客户提供更加快速、准确的个性化服务，同时降低服务成本、提升业务效率、管控业务风险。

三是建立并不断完善在全行范围内持续推进金融科技集成应用的机制，推动新一代核心系统在全行的推广应用。金融科技战略是全行共同的事情，在分行层面，进一步组织分行应用新一代系统进行优秀案例推广；在总行层面，重点抓好企业级应用项目的研究开发。最终形成一套从项目创意提出、需求设计、系统开发，到维护优化的全行全方位积极参与金融科技应用的激励体系，尤其是 KPI 考核要增加推动科技金融创新业务落地的相关内容。

四是探索建行金融科技人才培养模式。依托规划中的上海金融培训学院（拟），利用上海开发中心和上海数据分析中心技术优势，设立中国建设银行科技人才培养基地。

六、优化人才工作政策制度，实施“人才兴行”战略

人才是推动高质量发展的第一资源。在新阶段实施“人才兴行”战略不仅是建设银行发展战略优化调整的重要组成部分，更是深化改革增添新一轮发展动力的重要内容。配合经济转型、业务调整，不断优化建行人才工作政策制度，造就一支适合高质量发展的人才队伍尤其重要。

建议建行持续优化人才工作政策制度，加快实施“人才兴行”战略。一是改进人才工作考核办法，加快成立各部门、分行人才工作领导小组，实施“一把手”组长负

责制，将人才工作列为落实党建工作责任制的重要内容。

二是加大重点领域人才培养和引进力度。采取多种形式加强金融科技、金融数据分析、网络金融、投资银行、风险管理等新兴和紧缺领域的人才培养；紧扣全行重大战略部署和重点业务人才需求，实行更积极有效的人才引进政策，加大“高精新缺”人才引进力度，对具有世界一流或国内顶尖水平的高层次人才及团队，实行“一事一议”的特殊政策。

三是积极开展人才培训工作。坚持“干什么学什么，缺什么补什么”的原则，有的放矢地开发教育培训项目、设计教育培训课程、创新教育培训模式、评价教育培训效果。

四是优化完善人才评价机制。结合建设银行实际，借助大数据分析，研究建行人才评价指标，开发人才测评工具和方法，建立并不断完善人才评价标准。

五是优化薪酬、福利、荣誉等多元化激励制度。在全行营造多劳多得、少劳少得、不劳不得的绩效考核分配文化，让价值创造者获得有效激励和保障。建立包括荣誉称号、奖金、奖品、休假疗养等多层次、多元化的奖励体系，加大人才表彰奖励力度。

六是提高专业人才管理水平。鼓励高素质专业技术人才通过提升专业技术能力晋升专业技术职务。适度加大战略与新兴业务领域客户经理、产品经理、风险经理等专业人才的聘任力度，对替代成本较高的资金交易、信息科技、风险计量等领域的人才专业技术职务聘任给予一定程度的倾斜。

三大战略助力旅游市场拓展策略研究

山东省分行　楚　栋

近年来，随着各种鼓励政策的不断推出，中国旅游业发展迅速，已成为国民经济增长最快的产业之一。党的十九大工作报告中指出："我国社会主要矛盾已经转化为人民日益增长的美好生活需要和不平衡不充分的发展之间的矛盾。"这一科学论断，对旅游产业的发展具有重要意义。旅游产业作为朝阳产业、绿色产业，更是服务人民美好生活的事业，必将迎来新一轮的快速、高质量发展。运用新一代工具优势，将"三大战略"与旅游产业进行有机结合，借力旅游产业的发展，促进建行业务提升，具有重要的现实意义。

一、旅游产业概况

（一）旅游产业发展情况

近年来，我国旅游业发展迅速，2017 年国内旅游总人数约 50 亿人次，同比增速 12.8%；当年旅游收入 5.40 万亿元，同比增速 15.1%；旅游产业对国内生产总值的综合贡献达 9.13 万亿元，占国内生产总值的 11.04%；旅游业直接就业达到 2 825 万人，间接拉动了 5 165 万人[①]。可以看出，旅游产业在国民经济中的作用已日渐显现（见图 5.51）。

（二）旅游产业参与主体

旅游业是一个完整的经济体系结构，由"食住行游购娱"等紧密相连的产业链组成。围绕这六大板块，旅游产业涵盖了众多的市场参与主体，主要有以下几类：

---

① 资料来源：王思思.2017 年国内旅游超 50 亿人次，旅游收入逾 5 万亿［EB/OL］，http：//news.163.com/18/0206/20/DA06C71500018AOR.html，2018－02－06.

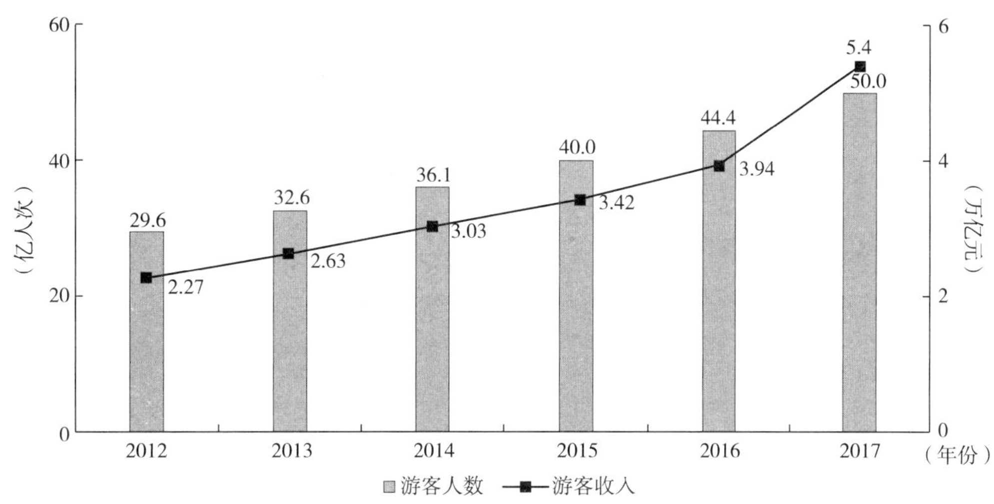

图 5.51　2012—2017 年国内旅游市场统计情况

资料来源：国家旅游局。

1. 政府

旅游产业的健康发展，离不开政府的扶持、管理和监督。在整个旅游产业中，政府扮演着推动者、管理者、监督者的角色。目前全国层面的旅游产业主管单位是国家文化和旅游部，在各省市主要是由各级旅游发展委员会或旅游局负责。

2. 旅游景区

旅游景区在整个旅游产业链条中处于最重要的地位，是旅游产业链条的辐射带动中心。旅游景区对游客的吸引力，直接决定了整个“食住行游购娱”链条的竞争力。优质的旅游景区如 5A 级景区，因其稀缺性，是一种宝贵的资源，值得建行加大投入，全力拓展。截至 2018 年 10 月，我国 5A 级旅游景区共计 258 家，其中江苏、河南、四川 3 省最多，分别为 23 家、17 家、13 家（见图 5.52）。①

3. 宾馆、饭店

宾馆和饭店作为旅游产业的配套单元，在一些旅游城市，其效益受淡旺季影响较大。淡季时，有可能因游客较少，出现门可罗雀的情况，急需寻找新的增收点。

4. 旅行社、导游

旅行社和导游在旅游产业中处在中间环节，充当了中介和服务者的角色。据不完

① 资料来源：百度百科．中华人民共和国国家旅游局公示国家 AAAAA 级旅游景区名单［EB/OL］，https：//baike. baidu. com/item/% E5% 9B% BD% E5% AE% B6AAAAA% E7% BA% A7% E6% 97% 85% E6% B8% B8% E6% 99% AF% E5% 8C% BA/3575094？fr = Aladdin，2018 - 10 - 17.

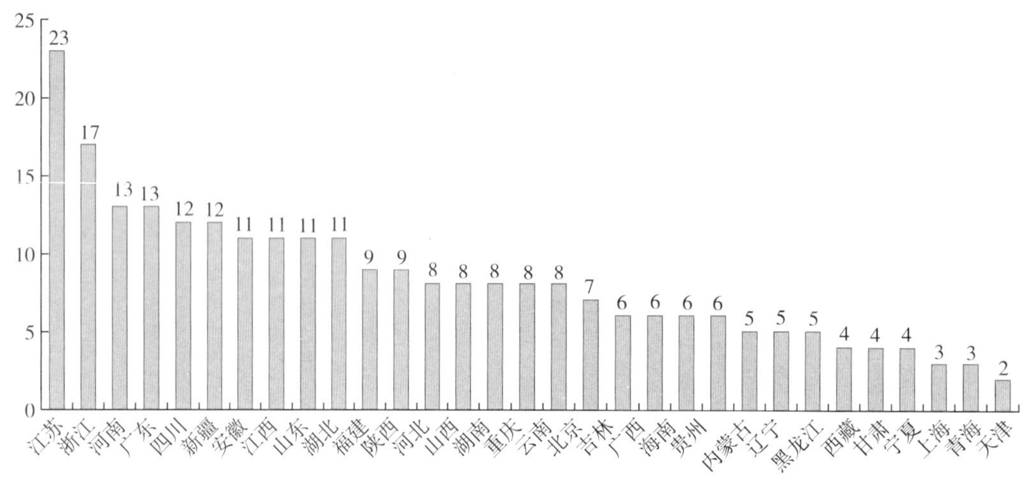

图 5.52　各省市 5A 级旅游景区数量（截至 2018 年 10 月）

全统计，全国共有旅行社约 2.74 万家①，导游约 80 万人②。受自由行、自助游、自驾游等趋势影响，以及旅游电商、景区电子导游等冲击，旅行社、导游的地位日趋边缘化。

5. 旅游电商

伴随国内互联网的迅速普及以及平台服务功能的日益完善，旅游电商已成为旅游产业中的重要参与者。第 42 次《中国互联网络发展状况统计报告》显示，2018 年上半年共有 3.93 亿网民通过在线进行旅行预订③，占所有网民的 49%；有 12.1% 的网民在线预订过旅游度假产品④。艾瑞数据显示，国内在线旅游度假市场集中度较高，途牛、携程、驴妈妈、同程四大平台占据了约 80% 的市场份额⑤（见图 5.53）。

6. 旅游纪念品企业

旅游纪念品是旅游产业的衍生品，目前各地企业对旅游纪念品的开发还存在参差不齐和同质化等问题，但真正具备特色的旅游纪念品，如当地老字号产品、非遗产品、土特产等仍然极具市场。

---

① 资料来源：新浪新闻．国家旅游局关于 2017 年第三季度全国旅行社统计调查情况的公报［EB/OL］，http：//news. sina. com. cn/o/2018 - 01 - 26/doc - ifyqyqni3316115. shtml，2018 - 1 - 26.

② 资料来源：新华日报．全国 80 万导游何以成为“弱势群体”［EB/OL］，http：//news. ifeng. com/a/20160229/47623667_0. shtml，2016 - 02 - 29.

③ 旅行预订：本报告中旅行预订定义为最近半年在网上预订过机票、酒店、火车票或旅游度假产品。

④ 资料来源：中国互联网络信息中心．《中国互联网络发展状况统计报告（第 42 次）》［EB/OL］，http：//www. cac. gov. cn/2018 - 08/20/c_1123296882. htm，2018 - 08 - 20.

⑤ 资料来源：艾瑞咨询．2018 年中国在线旅游度假行业研究报告［EB/OL］，http：//report. iresearch. cn/report/201805/3214. shtml，2018 - 05 - 21.

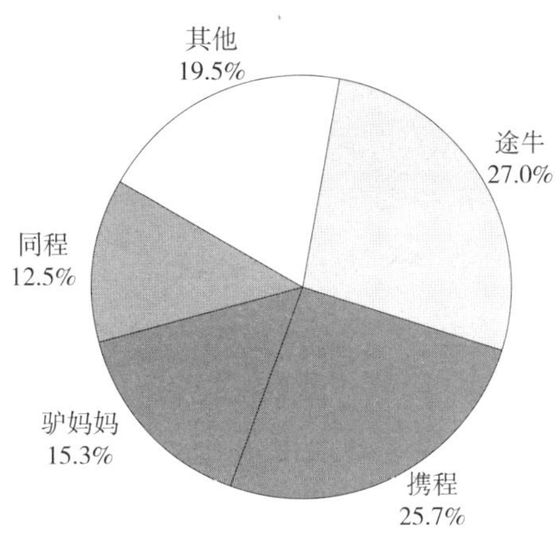

图 5.53　2017 年国内在线旅游度假市场占比情况（按交易规模划分，自营类）

7. 交通出行相关企业

交通出行是旅游中的重要一环，目前主要的交通出行方式包括飞机、铁路、长途汽车、租车以及自驾等。值得注意的是，自驾已经成为中国家庭出游的主要方式。根据国家旅游局统计，2018 年春节期间，全国游客采用自驾方式出游的比例已近 50%[①]。

8. 其他

目前全国各地正在推进全域旅游发展，农家乐、渔家乐、民宿等也正呈星火燎原之势，不断丰富着旅游产业链。

二、“三大战略”助推旅游市场拓展策略

围绕着旅游产业链条的七大类市场主体，建行从总行到分支行都在进行着有益的探索，涌现出了一批成功案例，取得了非常好的效果。借助新一代系统的强力支撑，将“普惠金融、住房租赁、金融科技”三大战略与旅游市场的拓展深度结合，还将创造更多价值，打造出更多的“建行样板”，具体包括如下七个方面。

（一）政府 + 金融科技

规范管理和促进发展是政府关注旅游产业的两个关键词。在规范旅游市场方面，多地政府都在打造旅游大数据系统，通过大数据实现对旅游市场的精细化管理，这其中就有建行金融科技平台的拓展机会。通过助力政府搭建旅游大数据管理平台，建行将实现对被管理景区的数据接入与整合，从而可以占据市场拓展的制高点。在促进发展方面，各地政府往往拿出大量的资源来助推旅游市场发展，如何整合好这些资源为

① 资料来源：叶玮 . 2018 年春节全国共接待游客 3.86 亿人次 自驾游占 50%［EB/OL］，http：//k.sina.com.cn/article_1663612603_ 6328b6bb020005u1h.html?from = travel，2018 - 02 - 02.

建行所用将成为制胜市场的法宝。如山东泰安分行，抓住当地旅游发展委员会大力推广“2018 年泰山国际登山节全球免费网络抢票活动”的有利时机，将活动承办网站“泰山惠玩网”内嵌至建行手机银行“悦享生活”频道，依托手机银行面向 3 亿手机银行用户广泛宣传，吸引了大量用户参加，赢得了多方赞誉。根据统计数据，2018 年 8 月 27 日 ~9 月 5 日，建行手机银行首页广告位共推广泰山国际登山节免费抢票活动次数超过 2.3 亿次，点击次数达到了 48.64 万次；在建行大力宣传推广下，合作伙伴“泰山惠玩网”10 天内收获了约 1 670 万网民的关注；免费抢票活动期间，共有 5.79 万张泰安各景区免费门票是从建行手机银行渠道抢到的，约占本次活动免费门票总票量的 2/3，价值约相当于 528 万元（总票量价值 800 万元），可谓取得了社会效益、经济效益双丰收，为各行拓展旅游市场提供了一种新的思路和借鉴（见图 5.54 和图 5.55）。

图 5.54　泰山惠玩网嵌入手机银行

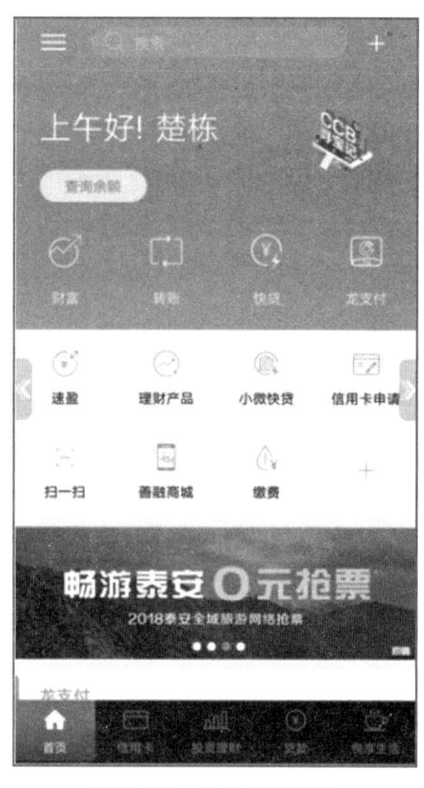

图 5.55　宣传抢票活动

（二）旅游景区 + 金融科技 + 普惠金融

旅游景区是旅游产业链中的核心企业，在门票支付、信贷支持、宣传推广、运营保障等多方面都有与建行合作的结合点。

1. 门票支付

目前各景区普遍需要线上、线下多渠道、多方式的门票支付解决方案，甚至不乏刷脸、指纹等先进的认证方式，这正是建行金融科技大显身手之时。龙支付、慧兜圈、龙 e 付可以满足各类景区线下购票的聚合支付需求，电子支付商户可以满足景区线上平台的支付需求；依托龙 e 付改造自助售票机，景区的无人售票需求一样可以轻松搞定。

2. 信贷支持

对于新建或扩建的景区，建行固定资产贷款、流动资金贷款可以直接予以支持；对于景区门票收益权、索道运营收费权等，还可配置资产证券化等投行产品。同时，围绕旅游核心企业的上下游，“e 游通”等网络银行产品一样可以切入产业链条，为众多企业提供普惠金融支持。云南分行为迪庆州旅游集团①设计推出的网络银行“e 游通”产品，就是依托核心企业向众多旅行社发放网络贷款，可以促进普惠金融的发展。

3. 宣传推广

当前景区众多，各个景区都在使出浑身解数、利用各种渠道对外推广。建行可与景区合作，共同开展龙支付满减、优惠购票等活动，既助力景区引流、扩大知名度，又推广了龙支付品牌，让游客获得实惠，真正打造出便民示范工程。

4. 运营保障

在旅游旺季，热门景区往往游客爆棚，旅游景区急切需要有志愿者参与到游客引导、次序维护等运营工作中来。对建行来说，这既是一个增进与景区联系的机会，又是建行积极履行社会责任、宣传金融知识、展现金融正能量的好时机。如山东泰安分行在五一、十一黄金周期间，发动青年员工广泛参与泰山景区志愿服务活动，助力泰山管委保障景区正常运营；同时，面向全国登泰山的游客，开展朋友圈转发“龙支付优惠购票 H5 页面”赠送遮阳帽活动，借力全国游客广泛宣传建行龙支付品牌及活动，收到了较好效果（见图 5. 56）。

（三）宾馆饭店 + 金融科技 + 普惠金融 + 住房租赁

利用慧兜圈、龙支付、龙 e 付，可以满足宾馆、饭店的聚合支付需求。对宾馆饭店行业中的小微企业、个体工商户，建行还可以提供小微快贷、账户云贷、个人快贷等普惠金融信贷支持。通过共同开展龙支付满减活动，可以助力宾馆饭店引流，提升人气。对于民宿、酒店式公寓等，住房租赁业务一样可以助力运营方精细化管理，实

① 迪庆州旅游集团是云南省迪庆地区（香格里拉）的旅游行业龙头企业，直接经营普达措国家公园景区，全额出资控股虎跳峡、梅里雪山、滇金丝猴 3 个国家公园。

图5.56　泰安分行“微蓝”志愿服务团队与游客打成一片

现最大收益。特别是在旅游淡季游客不多时，运营方完全可以在建行住房租赁平台发布房源，面向本地租客出租，获取租金收益。

（四）旅行社、导游+普惠金融+消费信贷

旅行社在接团、带团的过程中，难免需要一定的资金支持，建行普惠金融、消费信贷等产品就可以派上用场，凭借随借随还、循环信贷等优势助力它们做好经营。旅行社是建行旅游分期的最佳推广伙伴，通过与旅行社共同推广旅游分期或商户分期（龙卡随付贷），可以在帮助境外游等大额消费客户减轻压力的同时，助力建行消费信贷业务发展。游客在旅行社选择购买旅游产品，特别是境外游产品时，还具有购买旅游意外保险的需求，这也是建信人寿、建信财险等子公司跟进销售的好时机。导游群体庞大，每个导游接触的游客众多，是个由点带面推广建行产品与服务的很好的“触点”。围绕导游客群设计个人金融产品或开展营销活动，通过导游对游客的推介、扩散，将起到事半功倍的效果，这也是值得建行深耕的重要个人客群。

（五）旅游电商+金融科技+网络保险

1. 线上支付

通过对接旅游电商平台，接入建行线上聚合支付服务，可以使建行成为旅游电商的线上收单行，获得收单收益。

2. 网络保险

嵌入场景营销，是网络保险获得较快发展的重要原因之一，建信人寿、建信财险等子公司可通过与旅游电商平台合作，在游客线上购买旅游产品时，嵌入营销意外险、航空延误险等险种，扩大市场份额。

（六）旅游纪念品企业+善融商务+普惠金融

1. 善融商务

引导旅游纪念品企业入驻善融商务，依托建行善融商务线上平台、网点 O2O 或旅游景区 O2O 等模式，可以助力企业做好产品推广，拉动销售。

2. 信贷支持

借力小微快贷、云税贷、支农贷款等普惠金融产品，建行可以对旅游纪念品、老字号、土特产等生产企业提供信贷扶持，助力各地做好旅游产业链条的延伸。

（七）交通出行+金融科技

1. 智慧出行

对于铁路、公路、飞机客运企业，建行已在购票领域与其有了很多合作，并持续开展了龙支付优惠购票等活动，吸引了广大游客使用建行支付产品。

2. 智慧加油

对于自驾游发展迅速的特点，建行可以围绕车主出行必需的加油环节做文章。2018 年，总行网络金融部开展的智慧加油活动，就是运用金融科技服务自驾出行的一个典范（见图 5.57）。

3. 智慧停车

旅游景区停车场车流众多，是建行切入无感支付、聚合支付的重要场景，能够覆盖较多的自驾游游客，在拓展旅游景区时应一并考虑。

三、相关建议

（一）整合资源，建立统一的旅游产业服务解决方案

依托新一代强大的金融科技服务能力，全国各分行都在打造服务当地旅游产业的解决方案，虽各具特色，但缺乏整合，尚未形成合力。建议总行全面梳理全行旅游产业服务案例，形成统一的业务解决方案和技术支持方案，并采取模块化方式，供各分行“点菜”，按需配置，自由组合，统一标准，最高效率地满足旅游产业各参与主体的需求，助力分支行拓展好旅游市场。

图5. 57　总行龙支付智慧加油活动

（二）打造品牌，树立旅游产业中建行的市场地位

服务好旅游产业，契合十九大报告精神，也与“中国建设银行，建设美好生活”的愿景相一致。目前全行在旅游产业的布局还比较散，还没有形成统一品牌。甘肃分行与天水政府合作推出了“净土平安卡”，并打造“一部手机游甘肃”的旅游品牌，就为全行提供一个样板和借鉴（见图5. 58）。建议总行统筹全行情况，打造出建行特色旅游品牌，提升市场影响力。

图5. 58　一部手机游甘肃

（三）打造爆款，建立建行的差异化特色

知名度高的旅游景区是整个旅游产业链的核心资源，更是稀缺资源。建议总行全面梳理全国各分行与知名旅游景区的合作情况。对一些建行独家合作或深度合作的景区，建议经过有选择、有侧重的筛选后，集中财务资源开展大力度优惠，将这些优质、稀缺资源打造成为建行渠道（如手机银行）或产品（如联名卡等）的“爆款”，形成差异化特色。同时，还应抓住一些重要的节假日、旅游活动等，借力外部资源打造“爆点”，如山东泰安分行借力泰山国际登山节，推出建行手机银行免费抢票活动，依托总行资源加大宣传力度，收到了较好的效益。

（四）挖掘商机，紧跟旅游产业延伸的新事物

旅游产业已不仅限于出游、休闲、娱乐，还在不断涌现出新的模式。如与教育相结合形成的“研学游”，与马拉松、铁人三项等体育赛事相结合形成的“赛事游”等，形式非常多样。目前，金融同业还没有特别清晰的业务合作模式，但由于参与其中的都是中高端客户、年轻白领、高收入家庭等，在报名、出行、纪念品购买、延伸服务等多方面一定蕴藏着巨大的商机。建议全行密切关注这些领域，抢先看透、找到结合点，运用“普惠金融 + 住房租赁 + 金融科技”，积极尝试与介入，探索盈利模式，使建行成为“新经济”的市场引领者和排头兵，为全行转型发展做出贡献。

新形势下陕北能源区金融助力供给侧改革策略研究

陕西省分行　陈引妮

陕北不仅是红色革命圣地，更是典型的能源依赖型地区，主要包括延安、榆林两市。随着《陕甘宁革命老区振兴规划》的有序推进，陕北借着资源的东风和改革的步伐，使得能源企业初具规模。但是产业发展粗放、集聚度低、结构单一、经济模式脆弱，在煤价、油价一路下跌的影响下，导致大量中小煤企资金紧张，甚至倒闭破产，极大地影响了陕北能源区网点的信贷资产质量和经营效益。

供给侧改革的提出，为地方经济的发展指明了方向，更对商业银行的转型发展提出了要求，特别是对建行能源区网点过好资产质量关、转型发展关及创新关提供了契机。面对经济金融新常态，我们应该主动适应新常态，主动引领新常态，不断创新创变发展模式，不断适应技术革新趋势下的金融生态环境。

从国外研究来看，供给经济学是20世纪70年代出现在美国的一个经济学流派，分为激进供给学派和温和供给学派，但是供给经济学仍然是一个待完善的经济学科。国家经济出现问题，原因是有效供给与需求不匹配，不应该生产的商品太多，而需要的商品太少。金德勒贝格尔（Kindleberger C P.，2001）在研究经济增长与不良贷款率、信贷风险防控等关系时，指出商业银行在出现危机前一般都是信贷规模大肆扩张。克莱尔（Clair，1992）研究指出，经济增长与不良贷款率具有正向相关关系。

我国的供给侧改革不同于国外的供给经济学，国外供给经济学重点强调的是税收在供给中的作用，而我国的供给侧改革是基于本国国内当前特定的经济环境提出的。当前，我国的经济增长速度放缓，产能过剩严重，不良贷款率上升，供求失去应有的均衡。中国经济发展面临逐步失去人口红利、生产方式转换、产能闲置、经济增长动力不足等问题，供给侧改革是解决这些问题的关键战略导向。曹国华和刘睿凡（2016）研究了供给侧改革背景下商业银行面临的机遇、挑战，以及指出了信贷业务风险防控的具体措施，商业银行应从供给入手，提高信贷配置效率，为供给侧改革提供信贷服务。中国经济要想实现继续高速增长，必须加强供给侧改革，提高生产要素利用能力，完善体制机制建设。供给侧改革势必会影响商业银行的信贷投放，合理的信贷投放可以有效促进产业的转型升级，还可以保证商业银行的资产质量。因此，供给侧改革是国家经济调整的一剂良药，但需要商业银行信贷投向来保驾护航。

商业银行承担着为我国工商业提供优质金融服务的神圣使命，在我国经济转型期，更要转变传统粗放的信贷投放模式和经营管理方式，以更加积极的姿态支持战略性新兴产业和科技创新企业，为我国经济结构的优化升级保驾护航，为培育经济发展新动力，激发创新创造活力，更为营造“大众创业，万众创新”的新气象提供金融支持。

一、陕北经济运行整体情况

近年来，以煤炭、石油等能源为经济发展主要支柱的陕北，在面临能源工业产品价格下跌时，各项经济指标增长率均呈现出下滑态势。以延安为例，2015 年延安市实现生产总值 1 198.636 亿元，按可比价计算，增长 1.7%，较上半年（-2.2%）和前三季度（0.3%）分别提高 3.9 个和 1.4 个百分点。在经历了煤炭“黄金十年”发展后，榆林经济社会迎来了巨大发展，连续多年成为陕西经济发展的重要支撑。但受经济下行的“严冬”考验，榆林进入了近年来少有的困难局面，突出表现在煤炭、石油等主要工业产品价格下跌严重，企业生产经营困难和工业经济增长乏力等方面，严重制约了榆林经济的进一步发展。经济形势的持续低迷、金融机构不良贷款率陡升，将会给陕北各县域、各行业带来极大影响，尤其是制约了各金融机构的进一步发展。

二、延安经济金融整体情况

延安市石油、煤炭、天然气蕴藏丰富，是国家重要的能源基地，也是陕北能源化工基地的重要组成部分。长期以来，石油是经济增长和财政收入的主要来源。21 世纪以来，延安依托石油资源优势，实现了跨越发展，经济总量迈入全省前列，人均 GDP 突破 1 万美元。“十三五”以来，延安加快经济转型，积极实施“高端能化强市，特色产业富民，文化旅游带动，生态环境提升，城乡一体发展”战略。

截至 2017 年年末，全市常住人口 226.31 万人，城镇化率 60.79%，实现生产总值 1 266.39 亿元，按可比价计算（下同）比上年增长 7.6%，人均生产总值为 56 086 元，非公有制经济实现增加值 364.78 亿元，占生产总值比重为 28.8%，较上年提高 2.7 个百分点。全市居民人均可支配收入 23 045 元，增长 9.1%。城镇居民人均可支配收入 33 168元，增长 8.1%；农村居民人均可支配收入为 11 525 元，增长 9.1%（见图 5.59）。

财政金融方面，全市地方财政收入 140.42 亿元，增长 7.6%；地方财政支出 353.28 亿元，增长 7.9%。2017 年年末金融机构存款余额 1 566.83 亿元，增长 7.9%，比年初增加 114.37 亿元。各项贷款余额 1 110.71 亿元，增长 19.8%，比年初增加 183.21 亿元。其中，短期贷款 278.26 亿元，比年初增加 73.80 亿元；中长期贷款

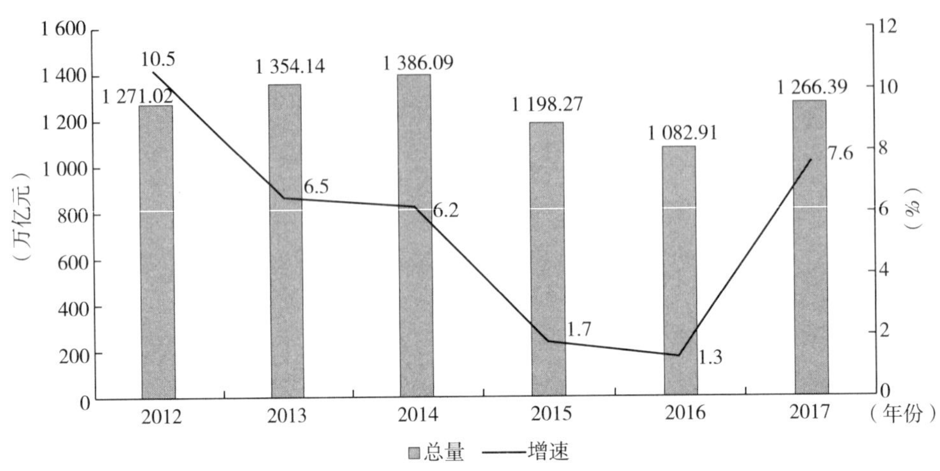

图 5.59　2012—2017 年延安市生产总值和增长速度

783.06 亿元，比年初增加 119.03 亿元。

学校医院方面，全市拥有延安大学和延安职业技术学院两所高校，拥有各类中小学 369 所，其中普通中学 114 所，普通小学 255 所。普通中学在校学生 12.76 万人，普通小学在校学生 20.89 万人。特殊教育学校 5 所，在校学生 369 人。幼儿园 579 所，在园幼儿 12.66 万人。全市初中毕业生升学率达到 95.05%。全市共有医院、卫生院 222 个，卫生技术人员 1.71 万人。

文化旅游方面，全年接待国内外旅游人数 5 059 万人次，增长 25.7%，其中海外旅游人数 3.95 万人次。实现旅游综合收入 298.7 亿元，增长 31.0%，其中外汇收入 380 万美元。

社会消费品零售额方面，全市实现社会消费品零售总额 284.65 亿元，比 2016 年增长 10.4%。从城乡看，城镇消费品零售额 223.17 亿元，增长 10.4%；乡村消费品零售额 61.48 亿元，增长 10.1%（见图 5.60）。

图 5.60　2012—2017 年延安市社会消费品零售额

新时期，根据延安市发展新规划，重点将在高端能化、农业现代化、文化旅游、城镇化建设、新经济等方面发力，在推进供给侧结构性改革的同时，也为建行客户拓展带来新机遇。

延安市充分发挥“两个明显优势”，以供给侧结构性改革为主线，着力推动质量变革、效率变革、动力变革，使发展质量和效益稳步提升。

工业经济提质增效。延安综合能源基地发展规划启动实施，延安至西柏坡、陕北至武汉等电力外送通道加快推进，富县煤油气资源综合利用项目实现中交，大唐热电联产正式向市区供热，“延安”青春岁月卷烟成功上市。

现代农业加快发展。积极推进以苹果为主的特色农业产业后整理，建成智能化选果线6条，新增冷气库储能10.5万吨，集中打造延安苹果、洛川苹果、梁家河苹果3个品牌，苹果产值达110亿元。蔬菜年产138.5万吨，畜禽养殖规模化率达到73.3%，林果、棚栽、养殖三大产业成为农民增收主渠道。

文化旅游产业深入推进。树立全域旅游理念，建成枣园·1938、北京知青馆、圣地河谷等项目，黄帝陵国家文化公园开工建设，南泥湾景区开发、宝塔山景区提升等快速推进，延安国际滑雪场建成开放，红色旅游景区列入全国创建5A级旅游景区预备名单，荣获2017年“十佳魅力城市”和“十大文化影响力城市”，接待游客突破5 000万人次，旅游综合收入近300亿元。

三、延安分行所处宏观环境PEST模型分析

（一）PEST模型简介

PEST分析法是指对企业所处宏观环境的分析，P是政治（Politics），E是经济（Economy），S是社会（Society），T是技术（Technology），详见图5.61。

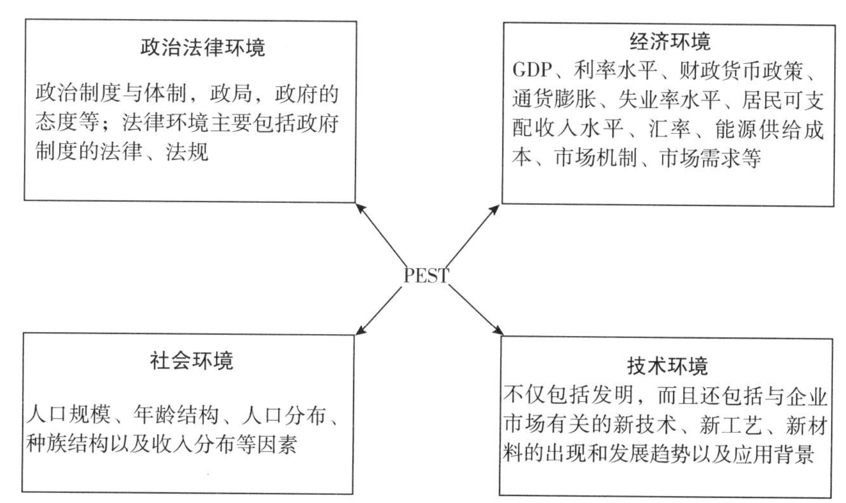

图5.61　PEST模型

（二） PEST 模型分析过程

根据延安分行所处的地域特色，结合实际，主要从政治法律环境、经济环境、社会环境及技术环境对建行进行了 PEST 分析，如表 5.49 所示。

表 5.49 延安分行 PEST 分析

政治法律环境	经济环境
• 与宏观经济运行状况、宏观经济政策和宏观经济结构调整高度相关 • 利率市场化脚步加快 • 互联网金融监管政策出台 • 财政账户清理政策出台	• 国际油价持续下跌，产量和利润双下降 • 房地产行业阶段性变化，资金吸纳能力变弱，资金由实入虚，进入资本市场 • 加快新区建设、黄河引水工程、延河治理工程等
社会环境	技术环境
• 本地居民储蓄意识依然很强，但理财能力相对不足 • 本地居民信用消费观念逐步形成，摆脱信用消费在观念上的束缚，有力促进了个人住房贷款、信用卡、个人消费贷款的发展 • 红色文化甚浓，地缘政治优势明显	• 信息技术的飞速发展使分行的管理创新和产品创新都实现了集成化、数据化和专业化 • 服务渠道进一步拓宽，智能网点建设速度加快 • 互联网金融的飞速发展，催生出更加满足客户的个性化服务，如善融商城、手机银行、劳动者港湾 App

面对复杂多变的经济金融形势，延安分行审时度势，全面分析区域经济状况，以供给侧改革为指引，以优化信贷结构为目标，全力优化信贷资产质量，积极部署金融助力供给侧改革。

1. 全面分析区域经济形势

国际油价持续萎靡不振，严重影响石油产业链上下游企业的资金回笼周期，潜在风险较大，违约概率上升，不良贷款增加。2008 年以前，石油价格最高时每桶达 140 美元以上，此后，缓慢下降，但 2014 年 7 月初，国际原油价格还在每桶 100 美元之上，到 2015 年，国际原油价格便暴跌至每桶 50 ~ 30 美元。权威机构预测，2018 年原油价格还将继续下跌，而延安开采石油的成本为每桶 65 美元左右，成本和收入严重倒挂。虽然建行加大了核心石油公司供应链融资的客户退出力度，采取优中选优的增量投放方式，但是由于基数较大，依然还有部分存量客户存在较大风险。

2. 以“三去一降一补”为行业调整方向

供给侧改革是战略引领，关键在于做好“三去一降一补”。作为金融机构，应以国家大政方针为出发点和落脚点，全面部署地方“一带一路”项目建设，创新信贷支持策略，提供绿色金融服务。延安经济结构单一，对煤炭、石油等能源依赖性强，再加上近年来煤油市场低迷和新能源革命，短期内能源价格不会反弹。因此，地方政府应该转变经济发展战略，金融机构应该积极支持地方经济发展，寻求新的利润增长点。

3. 重点挖掘区域特色项目

延安作为革命圣地，有着得天独厚的红色基因和政治优势，中央和地方在政策制定和经济支持上都会向老区倾斜。近年来，延安上马了一批具有红色意义的工程，如圣地河谷、东方红广场等，延安分行要充分利用近年来的发展基础，积极介入，不仅可以优化建行信贷结构，而且还有力地支持了地方经济的发展。当前，建行应该积极和总省行沟通，上下联动，加快介入延安新区建设，力争在客户数量与贷款规模上有较快增长，为其提供全方位的信贷支持。

4. 尽早尽快退出产能过剩行业

从区域经济结构和形势来看，建行须尽快退出煤炭、石油、地产、小贷公司及零售等行业，抢抓机遇，重点支持关乎民生的基建、水利、绿色农业等，为区域经济结构调整和优化贡献力量。但是也不能一刀切，要采取优中选优的举措，支持那些发展势头好、抗风险能力强、对地方经济贡献大的传统企业，为这些企业的转型发展提供资金和金融支持。

四、金融助力供给侧改革的具体策略

供给侧改革作为国家经济结构调整的重大战略，金融机构必须毫不动摇地跟进和支持。在深刻理解供给侧改革目的的基础上，金融机构应顺势而为，择优而栖，以积极的信贷投放方式支持中央和地方优化劳动力、土地、资本及创新等供给，创新经营管理方式，积极推进“互联网 +”与金融的深度融合，做好风险管理，保障客户的资金安全，化解风险，以更优质的互联网金融产品迎合消费者的需求，为我国经济结构优化做出应有贡献。

（一）深刻领悟供给侧改革的内涵

对供给侧改革的深刻理解关乎商业银行改革的方向。在供给侧改革背景下，商业银行要以“三去一降一补”为信贷行业调整方向，逐步压缩和退出产能过剩行业信贷资源，下大力气营销地方基建项目，抓住战略新兴行业发展机遇，积极给予信贷支持，为我国经济结构调整优化服务。

（二）积极优化信贷投放方式和结构

信贷是商业银行的核心优势。商业银行应该抓住国家供给侧改革机遇，以改变信贷投放方向为手段，以调整信贷结构为目的，积极部署信贷资源配置，减少产能过剩和高污染行业的信贷投放，把战略新兴产业作为重点投放领域，支持我国经济发展水平走向中高端。从延安区域经济情况来考虑，建行应紧跟政府步伐，全方位助力供给侧改革，大力支持地方经济结构调整，减少对石油、煤炭的依赖度，确保区域经济健康有序运行。

（三）抢抓区域重点项目和创新领域市场

商业银行应该根据所属区域经济发展特点，制定具有针对性的发展措施，特别是要挖掘所在地区的重点项目、特色项目及绿色项目，重点营销。商业银行应该以服务实体经济为天职，尤其是要解决好中小企业筹资难问题，积极营造“大众创业，万众创新”新气象。延安作为革命的圣地，有着得天独厚的政缘优势，一批批重点项目也在陆续开展。建行应在重点项目营销上锁定目标，上下联动，重点突破，以支持地方经济的同时，也能改善建行信贷行业分布的科学性。

（四）全力打造“移动银行”

未来的银行就是移动银行。在供给侧改革背景下，商业银行也要在供给侧发力，不断创新金融产品设计思路，优化产品销售渠道，推陈出新，缩短服务距离和时间，满足个人和单位客户对金融服务的需求，提升服务质效。同时建行应在产品设计上兼顾区域特色，以匹配不同人群的差异化偏好。

（五）全面优化人力资源结构

人力资源是商业银行发展的关键。在当前经济金融环境下，商业银行面临多重压力，尤其是人员流失。从发展角度来说，商业银行培养一名优秀的人才需要人、财、力，还有时间，但由于目前商业银行面临的金融脱媒、互联网金融、利率市场化等的冲击，导致部分员工对商业银行的前景产生担忧。因此，商业银行必须不断调整发展方向，优化人力结构，不顾一切谋发展，想方设法留人才，只有人才留住了，才能推动商业银行进一步发展。

五、总结

钱穆先生曾经说过：“在现实中发现问题，从历史中寻找答案。”在我国经济进入转型期和阵痛期时，为避免进入经济发展停滞陷阱，我国适时提出了供给侧改革，来优化经济结构，使得经济发展逐步走向中高端。而金融作为国家经济发展的重要支撑和保障，在关键时刻，要以国家战略调整为契机，毫不动摇地给予全面金融支持，同时建行要转变经营发展思路，把供给侧改革作为金融机构战略转型的重要机遇，积极支持创新型企业，优化信贷结构，扭转不良率飙升的态势，为国家创新发展奠定基础。

关于建行与电子政务平台合作策略的调查研究

河南省分行　黄　磊　王素娟　郝长江

一、“互联网＋政务服务”是一场深刻的社会变革，商业银行应当积极应对

近年来，在全面深化改革的背景下，国家从政策层面部署简政放权、放管结合、优化服务（简称“放管服”），以期用政府减权限权和监管改革，换来市场活力和社会创造力的释放。在“放管服”改革的实施路径方面，国务院将“互联网＋政务服务”定义为“深化放管服改革的关键环节”，并对“互联网＋政务服务”进行了高规格、高频次的安排部署。

（一）国家频繁出台政策，强力推进“一网、一门、一次”改革

自2016年以来，国家密集出台“互联网＋政务服务”的政策文件，从试点运行到全面推广、从“一号一窗一网”到“一网、一门、一次”、从审批便民化到全国一体化平台建设均做出了详细的部署，具体文件及关键词如表5.50所示。

通过分析表5.50中的相关文件，可以总结出以下内容。

1. 互联网＋政务服务的安排部署是一个循序渐进的过程

从地域范围上看，2016年4月，国家部署“互联网＋政务服务”信息惠民试点，9月部署各省市、国务院有关部门建设政务平台，12月部署建设覆盖全国的政务平台，范围由试点扩大到省市再到全国；从实现目标上，从看“一号一窗一网”到“一网通办”和“一网、一门、一次”，网上政务服务的要求逐步提高，体现出国家在各地实践基础上不断完善网上政务服务的标准，不断修正实施目标。

2. 互联网＋政务服务的实施期限明确

2017年年底，各省市建成省级政务平台，2018年年底国家级政务平台建成，2019年省市与国家级平台对接完成，2022年年底全面实现“一网通办”。一是明确了各级政府的实施期限，二是明确了远期的实施目标是全面实现“一网通办”，既有时限上的紧迫性，又考虑到“一网通办”实施过程的复杂性，按照先搭平台、再循序实现“一

网通办”的步骤进行，由简入繁、由易到难。

表 5.50 国家政策文件摘录

颁布日期	文件名称	关键词句
2016 年 4 月	国务院办公厅关于转发国家发展改革委等部门推进“互联网 + 政务服务”开展信息惠民试点实施方案的通知（国办发〔2016〕23 号）	加强政务信息资源跨部门、跨层级互通和协同共享，试点地区实现“一号一窗一网”目标
2016 年 9 月	国务院关于加快推进“互联网 + 政务服务”工作的指导意见（国发〔2016〕55 号）	2017 年年底前，各省（区、市）人民政府、国务院有关部门建成一体化网上政务服务平台
2016 年 12 月	国务院办公厅关于印发“互联网 + 政务服务”技术体系建设指南的通知（国办函〔2016〕108 号）	建成覆盖全国的整体联动、部门协同、省级统筹、一网办理的“互联网 + 政务服务”技术和服务体系
2017 年 5 月	国务院办公厅关于印发政务信息系统整合共享实施方案的通知（国办发〔2017〕39 号）	有效推进政务信息系统整合共享，切实避免各自为政、自成体系、重复投资、重复建设
2017 年 7 月	国家发展改革委关于印发“十三五”国家政务信息化工程建设规划的通知（发改高技〔2017〕1449 号）	基本形成满足国家治理体系与治理能力现代化要求的政务信息化体系，构建形成大平台共享、大数据慧治、大系统共治的顶层架构
2018 年 5 月	国务院办公厅关于深入推进审批服务便民化的指导意见	全面推行审批服务“马上办、网上办、就近办、一次办”，有条件的市县和开发区 80% 以上审批服务事项市县网上能办
2018 年 6 月	国务院办公厅关于印发进一步深化“互联网 + 政务服务”推进政务服务“一网、一门、一次”改革实施方案的通知	构建全流程一体化在线服务平台，推动企业和群众办事线上“一网通办”（一网），线下“只进一扇门”（一门），现场办理“最多跑一次”（一次），让企业和群众到政府办事像“网购”一样方便
2018 年 7 月	国务院关于进一步加快推进全国一体化在线政务服务平台建设的指导意见	2018 年年底前，国家政务服务平台主体功能建设基本完成；2019 年年底前，国家政务服务平台上线运行，各省（自治区、直辖市）和国务院有关部门政务服务平台与国家政务服务平台对接；2020 年年底前，各省（自治区、直辖市）和国务院有关部门政务服务平台应接尽接，政务服务事项应上尽上；2022 年年底前，政务服务事项全部纳入平台办理，全面实现“一网通办”

（二）国家电子政务外网已实现纵向贯通，一体化平台显现雏形

按照国家信息中心的通报，2018 年 6 月底，全国政务服务外网纵向贯通网络体系已基本形成，全国接入县（市、区、旗）总数为 2 734 个，区县级覆盖率达到 95.9%，用户接入网络平均可用率为 99.91%。可见，在“互联网 + 政务服务”的

热潮中，不论政务网办事项能够实现多少，全国范围内政务办事的外网体系基本成型，已经解决了政务服务网“有”和“无”的问题，下一步重点解决“办得成、办得好”的问题。

（三）“互联网＋政务服务”的影响力将遍及社会各个层面

“互联网＋政务服务”是国家“互联网＋行动计划”在政务领域的重要体现。在各地政务服务网未建成之前，政府相关厅局已经开始了“互联网＋”的相关尝试。例如海关总署在全国部署的网上缴纳关税的财关库银系统、国土资源部门部署的土地网上招拍挂系统等，这些系统将线下不规范、不透明的政务办事流程改造成了线上规范、透明的办事流程，影响了进出口、土地开发以及周边行业的行政申请流程，改变了某一领域、某一行业的办事规则和生态。作为“互联网＋政务行业应用”的整合者，“互联网＋政务服务”平台影响的行业、用户、群众的范围更加广泛，其不仅提高了政府受理依申请行政事项的效率、政府监察的透明度和有效性，更影响了需要在平台上办事的群众、企业的办事习惯，释放了市场活力，还影响了相关中介公司、相关行业从业人员（例如代理办证等）的行业生存与发展。

“互联网＋政务服务”影响深远，是政府向市民社会的另一种形式的权力让渡，实质是“政府自我革命，要削手中的权、去部门的利、割自己的肉”。

（四）商业银行必须积极应对“互联网＋政务服务”的推广和竞争对手的跨界竞争

在“互联网＋政务服务”平台建设中，互联网公司有着天然的优势，主流第三方支付机构以前所未有的力度参与其中，以平台建设的便利条件，直接撬动商业银行赖以生存的政府机构客户基础，并以“平台模式”跨界抢占个人客户、公司客户。

以“阿里系”参与河南政务服务网为例，支付宝利用其参股企业承建河南政务服务网的机会，在各家商业银行未参与的情况下率先开通了非税电子缴费入口，布局河南省非税资金和账户。同时，通过政务服务网开通支付宝用户互认、支付宝扫码登陆、支付宝付款等方式，意图打通用户登录、支付等环节，通过扩大适用场景、黏住个人客户和局委客户等方式，最终实现对非税资金、政府局委资金、个人客户的抢夺。

可见，在“放管服”改革、推进“互联网＋政务服务”的背景下，政务行业和相关行业的生态将会重塑，商业银行面临的跨界竞争将更加激烈，直接影响商业银行赖以生存的对公客户基础，也间接影响了对私客户，商业银行在这个趋势下必须积极应对。

二、河南省电子政务快速推进，建行提早介入并已实现多点突破

（一）近两年河南省“互联网+政务服务”发展浅析

自2017年年初起，河南省电子政务平台（下称省平台）建设提速，省政府连续出台多项政策文件，从省平台建设、市县乡政务平台建设两个维度对“互联网+政务服务”进行了详细安排。

从各项政策文件确定的目标来看，河南省“互联网+政务服务”可粗略分为两个阶段。第一阶段是2018年3月前，主要解决省、市、县三级电子政务平台的建设问题，其中以2017年9月底河南政务服务网上线、2017年年底实现省市县三级贯通为主要节点；第二阶段是2018年4月起，全省电子政务平台建设的重点转向行政权力事项的梳理上线和实现“一网通办”方面，其关键节点是《深化“一网通办”前提下“最多跑一次”改革推进审批服务便民化实施方案》的印发（见表5.51）。

表5.51 河南省政策文件摘录

颁布日期	文件名称	关键词句
2017年1月	河南省人民政府省长办公会议纪要	2017年年底前，省电子政务平台全面运行，具备网上审批、综合服务、工作督查和其他相应功能，并结合大数据开发，逐步推动商业模式应用。分阶段目标是：2017年3月底前，省电子政务专有云平台第一阶段基本建成，省级实体政务服务大厅和网上政务服务平台上线运行，省政府门户网站在原有基础上优化提升；6月底前，网上行政审批覆盖各省辖市和有条件的县（市、区）；9月底前，网上行政审批覆盖省、市、县三级；2017年年底前，网上行政审批覆盖省、市、县、乡四级
2017年2月	河南省人民政府办公厅关于印发2017年全省电子政务服务平台建设总体工作方案的通知	到2017年年底，电子政务服务平台有效运行，主要电子政务应用系统互联互通，省、市、县、乡四级具备网上行政审批能力，群众关注的重点民生服务事项实现网上办理
2017年4月	河南省人民政府关于印发河南省推进国家大数据综合试验区建设实施方案的通知	开展“互联网+政务服务”。梳理规范公共服务事项，简化优化办事流程，建设省、市、县、乡四级联动的河南省网上政务服务平台
2018年3月	关于印发河南省2018年“互联网+政务运行”工作方案的通知	2018年年底实现“五个100%”，即非涉密依申请行政权力事项100%在线办理；便民服务事项行政村100%全覆盖；全省统一部署、统一功能架构的重大应用系统100%与省网上政务服务平台对接；“一次办妥”清单事项100%完成；省直部门符合条件的非涉密政务信息系统100%向省政务云转移

（续表）

颁布日期	文件名称	关键词句
2018 年 5 月	河南省政务公开与政务服务领导小组关于印发河南省“平台之外无审批”实施方案和河南省政务服务“一次办妥”实施方案的通知	按照“成熟一批、实施一批、压茬推进”的原则，每季度公布一批“一次办妥”事项清单，2018 年 6 月底前，试点部门和市、县一批办件量大、涉及面广的重点事项“一次办妥”率先实现突破；2018 年 12 月底前，列入清单的事项 100% 实现“一次办妥”
2018 年 7 月	中共河南省委办公厅河南省人民政府办公厅关于印发《深化“一网通办”前提下“最多跑一次”改革推进审批服务便民化实施方案》的通知	在“一网通办”方面，2018 年 7 月底前，各地各部门审批服务办事系统要全部“联上”河南政务服务网，实现网络通；8 月底前，各地各部门审批服务办事系统与河南政务服务网要全部“打通”，实现数据通、业务通；9 月底前，部分审批服务事项网上“能办”；年底前，省级审批服务事项网上可办率达到 90%，市县级审批服务事项网上可办率达到 70% 在“只进一扇门”方面，2018 年年底前，市县级审批服务事项进驻综合性实体政务大厅比例达到 70%，50% 以上审批服务事项实现“一窗”分类受理；2019 年年底前，除对场地有特殊要求的事项外，审批服务事项进驻综合性实体政务大厅基本实现应进必进，70% 以上审批服务事项实现“一窗”分类受理 在“最多跑一次”方面，2018 年年底前，企业和群众到政府办事提供的材料减少 30% 以上，省市县各级 30 个高频事项实现“最多跑一次”；2019 年 6 月底前，企业和群众到政府办事提供的材料减少 60% 以上，省市县各级 100 个高频事项实现“最多跑一次”，年底前基本实现企业和群众到政府办理审批服务事项“最多跑一次是原则、跑多次是例外”

1. 省级电子政务平台

河南政务服务网（下称该平台）是省政府主导，常务副省长牵头，省政府办公厅、省发改委负责搭建的全省一体化网上政务服务平台。该平台采用政府购买服务形式建设，由河南省投资集团出资，河南云政数据管理有限公司承办。

该平台的建设目标是一点接入、实现全省各级政府政务服务的网上办理。该平台已经于 2017 年 9 月上线，采用省市两级分建的模式，其中省直单位事项由河南政务服务网集中办理（所有省直部门，所有非涉密行政权力事项必须在线办理），各省辖市可以建设自己的政务服务平台（不鼓励县域自建），但必须与河南省政务服务网对接。2017 年年底，该平台实现省市县三级贯通，2018 年 6 月实现省市县三级统一认证、统一入口。

2. 各地市电子政务平台

全省各地市电子政务平台牵头单位不一，部分地市由当地行政服务中心（行政便民审批中心、市民之家）牵头建设，如安阳、洛阳、商丘等地；部分地市由数字城市办公室牵头建设，如郑州市；部分地市由政府办公室牵头建设，如平顶山市。总体来说，各地市行政服务中心作为行政审批的牵头单位，在职能上与电子政务平台有着天然的契合，各地也多以行政服务中心作为牵头单位。

在建设进度方面，各地市、直管县均实现了与省平台的对接，实现了“统一身份认证”（各地平台与省平台用户互通）、“统一入口”（各地平台均通过省平台统一门户网站、App登录）。但是，各地市“一网通办”的实施进度和政务服务外网的实用性表现不一。

按照省政府“一网通办”通报（2018年9月底），省政府对电子政务平台主要考核网上可办事项、一网通办事项等9项指标，其中网上可办事项、一网通办事项是关键指标。从各地市的表现来看，在网上可办事项方面，排名最高的商丘市为578项，排名最低的鹤壁市为216件，安阳市排名全省第二；从一网通办事项来看，排名最高的南阳市为212件，排名最低的驻马店市为64项，安阳市排名全省第四（见表5.52）。

表5.52　省政府一网通办最新通报（2018年9月）

序号	单位	审批服务事项（项）			网上可办事项（项）				一网通办事项（项）			
		通用目录事项总数	行政审批事项总数	公共服务事项总数	总数	行政审批事项	公共服务事项	排名	总数	行政审批事项	公共服务事项	排名
	合计	28 922	24 218	4 704	10 031	9 760	271		2 910	2 761	149	
	省辖市	18 222	15 108	3 114	7 625	7 416	209		2 235	2 137	98	
1	郑州市	1 011	838	173	373	368	5	12	144	139	5	6
2	开封市	1 011	838	173	517	490	27	5	112	106	6	10
3	洛阳市	1 011	838	173	465	455	10	7	159	154	5	5
4	平顶山市	1 011	838	173	419	408	11	10	117	111	6	8
5	安阳市	1 011	838	173	570	544	26	2	181	176	5	4
6	鹤壁市	1 011	838	173	216	209	7	18	82	78	4	15
7	新乡市	1 011	838	173	312	307	5	16	86	81	5	13
8	焦作市	1 011	838	173	474	467	7	6	95	89	6	12
9	濮阳市	1 011	838	173	463	457	6	8	114	108	6	9
10	许昌市	1 011	838	173	374	366	8	11	107	104	3	11
11	漯河市	1 011	838	173	551	536	15	4	198	190	8	3
12	三门峡市	1 011	838	173	367	362	5	14	86	81	5	13
13	南阳市	1 011	838	173	562	543	19	3	212	204	8	1
14	商丘市	1 011	838	173	578	550	28	1	123	117	6	7
15	信阳市	1 011	838	173	330	325	5	15	73	68	5	17
16	周口市	1 011	838	173	368	359	9	13	77	72	5	16
17	驻马店市	1 011	838	173	261	253	8	17	64	59	5	18

（续表）

序号	单位	审批服务事项（项）			网上可办事项（项）				一网通办事项（项）			
		通用目录事项总数	行政审批事项总数	公共服务事项总数	总数	行政审批事项	公共服务事项	排名	总数	行政审批事项	公共服务事项	排名
18	济源市	1035	862	173	425	417	8	9	205	200	5	2
省直管县（市）		10700	9110	1590	2406	2344	62		675	624	51	
1	巩义市	1070	911	159	247	241	6	4	65	60	5	6
2	兰考县	1070	911	159	257	252	5	3	128	123	5	1
3	汝州市	1070	911	159	221	215	6	6	73	68	5	4
4	滑县	1070	911	159	190	185	5	8	55	50	5	7
5	长垣县	1070	911	159	230	223	7	5	74	67	7	2
6	邓州市	1070	911	159	383	378	5	2	72	67	5	5
7	永城市	1070	911	159	441	430	11	1	74	70	4	2
8	固始县	1070	911	159	140	135	5	9	51	46	5	8
9	鹿邑县	1070	911	159	199	194	5	7	44	39	5	9
10	新蔡县	1070	911	159	98	91	7	10	39	34	5	10

3. 政务平台承建方情况

电子政务平台的建设是一项极为专业的系统性工程，平台的承建方在平台建设、运营过程中承担着较其他“互联网 +”项目更多的义务，并可能代表政府方行使一些与平台建设相关的行政管理职能。

（1）省级电子政务平台承建方情况。云政公司是省投资集团下属子公司河南信息产业投资集团出资设立，专门从事政务服务网建设、政务数据共享工作的孙公司，该公司受省投资集团的领导和省发改委的指导，负责承建的具体事务。云政公司作为省级电子政务平台的“总承包商”，运用招标采购等形式将项目“分包”给杭州数梦工场等公司进行具体承建。

目前，云政公司正在推进河南政务服务网、河南政务云平台、统一证照平台、数据共享平台四大平台建设。其中政务云平台建设目标是采用云端服务的形式集中省级各厅局的信息系统，搭建全省统一的政务云平台；统一证照平台建设的目标是收集公安部门等多部门关于身份认证的数据，在统一平台上开展自然人、法人等单位的身份认证；数据共享平台的建设目标是汇总省直单位各项数据（例如测绘、地理信息、环保规划、人口信息、建筑规划等），建立统一的基础信息库，为各级政务服务、便民服务提供数据支持。

为了做好政务服务网的运营推广，河南信息产业投资集团与杭州数梦工场等公司联合成立了河南云数聚科技有限公司。该公司与云政公司在职能上有如下划分：云政公司负责电子政务平台的建设，建设结束后交由云数聚公司运营维护。

（2）各地市承建方情况。由于河南电子政务平台采用省市分建模式，各地市在选定承建方方面有自主权，其中，江苏国泰新点、深圳太极云软件、福建南威等国内一线软件供应商占有较大的市场份额。目前，这些承建方大多数与建行有合作关系，这是建行与电子政务平台合作的有利条件（见表5.53）。

表5.53　各地市电子政务平台信息

地市	合作银行	承建软件公司	PC端网址	App端	微信公众号
郑州	暂无	深圳太极云软技术股份有限公司	http：//m. public. zhengzhou. gov. cn/	i郑州	i郑州
洛阳	暂无	河南中兴网信科技有限公司	www. luoyangzw. gov. cn	洛阳政务服务	洛阳政务服务
开封	开封农商行	深圳太极云软技术股份有限公司	www. kfzwfw. gov. cn	开封政务服务	开封政务服务
安阳	建行	建行	www. aysmzj. gov. cn	安阳市民之家App	安阳市民之家
濮阳	暂无	福建南威	www. pyxzfw. gov. cn	暂无	暂无
鹤壁	鹤壁农商行、建行	江苏国泰新点有限公司	www. hnzwfw. gov. cn 河南政务服务网页面	暂无	暂无
焦作	暂无	福建南威	www. hnzwfw. gov. cn 河南政务服务网页面	暂无	暂无
济源	建行	江苏国泰新点有限公司	zwfw. jiyuan. gov. cn	暂无，新点开发中	暂无，政府开发中
新乡	暂无	大铂金科技有限公司	www. xxsxzfwzx. gov. cn	新乡政务	新乡政务服务
三门峡	暂无	崤云公司（当地政府成立）	无	暂无	暂无
商丘	华商银行	科大讯飞有限公司	wszw. shangqiu. gov. cn	商丘便民网	暂无
漯河	暂无	江苏国泰新点软件有限公司	lh. hnzwfw. gov. cn 河南政务服务网页面	暂无	暂无
许昌	暂无	浪潮	shenpi. xuchang. gov. cn	暂无	暂无
平顶山	平顶山银行	哈工大集团重庆普耀信息产业发展有限公司	pds. hnzwfw. gov. cn 河南政务服务网页面	暂无	暂无
驻马店	暂无	中国联通公司	www. zmdzwfw. gov. cn	天中e站	暂无
南阳	暂无	深圳太极云软技术股份有限公司	zwfw. nanyang. gov. cn	暂无	暂无

（续表）

地市	合作银行	承建软件公司	PC 端网址	App 端	微信公众号
信阳	暂无	科大讯飞有限公司；福建榕基软件有限公司	www. xyxzspfw. gov. cn	暂无	信阳智慧政务
周口	暂无	中国联通公司	zk. hnzwfw. gov. cn 河南政务服务网页面	如意周口人	周口政务服务
郑州航空港区	建行	暂无	暂无	暂无	暂无

（二）建行与全省电子政务平台的合作情况

1. 与省级电子政务平台的合作情况

2018 年 4 月 17 日，建行与河南省发改委签订《共同推进“互联网＋政务服务”合作框架协议》，约定在全省电子政务平台共建等方面开展合作；6 月、8 月，建行与河南云政数聚管理有限公司相继签订了框架合作协议和统一支付系统合作协议；8 月 11 日，建行政融支付平台嵌入河南政务服务网正式上线，首批上线 8 个项目，标志着建行与河南省级电子政务平台合作的落地。

8 月 11 日上线后，建行启动了非税缴费端口对接、第二和第三批费项上线、全渠道打通等工作，目前正在积极推进。

2. 与各地市电子政务平台合作情况

一是为安阳市政府建设了“智慧城市政务服务平台”，该平台上收总行后于 2018 年 4 月 21 日正式上线运行，5 月 7 日总行在安阳召开了平台上线发布会，将平台正式推广至全国。安阳智慧城市政务服务平台已经成为全国智慧政务的一面旗帜，目前平台注册用户 47.6 万户，累计办件 377 万余件，在省政务平台考核中，该平台稳居第一方阵，一网通办实现率、网上可办实现率等指标位居全省第一。同时，安阳分行通过该平台实现了存款新增、账户开立和数据挖掘等，带动了分行整体业务的健康发展。例如加速推动公共资源交易合作市县全覆盖，实现全辖 6 家交易中心独家线上合作，日均存款新增达到 4.79 亿元；开通水电气暖、通信、有线等 35 项便民缴费和查询服务，累计通过平台缴费金额近千万元；为安阳智慧人社提供唯一入口，将龙易付成功嵌入安阳公安网，短短 50 天已实现资金入账 305 万元，交易笔数达 5 万余笔。

二是全省各地市智慧政务多点突破。济源、鹤壁、兰考、郑州二七区已与建行签订政务平台合作协议，洛阳、平顶山、南阳、郑州自贸区等地达成合作意向，目前正在推进系统对接。

（三）建行参与“互联网+政务行业应用”情况

截至2018年9月底，建行参与了18个行业的24项“互联网+政务行业应用”，其中19个行业应用已上线。建行参与这些行业的模式有三种：一是建行承建或通过建行“新一代”系统直接提供服务，例如国库集中支付电子化系统、善行宗教事务服务平台、党群综合管理平台、公益教育平台等；二是建行替政府方采购第三方的软硬件设备，并将建行银企直连等产品接入，与第三方共同为政府方提供行业应用服务，例如法院案款管理系统、公共资源交易系统、国土系统等；三是政府主导建立平台，建行接入，例如非税电子化系统（见表5.45）。

表5.54　建行参与互联网+政务行业应用情况

政务行业	建行参与的“互联网+政务行业应用”	建行参与模式	完成状态
1. 社保部门	1. 智慧人社	与第三方软件公司合作	在建
	2. 社保联合收付系统	全建	已上线
	3. 社保跨行代发系统	全建	已上线
2. 财政部门	4. 代理非税收入系统	政府主导、建行配合	已上线
	5. 国库集中支付电子化	全建	已上线
3. 法院	6. 法院诉讼费网上缴费系统	与第三方软件公司合作	在建
	7. 法院案款管理系统	与第三方软件公司合作	已上线
4. 司法部门	8. 狱管资金系统	与第三方软件公司合作	已上线
5. 国土部门	9. 土地招拍挂网上交易系统	与第三方软件公司合作	已上线
6. 公共资源交易中心	10. 公共资源交易系统	与第三方软件公司合作	已上线
7. 工商管理部门	11. 工商注册信息直联	全建	已上线
	12. 工商E认证、企业登记全程电子化帮办	与第三方软件公司合作	已上线
8. 民政部门	13. 民政E线通	全建	已上线
9. 公安部门	14. 行政事业性收费平台（交警罚没、驾照考试、出入境等）	与第三方软件公司合作	已上线
	15. “互联网+公安”系统	与第三方软件公司合作	正在对接
10. 教育部门	16. 公益教育平台	全建	已上线
11. 卫生计生部门	17. 三医联动平台	与第三方软件公司合作	在建
12. 宗教管理部门	18. 善行宗教事务服务平台	全建	已上线
13. 商务部门	19. 资金监管易（商业预付卡、典当行）	全建	已上线
	20. 跨境E+	全建	已上线
14. 住建部门	21. 住建厅信息化系统	与第三方软件公司合作	在建
15. 供销社	22. E采通	全建	正在对接

（续表）

政务行业	建行参与的“互联网+政务行业应用”	建行参与模式	完成状态
16. 各级党组织	23. 党群综合管理平台	全建	已上线
17. 各级工会组织	23. 党群综合管理平台	全建	已上线
18. 养老机构	24. 安心养老平台	全建	已上线
19. 其他部门	25. 根据需求定制开发		

总体来说，近年来，建行在全省电子政务平台建设和“互联网+政务行业应用”方面介入早、成效大，紧跟政策导向、顺应发展趋势，不仅树立了建行系统全国智慧城市政务服务平台的标杆，还成功签订了省级政务平台合作的“首单”，实现了全省电子政务平台合作的多点突破，实现了多个政务行业的深耕细作。这些成绩的取得，得益于总行金融科技 Top+战略的实施，也充分体现了金融科技 Top+战略的及时性、准确性。

三、建行在“互联网+政务服务”热潮中的机遇、收益和挑战

“互联网+”是一项涉及面广、影响深远的社会变革，“互联网+政务服务”是这一变革在政务领域的体现。在这一变革中，互联网经济和金融科技将彻底改变金融领域竞争格局。这一变革蕴含着巨大的业务发展机遇，也带来了跨界竞争、不进则退的严峻挑战。

（一）面临的机遇

1. “互联网+政务服务”是一个新的领域，建行提前布局能够抢占先机

从国家政策和河南省电子政务平台建设情况来看，河南省内的电子政务平台建设起步晚，相关方的利益格局尚未完全定型。在“互联网+政务+金融”方面，除了建行在安阳走出一条成功的道路外，其他金融机构尚未有如此力度和顶层设计。就河南省的情况而言，电子政务平台是一个新兴的领域，短时期内平台的使用率不高、带来的收益不明显，但建行需要以“搭平台、建生态、围市场”的经营方式，提早“跑马圈地”，越早进入，谈判的成本越低，布局难度越小。

2. 政府“触网”带来机构客户需求的变化，是建行拓展政府机构客户的重要机遇

在“互联网+政务服务”的催化下，政府的厅局委办将政务办事流程移到互联网上，其金融需求也由线下移至线上。以公共资源交易系统为例，系统上线前，其招投标的信息流和资金流不统一（招投标发布在网上、投标保证金缴纳在线下）；系统上线后，招投标的资金流和信息流统一，其金融需求由线下的账户资金管理升级为线上的保证金缴纳、退还、结息、入库等需求。在这一需求变更的过程中，建行可以抓住机

遇，通过系统手段维护、拓展政府机构客户。

3. 群众政务办事习惯的改变，为建行抢占流量入口获客活客提供了难得的机遇

按照电子政务平台的建设规划，未来将实现“平台之外无审批”，个人、企业的依申请政务事项几乎全部移至电子政务平台。平台将汇聚个人、企业客户政务办事“刚性需求”，形成巨大的“流量入口”。抢占这一“流量入口”，将为建行以“平台模式”获客活客提供无限可能。

（二）带来的收益

与电子政务平台的合作，是落实金融科技战略的重要支点，能够在“互联网+政务”领域延伸建行的产品和服务，实现“渠道无界化”，带来的具体收益如下所述。

1. 账户与资金

建行参与互联网+政务服务的直接收益是账户与资金，一是能够带动机构客户账户开立和资金沉淀，例如带动入驻平台的厅局委办账户的开立。政务平台不仅有各单位政务办事项的整合，还有部分局委“重大行业应用”的接入，以安阳市民之家为例，其接入了安阳人社的智慧人社项目和公共资源交易系统，建行可通过平台“顺藤摸瓜”，营销相关局委的账户开立和存款增长；二是能够带动公共服务行业客户的账户开立和资金沉淀，通过共建电子政务平台，打通水电气暖、服务中介等公共服务事项，营销公共服务单位在建行的开户，进一步拓展建行在民生服务领域的市场份额。

2. 线上建行

通过建行直销银行、账户出海等系统和平台的接入，实现电子政务平台用户在政务服务网上办理金融业务，实现建行渠道的延伸，带来个人、企业用户的增长。

3. “数矿”资源

一是在建行为政府“代建”政务平台的模式下，掌握政务服务的全量数据资源，为用户勾画“脸谱”，以便于精准营销，例如通过查询住建系统的新房买入数据，结合该客户在建行系统内的账户来往等数据，有针对性地向用户推送建行家装分期等服务。二是在建行政融支付嵌入政务平台的模式下，通过用户在政务事项中的支付数据，能够将通过平台用户政务办事与建行掌握的用户数据结合，进行精准营销。政务办事、政务支付数据是宝贵的“数矿”资源，其应用的前景非本文能够总结，相信在大数据手段越来越融入社会生活的情况下，这一“数矿”资源能够得到更多的挖掘。

4. “用户”变“客户”

按照互联网企业的推广策略，“搭平台”是商业模式的第一步，平台流量越大、用户黏性越高，平台未来盈利的前景越广阔。据不完全统计，目前互联网平台获取单个活跃用户的成本为近百元，而电子政务平台有着天生的政府背书，由于“平台之外无审批”等政策，其获取用户的成本低于互联网市场的成本。建行在实现与电子政务平台“用户互认”后，无形中将平台“用户”转化为“潜在客户”。在“用户”变“客户”的道路上，建行还有很长的路要走，但是，建行成功介入电子政务平台，就已经走出了“平台模式”中“搭平台”这一步，为下一步寻找盈利点创造了条件。

（三）面对的挑战

1. 互联网企业版图扩张，侵蚀建行对公客户基础

近年来，互联网巨头开始大张旗鼓地与各地方政府开展公共服务领域的合作，抓住政府关注的“非现金城市”“智慧城市”“互联网+政务服务”等热点，以低价无偿方式与政府签约。例如2017年6月19日天津市政府与支付宝旗下蚂蚁金服签订合作协议，推进天津建设“无现金城市”；2017年12月26日，腾讯公司与河南省公安厅签订战略合作协议，共同推进互联网与警务工作的深度融合，助推“智慧公安”建设。表面上看，互联网巨头与政府合作搭建公共服务或政务服务平台，与银行业务的关联度不大，但是一旦互联网公司把控住平台入口后，其后跟进的支付结算、城市服务、在线金融等服务将牢牢占据主动权，将商业银行在政务行业积累多年的合作关系逐步蚕食。目前，互联网巨头已经在零售支付市场占据主导地位，其对“互联网+政务服务”的布局，是对银行赖以生存的对公客户根基的冲击。

可见，这些互联网巨头正在以传统商业银行不易察觉的“温水煮青蛙”的方式，布局公共服务和政务服务领域，侵蚀建行政府机构客户根基。

2. 电子政务领域专业性强，传统打法已不能适应

电子政务平台的建设不仅仅是“搭平台”，更是行政办事流程的重塑，涉及政务办事项的梳理和整合，需要政府各职能部门的全面参与，且大多数事项涉及厅局委办的内部行政审批、行政授权等专业事项，专业性很强。传统商业银行主要“通过向客户提供存贷汇等金融产品和服务获得风险报酬”，对新兴的互联网+政务服务领域不熟悉、不专业，如果没有多年政务服务经验的积累，银行很难把握政府方的真实需求，不了解政府平台的实际情况，无法参与其中。

在“互联网+”领域流行着“社群模式”（如微信）、“平台模式”（如腾讯）、“长尾模式”（如天弘基金）、“免费模式”（如360杀毒软件）、“O2O模式”（如小米）的营销策略，但建行对这些策略的使用并不熟悉，而传统的营销策略又不能适应“互联网+政务”领域，因此急需新的打法、新的营销策略。

四、建行应对策略及下一步工作建议

推广智慧城市政务服务平台，深度参与“互联网+政务服务”，是应对“互联网+”

热潮和跨界竞争的必然选择。下一步，建行要落实“科技驱动、能力开放、平台生态”的金融科技 Top + 战略，深度参与全省“互联网 + 政务服务”，抓住省平台这个关键，做好平台推广上线、省市业务融合、金融板块嵌入、线上线下一体等工作，探索行业事项梳理中的业务机遇，研究获客活客的方法路径，最终实现银政互利共赢。

（一）以科技驱动为核心，做好智慧城市政务服务平台在全省的推广

1. 对症下药，针对地市平台情况采用两种营销方式

目前，河南省电子政务平台采用省市分建模式，省平台提供技术标准、统一入口、统一身份认证，地市自建政务网上办事系统并接入。从各地市接入情况来看，鹤壁、焦作、漯河、平顶山、周口、三门峡6个地市没有单独的政务门户，其余12个地市均有单独的政务门户网站或 App，针对这种情况，建行在营销策略上应有所区别。

针对没有单独门户网站的6个地市，因为使用省平台统一入口，建行要重点做好在省平台上部署涉及6个地市的产品和服务，通过直接调用省平台服务的形式实现对6个地市的覆盖。

针对有单独门户网站的12个地市，要加强对当地政务服务平台的研究，采用省平台部署地市服务事项和直接对接地市平台两种方式进行营销推广。重点关注当地政务服务门户的使用情况，对于使用频次较高的平台，重点做好与地市自有平台的对接；对于使用频次较低且以省平台统一入口为建设重点的地市，重点做好通过省平台直接部署地市服务事项。

2. 线上线下一体，做好实体大厅与网上政务平台营销的相得益彰

现阶段，河南全省政务办事项中能够实现“一网通办”的比率不到20%，各地实体政务服务大厅仍然承担着大部分的政务办事项。因此，线下实体大厅的营销仍然重要。一是要通过网上政务平台的合作撬动与行政服务中心的全面合作，通过行政服务中心协调入驻单位的合作；二是通过线上政融支付平台的布局，切入线下窗口业务，通过 STM 布放、打通政务服务一体机等方式，争夺实体大厅入驻单位的账户和支付结算渠道。

（二）以平台生态为抓手，深度挖掘“互联网 + 政务 + 金融”内涵

根据《国务院关于进一步加快推进全国一体化在线政务服务平台建设的指导意见》，国家、省、市、县电子政务平台的一体化是大势所趋。建行在做好各地市推广的同时，更要把握好“一体化”的深刻内涵，挖掘与省电子政务平台的深度合作，拓展业务场景，做好省、市、县业务融合。

一是做好政融支付系统嵌入政务办事项。政务平台的核心是“一网通办”，建行介

入省级平台建设的切入点是通过金融功能的嵌入协助政务实现“一网通办”。因此，下一步要做好政融支付系统与省非税网上缴费系统的对接，确保建行支付渠道与政务办事项非税缴费的打通。目前，省非税网上缴费系统采用全省统建模式，建行与省非税局一点对接、全省通用，但是，省非税局主导的网上缴费功能尚未嵌入政务办事项，导致“一网通办”大打折扣。在可预期的未来，非税缴费将会逐步嵌入政务办事项中，建行要紧盯这一进程，确保早日接入。

二是做好省平台“便民缴费”项的批量上线。政务服务、公共服务是电子政务平台提供的两项主要服务，其中公共服务与建行对接的部分主要是“便民缴费”事项。目前，建行已上线郑州、洛阳等地的25个费项，下一步要快速推进，确保各地市缴费事项“应上尽上”。通过在省平台布局地市项目，实现省政务平台统一门户向各地市提供服务。

三是在省平台开辟“直销银行”，实现建行“渠道无界化”。目前，建行与省平台正在推进“惠民金融”（名称暂定）板块的合作，省平台将开辟专栏，嵌入建行直销银行、企业贷款、保险、理财、信用卡、劳动者港湾等18类产品和服务，将“线上建行”融入省平台，并通过省平台统一门户入口，将“线上建行”推广至各市县（见表5.55）。

表5.55　拟嵌入河南政务服务网的产品和服务

板块	产品名称	是否全程在线办理
1. 企业贷款	网络E信通	是
1. 企业贷款	惠懂你	是
1. 企业贷款	小微快贷	是
2. 信用卡	信用卡在线申办	是
2. 信用卡	消费分期	是
3. 保险	龙行无忧保险产品计划	是
3. 保险	龙行乐享百万身价B款保险产品计划	是
3. 保险	龙耀一世B款终身寿险	是
3. 保险	建信优享瑞盈1号年金保险	是
3. 保险	康乐人生B款保障计划	否
3. 保险	龙安e生医疗保险	是
3. 保险	团体一年定期寿险	否
3. 保险	团体意外伤害保险B款	否
3. 保险	安康无忧	否
4. 理财	各类个人理财产品	是
5. E账户	直销银行	是
6. 劳动者港湾	劳动者港湾	是

四是探索与省平台合作的应用场景。政融支付系统的嵌入，既是建行与省平台合作的核心，又是合作的开端。省平台是一个开放共享、合作共赢的平台，其应用场景在不断布局和完善中，例如审车业务、医疗保险信息互通业务等将陆续在省平台上线。下一步，建行要积极介入这些应用场景，在省平台上实现金融的多场景应用。

（三）关注政务行业事项梳理，寻找合作切入点

电子政务平台的建设是一项系统性工程，政府职能部门需要梳理本行业相关的政务事项并挂入电子政务平台。目前，河南省编办制定了统一的政务事项目录，各职能部门在这个框架内对政务行业事项的流程进行设计、优化和上线。现阶段河南省电子政务平台的工作重心是各市县、各职能部门梳理政务行业事项并“挂网”，省政府对各地市、直管县和省直部门“网上可办”和“一网通办”事项进行月度通报和考核。

各级政府及政府职能部门政务事项“上网”的过程，也是建行开拓银政合作新领域的机遇。以河南省住建厅项目为例，为落实省政府“互联网+政务服务”的要求，省住建厅加快推进全省住建管理平台建设，建行积极介入并一举签订合作协议，实现与省住建厅在平台共建、数据共享、农民工保证金业务等方面的战略合作。下一步，建行要密切关注省直相关厅局在“互联网+政务服务”领域的进展和需求，通过系统共建等方式介入，寻找业务机遇，拓展“互联网+政务+金融”的适用场景（见表5.56）。

表5.56　省直厅局政务事项“一网通办”情况

序号	省直部门	通用目录事项总数	网上可办事项（项）	一网通办事项（项）
1	省发展改革委	53	53	36
2	省教育厅	42	24	24
3	省科技厅	41	12	12
4	省工业和信息化委	27	23	21
5	省公安厅	17	12	3
6	省民政厅	38	31	11
7	省司法厅	38	3	2
8	省财政厅	4	4	4
9	省人力资源社会保障厅	107	39	17
10	省国土资源厅	51	50	34
11	省环保厅	25	25	13
12	省住房城乡建设厅	89	89	69
13	省交通运输厅	44	25	14

（续表）

序号	省直部门	通用目录事项总数	网上可办事项（项）	一网通办事项（项）
14	省水利厅	19	17	6
15	省农业厅	41	39	34
16	省林业厅	21	20	13
17	省商务厅	22	10	5
18	省文化厅	24	4	4
19	省卫生计生委	80	32	27
20	省政府外侨办	7	4	1
21	省工商局	56	45	45
22	省质监局	15	13	9
23	省新闻出版广电局	59	50	49
24	省体育局	6	6	6
25	省统计局	2	2	2
26	省旅游局	6	5	4
27	省粮食局	7	2	1
28	省安全监管局	13	7	4
29	省食品药品监管局	102	93	87
30	省人防办	25	2	2
31	省政府金融办	15	1	0
32	省政府发展研究中心	1	1	1
33	省气象局	6	0	0
34	省税务局	4	4	1
35	省国防科工局	3	3	1
36	省测绘局	11	10	8
37	省畜牧局	33	32	27
38	省文物局	40	29	23
39	省农机局	8	2	1
40	省残联	1	1	1
41	省档案局	8	6	3
42	省煤监局	6	6	6
合计	1 217	836	631	

（四）探索政务平台获客活客方法，助力金融科技“渠道无界化”

“搭平台、建生态、围市场”是互联网领域的常用策略，其目的是实现“获客活客”等营利目的。建行与电子政务平台的合作可以借鉴这一策略，通过合作带动建行金融科技“渠道无界化”的实现。其中，介入政务平台建设是“搭平台”和“围市场”，围绕政务平台建设多场景行业应用是“建生态”，最终要实现“获客活客”。目前，建行与电子政务平台的合作处于“搭平台”和“围市场”的阶段，“建生态”和“获客活客”是下一阶段的重点目标。

在“建生态”方面，重点是借助电子政务平台的政府背书，围绕政务事项和公共服务事项搭建多场景的行业应用。下一步要寻找应用场景，探索与省平台在多场景行业应用方面的深度合作，例如省平台近期推进的审车服务、大河读书、医院保险系统直连等场景，均是这一领域的有益探索，建行可探索介入。

在“获客活客”方面，重点是探索政务平台用户如何转变为建行客户。与常用的互联网平台相比，政务平台用户的特点是“低频次、高黏度”，即用户使用平台的次数少，但是平台对用户不可或缺。针对这一特点，建行营销思维应跳出平台自身，从大数据、政务 + 金融事项融合等方面抓客户，一是通过“数矿”资源的挖掘进行精准营销，二是探索政务办事项与金融服务的整合，即政务办事联动金融服务，用户在政务办事的同时，平台联动金融服务，实现政务 + 金融事项的融合。安阳智慧城市政务服务平台在“获客活客”方面做出了有益探索，例如该平台抽取社保相关数据，针对这些用户推送建行相关产品和服务，取得良好效果。“获客活客”是一个开放式命题，其实现方式多样，需要在实践中不断摸索、总结、完善。

（五）借助建行集团战略协同力量，探索与省平台的资本合作

由于电子政务平台建设的专业性和复杂性，平台承建方较其他项目有更大的话语权，与平台承建方的合作是建行与电子政务平台合作的重要一环。同江苏国泰、深圳太极、福建南威等国内一线厂商不同，省平台承建方云政及云数聚公司是近两年刚成立的新公司，建行有入股的可能性。为促进与省平台的深入合作，建行可以探索与建信资本等集团子公司战略协同，共同推进入股省平台承建方等事宜，通过资本合作等方式进一步密切与省平台的合作。

总体来说，“互联网 + 政务服务”是一项系统性工程，建行深度介入电子政务平台的建设、运营和推广，对建行应对跨界竞争、打造领先优势有着重要意义。在总行金融科技 Top + 战略的指引下，建行将运用互联网思维，以平台战略为支撑，在履行国有大行社会责任的同时，抓住跨越发展的历史机遇，在“互联网 +”的时代背景下，奠定可持续发展的坚实基础。

资管新规后的银行理财业务发展分析

湖北省分行 张 炜

自 2005 年《商业银行个人理财业务管理暂行办法》发布以来，银行理财业务 13 年来一直处于暂行办法加各种补丁的监管框架之下。2014 年、2016 年虽然分别出台过两次理财业务监督管理办法的征求意见稿，但最终都未正式实施。在资管新规发布后，银行理财业务出现了停滞不前的现象。从发行数据来看，产品新增出现负增长，主要业务以存量为主；在新规背景下，中小银行处于业务停止状态，市场上符合新规的产品发行较少。银行机构与非银机构之间的各种业务合作也由于细则的未落地而大幅度减少。这种“停滞”的状态直接导致了理财规模的萎缩。

根据银保监会消息，2018 年 5 月末银行业理财业务余额为 22.28 万亿元，6 月末余额为 21 万亿元，较 5 月减少 1.28 万亿元，上半年累计减少 1.17 万亿元。其中同业理财的规模和占比持续下降，截至 5 月末，在上年减少 3.4 万亿元的基础上，继续缩减 1.2 万亿元，同业理财业务已累计削减 2/3 以上，5 月末余额约为 2.05 万亿元。理财业务第二季度收缩的主要原因是细则的未落地所导致的市场观望而产生的业务基本停滞。

一、资管新规后银行理财面临的强监管形势分析

（一）表外理财纳入 MPA 考核，促进理财业务规范健康发展

1. 主要内容

央行在 MPA（宏观审慎评估体系）中增加了表外理财资金运用项目，扩大了广义信贷的统计范围。其表外理财资金运用余额等于该表中的资产余额减去现金余额与存款余额之和。

2. 主要影响

其影响主要体现在两方面：一是广义信贷增速方面，二是宏观审慎资本充足率方面，如表 5.57 所示。

表 5.57　表外理财纳入广义信贷的影响

指标名称	全国系统重要性机构	区域性系统重要性机构	普通机构
广义信贷	增幅与目标 M2 增速偏离不超过 20 个百分点为 60 分，否则为 0 分	增幅与目标 M2 增速偏离不超过 22 个百分点为 60 分，否则为 0 分	增幅与目标 M2 增速偏离不超过 25 个百分点为 60 分，否则为 0 分
资本充足率	[C*，+∞)，80 分；[C* −4%，C*)，48～80 分；[0，C* −4%)，0 分	[C*，+∞)，80 分；[C* −4%，C*)，48～80 分；[0，C* −4%)，0 分	[C*，+∞)，80 分；[C* −4%，C*)，48～80 分；[0，C* −4%)，0 分

宏观审慎资本充足率由 4 个指标决定：最低资本充足率，按照《商业银行资本管理办法》的相关要求执行，目前商业银行最低资本充足率为 8%；系统重要性附加成本，根据不同类型的银行（全国系统重要性机构、区域性系统重要性机构、普通机构）设定相应的数值，对于全国系统重要性银行、区域性系统重要性银行的附加资本设置为 1%，普通机构按照公式 0.5% +（1 −0.5%）×（资产规模/区域内最大资产规模）计算；储备资本；逆周期资本缓冲，MAX｛整体信贷顺周期贡献参数 × [广义信贷增速 −（目标 GDP + 目标 CPI）]，0｝。表外理财纳入广义信贷，通过逆周期资本缓冲对宏观审慎资本充足率产生影响。

（二）出台资管新规，加强对银行理财业务监管

为了守住不发生系统性金融风险的底线，促进银行理财业务持续稳健发展，2018 年 3 月 28 日，《关于规范金融机构资产管理业务的指导意见》（以下简称“资管新规”）经中央全面深化改革委员会第一次会议审议通过。

1. 主要内容

整体上看，新规严格限制投资范围、投资通道，通过去影子银行、去通道、加强表外监管、降低期限错配等措施，防范银行理财业务发展过程中暴露的金融风险。具体措施较为严格，监管力度明显加大，全面落实后预计将给银行理财业务带来多方面的重大影响。

“资管新规”与以往出台的资管监管政策相比，原由三会分别监管的各类资管产品实现了“五统一”：一是统一资产管理业务的定义和资管产品的范围、分类；二是统一合格投资者的标准；三是统一资管产品杠杆比例要求；四是统一资本约束和风险准备金计提标准；五是统一资管产品数据统计格式、口径及路径等统计制度。核心内容包括以下几项：

（1）禁保本及破刚兑。金融机构开展资产管理业务时不得向投资者承诺保本保收益，不得开展表内资产管理业务。

（2）限非标及控规模。禁止投资非标准化商业银行信贷资产及其收益权。非标准化债务资产投资应当符合有关金融监管部门的配额管理规定，并逐步缩小规模。

（3）禁止多级嵌套。除 FOF（基金中的基金）、MOM（管理人的管理人基金）和单层分包业务外，资管产品不得投资于其他资管产品，不得为发行的资管产品提供扩大投资范围、绕过监管的渠道服务。

（4）投资范围与集中度。固定收益资产、非标准资产、公开发行上市股票、非上市股权、金融衍生品和境外资产是资管产品的合法投资品。资管产品投资单一证券的市场价值或证券投资基金的市场价值不得超过资管产品净资产的 10%，私募股权产品除外；各资管产品投资单项资产的市场价值或证券投资基金的市场价值不得超过证券市值或证券投资基金市值的 10%。

（5）禁止资金池，要求独立托管。金融机构不得参与资金池业务，包括滚动发行、集体经营、期限错配和单独定价功能，资管产品由第三方托管机构托管。

（6）自营和代客业务分离。金融机构不得用自有资金购买机构或资产管理子公司发行的资管产品，不得提供任何直接非标准资产或股权资产，不得提供明示或暗示的担保或回购承诺。如果出现风险，金融机构不得以自由资金垫付。

2. 主要影响

（1）通过设定银行资产管理门槛，加大对投资终端的限制，实施第三方托管和累计风险准备金等，银行资产管理业务的运营成本将增加，这将减缓业务发展速度。

（2）每只资产管理产品必须由第三方进行托管。

（3）对银行理财业务资金管理、产品发售等影响很大，使银行理财必须改变当前大规模进行资金池期限错配的操作管理方式和策略，提高自身管理投资能力，这也是对整个银行理财发展的严峻挑战。

（4）投资范围的限制也将使得商业银行减少非标准和股权资产的配置。债券资产配置的压力将增加，总收益率将下降，从而迫使银行理财降低资本成本。

（5）资产证券化是非标转标的主要手段。

（6）允许银行委外，但对嵌套有限制，以防止金融机构之间的风险传染。

（7）预计未来大多数银行将设立资产管理子公司以避免净资本限制。

2018 年 7 月 20 日，中国银保监会发布《商业银行理财业务监督管理办法（征求意见稿）》（简称《理财办法》），整体内容上与资管新规保持一致，没有超出预期的条款，具体内容如表 5. 58 所示。

表 5.58 《理财办法》重要条款列示

角度	重点内容列示
销售管理要求	• 降低公募理财销售起点从 5 万元至 1 万元，拉近与公募基金距离，有利于降低公募理财销售的难度，增加竞争力 • 双录要求保留；销售渠道仅限于吸收存款的银行业金融机构
投资范围	• 没有明确区分公私募，允许公私募理财产品投资各类公募证券投资基金 • 明确公募理财可以投资非标，但投资上市公司股票还需另行制定
非标投资	• 总量上进行"35% 和 4%"的限制，单只公募理财产品投非标准资产的比例无限制 • 增加 10% 的集中度限制，与大额风险暴露政策目的一致，防范集中度风险
委外与投顾	• 提出理财投资合作机构的概念（包括委外与投顾机构），必须是具有专业资质并受金融监督管理部门依法监管的金融机构或银行业监督管理机构认可的其他机构 • 对于公募理财是否可以委托给私募证券资管产品没有禁止也没有明确要求，目前来看合作路径依然存在
登记托管	• 银登中心对理财产品的发行信息、募集情况、投资资产、投资者信息等内容进行登记，初步实现理财产品的全流程集中统计，有利于真正实现理财业务的穿透式监管和运作管理的全面动态监管
保本理财处置	• 明确保本理财按照结构性存款或其他存款规范管理 • 发行结构性存款必须具备衍生品交易业务资格

（三）进一步完善资管产品增值税纳税规则

财政部、税务总局连续发布财税〔2016〕36 号（简称"36 号文"）、财税〔2016〕140 号（简称"140 号文"）以及财税〔2017〕2 号文件，基本明确了银行资管产品增值税征收相关内容。

1. 主要内容

（1）36 号文主要内容。明确"销售金融服务"包括贷款服务、金融商品转让、直接收费金融服务和保险服务 4 类，前 3 类与银行资管有关。明确了"营改增"过渡期相关税收减免政策。

（2）140 号文主要内容。140 号文进一步明确了投资者在金融商品持有期间（含到期）取得的非保本收益，不征收增值税。明确了纳税人购入基金、信托、理财产品等各类资管产品持有至到期不属于金融商品转让。另外明确在资管产品运行过程中的增值税纳税人为资管产品管理人。

（3）财税〔2017〕2 号文主要内容。明确在资管产品运营过程中以资管产品管理人为增值税纳税人的有关规定的政策执行起始时间为 2017 年 7 月 1 日。起始日之前已纳税额可从起始日后计算的增值税应纳税额中抵减。

按照税收政策精神，银行理财业务涉及增值税纳税行为的主体主要包括理财产品、银行、投资者、第三方机构，具体如下所述。

理财产品。理财产品作为特殊目的载体（SPV），在其生命周期内存在的应税行为主要包括“贷款服务”及“金融商品转让”。可适用的增值税税收优惠主要包括金融同业往来、国债、地方政府债、金融债的利息收入免征增值税、持有或持有至到期的金融商品取得的非保本收益不征收增值税等。

银行。银行作为产品管理人和资产管理相关金融服务的提供者，按照约定从理财产品取得托管费、销售费、管理费等中间业务收入，属于“提供应税金融服务”。

投资者。保本产品购买人因获得保本收益，其应税行为属于“贷款服务”，应就其取得收益缴纳增值税。目前，银行不负责代扣代缴理财产品购买者应缴税款。

第三方机构。银行理财业务涉及的第三方机构主要包括理财产品支付给第三方机构的管理费，第三方机构的应税行为同属“提供应税金融服务”，应由中介各自就此部分收入缴纳增值税。

2. 主要影响

（1）明确了银行理财作为纳税主体的地位。140 号文明确了资管产品管理人作为增值税纳税人，为资管产品运营过程中发生的增值税应税行为进行增值税缴费，使得税收征收工作更为便利。而政策解读文件明确规定管理人收取的管理费、运用资管产品资金进行投资时所产生的增值税均由管理人缴纳，这一规定及对征税范围的完善，将对整个银行资管业务造成重大影响。

（2）固定收益类资产利息收入需要缴税，但利率债等部分资产免予征收。政策明确在银行理财投资中占据重要地位的固定收益类资产利息收入需缴纳增值税，如信用债、非标类投资、股票质押回购等，但国债、质押式回购、地方政府债、金融债、同业存款、同业存单、央票等债券的利息收入免征增值税。

（3）金融商品转让应缴纳增值税。这对银行理财而言，所有股票、债券等资产的资本利得收入均需缴纳增值税，没有豁免。

（4）补充明确“保本收益”的范畴及保本需缴纳增值税、非保本不缴纳增值税。对于底层投资品及资管产品的增值税征收明确为投资明确带有保本承诺的资产需缴纳增值税。

（5）资管产品持有至到期不缴纳增值税。

（四）规范信贷资产收益权转让业务

2016 年银监会下发了银监办发〔2016〕82 号文件（简称“82 号文”）。

1. 主要内容

银行应在信贷资产收益权转让后按照原信贷资产计提资本。信贷资产收益权出让方银行应按照会计处理和风险实际承担情况计提拨备，不得通过本行理财资金直接或间接投资本行信贷资产收益权，不得以任何形式承担显性或隐性回购义务。对机构投资者资金来源应当穿透。银行非标理财产品在银登中心完成转让和集中登记的，其资产不计入非标准化债权资产。

2. 主要影响

82 号文强调信贷收益权会计出表而监管不出表的思路，也同时表达了监管层防范金融风险的决心。在业务规范后，银行理财业务不能再以创新之名，行监管套利之实，而是应通过业务创新充分体现国家经济发展导向，推动理财业务健康有序发展。

（五）明确理财信息登记要求

根据 2016 年银监会创新部的工作要求，为全面加强理财投资风险监测，切实做好理财产品投资资产的信息登记工作，结合登记情况，中央国债登记结算公司于 2016 年 6 月发布《关于进一步明确理财投资信息登记要求的通知》（中债字〔2016〕76 号）。

1. 主要内容

一是按月度统计资产管理计划分类，并按穿透前和穿透后分别统计；二是严格做好资管计划类资产的信息登记工作；三是准确登记资产分类；四是准确登记资产明细信息；五是不得漏报拆入、正回购等负债信息；六是注意核对通过理财登记系统登记的明细信息与月度统计表总量信息在计算口径、统计时点和结果上的一致性。

2. 主要影响

通知发布后将进一步加强监管机构对理财投资的监测力度，监管机构将准确掌握穿透后的底层资产配置，同时明确了理财信息的登记要求，有效规范银行业理财登记体系，帮助银行业金融机构深入理解登记内容，提高登记质量，加快推进银行理财业务标准化进程。

三、当前银行理财业务面临的挑战和措施

（一）面临的挑战

银行理财业务规模占比为资产管理行业最大部分，但其经营模式、大类资产配置、盈利模式、系统建设、基础管理等还存在一些较为薄弱的方面，是银行理财业务未来发展面临的重要挑战。

1. 银行理财法律地位仍有待明确

法律上的缺位，使得银行理财产品在风险隔离、过手机制等方面无法真正完善，利率风险、市场风险、信用风险也无法真正传递给投资者，刚性兑付的压力依然存在。

2. 投研能力亟待提高，投研队伍建设尚待加强

近年来银行理财业务发展虽然较快，但整体而言，投资的主动管理能力较为粗放，距离精细化、专业化的主动投资管理水平还有一定差距。很多银行的理财业务尚未形成较为专业化的投研团队，导致银行理财业务的资产配置能力、产品创新能力不足，使得资产整体收益水平较证券、基金等市场化的资管子行业有一定差距。在当前宏观形势日趋严峻、市场监管日趋严格、行业竞争日趋激烈的背景下，投研能力以及交易能力的差距将成为决定商业银行理财业务竞争力提升的关键因素。从近年来银行理财业务资产配置发展趋势来看，标准化资产的配置比例越来越高，而投研能力是标准化资产投资不可缺少的一环。

3. 薪酬激励约束机制有待进一步完善

目前银行理财从业人员的薪酬体制与市场有较大差距，无法留住或吸引优秀人才，在一定程度上制约了银行理财业务的发展。如何在传统商业银行的组织管理框架下建立健全有效的激励约束机制，就成为推动银行理财业务发展过程中需要重点研究的问题之一。银行理财业务作为传统商业银行衍生出来的重要的中间业务，其激励约束机制既不能完全照搬其他非银行金融机构的现有体制机制，也不能延续传统银行的现有体制机制，需要结合银行理财业务的发展实践，在激励约束机制方面进行创新设计，进而使银行理财业务的发展既能满足商业银行作为一个整体发展的需要，也能满足在大资管市场竞争的需要。

（二）改进措施

银行理财业务面对上述各种挑战，要以问题为导向，通过与监管机构的积极沟通、自身核心竞争能力的建设、与外部机构的大力合作，逐步适应和解决发展过程中面临的各种问题。

1. 资产管理业务应回归本源，明晰角色和定位

一个回归本源的银行资管行业，其定位应为传导、分散、匹配风险，而非承担和消除风险。具体而言，比照欧美健全的体系，均应包含具备以下特征的三层架构：一是资本市场层，为银行理财业务提供合格的、丰富的、能够长期持续创造价值的基本投资品；二是资管产品层，是资产管理机构努力发挥专业价值的位置，其目标是分散、降低投资组合的非系统性风险；三是资金管理层，即财富管理层，其功能是提供契合客户自身特点的财富增值方案、现金流支出匹配方案和风险管理方案。

2. 统一监管标准，加强功能监管，引导转型

伴随监管政策的变化，国内资产管理行业实施功能监管指日可待，监管政策的出台对于银行理财业务的持续稳健发展是非常重要的。完善资产管理行业的监管框架，

按照产品本质特征进行一般性、功能性的定义和分类，确保同类型产品的监管逻辑一致。同时，在统一规定的基础上尽快推动相关立法的完善，将核心标准通过法律的形式长期固化。只有不断完善监管体系，银行理财业务才能实现有效转型。

3. 更加注重大类资产配置和策略研究

大类资产配置的前提是全资产经营，银行资管在资产端要从货币、类信贷、债券向全资产经营转型。在实现全资产经营的前提下，基于市场研究和策略研究实现资产组合管理，综合运用投资时钟原理，把握大类资产轮动形成的市场机遇，平衡风险与收益。而有效进行大类资产配置的重要前提是对宏观经济周期的深入研究。

4. 加快投研体系建设，夯实核心竞争力

加大银行理财业务投研体系建设。一是宏观和利率市场研究，包括跟踪新常态下国内经济形势、经济政策的变化；把握利率变化时机，提升自主投资能力；做好市场预判，及时调整债券投资策略。二是 FOF 和 MOM 研究，包括加强委托投资策略的研究，提高管理人选择和策略选择的科学性。强化投前、投中的业绩归因分析，为投后管理提供决策参考。三是信用研究，建立信用评级团队，为信用类资产投资提供决策参考，预防和化解信用风险。四是资本市场研究，合理预判和把握资本市场波动，积极调整资本市场业务的风险准入、投资策略和对冲策略。

（三）2018 年理财业务发展方向

1. 净值型产品成竞争焦点，预期收益型产品仍是主流

随着资管新规的逐步落地，资管业传统的行业分类监管模式将逐步被打破，功能性监管或将成为主流。在“大资管统一监管”的框架下，银行理财的发展方向继续向“调结构、稳风控”方向转变，理财规模增速将进一步放缓。同时，理财产品仍承载刚性兑付压力，如何使理财产品回归资产业务的本质，如何打破刚性兑付的软约束，成为摆在各家商业银行面前的一项亟待解决的问题。

由于普通大众投资者对于预期收益型理财产品的认可度和接受度较高，对于净值型理财产品，尤其是在净值发生回撤时，对于净值型理财产品的销售和投资者对于净值型理财产品的接受和认可还有很长的一段路要走，需要继续深化投资者教育。

2. 挖掘资产证券化投资机会

相较于传统的债券产品，资产证券化产品溢价优势比较明显，资产证券化品种成为目前各家银行大类资产配置的重要理财产品。统计显示，2017 年共发行资产证券化产品 134 只，发行规模达到 5 977.29 亿元，总发行规模和发行数量均明显高于 2016 年。

资产证券化受到银行资管的青睐，是因为两者的对接有着天然契合度，银行理财

“非标转标”的动力能为资产证券化的大发展带来巨大空间。股份制银行、城商行等非标转标的需求旺盛，资产证券化则是非标准化债权向标准化债权转变、实现直接融资的重要手段。作为发起机构，银行资管可以将本行理财资金投资的债权类资产打包出售给特殊目的载体，实现资产剥离，并作为委托人牵头整个 ABS 项目的落地。作为证券化资产的投资者，银行理财资金可以投资资产证券化产品。

3. 委外投资模式进一步发展成熟

在目前的监管环境中，发展 MOM 和 FOF 成为银行理财的一个重要方式。在高收益资产陆续到期且投资限制越发严厉的背景下，获取具有竞争力的收益率难度日益增加，在日渐困难的投资局面中，MOM 和 FOF 能一定程度地帮助银行理财投资降低波动率、提升收益率。因而从长远看，类似 FOF、MOM 等模式对于大资金管理更具优势，有可能演变成银行理财的一种重要的投资模式，随之带来的便是委托投资市场的进一步扩张和成熟。

第一，银行理财委外筛选机制将进一步标准化、完善化，对委外机构的风险控制能力也将进一步加强。零碎粗放的委外机构甄别将持续完善为较为系统标准的筛选流程，对银行的风险控制能力的要求加大，委外审查风控将更为精细化、专业化、完善化和成熟化。

第二，对委外机构一是建立健全稳定的投研、交易、风控团队；二是建立绩效归因评价体系，适时对委外机构投资业绩进行归因分析；三是完善信息披露制度，对投资策略执行情况、资产持仓情况、风险变动情况进行及时的信息披露。

第三，银行理财从主动投资到委托投资，从单一债券投资到对多类资产及产品的投资。这一变化将更多地开始考验银行理财对大类资产轮动节奏的把握、组合配置管理能力、对委外机构和产品的筛选能力和风控能力的强弱。

风险管控篇

普惠金融风险底线评估：基于压力测试技术

总行风险管理部　王　林

一、引言

压力测试（stress test）是用来评估异常但又可能发生的宏观经济或事件冲击下，对金融体系整体或某些特定资产组合脆弱性进行定量影响评估的技术总称。在具体业务领域，压力测试具有能前瞻性评估某些小概率事件对商业银行经营或其所拥有的投资组合可能造成的影响的优势；另外，商业银行压力测试能帮助金融监管者更好地进行特定金融机构的信用风险等领域的监管工作。目前，全球主要国家监管当局均要求所属银行定期进行压力测试的工作，例如美联储每年均针对境内的主要银行业机构开展银行业压力测试（CCAR）。自20世纪90年代国外先进商业银行开展压力测试工作以来，压力测试的理念和方法体系在全球银行业中得到广泛应用，目前，其作为评价极端风险和尾部风险的重要工具，成为进行前瞻性风险管理的有力工具。

自2008年美国爆发次贷危机以来，我国为了推动经济转型发展，更好促进就业，提高经济发展的质量和内涵，采取了一系列措施鼓励商业银行支持普惠金融业务发展。但受国外需求萎缩，人民币单边升值，以及石油、黄金等大宗商品价格的剧烈波动，企业的用工成本持续上升等众多因素影响，全国小微企业整体发展趋缓，尤其是钢贸、联保联贷等业务受到的冲击尤为严重，使小企业的发展受到空前的严峻挑战。因此，如何更好地识别普惠金融业务在极端宏观经济下的信用风险特征，合理评价商业银行能够承受的风险底线，具有十分重要的理论和现实意义。本文通过采用“自上而下”的压力测试技术和方法，测量不同压力情景下的宏观因素下行对普惠金融业务中的核心组成部分——小微企业信贷业务资产质量的影响，并运用蒙特卡洛模拟方法，合理评估不同置信区间水平下商业银行小微企业信贷业务的风险底线和可承受的风险上限。

二、相关研究综述

从内容上看，商业银行压力测试研究主要分为理论研究和具体实证研究两方面。

在压力测试的理论和研究方面，威尔逊（Wilson，1997）和默顿（Merton，1974）研究的内容和框架是开展相关工作研究的先导者和探索者，同时也是研究学者开展压力测试理论和方法研究的重要参考依据。威尔逊（1997）主要利用逻辑回归（Logit）方法转换工业部门的违约概率，将（0，1）分布变量转变成连续的线性变量，并将转换得到的指标与 GDP、失业率等宏观经济变量构建回归模型，然后根据宏观经济指标的压力情景，进行不同宏观经济冲击下的违约率分布预测。此后，博斯（Boss，2002）、维罗莱宁（Virolainen，2004）和翁（Wong，2008）等学者，分别以威尔逊模型为基础，对模型的方法进行了优化和改进，并采用不同的实证对象，分别对澳大利亚、芬兰、中国香港银行体系进行了压力测试实证研究。对于以威尔逊研究的方法为基础的压力测试工作，由于是基于整体资产组合的压力测试，可以称之为“自上而下”的压力测试。而默顿主要基于期权定价的基本原理，将各上市公司的股票价格波动和价值变化作为评价的出发点，与宏观经济要素变化的具体反应进行回归，由此构建以公允价值计量的资产价格变动相关理论与违约概率模型结合的压力测试模型，将公司价值低于负债规模作为违约的触发点。与以威尔逊研究的方法为基础的“自上而下”的压力测试相对应，默顿模型是商业银行开展此类压力测试的模型，也称为“自下而上”的压力测试。

在国内压力测试方面，研究的主要内容涉及三个方面。一是重点进行压力测试理论的研究。这一部分以介绍和梳理国外相关理论体系为主。高扬、王林（2016）首次将 Z-Shift 转换矩阵方法应用于我国商业银行的压力测试体系中，由于此方法为美联储开展大型银行 CCAR 压力测试模型的应用方法之一，因此具有较强的理论研究意义，该压力测试框架以威尔逊压力测试模型为基础模型，对我国商业银行开展信用风险压力测试的“自上而下”模型进行了体系设计和方法应用，并基于 Z-Shift 转换矩阵，进行压力结果的细化应用和资产组合的传导。二是以对国外监管机构和大型银行压力测试体系先进经验介绍为主，引入全球领先的压力测试理念和思路。王林（2015）基于美联储 2015 年公布的新一轮银行业压力测试结果，分析了 31 家在美主要银行控股公司在假设不利（adverse）和极端不利（severely adverse）两种情景下的资本抵御宏观经济和金融市场风险的冲击，并从方法和应用实质上分析了美联储压力测试的方法特征及发展趋势，对提升我国商业银行压力测试的技术水平，更好地配合相关领域的转型发展工作具有借鉴意义。三是利用相关压力测试模型，针对我国商业银行各风险计量领域，进行具体的压力测试实证方面的研究。例如，谭晓红、樊纲治（2011）以不良贷款率为因变量，构建评估商业银行信用风险的评价指标，采用表面无相关 SUR 模型对我国不同类型商业银行，如国有商业银行、股份制银行、城市商业银行和农村商业银行等分别进行了信用风险的宏观压力测试。

从商业银行压力测试开展的现状看，尚未开展过在普惠金融业务的信用风险专项压力测试工作。因此，本文的贡献在于：基于我国商业银行在普惠金融业务发展方面的特征，建立 SUR 模型分析相关风险因素变动对业务资产质量的不同影响；并运用目前前沿的蒙特卡洛模拟方法，模拟商业银行普惠金融业务在压力情景下的损失分布，定量分析相关的抗风险能力。

三、普惠金融业务信用风险压力测试实证研究[①]

（一）模型构造

本次测试采用 SUR 回归方程组进行，相关模型系统可由如下方程组表示：

$$y_t = f(x_1, x_2, \cdots, x_n, \beta, v_t) \tag{1}$$

$$x_{it} = \alpha_{i,0} + \sum_{j=1}^{k} \alpha_{i,j} x_{i,t-j} + \varepsilon_{i,t} \tag{2}$$

$$\mathrm{E} = \begin{bmatrix} v_t \\ \varepsilon_t \end{bmatrix} \sim N(0, \Sigma) \ \Sigma = \begin{pmatrix} \Sigma_v & \Sigma_{v,\varepsilon} \\ \Sigma_{\varepsilon,v} & \Sigma_\varepsilon \end{pmatrix} \tag{3}$$

其中，方程（1）刻画了普惠业务 MPD 变化情况与各个风险因子间的关系，式中 y_t 为普惠业务 MPD 的变化率，x_i 为各个风险因子，β 为参数向量，v_t 为残差。方程（2）表示了各因子本身的动态 AR 过程，$\varepsilon_{i,t}$表示因子 x_i 自回归方程的残差。方程（3）表示了各个方程之间的相互影响，N（0，Σ）表示均值为0，方差为Σ的多维联合正态分布。

方程（2）描述了各风险因子的时间序列动态过程，即考察各因子同比增长率的当期值和其自身的滞后值之间有何内在联系，它们与方程（1）共同反映了普惠业务 MPD 与各因子间的传导关系。

方程（3）表示的则是前述各方程随机扰动项的方差—协方差矩阵，刻画了各因子间以及各因子与不良率变化间的交互影响。

在整个方程系统的估计过程中，采用了逐步回归的方法，并在信息重叠的因子中选择解释力度最高的因子，以得到最后的模型结果。

（二）指标选择

在本次测试中，主要考虑了两类风险因子：宏观经济因子和普惠客户经营状况因子。

---

① 相关数据在本文发表过程中均进行了一定处理，只为反映研究方法，不代表真实的业务数据和情况。

1. 全国宏观经济因子

结合国内外宏观信用风险压力测试的经验和专家的分析，本次测试中备选的宏观经济风险因子包括：国内生产总值（GDP）、全国工业增加值、全国社会消费品零售总额、全国进出口总额、全国居民消费价格指数（以下简写为“全国 CPI”）、全国工业品出厂价格指数（以下简写为“全国 PPI”）、货币供应量 M2、银行间市场同业拆借利率、人民币兑美元汇率、铁矿石价格指数、煤炭价格指数以及布伦特原油期货价格指数这 12 个指标。宏观经济数据均来自国家统计局公布的数据。

2. 普惠客户经营状况因子

与全国宏观因子的选择相匹配，结合普惠业务运行的具体情况，本次测试选择的经营状况因子包括：企业家信心指数、制造业采购经理指数、制造业企业景气指数、新订单指数、新出口订单指数共计 5 个指标。相关数据均来自国家统计局公布的数据。

（三）数据处理

1. 定义压力测试目标

本次压力测试以普惠业务的信用风险作为测试目标。在标准化的压力测试中如：威尔逊（1997）、博斯（2002）、维罗莱宁（2004）和香港金融管理局季报（2006）等，通常用新发生违约率作为反映对公信贷资产宏观信用风险状况的指标。具体来看，新发生违约率又可分为以违约客户数计算的新发生违约率（MPD_1）和以违约金额计算的新发生违约率（MPD_2）。

以违约客户数计算的新发生违约率（MPD_1）为：

$$MPD_1 = \frac{\text{当期内违约客户数}}{\text{期初正常客户数}} \tag{4}$$

其中，期初正常客户数为截至考察期期初未发生违约的客户总数，当期内违约客户数为在考察期内发生违约的客户数量（即期内新增违约客户数）。

以违约金额计算的新发生违约率（MPD_2）为：

$$MPD_2 = \frac{\text{当期内违约金额}}{\text{期初正常信贷余额}} \tag{5}$$

其中，期初正常信贷余额为截至考察期期初未发生违约的信贷余额，当期内违约金额为在考察期内发生违约的金额（即期内新增违约金额）。

由于商业银行不良率指标中，不良贷款通常经过多次的剥离和核销操作，因此使得不良率出现多次明显的非经济因素引致的跳跃，经测算，采用以违约客户数权重的新发生违约率（MPD_1）更具有代表性，可以作为普惠业务信用风险状况的测度指标。

2. 对 MPD 的 Logit 转换

令 MPD_t 表示 t 时刻银行的不良贷款率，由于其值介于 0 与 1 之间，以其 Logit 变换值 y_t 作为回归因变量，即：

$$y_t = ln\left(\frac{1 - MPD_t}{MPD_t}\right) \tag{6}$$

此时，$-\infty < y_t < +\infty$，且 y_t 与 MPD_t 有明显的反向关系，y_t 越高，信贷风险状况越好。y_t 可以看作是银行的稳健性指标。

3. 确定样本时间长度

在可能获取相关风险因子的情况下，为保证统计检验的可靠性和结果的合理性，并充分反映最新的风险特征，采用相关季度数据进行样本构建。为了尽量提高统计结果的可靠性，同时考虑 2008 年金融危机时的宏观经济状况，采用了从 2007 年第一季度至 2014 年第四季度共计 32 个数据点。

4. 业务数据处理

为使数据满足统计分析的要求，对数据进行相关处理，以满足计量模型的需要。第一，由于回归模型假设随机扰动项服从正态分布，必须保证数据转化为在 $-\infty$ 到 $+\infty$ 上取值的时间序列；第二，将所有的序列转换为平稳序列。

对于因变量 MPD，由于采用的是对数差分计算，满足 $-\infty$ 到 $+\infty$ 的取值范围。对该序列进行 ADF 单位根检验并对序列的时间趋势进行检验，检验结果均表明，因变量序列为平稳序列，可以用来建模。

本次分析所考察的 17 个自变量中，相关数据处理过程如下所示。

第一步，将数据中所有的当年累计值转化为当季新增值。

第二步，计算各因子的对数同比变化率，剔除季节效应的影响，即：

$$\text{同比增长率} = \ln(\text{因子 } t \text{ 期的新增值}) - \ln(\text{因子 } t-12 \text{ 期的新增值}) \tag{7}$$

第三步，对上述同比增长率进行 ADF 单位根检验和时间趋势检验。如果序列存在一个单位根非平稳，则对平稳序列进行普通一阶差分；经检验，本次测试的所有同比增长率不存在需要二阶差分的情况。

第四步，对处理后的所有序列再次进行 ADF 单位根检验和时间趋势的检验，检验结果表明，各个自变量均为平稳序列，可用于建模。

（四）模型构造结果

1. 单因子回归

方程系统构建的第一步是用 y_t 对各个风险因子的当期和滞后一期进行单因子回归，

使用 NW 方法初步筛选出对普惠业务 MPD 变化具有影响的因子。因子初步筛选结果表明，以 10% 为显著性水平，候选因子中与因变量有显著关系的因子为：国内生产总值（GDP）、制造业企业家信心指数（QYXX）、制造业采购经理指数（CGJL）共计 3 个指标。

2. SUR 模型估计结果与分析

（1）SUR 模型估计结果

从表 6.1 中可以看到，在估计结果中，各项系数的正负号符合经济学意义。

表 6.1　方程系统的 SUR 估计结果

	因变量			
自变量	y_t	$LnGDP_t$	$QYXX_t$	$CGJL_t$
常数项	0.7378****			
$LnGDP_t$				
$QYXX_t$				
$CGJL_t$	0.1922****			
$LnGDP_{t-1}$		0.8362****		
$QYXX_{t-1}$	0.2817****		1.4914***	
$CGJL_{t-1}$				0.7255****
$LnGDP_{t-2}$	0.3025****	0.5125****		
$QYXX_{t-2}$			0.7144***	
$CGJL_{t-2}$				0.3981****
y_{t-1}	0.9108****			
y_{t-2}				
调整后的 R^2	0.9647	0.9717	0.9392	0.9101
DW 值	2.1142	1.799453	1.599973	1.98704
样本数目	32	32	32	32

注：（1）**、*** 及 **** 分别表示 10%、5% 及 1% 的显著性程度。
（2）调整后的 R^2 为 OLS 估计所得值。

将上述结果写成方程的形式为：

$$\begin{cases} Y_t = 0.7378 + 0.3025 \times LnGDP_{t-2} + 0.1922 \times CGJL_t + 0.2817 \times \\ QYXX_{t-1} + 0.9108 \times Y_{t-1} + \varepsilon \\ LnGDP_t = 0.8362 \times LnGDP_{t-1} + 0.5125 \times LnGDP_{t-2} + \nu_1 \\ CGJL_t = 1.4914 \times CGJL_{t-1} + 0.7144 \times CGJL_{t-2} + \nu_2 \\ QYXX_t = 0.7255 \times QYXX_{t-1} + 0.3981 \times QYXX_{t-2} + \nu_3 \end{cases} \tag{8}$$

其中第一个方程给出的是商业银行普惠业务信贷资产质量变化和风险因子之间的关系，各因子前的系数代表了该因子对因变量变化的影响方向与影响程度。可以看到，经系统模型筛选后，统计结果表明与MPD变化有显著关系的因子只剩下3个：国内生产总值（GDP）、企业家信心指数（QYXX）、制造业采购经理指数（CGJL）。其中，国内生产总值提前两期对普惠业务信贷资产质量产生影响。制造业采购经理指数当期对普惠业务信贷资产质量产生影响。企业家信心指数提前一期对普惠业务信贷资产质量产生影响。

从影响方向看，各因子对不良贷款变化率的影响均显著为负。这意味着，当国内生产总值提前两期出现下降，小型企业景气指数下行，企业家信心指数提前一期下降时，将对普惠业务信贷资产质量产生影响。

（五）执行压力测试

1. 压力情景设计

压力情景设计可以分为历史情景、系统情景和专家情景3种方法。根据我国宏观经济发展的阶段和特征，此次压力测试采用历史情景法确定最可能发生的轻度压力情景（情景一），采用专家情景法判断中度和重度压力情景（分别称情景二、情景三）。

第一，历史情景法。所谓历史情景法即采用历史上曾经发生过的极端情形进行压力测试。因此，采用整体建模样本2007年第一季度至2015年第四季度的各变量最低值作为情景一（轻度压力）：国内生产总值较上季度降至6.6%，企业家信心指数降至83.9，采购经理人指数降至41.2。

第二，专家情景法。基于相关机构对中国经济的预测，并征求相关业务领域专家和专业人士的意见，设计的两种压力冲击情景如下：

情景二（中度压力）：国内生产总值较上季度降至6.0%，企业家信心指数降至80，采购经理人指数降至40。

情景三（重度压力）：国内生产总值较上季度降至5.0%，企业家信心指数降至70，采购经理人指数降至35。

为充分反映宏观经济风险因子对不良贷款率的影响，本次压力测试采用回归预测法与蒙特卡洛模拟两种压力测试方法。回归预测法侧重于对未来趋势的分析，是线性的点估计；蒙特卡洛模拟产生大量的不良贷款率在压力情境下的可能取值，再通过模拟出的数据，利用分位数方法求出不良贷款率在给定置信水平下的VaR值，可以看出未来不良贷款率的可能分布情况。

2. 回归预测法的压力测试结果分析

回归预测法压力测试先是对宏观经济变量压力情景进行设定，然后利用回归分析估计出主方程的系数，从而得到各宏观经济风险变量的影响程度，最后代入压力情景下各变量的取值，计算出 Yt，再通过 Logit 变换得到不良贷款率的取值（见表 6.2）。

表 6.2　回归预测法压力测试结果

压力情景	轻度压力	中度压力	重度压力
不良贷款率	3.56	5.41	7.82
不良率变动	—	1.85	4.26

3. 蒙特卡洛模拟法的压力测试结果分析

首先将之前估计得到的信用风险传导模型系统的协方差矩阵 Σ 进行 Cholesky 分解，得到满足 $\Sigma = AA'$ 的 $(n+1) \times (n+1)$ 阶矩阵 A；然后随机生成独立的服从标准正态分布的 $(n+1)$ 维向量 Z_{t+1}，代入 $E_{t+1} = AZ_{t+1}$，即可得到 t+1 时刻 $(v_{t+1},\ \varepsilon_{t+1})'$ 的模拟值；再将 ε_{t+1} 以及已知的 Xt、X_{t+1} 代入之前估计得到的各自变量自回归方程，即可得到各风险指标的 t+1 期的模拟值；最后，将 v_{t+1} 的模拟结果以及前一步得到的 X_{t+1} 代入之前模型中的主回归方程，就可以得到 Y_{t+1} 的一个模拟值，再由 Logit 变换即可以得到新发生违约 MPD_{t+1} 的一个模拟结果。

以上 4 步给定了根据 t 时刻信息来模拟未来 t+1 时刻不良贷款率的方法。每次模拟都可以得到 MPD_{t+1} 的一个模拟值，重复 1 万次，就可以得到 MPD_{t+1} 的一个概率分布，并相应计算期望不良贷款率和 VaR 值。

根据前述压力情景和模拟步骤，本次压力测试计算了轻、中、重 3 种压力情景下不良贷款率的期望值、90% 分位数、95% 分位数和 99% 分位数。期望值表示 1 万次模拟得到的不良贷款率的平均值；90%、95% 和 99% 则分别表示 1 万次模拟后得到的不良贷款率分布的 90%、95% 和 99% 分位数，即本质上的 VaR 概念。以表 6.3 重度压力情景下得到的不良贷款率 99% 分位值 16.59% 为例，它意味着在最不利的重度情景下，我们有 99% 的把握认为未来一年内商业银行普惠业务的不良贷款率不会超过 16.59%，或者说只有 1% 的可能会超过 16.59%（见图 6.1）。

表 6.3　蒙特卡洛模拟法压力测试结果

压力情景		轻度（%）	中度（%）	重度（%）
不良贷款率	均值	3.56	5.41	7.82
	90% 置信区间	5.54	7.09	10.69
	95% 置信区间	8.34	9.44	14.65
	99% 置信区间	11.38	14.19	16.59

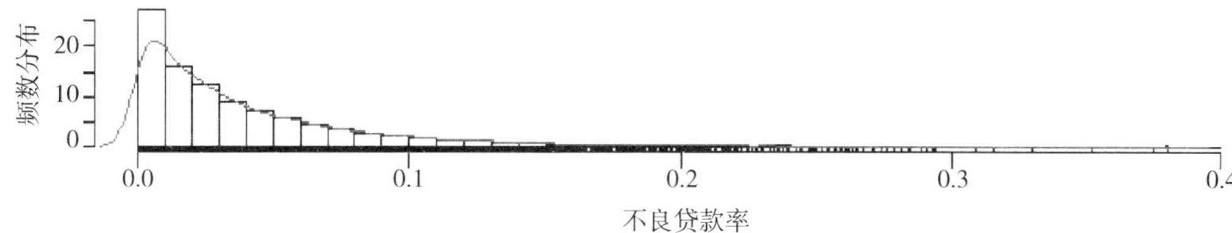

中度情景下不良贷款率的分布

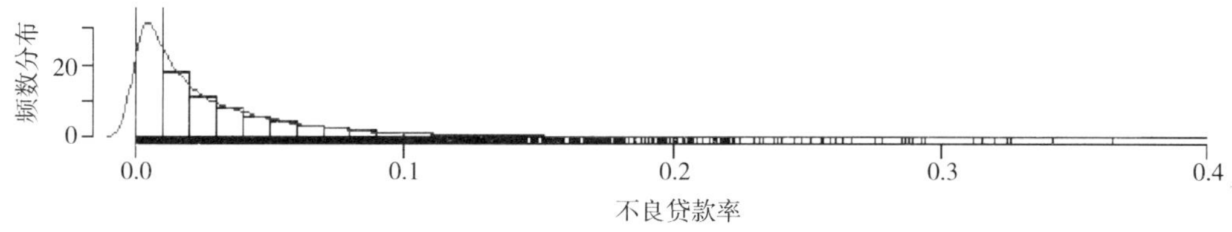

轻度情景下不良贷款率的分布

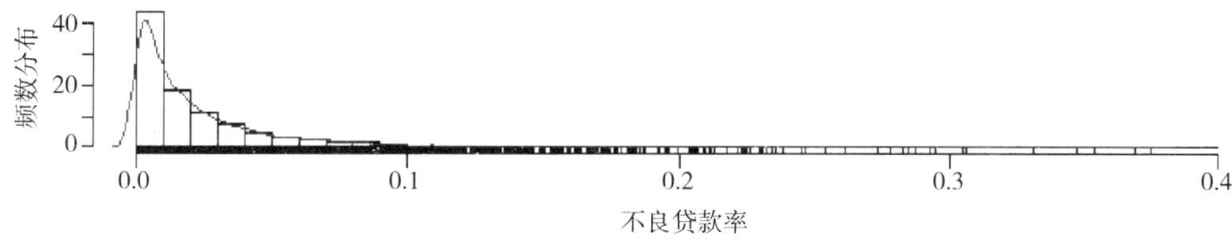

图 6.1　不良贷款率蒙特卡洛模拟分布

四、总结及建议

本文通过建立信用风险的 SUR 模型，对商业银行的普惠业务不良贷款进行了压力测试，测试结果表明，经济下行、企业主信心不足以及采购经理人指数的下降，对普惠业务整体的信贷资产质量产生负面冲击。在 3 种压力情景之下，由宏观压力测试模型预测出的不良贷款率都呈现出明显的上升趋势，说明国内生产总值、企业家信心指数、采购经理人指数出现下降，都是普惠业务风险趋势上行的前期指标，都提示未来商业银行不良贷款率的增加，使得商业银行普惠业务信用风险增大。尤其是在重度压力下，不良率均值为 7.82%，并有一定概率会突破 10%。因此，采用压力测试工具，对于评估商业银行普惠业务抵御系统性极端不利冲击的能力，合理估计信贷资产质量具有积极的意义。

但是从此次压力测试情况看，由于过去多数银行忽视普惠业务发展，以及经济一直呈较快速度发展，我国商业银行在普惠业务中的相关数据积累不充分，部分通过业务经验判断应该具有较强预测能力的指标在实际中与风险状况趋势不符，在一定程度上制约了普惠业务压力测试实践的应用。因此，建议我国商业银行采取如下手段，提高普惠业务风险管理能力。

一是随着我国采用各种政策鼓励商业银行发展普惠金融业务，以及各项数据存储长度和质量的提升，商业银行可以尝试采用更具有宏观指导意义的指标进行普惠金融业务信用风险压力测试，并逐步进行压力测试与其他风险管理方法的整合，提高压力测试结果对商业银行普惠金融业务发展的影响力和预测力，推动普惠金融业务更好地发展；二是利用大数据、人工智能、机器学习等新技术、新方法，推动普惠金融业务发展转型，提升业务经营水平和发展效率；三是改变传统的风险评价模式，由注重财务报表评价、注重押品等方面向注重履约能力评价转换，加大对客户第一还款源的评价和监控能力。

同业特殊目的载体投资业务对商业银行绩效的影响

——基于39家上市银行年度数据的实证研究

总行财富管理与私人银行部　徐　超

一、引言

2008年以来，我国利率市场化进程加快、银行业竞争日趋激烈，商业银行积极开展金融创新，寻求新的盈利增长点，其中，同业业务成为商业银行重要的新兴业务之一，其间也经历过多次监管规范。

2013年至2014年年中，部分商业银行为减少资本、拨备计提以及信贷规模管控等监管约束，通过同业业务中的买入返售科目大量开展非标准化债权投资业务，引起了监管关注，为此，人民银行等五部委于2014年5月联合发布了《关于规范金融机构同业业务的通知》（银发〔2014〕127号，以下简写为127号文），对同业业务进行规范：清理“买入返售”项下的非标债权资产，规定具有合理公允价值和较高流动性的金融资产才能纳入“买入返售”科目，禁止三方合作业务纳入“买入返售”科目，并设定了金融机构同业融资比例上限；允许商业银行以同业投资特殊目的载体方式开展非标债权投资，并要求按照“实质重于形式”原则计提资本和拨备。127号文推出执行后，政策效果显著：41家上市银行① 2014年年底买入返售业务余额5.48万亿元，较2013年同期下降13.7%；而承载同业投资特殊目的载体的应收款项类投资持续保持快速增长，2014年年底余额7.57万亿元，较上年增长64.6%。

从2017年年初起，银监会针对近年来商业银行金融创新过程中存在的问题与风险，进行了“三违反、三套利、四不当、十乱象”专项监管行动，其中，对同业殊定

① 资料来源于41家在A股或H股的上市银行的公开报告，41家上市银行为工商银行、建设银行、中国银行、农业银行、交通银行、邮政储蓄银行、招商银行、浦东发展银行、民生银行、兴业银行、平安银行、中信银行、华夏银行、光大银行、浙商银行、南京银行、宁波银行、北京银行、江苏银行、杭州银行、上海银行、成都银行、贵阳银行、重庆银行、重庆农商银行、郑州银行、天津银行、盛京银行、青岛银行、锦州银行、徽商银行、哈尔滨银行、广州农商银行、江阴银行、张家港银行、常熟银行、九台农商银行、无锡银行、吴江银行、中原银行以及甘肃银行，后同。

目的载体投资业务存在的多层嵌套、穿透管理不到位、资金投向合格性审查不严格、资本及拨备计提不充足等问题进行了重点规范。政策执行后，同业特殊目的载体投资业务规模逐步下降：41 家上市银行 2017 年年底应收款项类投资余额 13.21 万亿元，较上年底下降 0.9 万亿元。

从近年来监管行动的重点看，基础资产主要为各类融资项目等非标准化债权资产的特殊目的载体投资业务是监管的重点，着重关注商业银行在特殊目的载体投资业务方面是否存在基础资产穿透管理不到位、多层嵌套藏匿风险、资金投向不合规以及资本拨备计提不到位的问题；这也反映出，同业特殊目的载体投资业务对商业银行经营带来了较大的潜在影响。现有研究多从商业银行整体的角度定性分析了同业特殊目的载体投资业务产生的影响（陈颖、段希文、孙晨正，2014），较少从商业银行的微观绩效层面定量分析实际的影响。本文首次从实证角度，以 39 家上市商业银行为研究对象，利用 2013—2017 年面板数据，对特殊目的载体投资业务对商业银行绩效的影响进行了分析研究，具有一定的创新性。

二、同业特殊目的载体投资业务简介及相关研究

（一）同业特殊目的载体投资业务简介

127 号文指出，同业投资是指金融机构购买（或委托其他金融机构购买）同业金融资产（包括但不限于金融债、次级债等在银行间市场或证券交易所市场交易的同业金融资产）或特殊目的载体（包括但不限于商业银行理财产品、信托投资计划、证券投资基金、证券公司资产管理计划、基金管理公司及子公司资产管理计划、保险业资产管理机构资产管理产品等）的投资行为。按照此定义，商业银行同业特殊目的载体投资是指，商业银行购买银行理财产品、信托计划、证券投资基金、证券公司资产管理计划、基金管理公司及子公司资产管理计划、保险业资产管理机构资产管理产品等特殊目的载体。通常，商业银行将同业特殊目的载体投资业务计入资产负债表中的“应收款项类投资”项下（童琳，2017）。

以通过特殊目的载体投资信托贷款的交易结构为例，商业银行自营资金（即同业投资）投资于证券公司、基金子公司等设立的资产管理计划，该资产管理计划投资于信托公司设立的单一资金信托计划，该信托计划向融资人发放信托贷款，到期由融资人清偿信托贷款本息，商业银行自营资金通过资产管理计划获得相关收益分配。交易结构见图 6.2。

该交易结构中，商业银行通过资管计划、信托计划向融资企业提供资金的行为属于同业特殊目的载体投资，不占用信贷规模，也不受到项目准入要求、资金受托

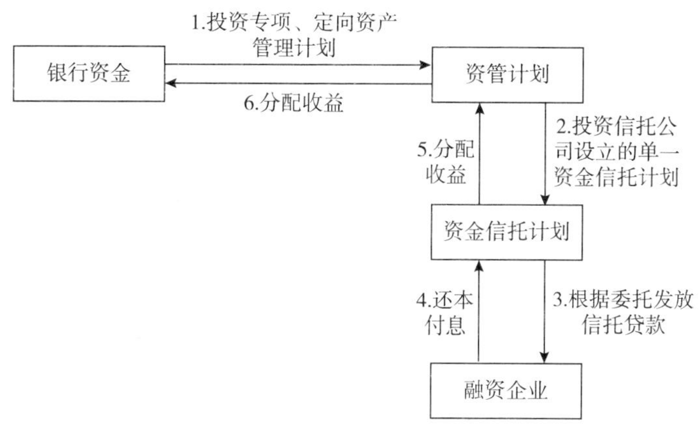

图6.2　委托贷款模式下的同业特殊目的载体投资业务交易结构

支付等信贷政策强制约束，在某种程度上增强了商业银行经营活动空间；同时，前述融资企业通常为商业银行自身的企业客户，可能因银行自身信贷额度不足、企业资质较信贷业务标准有瑕疵、融资需求较为急迫等原因，商业银行选择通过同业特殊目的载体投资向融资企业提供资金支持，商业银行实际控制着融资项目与融资资金这两端，特殊目的载体以及证券公司、信托公司主要充当连接银行项目与银行资金的“通道”。

127号文出台后，同业特殊目的载体投资业务快速发展，已成为近年商业银行重要的经营增长点之一，对商业银行经营影响愈发明显：截至2017年年底，41家上市商业银行应收款项类投资总额13.21万亿元，较2013年年底增长了187.2%，是同时期商业银行信贷规模增幅的3.24倍；占同期商业银行总资产的比例为7.9%，较2013年年底大幅提高了3.6个百分点。

（二）现有的相关研究

现有研究主要集中在同业业务整体分析方面，邵汉华、杨俊、廖尝君（2015）分析了商业银行同业业务扩张对货币政策传导的影响，研究发现，随着同业业务比重的提高，商业银行信贷对货币政策敏感性降低，同业业务扩张显著地弱化了银行信贷渠道的传导；吴军、黄丹（2015）从规避金融管制角度分析了商业银行同业业务的发展情况，他认为，资本监管压力、贷存比限制、经营压力以及资产质量考核是推动同业业务发展的重要因素；翟光宇等（2015）利用上市银行数据分析了同业业务扩张对商业银行经营风险的影响，分析认为，同业业务兴起的原因主要是规避存贷比、资本计提等监管约束以及获取更多利润，但增加了银行间的传染风险、流动性风险和信用风险。

也有学者对同业业务的部分业务品种进行了研究分析。陈颖、段希文、孙晨正

（2014）对新型同业业务的潜在风险传染效应进行了研究，研究发现，商业银行新型同业业务存在风险传染效应，国有大型银行对同业资产损失的吸收能力有所加强，风险传染效应有所减弱。祝继高、胡诗阳、陆正飞（2016）分析了同业业务中的买入返售业务对商业银行经营绩效的影响，研究发现，买入返售业务规模占比越高，商业银行潜在经营风险就越高。董瑾杰（2018）研究了同业非标对金融稳定的影响，研究发现，大量同业非标资产通过股权及其他投资进入广义信贷，对宏观审慎监管和货币政策产生影响。

三、同业特殊目的载体投资对商业银行绩效的定性分析

在商业银行盈利能力方面，同业特殊目的载体投资业务可协助商业银行规避信贷规模管控等监管约束，扩大了可贷资金投放规模，增加了商业银行的经营收益来源，提高了商业银行资金运营效率；也存在因监管约束不足、内部管理有所放松、基础资产准入门槛降低，从而导致产生的新增收益不能覆盖对应的额外成本，最终降低了商业银行盈利能力的可能性。需要说明的是，同业特殊目的载体投资业务属于商业银行的表内投资业务，商业银行持有的特殊目的载体为表内生息资产，投资产生的收益属于利息收入。

在商业银行经营风险方面，同业特殊目的载体投资业务也带来了以下风险：一是基础资产带来的信用风险，商业银行投资的各类特殊目的载体，穿透后的基础资产多为融资项目等非标准化债权资产，最终这些基础资产可能产生到期难以兑付的信用风险，尤其是由于同业特殊目的载体投资的基础资产未纳入信贷业务范畴，受到的监管约束较少，在项目资质审查、风险评估等内部风险管控措施方面可能有所弱化，从而进一步加大了潜在的信用风险；二是不透明风险，由于商业银行同业特殊目的载体投资业务涉及主体数量较多、流程环节较复杂、信息披露可能不及时，导致商业银行难以真实全面了解到实际业务过程中的客观真实情况、风险特征，导致风险管理不到位、潜在风险情况了解不充分等；三是操作风险，商业银行在同业特殊目的载体投资业务过程中，由于经营人员在资金交易、信托公司等“通道机构”管理，基础资产筛选识别，投后管理等业务环节不遵守有关制度规章，导致了相关风险事件发生。上述风险最终将增加商业银行的风险，对实际经营产生负面影响。

四、同业特殊目的载体投资对商业银行绩效的实证分析

前文通过定性分析的方式论述了商业银行同业特殊目的载体投资业务对商业银行经营绩效的影响。本文继续用计量方法实证研究同业特殊目的载体投资业务对商业银行经营绩效产生的影响。

（一）模型设定与变量定义

本文借鉴了国内外有关研究商业银行经营绩效（薛超，2014；李志辉，李梦雨，2014；孟晓霞，2016）的方法，检验同业特殊目的载体投资业务与银行绩效之间的关系，运用普通面板数据模型，对以下公式进行回归：

$$Profit_{it} = \alpha_i + \beta_1 CF_{it} + \beta_2 TA_{it} + \beta_3 CAR_{it} + \beta_4 CA_{it} + \beta_5 CTI_{it} + \beta_6 GDP_{it} + \varepsilon_{it} \quad (1)$$

$$RISK_{it} = \alpha_i + \beta_1 CF_{it} + \beta_2 TA_{it} + \beta_3 CAR_{it} + \beta_4 CA_{it} + \beta_5 CTI_{it} + \beta_6 GDP_{it} + \varepsilon_{it} \quad (2)$$

其中，$i=1$，2，…N 为横截面的个数，代表 N 家商业银行；$t=1$，2，…，T 表示 T 年的时间序列。

模型中涉及的主要变量定义如下所示。

1. 银行绩效的度量

Profit：银行的盈利性指标。盈利性指标主要用于衡量商业银行运用资金赚取收益的能力。本文分别选取净资产收益率（ROE）和净息差（NIM）作为盈利性指标。

其中，净资产收益率是指税后利润与平均净资产的比率，可以反映出商业银行扣除风险拨备、税收等因素后的实际盈利能力；净息差是指商业银行所有的净利息收入与全部生息资产的比率，该指标可以反映出商业银行在计提拨备前资产端的定价能力。

RISK：银行的风险指标。风险性指标主要用于衡量银行收入的不确定性，根据巴塞尔委员会对银行风险的分类，主要包括信用风险、市场风险和操作风险等。鉴于信用风险是我国商业银行面临的最主要风险，因此我们选择不良贷款率（NPLR），即次级类贷款、可疑类贷款与损失类贷款三者之和与各项贷款总额的比率，作为商业银行风险的度量指标。

2. 同业特殊目的载体投资业务的度量指标

商业银行在 2013 年通过买入返售业务科目大量开展特殊目的载体投资业务，2014 年 5 月 127 号文发布之后，改计入应收款项类投资科目，因此，对于没有精确披露 2013 年年底同业特定目的投资业务数据的商业银行，本文以买入返售业务数据作为衡量 2013 年年底商业银行同业特殊目的载体投资业务规模，以应收款项类投资数据作为衡量 2014—2017 年商业银行同业特殊目的载体投资业务规模。

将同业特殊目的载体投资业务规模在同期商业银行总资产中的占比作为该银行同业特殊目的载体投资业务的度量指标。

3. 控制变量

在控制变量的选取方面，已有文献发现资产规模、成本收入比、贷存比、权益资本占比以及资本充足率是影响银行绩效的重要因素（张健华、王鹏，2011；Martin、

Parigi，2013；徐斌，郑垂勇，2018），因此本文将上述因素作为控制变量，采用银行总资产的对数（TA）、成本收入比（CTI）、贷款总额与存款总额的比率（LD）、股东权益与总资产的比率（CA）以及资本充足率（CAR）5 个变量作为银行特征的控制变量。同时，由于银行业是一个强周期性行业，经营绩效跟宏观经济大环境有很大关系，因此，以当年的 GDP 增速作为宏观经济的控制变量，其中，对于在局部区域经营的区域性商业银行，选择当年度经营区域的 GDP 名义增速，而对于在全国范围内经营的全国性商业银行，选择当年度全国 GDP 名义增速（见表 6.4）。

表 6.4　回归变量定义

变量名称	符号表示	变量解释
盈利性指标	Profit	净息差（NIM）、净资产收益率（ROE）
风险指标	RISK	不良贷款率（NPLR）
特殊目的载体投资指标	CF	同业特殊目的载体投资规模占总资产的比例
资产规模指标	TA	年末总资产（取对数）
成本收入比	CTI	营业费用与营业收入的比值
存贷比	LD	年末贷款余额与存款余额的比值
权益比率	CA	所有者权益与总资产的比值
资本充足率	CAR	资本金额与表内外加权资产期末总额的比值
地区经济发展水平指标	GDP	全国或各地区年度名义 GDP 增长率

（二）数据来源及描述性统计

本文研究对象为我国 39 家[①]上市商业银行，样本研究区间为 2013—2017 年，时间跨度为 5 年，截面个数为 39 个，属于短面板数据类型。

回归模型所用的宏观经济变量——GDP 名义增长率通过国家统计局、相关地区统计局网站上公布的数据计算得出。商业银行的净息差、净资产收益率、不良贷款率、存贷比、成本收入比、资本充足率、权益比例、总资产、同业特殊目的载体投资业务规模等数据来源于万得数据库及年报；同业特殊目的载体投资业务规模占比根据万得数据库及年报数据计算整理得出。

39 家样本商业银行中，按照经营区域大小划分，可以分为 15 家全国性商业银行（5 家国有商业银行、1 家邮政储蓄银行，以及 9 家全国股份制商业银行）和 24 家区域性商业银行（城市商业银行和农村商业银行），描述性统计结果如表 6.5 所示。

---

① 前述 41 家上市商业银行中，有 2 家银行（中原银行、甘肃银行均为区域性的城商或农商银行）在 2013—2017 年存在数据不全的情况，因此剔除出研究样本，从而研究对象为剩余的 39 家上市商业银行。

表6.5 主要变量的描述性统计

变量	全样本		全国性商业银行		区域性商业银行	
	均值	标准差	均值	标准差	均值	标准差
NIM	2.495	0.520	2.336	0.341	2.594	0.586
ROE	14.869	3.231	15.183	2.855	14.672	3.442
NPLR	1.272	0.413	1.343	0.395	1.228	0.419
CF	0.129	0.101	0.119	0.097	0.137	0.102
TA	9.242	1.654	10.967	0.894	8.164	0.957
CTI	30.760	6.660	31.328	7.632	30.406	5.981
LD	0.670	0.121	0.741	0.131	0.626	0.091
CA	0.067	0.012	0.065	0.011	0.069	0.012
CAR	12.731	1.306	12.491	1.416	12.882	1.214
GDP	8.430	4.117	8.890	1.567	8.138	5.087

描述性统计指标显示，全样本商业银行的同业特殊目的载体投资业务占比平均为12.9%，而全国性商业银行平均为11.9%，比全样本商业银行要低1个百分点；区域性商业银行平均为13.7%，比全样本商业银行平均要高0.8个百分点，较全国性商业银行平均高1.8个百分点。平均而言，区域性商业银行的同业特殊目的载体投资业务占比更高。

为保证模型检验的有效性，还对实证模型中自变量的多重共线性情况进行了分析。以全样本商业银行为例，表6.6的相关系数矩阵显示，自变量之间不存在明显的多重共线性情况。

表6.6 全样本自变量相关系数矩阵

自变量	CF	CA	CTI	LD	TA	CAR	GDP
CF	1.0000	-0.3029	-0.2754	-0.2346	-0.0468	-0.4369	-0.3326
CA	-0.3029	1.0000	-0.0897	0.3186	-0.2309	0.6333	0.0209
CTI	-0.2754	-0.0897	1.0000	-0.1981	-0.1077	-0.0351	0.2032
LD	-0.2346	0.3186	-0.1981	1.0000	0.3602	0.0870	-0.1234
TA	-0.0468	-0.2309	-0.1077	0.3602	1.0000	-0.0731	-0.2926
CAR	-0.4369	0.6333	-0.0351	0.0870	-0.0731	1.0000	0.1052
GDP	-0.3326	0.0209	0.2032	-0.1234	-0.2926	0.1052	1.0000

对全国性商业银行、区域性商业银行样本，自变量相关系数矩阵为类似结果，限于篇幅不再列出。

（三）实证结果

1. 同业特殊目的载体投资业务对商业银行盈利的实证结果

本文分别选择净息差（NIM）和净资产收益率（ROE）为因变量，利用模型 1 依次对全样本商业银行、全国性商业银行样本以及区域性商业银行样本进行了实证检验。

表 6.7 是对商业银行净息差（NIM）的回归分析结果，模型 1 为所有变量的回归结果，研究发现，特殊目的载体投资业务占比与商业银行的净息差水平呈正相关关系，说明特殊目的载体投资业务提高了商业银行资产端的定价水平，但不同类别的银行差异较大，对于全国性商业银行来说，特殊目的载体投资业务占比与其净息差呈负相关关系，说明特殊目的载体投资业务降低了全国性商业银行的资产定价水平；而对于区域性商业银行来说，特殊目的载体投资业务占比与其净息差呈正相关关系，说明特殊目的载体投资业务提高了区域性商业银行的资产定价水平。在控制变量方面，总资产、成本收入比、权益比例、资本充足率等变量的回归结果不显著，或者与现有研究、预期相一致；贷存比系数显著为负，可能的原因是随着利率市场化的推进，传统贷款利率下浮较为明显，降低了资产定价水平；GDP 增速的系数显著为负，可能的原因是经济增速放缓时，银行出于风险补偿原因，通常会提高信贷利率。模型 2 和模型 3 为在模型 1 的基础上，分别调整银行控制变量后的回归结果，总体结果与模型 1 类似。

表 6.8 是对商业银行净资产收益率（ROE）的回归分析结果，模型 1 为所有变量的回归结果，研究发现，不管是全样本商业银行、全国性商业银行还是区域性商业银行，特殊目的载体投资业务占比与商业银行净资产收益率水平均呈现负相关关系，说明特殊目的载体投资业务降低了商业银行的盈利能力。在控制变量方面，总资产、成本收入比、权益比例、资本充足率、GDP 增速等变量的回归结果不显著，或者与现有研究、预期相一致；贷存比系数显著为负，可能的原因是随着利率市场化的推进，传统信贷业务的经营绩效下降。模型 2 和模型 3 为在模型 1 的基础上，分别调整银行控制变量后的回归结果，总体结果与模型 1 类似。

表 6.7　对因变量为净息差（NIM）的回归分析结果

	全样本商业银行			全国性商业银行			区域性商业银行		
	模型 1	模型 2	模型 3	模型 1	模型 2	模型 3	模型 1	模型 2	模型 3
CF	0.468*	0.60**	0.47*	-1.37***	-1.34***	-1.35***	0.69*	0.88*	0.66
	(1.73)	(2.08)	(1.74)	(-3.65)	(-3.41)	(-3.80)	(1.80)	(1.82)	(1.37)
TA	-1.10***	-1.03***	-1.09***	-0.26***	-0.24***	-0.26***	-1.18***	-1.11***	-1.18***
	(-17.25)	(-15.93)	(-17.35)	(-4.23)	(-3.79)	(-4.32)	(-13.86)	(-12.96)	(-13.91)

（续表）

	全样本商业银行			全国性商业银行			区域性商业银行		
	模型 1	模型 2	模型 3	模型 1	模型 2	模型 3	模型 1	模型 2	模型 3
CTI	-0.04***		-0.03***	-0.02***		-0.02***	-0.04***		-0.04***
	(-6.35)		(-6.34)	(-3.11)		(-3.14)	(-5.63)		(-5.62)
LD	-0.66***	-0.81***	-0.67***	-2.14***	-1.91***	-2.22***	-0.97**	-1.33**	-1.01**
	(-3.37)	(-3.42)	(-3.66)	(-6.00)	(-5.23)	(-7.69)	(-2.10)	(-2.36)	(-2.21)
CA	-0.62	-0.77		-1.91	0.41		-1.97	-3.10	
	(-0.25)	(-0.27)		(-0.32)	(0.07)		(-0.60)	(-0.82)	
CAR	0.001	0.005	-0.002	0.021	0.001	0.014	-0.007	0.02	-0.01
	(0.07)	(0.29)	(-0.11)	(0.62)	(0.03)	(0.51)	(-0.29)	(0.78)	(-0.76)
GDP	-0.02***	-0.03***	-0.02**	-0.04***	-0.05***	-0.04***	-0.01**	-0.02*	-0.01**
	(-3.64)	(-5.07)	(-3.65)	(-2.86)	(-3.89)	(-2.88)	(-2.18)	(-3.01)	(-2.23)
cons	14.30***	12.73***	14.28***	7.66***	6.93***	7.63***	14.39***	12.48***	14.37***
	(24.58)	(23.33)	(24.59)	(11.88)	(10.97)	(12.17)	(17.04)	(15.00)	(17.09)
N	195	195	195	75	75	75	120	120	120
adj. R^2	0.765	0.648	0.714	0.585	0.539	0.587	0.645	0.619	0.626
F	31.17	25.74	31.70	15.89	15.41	18.58	22.70	19.69	23.64

注：（1）根据不同模型的检验显示，全样本商业银行、区域性商业银行样本，适合个体固定效应模型；全国性商业银行样本，适合个体随机效应模型。

（2）括号内为 t 检验值，***、** 和 * 分别代表在 1%、5% 和 10% 的显著性水平上显著。

表 6.8　对因变量为净资产收益率（ROE）的回归分析结果

	全样本商业银行			全国性商业银行			区域性商业银行		
	模型 1	模型 2	模型 3	模型 1	模型 2	模型 3	模型 1	模型 2	模型 3
CF	-4.66***	-4.68***	-5.34***	-13.82***	-13.27***	-12.02***	-5.37**	-4.76**	-6.07**
	(-2.94)	(-3.53)	(-3.13)	(-5.46)	(-5.26)	(-4.58)	(-2.10)	(-2.59)	(-2.17)
TA	-5.73***	-5.31***	-5.71***	-2.20***	-2.04***	-2.25***	-6.14***	-5.27***	-6.18***
	(-15.38)	(-17.60)	(-14.61)	(-5.05)	(-4.76)	(-5.00)	(-10.87)	(-14.77)	(-10.54)
CTI	-0.10***		-0.08**	-0.158***		-0.155***	-0.299***		-0.28***
	(-2.93)		(-2.47)	(-4.41)		(-4.06)	(-5.55)		(-5.00)
LD	-12.27***	-13.20***	-15.17***	-18.74***	-16.59***	-23.01***	-13.20***	-14.39***	-16.93***
	(-8.42)	(-9.92)	(-9.93)	(-7.76)	(-7.01)	(-10.78)	(-4.22)	(-4.91)	(-5.38)
CA	-75.91***	-69.83***		-115.3***	-94.60**		-75.13***	-68.66***	
	(-4.71)	(-5.00)		(-3.18)	(-2.62)		(-3.08)	(-3.39)	
CAR	-0.22**	-0.27***	-0.43***	0.17	-0.03	-0.22	-0.37**	-0.23*	-0.59***
	(-2.20)	(-2.96)	(-4.71)	(0.76)	(-0.14)	(-1.11)	(-2.20)	(-1.89)	(-4.11)

（续表）

	全样本商业银行			全国性商业银行			区域性商业银行		
	模型1	模型2	模型3	模型1	模型2	模型3	模型1	模型2	模型3
GDP	-0.002	-0.02	-0.0002	0.23**	0.10	0.27***	-0.03	-0.05	-0.04
	(-0.04)	(-0.71)	(-0.007)	(2.62)	(1.22)	(2.79)	(-0.67)	(-1.22)	(-0.89)
cons	87.66***	81.66***	86.68***	63.10***	57.09***	63.62***	94.03***	75.44***	92.91***
	(24.45)	(32.17)	(22.55)	(14.02)	(13.33)	(13.51)	(16.79)	(21.37)	(16.37)
N	195	195	195	75	75	75	120	120	120
adj. R^2	0.775	0.698	0.652	0.671	0.622	0.632	0.609	0.615	0.589
F	31.13	39.91	26.50	22.41	20.84	22.43	17.85	22.42	16.32

注：（1）根据不同模型的检验显示，全样本商业银行、区域性商业银行样本，适合个体固定效应模型；全国性商业银行样本，适合个体随机效应模型。

（2）括号内为t检验值，***、**和*分别代表在1%、5%和10%的显著性水平上显著。

综合以上研究显示，对区域性商业银行而言，开展同业特殊目的载体投资业务有助于提高其拨备前的资产定价水平，但综合考虑拨备等风险因素后，反而降低了净资产收益率水平。对全国性商业银行而言，同业特殊目的载体投资业务不仅降低了其拨备前的资产定价水平，同时也降低了综合风险等因素之后的净资产收益率水平。因此，研究认为，同业特殊目的载体投资业务降低了商业银行的实际经营绩效，原因可能是商业银行通过同业特定目的载体提供融资的基础资产，多为不完全符合商业银行既有政策要求，潜在风险较大，虽然提高了融资定价水平，但仍难以覆盖产生的经营成本，最终对商业银行实际盈利产生负面影响。

2. 同业特殊目的载体投资业务对商业银行经营风险的实证结果

本文选择不良贷款率（NPLR）作为衡量商业银行经营风险的因变量，利用模型2，依次对39家全样本商业银行、15家全国性商业银行样本以及24家区域性商业银行样本进行实证估计。

表6.9是对商业银行不良贷款率（NPLR）的回归分析结果，模型1为所有变量的回归结果，研究发现，不管是全样本商业银行、全国性商业银行还是区域性商业银行，特殊目的载体投资业务占比与商业银行不良贷款率均呈现正相关关系，说明特定目的载体投资业务增加了商业银行的经营风险。控制变量的回归结果不显著，或者与现有研究、预期相一致。模型2和模型3为在模型1的基础上，分别调整银行控制变量后的回归结果，总体结果与模型1类似。

表6.9　对因变量为不良贷款率（NPLR）的回归分析结果

	全样本商业银行			全国性商业银行			区域性商业银行		
	模型1	模型2	模型3	模型1	模型2	模型3	模型1	模型2	模型3
CF	0.41*	0.66*	0.42*	1.08***	1.09***	0.96***	0.92***	0.87***	0.92***
	(1.73)	(1.84)	(1.81)	(3.21)	(3.07)	(2.94)	(3.58)	(3.43)	(3.64)
TA	0.41***	0.66***	0.63***	0.34***	0.34***	0.34***	0.50***	0.51***	0.50***
	(12.36)	(13.23)	(12.35)	(6.33)	(6.02)	(6.58)	(9.46)	(9.87)	(9.53)
CTI	-0.01***		-0.01***	-0.009		-0.0007	0.007		0.007
	(-2.68)		(-2.86)	(-0.20)		(-0.15)	(1.17)		(1.20)
LD	1.67***	1.64***	1.81***	2.60***	2.61***	2.90***	0.86**	1.03***	0.85**
	(7.48)	(7.21)	(8.92)	(8.13)	(7.92)	(11.04)	(2.43)	(3.17)	(2.53)
CA	2.99	3.61*		8.23	8.35		-0.24	-0.25	
	(1.40)	(1.68)		(1.63)	(1.62)		(-0.09)	(-0.11)	
CAR	0.0001	-0.001	0.01	-0.05	-0.05	-0.02	0.03	0.02	0.03
	(0.01)	(-0.05)	(1.09)	(-1.59)	(-1.58)	(-0.92)	(1.57)	(1.24)	(1.86)
GDP	-0.01***	-0.02***	-0.015***	-0.07***	-0.07***	-0.07***	-0.004	-0.04	-0.04
	(-2.98)	(-3.53)	(-3.10)	(-5.93)	(-5.98)	(-6.04)	(-1.06)	(-0.88)	(-1.05)
cons	-5.46***	-6.08***	-5.49***	-3.68***	-3.70***	-3.69***	-3.99***	-3.92***	-4.00***
	(-11.38)	(-14.22)	(-11.44)	(-4.43)	(-6.50)	(-6.61)	(-7.33)	(-8.21)	(-7.34)
N	195	195	195	75	75	75	120	120	120
adj. R^2	0.739	0.631	0.617	0.684	0.681	0.669	0.616	0.589	0.539
F	23.49	22.74	23.71	23.85	28.09	26.00	18.58	19.85	19.49

注：（1）根据不同模型的检验显示，全样本商业银行、区域性商业银行样本，适合个体固定效应模型；全国性商业银行样本，适合个体随机效应模型。

（2）括号内为t检验值，***、**和*分别代表在1%、5%和10%的显著性水平上显著。

以上实证分析发现，不论对全国性商业银行还是区域性商业银行来说，同业特殊目的载体投资业务与商业银行的信用风险之间存在着显著的正相关关系，即商业银行同业特殊目的载体投资业务占比的提高增加了商业银行的信用风险。

本文还对回归方程进行了稳健性检验，如取ROA替换ROE，取工业增加值增速替换GDP名义增速，均取得类似结果，限于篇幅不再列出。

五、结论与政策建议

本文运用我国39家商业银行2013—2017年平衡面板数据进行回归分析，研究了同业特殊目的载体投资业务对商业银行绩效的影响。结果显示，商业银行开展同业特殊目的载体投资业务降低了商业银行的盈利能力，增加了经营风险。可能的原因是，商业银行，尤其是区域性商业银行，通过同业特殊目的载体投资业务绕开了相关信贷业务管理制度与规定，降低了基础资产项目的准入标准和门槛，为部分不符合现行信贷及监管政策的项目提供了融资，且后续管理不到位，潜在信用风险较大，降低了商业银行的经营绩效，增大了商业银行的经营风险。为此，提出以下政策建议。

一是要强化基础资产的经营管理工作。建议商业银行在开展同业特殊目的载体投资业务过程中，在基础资产准入评估等方面，要严格按照行内信贷业务的标准、流程与要求开展，审慎评估、了解基础资产的现金流、抵质押、信用风险等真实情况，把好基础资产的准入关；按照“实质重于形式”的原则，根据基础资产的真实情况，准确计提资本与拨备，确保经营指标能真实反映基础资产的情况；按照信贷业务贷后管理的有关制度要求，强化后续管理，及时跟踪、评估基础资产风险特征变化情况，尽早发现潜在风险苗头，采取有效应对措施。

二是推进同业特殊目的载体投资业务转型。建议在监管政策上，通过提高投资非标准化债权资产的拨备、资本计提标准，限制非标准化债权资产投资比例上限，禁止多层嵌套等方式，鼓励直接投资金融机构同业发行的债券等标准化资产，逐步推动商业银行同业特殊目的载体投资业务转型成为真正的投资业务。

商业银行客户财务分析框架研究

建行大学华东学院　冯文滔

一、导言

目前，大部分公司财务分析都是站在投资者或企业管理者视角展开的，其财务分析的目的是为投资者筛选优质公司提供某种手段或者帮助 CEO（首席执行官）、CFO（首席财务官）做好企业财务管理工作，而并非站在商业银行视角进行信贷决策分析。在没有明确“谁在分析”或“分析为了谁”的前提下，我们就难以回答另一个重要问题：怎么分析？有鉴于此，商业银行客户财务分析存在分析主体不明确、财务指标分析难以与企业业务有效结合、常常依靠经验或常识做出主观判断等问题，归根到底是因为没有建立一个系统的财务分析框架。因为缺失一般性的财务分析框架，客户经理或行长在客户财务分析时采取“头痛医头，脚痛医脚”的方式，很可能导致盲人摸象、以偏概全的决策风险。

二、研究背景综述

本节主要包括商业银行客户财务分析的培训现状和财务分析理论概述两个模块，详细阐述了客户财务分析的培训现状以及财务分析理论体系的发展情况，为建立银行客户财务分析框架奠定文献基础。

（一）信贷培训相关文献

就我目前所掌握的资料来看，建行自 1997 年以来，分别于 2000 年、2005 年编写和修订了《信贷管理：信贷人员如何分析企业财务报表》岗位培训教材，内容主要围绕 3 张报表和 3 种能力（偿债、盈利和营运）展开。此外，建行对公业务条线从 2004 年开发第一套《公司业务客户经理培训教材》开始，分别于 2013 年、2015 年、2016 年完成了对公信贷持证上岗资格考试《客户经理篇》教材的编写和修订工作，教材在内容上没有单列财务分析模块，而是置于《客户识别与选择》一章，将财务分析的内涵更多地拓展到了企业的生产经营和外部环境。建行在客户经理的财务分析培训方面体现了一定的系统性、专业性和前瞻性。在其他商业银行的对公信贷培训中，财务分析培训则比较零散，缺乏系统性。在信贷岗位培训中，交通银行（1999）、中国银行（2005）、北京农商银行（2012）等都不约而同地将财务分析集中在“如何阅读企业资产负债表”“如何阅读企业利润表”“如何阅读企业现金流量表”“财务比率分析”“财务趋势分析”等传统财务分析框架之中。

（二）财务分析理论文献

就我目前所掌握的资料来看，相关文献主要以教材专著为主，国外的译著主要有：施利特和皮勒的《财务诡计》（2012）、帕利普和希利的《经营分析与估值》（2014）[①]、希金斯的《财务管理分析》（2015）、斯蒂芬佩因曼的《财务报表分析与证券估值》（2016）。国内的著作主要有：黄世忠的《财务报表分析：理论·框架·方法与案例》（2007）、陆正飞的《财务报告与分析》（2014）、池国华的《财务报表分析》（2017）等[②]。就学术论文层面，针对财务分析框架的基础性研究鲜见，主要是中国会计学会财务管理专业委员会、会计基础理论专业委员会的一些学者仍在砥砺前行。李心合和蔡蕾（2006）、叶康涛等（2014）、张婷婷和张新民（2017）的研究都直接将矛头指向基于财务指标的财务分析方法的缺陷，强调财务分析内涵应该进一步拓展到企业战略层面。

综上所述，传统财务分析方法已经比较成熟，现代财务分析方法也在不断完善之中，但仍存在一些相见不相识的鸿沟需要商业银行谨慎对待。一方面，作为债权人的商业银行如何进行客户财务分析？在关注商业银行作为财务分析需求主体方面，很少有理论性专著直指商业银行，如果商业银行不加区分地借鉴相关财务分析思路，必然导致理论分析与实务操作脱节。另一方面，早期商业银行财务培训主要依赖外部高校专家，尤其是财经类高校的研究成果，很多培训内容直接移植自经典财务分析甚至是财务管理学专著，在缺乏商业银行内部需求调研的情况下，也就难以设计出真正符合商业银行自身业务发展需要的财务分析框架。

三、基于客户经理和基层管理者的调研

在相关文献分析的基础上，我首先以银行客户经理和基层管理者两个层级作为调

---

① 作为“哈佛财务分析框架”或者“战略财务分析框架”的提出者，哈佛大学的帕利普和希利两位教授在财务分析的框架体系构建方面做出了开创性的贡献。

② 国内关于财务分析的教材汗牛充栋，由于我个人能力有限，无法穷尽，难免挂一漏万。此外，还有类似“如何读懂财报”“财报就像一本书”“财报那些事儿”等大众读物，尽管没有系统的理论体系，但自成一家，也可作为财务分析的有益参考，不再赘述。

研对象，以客户财务分析培训需求摸底作为调研目的，针对2016年客户经理培训班部分学员、基层机构负责人培训班和网点负责人培训班部分学员进行问卷调研①。现对相关调研数据分析如下。

（一）基于客户经理的调研

调研样本选自2016年客户经理培训班部分学员，描述性统计如表6.10所示。样本的性别比例为男性客户经理占比为58%，女性为42%；平均年龄大约36岁，77%的客户经理学历为本科，在建行平均工作时间约为5年；获得财务与会计相关学位（含辅修）或者拥有财会相关资质证书的人数占比为78%。在财务分析能力的自我评价上，客户经理样本组对于“自我总体评估”的结论均值是“一般”，略靠近“不满意”（均值为3.13）；在各个细项上，客户经理的自我评估值均值还是徘徊在“不确定”上，但比起整体财务分析能力而言，更偏向“同意”自己有相应的分析能力（各项均值都小于3.13）。

表6.10　客户经理样本描述性统计

变量	样本数	均值	标准误	最小值	中位数	最大值
性别	269.00	0.58	0.50	0.00	1.00	1.00
年龄	269.00	1.60	0.78	1.00	1.00	4.00
学历	269.00	2.06	0.48	1.00	2.00	3.00
工作时间	269.00	1.89	1.10	1.00	1.00	4.00
学位及证书	269.00	0.78	0.41	0.00	1.00	1.00
总体评价	269.00	3.13	0.90	1.00	3.00	5.00
年报结构	269.00	2.90	0.95	1.00	3.00	5.00
重要信息	269.00	2.74	0.81	1.00	3.00	5.00
非财务	269.00	2.91	0.80	1.00	3.00	5.00
资产负债表	269.00	2.74	0.81	1.00	3.00	5.00
利润表	269.00	2.71	0.76	1.00	3.00	5.00
现金流量表	269.00	2.80	0.77	1.00	3.00	5.00
钩稽关系	269.00	2.86	0.83	1.00	3.00	5.00

（二）基于基层管理者的调研

调研样本选自2016年基层机构负责人培训班和网点负责人培训班部分学员，描述

① 本次客户经理样本来自江苏、浙江、上海、广西、云南、贵州6家兄弟分行；基层管理人员样本取自总行培训项目，涵盖建行37家一级分行的基层管理者。

性统计如表6.11所示。本次调研结果表明，银行基层管理者大部分年龄在46岁左右，本科学历占比为82.95%，大部分基层管理者都是主持全面工作；获得财务与会计相关学位（含辅修）或者拥有财会相关资质证书的人数占比高达89%，其中，近20%的学员已具备中级会计职称，具备中高级财务会计技能。在客户财务分析能力的自我认知方面，基层管理者样本组对于“自我总体评估”的结论均值是“一般”，略靠近“满意”（均值为2.92）；在各个细项上，基层管理者样本组的自我评估值与客户经理样本组类似，自我感受也是略好于“总体评价”（各项均值都小于2.92）。

表6.11　基层管理者样本描述性统计

变量名称	变量数	均值	标准误	最小值	中位数	最大值
性别	88.00	0.51	0.50	0.00	1.00	1.00
年龄	88.00	2.55	0.69	1.00	3.00	4.00
学历	88.00	1.90	0.40	1.00	2.00	3.00
分管工作	88.00	3.31	1.08	1.00	4.00	5.00
对公类型	88.00	2.60	0.93	1.00	3.00	5.00
学位及证书	88.00	0.89	0.32	0.00	1.00	1.00
总体评价	88.00	2.92	0.86	1.00	3.00	5.00
年报结构	88.00	2.78	0.72	1.00	3.00	5.00
重要信息	88.00	2.64	0.73	1.00	3.00	5.00
非财务	88.00	2.83	0.75	1.00	3.00	5.00
资产负债表	88.00	2.76	0.66	1.00	3.00	5.00
利润表	88.00	2.70	0.66	1.00	3.00	5.00
现金流量表	88.00	2.76	0.63	1.00	3.00	5.00
钩稽关系	88.00	2.77	0.64	1.00	3.00	5.00

（三）调研结论

首先，调研数据表明，无论是客户经理还是基层管理人员，都具备了进行财务分析的基础会计知识（拥有基础财务会计背景的人数占比分别为78%和89%），这显然与“行内对公客户经理或行长缺乏基本会计知识”的传统认知不符，以初、中级财务会计知识为主的财务培训已不能满足行内对公业务发展的要求。其次，无论是客户经理还是基层管理人员，都不约而同地表现为：对自身“总体”财务分析能力觉得“一般”，但细项财务分析能力认为“还行”。可能还是因为“头痛医头，脚痛医脚”的顽疾挥之不去，在学员的脑海中没有建立起系统化的财务分析框架，从而无法将已有的经验和分析技巧整合到一个统一的分析框架中。最后，在基层管理人员样本组中，我发现88.64%的学员认为“需要”财务分析培训，30%左右的学员表示“非常需要”财务分析培训①。

四、财务分析的一般框架

在回顾相关文献资料和需求调研的基础上，我认为，商业银行的财务分析思路可以在以下几个方面进行完善。

首先，明确分析主体。我认为一般性财务分析框架可以囊括不同财务分析主体，但是需要注意不同主体之间的同构性。比如：大股东注重企业发展战略与长期绩效，可类比商业银行发放的长期贷款（固定资产、项目贷款等），关注的焦点应该是企业持续的利润创造能力；中小股东更加看重企业带来的现实利益，与短期贷款（流动性贷款等）类似，需要关注企业短期内现金流的创造能力。无论是关注利润表还是现金流量表，企业的盈利能力和现金流创造能力最终的来源还是企业业务的发展，也就是对资产负债表中资产和资本的综合运用。

其次，采用结构化方法。传统财务分析框架主要纠结于财务会计报表的解读，按照每一项财务会计项目或会计科目展开，在某种意义上既加大了分析的难度（对会计准则掌握程度要求很高），又降低了财务分析与信贷决策的相关性。因此，要适当进行财务报表项目的归类，进行结构化的多层次分析，关键是抓主要问题。比如：要分析企业的经营能力就应该主要针对经营性资产进行分析，包括针对存货、商业债权、货币资金、固定资产、无形资产等经营性资产的真实性情况和实际运用情况及其与企业内外部环境的匹配程度的分析。

最后，注重基本情况分析。一个企业所处行业情况、竞争战略选择以及公司治理情况等都是决定形成什么样财务报表的前提。比如：如果企业在商业模式选择方面出现“两头吃”的情况，像国美、苏宁或者亚马逊等企业，就不能单看利润表，其现金流占用才是这类型企业生生不息的关键；股权结构作为公司治理的核心要素，体现了公司高层之间的权力制衡情况，有什么样的股权结构就会什么样的公司战略，从而就会选择什么样的人去管理公司，也就决定了企业的生产经营管理情况，反映在最终的财务报表上，好比2010年丰田“召回门”事件、真功夫上市失败事件等，就不单是企业生产经营出现了问题。

综上所述，我按照基本情况分析、审计报告分析、经营投资分析的思路构建了商

① 在一次客户经理调研中，我曾做过培训需求调查，结果99%的客户经理认为“需要”财务分析培训，75%的客户经理认为“非常需要”财务分析培训。这可能是由于财务分析是从事信贷业务的客户经理必须掌握的看家本领，相关培训需求应该是刚性的。因此，本次调研没有就客户经理的财务分析需求再单独设问。

业银行客户性财务分析框架，如图6.3所示。该框架本身既具有一般财务分析的特点，也满足商业银行客户财务分析的基本要求，主要表现在：以基本情况分析作为财务分析的前提，将传统的客户“基本情况调查”纳入财务分析中，是对一般财务分析方法在商业银行层面的拓展；强调对审计报告的解读，深入挖掘审计报告的出具背景、更换事务所形式、审计定价合理性等信息，为财务会计报告的会计信息质量提供参考依据；从经营或投资的视角来看企业的主要财务会计报表，结合商业银行信贷业务作为分析切入点。

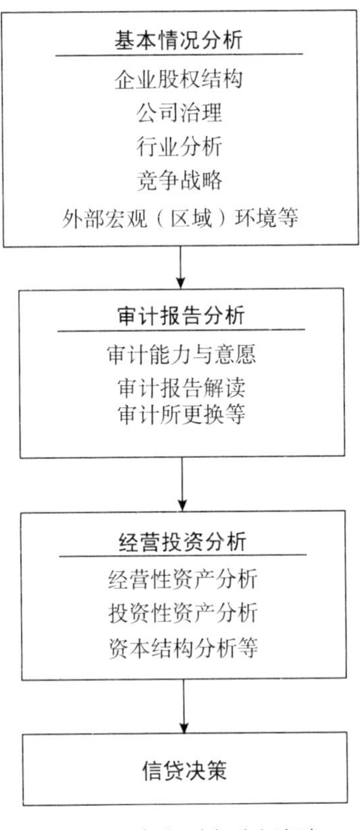

图6.3　客户财务分析框架

（一）基本情况分析

基本情况分析主要是了解客户的战略，包括股权结构、公司治理、竞争战略、行业和宏观（区域）环境等方面。其中，股权结构分析需要掌握实际控制人性质、资本结构配置、投票权与现金流权比率、离岸股权结构等知识点；行业分析是对战略分析的展开，同时又是战略形成的主要影响因素；竞争战略分析主要以波特的竞争战略分析为主，同时结合SWOT模型、波士顿矩阵等工具进行分析；外部宏观（区域）环境变化是同一区域的所有行业、所有企业共同面对的风险因素。银行客户经理和基层管理者应重点掌握行业分析和竞争战略等分析工具，并运用工具分析目标客户的行业地位和竞争战略，从而对企业所面临的各类宏观、行业、区域和法律法规风险有一个整体把握。

（二）审计报告分析

财务报表数据是经过一系列复杂、精准的会计程序加工后生成的财务信息。因此，在进行财务报表分析之前，理论上应有一个会计分析环节。但是，一方面，根据前文调研的结果，大约70% ~80%的客户经理和基层管理者已经具备基础财务会计知识，20% ~30%的客户具备中高级财务会计知识；另一方面，某些财务会计准则确实存在说法不统一、理论基础不明确、实务操作千差万别等一系列问题，加之相关监管机构（证监会、财政部）的说辞也经常不一致，因此，对于普适性的会计知识可以适当简化，对于专业化程度很高的会计准则完全可以单独开课讲解。本文所建立的财务分析框架主要是基于财务报告中注册会计师出具的审计报告，在整体上对企业财务报表的会计质量做出初步判断。

综上所述，审计意见的分析应该结合审计师、审计所的风险偏好等一起分析。任何审计意见都是风险和收益权衡的结果，因此审计师出具审计意见的能力和意愿就是分析的关键点。与此同时，审计所性质、近 3 年审计收费情况、审计所国际化程度、审计所区域性质等也是审计报告质量的重要影响因素。

（三）经营投资分析

目前，企业客户的基本财务报表一般包括资产负债表、利润表、现金流量表和所有者（股东）权益变动表。从基本关系来看，资产负债表的货币资金项目理论上可以打开为一张现金流量表，未分配利润项目可以倒推出一张利润表，股东权益变动则是对资产负债表所有者权益项目的细化；从企业业务发展来看，无论是生产经营还是投资，企业都离不开对资产的投入和运用，由此才能创造出利润和现金流；从会计准则的发展来看，资产负债表观已经成为当前国际会计准则委员会和美国会计准则委员会难得达成一致意见的点。因此，以企业的资产负债表为基础，联动利润表、现金流量表进行财务分析，具有理论和现实的双重意义。

在资产负债表中，资产和负债通常是按流动性从高到低依次列示。资产按照流动性可分为两类。一类是流动资产，一般来说是指一年以内或者一个经营周期内可以变现的资源：货币资金、以公允价值计量且其变动计入当期损益的金融资产、衍生金融资产、商业债权（应收账款、应收票据、预付款项、其他应收款等）和存货。另一类是长期资产（非流动资产），一般来说是一年或者一个经营周期以上才可变现的资源：

投资类资产（可供出售金融资产、持有至到期投资、长期股权投资等）、固定资产（投资性房地产、固定资产、在建工程等）和无形资产等。然而，站在企业业务发展的角度，资产必须是可以为企业利润做出贡献的，按照这种方式可以将企业的资产分为经营资产和投资资产。经营资产主要包括商业债权（预付款项、应收票据和应收账款）、存货、货币资金、固定资产和无形资产；投资资产主要包括持有至到期投资、长期股权投资等投资资产，还可能包括一些没有明视为投资但实际上是控制性投资的项目。此外，资产负债表的右方可以统称为企业的“资本”，包括债务资本和股权资本，企业的资本分析有助于了解企业的融资成本、股东权益、与资产的匹配程度等信息。

综上所述，站在企业业务发展的角度，将资产分为经营和投资两种类型，有助于以商业银行作为主体的客户财务分析方法进一步提升和完善。因为，在区分经营性资产和投资性资产的基础之上，如果从现金流量表角度理解，实际上区分出了企业的“经营活动”和“投资活动”，并且资产负债表的“资本结构”分析也解释了企业的“筹资活动”；如果从利润表的角度理解，实际上区分出了“主营业务收入”和“投资收益”带来的利润贡献。对于商业银行信贷分析而言，有助于客户经理从企业业务发展层面深刻理解企业财务数据，并且这种划分有助于商业银行按照不同对公信贷产品（流贷、固贷等）开展更具针对性的客户财务分析。

五、结论

通过文献回顾和实地调研，本文提出了一个基于商业银行的财务分析框架，相关研究结论和有待完善之处如下。

（一）研究结论

首先，本文整理出一套以商业银行为分析主体的财务分析框架，该分析框架纳入了基本情况分析、审计报告分析和经营投资分析等关键点，形成前后逻辑一致的系统性分析框架，是对财务与非财务分析方法的有效整合，为客户经理提供了一个简洁有效的财务分析思路。其次，本文强调了“基本情况分析”在财务分析中的重要性，梳理了股权结构、公司治理、行业与竞争战略、宏观（区域）环境的分析方法。再次，本文着重指出资产负债表分析在财务分析中的重要地位，并且将经营资产和投资资产的划分作为商业银行财务分析的有效手段，有助于客户经理理解财务报表与企业业务之间的关联关系，从而做出正确的信贷决策。

（二）有待完善之处

一方面，本文没有涉及商业银行企业客户的规模、所处行业以及集团（单一客户）

的分类，未来的研究可以进一步将一般性的财务分析框架嵌套入不同规模、行业和母子公司的客户分析中，将更加具有针对性，但是这并不妨碍该财务分析框架在客户财务分析中的普适性。另一方面，限于时间和精力有限，我没有提供具体的企业案例分析，在实际的培训授课时，可以增加企业案例，有助于客户经理更好地理解和掌握该财务分析框架。

资产负债表与现金流量表的“第二钩稽关系”

建行大学华东学院　冯文滔

一、引言

财务报告真实性核查是指在贷前调查和贷后管理环节，通过对客户财务报告的形式核查，报表间钩稽关系、主要科目等事项的实质性内容核查，以及与历史数据的比对，了解客户真实财务情况，判断客户是否账表相符、账实相符。其中，钩稽关系复核是客户财务报告真实性核查的一种重要且高效的方法，以下是客户经理经常会引用的一个经典钩稽关系公式（后文简称 FIRST）①：

期末货币资金余额 - 期初货币资金余额 = 当年现金及现金等价物的净增加额

客户的财务报表是否必须满足这一钩稽关系？为什么不满足？中国会计准则（CAS）、国际会计准则（IAS）和美国会计准则（ASC）对此如何解释？资产负债表和现金流量表之间是否有一个更加符合中国实际的钩稽关系？本文将从 FIRST 的适用现状、会计准则差异入手，解读其使用前提，同时提出一个更加适合中国企业财务报表分析的“第二钩稽关系”公式。

二、FIRST 适用现状

本文以 CSMAR 数据库作为样本来源，选取 2001—2015 年沪深两市主板上市公司作为总体，为保持数据原貌，剔除货币金融行业和缺失值，最终获得 19 047 个样本观测值，其中满足 FIRST 钩稽关系的上市公司观测值为 1 843 个，如表 6.12 所示。

---

① 我将该公式简称为 FIRST，意指资产负债表和现金流量表的“第一钩稽关系”，区别于后文所提出的 SECOND（第二钩稽关系）。

表6.12 FIRST的适用性分析

年份	公司数A	占比A（%）	公司数B	占比B（%）
2001	145	7.87	1 035	14.01
2002	163	8.84	1 111	14.67
2003	172	9.33	1 173	14.66
2004	172	9.33	1 230	13.98
2005	153	8.30	1 274	12.01
2006	176	9.55	1 269	13.87
2007	125	6.78	1 274	9.81
2008	152	8.25	1 288	11.80
2009	118	6.40	1 283	9.20
2010	106	5.75	1 294	8.19
2011	108	5.86	1 316	8.21
2012	87	4.72	1 346	6.46
2013	79	4.29	1 363	5.80
2014	44	2.39	1 370	3.21
2015	43	2.33	1 421	3.03
合计	1 843	100.00	19 047	9.68

资料来源：CSMAR数据库。

如表6.12所示，公司数A是每年满足FIRST的上市公司观测值，公司数B是每年总的上市公司观测值，占比A是满足FIRST的上市公司在各年的分布，占比B是满足FIRST的上市公司占当年上市公司总数的比例。从趋势来看，满足FIRST的上市公司比例从2008年以后逐年下降，2015年达到历史新低的3.03%。从总量来看，2001—2015年平均有9.68%的上市公司满足FIRST，其中，2002年的占比最高，达到14.67%。与此同时，我计算了上市公司被出具“非标”审计意见的比例，平均结果占样本总量的8.82%。也就是说，满足FIRST的上市公司平均比重几乎与被出具“非标”审计意见的上市公司比重接近——满足FIRST与被出具“非标”审计意见一样成为一种小概率事件。因此，如果银行客户经理直接采用FIRST分析资产负债表和现金流量表的钩稽关系，并以此作为判断企业财报真实性的依据，那就很值得商榷了。

三、会计准则比较

FIRST的适用性问题可能需要追本溯源，我认为可以从会计准则层面做进一步分析。就目前世界上主流的会计准则选择而言，主要是在国际会计准则和美国会计准则之间相互争胜，双方的所谓“协调”也颇具博弈意味。总体而言，无论是美国会计准则还是国际会计准则，其资产负债表的披露都不会提及“货币资金”这一称谓，而是直接披露“现金”“现金等价物”或兼而有之。

以《国际会计准则第1号财务报表列报》（简写为IAS1）和《国际会计准则第7号现金流量表》（简写为IAS7）的披露要求为例，IAS1明确“现金及现金等价物”的定义应参考IAS7的解释：“现金，指库存现金和活期存款；现金等价物，指期限短、流动性强、易于转换成已知金额的现金，并且价值变动风险很小的投资。”可以看出，一方面，IAS将资产负债表中的“现金”和现金流量表中的“现金”等量齐观，即能够进入现金流量表的“现金”是不存在使用受限这种情况的，资产负债表中披露的“现金”当然也不包括使用受限的现金。IAS没有直接提及“使用受限的现金”的概念，这可能导致诸如“定期存款”应否以及如何纳入现金流量表等问题，但仍可推知，IAS实质上将“使用受限的现金”排除在资产负债表中所披露的“现金”范畴以外。另一方面，在IAS1中，国际会计准则明确“现金及现金等价物”属于“财务状况表”（即资产负债表）中应当包含的单列项目之一，同时，IAS7指出“主体持有现金等价物只是为了满足其短期现金承诺的需要，而不是为了投资和其他目的”。也就是说，IAS未将“现金等价物”单独视为一项投资或者说仅仅视为一项“特殊”的投资，在披露时并入“现金及现金等价物”。综上所述，在采用国际会计准则进行报告披露时，对比我国资产负债表中的“货币资金”项目，国际会计准则实际上是将现金流量表中的“现金及现金等价物”直接反映到资产负债表中。

以美国会计准则《美国会计准则第210号资产负债表》（ASC210）和《美国会计准则第230号现金流量表》（ASC230）的披露要求为例：ASC210明确指出资产负债表中的“现金可以随时变现，任何形式的受限制的现金都不得计入，除非在一个生产经营周期内可以变现，并且受限制的现金不能计入流动资产”，同时也明确资产负债表中有关“现金”的定义应直接参考ASC230。在ASC230中，非常具体地说明了像最低存款余额这一类使用受限制的现金绝对不能入现金流量表。可以看出，虽然表述不尽相同，但ASC与IAS对资产负债表中“现金”披露的理解在“排除对象”方面都是相同的：“使用受限的现金”被排除在外。此外，ASC在《美国会计准则第320号股权与债权投资》（ASC320）中进一步明确了“现金等价物”作为一项投资的定义和处理方法。由此可见，ASC对“现金等价物”在资产负债表中的披露迥异于IAS，不是将其纳入“现金及现金等价物”，而是分别按照“现金”和“现金等价物”各自披露。比如：自购买之日起3个月内到期的美国短期国债会直接以“TREASURY BILLS”在资产负债表中披露，列在“CASH”之后，此时CASH和TREASURY BILLS的期末合计数方才等于现金流量表中的“现金及现金等价物”的期末余额。

以CAS为例，尽管我国会计准则与国际会计准则实质性趋同，但在“货币资金”项目上却有一定的自身特点。无论在2014年《企业会计准则第30号财务报表列报》（CAS30）还是《企业会计准则：应用指南2006》（后文简写为《应用指南2006》）中，都明确“货币资金”应当作为单独列示的项目在资产负债表中反映，主要包括企业期末持有的现金、银行存款和其他货币资金等总额。《企业会计准则第 31 号现金流量表》（CAS31）给出了“现金”和“现金等价物”的定义：“现金，是指企业库存现金以及可以随时用于支付的存款；现金等价物，是指企业持有的期限短、流动性强、易于转换为已知金额现金、价值变动风险很小的投资。”然而，CAS30 和 CAS31 都没有明确“使用受限的现金”能否在“货币资金”项目中反映，由此导致在实务操作中，“使用受限的现金”当然地进入了“货币资金”项目，这也就区别于 IAS 和 ASC 的披露要求。此外，从“货币资金”项目所包括的总账一级科目和“现金等价物”的定义可以看出，“货币资金”没有包括“现金等价物”，并且“现金等价物”直接被视为一项短期投资。《应用指南 2006》中称其主要指债券投资，比如从购买之日起 3 个月内到期的国库券。

通过以上分析可以看出，如果按照国际会计准则的披露要求，上市公司肯定满足 FIRST，因为资产负债表与现金流量表之间在“现金及现金等价物”的披露方面完全一致，FIRST 与其说是钩稽关系验证，不如说是对准则披露要求的验证；如果按照 ASC 的披露要求，相关钩稽关系分析只需多做一步，将资产负债表上的“现金”与随之披露的“现金等价物”（如果有）加总后再与现金流量表中的净增加额交叉核验，也必然满足 FIRST。但是，如果按照 CAS 的披露要求，应该如何进行资产负债表与现金流量表之间钩稽关系的验证呢？

四、第二钩稽关系

由前文分析可知，FIRST 公式左右相等的前提，也是 IAS 和 ASC 都共同强调过的，即资产负债表中的“现金”必须是不受使用限制的。但是，根据中国会计准则的披露要求：其一，资产负债表的“货币资金”项目中会包含“使用受限的现金”，这就导致了公式 FIRST 必然难以平衡，并且无法简单地通过当期受限货币资金进行调整，因为期初货币资金又是上一年的期末货币资金，可能也需要调整，上一年的期初货币资金又会涉及上上一年的期末货币资金，如此类推至无穷无尽；其二，“现金等价物”不包括在“货币资金”中，但又不像 ASC 那样直接披露，而是可能置于其他金融工具中，这又可能导致钩稽关系分析的难度进一步加大。因此，在本文第二部分的经验分析中，只有 9.68% 的主板非金融类上市公司满足 FIRST 实则是完全可以接受的，因为既没有剔除使用受限的“货币资金”，也没有加入“现金等价物”，FIRST 必然无法平衡，如果平衡了，反倒是小概率事件①。基于此，我试图推导一种更为合理的资产负债

---

① 根据 CAMAR 数据库信息，在上市公司严格的披露要求下，每 10 家公司中至多也只有一家满足 FIRST 钩稽关系，那么，实际业务操作中，客户经理对于满足 FIRST 的财报反而应更加关注。

表和现金流量表“第二钩稽关系”公式（后文简称SECOND）。

首先，将资产负债表中的“期末货币资金余额”划分为“期末使用受限的货币资金余额”和“期末使用不受限的货币资金余额”，即：

期末货币资金余额 = 期末使用受限的货币资金余额 + 期末使用不受限的货币资金余额 （1）

其次，将现金流量表中的“期末现金及现金等价物余额”划分为“期末现金余额”和“期末现金等价物余额”，即：

期末现金及现金等价物余额 = 期末现金余额 + 期末现金等价物余额 （2）

公式（1）和公式（2）都是无须任何前提的恒等式，对二者做减法，用公式（1）减公式（2），得到：

期末货币资金余额 - 期末现金及现金等价物余额 = 期末使用受限的货币资金余额 + 期末使用不受限的货币资金余额 - 期末现金余额 - 期末现金等价物余额 （3）

在公式（3）中，等式左边的项目可以从资产负债表和现金流量表中直接获取，关键是如何分析公式（3）的右边部分。尽管中国会计准则没有限制“使用受限的现金”进入“货币资金”项目，但至少明确了两点：其一，“使用受限的现金”不能入现金流量表，也就是说我国上市公司的现金流量表中不可能有使用受限制的现金；其二，“货币资金”项目包含现金、银行存款以及其他货币资金等总账一级科目（个别大型上市公司可能还有自己的财务公司，因此还可能会包括法定存款准备金和超额存款准备金），但不包含短期投资项目，因此，“现金等价物”一般不会放在“货币资金”项目中核算（由于本文仅针对报表层面做钩稽关系讨论，因此不涉及“现金等价物”的具体确认，但在单个案例分析时需要考虑）。根据对CAS这两点披露要求的理解，可以推知：公式（3）右边的“期末使用不受限的货币资金余额”与“期末现金余额”相等。因此，我们得到资产负债表和现金流量表的“第二钩稽关系”（SECOND）：

期末货币资金余额 - 期末现金及现金等价物余额 = 期末使用受限的货币资金余额 - 期末现金等价物余额 （4）

SECOND主要反映的是CAS框架下报表层面的钩稽关系。我通过具体财务分析案例来简要说明如何运用SECOND进行财务报表钩稽关系分析。以万科2015年年报为例，我们首先采用FIRST公式分析，“期末货币资金余额 - 期初货币资金余额”等于 -9 534 872 359.60元，与万科2015年的“现金及现金等价物的净增加额” -9 905 698 500.36元不相等，不满足FIRST。但是，正如前文所述，这并不能说明万科年报就一定存在问题。我们再来验证万科年报是否满足 SECOND 公式。SECOND 等式的左边一般可以直接计算得到，由万科 2015 年年报可以算出“期末货币资金余额 - 期末现金及现金等价物余额”（53 180 381 016. 34 - 62 715 253 375. 94）等于 1 432 759 850. 40 元。在对 SECOND 等式的右边进行分析时，通常我们需要查询万科年报的附注信息。万科在 2015 年的财报附注中披露“货币资金”中的银行存款含有受限使用 3 个月以上的资金 1 432 759 850. 40 元，同时其合并资产负债表中无其他短期投资，即“期末现金等价物余额”等于 0。那么，万科的 2015 年的资产负债表和现金流量表就满足了我所提出的 SECOND 钩稽关系。

应该说，FIRST 是一种在财务报表分析中的重要钩稽关系，但是其运用强烈依赖于会计准则的披露规定，需要排除使用受限的现金以及纳入现金等价物余额，这是投资者、债权人以及政策制定方都值得关注的问题。SECOND 则是在目前我国会计准则下更加一般化的钩稽关系：（1）SECOND 将使用受限的现金、现金等价物纳入钩稽关系分析中，弱化了 FIRST 强烈依赖的“不受限”前提；（2）SECOND 所包含的资产负债表和现金流量表项目皆为期末的时点数据，不涉及期初以及其他以前期间相关项目的调整，公式成立与否直接由数据本身在年报中的可获得性决定；（3）SECOND 等式的左边取自“显性”的项目，右边则是“隐性”的项目（财报附注），实现了财务报表分析中“显性”信息与“隐性”信息的交叉检验。

五、结论

综上所述，立足于银行客户财务报表分析视角，我从财报披露层面，透过“货币资金”项目在不同会计准则披露要求下的比较，推导出更加符合中国会计准则披露要求的 SECOND 钩稽关系公式，即：期末货币资金余额 - 期末现金及现金等价物余额 = 期末使用受限的货币资金余额 - 期末现金等价物余额。并就具体案例做了简要剖析。同时，我也注意到，伴随我国会计准则与国际会计准则的实质性趋同，以及一些 A + H 股上市公司按照国际会计准则的要求在报表中直接披露“现金及现金等价物”而不是“货币资金”，这样便完全满足 FIRST 钩稽关系，但这并不妨碍目前选择 SECOND 公式进行国内公司财务报告真实性核查的普适性。

商业银行内保外贷业务发展探究

——基于银行、民营企业与监管三方利益平衡的视角

总行信贷管理部　刘　翔

近年来，受廉价劳动力、贸易壁垒突破和先进技术需求因素的影响，我国民营企业掀起了一股境外发展热潮。实践证明，民营企业的境外发展离不开改革开放政策与金融资源配给，而金融业务发展也要服务于国家战略部署。随着国家"一带一路""走出去"战略的稳步推进，商业银行的跨境金融业务呈现出蓬勃发展之势。其中，作为重要的跨境融资性业务，内保外贷业务的签约额、签约量均实现快速增长，在解决民营企业境外融资难、成本高，落实国家"走出去"发展战略等方面发挥着积极作用。截至2018年上半年，我国境内投资者共设立境外企业超过4万家，对外直接投资累计净额超过1.5万亿美元，对3 617家境外企业进行非金融类直接投资，累计实现投资571.8亿美元，同比增长18.7%①。境外企业日益增长的发展需求，推动境内母公司（或总公司）开展内保外贷业务。同时，多项监管政策的相继出台，从额度占用、资金回境、办理流程等方面为内保外贷业务的发展"松绑"，政策红利得到有效释放。但在内保外贷业务迅速发展的过程中，也暴露出诸多违规操作、风险防范滞后等问题，客观上形成了一定的风险敞口与潜在隐患。2017年下半年，监管机构以窗口指导的方式逐步加强对商业银行内保外贷业务的监管，释放出风险管控的强烈信号。2018年以来，外管局相继发布外汇违规案例，其中内保外贷违规案例23起，占比达17.04%，共计罚没金额1.08亿元②。要有效防范内保外贷业务风险，发挥金融服务对民营企业境外业务拓展的支持作用，需要从业务自身特点入手，把握业务开展的内在逻辑，厘清业务实践中存在的问题症结，寻求切实可行的方法路径，实现主动管控风险，管理全面覆盖，确保内保外贷业务高质量发展，助力民营经济迈向国际化的新征程（见表6.13和图6.4）。

---

① 资料来源：中华人民共和国商务部网站，http：//www.mofcom.gov.cn/。

② 资料来源：外汇管理局门户网站，http：//m.safe.gov.cn/safe/。

表 6.13 近期内保外贷监管政策梳理

时间	文件名称	发文机构	主要规定
2014 年 6 月	《跨境担保外汇管理办法》	外管局	取消了内保外贷的审批环节、担保额度控制等限制性条件
2017 年 1 月	《关于全口径跨境融资宏观审慎管理有关事宜的通知》	人民银行	降低金融机构办理内保外贷额度的占用，由原来的 100% 调整至 20%
2017 年 1 月	《关于进一步推进外汇管理改革完善真实合规性审核的通知》	外管局	允许内保外贷项下资金调回境内使用
2017 年 1 月	《关于规范银行业服务企业走出去 加强风险防控的指导意见》	银监会	银行业金融机构开展内保外贷等跨境担保业务，应加强融资第一还款来源分析，审慎评估借款及担保主体的风险承受能力
2017 年 12 月	《关于完善银行内保外贷外汇管理的通知》	外管局	细化了内保外贷交易中担保履约可能性的审核原则及要点
2017 年 12 月	《企业境外投资管理办法》	发改委	审核内保外贷业务可能涉及的境外投资行为的政策合规性
2018 年 2 月	《关于规范保险机构开展内保外贷业务有关事项的通知》	外管局	明确了保险机构开展内保外贷业务的具体规范和要求

资料来源：根据北大法宝数据库资料整理所得。

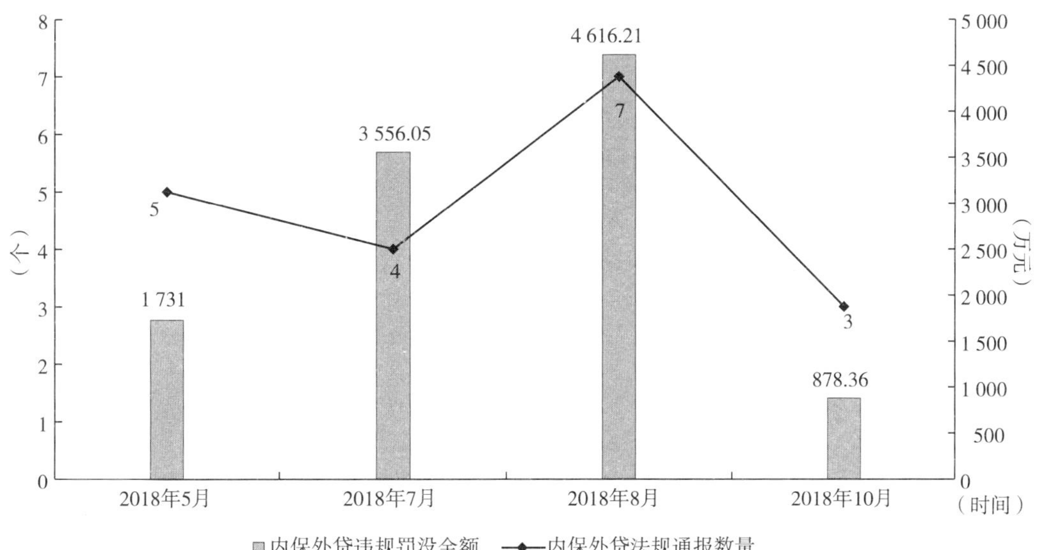

图 6.4 截至 2018 年 11 月内保外贷业务监管通报情况

资料来源：根据外汇管理局发布的监管通报整理所得。

一、内保外贷业务的发展现状与特点

内保外贷业务是境内银行在申请人提供足额保证金的前提下出具融资性保函或备

用信用证，由海外银行机构向境外企业发放贷款的境内外、表内外业务组合，即“内保＋外贷”。相较于境外投资、境外放款政策，内保外贷业务手续简便、管理宽松，无须经过相关部门审批，成为境内企业寻求海外发展的重要融资渠道，为境外企业提供成本较低的资金支持。对境内银行而言，内保外贷业务有全额保证金支持，属于低风险业务，其资本占用较流动资金贷款低，能增加银行的中间业务收入，改善财务报表状况。同时，境内外联动合作能为海外机构提供相对优质的业务，增加境外贷款投放，助力其海外业务拓展。在监管层面，内保外贷业务符合当局鼓励的“人民币跨境贸易业务结算”导向，是国家战略落实与对外开放新格局形成的应有之义。因此，内保外贷业务近年来呈现快速增长态势，2016 年、2017 年，商业银行内保外贷余额同比分别增长 46% 和 21%①。总体而言，内保外贷业务呈现出以下特点。

一是低信用风险与高操作风险并存。内保外贷业务属于低风险业务，低风险业务并不能简单地理解为风险水平较低，准确地说，应当是较低的信用风险、较高的操作风险。内保外贷业务通常需要境内企业提供全额保证金，可视情况增加风险缓释措施，基本可以覆盖当期的信用风险敞口。业务实践中，内保外贷不良率远低于普通贷款，信用风险较低。但不容忽视的是，内保外贷业务涉及境内外金融机构、企业等多个主体，历经申请、开立保函、境外放款、资金回收或保函履约等多个环节，违规操作的空间较大，如交易背景不真实变相跨境套利、擅自改变资金用途等。主体多、流程长、监管政策频出大大增加了内保外贷业务的合规操作风险。

二是负债境内化与资产境外化趋向。内保外贷业务涉及跨境币种错配和资金流动，其反担保形式通常为人民币存款或境内具有相当价值的押品，担保标的为美元等外币债务。在美元低息周期及人民币升值预期下，企业实际控制人可以通过控制内保外贷履约与否，“切割”境外资产和境内负债，实现资产的跨境布局。近年来商业银行内保外贷履约额呈现上升趋势，2016 年、2017 年履约额分别同比增长了 90% 和 48%②，使得担保项下的资金流向境外。

三是表内业务与表外业务结合。内保外贷业务涉及境内保函或备用信用证开立业务和境外贷款业务，其中保函开立业务属于表外业务，境外贷款业务属于表内业务。表内外业务相结合甚至发生转化，在一定程度上增加了内部管理的难度。同时，在内保外贷业务实践中，不断涌现出组合创新模式，如内保外购、内保外债等模式，应用到诸多表内外产品组合中。业务模式和产品组合的叠加，在内保外贷业务创新发展的同时也带来了诸多管理挑战。

---

① 资料来源：荣蓉、韩英彤．继续支持真实合规内保外贷业务的开展［J］．中国外汇，2017（18）．

② 资料来源：同上。

二、内保外贷业务中信贷配给的内在逻辑

内保外贷业务开展过程中，监管层、商业银行与民营企业三方的基本关系是：监管层通过内保外贷监管政策的制定直接干预影响商业银行，以达到监管目的。商业银行需要在满足监管的前提下获得利润并有效地控制风险。民营企业需要获得合理资金成本下的融资支持以实现发展，一定程度上与监管层的政治意图相契合，如推动经济增长、增加就业等。三方主体之间形成相互影响的关系闭环（见图6.5）。

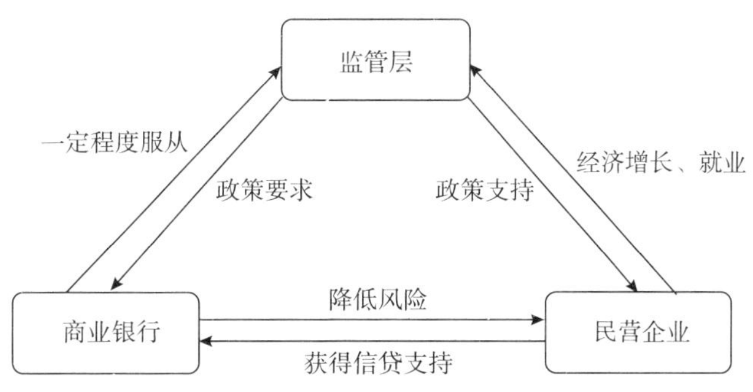

图6.5　监管层、银行、民营企业三方关系示意

值得注意的是，监管层、商业银行和民营企业各自的动机与行为存在差异，导致三方的利益博弈会出现相应的调整和变化。商业银行面向企业开展内保外贷业务，包括国有企业和民营企业，这涉及两者间的信贷配给关系。相较于境内信贷业务，海外贷款业务无论是尽职调查还是贷后管理都更具难度，商业银行在业务操作中为防范和规避金融风险，倾向于较为稳定的国有企业，而警惕高风险的民营企业。另外，相较于国有企业，民营企业利用内保外贷业务模式实现境内资产转移或变相套利的动机更为强烈。随着高质量发展要求的提出以及市场的日趋成熟，金融资源配置在注重安全稳定的同时也关注经营效率。面临改革的国有企业不再是市场的“独宠”，民营企业的整体质量和经营水平在不断提升。

具体而言，商业银行的信贷配给效用函数可描述为：$U=f(S, P)$。其中U是商业银行的效用，S是国有企业的经营稳定与产出增长状况，P是民营企业的融资风险。不难发现，商业银行的效用函数是国有企业经营状况的增函数，是民营企业融资风险的减函数，即$\partial U/\partial S>0$，$\partial U/\partial P<0$。要使得商业银行的效用达到最大，就要力求S不断上升，P持续下降，这也正是监管层的意图所在。因此，要加大民营企业的信贷力度，降低内保外贷的业务风险，其关键在于信息不对称和金融抑制背景下的企业状况和市场波动的甄别问题，而这依赖于监管明确导向、企业诚实守信、银行合规经营。如有某一方为降低自身成本采取于己最佳的策略，往往会使整体偏离帕累托最优。简

言之，民营企业的信贷资源配给是市场发展和主体资质变化的结果，要有效提升内保外贷业务质效，应着力于构建利益平衡机制下的风险控制体系，增加民营企业的违规成本、减少监管层的管理成本、降低商业银行的风险水平。尽管在短期、局部看这并非是最优策略，却能实现长期、整体的最大效用。

三、内保外贷业务发展存在的问题

商业银行内保外贷业务自2001年发展至今，先后经历了业务试水、规模增长、质量提升等阶段，银行机构对内保外贷业务的开展日益娴熟。但不容忽视的是，内保外贷风险管理过程中仍然存在诸多问题，制约着业务的健康发展。

（一）认识盲点：全面风险管理思维缺位

内保外贷业务风险管理不是单一风险的防范，而是多种风险的应对，通常涉及信用风险、市场风险、汇率风险、合规风险等。而实践中，多数商业银行容易出现重信用风险、轻政策合规等风险的情况，对风险认识不足。其主要原因在于：一是业绩驱动且有全额保证金质押，使得商业银行的风险管理认识出现松懈；二是跨市场、多币种、多模式的业务维度增加了风险复杂度，单一的风险管理方式滞后于应对风险变化的现实需要；三是全面风险管理理念尚未深入各个业务环节，思维方式的革新仍有待于政策宣导和要求落实。全面风险管理认识上的盲点在一定程度上影响了内保外贷业务风险防控的导向，容易形成风险隐患。

（二）能力弱点：主动风险管理能力不足

内保外贷业务充分调动境内外要素市场与金融市场资源，面对的风险管理环境相对复杂。针对市场环境变化、监管政策差异、利率汇率波动等挑战，商业银行往往陷入被动应对的境地，监测关口滞后，提前管控主动性不强，缺乏主动管理风险的能力。如境内银行对于境外借款人的尽职调查客观上存在一定困难，导致其对境外市场重要信息掌握不足，难以及早识别异常风险；缺乏大额、高频履约业务的监测机制，内保外贷业务趋势变化、结构特征等情况难以及时有效掌握等。面对跨市场、跨币种的内保外贷业务，多数商业银行目前仍处于被动管控风险的阶段，主动管理能力欠缺，一旦风险爆发则为时已晚。

（三）流程漏点：流程管控体系亟待完善

信贷管理流程的规范性、完善性对管理成效有着至关重要的影响。内保外贷业务由境内银行办理、境外银行放款，贷前、贷中、贷后环节的机制建设和衔接有效性不足，流程环节中的约束反馈作用不强。在贷前阶段，境内银行缺乏对内保外贷境外债务人主体资格、还款来源、借款资金用途、境内担保人等真实情况予以核查，风险评估机制相对弱化；在贷中阶段，多数境外银行尚未建立独立的放款管理机构，放款环节一般是由风险经理进行平行操作，风险管控效果受到影响；在贷后阶段，操作流程较为粗放，管理实效欠佳，跟踪预警机制亟待完善，对发生异常变化的业务反馈不及时，轨迹管理有待加强。流程管控体系上的疏漏使管理成效大打折扣，让风险有机可乘。

（四）机制痛点：关联共享机制尚未形成

内保外贷业务涉及多主体、多环节、多市场，其管理效能受制于信息的数量与质量。目前，内保外贷业务中“信息孤岛”问题突出。商业银行内部管理部门间对于内保外贷业务数据存在统计口径不一致、传递不及时等问题，极大地增加了业务管理成本；各商业银行间缺乏必要的信息共享平台，对于内保外贷履约企业信息披露不足，给履约企业进行跨行套利提供了可能；各个业务间的信息尚未有效关联，境外债务人未清偿之前内保外贷债务的，并不影响其申请新的内保外贷业务，这也给循环套利创造了空间。不难发现，各部门、银行、业务间信息的孤立通常会造成管理上的脱节，关联共享机制的缺位使得各主体的信息资源难以得到整合，形成“信息壁垒”“数据烟囱”，最终将陷入“管理未至，风险已来”的被动局面。

四、对内保外贷业务发展的相关建议

（一）积极建立全面风险管理思维方式

风险管理是银行价值创造的基石，是一项系统性工程。内保外贷业务的风险管控不能仅仅关注单一或某种风险，应当跳出传统思维，树立全面风险管理理念，开阔风险管理思路，广泛收集客户、市场、政策等各类信息数据，积极应对信用风险、市场风险、汇率风险等内保外贷业务可能存在的风险隐患。同时，落实全面风险管理要求，加强内保外贷业务发展趋势、结构变化、区域分布、资产质量、经济资本等方面的研究，紧扣问题导向，督促靶向整改，提升管理效能，定期形成内保外贷业务专题分析报告。通过政策传导，积极引导各级机构理性、合规地开展内保外贷业务，履职尽责，不留死角，增强全面驾驭风险的本领。

（二）稳步提升主动管理风险的能力

掌握风险管控主动权的关键在于管控能力与管理需求的匹配。针对内保外贷业务，要明确导向、紧抓关键、夯实基础，提升主动管理风险的专业能力。一是要研究遵循市场规律。比如，作为跨境融资担保业务，内保外贷与汇率等价格因素紧密联系。从市场经验看，内保外贷签约量集中在人民币升值期间而担保履约量的峰值则出现在人民币贬值期间，市场趋势的研判为内保外贷业务管理提供了相对合理的时间区间和管理重点。二是要关注关键领域的异常现象。内保外贷违规套利通常会有异常的表征，如保证金账户到期日不能覆盖保函有效期则可能存在提前履约倾向；快投快出、母小子大、大额非主业投资、保证金资金来源不明等表明境外投资套利行为的可能性。三是要加强协同控险力度。明确内保外贷业务境内外银行机构的风险责任，境外机构应协助境内机构做好境外尽职调查与跟踪管理，推进集团内部信息共享与风险信号传导，放大风险管理“1 +1 >2”的倍增效应。

（三）持续优化流程管控体系

商业银行要做实贷前、贷中、贷后管理“三道防线”，强化银行内部控制约束机制，持续优化管控流程。在贷前阶段，落实展业“三原则”要求，择优遴选客户，加强客户资质、业务真实性、资金来源的审核力度，建立内保外贷履约风险的评估制度，对履约倾向、履约条件进行审查，提高合规性与审慎性。同时，积极关注资金用途，要符合国家战略方向与银行信贷政策，优化信贷投向，有效防范“灰犀牛”“黑天鹅”。在贷中阶段，强化授信审批实质性风险判断，将经济资本占用和 RAROC 指标作为授信审批重要依据，确保内保外贷业务质量。建立相对独立的放款流程机制，加强放款审核等环节控制，及时跟踪借款资金流向，及早发现套利行为或资金违规使用情况。在贷后阶段，完善跟踪预警机制，持续监测核查，对大额、高频履约、异常变动业务进行重点监管，并尽可能将监测关口前移，在实质性风险之前预警防范，将贷后跟踪情况作为后续授信审批、放款审核等环节的要件，提升内保外贷业务管理的精细化、专业化水平。

（四）形成有效的关联共享机制

信息是业务管理的重要依据，也是质效提升的有效手段。内保外贷业务管理要着力打通信息鸿沟“最后一公里”，依托大数据技术建立高效互通的关联共享机制，运用信息化手段感知业务态势、畅通信息渠道、辅助科学决策。通过共享机制，加强内保外贷履约企业的信息披露，汇总分析履约企业的情况，避免履约企业利用银行间信息不对称进行套利。建立内保外贷关联机制，境外债务人未清偿之前内保外贷债务的，境内企业未经批准不得办理内保外贷相关业务，从而减少循环套利的操作空间。同时，推动机制运行常态化，不断适应错综复杂的金融环境，在信息的交织、传递、组合和导入中实现信息资源整合、管理资源集聚，实现内保外贷业务风险、收益和资本之间的平衡。

五、总结

党的十九大以来，“对外开放新格局”的概念已经成为全面深化改革的重要概念①。金融服务要回归本源，服务实体经济，更好地体现了我国民营经济和金融法治发展中的主体意识和问题意识。在内保外贷业务活动中，商业银行、民营企业、监管层都会基于不同立场而产生不同价值取向，而业务理念和制度层面的变迁则展现出了金融服务对多元话语和价值的规范与统一，更确切地说是多元视角下的一种制度和管理上的平衡。我国内保外贷业务目前仍处于快速发展过程中，要突出主体意识和问题导向，加快风险理念、管理能力、制度体系的建构并不断完善，增强驾驭风险的本领。唯有如此，才能使内保外贷业务获得更多主体的认同，让民营企业在开放的市场生态中实现发展。

① 资料来源：舒米．中国金融：引领全面开放新格局［J］．时代金融，2018（1）．

论中国金融防风险背景下的政策选择

——基于近40年中日经济的比较分析

建信期货　翟贺攀

一、背景及意义

2017年10月18日，习近平总书记在党的十九大报告中提出，要坚决打好防范化解重大风险、精准脱贫、污染防治的攻坚战，使全面建成小康社会得到人民认可、经得起历史检验。

2018年3月5日，提请十三届全国人大一次会议审议的政府工作报告将三大攻坚战的任务具体化：推动重大风险防范化解取得明显进展、加大精准脱贫力度、推进污染防治取得更大成效。

2018年是中国改革开放40周年，40年来中国经济和社会发展取得举世瞩目的成就，同时在经济和社会领域也存在一些亟须加强和改进的问题。改革开放步入深水区，改革的难度加大，开放面临更多的不确定性，中国经济的转型升级需要在更高的层面来规划和实施。正是在这样的背景下，中央把防范化解重大风险摆在了三大攻坚战的首位。

回顾40年来中国改革开放的历史进程，我们发现，我们近年来经历过的事件和问题——经济快速发展后L型增长，城市化、资源紧张与房价高企，贸易摩擦与贸易战，人民币大幅升值后有所贬值，人口红利消失、人工成本上升与老龄化，经济“脱实向虚”与金融风险加大等，与日本近40年来的前期有诸多相似之处。通过考察近40年日本经济的发展历程，借鉴其成功转型经验，反思其历史教训，可以为我们今天做好防范化解金融领域重大风险提供有益的帮助。

二、中国改革开放40年与日本近40年前期的相似性

（一）经济快速发展后L型增长

中国方面，1978—2007年，按不变价格计算，GDP年均增长率为10.04%。而

2008—2017 年，以不变价格计算的 GDP 年均增长率回落至 8. 26%，甚至 2015—2017 年均保持 7% 以下的增幅，改革开放后中国经济 30 年的高速增长被近年来的 L 型增长取代。

日本方面，1978—1988 年，按不变价格计算，GDP 年均增长率为 4. 46%。而 1989—2017 年，以不变价格计算的 GDP 年均增长率回落至 1. 34%，甚至亚洲金融危机时期的 1998 和 1999 年以及全球金融危机时期的 2008 年、2009 年乃至 2011 年均有负增长，泡沫经济爆发和破灭后日本经济长期保持低速增长，被部分学者描述为“失去的 20 年”甚至“失去的 30 年”（见图 6. 6）。

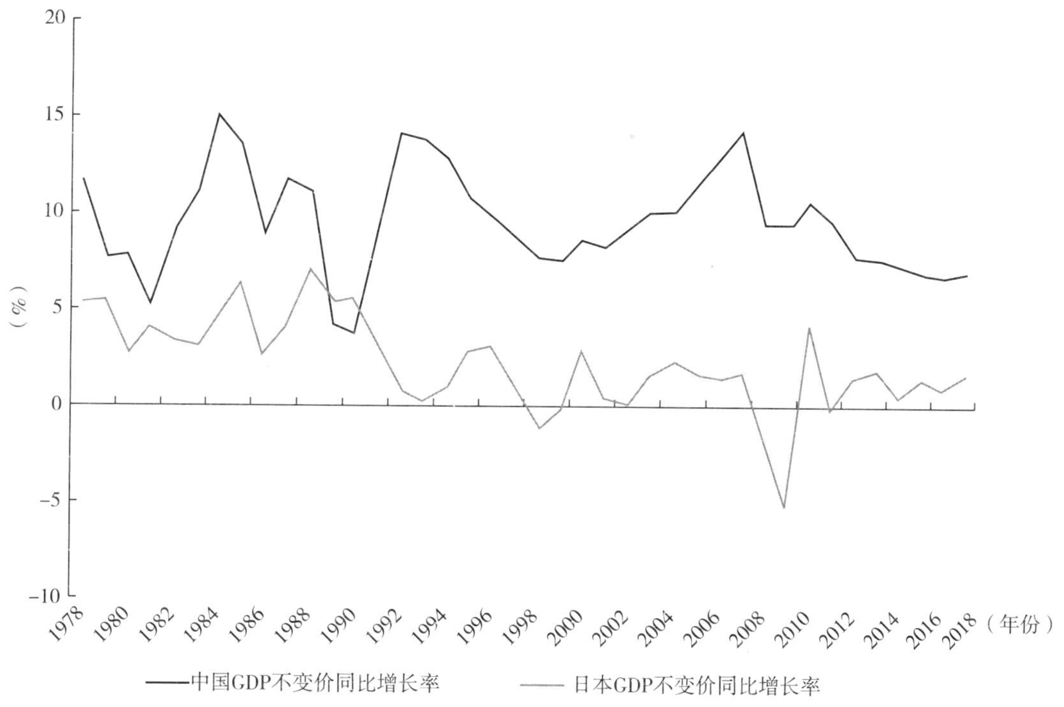

图 6. 6　中国与日本近 40 年的 GDP 增长率

资料来源：万得资讯，建信期货研究中心。

（二）城市化、资源紧张与房价高企

中国方面，1950—1964 年，联合国发布的中国城市化率从 11. 80% 逐步攀升至 18. 30%；1965—1973 年，小幅回落至 17. 18%；1974—1978 年，再度上升，但增幅较小，1978 年至 17. 90%；1979 年以后几乎一路快速上升，2011 年突破 50%，2018 年达到 59. 15%。

日本方面，1950—1975 年，联合国发布的日本城市化率从 53. 40% 快速上升至 75. 72%；随后的 1976—2000 年，陷入低速增长阶段，2000 年至 78. 65%；2001—2010

年增速提高，年均增长 1.22 个百分点，2010 年至 90.81%；2011 至今年均增长仅为 0.08 个百分点，2018 年达到 91.62%（见图 6.7）。

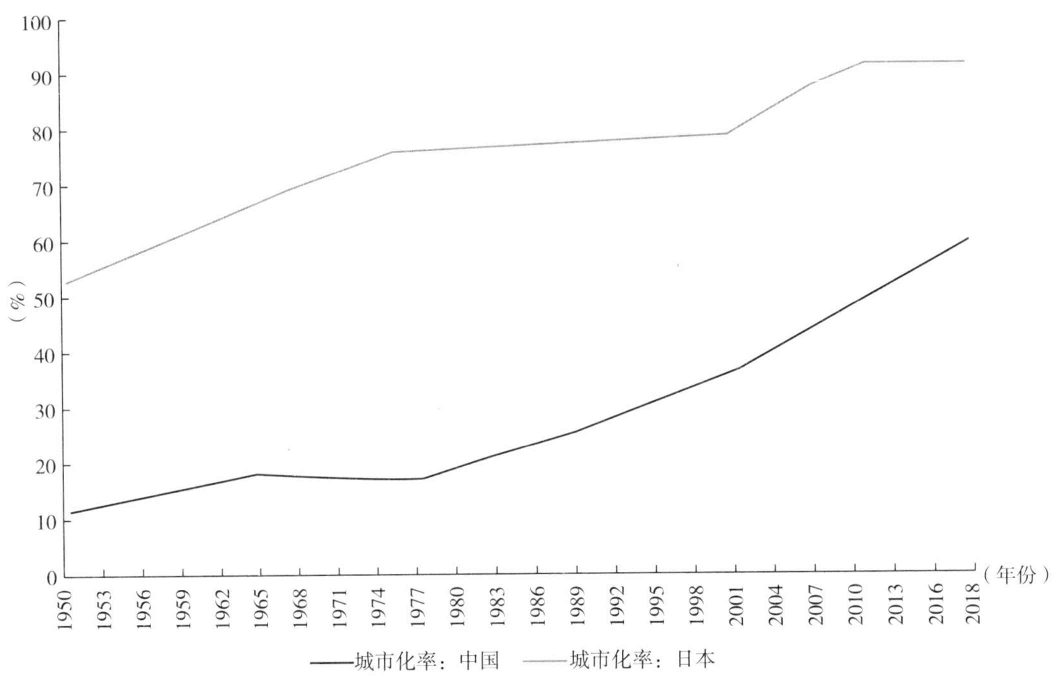

图 6.7 中国与日本近 69 年城市化率

资料来源：万得资讯，建信期货研究中心。

由上述数据可见，1979—2018 年改革开放 40 年里，中国城市化率快速上升的阶段与 1950—1964 年日本城市化率快速上升的阶段具有较大相似性。城市化率的快速提升，带来城市核心区用电、用水和房地产等方面的紧张。2004—2011 年，在用电高峰季节，京津冀地区、上海、江苏、浙江、安徽、湖南、河南、江西、重庆等地多次出现“电荒”。而日本则是在 1973 年石油危机之后，通过大力发展核电，缓解了其用电紧张局面。

经合组织（OECD）发布的成员国季调后实际房价指数显示，以 2010 年房价为 100 计算，2018 年第二季度中国季调后实际房价指数已经上升至 126.90，也就是说，2018 年第二季度中国实际房价较 2010 年已上升 26.9%。而日本的季调后实际房价指数在 1960 年以来则经历了两次大的上升周期、一次较短的回调周期和一次漫长的下跌周期：1960 年第一季度至 1973 年第四季度，自 28.42 快速上升至 134.78；1974 年第一季度至 1977 年第三季度，回落至 95.29；1977 年第四季度至 1990 年第三季度，再度上升并创下新高 174.07；1990 年第四季度至 2009 年第三季度，大幅下滑至 96.06；2009 年第四季度以来有所回升，2018 年第二季度至 106.11（见图 6.8）。

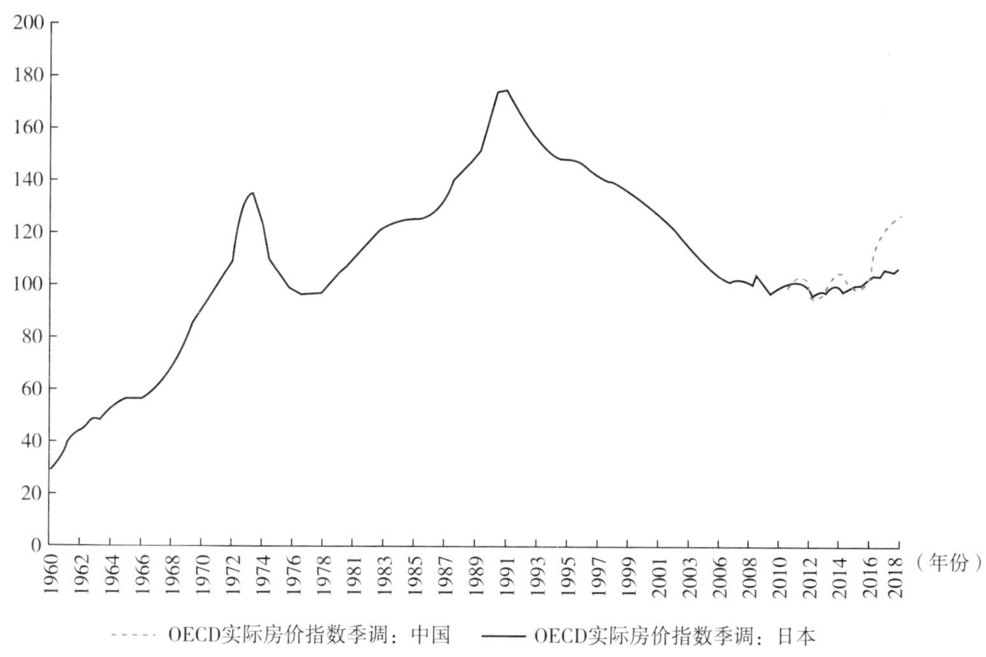

图 6.8　中国与日本近年来实际房价指数

资料来源：万得资讯,. 建信期货研究中心。

从上述数据可以看出，2010 年以来中国房价的走势与日本 1977—1990 年房价走势具有高度相似性。至于 2018 年以后中国房价的走势会不会重演 1990 年以后日本的房价走势，不仅取决于中日两国土地资源的特殊性、人口流动的差异性，更取决于两国经济政策的选择。

（三）贸易摩擦与贸易战

1. 近年来美国对中国的主要贸易措施

20 世纪 90 年代，美国曾 3 次对中国进行“特别 301 调查”，分别是 1991 年、1994 年和 1996 年。

2009 年，美国钢铁工人联合会向美国国际贸易委员会提出申请，对中国产乘用车轮胎发起特保调查。随后，美国国际贸易委员会以中国轮胎扰乱美国市场为由，建议美国在现行进口关税的基础上，对中国输美乘用车与轻型卡车轮胎连续 3 年分别加征 55%、45% 和 35% 的从价特别关税。

2010 年 10 月，美国贸易代表办公室宣布，应美国钢铁工人联合会申请，将按照《美国贸易法》第 301 条款，对中国政府所制定的一系列新能源政策和措施展开调查。这是美国自中国加入 WTO 以后首次动用“301 条款”对其他经济体贸易行为进行调查。

2012 年 10 月 8 日，美国众议院发布调查报告，以国家安全为由，阻止中国两家通信设备制造商华为和中兴进入美国系统设备领域。

2012 年 10 月 10 日，美国商务部终裁判定，中国向美国出口的晶体硅光伏电池及组件存在倾销和补贴行为。

2018 年 1 月，特朗普政府宣布“对进口大型洗衣机和光伏产品分别采取为期 4 年和 3 年的全球保障措施，并分别征收最高税率达 30% 和 50% 的关税”。

2018 年 2 月，特朗普政府宣布“对进口中国的铸铁污水管道配件征收 109.95% 的反倾销关税”。

2018 年 2 月 27 日，美国商务部宣布“对中国铝箔产品厂商征收 48.64% ~ 106.09% 的反倾销税，以及 17.14% ~80.97% 的反补贴税”。

2018 年 3 月 9 日，特朗普正式签署关税法令，“对进口钢铁和铝分别征收 25% 和 10% 的关税”。

2018 年 3 月 22 日，特朗普政府宣布“因知识产权侵权问题对中国商品征收 500 亿美元关税，并实施投资限制”。

2018 年 4 月 4 日，美国政府发布加征关税的商品清单，将对中国输美的 1 333 项 500 亿美元的商品加征 25% 的关税。

2018 年 4 月 17 日，美国商务部部长罗斯宣布，对产自中国的钢制轮毂产品发起反倾销和反补贴调查（即“双反”调查）；美商务部还初裁从中国进口的通用铝合金板存在补贴行为。

2018 年 5 月 29 日，美国白宫宣布将对从中国进口的含有“重要工业技术”的 500 亿美元商品征收 25% 的关税。其中包括与“中国制造 2025”计划相关的商品。

2018 年 6 月 15 日，美国政府发布了加征关税的商品清单，将对从中国进口的约 500 亿美元商品加征 25% 的关税，其中对约 340 亿美元商品自 2018 年 7 月 6 日起实施加征关税措施，同时对约 160 亿美元商品加征关税开始征求公众意见。

2018 年 7 月 6 日 00：01（北京时间 6 日 12：01），美国开始对第一批清单上 818 个类别、价值 340 亿美元的中国商品加征 25% 的进口关税。作为反击，中国也于同日对同等规模的美国产品加征 25% 的进口关税。

2018 年 7 月 10 日，美国政府公布进一步对华加征关税清单，拟对约 2 000 亿美元中国产品加征 10% 的关税，其中包括海产品、农产品、水果、日用品等项目。

2018 年 8 月 2 日，美国贸易代表声明称拟将加征税率由 10% 提高至 25%。

2018 年 8 月 8 日，美国贸易代表办公室（USTR）公布第二批对价值 160 亿美元中国进口商品加征关税的清单，8 月 23 日起生效。最终清单包含了 2018 年 6 月 15 日公布的 284 个关税项目中的 279 个，包括摩托车、蒸汽轮机等产品，将征收 25% 的关税。

2018 年 8 月 23 日，美国在 301 调查项下对自中国进口的 160 亿美元产品加征 25% 的关税。

2018 年 9 月 17 日，特朗普政府表示，将对约 2 000 亿美元的中国商品加征关税，对上述中国商品加征的 10% 关税将于 9 月 24 日生效，年底税率将上调至 25%。关税将影响从行李箱到海鲜水产等数千种商品，特朗普激进关税政策的影响将首次扩大到范围更广的美国消费者。

2. 1957—1995 年日美贸易战

日美贸易战开始于 20 世纪 60 年代，激化于 70 年代，高潮于 80 年代，基本上对应于日本制造业的重生、崛起和兴盛 3 个阶段。从 20 世纪 60 年代至 90 年代这 30 多年间，日美之间爆发了无数次贸易争端，其中行业层面的大型贸易战共有 6 次，宏观层面的贸易战有 2 次。

1957—1972 年的纺织品战。日本纺织品从 20 世纪 50 年代开始抢占美国市场，是最早进入美国贸易保护者视线范围内的日本商品。1957 年开始美国密集通过限制日本纺织品的相关贸易法案，最终以日本“自愿限制出口”的承诺而平息争端。

1968—1978 年的钢铁战。日本钢铁行业继纺织行业之后，在 20 世纪 70 年代成为对美出口的主要部门，遭到美国钢铁行业工会的强烈抵制。1977 年美国发起反倾销起诉，日本再次以“自愿限制出口”妥协。

1970—1980 年的彩电战。20 世纪 70 年代，日本家电行业崛起，在 70 年代后期取代钢铁行业成为最大出口部门，一度对美出口占彩电出口的 90%，在美国彩电市场占有率达三成。1977 年美日签订贸易协议，日本再次“自愿限制出口”。

1979—1987 年的汽车战。此次贸易战在日美贸易战中最为激烈。20 世纪 80 年代，日本汽车继家电行业之后，成为日本赚取贸易顺差的核心产业，对美出口急剧上升，导致全美范围内的抗议潮。最终以承诺日本汽车厂家赴美投资、自愿限制出口、取消国内关税等措施告终。

1987—1991 年的半导体战。日本借助低价芯片对美国产业造成冲击，美国通过反倾销、反投资、反并购等手段进行贸易保护，最高时对相关产品加收 100% 的关税。最终以日本对美出口产品进行价格管制等手段结束。

1980—1995 年的电信战。1985 年美日共同启动电信行业开放，移除日本在电信行业的贸易壁垒，日本电信市场系统性对外开放。

（四）货币大幅升值后有所贬值

1985 年 2 月至 1995 年 4 月的 10 年间，美元兑日元汇率自 262.79 大幅走低至 80.61，日元升值幅度达 69.3%，这与 2005 年 7 月至 2015 年 6 月的近 10 年间美元兑人民币汇率自8.2765大幅下滑至6.1104，人民币升值26.2%具有较大相似性。在随后的数年里，人民币和日元都有所贬值，但贬值幅度与其前期升值幅度相比，都相对有限。人民币和日元的升值，吸引国际资本直接或间接流入所在国，推动了所在国资产价格特别是不动产价格的上升（见图6.9）。

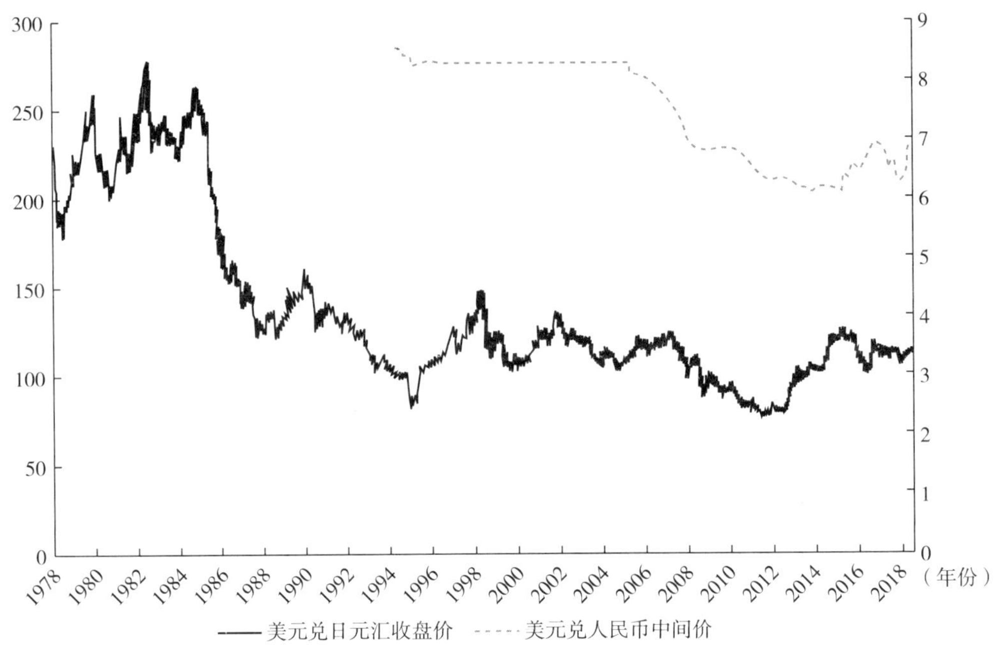

图6.9 中国与日本兑美元汇率变化

资料来源：万得资讯，建信期货研究中心。

（五）经济“脱实向虚”与金融风险加大

衡量经济是否“脱实向虚”，有一个较为简便的指标，即广义货币供应量（M2）与国内生产总值（GDP）的比率。1961—1994年的33年间，日本M2/GDP比率自0.49逐步攀升至2.01；而1985—2015年的30年间，中国M2/GDP比率自0.57逐步攀升至2.02。就单位货币供应量产生的GDP来说，中国与约20年前的日本有非常大的相似性，即更多的货币资金流向金融部门，在金融体系内部从事不产生实际价值的套利活动，拉长资金流链条，挤压实体经济融资空间，提高实体经济融资成本，经济“脱实向虚”的迹象明显（见图6.10）。

随着经济金融化的深入发展，经济“脱实向虚”会导致实体经济效益逐步下滑，利润率走低，投资日益萎缩，生产要素需求疲弱，资金流向有更高收益的虚拟经济，这将进一步强化“脱实向虚”，使实体经济更加脆弱，而巨量资金堆积在金融部门也将加大经济周期作用下的经济运行风险。基于此，我们把防风险放在三大攻坚战的首位，

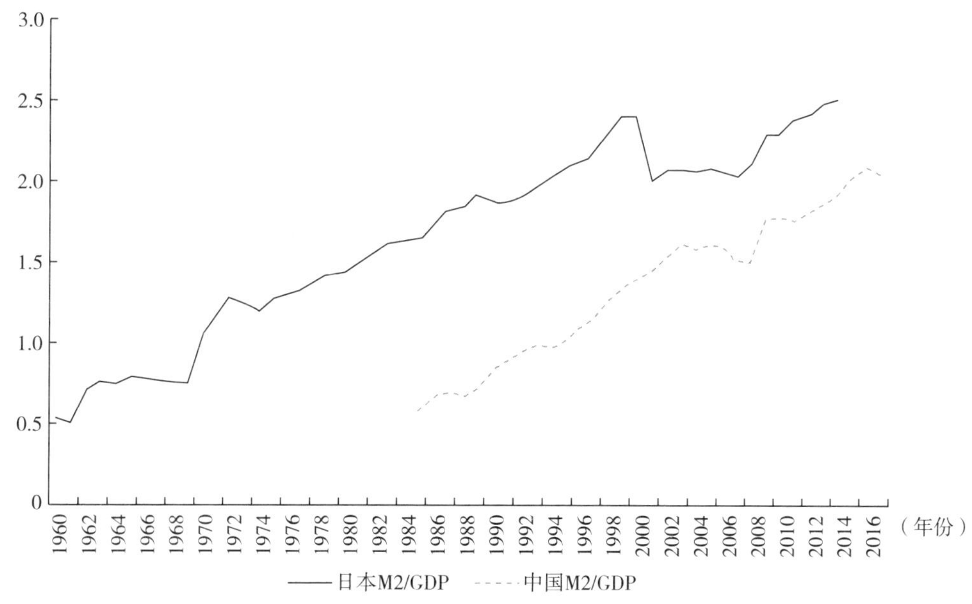

图 6.10　中国与日本近年来 M2 与 GDP 比率

资料来源：万得资讯，世界银行，建信期货研究中心。

切实扭转经济“脱实向虚”的运动轨迹，通过振兴实业这个根本来实现中华民族的伟大复兴。

三、日本泡沫经济的教训与成功转型的经验

（一）日本泡沫经济的教训

1. 面对美国发起的贸易战和本币升值要求轻易妥协

每当美国国内经济或社会领域出现这样或那样的问题的时候，活跃在美国政治舞台的政治家或政客们，就喜欢把民众的注意力引向国外。20 世纪 60 至 80 年代，日本经济快速崛起，超越西欧发达国家，成为仅次于美国的全球第二大经济体且发展速度惊人。随着 1980 年以后美国经济出现巨额财政赤字和贸易赤字，美国贸易保护主义抬头，日本不幸沦为美国对外政策首当其冲的国家。美国相继颁布“超级 301 条款”和“综合贸易法”对日本进行施压，逼迫日本在贸易领域主动降低出口，在外汇管制领域放弃稳定汇率（1971 年之后日元兑美元升值 30%）。从 1985 年 9 月《广场协议》签订到 1995 年日元兑美元升值更是达到 50%。面对美国发起的贸易战和本币升值要求，日本的轻易妥协让其付出惨痛的代价：为对冲日元升值对出口的影响，日本央行在《广场协议》之后至 1987 年 3 月连续 5 次下调公定贴现率，给偏热的日本经济“火上浇油”，为泡沫经济的产生和破灭提供了充分的内部（连续降息后快速加息）和外部

(大幅升值后国际资本涌出)的条件。

2. 货币政策过度关注外部目标，而忽视内部均衡增长和充分就业

纵观20世纪80年代日本央行的货币政策，尽管日本是外向型经济体，需要高度重视汇率和外贸等经济指标，但忽视内部均衡增长和充分就业的内部目标，是其政策失误的重要方面。

从日元升值的效果来看，其本身对于日本对外贸易的影响有限：尽管1986年以其本币计算的出口增幅由前一年的3.9%大幅下降至16.98%的负增长，但1987年日本GDP增幅快速回升，1988年其GDP增幅创下6.8%的新高。1986—1991年，日本经济甚至创下第二次世界大战后第二个最长的景气纪录。正是日本经济决策者对其国内状况判断失误，造成了其经济过热后“硬着陆”——连续降息导致流动性过剩，同时本币升值和放松外汇管制引发国际资本涌入，大量资本从其国内实体经济或国外转出，投资到日本股市和房地产领域，催生资产泡沫急剧膨胀，为其后来泡沫经济的破灭埋下伏笔。

3. “急刹车”导致泡沫经济破灭

直到20世纪80年代后期，日本当局才意识到经济过热、泡沫已经膨胀到不易收拾的地步。日本经济决策者错误地采取了“急刹车”措施给经济降温：1989年5月，日本央行调高公定贴现率0.75个百分点至3.25%，随后连续两次上调公定贴现率至1990年3月的4.25%，同时开始限制银行贷款增长规模。大力度收紧货币政策的措施和金融市场预期方向的改变，导致流动性锐减，股市和房地产价格暴跌，日本泡沫经济破灭。

4. 缺乏逆周期调节和稳预期的措施

第二次世界大战以后，主要发达经济体爆发经济危机的时间跨度和影响深度都比战前有明显减弱，这主要归功于政策制定者运用凯恩斯宏观经济理论和新古典经济理论，对经济周期采取逆周期调节。而随着信息和通信技术的快速发展，全球金融市场受交易者预期因素的影响日益加强。如何合理引导民众预期成为政策制定者必须重点考虑的内容。合理引导预期将有助于政策效果的提升和政策目标的实现，而忽视预期因素，将导致政策效果大打折扣，甚至出现与政策目标相反的效果。

无论是20世纪80年代日本泡沫经济的产生、放大、膨胀时期，还是20世纪90年代之后的抑制泡沫、经历阵痛时期，日本经济政策决策者都缺乏有效的逆周期调节和稳预期的措施，结果导致泡沫不断自我实现式的膨胀后预期崩溃，给金融市场和实体经济带来不可估量的影响。自1990年日本泡沫经济破灭至2010年，被部分学者描述为日本“失去的20年”——经济长期低速增长、消费意愿低迷、实体经济不振。

但实际情况并非如此，进入21世纪以来，日本经济苦练内功，在精密制造、生物医疗、人工智能等方面成功转型，并通过积极拓展海外投资的方式增加本国财富。

（二）日本成功转型的经验

1. 高度重视理论创新和技术创新

1949—2018 年的 70 年间，日本有 26 位科学家获得诺贝尔奖（见表 6.14）。

表 6.14　1949—2018 年获得诺贝尔奖的 26 位日本科学家名单

序号	年份	科学家	获奖类别
1	1949	汤川秀树	诺贝尔物理学奖
2	1965	朝永振一郎	诺贝尔物理学奖
3	1968	川端康成	诺贝尔文学奖
4	1973	江崎玲於奈	诺贝尔物理学奖
5	1974	佐藤荣作	诺贝尔和平奖
6	1981	福井谦一	诺贝尔化学奖
7	1988	利根川进	诺贝尔医学生理学奖
8	1994	大江健三郎	诺贝尔文学奖
9	2000	白川英树	诺贝尔化学奖
10	2001	野依良治	诺贝尔化学奖
11	2002	小柴昌俊	诺贝尔物理学奖
12	2002	田中耕一	诺贝尔化学奖
13	2008	南部阳一郎（美国籍）	与益川敏英和小林诚共同分享 2008 年的诺贝尔物理学奖
14	2008	小林诚	与益川敏英和南部阳一郎共同分享 2008 年的诺贝尔物理学奖
15	2008	益川敏英	与小林诚和南部阳一郎共同分享 2008 年的诺贝尔物理学奖
16	2008	下村脩	诺贝尔化学奖
17	2010	根岸英一	诺贝尔化学奖
18	2010	铃木章	诺贝尔化学奖
19	2012	山中伸弥	诺贝尔生理或医学奖
20	2014	中村修二	诺贝尔物理学奖
21	2014	赤崎勇	诺贝尔物理学奖
22	2014	天野浩	诺贝尔物理学奖
23	2015	大村智	诺贝尔生理学或医学奖
24	2015	梶田隆章	诺贝尔物理学奖
25	2016	大隅良典	诺贝尔生理学或医学奖
26	2018	本庶佑	诺贝尔生理学或医学奖

资料来源：https：//www. nobelprize. org/。

2018 年 1 月，全球领先的智能信息服务商科睿唯安（Clarivate Analytics）公布了

《2017 年全球百强创新机构》的调研报告，在全球企业创新排名的前 100 名榜单里，日本以 39 家高居榜首，超过美国的 36 家（其次是法国 7 家，德国 4 家，韩国 3 家，瑞士 3 家，荷兰 2 家，中国台湾 2 家，中国大陆、芬兰、瑞典、爱尔兰各 1 家）。该榜单在 2014 年之前一直是美国第一名，2015 年之后被日本超越。中国大陆科技公司华为是继 2014 年、2016 年后第三次登榜，同时也是中国大陆 2017 年唯一登入此榜的企业。

早在 2013 年，麦肯锡发布的研究报告就指出，有望改变生活、商业和全球经济的十二大新兴颠覆技术分别是：移动互联网、人工智能、物联网、云计算、机器人、次世代基因组技术、自动化交通、能源存储技术、3D 打印、次世代材料技术、非常规油气勘采、资源再利用。日本全力投入应用于未来的新技术，且在大多数领域已经做到了世界前三。某些科研已经做到了世界第一，如大数据云计算、新材料、资源再利用、能源存储、机器人等。全球顶尖的高科技公司，如三星、英特尔、苹果、高通等，若没有日本的高精度设备、配件及解决方案，这些顶尖的高科技公司的发展至少要倒退 10 年。

日本在理论创新和技术创新领域的领先地位，源于四个方面：一是研发经费占 GDP 比例世界第一；二是由企业自主研发经费占总研发经费的比例世界第一；三是核心科技专利占世界 80% 以上；四是专利授权率高达 80%，专利申请质量高。

2. 突破国内资源局限，在全球范围内配置资本、土地、劳动力和技术

许多学者考察日本经济，受制于 GDP 的传统思维，却忽视 GNP（国民生产总值）对于一个国家或地区的居民来说更有衡量财富的意义。日本长期坚持为企业减税的政策，鼓励国内资本输出。

2018 年 5 月，日本公布 2017 年日本对外资产余额及对外负债余额。其中日本政府、企业及个人在海外持有的对外资产余额增至 1 012.43 万亿日元（约合人民币 58.52 万亿元），首次突破千万亿大关，是日本国内 GDP 的 1.85 倍，约占中国 GDP 的 71%。

四、对中国金融防风险的政策建议

通过近 40 年中日经济的比较分析，特别是吸取日本泡沫经济时期的政策教训，借鉴日本进入 21 世纪后的成功转型经验，我们针对目前中国金融防风险的重大任务，提出如下政策建议。

（一）货币政策

（1）及时关注经济运行的变化趋势，避免政策滞后带来的治理困难。

（2）逆周期调节要松紧适度，切忌“急刹车”“猛踩油门”。

（3）合理引导预期，因为在经济金融化时代，货币政策效率与民众预期关系紧密，运用好预期管理，货币政策才能事半功倍。

（4）去杠杆政策需择时，在经济增长下行周期应给予适当放松或缓和。

（5）在内外政策目标的选择上，货币政策应把内部均衡增长和充分就业的目标放在首位。

（二）贸易政策

（1）对美欧发达经济体出口，将面临贸易保护主义抬头的风险，中国应在“一带一路”倡议的指导下积极拓展与相关国家或地区的经济技术合作，以降低贸易风险。

（2）通过自贸区、自贸港以及降低部分贸易品关税等方式，降低通关和物流成本，在多边贸易谈判遭遇挫折的形势下，加强与主要经济体的自贸区谈判，就跨国、跨区域生产要素和商品流通达成更广泛的协议。

（3）在做好经常账户监管的同时，更加注重资本项目的渐进式开放，对国际资本流动加强识别和管理，通过政策引导，使国际资本流向趋于合理、规模适度可控。

（三）汇率政策

（1）人民币汇率政策要遵循国家的战略目标选择，实行有管理的浮动汇率制度，避免过度的单边走势给实体经济和对外贸易产生较大的冲击。

（2）合理引导贬值预期，在重大关口或重要事件发生前后，守住不发生系统性风险的底线。

（3）人民币汇率政策应保持在合理均衡水平上的基本稳定，着眼于给中长期经济发展提供良好的外部环境和汇兑条件，避免因为外部政治势力或内部企业压力而轻易改变汇率政策。

（四）财政政策

（1）相比于货币政策，财政政策具有更大的政策空间，在补短板、惠民生等领域发挥更大的作用。

（2）可以实行差异化减税降费，比如对于小微企业、科技型初创企业、民生和基建领域的企事业单位等，关键要做到标准透明、公平公开。

（3）加大对于基础理论和技术方面的创新活动的投入力度，决定一个国家竞争力的关键还是科技、教育和人才，财政政策要更多地向这些方面倾斜。

（五）社会政策

（1）在中国人口红利逐步消失的阶段，社会政策要提早对工资、物价上涨和人口老龄化做好预案，鼓励生育的政策要加快落实，关注老龄化带来的消费变化，通过基础设施领域和其他社会资源的合理分配加以积极应对。

（2）制定和执行好污染防治和精准扶贫等配套政策，保障社会公平发展，不能以牺牲环境和部分同胞的利益为代价。

（3）做好住房、医疗、生育、养老、交通等其他社会领域的共同发展任务，通过信息化和优化资源配置，降低民生成本，提高民众幸福感。

中国资产证券化对系统性风险的影响

陕西省分行　赵轶一

一、中国资产证券化的发展

（一）资产证券化的起源

资产证券化起源于美国。1970 年，美国第一次将抵押贷款进行组合，从而将一定存量的资金转换成了证券。房贷转付证券由此产生，并实现了该项证券的交易，从此之后资产证券化开始在西方发达国家的资本金融市场作为一种新型的金融工具发展开来。其实质内涵是将一定存量的资本，通过一定的方式分割和组合而转换成证券的形式，在金融市场上实现交易。

2005 年，我国的资产证券化才算是真正开始试点工作①，落后美国等国家 30 多年。这第一次试点，发行了中国建设银行的房屋抵押支持债券和国家开发银行的现金流抵押证券。这次资产证券化发行证券共计 72 亿元，之后我国各个商业机构开始陆续进行资产证券化的投放工作。然而，我国资产证券化发展的脚步是缓慢的，而且在发展的过程中基本上有将近 90% 的融资渠道是从我国的商业银行而来的。证券发行的投资者比较单一，结构也比较简单。证券发行的市场也存在流动性差、风险高的问题。这些情况都导致我国资产证券化发展进程缓慢，不管是从时间上还是发展程度上都远远落后于美国等资本主义国家。

（二）中国资产证券化的现状

1. 产品发行明显加速

我国的资产证券化采用的是信托的方式②。被证券化的资产将通过信托机构进行某

① 由人民银行、银监会等 10 个部委组成试点工作小组。

② 信托是一种理财方式，也是一种涉及委托人、受托人、受益人的法律行为。

种信托，以换取相应的收益权证，然后信托机构以证券产品的形式销售给投资者。近年来，我国资产证券化发行产品的速度有了明显快速增长的情况，相关数据表明，截至2014年9月，该段期间共累计发行了51只信贷资产证券化产品。2014年前三季度的累计金额达到了2 075亿元。其中包含了CLO（抵押贷款债券）发行的产品40只，该部分金额约占全部金额比例的88%，而ABS（资产支持债券）同时也发行了8只，所占比例为7%，MBS（住房抵押贷款支持债券）发行1只，所占比例较小，仅有3%；其他类型资产证券化产品各1个，金额均为总金额的一个百分点（见表6.15）。而在2012年以前，这些产品的发行金额量累计仅有667.8亿元，可以看出从2012年我国重启了资产证券化发行以后，资产证券化产品在发行量、普及范围上有了很大幅度的提升，其中，在数量上多达第一轮资产证券化的产品发行量总量的3倍。

表6.15　2014年前三季度我国资产证券化产品发行数量统计

类型	数量	金额（万元人民币）
CLO	40	18 187 308.81
Auto-ABS	8	1 514 378.92
RMBS	1	681 423.77
消费贷款 ABS	1	263 085.52
融资租赁资产支持证券	1	101 233.59
合计	51	20 747 430.60

2. 以信托资产为主，方式单一

我国资产证券化的发行产品开始不断丰富，逐渐向多元化发展，但是目前仍然以信贷产品为主。信贷产品除了常见的信贷资产类型外，又新增了Auto-ABS（汽车贷款）、个人住房抵押贷款等，但是资产证券化的方式仍然比较单一（见图6.11）。

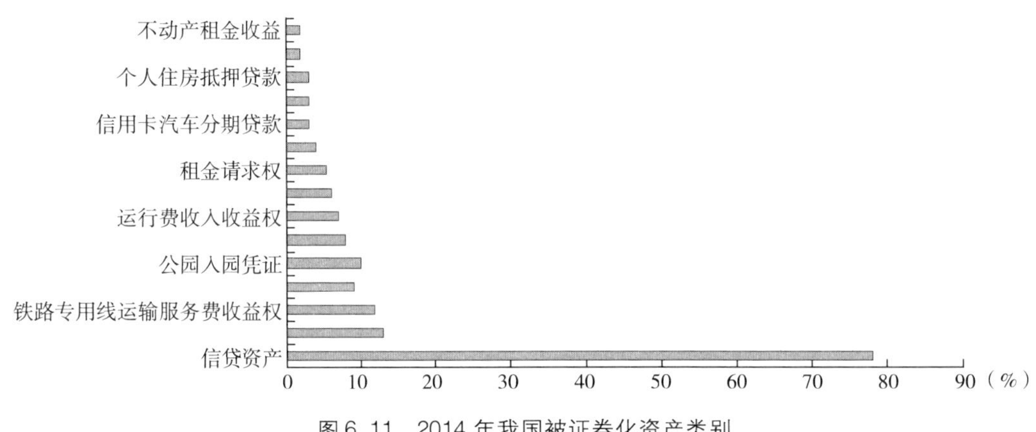

图6.11　2014年我国被证券化资产类别

通过图6.11可以看出，目前在我国，信贷类产品占据资产证券化的主要结构。2014年，我国信贷资产证券化总量已经占当年资产证券化总量的将近80%，而其他类型基本上处于10%左右的水平，各个商业银行也更加偏重对于信贷类资产证券化产品的发行。其中的原因与信贷资产的独立性原理有关。也就是说，对于发起人而言，证券化资产可以被分隔于其自有财产之外，即便发起人破产了也不会将该部分资产作为破产的财产进行清理，可以实现破产隔离的效果。所以商业银行对于资产证券化产品的偏好更加倾向于信贷类资产产品。

3. 没有专门的担保机构

为了能够最大限度地吸收来自我国投资者的更多投资，从而全面降低我国资产证券化产品的发行成本，资产证券化常常是通过信用等级评价制度，用较高的信用等级来赢取更多的资产支持证券化资产。① 在我国运用信用等级来对资产证券化进行保护的相关方法主要有两种：一种是外部第三方的方法，另一种是内部的方法。

外部第三方的方法主要是第三方通过我国相关的法律法规的规定，在明确了自身应该承担的责任和义务之后，信用担保主要面向证券化交易以及参与其中的其他机构提供。通常情况下，第三方要为此担保活动承担一定程度的风险，一般采用的主要方式是通过保险公司提供相应担保的书面证明以及相关的信誉程度的评级证明等。内部法是指通过对资产化证券进行有限偿还的债券重组，从而来提高信用级别，或者是采用连带的方式将发起人与更多的责任人联系在一起，从而获取更高的信用级别。

相比我国，国外资本主义发达国家的资产证券化则是由抵押贷款协会、抵押公司、国民抵押协会等专门的组织完成。这些组织以信用担保的方式，以住房抵押贷款的证券化等为对象，为其提供信用等级的升高。而政府部门则在整个过程中起监督和管理的作用，不直接参与相应的证券化活动。

4. 市场流动性差

从各种债券的发行总量上来看，我国资产支持证券的发行市场可说是规模较小，且交易表现不活跃（见图6.12）。在我国进行资产证券化发行以前，曾有相当一部分学者认为随着我国经济政策的进一步放宽松，我国的资产证券化将会在2006年时就达到1 500亿元，然而这一乐观的预计并没有实现，一直到2013年我国的资产证券化重启以后才一举达到并突破这个数据②。然而，通过图6.12可以看出资产支持证券在我国全部的债券中仅有2.35%的比例，这一比例相对而言微乎其微，远远不能发挥资产证券化的作用。

---

① 国际上最权威的信用评级机构为：标准普尔公司、穆迪投资服务公司、惠誉国际信用评级公司。

② 2012年我国资产证券化试点投入500亿元，2013年投入3 000亿元，到2014年年初累计存量达到4 000亿元。

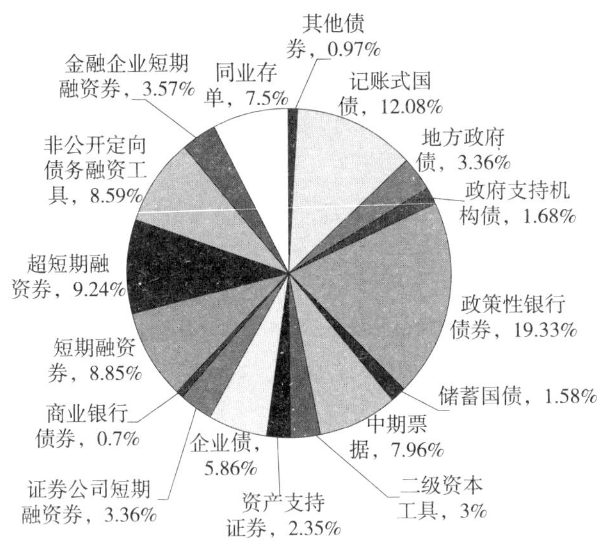

图 6. 12　2014 年各种债券累计发行比例

而美国早在 2006 年的时候其资产支持的债券发行量就已经达到债券市场总量的 52%，其中未偿还债券比例也占 31%，是美国最主要的固定收益债券品种。相比我国的资产支持证券，美国的资产支持证券早已经在 2006 年就进入了规模大、活跃度高的高度发展阶段（见表 6. 16）。

表 6. 16　2006 年美国资产支持证券的发行量、交易量和未偿余额　（10 亿美元）

MBS 发行量	2 003
ABS 发行量	1 252
MBS 日成交量	255
MBS 未偿余额	6 492
ABS 未偿余额	2 130

二、存在的问题

（一）投资主体单一

当前，我国可以进行资产证券化产品投资的主体主要有 9 个类型，分别是特殊结算成员、商业银行、信用社、非银行金融机构、证券公司、保险机构、基金、非金融机构以及境外机构。我国对于资产证券化产品投资主体的限制是造成我国证券化产品市场活跃度低的一个重要原因。

普遍说来，住房抵押贷款的证券化产品都具有很明显的长期性、高收益、风险小并且流动性强的特点，在很大程度上可以满足老年人养老保险基金和保险公司等的投资需求，但是我国当前的证券化产品的主要投资者以商业银行和基金为主，而保险公司的参与度却十分低。我国的养老基金所覆盖的人群范围远远小于保险公司，因此，保险公司对于资产证券化产品投资参与的力度也在一定程度上反映了我国养老保险制度的不完善。相比而言，国外大多数国家的保险公司在证券化过程中扮演了关键角色，成为资产支持证券最大的投资者。

通过图 6. 13 可以明显看出，在资产支持证券一栏中商业银行持有 1 770. 22 亿元，而保险公司仅持有 36. 35 亿元，我国在投资者结构中明显表现出不平衡的偏向，这对于我国国民的生活保证具有不利的潜在影响。

表 6. 17　2014 年年底在中央结算公司登记托管的主要券种持有者构成

种类	2014 年同比增幅（亿元，%）								
	特殊结算成员	商业银行	信用社	非银行金融机构	证券公司	保险机构	基金	非金融机构	境外机构
记账式国债	18 439. 28	59 567. 10	751. 78	260. 00	290. 83	3 050. 94	947. 68	5. 10	2 214. 53
	2. 28	10. 71	6. 84	0. 00	307. 38	5. 21	-2. 89	-73. 58	63. 16
地方政府债	98. 35	11 471. 80	22. 10	0	1. 75	6. 60	17. 10	0	5. 80
	-2. 53	35. 25	-3. 07	0. 00	483. 33	-24. 14	1 454. 55	0. 00	0. 00
政策性银行债券	169. 10	78 046. 69	2 842. 57	74. 70	217. 64	6 141. 73	9 702. 05	3. 40	2 385. 17
	50. 31	8. 20	16. 53	143. 32	20. 70	-0. 45	38. 42	-81. 01	109. 63
央行票据	499. 40	3 624. 32	0	0	0	0	0	0	185. 00
	-14. 41	-24. 25	0. 00	0. 00	-100. 00	-100. 00	-100. 00	0. 00	80. 78
企业债	10 582. 70	6 659. 87	1 145. 90	129. 32	1 026. 36	3 099. 09	6 319. 42	31. 35	69. 87
	63. 03	15. 19	3. 75	10. 42	48. 13	-9. 63	16. 97	-21. 17	71. 89
资产支持证券	58. 16	1 770. 22	7. 34	50. 24	38. 78	36. 35	726. 22	0. 30	1. 32
	485. 14	1 184. 85	167. 86	25 022. 00	970. 05	627. 02	6 049. 18	0. 00	0. 00
商业银行债券	12. 70	4 071. 64	124. 82	32. 90	17. 35	5 750. 84	2 491. 71	23. 20	8. 50
	-62. 20	0. 35	-1. 41	-22. 18	-29. 41	-4. 48	-3. 42	-49. 01	13. 33
政府支持机构债	142. 59	5 712. 35	272. 15	52. 73	83. 72	3 318. 74	1 388. 76	0. 26	53. 56
	13. 19	15. 56	0. 33	-15. 74	-16. 49	3. 43	29. 82	-87. 51	20. 90

（二）专业担保机构建立不完善

我国所实行的资产证券化投资吸引的方式是以保险公司等第三方机构或者是采用内部化的方法来增加信用等级的评定。然而，我国实行信用等级评定时所认定的信用等级与担保机构的信用等级直接挂钩，即不能超越担保机构的信用等级。如果一个保险公司的信用等级是 AAA，则由该机构进行担保的证券化投资信用等级也只能为 AAA，而不能有更高的级别。这种不健全的机构或者说是制度，对我国资产支持证券化投融资的发展造成了很大的阻碍。

通过前文的分析我们可以看出，美国等发达国家具有专门的信用等级较高的信用担保机构，通过专业的信用担保机构对证券化投资进行信用担保，一方面可以在很大程度上提高信用等级，另一方面也可以大大降低寻找高等级担保机构的时间和成本，进而削减了证券发行的成本。然而，我国尚没有建立比较专业的大型专门从事信用担保的脱离政府的机构，当前已有的一些担保机构在很大程度上受制于政府部门，不能够独立进行信用的担保。

（三）一级市场受限制，二级市场尚未形成，流动性差

从当前资产证券化的一级市场来看，由于各方面法律法规制度的不健全，通过调整资产负债结构、增加资产流动性等证券化的方法尚不能得到有效的实施，这就造成当前我国一级市场上资产证券化出现种种尴尬现象。同时，投资者数量相对而言较少，主要以商业银行为主，而相继而来的商业银行的投资必然会造成收益水平的提高，银行势必会出现亏损的现象。

在二级市场上，资产支持证券的交易量相当小，很少有机构会通过在二级市场进行资产支持证券产品的相关交易活动，大多数的投资者都选择将产品一直持有到期。虽然企业专项信贷资产支持的证券在很大程度上具有很有潜力的市场空间，但是证券的出售仍然存在很严重的交易对象难以寻找的难题，同时资产支持的证券尚不支持回购的情况，因此二级市场上资产支持的证券基本上没有市场，资产证券化的流动性很差。

三、对系统性风险的影响

目前中国的资产证券化仍处于发展不成熟、市场不活跃，却开始高速发展的阶段。根据美国等资产证券化程度发达的国家的历史经验，我国在发展资产证券化的过程中有可能遇到诸多问题，会对金融稳定性等方面造成影响。未来资产证券化的发展前景巨大，导致对中国资产证券化的发展及其产生的影响进行研究是很有必要的。在此，本文仅简要讨论中国资产证券化对系统性风险的影响。

资产证券化，换种说法，就是解决流动性问题的一种金融创新。“金融创新，是突破金融业多年传统的经营局面，在金融工具、金融方式、金融技术、金融机构以及金融市场等方面进行明显的创新、变革。”① 金融创新这股浪潮不可阻挡地兴起繁荣，它的迅猛发展之势给整个金融体制、金融宏观调控乃至整个经济都带来了深远影响。资

① 资料来源：黄达．金融学（第三版）［M］．北京：中国人民大学出版社，2012.

产证券化同时也是金融市场与金融中介的关键连接点，其意义远远超出解决流动性问题的范围。同时我们也应该看到，联结金融市场和金融中介的证券化在化解某些风险时有可能带来其他风险，即所谓“双刃剑”。2007 年生发于美国的次贷危机就是最好的例子和证明。这也说明，资产证券化与系统性风险息息相关，它们之间似乎存在着某种机制，影响着后者的形成、积累和传导。

（一）系统性风险的定义

在对金融体系系统性风险测度之前，首先需要界定系统性风险的概念。目前，“系统性风险”已然成为学术界的热点话题。金融监管部门也对其投入了大量关注和研究力度。但究竟如何划分系统性风险、系统性风险具体包含哪些种类的风险，还没有形成一个能被普遍肯定、接受的明确统一的定义。这从一定程度上反映了学术界对系统性风险研究的欠缺，以及系统性风险这一问题本身的客观复杂性。20 世纪 50 年代，美国经济学家马科维茨认为，系统性风险是整个经济体系产生的并且无法通过分散化投资进行消除的风险，因此又叫不可分散风险。这一观点显然是从微观角度上对系统性风险的定义。随着金融危机的爆发频率变高，学术界越来越多地从宏观角度来关注或研究系统性风险。

就目前已存在的研究成果来说，对系统性风险的定义主要从三个角度展开。第一，从风险传染的角度，哈特和津加莱斯（Hart and Zingales）认为系统性风险是指金融体系内机构倒闭或市场崩溃这样的尾端事件，从一个机构传染到多个机构、从一个市场蔓延到多个市场，导致损失在金融体系内不断扩散，并对实体经济造成冲击的风险。第二，根据危害范围的大小，将系统性风险定义为威胁整个金融体系以及宏观经济的事件。[①] 欧洲央行认为，系统性风险是金融体系极度脆弱，金融不稳定大范围发生，导致金融体系运行困难，从而经济增长遭受巨大损失的风险。第三，从影响实体经济的角度，20 国集团财长和央行行长报告将系统性风险定义为可能对实体经济造成严重负面效应的金融服务流程受损或遭受破坏的风险。国际货币基金组织等认为系统性风险是金融体系部分或全部遭受损失时，大范围金融服务被中断从而对实体经济造成恶劣影响的风险。[②]

（二）影响机制

资产证券化之所以能对系统性风险产生影响，很大程度上与资产证券化本身的基

---

① 贝尔南克（Bernanke，2009）提出该观点，认为防范系统性风险的措施有：加强对“大而不倒”金融机构的监管，改革基础设施和防止政策周期性。

② 资料来源：白雪梅，石大龙．中国金融体系的系统性风险度量［J］．金融市场，2014，6：76－77.

本功能或运行机制有关。分析其中的影响因素，能进一步阐明资产证券化对系统性风险的影响机制。

1. 与资产证券化的运作机制有关

资产证券化的发展面临着被证券化资产的种类增加和复杂化的必然趋势，会导致对资产定价、风险评估的难度加大，系统性风险便由此产生。随着市场利率的变化，不同资产的价格也会存在不同方向的变化。其中，不同被证券化资产的种类不再单一，价格期限关系不同，对利率的敏感度不同，也会加大定价难度。当资产定价存在偏差，也反映了市场不是完全有效的，市场价格不能完全反映市场信息，市场中的信息披露机制存在一定的问题，信息披露不完全，这也是风险形成的因素之一。更进一步说，信息不对称导致的代理问题也是系统性风险的来源之一。信息披露这一行为往往需要很高的成本，当市场参与者对这项成本的评估结果是信息分析的成本要高于期望的收益时，市场参与者就会放弃对信息的分析行为。这一过程的发生也是造成市场中的评级机构垄断的原因。而评级机构的垄断不仅使信息不能充分披露，也在很大程度上加大了道德风险。在资产证券化运作进程中，若信息不对称程度过大，甚至每两个市场参与者之间都存在信息不对称的问题，那么就间接说明每两个参与者之间都存在委托代理问题。严重复杂的委托代理问题会造成严重的逆向选择，加大系统性风险。

2. 资产证券化的基本功能对系统性风险的增加有促进作用

资产证券化的完成，意味着流动性的增加，同时在一定程度上具有风险转移的功能。资产证券化的最初产生，可以说就是为了解决缺乏流动性的问题。随着资产证券化的程度变化和不断发展，资产证券化又在渐渐降低融资成本，在优化资源配置以及提高资本充足率方面发挥了重要作用。流动性的增加，往往意味着贷款机构放贷的比例增大，意味着对贷款人的资信评级和财务状况调查放松，对其基础资产的情况监督放宽。这一系列过程反映出道德风险的增加，从而更易产生资产价格的泡沫。在资产证券化的过程中，风险会不断转移，风险的承担者越来越多、范围越来越广，同时金融创新使衍生品层出不穷，这都使得风险在不断转移的过程中增长，系统性风险不断积累。

3. 被证券化资产的价格波动导致系统性风险的爆发

资产证券化的定价基础是被证券化资产的价格，这就说明被证券化资产的价格变动对诸如资产证券化产品等衍生品的价格变化起决定性作用。这也意味着如果经济出现反向波动，会影响到被证券化资产的价格，使其价格下跌，评级下降。经济趋冷本身也意味着资产证券化的功能缺失，市场对证券化产品的需求减少，出现所谓的“投资约束”①。如此，整个市场负向波动加大，到一定程度时就会引起系统性风险的爆发。

（三）对资产证券化程度和系统性风险的测度

如果要量化分析资产证券化造成的系统性风险，那么对资产证券化程度和系统性风险的度量都必不可少。而本文研究资产证券化对系统性风险的影响，出发点是从传导机制来说明影响的存在，因此，对于量化研究只提出可行性办法的说明，并不对两者进行回归分析。

在对系统性风险的度量中，VaR 技术是一种颇受信赖的方法。VaR 产生于 1994 年，是一种用标准统计技术来对金融风险进行估计的方法，可被定义为：一种可以在正常的市场环境下，给定时间区间和置信度水平，预计某种资产或资产组合最大损失的方法。VaR 技术的局限性在于，它表明的是一定置信度内的最大损失，但并不能绝对排除发生高于这个损失的可能性；它更不能代替好的管理、经验和判断，只是一个工具，并不具备决策的品格。2008 年，CoVaR 作为一种更好的测度金融体系系统性风险的方法而被提出，它弥补了传统 VaR 方法在进行线性回归分析时对尾部损失的测度不充分的问题，因此这种方法的可信度更高。②

不论是 VaR 方法还是 CoVaR 方法，都对数据要求较多、较严格，操作方法也更复杂。如果需要简化分析，beta 值也可用来直观衡量系统性风险。③ 本文给出了一组 beta 值来衡量系统性风险。如表 6.18，是 2006—2015 年这 10 年间中国证券市场所有上市股票的 beta 均值。④

表 6.18　2006—2015 年中国证券市场的 beta 均值

年份	2006	2007	2008	2009	2010	2011	2012	2013	2014	2015
beta	0.983	0.961	1.074	1.052	1.081	1.184	1.253	1.090	0.979	1.155

对于资产证券化程度的衡量，一般有资产证券化率，即被证券化资产与总资产之比。这里说的资产证券化率，一般指的是信贷资产证券化率。而对资产证券化率的解释，还有一种社会资产证券化率的说法，即社会资产证券化程度 = A 股市场市值/GDP。这种说法对资产证券化程度的衡量与本文探讨的范畴有出入，但是，从宏观角度出发，

① 投资约束通常指投资人自行承担投资风险并约束自身投资行为的机制。

② CoVaR 方法由阿德里安和布伦纳迈尔（Adrian and Brunnermeier）提出。在 2007—2009 年，对系统性风险的测度方法主要有两种：综合指数法和早期预警法。

③ 这里可以将整个金融市场的 beta 作为 1。

④ 此 beta 为所有个股的 beta 之和与个股总数之比（国泰君安数据库）。

社会资产证券化率用于衡量证券市场发展程度似乎更为贴切。

由于中国资产证券化发展水平的限制，关于信贷资产证券化率的数据较难掌握，故本文仅列出对中国10年间的社会资产证券化程度的简要分析。巴菲特曾对这一证券化率给出了自己的见解，他认为这一数值在70% ~80%是一个合适投资的信号，而逐渐增加的数值意味着逐渐递增的风险，当逼近200%时，这就成了一个高危信号。如表6.19所示，在2007年，中国证券化率超过了100%，达到大约120%，似乎对之后发生的全球金融危机有印证作用。这也说明，该证券化率虽然不完全吻合本文着重讨论的资产证券化范畴，但是其作为衡量资产证券化程度的诸多方式之一，也与系统性风险的关联密不可分，不可忽略其重要的警示作用。这也间接说明，不管从宏观还是微观角度，资产证券化与系统性风险的联系都必然存在。

表6.19　对社会资产证券化程度的测度

年份	市值（亿元）	GDP（亿元）	证券化率（%）	年份	市值（亿元）	GDP（亿元）	证券化率（%）
2006	88 909	217 657	40.85	2011	213 800	484 124	44.16
2007	325 799	268 019	121.56	2012	229 100	534 123	42.89
2008	120 990	316 752	38.20	2013	237 600	588 019	40.41
2009	243 084	345 629	70.33	2014	371 100	635 910	58.56
2010	264 300	408 903	64.64	2015	417 926	676 708	61.76

四、基于中国资产证券化发展现状提出的几点对策

（一）加强金融监管

在资产证券化深入过程中，风险不断分散化，总信贷供给内生性地扩张，容易引发系统性风险。《巴塞尔协议Ⅲ》非常重视对系统性风险的管理，要求对证券化资本更加注重审慎并且更具有风险敏感性。①

自次贷危机爆发以来，学术界对它产生的原因、危害都进行了许多研究。由于次贷危机通过资产证券化产品的形成这一方式来传播，使人们很容易对资产证券化的认识产生误解，认为资产证券化对次贷危机的发生产生了必然的影响。事实上，资产证券化作为一种工具，存在如何运用的问题，从解决问题的角度考虑，也就是说，合理的运用能发挥其优势作用，而不当的运用就会招致风险。所以，这二者的存在在如今

① 《巴塞尔协议Ⅲ》于2010年发布，它对资本充足率提出了更细致详尽的要求，对资本的定义更加严格，要求各项指标要在2019年全面完成。

的金融发展过程中有很大的关联性，但是次贷危机的出现并不一定是资产证券化的必然，而很大程度上是在监管缺失的情况下某些机构对资产证券化的不当运用所导致的。因此，为了对系统性风险进行更有效的管理和把握，防止金融危机的爆发，我国对金融监管的关注进一步加强。广义的金融监管被定义为除监管当局的监管外，还囊括了金融机构内部控管和稽查、来自行业自律性组织的监管以及社会中介组织的监督等。

目前，中国的金融监管模式采用的是“一行两会”的分业监管模式。[①] 随着金融创新的推进，金融行业内的相互影响会不断加大，过度的金融创新导致系统性风险的加大，传统的监管模式将不再适应新发展的需要。在2008年的国际金融危机后，人们更意识到传统的以微观审慎为基础的金融监管收效甚微，开始着重实施宏观审慎监管。宏观审慎模式是近年来与中国金融监管密切相关的概念，它是一种以维护金融体系稳定为目的，以防止金融体系对经济体系的负外部溢出为途径，从而采取的一种自上而下的宏观监管模式，对于另一个与金融体系相关的顺周期性问题，建立宏观审慎框架也有所裨益。它将有助于降低银行业乃至整个金融体系的顺周期性，进而增强金融体系的稳定性及其应对系统性风险的能力。

放眼全球，为对系统性风险进行更有效的监管，20国集团峰会于2009年4月做出决议，决定设立全球金融监管机构——金融稳定委员会（FSB）。[②] 金融稳定委员会也对金融体系系统性风险做出了解释，认为一些风险因素（如经济周期、国家宏观经济政策的变化、来自外部的金融冲击等）能引起一个国家的金融体系产生强烈波动的可能性，并且这种风险对国际金融体系乃至全球实体经济都会产生巨大的负外部效应。金融稳定委员会还认为，系统性风险无法通过风险管理手段得以削弱或消除，最有效可行的办法就是通过积极有效的监管，防止其积累甚至爆发。

（二）应对资产证券化自身发展的具体措施

除了对中国资产证券化所引致的系统化风险要采取积极的金融监管对策之外，为了应对中国资产证券化的自身发展，使其迈向良性发展的轨道，以更好地促进中国金融业的繁荣稳定，以下也提出了几点具体措施。

1. 扩大投资主体

通过前文中的分析可以看出，在我国当前的金融结构中，投资的主体太过单一，而且投资的产品也过于单一，这就造成大量的资金和投资者只拥有少数的投资品种，

---

① “一行两会”中的“一行”是指中国人民银行，“两会”是指中国证监会、中国银保监会。

② 20国集团成员包括：美国、日本、德国、法国、英国、意大利、加拿大、俄罗斯、欧盟、澳大利亚、中国、南非、阿根廷、巴西、印度、印度尼西亚、墨西哥、沙特阿拉伯、土耳其、韩国。除了金融稳定委员会之外，金融监管职能的国际协调组织还有巴塞尔委员会、国际证监会组织、国际保险监管官联合会等。

将会导致我国金融结构的进一步恶化。针对这一情况，我国应当扩大投资主体，将当前的以商业银行为主的资产支持证券化投资转型为以商业银行、基金、保险机构三者并行的模式，尤其是应当大大提高保险机构的投资比例。养老保险制度是我国居民生活的保障，然而相当一部分居民并不能够享受社会福利，尤其是不具有养老保险金的社会福利，保险机构可以通过一定的模式对我国居民的养老保险提供很大的帮助。因此，保险机构应当加强对资产支持证券的投入比例，通过开发新的产品使我国大量的居民都能够受益。商业银行的主体地位可以保持，同时商业银行应该起到带头作用，将资产支持的证券进一步推广，扩大我国的资产支持证券在证券中的总体比例，提高资产证券化的规模。

2. 设立专门的信用担保机构

信用担保机构是我国资产证券化投融资的重要机构，然而我国的资产证券化信用担保机构尚没有一个完善的体系，一方面没有具有规模的专业机构，另一方面政府机构不能为证券化进行担保。因此，为了能够进一步保证我国的资产证券化顺利开展，必须立即建立起有效的信用担保机构。本文建议我国借鉴国外的先进经验，通过设立专业从事信用担保活动的担保协会或者以法律的形式准许我国政府机构进行信用担保，通过专业的机构和政府部门的优势地位，以及对信息的收集和把握来进一步提高资产支持证券化的市场流通性。

同时，本文建议采用政府担保逐步向专业担保机构转型的模式。首先，在政府机构中成立专门进行担保活动的下属单位，通过借助我国政府机构的特殊地位以及已经建立起来的信誉度来促进当前市场中资产支持证券的流通；其次，在机构发展到可以自主盈利的情况下，将单位分出去形成一个专业的信用担保公司，政府从担保活动中独立出来不再参与担保活动，而仅仅对担保活动起引导和监督的职能。通过该方法的执行不断推动我国信用担保机构的建设，从而促进我国资产支持证券的流动，提高流动性。

3. 积极培养二级市场

资产证券化受到利率的影响作用很大，因此，要培养二级市场的首要措施是加快利率市场化的速度。我国当前的利率市场并没有完全实现市场化，因此在很大程度上，金融机构的利率并不能够完全依据当前资本市场的货币供求关系以及客户的信用风险来进行个性化的制定，而住房抵押贷款被银行归类于优质信贷资产之一，对于金融机构而言，缺乏实行证券化的有效动力。而在利率实现市场化以后则可以使银行通过增加中介服务来获取收入，能够在很大程度上提高资产的流通，降低金融机构完全承担信贷风险的局面。

其次，二级市场的建设还要同时加强固定利率的贷款。资产证券化起源于美国的固定资产贷款，而我国也正是因为受到浮动利率贷款的影响，从而导致银行对资产证券化参与的动力不足，因此不断加强对固定利率贷款的推行有助于资产证券化市场的发展。

最后，针对信贷资产及其证券化产品，应大力加强囊括了其信息的数据库的建设。担保机构在进行信用担保时必须通过对历史数据的分析进行信用等级的评定，如果没有完善的信息化数据系统，则会给信用担保机构的信用评级活动带来很大的困扰以及限制。因此，加强对信贷资产以及证券化产品信息数据库的建设，准确收录以往的数据信息，可以提高信用等级评价活动的便利度，从而间接促进资产证券化市场的发展。

4. 完善法律法规建设

法律法规是一切经济活动的准绳，没有法律法规的金融市场是混乱的，一旦出现了问题就很难有明确的解决方案。我国必须对资产证券化的法律法规进行完善，对当前已经出现的资产证券化问题进行法律法规的制定，并通过国家强制力保证实施，从而促使我国资产证券化市场的有序进行。法律体系的建设是一个长期的过程，必须不断地实践和修正，通过长期的努力建立一套适合我国国情的有效的法律制度体系，保证我国资产证券化市场的有序、优质发展。

五、总结

我国的资产证券化起源于 1992 年三亚市丹洲小区将 800 亩地作为发行标的物，从而将其销售并获得了 2 亿元的地产投资券。2005 年国家正式进行了资产证券化的试点工作，2012 年又重启了资产证券化活动。从我国资产证券化发展的历程来看，在第一次试点工作时国内众多的学者和机构对其抱有较大的期望，然而并没有取得良好的发展。2012 年至今，我国的资产证券化以成倍的速度增加，开始进入了高速发展的阶段。但是需要看到的是，在高速发展的同时也暴露出了一系列的问题，本文通过分析总结出我国当前资产证券化存在的主要问题是：投资主体过于单一、没有专门的担保机构、流动性差。而更重要的也更具有现实意义的是，对资产证券化是否引致系统性风险的研究。自次贷危机爆发以来，对资产证券化的思考一直存在着对系统性风险的影响的考量。本文分析了资产证券化对系统性风险的影响机制，介绍了能够量化二者的具体方法。最后，本文阐述了资产证券化对系统性风险的影响确实存在，但不是引发次贷危机等金融风险的必然原因，这其实也是在金融监管不完备的背景下发生的。在资产证券化程度必然深化的金融环境下，以金融监管为主的监管机制是对系统性风险的主要防范措施。另外，本文也就资产证券化要如何深入发展提出了针对性的建议，希望通过这些对策建议的实施，能够使我国资产证券化的发展更上一个台阶，从而进一步促进我国金融市场的发展。

不良资产证券化研究

大连市分行　翟志亮

不良资产证券化（NPAS）发展已有20多年的历史，以曾经深受银行不良资产困扰的美国、日本和韩国最为活跃。近几年，随着我国经济下行期运行，不良资产规模日益增加，已成为困扰我国金融业发展的重要因素。因此，为缓解不良资产压力，监管部门于2006年和2016年先后进行了两次不良资产证券化的试点。

一、引言

资产证券化是指发起人将未来可产生稳定现金流，但目前缺乏流动性的特定资产组合，打包形成特殊目的载体（SPV），通过发行可交易证券在金融市场上进行出售的一种融资方式。

由此可见，只要未来可形成稳定现金流的资产，都可以进行证券化。单笔不良资产虽然暂时不能按时偿还本息，但通过将不同行业不同地区的大量不良资产，经过结构化分层等安排，形成特定资产池，通过风险的内在抵消，降低整体风险后，可形成稳定的本息回收率。因此，为缓解商业银行不良贷款压力，调整资产负债结构，我国于2005年开始推进不良资产证券化业务。

（一）我国不良资产证券化的进程

2006年10月，为缓解不良资产压力，银监会提出了不良资产证券化试点，首批试点企业为四大资产管理公司。2006年12月，推出信元2006—1优先级重整资产支持证券和东元2006—1优先级重整资产支持证券两个不良资产证券化产品。

2008年，受美国次贷危机影响，我国暂停了资产证券化试点业务。随着经济增长放缓，商业银行不良贷款问题日趋严重。2016年，为缓解商业银行不良贷款压力，监管部门重启不良资产证券化试点，批准中国建设银行、招商银行等5家股份制商业银行作为试点，共计发行不良资产证券化产品约500亿元，处理不良资产共计2 000亿元。

（二）我国不良资产证券化的特点

不良资产证券化的产品模式等同于普通资产证券化：第一，信托公司购买商业银行的不良资产组合；第二，信托公司对不良资产组合进行分层和结构化处理；第三，增信机构对资产组合进行内部增信和外部增级；第四，评级机构对资产组合进行信用评级；第五，发行机构向投资者发售证券化产品。

虽然不良资产证券化产品与普通资产证券化产品模式基本相同，但在具体操作上，还存在以下差异。

1. 基础资产不同

普通资产证券化产品，其基础资产一般为银行正常类贷款，即可以按时还本付息的优质贷款，其在未来可以形成稳定的现金流。而不良资产证券化的基础资产，则是需要通过法律诉讼、对抵押物评估拍卖等法律流程后，对不良资产的处置情况有个预期，进而形成未来的现金流，具体如下所示：

（1）不良资产证券化其基础资产未来的现金流，需通过对抵质押物的评估拍卖、担保人及借款人的资产处置而得来，非正常经营的现金流。

（2）受不良资产处置过程的影响，其基础资产的还款时间和还款额度具有不确定性，未来现金流不稳定，因此对基础资产的分层及结构设计要求较高。

（3）不良资产受经济周期影响较大。

从过往发行的不良资产证券化产品来看，其基础资产多为抵押率较高、抵押物较易变现、担保人还款能力较强的不良贷款。

2. 增信方式不同

普通资产支持证券，由于其基础资产较好，一般只采用内部增信的方式，不需要外部增级。由于不良资产证券化产品的基础资产是银行不良贷款，因此其未来的现金流具有不确定性，通常需要同时使用内部增信和外部增级两种方式。

内部增信主要采用优先、次级分层的方式，不良资产证券化的次级比例要高于普通资产证券化产品。从已发行的不良资产支持证券来看，次级的平均比率约为29%。

对于外部信用增级，主要指由次级债券的投资者对优先级投资者提供流动性支持。例如中国银行发行的“16中誉1期”不良资产支持证券，其资产服务顾问和外部流动性支持机构均由信达资产管理公司担任。因此，“16中誉1期”的优先级风险较低，其获得了超过3倍的超额认购，最终以101元溢价发行。

3. 投资者不同

与普通资产证券化产品相比，不良资产证券化次级收益具有不确定性，其投资风险较高，因此，只有拥有处理不良资产丰富经验的投资者才可能投资次级证券，其投资者范围较小。从已发行的几只不良资产证券化产品来看，其次级投资者均为私募基金或四大资产管理公司。如已发行的招商银行不良资产证券化产品，其次级证券投资者为私募基金。

4. 次级证券投资人的职能不同

普通资产证券化产品中，次级证券投资人不参与现金流的回收工作，其由资产服务机构完成。但在不良资产证券化产品处置过程中，由于次级投资人拥有专业的不良资产处置能力，因而其通常作为资产服务顾问，加入基础资产的处置中，并收取一定的顾问费。

5. 服务机构的激励制度不同

在普通资产证券化产品中，服务机构按照产品规模收取固定的报酬。不良资产证券化的资产服务机构，其处置能力和积极性对产品现金流的回收起到至关重要的作用，因此其报酬具有以下特点：（1）在偿付优先级证券利息之后，才能支付服务机构报酬，个别情况下服务机构的报酬支付甚至在偿付优先级本息之后；（2）根据不良资产回收难易程度不同，有的服务机构可收取浮动报酬，即当基础资产现金回收比例超过预先约定的水平时，服务机构可按一定比例获得超额部分的收益。

6. 信息披露的要求不同

依据现有监管制度规定，普通资产证券化产品只需对发行信息、基础资产、交易结构等信息进行披露。对于不良资产证券化产品，根据中国银行间交易商协会于2016年4月19日发布的《不良贷款资产支持证券信息披露指引（试行）》的规定，发行人需详细披露不良资产的抵押品、担保人以及服务机构对不良资产处置的经验及能力情况等。

二、不良资产证券化的国际比较及启示

（一）美国不良资产证券化的模式分析

美国在20世纪80年代爆发了两次破产风潮，为稳定金融和经济秩序、防止危机大规模蔓延，政府于1989年8月9日成立了临时机构（重组信托公司，简写为RTC），负责处置和管理不良资产。经过6年多的操作，RTC用资产证券化的方式处理不良贷款超过4 500亿美元，为美国未来经济的繁荣发展打下了良好基础。

美国不良资产证券化的操作过程为：第一步，选择合适的不良资产，建立资产池；第二步，选择专业机构成立经营公司；第三步，根据资产池的情况，合理分层和切割债券；第四步，证券的发行。

RTC通过将不良资产进行证券化的方法，获得了现金，盘活了银行不良资产，具

有开创意义。

（二）日本不良资产证券化的模式分析

受地产泡沫及亚洲金融危机影响，日本银行业不良资产剧增。为缓解不良贷款，日本政府于 1999 年 10 月 25 日推出了亚洲首例不良资产证券化项目。高盛公司和投行摩根大通既是证券发起人、投资者，也是基础资产的服务商、承销商。此笔不良资产证券化产品的基础资产为 700 多套房屋不良贷款，发行规模约为 210 亿日元。

在处置不良资产方面，日本政府更重视制度的建立。如 1990 年先后出台了《金融机构重组方针》《重建金融机构机能紧急措施法》《金融系统稳定化对策》《过度银行计划》等，明确了对不良资产处置的基本方法。

同时，日本政府于 1998 年设立了金融再生委员会和金融监督厅，全面负责清理 146 家银行的不良资产。由于日本政府对债权管理过于严格，导致出现虽然进行了证券化处理，但不良贷款余额未减反增的情况。

（三）韩国不良资产证券化的模式分析

亚洲金融危机同样使韩国金融机构产生了大量的不良资产，韩国政府运用资产证券化的方式，有效化解了不良资产，其对我国不良资产的处置具有借鉴意义。

韩国政府积极开展金融重整计划，于 1997 年 12 月接受了国际货币基金组织提供的援贷协议，金额约为 583 亿美元。对于不良资产证券化的推进，其先从法律制度入手，制定了《有效处理金融机构不良资产及成立韩国资产管理公司的法案》，设立了金融监督委员会和韩国资产管理公司（KAMCO），负责不良资产处置方案的拟定与执行。

KAMCO 于 1999 年 6 月推出不良资产证券化产品，金额约为 3 200 亿韩元，其基础资产为 5 个地方银行的不良贷款。韩国政府利用证券化手段处理的不良资产占总不良资产的 20%，其具体过程如下所示。

1. 构建资产池

韩国不良资产证券化产品的基础资产一般由多家银行的不良贷款组成。

2. 信用增级

韩国多采用超额担保和基础资产打折的方式对证券进行信用增级。

3. 发行和流通

韩国政府通过设立境内外两个证券公司，进行产品的销售。

（1）在开曼群岛注册韩国资产基金有限公司。

（2）为实现销售与破产隔离功能，设立韩国第一证券化公司。

具体操作为，韩国资产基金有限公司购买韩国第一证券化公司所持有的不良资产组合和卖出期权。随后，韩国资产基金有限公司发行浮动利率证券，并销售给境外投资者。之后，韩国资产基金有限公司利用卢森堡证券交易所，将其发行的证券上市，合格机构投资者可购买该证券。

三、我国对不良资产证券化的需求

（一）缓解银行不良贷款压力

近几年，受宏观经济结构调整及经济周期下行的影响，我国商业银行的不良贷款余额和不良贷款率不断上升。截至2016年年底，商业银行不良贷款余额达15 123亿元，较上一年增长2 379亿元；商业银行不良贷款率为1.74%，已接近2%的风险警戒线。

一方面，商业银行不良贷款余额持续上升，将严重侵蚀商业银行的利润及资本。如果不良贷款的增长速度过快，将会导致银行超额拨备减少。同时，拨备的增加将直接导致净利润减少，即核心一级资本直接减少。

另一方面，商业银行传统处理不良资产的方式和手段，都无法及时有效地化解不良贷款。运用证券化的方式处理不良贷款，既可加快不良资产处置效率，又可盘活不良资产。

（二）提高不良贷款处置效率与效益

从效率上来说，不良资产证券化为商业银行提供了一个快速、有效、合规的，使不良资产出表的方法。同时，不良资产证券化将表内的不良资产转换成了表外的中间业务收入，盘活了银行存量资产。

从效益上来说，传统的不良资产处置方式是将不良资产转让给四大资产管理公司，价格基本为二至三折。但通过不良资产证券化，部分银行可获得更高的利润。例如，中国建设银行在2008年发行的重整资产支持证券，由于其既是发起机构，又是资产服务商，根据实际不良资产处置情况，建行最终回收率达到了44%，远远超过传统的二至三折。

（三）满足多元化投资需求

随着社保基金、险资、证券投资基金等投资机构的发展，其需要更为多样化的投资渠道来满足其投资需求。目前，固收市场上，标准化的资产证券化产品由于其信用评级普遍较高，一般均为AA+以上，因此收益率相对较低，无法满足投资者的需求。同时，非标信贷类产品虽然收益较高，但风险过大。

不良资产证券化产品，其基础资产经过专业的分层后，具有分散性相对较好、收益相对较高的特点。其分层结构的设计及收益的梯次，可以满足投资者多元化的投资需求。

四、案例分析

中誉 2016 年第一期不良资产支持证券（简称“16 中誉 1 期”）。

（一）基础资产

中国银行山东省分行的 72 笔不良贷款，本息余额约为 12.54 亿元。其中，可疑类贷款占比为 3.31%，次级类贷款占比为 96.69%。最大借款人未偿贷款本息余额约为 5 亿元，占比 40.46%。前五大借款人的未偿贷款本息余额约为 9 亿元，占比 71.83%。从整体情况来看，不良贷款集中度较高。

同时，此期产品的不良资产多以抵质押贷款为主，金额约为 10.19 亿元，占比 81.29%，因此抵质押物的变现情况将是产品的主要回款来源。

（二）证券发行信息

发行规模 3.01 亿元，其中优先级 2.35 亿元，占比 78%，票面利率 3.42%（固定利率，每半年付息），加权平均期限 0.91 年，评级 AAA。次级 0.66 亿元，占比 22%，加权平均期限约为 2.62 年。

（三）增信措施

本产品具有内部信用增级和外部信用增级措施。

内部增信主要采取优先和次级的分层安排，同时还设立了流动性储备账户。外部增信主要是发生支付风险时，次级债券投资者依据信托设立时的约定，提供一定金额的流动性支持款项。同时，当基础资产回收的现金无法偿付优先级本息时，由次级证券持有者支付不足部分。

（四）交易模式

交易模式详见图 6.13。

五、我国资产证券化发展的制约因素

我国资产证券化发展还处于初级阶段，虽然有较高的现实需求，但由于技术和外部制度体系的不完善，将会制约不良资产证券化的发展。

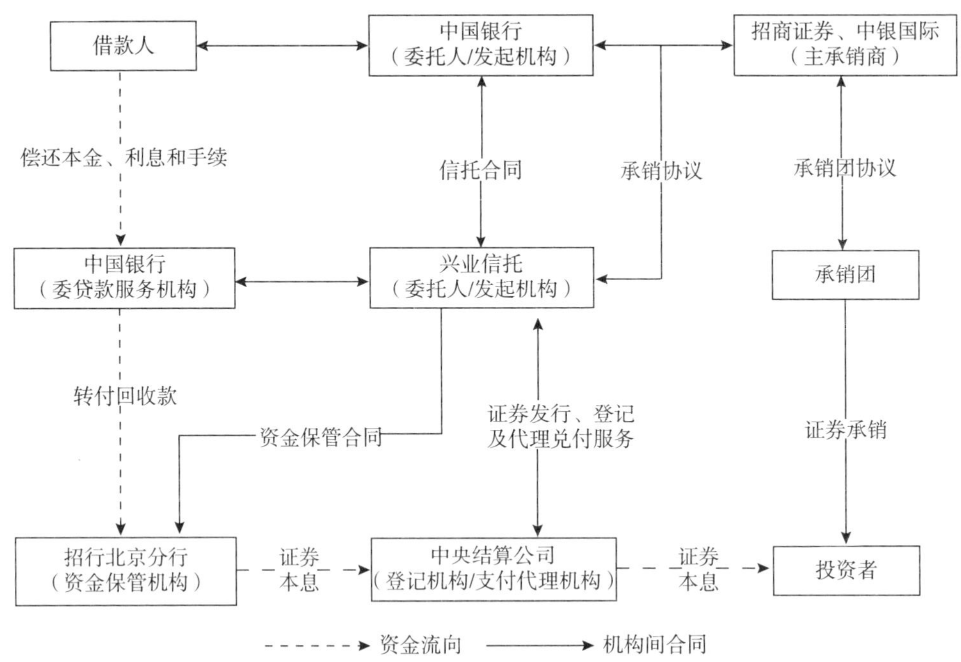

图 6.13　交易模式示意

资料来源：中誉 2016 年第一期资产支持证券发行说明书。

（一）信息披露体系不健全

由于不良资产证券化产品的基础资产为不良资产，因此其违约风险较大，对信息披露要求更高。从美国资产证券化的成功经验来看，其对信息披露制度的不断补充和完善，促使其快速发展。现阶段我国信息披露体系还不健全，现有产品的信息披露及监管政策还不明确，对基础资产信息披露不足。

（二）流动性不足

目前，我国不良资产支持证券的发行还仅限于试点，市场流动性明显不足。首先，受政策影响，不良资产支持证券发行规模较小，基础资产均为银行不良资产贷款，因此产品风险较高，无法满足投资者的需求。其次，从国外的发展经验来看，机构投资者是不良资产支持证券的主要投资者，而目前，我国保险、基金、券商等机构投资者发展还不完善，因此不良资产证券化市场缺乏活力，流动性不足。

（三）相关规章制度不健全

目前，我国在法律法规、会计准则及税收制度方面，对不良资产证券化的规定都不完善。同时，还存在税负过重、抵押权变更环节效率低下等问题，严重阻碍不良资产证券化的发展。

六、对我国不良资产证券化发展的建议

不良资产证券化是提高不良资产处置效率的有效手段，要尽快消除制约我国不良资产证券化发展的障碍，大力推动不良资产证券化发展。

（一）完善信息披露制度

已发行的不良资产证券化产品，基础资产主要为商品房，对公、小微企业以及信用卡不良贷款等。未来可能出现更多种类的不良资产证券化产品。《不良贷款资产支持证券的信息披露指引（试行）》是不良资产证券化的信息披露依据，但该指引只对基础资产的抵押物和担保情况提出了披露要求，且规定较笼统。为了推进不良资产证券化的发展，使投资者更加清楚地了解基础资产的真实情况，需要监管部门将不良资产的信息披露制度进行细化，对不同类型的基础资产进行有针对性的信息披露。

（二）增强二级市场流动性

为解决我国不良资产证券化流动性不足的问题，可以从以下四个方面入手。

第一，要培育和鼓励机构投资者（如证券、保险、基金等）参与不良资产证券化的投资，打破现有的银行业互持现象。同时，政府要出台相应政策，扩大机构投资者的投资权限，使其成为不良资产支持证券的主要投资者，从而降低不良资产支持证券的非系统性风险，提高流动性。

第二，建立投资者保护机制，提高市场透明度，保护投资者利益。

第三，参考做市商制度，鼓励有证券化经验的机构参与不良资产证券化，提高二级市场流动性。

第四，参照美国经验，为不良资产证券化产品注入国家信用，提高其信用级别，增加流动性。比如，设立政府基金，在处置不良资产过程中，当其回收的现金无法支付债券本息时，基金对优先级证券的持有者提供偿付保证。

（三）培育次级证券投资市场

目前，我国不良资产证券化还处在试点阶段，四大资产管理公司是次级证券的主要投资者，其他投资者对其了解和参与程度不足。

从国外的发展经验来看，次级证券的投资者不仅仅是有丰富经验的资产管理公司，还可以是各类金融机构（如投资银行、证券公司、对冲基金等）。虽然发展和培育次级证券投资者的过程很漫长，但通过不断推广及建立严格的投资、信息披露制度，次级

证券的投资群体将逐步扩大。

（四）充分发挥服务机构作用

针对不良资产证券化的特点，最大限度地发挥服务机构的作用，促进不良资产证券化发展。

第一，建立独立的第三方估值体系。由于第三方估值体系独立于产品之外，其只依据不良资产的实际情况进行估值，因此其不受利益左右，可以为投资者提供有效、公正的价格参考。尤其是对于像不良资产支持证券这种交易不活跃的债券，第三方估值体系可以最大限度地反映债券的收益与风险。

第二，建立良好的信用评级和增级体系。不良资产支持证券评级难度较大，需要从业经验丰富、公信力较高的评级机构。一方面，通过引入外部竞争者的方式，促进评级机构快速提高业务水平；另一方面，通过自律组织或监管制度等方式，规范评级机构的发展及业务操作。

第三，完善服务机构的激励约束机制。不良资产证券化中，服务机构的业务水平及尽职情况直接影响不良资产的处置结果，因此，建立有效的激励约束机制，可有效提高不良资产证券化的处置效率。

（五）完善相关规章制度

针对不良资产证券化出台更为明确的会计、税收、法律法规等准则，统一目前会计、税务、不良资产转让等操作。同时，在我国不良资产证券化的起步阶段，应尽量避免重复征税，为推动不良资产证券化发展，可适当考虑对其投资者给予一定的税收优惠。

中小企业普惠金融发展中风险管控策略研究

山西省总审计室　温岳中

普惠金融是指能有效、全方位为社会所有阶层和群体提供服务的金融体系，即让所有老百姓享受更多的金融服务，更好地支持实体经济发展。中小企业普惠金融是我国解决中小企业融资难、融资贵的重大举措，但客观上该业务具有收益低、成本高、风险大等特征。如何实现风险与收益的平衡成为商业银行中小企业普惠金融业务发展中的一大难题。

一、中小企业普惠金融业务发展面临的困难与挑战

（一）尚未形成有效的管理模式

目前，普惠金融业务的发展受政策影响因素较大，在不同区域的发展差异较为明显。商业银行虽完成了普惠金融专职管理机构的设置，但各项管理工作仍在探索阶段，管理架构、配套政策、业务流程、人员配备等都需要进一步改善和优化。

（二）尚未建立健康的业务发展模式

中小企业普惠金融业务的发展多体现在“量”上，面临中小企业不良率高、银企信息不对称等难题，尚无有效的解决途径。中小企业信贷业务风险管理变得非常复杂，高成本、高风险与低收益相对立的矛盾非常明显。商业银行在中小企业业务发展过程中有着明显的阶段性，快速发展与不良率上升常常相伴，而不良率上升必然导致中小企业信贷业务的收紧，无法满足我国中小企业普惠金融发展的要求。

（三）尚未健全业务发展的配套政策

我国现有的有关普惠金融发展的支持政策略显不足，法治框架、信用体系的建立等还不完善，未能最大限度地引导和激励商业银行发展中小企业普惠金融的积极性。

二、中小企业普惠金融业务风险管控策略研究

银企信息不对称、抗风险能力弱、风险与收益不匹配是各商业银行不愿发展中小企业普惠金融业务的重要原因，寻求有效途径解决中小企业风险管控是必经之路。本文结合中小企业业务发展状况，探索用线上产品思维解决线下业务①发展问题的新模式，试图通过大数据研究方法，对客户进行定量及定性分析，对线下中小企业信贷客户进行分类管理，并通过政策引导实现客户的良性发展。

一是构建量化模型，对客户进行科学分类管理。运用线上产品思维方式对传统线下客户进行分类，实行名单制管理，为今后客户日常管理、办理续贷业务等提供参考。如根据客户日均存款、结算量、资产分类、逾期欠息情况等进行定量分析，根据行政处罚信息、人行征信信息、银行内控名单、工商法院信息等进行定性分析。

二是根据客户分类结果实行差别化定价政策。按照量化模型对客户分类的结果通过制定差别化的信贷政策引导客户良性发展。对分类结果较好的客户给予利率、额度、期限等方面的政策优惠，使客户主动提高对我行的贡献度，增加客户黏性。如通过利率的提升和下调、额度的增加与减少、期限的延长与缩短等，实现客户差别化管理。

三是建立贷后管理、客户维护、产品营销等综合化激励约束机制。完善信贷业务关键规定动作管理机制，深化风险预警系统应用，在重视贷款发放的同时，积极强化存量贷款管理，向主动风险管控要效益。

三、客户风险管控策略的具体实施方法

通过对客户日常数据进行赋值计算，划分客户标准，结合行业政策、信用信息等确定客户分类。在客户分类基础上制定差别化政策，进行客户管理，最终达到客户良性引导的目的，具体步骤如下所示。

（一）指标确定

将客户分类指标归类为结算度、贡献度和风险度 3 个维度，每个维度细分为高、中、低 3 档，并对各项指标给予不同的赋值，如表 6. 20 所示。

---

① 线上业务指的是互联网渠道业务模式，线下业务指的是传统信贷业务发展模式。

表 6.20　客户分类指标及赋值

序号	指标	分类	标准	赋值
1	贡献度（存贷比）	高收入	≥20%	30
2		中收入	5% ~20%	20
3		低收入	<5%	10
4	结算度（单位贷款贷方结算覆盖率）	高结算	≥5 倍	30
5		中结算	2.5 ~5	20
6		低结算	<2.5	10
7	风险度（逾期次数）	低风险	正常客户（个别发生过 1 次短暂逾期）	30
8		中风险	再融资及关注类客户	20
9		高风险	欠息≥3 次，或不足 3 次、但最高逾期天数≥25 天	10

注：表中数字仅作举例说明，不具有参考意义，各商业银行要根据实际情况进行制定。

（二）数值计算

通过为结算度、贡献度和风险度的不同档次进行赋值，并给予相应的权重系数，计算得出每个客户的分数，确定“进、保、压、退”的客户分类。

计算分值的公式为：

分值 Y = 贡献度 × 权重系数 X1 + 结算度 × 权重系数 X2 + 风险度 × 权重系数 X3。

鉴于风险重要性考虑，本报告设系数①为 X1 =0.2 ，X2 =0.2，X3 =0.6。

（三）初步分类

根据数值计算的结果，确定对客户采用的相应策略（见表 6.21）。

表 6.21　客户分类标准

指标名称 / 分类	进	保	压	退
分值 Y	≥26	20≤Y <26	14≤Y <20	<14

注：表中数字仅作举例说明，不具有参考意义，各商业银行要根据实际情况进行制定。

（四）分类调整

在定量分析分类结果的基础上，结合企业的行业性质、失信被执行人信息、银行内控信息、反洗钱信息、核销信息、行政处罚信息，以及企业主的失信被执行信息、

① 系数可根据实际需要进行调整，仅供参考。

信用卡核销信息、反洗钱信息等信息，降低客户分类档次或直接纳入/退出客户分类。同时，为体现审慎原则，模型测算出客户分类，需要进一步结合 RAROC 值，进行分类结果调整。如对于达不到盈亏平衡点的客户，需要降低档次。

（五）差别化政策

各商业银行可以根据分类结果，讨论制定差别化信贷政策，主要包括额度、期限、利率、担保、循环额度等政策（见表 6. 22）。

表 6. 22　不同分类客户差别化政策

客户政策	进	保	压	退
额度政策	结合客户需求可适当增加额度	结合客户需求，不超过存量	压缩额度 10%	压缩额度 20%
期限政策	结合订单按需设定，最长 12 个月	结合订单按需设定，最长 12 个月	结合订单按需设定，最长 9 个月	结合订单按需设定，最长 6 个月
利率政策	上浮不低于 10%	上浮不低于 20%	上浮不低于 30%	上浮不低于 40%
担保政策	可不追加担保	适量增强缓释措施	增强缓释措施	增强缓释措施
循环额度	可循环额度		不可循环额度	

注：表中数字仅作举例说明，不具有参考意义，各商业银行要根据实际情况进行制定。

四、客户风险管控建议

一是持续跟踪分类客户，确保客户策略落地实施。分类方法的研究旨在对业务的发展进行指导及提供参考，在今后客户管理时要持续跟踪其使用及适用情况，确保分类策略结果的落地实施。切实退出高风险客户，引导低风险客户实现良性发展，提高优良客户黏性及对建行贡献度。

二是结合风险预警信息，强化客户风险日常监督。随着普惠金融战略的实施，客户模式由“双大”向“双小”转变，今后中小企业客户管理应结合各商业银行风险预警等系统进行，更多地由“人控”向“机控”转变，对于出现风险苗头的客户，应及时做好风险防控及应对，确保信贷资产安全。

三是动态调整分类指标，及时优化分类方法。本报告中分类指标的选取并非最优的分类体系，在实际运用时要根据客户整体情况、行业政策等进行调整优化，确保分类方法的有效性和可操作性。

五、总结

中小企业普惠金融业务的发展是一项系统性、长期性工程，需要政府、监管机构、商业银行等的通力合作。随着我国普惠金融战略的推广和深入实施，普惠金融经营管理体系、支持政策、配套设施都将逐步完善和优化。我国的中小企业数量庞大，未来发展前景非常广阔。从商业银行的角度来看，在日趋激烈的竞争环境下，中小企业将成为其今后的主流客户，但同时中小企业信贷风险管理水平也是对各商业银行的一大挑战，各商业银行需要强化内控管理，通过全方位的努力来提升信贷风险管理水平。

金融科技业务创新中合规管理的若干思考

——内控合规视角

浙江省分行　方　圆　洪　江

一、金融科技简介

（一）基本概念

金融科技“Fintech”是 Financial Technology 合并后的缩写，泛指技术进步驱动的金融创新。金融稳定理事会在 2016 年首次发布的《金融科技的全景描述和分析框架报告》（FSB，2016）中对金融科技做了初步定义，即指利用大数据、云计算、区块链、人工智能等前沿技术进行金融创新，通过新技术、新方式，创造新的金融业务模式、应用、流程或产品，降低金融交易、融资成本，减少无效劳动和信息不对称，提升服务效率。

本文所探讨的“金融科技”，是指对银行业务中的数字化或电子化运用，如网上银行、手机银行等，同时也是指可以应用于金融领域的各类新技术，如分布式账户、云计算、大数据，以及其涉及的新业务。

（二）发展阶段

根据巴曙松等人的研究，将金融科技划分为三个阶段。第一个阶段为金融 IT 阶段（金融科技 1.0 版）。银行通过传统 IT 的软硬件的应用来实现办公和业务的电子化、自动化，提高业务效率。第二个阶段为互联网金融阶段（金融科技 2.0 阶段）。主要变革了传统金融交易渠道，出现各类业务的在线平台，实现信息共享和业务融合，代表性的包括 P2P（个人对个人）网络借贷、互联网保险和基金等。第三个阶段是金融科技 3.0 阶段。银行通过大数据、云计算、人工智能、区块链这些新技术来进行客户识别、风险定价模型、投资决策等过程，代表技术有大数据征信、智能投顾、供应链金融等。

（三）业务模式

巴塞尔银行监管委员会将金融科技分为四大类，包括支付结算、存贷款与资本筹集、投资管理、市场设施（见表6.23）。

表6.23　金融科技业务模式分类

支付结算	存贷款与资本筹集	投资管理	市场设施
·零售类支付	·借贷平台	·智能投顾	·跨行业通用服务
移动钱包	借贷型众筹	财富管理	客户身份数字认证
点对点汇款	线上贷款平台	·电子交易	多维数据归集处理
数字货币	电子商务贷款	线上证券交易	·技术基础设施
·批发类支付	信用评分	线上货币交易	分布式账户
跨境支付	贷款清收		大数据
虚拟价值交换网络	·股权融资		云计算
	投资型众筹		

上述业务分类中，“支付结算”、“存贷款与资本筹集”和“投资管理”的业务模式具备较强的金融属性，一般纳入金融业务和金融监管。“市场设施”通常被利用到对金融机构提供的服务中，不具备金融行业的特性，但随着科技与金融的深入融合，各类金融科技设施对金融机构的稳健运行带来越来越重要的影响，监管机构已经加强了关注。

二、现实作用与风险挑战

当前，金融机构拥抱金融科技的姿态和步伐不断加大，建设银行更是将其作为住房租赁、普惠金融等一系列市场战略的重要支撑和基础，但也应清醒地认识到金融科技给商业银行带来的影响和挑战。

（一）积极作用

作为金融与科技的桥梁，金融科技对于加强银行的服务供给、提升服务效率、增强风险管控能力、促进转型等方面具有重要作用。

1. 更好地提高银行服务效率

金融科技技术具有全天候、跨地域的特性，能在时间和空间方面弥补传统金融服务的空隙，也具备标准化操作、简化交易、快速响应、海量服务等特征。

2. 能显著提高主动营销和精准营销能力

依托数据采集、整合和分析，在客户识别、挖掘客户线索、客户需求智能分析和产品匹配等方面，使银行能更好地“了解自己的客户”，提升客户画像精准度，便于锁定目标群体。

3. 能提供智能化决策和合规风险管理能力

通过模式识别、数据抓取、关键信息分析、自动成文报告、动态跟踪、舆情分析等技术，运用于业务前、中、后各环节，可与银行尽职调查和专业经验深度融合，最大限度提供更科学合理、风险可控的决策支持。

4. 是银行创新的重要手段和途径

为银行再造业务流程和交易方式、创新产品和服务、重构业务格局提供良好的技术支撑，通过对支付、理财、智能投顾等业务的深度挖掘和利用，有助于推动经营的开放性和普惠性。

5. 有助于加快网点物理转型

进一步优化网点人员配置，减轻可被机器替代的标准化、操作性和重复性劳动压力，建立智能专业咨询系统支持员工提供个性化、定制化和更为专业化的服务。同时，为网点加速业务延伸、业务引流和提升获客方面的转型提供技术基础。

（二）潜在风险与特征

1. 改变了风险的权重和分布

一方面，在银行传统业务体系中，主导风险主要体现为信用风险，金融科技在一定程度上提高了银行的合规风险管理能力，但另一方面，金融科技业务实质上已经改变了银行主要风险分布。主要体现为：一是数据风险，以“数据分析”和“云计算”作为业务基石存在系统性偏误风险，将会出现一连串负面效应和损失；二是技术风险隐蔽性高，对技术风险的预判和防范要求随之升高，一旦风险爆发和蔓延，银行及客户易于陷入被动局面；三是容易出现技术风险和操作风险交叉叠加的现象。

2. 系统性风险概率提升

面对高度网络化、数字化、移动端、分布式的金融科技体系，增加机构之间的关联性，也增加了金融体系的复杂性，金融风险较大的突破了地域限制，业务风险一旦爆发，便可能迅速演变为大规模的系统性风险，这就对银行具备与之匹配的合规管理、风险控制能力及技术资源提出了更高的要求。

3. 为洗钱和恐怖融资提供便利渠道

这主要是由参与主体的多元性以及带来的信息不对称所引发的。金融科技发展促进了银行业务从线下到线上的延伸，并深入社会各个领域，参与主体的多元性、极强的隐秘性，以及交易双方的虚拟身份加大了银行对身份确认和交易确认的难度，这就为洗钱和恐怖融资提供了极有利的犯罪渠道。

（三）合规工作面临的挑战

1. 对内控合规专业能力形成挑战

内控合规部门可能难以快速配备相应的管控资源，包括人才资源（同时理解系统语言和业务语言的专家）和科技监管资源（监控手段、预警工具等）；也难以及时更新知识结构，对游离在监管政策之外，或变相规避监管的金融科技业务，无法识别潜在风险，从而影响内控的有效性。

2. 增加风险监测和合规管控难度

部分大量运用去中心化和金融脱媒手段的金融科技业务，会存在交易活动脱离中央清算机制、不受最终收益客户管控的可能性，增加了交易各方的风险敞口，为风险监测带来较大压力。而大数据应用行为本身的合规性及监控手段也没有形成较为完善的内控体系，缺乏有效工具。

3. 对员工行为管理提出更高要求

虚拟环境下的信息不对称、交易不透明、身份不确定、业务违规隐蔽性强还容易引发员工道德风险，因而给员工行为管理带来难题。

三、怎样守住金融科技业务的创新关口

金融科技对我国深化金融改革创造了历史性的发展新机遇，纵然存在诸多的风险和挑战，但迅猛发展的趋势已经势不可挡。随着建行大力发展科技金融业务，也迎来了相关业务创新的高潮，对创新过程中的合规管理提出了更高更迫切的要求。结合这类业务的特性，合规管理在创新关口应注重把握以下几个方面的工作。

（一）业务上市前——合规评审机制

“要把金融猛兽关在合规的禁锢边界中。”科技金融本身作为新兴的金融形态，还没有经历足够多的市场检验和历史考验，尚没有一套成熟有效的预警、管控、干预和应急处置体系和经验。所以要在科技金融产品上市之前，尽可能地揭示或有风险、合规漏洞，弥补业务流程、管理措施的缺陷。所以，目前建行初步建立起的创新产品的合规性审查和洗钱风险评估机制就显得尤为重要，是科技金融业务创新面市前的最后一道内控关口。

合规性审查与洗钱风险评估是相对独立的两项评审措施：合规性审查主要涉及新产品的外规内规遵循性，产品设计中的制度风险、法律风险、操作风险、流程风险、声誉风险和相应的风险管控措施；洗钱风险评估专项评估新产品的洗钱风险漏

洞和风险等级，出具相应的防控建议。两项工作宜集中在一个牵头部门，进而通过组建各业务部门专家团队、聘请外部评审、召开专家会议等形式进行创新产品的评审。应明确：合规性审查和洗钱风险评估如有一项不通过的，新产品将不能面市。

（二）合规管控的重点

在对金融科技创新产品进行合规性审查和洗钱风险评估时，应关注以下几点。

1. 对法律法规、规章制度的遵循性

首先是审查对国家层面的法律法规和监管机构的政策的遵循性，清醒地认识到违法违规带来的处罚和损失，重点关注是否存在以“新瓶装旧酒”的方式逃避监管，规避国家宏观调控政策限制的情况，重点关注相关监管制度和规范是否及时跟进。其次是审查对建行（包括总行和一级分行）规章制度的遵循情况，创新中如存在制度的理解差异、执行标准差异，需尝试突破性的设计时，应取得相应的支持性依据，如监管批复、总行批复、高层或行内决策等。

2. 辨别创新类型

首先要进行创新的实质性辨别，应区分真实创新与部分以流程细节完善、系统功能微调形成的名义创新；其次是细分金融科技创新的类型，分清类型是为了更科学有效地运用业务领域的知识开展有针对性的评审，可将上述文中提及的巴塞尔银行监管委员会的分类（表6.23所示内容）用作参考。

3. 穿透性原则，把握创新业务本质

业务形态多样化、业务品种组合化是金融科技创新业务的特点之一，但科技在产品设计和业务模式上的运用并不能改变支付清算、借贷融资等金融业务的根本属性，其风险本质特征和监管要求遵循性的本质并未变化。所以，在审查时应按照“实质重于形式”的原则，以穿透式的视角从交易对手、贸易背景、资金来源和流向、支付路径、中间环节等方面辨别业务本质。比如现在市场上存在的车牌“无感支付”业务，改变了交易渠道和形式，资金清算的流转方向并未变化，而当中车牌与付款账户关联的真实性、账户签约与自动扣缴的合规性、账户受益人的资金安全等问题才是我们应该穿透把握的合规风险部分。

4. 形式合规与实质合规同等重要

从形式合规来看，金融科技业务创新成果必须纳入全行产品库和合规风险管理体系中，所以在审查时应重点关注其配套的业务制度、产品办法、操作规程（手册）、合同协议，避免新业务无章无序运行。从实质合规来看，一是关注创新产品设计、授权审批、业务运行及效果预测中存在的制度性、机制性、系统性缺陷和受控状态；二是关注风险缓释及控制措施、操作风险管理、人员管理中的合规薄弱点；三是关注创新产品运营和管理中，是否存在行内部门职责不清、任务不明的现象。

5. 重视并加强反洗钱工作

2018年10月，国家“一行两会一局”齐亮相，出台重磅制度，将金融机构反洗钱和反恐怖融资监管提升到新高度，在此背景下，金融科技业务必然是今后的监管重点。所以在进行洗钱风险评估时，一是要关注产品中的客户准入政策、产品设计开发、业务流程构建是否嵌入洗钱风险控制措施；二是要对风险等级进行识别与划分，不仅要考虑金融产品的固有风险，而且应根据等级分类，结合当前市场的具体运行状况进行跟踪和动态调整，建立重评估机制；三是进行对公、对私客户独立且差别化的评估，同一产品同时涉及公私客户的，须在分别评估后取相对高的等级作为结论依据；四是跟进金融科技创新的产品部门是否就风险评估结果制定适合的风险控制措施，有效防范客户利用建行产品从事洗钱和恐怖融资活动的风险。

6. 加强对员工行为和操作风险的防范措施

从创新产品相匹配的制度、系统运作、操作流程、岗位责任等角度，加强关注有无明确的岗位职责和操作说明，操作中岗位间的制约是否完善，系统授权是否等级分明等，充分揭示人为因素及其带来的合规风险和道德风险。

7. 关注消费者权益保护和声誉风险

金融科技业务一旦风险暴露，极易引起大规模的负面效应和群体性事件，所以在评审时要特别关注消费者权益保护相关措施有无设计和明确，突发事件应急处置和声誉处理措施是否具备，是否有应急预案。

（三）业务上市后——基于风险等级的跟踪监控

基于合规性审查和洗钱风险评估出具的“风险等级”评定，根据科技金融创新业务的实际运作情况，对中高风险、高风险的业务进行跟踪和监控，重点关注是否存在违规操作、放大信用风险的问题。一些金融科技业务的设计和制度可能完备，但在营销和运行过程中，因其多由机控、系统操作，可能存在人为的弱化管理、弄虚作假、不严格执行产品设计条款，因此带来信贷风险及其他合规风险失去控制或被放大的隐患。

还可以借鉴国外“监管沙盒”“指导窗口”等监督管理的经验，使创新的机构和产品能在范围可控、风险可控的前提下开展产品测试和试点，给金融科技创新留有一定的容错空间和观察期。

四、案例与实务

（一）业务案例介绍

某分行拟开展“×付宝商户收单集合平台”[①] 业务，计划通过商户营销，大力推广“×付宝集合平台”的设备和结算业务。

模式一：个人与商户间的小额交易。商户安装这一设备，个人客户安装“×付宝”手机软件，商户就能通过设备进行客户付费结算，同时客户也将获得一定的优惠和回馈。

模式二：商户与商户间的大额交易。双方商户都安装这一设备，收单商户发起收款流程，收单设备生成二维码，通过手机端发送二维码及本次交易密码至付款商户，付款商户用己方设备扫描二维码，输入接收到的交易密码进行支付。

（二）评审中揭示的风险点

在合规性审查和洗钱风险评估过程中，注意到以下几方面的风险点。

1. 支付风险

快捷支付、二维码支付、非接触式支付等新型支付手段存在资金被盗的风险，如客户手机丢失，手机信息及短信验证码被不法分子获得，可直接使用二维码在商户支付时进行线下消费。

2. 软件应用端风险

如果二维码支付、非接触式支付应用软件的身份认证及登录控制不严格规范，不法分子容易在熟悉客户个人信息前提下冒充客户使用二维码支付和非接触式支付方式。尤其是在“商户—商户”的模式下，客户将面临大额损失。

3. 二维码技术含量及场景安全性风险

二维码的技术门槛很低，编译和发布较为简单，如果应用场景里设备摆放环境随意而不受监控，不法分子将会偷换商户收款二维码来盗取资金。

4. 反洗钱客户身份识别风险

该业务采用非面对面开立Ⅱ类账户及Ⅲ类账户，冒名开户风险较大，一旦成功开户，便可通过支付机构的支付账户进行转账消费，或是完成资金盗取。

（三）评审建议

根据评审的风险点，提出以下改进建议。

---

① 根据文章论述需要，对产品名称及相关功能进行了处理。

1. 加强商户管理

应当根据《银行卡收单业务管理办法》《关于银行卡收单业务的风险提示》等监管文件，加强商户管理，并要求将设备放在监控覆盖区域。

2. 改进并组合使用多种支付验证方式

除二维码和短信密码外，建议设定静态支付密码、指纹（动态人像）识别、手机安全数字证书等。

3. 加强电子渠道Ⅱ、Ⅲ类账户开户审核

完善客户身份识别工作，防范洗钱和恐怖融资风险、伪卡交易等负面行为。

4. 充分告知风险，配备应急预案

针对该业务可能出现的主客观风险，对商户和客户进行充分告知，保障消费者合法权益，维护建行声誉。

五、科技合规展望

金融科技的发展必将推动合规管理的科技化运用，也就是通过监管科技（Regtech）提升合规管控能力。应充实合规部门科技资源，或建立专门的监管科技团队，借助信息科技系统工具加强动态监管、预测分析，着力解决金融科技业务发展与合规管理信息不对称的难题，引入人工智能、机器学习技术进行跟踪、监测、识别和预警，提高合规管控的质量和效率。金融科技与监管科技都依托大数据及数据分析，这为两者共同发展、相互完善提供了坚实的基础。

六、总结

“Fintech”也好，“互联网+金融”也罢，金融科技再“炫”也不会改变金融中介的事实，发挥的都是金融功能。我们应该大胆拥抱、小心应对，平衡金融科技创新与合规风险管控，把发展与合规作为一个有机的整体来考虑。一方面，要清醒认识到：金融科技和金融科技创新都是新事物，都存在对传统金融工具的革新和突破，没有绝对的安全和零风险，过度注重安全措施而忽视发展和效率，会限制金融科技创新的活力。另一方面，更要深刻明白：内控合规应是金融猛兽身上无形的项圈，通过严格审查、密切监管、及时指导或中断等手段，避免出现盲目追求效率、肆意突破底线、变相绕开监管等不良金融科技创新行为。

破产程序中银行保证债权的止息规则

江苏省分行　曹婷婷

一、问题的提出

2015 年 1 月 1 日，A 公司与建行签订 1 年期流动资金贷款合同，借款本金 5 000 万元，年利率为 4.35%，罚息年利率为正常年利率的 1.5 倍。同日，B 公司与建行签订保证合同，为 A 公司在建行的借款、利息、费用等方面提供连带责任保证担保。其间 A 公司正常付息，直至 2015 年 10 月 10 日，建行因 A 公司无力偿还债务而向法院提出 A 公司破产的申请，同日法院受理了该申请。

《担保法》司法解释第 44 条规定："保证期间，人民法院受理债务人破产案件的，债权人既可以向人民法院申报债权，也可以向保证人主张权利。"也就是说，在上述案例中，建行作为债权人有着一定的选择权。在多种选择中债权人将如何实现自身权益的最大化？破产程序中，银行的保证债权该适用什么样的止息规则？

（一）债权人未申报债权，直接向保证人主张权利

如果在上述案例中，建行选择直接向保证人主张担保债权的实现，同时将这一选择通知到保证人 B①，那么保证人 B 则可以根据《企业破产法》赋予其的求偿权和将来求偿权②向 A 公司的破产管理人申报债权。在这种选择下，债权人并未参与到破产程序中，那么《企业破产法》停止计息的规定也就不应该对债权人生效，而债权人主张的保证责任也必须是包含所有利息的完全债权。那么，保证人应该在什么范围内申报债权呢？

（二）债权人申报债权的同时也向保证人主张权利

目前的司法实践中，有一种观点认为债权人不能在申报债权的同时向保证人主张

---

① 《担保法》司法解释第 45 条规定：债权人知道或者应当知道债务人破产，既未申报债权也未通知保证人，致使保证人不能预先行使追偿权的，保证人在该债权在破产程序中可能受偿的范围内免除保证责任。

② 《企业破产法》第 51 条第一款规定了求偿权，第二款规定了将来求偿权。

权利，因为这样做的结果很可能会导致双重受偿，债权人既在破产程序中得到部分清偿，又在保证人处实现保证债权。但是事实上，如果债权人未在保证期内向保证人主张权利的话，也会存在丢失保证债权的风险。为了避免双重受偿的可能性，目前司法实践中也存在两种做法：一种是判决保证人在破产程序终结后履行保证责任；另一种是直接判决连带责任保证人承担保证责任，在保证人承担保证责任即做出清偿后再由保证人作为债权人申报债权。保证人承担的保证责任是否包括破产受理之日起的利息呢?

（三）破产程序终结但债权人没有得到完全受偿的情况下，债权人应在破产程序终结后6个月内向保证人主张权利

《担保法》司法解释第44条第二款及《企业破产法》第124条都规定了债权人在破产程序中未得到清偿的债权可以继续要求保证承担保证责任。同样的，保证人是否需要承担债务人进入破产程序之后的利息呢?

（四）破产程序开始于民事执行阶段

在实践中，还存在着这样一种可能，在债务人破产程序开始之前，债权人已经在生效判决中被确认了债权及担保债权，且已经进入了执行程序。根据《企业破产法》第19条及第20条的规定，在法院受理债务人的破产程序后，针对债务人的诉讼程序包括执行程序应当中止，在管理人接管债务人的财产后再恢复。那么，债权人申请恢复对实现担保债权时是否包括未偿付的利息呢?

显然，在上述四种选择中，都存在着破产程序中银行保证债权是否包含停止计息后的利息问题。大部分的司法实践认为保证人不承担破产受理之后的主债务利息，而大部分的学者则认为其应当偿付破产受理日之后的主债务利息。

二、破产程序中银行保证债权随主债权停止计息

认为保证人不偿付破产受理之后的主债务利息也即破产程序中银行保证债权随主债权停止计息的司法实践大都持以下观点。

（一）保证具有从属性

因为保证具有从属性，所以主债权停止计息，保证债权也停止计息。保证具有从属性体现在4个方面：成立具有从属性、范围具有从属性、变更和消灭具有从属性、转移上具有从属性。接下来主要从第二个方面讨论。保证在范围上具有从属性，是指保证的责任范围不能大于主债务，只能小于或者等于。根据《企业破产法》规定，在主债务人被法院受理破产之日即停止计息，这时主债务的范围是未受偿的本金及至停

息之日止的利息。这时，根据保证范围的从属性，银行享有的保证债权也只能停止计息，保证人只对未受偿的本金和至停息之日止的利息承担保证责任。这一点也可以从《担保法》上对保证范围的规定得到佐证，《担保法》第21条规定："保证担保的范围包括主债权及利息、违约金、损害赔偿金和实现债权的费用。"可以肯定的是，保证担保的范围应当限于主债务人的责任范围，在主债务人被法院受理破产后，根据停止计息的规定，其后的利息主债务人已经不用承担，不在主债务人责任范围内的利息也更不在保证担保的范围。

另外，依据保证人的抗辩权，在企业进入破产程序后，债权人不得再向债务人主张破产程序开始后的利息，也即债务人可以依据《企业破产法》第46条而对抗债权人的利息请求，此时，债务人享有抗辩权，《担保法》第20条规定保证人享有债务人的抗辩权，那么保证人就可以根据抗辩权来对抗债权人的利息请求权。

（二）债权人和保证人的利益平衡

担保制度得以有效运转，在于债权人的风险转移以及担保人取得追偿权两大功能，担保制度缺少上述两大功能的任何一项都将不能存续。① 一方面，在《担保法》和《担保法》司法解释②赋予债权人选择权的情况下，如果债权人选择直接向保证人主张权利，则保证人应当承担的是全部的保证责任，不受《企业破产法》停止计息规则的影响，而且保证人也可在破产程序中行使其追偿权；如果债权人选择直接申报债权，则应根据《企业破产法》规定，受到停止计息规则的约束。那么在债权人有自主选择的情况下，应该由债权人自身权衡利弊并承担相应的后果。如果允许债权人参与破产程序申报债权，之后也可以要求保证人偿付破产程序之外的利息，那么就是将债权人行使选择权后产生的不利后果强加给了保证人，恐怕是侵害了保证人的利益。另一方面，法院受理破产案件后停止计息，债权人遭受的仅仅是小部分利息损失，其仍可以从破产管理人及保证人处得到清偿。而如果不对保证人停止计息，则损害了保证人的追偿权，这样轻易地剥夺保证人的追偿权将严重动摇保证制度的有效运行，侵害了保证人的权利。

三、破产程序中银行保证债权不随主债权停止计息

认为保证人应当偿付破产受理之后的主债务利息也即破产程序中银行保证债权不随主债权停止计息的学术界大都持以下观点。

---

① 资料来源：夏群佩，洪海波．主债务人进入破产程序后连带保证人的责任范围［J］．人民司法（案例），2017（14）．

② 《担保法》第32条和《担保法》司法解释第44条。

（一）停止计息规则的立法目的

停止计息规则的立法目的在于调整破产程序中多个债权人之间的关系，是为了保证破产程序能够顺利进行而做的一种特殊规定。“附利息的债权如果在破产程序开始后仍处于计息状态，则它们的数额在程序期间处于变动状态。”[①] “为了破产程序的顺利进行，有必要在债权人申报债权时确定债权的具体数额”。[②] 因为破产程序是一个较长期的过程，破产债权的确认也需要相当长的时间，如果不停止计息，破产债权将会不断地出现和累积，将永远没有一个确定的数字，破产程序无法终结，债权人也无法尽快得到清偿。停止计息的规则是为了让破产程序顺利进行，并非为了减轻保证人责任，因此并不适用于保证人。另外，保证人承担破产程序期间产生的利息本就是保证制度的应有之义，在其风险预判之内。保证制度是为了保障债权人的权利，为了能让债权人在债务人不能偿还债务时降低损失，显然债务人破产是债权人在保证制度中防范的主要风险。

（二）保证从属性的突破

保证具有从属性，但在特殊情况下也是可以突破的。一是破产重整突破从属性。《企业破产法》关于重整的条款明确规定重整计划不影响债权人对债务人的保证人和其他连带债务人所享有的权利。在破产重整中，大都会对债务人的债务进行减免，也可能迟延、分期履行、放弃抵押权利等，如果从保证的从属性上说，保证责任将得到相应的免除。然而《企业破产法》已经明确，保证责任不受重整计划的影响。“如因债权人在重整计划中不得已而减免债务人的部分债务，便相应减轻保证人和其他连带债务人的责任，就与担保设立的宗旨相违背”[③]。二是破产和解突破从属性。《企业破产法》第 101 条明确了和解协议不对保证债权产生影响。类似于破产重整的规定，《企业破产法》认为和解协议对主债务人的债务免除并不同于《民法》上的债务免除，因为《企业破产法》程序上的免除不对具有从属性的保证债权产生影响。三是破产清算分配后的从属性突破。《企业破产法》第 124 条规定在破产清算分配后，主债务人的债务予以免除，但保证人仍应当承担全部的保证责任。在破产程序中，保证仍应发挥其保证制度的作用，突破其对主债务的从属性。

（三）选择权下权利不应被削减

王欣新教授早在 1998 年的文章中就提到过债权人在破产程序中有申报债权或者不

① 资料来源：王卫国．破产法精义［M］．北京：法律出版社，2007.

② 资料来源：中华人民共和国企业破产法释义及实用指南［M］．北京：中国民主法制出版社，2006.

③ 资料来源：中华人民共和国企业破产法释义及实用指南［M］．北京：中国民主法制出版社，2006.

申报债权直接向保证人追偿的选择权，如果债权人选择不申报债权，那么他可以向保证人要求承担完全的保证责任；而如果在债权人选择申报债权时他就要损失部分的利息（法院受理破产申请之后的利息）求偿权，显然此时债权人的权利被削减了，债权人参加破产程序也将失去积极性。许德风教授也认为①，《企业破产法》停止计息的规定不表示主债务的减少，更不免除保证人责任，这项规定不排除债权人可以在未完全受偿时向保证人追偿利息的权利，债权人如果不申报债权而直接向保证人要求承担保证责任的话，保证人应承担全部的保证责任，包含停止计息后的利息。两位学者都认为，在债权人有参加破产程序或者直接向保证人追偿的选择权时，无论债权人选择如何，他的权利都不能因此被削减。

四、冲突的解决

司法实践和学者基本持完全相反的观点，是因为存在着破产债权和一般债权。《企业破产法》第 107 条和第 124 条规定了破产债权：从法院受理破产申请之日至破产程序终结期间的债权为破产债权。回到规定止息规则的第 46 条，其立法目的在于方便确定破产债权的范围，是为了破产程序的顺利进行，这是一条针对破产债权的程序性规定，停止计息的对象也指的是破产债权。在债权人申报债权进入破产程序后，这一《企业破产法》的程序性规定对债权人和债务人（进入破产程序后称为破产人）生效。但是这一效力却并不及于保证人，因为保证人没有参与其内，他们之间的权利义务关系不受《企业破产法》程序性规定调整，而从属于民商事制度，也就是说保证人担保的债权就是民商法意义上的一般债权。在债权人没有申报债权的时候，他们之间也就没有形成破产法律关系，更遑论要适用《企业破产法》的程序性规定。所以，学者认为不应当停止计息是因为一般债权自始至终未发生过变化，司法实践认为应当停止计息是因为一般债权进入破产程序后其利益受到削减而成为破产债权。

事实上，要解决这一冲突，我们应该引进一个新的概念：劣后债权。将破产程序开始后的债权利息列为劣后债权，它是破产债权的一部分，这时候司法实践上的破产债权数额将等同于学者认为的一般债权的数额。而在受偿顺序上，劣后债权将列在所有债权清偿的最后顺位。这一清偿顺序不仅仅适用于一般的破产清算程序，还适用于破产重整程序、破产和解程序。当债务人的财产不能够清偿所有债权人的本金金额时，破产程序开始后的利息作为劣后债权自然不必清偿；但当通过破产清算的拍卖或者破产重整、和解程序时，往往会因为最大程度实现了企业的财产价值而使得仍有可能对劣后债权进行清偿。

---

① 资料来源：许德风．破产法论：解释与功能比较和视角［M］．北京：大学出版社，2015.

当然，为了延续止息规则确保破产程序顺利进行的功能，法律还应当规定在破产重整计划或者和解计划得以通过时，劣后债权无表决权；在进入破产程序后，规定统一的利率水平来计算利息，避免由于不同债权人不一致的利息计算标准而导致各债权人之间的利益失衡。

最后，在未有法律规定劣后债权前，银行为了最大限度地维护自身利益，可以在向破产管理人申报破产债权的同时对保证人提起诉讼，并申请诉前财产保全，即便是诉讼会被中止，也避免了保证人财产的不利转移和保证期间的失效。并且，在向保证人追偿时，应有理有据地提出对破产程序开始后的利息请求。